Trusts Textbook

Trusts Textbook

SECOND EDITION

Gary Watt MA (Oxon), Solicitor
Senior Lecturer, University of Warwick

OXFORD
UNIVERSITY PRESS

OXFORD
UNIVERSITY PRESS

Great Clarendon Street, Oxford OX2 6DP

Oxford University Press is a department of the University of Oxford.
It furthers the University's objective of excellence in research, scholarship,
and education by publishing worldwide in

Oxford New York

Auckland Cape Town Dar es Salaam Hong Kong Karachi
Kuala Lumpur Madrid Melbourne Mexico City Nairobi
New Delhi Shanghai Taipei Toronto

With offices in

Argentina Austria Brazil Chile Czech Republic France Greece
Guatemala Hungary Italy Japan Poland Portugal Singapore
South Korea Switzerland Thailand Turkey Ukraine Vietnam

Published in the United States
by Oxford University Press Inc., New York

British Library Cataloguing in Publication Data
Data available

Library of Congress Cataloging in Publication Data
Data available

Typeset by Newgen Imaging Systems (P) Ltd., Chennai, India
Printed in Great Britain
on acid-free paper by
Antony Rowe Limited, Chippenham, Wiltshire

ISBN 0–19–928444–X 978–0–19–92844–3

1 3 5 7 9 10 8 6 4 2

PREFACE

Despite its mediaeval origins, the trust concept boasts a multiplicity of contemporary uses and these will form the main focus of this book: trusts in commerce, insolvency, pensions and cohabitation figure prominently. Indeed, my greatest satisfaction in more than a decade of teaching the law of trusts has been to demonstrate that a subject which students sometimes expect will be archaic, insignificant and impenetrable is in fact highly relevant to contemporary commercial and family life, and, most importantly, is interesting and can be clearly understood. The reader might even conclude, as I have, that the flexibility and utility of the trust goes beyond that of any other legal creature. Thus, within this volume you will discover whether a trust to promote the works of the classical composer Delius is charitable and, at the other extreme, whether the manager of a young and vulnerable pop-star owes their protégé a trust-like ('fiduciary') duty.

Just as the substance of this book emphasises that which is current and relevant to the modern world, so also the form of the book takes advantage of the latest advances in teaching and learning. The use of exercises, questions, diagrams and end-of-chapter summaries is designed to reinforce learning at every stage and the accompanying Online Resource Centre provides regular updates to the text and useful links to supplementary materials. The book provides clear guidance on the subject, but the student is not spoon-fed; rather he or she is shown where to find the spoon and how to feed himself or herself. There is enough in this book and the accompanying Online Resource Centre to satisfy the demands of typical undergraduate degree courses in trusts, but if the student is hungry for more he or she may wish to consult books which address current debates in even more depth. My own textbook *Trusts and Equity*, also published by Oxford University Press, is one. For even greater depth the student may consult specialist monographs on particular areas of the subject (Lionel Smith on *The Law of Tracing* and Robert Chambers on *Resulting Trusts*, both published by Oxford University Press under the Clarendon Press imprint, are excellent examples). The leading journals on the subject (for example, *The Law Quarterly Review* and *The Conveyancer and Property Lawyer*) may also be consulted. There is a dedicated Online Resource Centre accompanying this book which contains periodic updates to the text and web links to useful primary sources and academic commentary. The reader might find this resource especially useful when it comes to following the progress of proposed reforms of the law. Thus, for example, when the Charities Bill 2004 eventually becomes law, a link to the Act will appear on the web site accompanying this book. The Bill (which consolidates, and makes minor changes to, definition of 'charity') is itself already covered in depth in the text.

Whatever course you take, I wish you every success in your studies.

Gary Watt
1st December 2005

OUTLINE TABLE OF CONTENTS

CONTENTS

TABLE OF CASES

TABLE OF STATUTES

Statutory Instruments

■ HOW TO USE THIS BOOK

This book will give students of trusts law a clear and accurate introduction to the subject. Our aim has been to make the material as accessible as possible for those students coming to the subject for the first time. To this end we have included a number of features throughout the text to allow for interactive use of the book by students, in testing their knowledge and checking their understanding.

An Online Resource Centre (www.oxfordtextbooks.co.uk/orc/watttextbook2e/) accompanies this book, featuring web links to statutes, cases, academic articles and other resources that complement the paper text. The Online Resource Centre also includes regular legal updates and answers to the Summative Assessment Exercises found at the end of the book chapters.

Chapter Objectives

Each chapter opens with a set of objectives to help students identify the areas they should understand by the end of the chapter

Question boxes ?

Questions are included throughout the text to encourage students to engage critically with the issues discussed. They also provide a useful means for students to test their knowledge while reading the chapter or during the revision process.

Exercises

Exercises are included throughout the text for students to test their understanding of the issues raised by key cases, and to encourage deeper reading and analysis of cases.

Key Extracts from Cases and Materials

Extracts from key cases and materials are included in boxes throughout the text to illustrate and reinforce key principles.

Chapter Summaries

Each chapter ends with a summary of the main issues discussed in the chapter. This is not intended as a substitute for reading the chapter, but rather as a section to refresh the student's memory on the key issues discussed.

Further Reading

Sources recommended in the text for additional reading assist the student to understand the important issues, and encourage a broader knowledge of the subject.

Summative Assessment Exercises

Each chapter ends with a 'Summative Assessment Exercise' that asks a question or sets up a scenario for students to assess and answer using the knowledge gained through reading the chapter. Full specimen answers to the Summative Assessment Exercises can be found on the Online Resource Centre (www.oxfordtextbooks.co.uk/orc/watttextbook2e/).

Glossary

A glossary ensures students are able to understand the terminology specific to trusts law.

Updates

Updates to the text can be found on the Online Resource Centre (www.oxfordtextbooks.co.uk/orc/watttextbook2e/). This indispensable resource allows students to access changes in the law that have occurred since publication of the book: students can keep up to date with new developments without buying a new book. Updates are available in pdf format, so can be printed for easy reference.

Web links

Annotated web links can be found on the Online Resource Centre (www.oxfordtextbooks.co.uk/orc/watttextbook2e/). The web links help students to research topics of particular interest and are checked regularly to ensure they remain up to date and relevant.

1 Introduction to equity and trusts

OBJECTIVES

By the end of this chapter you should understand:

1 The historical development of equity

2 The theoretical and functional distinction between equity and the common law

3 The maxims and doctrines of equity and their correct usage

4 The distinction between the remedial and institutional roles of equity

5 The place of equity in the modern world and its possible future development

1.1 Introduction

As you come to study this subject, you should already be aware that English law is based on case law and precedent to a greater extent than the code-based law of Germany, France and other European states. English law is said to be a common law system. Where the law is code-based there is said to be a civil law system. However, within our common law system the term 'common law' is given at least two other meanings. The first contrasts common law (that is, case law) with statutory law. The second contrasts common law (the law of crime, contract, tort, etc whether it takes the form of statute or case law—the latter originating largely from the court of the King's Bench) with equity.

This terminology is inevitably a little misleading, for we will see that equity is not so much a separate branch of law as a distinctive feature of all law. Wherever any right or power exists at common law (in the latter sense of that term), the role of equity is to restrain the exercise of the right and to keep the power in check. In this way, even the most complete form of ownership acknowledged at law, that of legal title to a fee simple absolute in possession, may be subject to another's equitable claim. Thus if the legal owner of the fee simple title to land invites a stranger to build a house upon it, having raised in that stranger a legitimate expectation that he will thereby acquire a beneficial interest in the land, and the stranger duly builds the house, equity restrains the legal owner from asserting absolute ownership against him (see 17.4).

Probably the single most important creature of equity is the trust. If title to any property is vested in a person as trustee for another, equity not only restrains the trustee from denying his trust and setting himself up as absolute owner, but imposes upon the trustee positive duties of good faith towards the other person (see **Chapters 11** and **12**).

However, equity should not be confused with morality. Equity is singularly uncritical of a vast range of social behaviour which might be regarded as immoral. Rather, equity confines itself to the restraint of unconscionable abuse of legal power and unconscionable assertion of legal title. Yet, even in that role, equity does not recognize every sharp, harsh or unkind assertion of legal title to be unconscionable. On the contrary, equity appears sometimes to encourage sharp practice. 'Gazumping' (see 1.3.1.1) and investing in ethically unsound companies (see 14.2) are sometimes imperative where such a course is likely better to serve the financial interest of the beneficiaries of the trust. Equity is not concerned to effect the just distribution of social resources. If 99 per cent of all wealth were in the hands of one per cent of the population this would be a great social inequality, but equity would have nothing to say on the matter. Again, to some extent the opposite is true, for it sanctions the use of trusts by the wealthy as a tax planning device, and even varies trusts to enable them to keep apace with fiscal changes. In short, equity fulfils the common law. It does not attempt to supplant it with a moral code.

It is sometimes said that equity operates as a 'gloss' on the common law. Equity is not, however, a mere 'gloss', for it looks to substance rather than form, enabling it to give effect to the true intentions of parties to a transaction where the strict legal position does not reflect those intentions (see 1.4.3).

1.2 The historical development of equity and trusts

For the student, an appreciation of the historical development of equity and trusts is crucial to a true understanding of the law as it currently is. What is more, the rational future development of the law depends upon an understanding of its origins. We will see through the course of this chapter that the future development of equity and trusts is very much a live issue.

1.2.1 The historical development of equity

The history of equity is characterized by its continual ebb and flow between compatibility and competition with the common law.

1.2.1.1 Medieval equity and the sixteenth century

In the twelfth century the royal court was largely itinerant. The itinerary of Henry I, for instance, took him as far afield as Carlisle, Norwich, Southampton and Normandy, all within the years 1119–23, whilst still allowing time to campaign war in Wales. Incidentally, the so-called 'White Ship disaster' occurred in the English Channel in 1120, killing Henry's two sons and many of the 'aristocracy' of the day (it was the twelfth century equivalent to the sinking of the *Titanic*). Effective government required that the King and his courtiers travelled the length and breadth of the realm collecting taxes, dispensing justice and generally asserting royal authority. One of the chief courtiers was the King's Chancellor, a learned cleric (usually a bishop), who would advise the King and his Council. The Chancellor was keeper of the King's Great Seal, and beneath him were the Chancery scribes who were responsible for the King's paperwork (or parchment work as it was then). These manuscripts of early Chancery proceedings were important not only for their influence in establishing coherence in the law, but for standardizing the English language, where previously there had been great regional variation. It can in fact be argued that '[t]he genealogy of modern Standard English goes back to Chancery, not Chaucer' (David Crystal, *The Cambridge Encyclopedia of the English Language*, CUP, 1995, p 41). Most other written material of the time was in Latin.

By the early fourteenth century the King's common law was fairly well established and where it caused injustice in individual cases, with consequent embarrassment to the King's conscience, the task of providing a just remedy fell to the Chancellor. By the end of that century the Chancellor was dispensing justice on his own authority from his base in Westminster, his concern being still to remedy the rigid common law position on grounds of conscience. The petitions to the Chancellor grew in number throughout the fifteenth century and the Court of Chancery, the Chancellor's court, grew. Nevertheless, Chancery was intimately involved with the common law throughout the period of its early development. Indeed, the medieval Chancellor as keeper of the King's seal was responsible for framing and issuing the writs upon which actions in the common law courts were commenced.

Competition with the common law followed, as throughout the sixteenth century increasing numbers of petitions were brought to remedy the harshness of the common law. Common law suits were at that time subject to technical and inflexible forms of action, with the result that a just cause might fail due to the lack of some formality. Chancery's ad hoc dispensation of justice in individual cases in the sixteenth century led Selden to suggest, famously, that for a time equity varied according to the size of the Chancellor's foot.

A similar observation led Lambarde, a sixteenth century Chancery lawyer, to muse:

> Whether it be meet that the Chancellor should appoint unto himselfe, and publish to others any certaine Rules & Limits of Equity, or no; about the which men both godly and learned doe varie in opinion: For on the one part it is thought as hard a thing to prescribe to Equitie any certaine bounds, as it is to make one generall Law to be a meet measure of Justice in all particular cases.

(Quoted in S F C Milsom, *Historical Foundations of the Common Law*, 2nd edn, London, 1981, p 94).

1.2.1.2 The emergence of modern equity

The competition between Chancery and the common law courts came to a head in the early seventeenth century with the *Earl of Oxford's Case*, reported at (1615) 1 Rep Ch 1. Chief Justice Coke had indicted a defendant in a common law action who had deigned to apply to Lord Chancellor Ellesmere for an injunction against a common law judgment on the grounds of fraud. Lord Ellesmere's response was to reason that such an injunction did not offend the common law courts at all, that it was effective merely *in personam* against the person who had been successful in the common law court: 'The office of the chancellor is to correct men's consciences for frauds, breaches of trust, wrongs and oppressions of what nature soever they be, and to soften and mollify the extremity of the law'. So 'soft and mollifying' was the effect of Chancery that if a person breached a Chancery injunction by enforcing his common law judgment, Chancery could imprison him for contempt! (Something similar still occurs today—in one recent case a fraudster was imprisoned for two years for breaching an equitable injunction that had frozen his assets (*Shalson v Russo* [2003] EWHC 1637 (Ch).)

In the end, the dispute between the Chief Justice and the Lord Chancellor was referred, in 1616, to King James I. The King resolved the dispute in favour of Lord Ellesmere, on the advice of his Attorney-General, Sir Francis Bacon. (Bacon went on, in fact, to succeed Lord Ellesmere as Chancellor.) So, Chancery, like so many other great institutions can trace its independence to a clash of political personalities!

In the eighteenth century equity matured like a good wine through the careful Chancellorship of, amongst others, Heneage Finch, Lord Nottingham, who has rightly been called the father of modern equity (Holdsworth, *History of English Law*, vi, p 547). The doctrine of clogs on the equity of redemption, which enables borrowers to redeem their mortgaged land, and the modern rule against perpetuities (see 6.3) find their source in his judgments and decrees. During the eighteenth century equity developed in a manner supplemental to the common law, rather than in competition with it. Chancery appears to have been a beneficiary of the so-called 'Enlightenment' philosophy which emerged in that century.

Somewhat a victim of its own success, by the early nineteenth century the Court of Chancery had become hopelessly busy, despite the appointment in 1729 of the chief Chancery Master, the Master of the Rolls, to sit as a second judge. In 1813 a Vice-Chancellor was appointed. There were now three judges presiding in Chancery, where once there had been the Chancellor alone. Yet the first Vice-Chancellor, upon being asked whether the three judges could cope, is said to have replied 'No; not three angels'.

***Bleak House*, 1852–1853, Charles Dickens**

Chapter 1 — In Chancery

. . . Fog everywhere. Fog up the river, where it flows among green aits and meadows; fog down the river, where it rolls defiled among the tiers of shipping and the waterside pollutions of a great (and dirty) city. Fog on the Essex marshes, fog on the Kentish heights. Fog creeping into the cabooses of collier-brigs; fog lying out on the yards, and hovering in the rigging of great ships; fog drooping on the gunwales of barges and small boats. Fog in the eyes and throats of ancient Greenwich pensioners, wheezing by the firesides of their wards; fog in the stem and bowl of the afternoon pipe of the wrathful skipper, down in his close cabin; fog cruelly pinching the toes and fingers of his shivering little 'prentice boy on deck. Chance people on the bridges peeping over the parapets into a nether sky of fog, with fog all round them, as if they were up in a balloon, and hanging in the misty clouds.

Gas looming through the fog in divers places in the streets, much as the sun may, from the spongey fields, be seen to loom by husbandman and ploughboy. Most of the shops lighted two hours before their time — as the gas seems to know, for it has a haggard and unwilling look.

The raw afternoon is rawest, and the dense fog is densest, and the muddy streets are muddiest near that leaden-headed old obstruction, appropriate ornament for the threshold of a leaden-headed old corporation, Temple Bar. And hard by Temple Bar, in Lincoln's Inn Hall, at the very heart of the fog, sits the Lord High Chancellor in his High Court of Chancery.

Never can there come fog too thick, never can there come mud and mire too deep, to assort with the groping and floundering condition which this High Court of Chancery, most pestilent of hoary sinners, holds this day in the sight of heaven and earth.

1.2.1.3 The procedural reforms of the nineteenth century

The Court of Chancery Act 1850 and the Court of Chancery Procedure Act 1852 were early attempts to wrestle with the procedural problems in the Court of Chancery. But the great step towards expediting the procedure of Chancery came when Lord Chancellor Selborne introduced the Judicature Act 1873 into Parliament. Ironically, it was due to administrative delays that the statute did not in fact come into force until 1875, when it was re-enacted with amendments. We now refer collectively to the Judicature Acts 1873–1875. By these enactments the Supreme Court of Judicature was established with concurrent jurisdiction to administer the rules of equity and law within a uniform procedural code.

Section 34 of the Judicature Act 1873 assigned the following matters to the new 'Chancery Division' of the Supreme Court:

- the execution of trusts
- administration of the estates of deceased persons
- the dissolution of partnerships and taking of partnership accounts
- the redemption or foreclosure of mortgages
- the raising of portions or other charges on land
- sale and distribution of proceeds of property subject to a lien or charge
- the rectification or setting aside or cancellation of written instruments
- the specific performance of contracts for real estate, including leases
- the partition or sale of real estates
- the wardship of infants and the care of infants' property

1.2.1.4 Equity in the twentieth century

In addition to this list, the Chancery Division of the High Court now has jurisdiction arising out of the wide-ranging 1925 scheme of property legislation (Law of Property Act 1925, Trustee Act 1925, Settled Land Act 1925, etc) and numerous other statutes, many of which we will be considering in detail throughout the remainder of this textbook.

And, of course, in addition to matters expressly assigned to Chancery, it should not be forgotten that, long before the Judicature Acts of 1873–1875, Chancery had a concurrent jurisdiction to award equitable remedies in response to actions of an essentially common law nature. Hence the decree of *specific performance* of contracts (see 1.3.4.1).

It is of vital importance to realize that the Judicature Acts did not do away with the distinction between law and equity. On the contrary, the 1925 property legislation is largely based on the ongoing fundamental distinction between legal and equitable title. But this is to take equity in its formal sense. Equity at its highest should be a feature of *all* law, whether it be in the Chancery Division or any other division of the High Court. In this vein Professor J H Baker has said of the post-Judicature Acts legal landscape:

> If, for reasons of history, equity had become the law peculiar to the Court of Chancery, nevertheless in broad theory equity was an approach to justice which gave more weight than did the law to particular circumstances and hard cases. The abolition of the historical, procedural distinction gave new emphasis to this broad view of equity . . . [today] . . . Chancery judges are the least likely to administer equity in the broad sense, because the type of work they do demands as much certainty as clear

> rules can provide. The Queen's Bench judges, on the other hand, are more given to the equitable approach, having inherited it from the jury. Paradoxically, as the equity of the Chancery has hardened into law, so the law has been dissolving into something like abstract equity . . .

One reason that the work of the modern Chancery Division is so dependent on certainty is that the majority of the business of the Chancery Division is now commercial in nature. Indeed, one of its leading judges has commented extrajudicially that 'a case concerning an express trust is something of a rarity nowadays' (Sir Peter Millett, 'Equity—the road ahead' (1995) 9 TLI 35 at 36).

1.2.1.5 The certainty–justice debate

It is often said that the development of law is characterized by the ongoing search for a balance between justice and certainty. Or to be more precise, a balance between justice in the individual case and that justice for the civilian population at large which flows from certainty in the law. We noted above that in the sixteenth century the Chancery was a fount of ad hoc justice, leading to the complaint that equity varied according to the length of the Chancellor's foot. The gradual move away from such ad hoc justice towards certainty led Bagnall J to suggest in *Cowcher v Cowcher* [1972] 1 WLR 425 at 431 that in modern times '[i]n the field of equity the Chancellor's foot has been measured or is capable of measurement'. He was careful to add, however, that '[t]his does not mean that equity is past child-bearing; simply that its progeny must be legitimate—by precedent out of principle'. Some few years later Browne-Wilkinson J expressed a similar view: 'Doing justice to the litigant who actually appears in court by the invention of new principles of law ought not to involve injustice to the other persons who are not litigants . . . but whose rights are fundamentally affected by the new principles' (*Re Sharpe* (a bankrupt) [1980] 1 WLR 219 at 227).

In modern times equity is alive and well, and as well at home in the King's Bench Division as in the Chancery Division. Wherever the rigours or limitations of the law create injustice in the individual case, equity will seek to provide a remedy. In doing so equity is always cautious to base its invention on established principle, and is mindful always that the best equity should have no detrimental effect upon innocent third parties and the population at large.

1.2.2 The historical development of the trust

The progenitor of the *trust* was the *use*. As early as the seventh and eighth centuries the common law had a form of *use* in relation to chattels and money, whereby money had and received by A for the use of B subjected A to common law obligations as to the use of the money had and received. If A refused to account to B, B could bring an action to account, an action which came to resemble something like an action for breach of trust (*Taillour v Medwe* (1320) *Year Books of Edward II, 14 Edward II* (Selden Society vol 104) (London 1988) p 39 and xi). This common law trust for the payment of money was enforced long before Chancery recognized trusts of land.

However, it was in relation to land that 'The use simply could not be fitted into the common law scheme of things, for the doctrine of estates and the doctrine of seisin left no place for the separation of beneficial enjoyment from legal title' (AWB Simpson, *An Introduction to the History of the Land Law* (Oxford: OUP, 1961) pp 164–5).

The *use* of land has existed since at least the early thirteenth century, and became an important device during the crusades. So, for example, when Guille de Pends left for battle he might well have left title to his landed estate in the name of a trusted friend, to be held for the use and benefit of Guille's family during his absence. The use might have read: 'I convey all my lands to Richard de Livers for the use of Lady de Pends and her children'. Nevertheless, the use of land, though recognized by Chancery, differed from the trust of land in one important respect, as Professor Simpson (*op cit* at p 170) has said:

> The use had originated as a personal confidence or trust placed by one person in the other, and even when a use became a species of property it continued to bear marks of this origin. Thus it never came to bind the land itself; rather, it was conceived to bind the conscience of persons into whose hands the land came.

In 1535, Henry VIII pushed through the Statute of Uses with a view to abolishing uses of land, the effect of the use having been to encumber the Crown's legal feudal entitlements (revenue-raising powers flowing from the Crown's status as legal 'Landlord') with equitable claims. The effect of the Statute of Uses was to transfer legal title (seisin and estate) to the person with the equitable claim, thus bringing the use to an end.

However, by the time of, and partly as a result of, the enactment of the Tenures Abolition Act of 1660, the economic imperatives underlying the Statute of Uses were no longer of importance. Simpson records (at pp 187–8) that:

> This was bound to have an effect upon its treatment by the courts. Very probably it accelerated the rise of the passive trust, which is the most notable of all the evasions of that ill-used Statute. By about 1700 it had become possible to create trusts which apparently differed only in name from uses, but which were not executed by the Statute. Such trusts were enforced in Chancery just as uses had been before 1535, so that the separation of legal and equitable ownership was again possible. Such trusts were created by a conveyance 'to A, unto and to the use of A, in trust for B', and by adopting this simple variant on the formula 'to A to the use of B' a conveyancer was allowed to create equitable estates just as he had been before the Statute.

The trust was not, however, a mere replication of the old use under a new name. Crucially, the trust did not have to be established *in personam* against every person into whose hands it came, rather the trust bound the land itself. In the Court of Chancery the *bona fide* purchaser for valuable consideration of legal title to the land would take free of the trust, and only then if he had purchased without notice of the trust (*per* James LJ in *Pilcher v Rawlins* (1872) 7 Ch App 259, 268–9). This person was known, accordingly, as 'Equity's Darling', and is sometimes still referred to as such today (see, for example, *Griggs Group Ltd v Evans* [2005] FSR 31; [2005] EWCA (Civ) 11 Court of Appeal, *per* Jacob LJ at para 7). Jeffrey Hackney (in *Understanding Equity and Trusts*, Fontana, 1987) has suggested that the Court of Chancery afforded this person special status because it had no *jurisdiction* to question the legal title of such a person. In other words, he suggests that equity's darling is in truth the darling of the common law.

In any event, the situation had been reached whereby the Court of Chancery acknowledged the existence of a separate equitable title under a trust which the equitable (beneficial) owner could enforce against the legal owner against whom the equitable right had been established (the trustee), and against third parties who acquired the legal title with notice of the equitable interest binding upon it. Where Chancery recognized two or more parties as having competing equitable claims of equal merit, the Chancery judge would apply the maxim *qui prior tempore est potior est jure*, giving priority to whichever claim came first in time (see 1.4.10, below).

The court's approach to disputes between legal owners and equitable owners and disputes between equitable owners *inter se* was neatly summarized in *Liverpool Marine Credit Co v Wilson* (1872) 7 Ch App 507 at 511: 'The legal owner's right is paramount to every equitable charge not affecting his own conscience; the equitable owner, in the absence of special circumstances, takes subject to all equities prior in date to his own estate or charge'.

Through this scheme of priority to claims in land, having its roots in the doctrine of notice and the equitable maxim *qui prior tempore est potior est jure*, Chancery created a law of property where previously there had existed only the common law concept of formal title. In the eighteenth and nineteenth centuries the trust was used extensively in relation to land to effect settlements according to which land could be kept within families for generation after generation. Changes in social attitudes, not to mention fiscal considerations and the onset of systemic inflation, have seen a dramatic decline in the use of trusts for this purpose. However, it is because of equity's willingness to acknowledge property behind legal title, that trusts, despite their origins as medieval land obligations, are nowadays asserted with regularity in modern commercial contexts and in particular in the context of insolvency. As Sir Peter Millett has said extrajudicially: 'It can no longer be doubted that equity has moved out of the family home and the settled estate and into the market place' ('Equity—the road ahead' (1995) 9 TLI 35 at 36). To this we now turn.

1.2.3 Equity and trusts in modern commercial contexts

In 1995 in *Royal Brunei Airlines v Tan* [1995] 3 WLR 64 (see 19.6), Lord Nicholls of Birkenhead observed that '[t]he proper role of equity in commercial transactions is a topical question'. It is, of course, but it is also a rather old one.

In 1927 Atkin LJ criticized the introduction of equitable principles into commercial sale of goods transactions as a migration 'into territory where they are trespassers' (*Re Wait* [1927] 1 Ch 606 at 635). Against this Sir Peter Millett has suggested (*op cit* 1.2.2 at 36) that '[t]he intervention of equity in commercial transactions, long resisted by common lawyers, can no longer be withstood'. On both sides of the modern debate there is an implicit assumption that the intervention of equity in the field of commerce is something of a new development. In fact, equity has always exercised a right of way through that particular field. Professor Baker observed in *An Introduction to English Legal History*, 3rd edn, 1990 (pp 119–21), that, throughout the fifteenth century, tort and commercial cases featured as prominently in Chancery as property disputes. He records that 'the typical petition complained of weakness or poverty or the abuse of position by an opponent'. It is interesting that some of the leading modern cases in which equitable principles have been developed still involve precisely the same kinds of plea. See, for instance, *O'Sullivan v MAM* [1985] QB 428 (12.2.1.2) where a pop star was granted equitable rescission of an unfavourable contract he had signed as a young and inexperienced artist when subject to the undue influence of his manager.

? QUESTION 1.1

Can you think of any reason why commercial purchasers of legal title should not be burdened with equitable interests of which they have notice?

If notice meant 'actual notice' there could hardly be any objection. But equity has long taken the view that notice includes matters that would have been revealed by reasonable inquiry, thus the purchaser of land will have 'constructive notice' of equitable interests he ought to have discovered (*Hunt v Luck* [1902] 1 Ch 428). Against the introduction of the equitable doctrine of constructive notice into commerce, Lindley LJ had this to say: 'In dealing with estates in land title is everything, and it can be leisurely investigated; in commercial transactions possession is everything, and there is no time to investigate title; if we were to extend the doctrine of constructive notice to commercial transactions we should be doing infinite mischief and paralyzing the trade of the country' (*Manchester Trust v Furness* [1895] 2 QB 539, 545). Of course, what Lindley LJ omitted to acknowledge is that land can also be an article of commerce.

As for the introduction of *trusts* into commerce, Bramwell LJ was as cautious as his learned brother Lindley LJ, and for much the same reasons: 'Now I do not desire to find fault with the various intricacies and doctrines concerned with trusts, but I should be very sorry to see them introduced into commercial transactions, and an agent in a commercial case turned into a trustee with all the troubles that attend that relation' (*New Zealand & Australian Land Co v Watson* (1881) 7 QBD 374, 382). We shall see in **Chapter 19** that commercial agents such as banks, solicitors, directors, etc can indeed be turned into trustees, or at the very least treated as if they were trustees, but there is no doubt a reluctance even today to extend equitable regulation into that sphere.

1.3 Equity and the common law

The history of the relationship between Chancery and the common law courts tends to highlight the *procedural* differences between the two systems of law. Since the Judicature Acts (see 1.2.1.3) those procedural distinctions have largely been done away with. Nevertheless, there still remain two distinct systems of law which seek to achieve different ends by different means, but at the hands of a single judge.

Sir Anthony Mason, 'The Place of Equity and Equitable Remedies in the Contemporary Common Law World' (1994) 110 LQR 238, 239.

Equity has yielded to the common law some ground that conceivably it might have claimed for itself. The boundless expansion of the tort of negligence, based on the existence of a duty of care to one's neighbour has, in all probability, stultified the development of equitable compensation for breach of fiduciary and other equitable obligations. Equitable compensation, of which I shall have more to say, is now coming to the fore but its long sleep since 1875 or, more accurately, 1914 (when *Nocton v Lord Ashburton* [1914] AC 932 was decided) may be attributed to the rise of negligence and the extended notion of the duty of care.

What are the reasons for the onward march of equity after the physicians had pronounced it incapable of childbirth? They are, I think, many and varied, some of them not being of general application. Two can readily be identified. First, there were the Judicature Act 1873 (UK) and its counterparts in other jurisdictions ('the Judicature Acts'). By providing for the administration of the two systems of law by the one system of courts and by prescribing the paramountcy of equity, the Judicature Acts freed equity from its position on the coat-tails of the common law and positioned it for advances beyond its old frontiers. Secondly, the ecclesiastical natural law foundations of equity, its concern with standards of conscience, fairness, equality and its protection of relation-ships of trust and confidence, as well as its discretionary approach to the grant of relief, stand in marked contrast to the more rigid formulae applied by the common law and equip it better to meet the needs of the type of liberal democratic society which has evolved in the twentieth century.

It is remarkable that the common law has remained for so long impervious to the beguiling charms of equity. More than 100 years elapsed after the introduction of the original Judicature Act before lawyers became receptive to the notion, still regarded as heretical by some Australian commentators, that equity and common law are capable of constituting together a single body of law rather than two separate bodies of law administered together.

? QUESTION 1.2

In the passage set out above, Sir Anthony Mason suggests that the neighbourhood principle in the tort of negligence might conceivably have been developed in equity rather than in the tort of negligence. Do you think this is right, bearing in mind the way that equity operated historically in relation to the common law?

The present writer would respectfully suggest that it is not. The neighbourhood principle in the tort of negligence prescribes a standard of care for the civilian population generally. Breach of that duty of care does not depend upon any pre-existing legal relationship between the claimant and the defendant to the negligence suit. In contrast, equity does not prescribe and never has prescribed minimum standards of civilian behaviour, let alone suggested a paradigm. In equity there is no gold standard of conscientious conduct equivalent to the objective opinion of the reasonable man in tort, the so-called 'man on the Clapham omnibus'. Equity does not concern itself with civil conduct generally, but only with conduct in relation to pre-existing legal rights, powers and duties. In short, there never is equity without law. As the maxim tells us, 'equity follows the law' (see 1.4.2).

Even where equity recognizes equitable property rights which bind the world at large (or, to be precise, the whole world with the exception of the so-called 'equity's darling' or 'bona fide purchaser of a legal interest without notice of the equitable property right' (see 1.2.2)), the equitable right has no existence independent of the common law. Consider, for example, a binding contract to purchase land (which is the equitable interest known as an 'estate contract'). It exists only because the legal owner who agreed to assign or grant the lease is bound in equity to hold his legal title in keeping with his promise. Another example is the trust itself, for example, a trust of land. The equitable beneficial interest under such a trust could not exist without same ultimate legal title to the land.

Sir Anthony Mason would, however, disagree with this 'dependent' representation of equity. He suggests that 'by providing for the administration of the two systems of law by the one system of courts and by prescribing the paramountcy of equity, the Judicature Acts freed equity from its position on the coat-tails of the common law and positioned it for advances beyond its old frontiers' ('The Place of Equity and Equitable Remedies in the Contemporary Common Law World' (1994) 110 LQR 238 at 239).

The problem with this larger view of the equitable jurisdiction, it is submitted, is that equity can too easily become confused with the quite distinct concept of morality. This is a distinction which the next section seeks to clarify.

1.3.1 Equity, common law and morality

It should be clear from the preceding discussion that equity is most certainly a branch of law and not a branch of morality. However, largely due to its ecclesiastical origins and the consequent concern for conscience, it is a branch of law that has a moral flavour not so evident in the common law (although Sir Peter Millett opined in *Trustee of the Property of FC Jones and sons (a Firm) v Jones* [1997] Ch 159 that it would 'be a mistake to suppose that the common law courts disregarded considerations of conscience'). Just one example of equity's concern with matters of conscience is the requirement that, in relation to investment, trustees should 'take such care as an ordinary prudent person would take who was minded to invest for the benefit of another for whom he felt *morally* obliged to provide' (*emphasis added*) (*per* Lindley LJ in *Re Whiteley*, see 11.3).

1.3.1.1 The limits of equitable 'morality'

Equitable morality is limited to the restraint of unconscionability in legal contexts

Equity will not enforce a bare moral promise (*Taylor v Dickens* [1998] 1 FLR 806, see also, 17.4). In fact, equity will sometimes encourage a trustee to break a non-legal promise ('gentlemen's agreement'), if to do so would be in the best financial interest of beneficiaries (*Buttle v Saunders* [1950] 2 All ER 193). How can this be reconciled with the fact that equity, being unable to countenance the breaking of a promise made in a *legal* contract will enforce the contract according to the maxim that *equity sees as done that which ought to be done* (see 1.4.8)? The answer is that equity is not concerned with moral conduct generally, but only with the moral exercise of *legal* power or position. A great deal of immoral conduct is prohibited neither in law nor equity. In fact, despite the ecclesiastical origins of equity, only three of the Ten Commandments (see Exodus chapter 20) are to be found today in English law, and even then in limited form. Equity cannot even claim the three survivors. 'Do not steal', 'do not kill' and 'do not accuse falsely' are to be found in the *common law*: as theft, homicide and perjury!

? QUESTION 1.3

Some years ago the late Diana, Princess of Wales, was secretly photographed while exercising in a gymnasium. She was photographed by the gym owner, whose guest she was, and the resulting images were sold by him to the tabloid press, allegedly earning him a small fortune. Legal proceedings against him were threatened, but never came to court. Do you think that equity would have required him to disgorge his ill-gotten gains?

In a court of morality there can be little doubt that the photographer would have been called to account for the proceeds of sale of the photographs. At common law, however, there was no cause of action against him. The Princess had been his guest, there had been no contract between them into which terms could be implied. What is more, there is no such thing in English law as a general tort of infringement of privacy (although, now that the Human Rights Act 1998 is in force, equivalent protection might ensue). In short, there was no legal relationship between the photographer and the Princess. Regardless of the lack of a relationship might it be said that the photographer had been unjustly enriched, and that the Princess should have had a cause of action on that basis alone? *Unfairly* enriched he may have been, but *unjustly* enriched in a legal sense, no. English law has only relatively recently acknowledged that A has a cause of action against B where B was unjustly enriched *at A's financial expense* (*Lipkin Gorman v Karpnale Ltd* [1991] 3 WLR 10). It is probably still some way off from acknowledging that enrichment may be unjust merely because it was acquired at the expense of someone else's privacy or reputation.

? QUESTION 1.4

Do you think it would it be right, in the view of such common law restraint, for equity to assume to regulate this type of wrong?

If the wrong committed through photographing the Princess had fallen into an accidental or technical lacuna in the common law, equity might legitimately have filled the hole as part of its 'supplemental' or 'concurrent' jurisdiction, to give effect to, and make sense of, the common law rules. The problem in this case is that the lack of a remedy was no mere oversight or imperfection within the scheme of legal regulation, the problem was that the wrong lay *beyond* the present boundaries of legal regulation. Equity is not the solution to the wrong in this type of case. Accordingly, the recent development of the equitable idea of 'breach of confidence' to fill this particular lacuna (see, for instance, the celebrated case of *Douglas and others v Hello! Ltd* [2001] QB 967, CA) is a situation in which equity (or at least the language of equity) has been inappropriately employed to perform a common law function. Indeed, the House of Lords has recently acknowledged that the equitable label 'breach of confidence' is inappropriate in this context. Lord Nicholls suggests that '[t]he essence of the tort is better encapsulated now as misuse of private information' (*Campbell v MGN Ltd* [2004] 2 AC 457, House of Lords, at paras 13–14). Although that message appears to have been overlooked in a recent appeal in the *Douglas v Hello* litigation (*Douglas and others v Hello! Limited and others* [2005] EWCA Civ 595, CA).

The question is whether equity, which has traditionally followed the common law, should go ahead of it, extending its boundaries. If we conclude that it should, there is a danger that we will have elevated equity to the status of free-standing moral guardian of society. The problem with this approach lies in choosing *whose* morality should hold sway. We might find ourselves thrown back to a time when justice varied according to the length of the judge's foot.

Equity is morally ambiguous because it is selective in its recognition of unconscionable behaviour as between different legal contexts

Sometimes commercial sharp practice goes unchecked by equity, even if oppressive, and even if advantage has been taken of a legal entitlement. So, for example, in *Liverpool Marine Credit Co v Hunter* (1867–68) 3 Ch App 479 the defendants, the owners of a ship subject to a mortgage, deliberately sent the ship to be sold in Louisiana, knowing that Louisiana did not recognize mortgages of ships. The claimant argued that the defendant had committed a positive fraud. The judge held (at 487) that the defendant owed no duty of care to the claimant: 'I do not . . . see how Equity could properly interfere to restrain the actions which, however oppressive . . . arose out of remedies employed by the plaintiff for the recovery of his debt, of which the law entitled him to avail himself'.

The fact must be faced that equity's scrutiny of conscince varies dramatically according to the context in which legal powers are exercised and duties discharged. In *Barnes v Addy* (1874) 9 Ch App 244, a case of alleged accessory liability against an agent who had acted for a trustee who had breached his trust, Lord Selborne said that 'strangers are not to be made constructive trustees merely because they act as the agents of trustees in transactions within their legal powers, *transactions, perhaps of which a Court of Equity may disapprove*' (emphasis added). He then went on to describe exceptional cases in which such agents would be liable (see **Chapter 19** to discover what they were).

When the same issues arose for consideration in the Privy Council in *Royal Brunei v Tan* [1995] 3 WLR 64 Lord Nicholls stated that:

> Unconscionable is a word of immediate appeal to an equity lawyer. Equity is rooted historically in the concept of the Lord Chancellor, as the keeper of the royal conscience, concerning himself with conduct which was contrary to good conscience. It must be recognised, however, that unconscionable is not a word in everyday use by non-lawyers. If it is to be used in this context, and if it is to be the touchstone for liability as an accessory, it is essential to be clear on what, in this context, unconscionable means.

1.3.2 The dualism/fusion debate

From the earliest times there was 'plenty of equity in the common law' (Radcliffe and Cross, *The English Legal System*, 3rd edn, 1954 at p 116), and where equity has petrified to the extent that it recognizes *rights* (that is, entitlements that do not depend upon the exercise of the court's discretion), for example, rights under express trusts, it may be fair to say that equity operates as if it were common law.

Nevertheless, the judicial and academic fracas still persists between the entrenched battle lines of dualism and fusion. Professor Ashburner set out the dualist position in his *Principles of Equity* (2nd edn, 1933), where he famously described the common law and equity as two streams of jurisdiction which 'though they run in the same channel run side by side and do not mingle their waters'. Regardless of the substantial merits of his analysis, Professor Ashburner's metaphor is not a particularly helpful one. The picture of two streams running in the same channel without mingling is a hard one to imagine. Half a century later, Lord Diplock took the metaphor to its logical conclusion when he stated, *obiter*, that 'it may be possible for a short distance to discern the source from which each part of the combined stream came, but . . . the waters of the confluent streams of law and equity have surely mingled now' (*United Scientific Holdings Ltd v Burnley Borough Council* [1978] AC 904 at 924–5).

The dualists took up arms again when Meagher, Gummow and Lehane, authors of the leading Australian textbook, *Equity, Doctrines and Remedies*, described their Lordships' decision in *United Scientific* as 'the low water mark of modern English jurisprudence' (2nd edn, 1984 at xi). To which Professor Peter Birks gave the following characteristically quotable response (*Civil Wrongs: A New World*, The Butterworth Lectures 1990–91, p 55):

> It is dangerous, not to say absurd, almost 120 years after the Judicature Acts, to persist in habits of thought calculated to submerge and conceal one or other half of our law . . . Meagher, Gummow and Lehane . . . did not attempt to say why the properties and dispositions of equity, which they rightly admire, should be confined to something less than the whole law. They did not attempt it because it cannot be done, any more than the courts might justify themselves in doing alpha justice on Mondays and Tuesdays and something less for the rest of the week.

In *Elders Pastoral Ltd v Bank of New Zealand* [1989] 2 NZLR 180 at 193, Somer J provided a more conciliatory summary of the current relationship between law and equity. It is a summary that nowadays finds approval in most quarters:

> Neither law nor equity is now stifled by its origin and the fact that both are administered by one Court has inevitably meant that each has borrowed from the other in furthering the harmonious development of the law as a whole.

1.3.3 Concurrent rights in equity and common law

The case of *Walsh v Lonsdale* (1882) 21 Ch D 9 addressed some interesting issues of relevance to this section. The facts were that a landlord and tenant had entered into a contract for a seven-year lease, the tenant had gone into possession, but the parties had forgotten to execute the formal deed needed for a valid legal lease. Despite the absence of the deed, the landlord claimed rent in advance in accordance with the contract and attempted to enforce his claim by exercising the *legal* right to distress for rent (which is the right to take and sell the tenants' goods *in lieu* of rent). The tenant claimed that in the absence of a *legal* deed there could be no *legal* right to claim rent in advance, and that rent should be payable in arrear, so he sought an injunction against the distress.

Sir George Jessel MR, one of the leading equity judges of all time, stated (at pp 14–15) that: 'There are not two estates as there were formerly . . . There is only one Court, and the equity rules prevail in it. The tenant holds under an agreement for a lease. He holds, therefore, under the same terms in equity as if a lease had been granted'. Ironically, the *tenant* had sought the aid of equity (in the form of an injunction), but the *landlord* actually received it (in the form of an equitable lease). Paradoxically, the landlord was permitted to exercise the traditionally *legal* right to levy distress for rent against the tenant of an *equitable* lease. Sir George based his judgment on the maxim that *equity sees as done that which ought to be done* (see 1.4.8).

For the purposes of our present inquiry, a strange result flows from the decision in *Walsh v Lonsdale*. The Law of Property Act 1925, s 54 provides that a lease for a term of not more than three years will usually be a valid *legal* lease without the need for any written formality at all. Included in this class of informal leases are periodic tenancies (for example, weekly, monthly or yearly tenancies, the period being determined by the period according to which rent is calculated).

? QUESTION 1.5

Suppose that a landlord had *contracted* to grant a tenant a 10-year lease at £300 per year, and that the tenant had taken possession of the leasehold premises. What right or rights would the tenant have in the land?

The answer is that the tenant would have a 10-*year lease in equity and* a concurrent *yearly periodic tenancy at law*. The periodic tenancy is a far less valuable right (being determinable at six months' notice) than the 10-year equitable lease, but would be a very useful additional entitlement should the equitable lease be lost because of failure to register it or because of substantial breach by the tenant of a term of the contract (see 1.4.6).

The case of *Barclays Bank v Quistclose Investments Ltd* [1970] AC 567 is another where common law and equitable rights were held to co-exist. The facts were, briefly, that Quistclose made a loan to a company (RR Ltd) on the brink of insolvency for the express purpose of paying a dividend that the company had declared in favour of its shareholders. Had the loan been repaid in the normal course of events, the case would have been just like any other in which common law contractual obligations had been discharged. However, the borrowing company became insolvent before the dividend had been paid. At that point one might assume, as did Barclays Bank, that Quistclose's contractual claim would have to join the queue of personal claims against the estate of the insolvent company. In fact, a majority of their Lordships favoured quite the opposite result.

Lord Wilberforce, delivering the leading speech, held that the arrangement gave rise to a primary trust in favour of the shareholders in whose favour the dividend had been declared, and a secondary trust in favour of Quistclose arising in the event of the company's insolvency. What type of trust this secondary trust might be is considered at 2.3.4.2. What is significant for present purposes is that a trust of *any* sort was held to exist *alongside* the common law contractual debt. Lord Wilberforce held (at p 582) that '[t]here is surely no difficulty in recognising the co-existence in one transaction of legal and equitable rights and remedies'. No doubt it has never been a difficulty to recognize the existence of concurrent legal and equitable rights, but whether as a matter of policy it *should* be recognized is quite a different matter.

? QUESTION 1.6

Can you think of any policy reasons for and against the decision in *Quistclose*?

The consequence of Lord Wilberforce's analysis was, of course, to take Quistclose out of the queue of general creditors and to promote its claim to the status of proprietary right. *Against* this it could be argued that the borrowing company had unfairly preferred Quistclose to its other creditors. In *favour* it could be argued that to save a company from insolvency is for the good of all its creditors, and is to the benefit of society generally, and that special protection should be advanced to those creditors who lend money to companies on the brink of insolvency.

1.3.4 Equity and contract

In the next chapter we will compare contracts with trusts. Our concern at this point is to understand the relationship between equity and the common law of contract. In relation to this it is crucial to accept that, although equity seeks to give effect to the substantial intentions of the parties to a contract (as the maxims put it, *equity imputes an intention to fulfil an obligation*, and *sees as done that which ought to be done*), it is not the role of equity to give parties more than they bargained for: '[a] fiduciary duty . . . cannot be prayed in aid to enlarge the scope of contractual duties' (*per* Lord Jauncey of Tullichettle in *Clark Boyce v Mouat* [1994] 1 AC 428 at 437).

1.3.4.1 Specific performance

It *is* legitimate, however, for equity to require contracting parties to carry out their mutual contractual promises. Equity achieves this by granting the remedy (sometimes called 'the decree') of specific performance. The remedy is awarded in the court's discretion. So if a claimant has committed a substantial breach of a term of the contract the decree might be refused (for *he who comes to equity must come with clean hands* (see 1.4.6)).

Equity orders the specific performance of contracts because *equity sees as done that which ought to be done* (see 1.4.8). As was observed in *Tilley v Thomas* (1867–68) 3 Ch App 61 at 72: 'contracts ought to be performed. To break them, and to propose compensation for the breach by damages, is not complete justice'. In a similar vein, Sir Peter Millett has commented extra-judicially (*op cit* at p 41) that:

> The common law remedy for breach of contract is an award of damages. The promisor's legal obligation is *either* to perform the contract *or* to pay damages at his option. He is free to break his contract if he chooses. But while the common law waits until the promisor has broken his contract and then awards damages for breach, equity adopts an entirely different approach . . . it refuses to countenance the possibility of breach.

Having said all that, where common law damages would provide an *adequate* remedy, specific performance will not be awarded. The court will only decree specific performance where 'it can by that means do more and complete justice' than the common law (*Wilson v N & BJ Rly Co.* (1874) 9 Ch App 279 at 284). For this reason a number of specific performance cases relate to land, for all land is unique and damages are therefore presumed to be inadequate compensation for breach of a contract to convey land.

Consider the case of *Beswick v Beswick* [1968] AC 58. The facts were that Mr B gave his coal merchant business to his nephew, in consideration of which the nephew agreed to look after Mr B's widow after Mr B's death, to the order of £5 per week. In due course Mr B died and his widow sought to enforce the nephew's promise. The House of Lords granted the equitable remedy of specific performance of the contract in favour of the widow, because the defendant had received the whole benefit of the contract and as a matter of conscience the court would ensure that he carried out his promise so as to achieve 'mutuality' between the contracting parties. However, the widow could not enforce the contract in her own person, but only in her capacity as Mr B's personal representative. The doctrine of privity of contract would not permit her to sue in her own right. The fact that the widow was suing in her husband's place meant that common law damages would have been merely nominal (the husband, being dead, had suffered no real loss); damages being inadequate, specific performance was ordered.

Incidentally, Lord Reid acknowledged that had the case involved a *trust* for the benefit of Mrs B, as opposed to a *contract* for her benefit, she would have been entitled to sue in her own person. However, counsel for Mrs B did not argue that there was a trust, and so their Lordships restricted their deliberations to the contract issue. (Note that the Contracts (Rights of Third Parties) Act 1999 (see 5.6) now permits persons in Mrs B's position (that is, an identified third party beneficiary of a contract) to enforce the contract in some cases.)

There is another significant twist in the tale of specific performance. According to the Chancery Amendment Act 1858 (known as Lord Cairns' Act), courts can award common law-type damages in lieu of an injunction or decree of specific performance (see, now, the Supreme Court Act 1981, s 50).

? **QUESTION** 1.7

It is said that specific performance of a contract will only be decreed where an award of damages for breach would be an inadequate remedy. How can this be reconciled with the fact that courts can award damages in lieu of specific performance?

The answer is that a court might be minded to award damages in lieu of specific performance where a claim for specific performance has failed. The procedure obviates the necessity for the pleadings to be amended.

Finally, it should be noted that there are some situations in which specific performance will generally not be decreed. Examples include contracts of personal service (see, for example, *CH Giles & Co Ltd v Morris* [1972] 1 WLR 307) and contracts requiring constant supervision (see, for example, *Cooperative Insurance Society Ltd v Argyll Stores (Holdings) Ltd* [1998] AC 1).

1.3.4.2 Restrictive covenants

It was established by Lord Cottenham, the Lord Chancellor, in *Tulk v Moxhay* (1848) [1943–60] All ER Rep 9, that whereas the common law of contract will only enforce the burden of a restrictive covenant (that is, a promise in a deed that is negative in substance such as 'I promise not to build on the land that you are selling to me') against the person who entered into the covenant (the original covenantor), equity may enforce the burden of the covenant against the covenantor's successors in title if they have notice of it. Lord Cottenham stated that: 'Nothing could be more inequitable than that the original [covenantor] should be able to sell the property the next day for a greater price, in consideration of the assignee being allowed to escape from the liability which he had himself undertaken'.

1.3.5 Equity and crime

The court of equity is not a court of punishment (see *Vyse v Foster* (1872–73) 8 LR Ch App 309 at 333). However, equity's traditional concern for matters of conscience has led to some interesting points of overlap with the criminal law. It has been suggested that where somebody profits from killing another, the ill-gotten gains are held by the killer as constructive trustee for those entitled under the deceased's will or intestacy. Certainly, it is well established that a killer will not be permitted to take the victim's property by will or intestacy (*Re Sigsworth* [1935] Ch 89), and if, the killer's innocent children were next-in-line to inherit under the victim's intestacy, they will receive nothing if the killer is still alive, with the result that the estate may pass to some more remote relative of the victim in ways the victim would never have intended. This seems unfair, so the Law Commission has recommended that where a potential heir is disqualified under this so-called 'forfeiture rule' the estate should be distributed on the assumption (somewhat unlikely in reality) that the killer had pre-deceased the victim (*The Forfeiture Rule and the Law of Succession* Report (Law Com No 295), 27 July 2005). (Incidentally, this presumption will apply not only to the potential heir who kills, but also to the potential heir who refuses the inheritance and to a potential heir who dies unmarried under the age of 18 but leaves behind children.)

It has also been held that criminal gains in the form of a bribe (*AG for HK v Reid*, see 16.4.1.1) are subject to a constructive trust in an appropriate case. Beyond this it seems certain that no branch of the civil law will actually enforce rights which have accrued to the person asserting them *as a result of* the crime of that person (*Cleaver v Mutual Reserve Fund Life Association* [1892] 1 QB 147). If equity takes note of criminal behaviour, then it is equally true that the criminal courts take notice of equity, if only in as much as dishonest breach of trust or fiduciary duty is an aggravating factor in cases of theft. (See *R v Clark* [1998] Crim LR 227.)

1.3.6 Equity and restitution

For present purposes we will adopt Professor Andrew Burrows' proposition that 'Restitution is the law concerned with reversing a defendant's unjust enrichment at the plaintiff's expense' (*The Law of Restitution*, 1993, Butterworths, p 1). An interesting example of a case in which restitution was awarded to reverse an unjust enrichment is *Cressman v Coys of Kensington* [2004] All ER (D) 69, Court of Appeal, in which the purchaser of a car mistakenly transferred with a valuable personalized number plate was liable to account for the value of the number plate because he knew of the mistake at the time of the purchase.

Supporters of the development of restitution as a coherent body of English law in its own right play down the distinction between the legal and equitable nature of restitutionary remedies and the routes to asserting them. The emphasis is upon remedial justice for the claimant, be it achieved by requiring the defendant to disgorge his unjustified receipts under, for example, a common law tort action for money had and received, or as a constructive or resulting trustee in equity. This aspect of restitution was met with some scepticism in *Westdeutsche Landesbank Girozentrale v Islington London Borough Council* [1996] 2 WLR 802 where Lord Browne-Wilkinson commented that 'the search for a perceived need to strengthen the remedies of a plaintiff claiming in restitution involves, to my mind, a distortion of trust principles'.

Nevertheless, the House of Lords in *Lipkin Gorman (a firm) v Karpnale Ltd* [1991] 3 WLR 10 did appear to acknowledge a general remedy of restitution based on the concept of unjust enrichment. In that case a partner in a firm of solicitors (the claimants) had used monies from the firm's client account in order to gamble at the 'Playboy' casino (run by the first defendant, Karpnale Ltd). The House of Lords decided that the casino had to pay back the monies it had received to the extent that it had been unjustly enriched by them. However, it did not have to pay back monies to the extent that it had changed its position in good faith as a result of receiving them (the so-called 'change of position' defence). It was permitted to deduct a sum equivalent to the winnings it had paid out to the fraudulent solicitor before making restitution to his firm.

***Lipkin Gorman (a firm) v Karpnale Ltd* [1991] 3 WLR 10, House of Lords**

Lord Goff of Chieveley:

In these circumstances it is right that we should ask ourselves: why do we feel that it would be unjust to allow restitution in cases such as these? The answer must be that, where an innocent defendant's position is so changed that he will suffer an injustice if called upon to repay or to repay in full, the injustice of requiring him so to repay outweighs the injustice of denying the plaintiff restitution. If the plaintiff pays money to the defendant under a mistake of fact, and the defendant then, acting in good faith, pays the money or part of it to charity, it is unjust to require the defendant to make restitution to the extent that he has so changed his position. Likewise, on facts such as those in the present case, if a thief steals my money and pays it to a third party who gives it away to charity, that third party should have a good defence to an action for money had and received. In other words, bona fide change of position should of itself be a good defence in such cases as these. The principle is widely recognised throughout the common law world. . . . The time for its recognition in this country is, in my opinion, long overdue.

According to one of the leading academic advocates of a substantive law of restitution, Professor Peter Birks, '[t]heir Lordships [in *Lipkin*] looked forward to the day in which there might be a synthesis of common law and equity relating to restitution of misapplied funds' (*Civil Wrongs: A New World*, The Butterworth Lectures 1990–91, pp 55, 56). Certainly this was the view of Lord Goff (the co-author, with Professor Gareth Jones, of *Goff and Jones on Restitution*). His Lordship, having accepted that the solicitors' claim was founded upon the unjust enrichment of the club, and that the club was entitled to defend that claim to the extent that it had changed its position in good faith, said:

> The recognition of change of position as a defence should be doubly beneficial. It will enable a more generous approach to be taken to the recognition of the right to restitution, in the knowledge that the defence is, in appropriate cases, available; and, while recognising the different functions of property at law and in equity, there may also in due course develop a more consistent approach to tracing claims, in which common defences are recognised as available to such claims, whether advanced at law or in equity.

(As to tracing, see **Chapter 18**.)

Ironically, if common law and equity do unite within an independent law of restitution, the effect might actually be to separate restitution, at least temporarily, from the rest of English law. This outcome will only be avoided if the restitution lawyers succeed in establishing a *universal* remedial interchange between law and equity, for restitution itself is not *all* law. The law of restitution addresses only a certain range of remedial concerns. It is not, for instance, concerned with compensation for loss. What is more, its prophylactic, as opposed to its remedial, function is relatively underdeveloped.

1.3.7 Equity and the common law duty of care

The duty to act carefully (the duty not to act negligently) has evolved from different origins at common law and in equity, but despite their distinct historical sources both are concerned with the same essential fault or 'tort'.

Base Metal Trading Ltd v Shamurin **[2005] 1 WLR 1157; [2004] EWCA Civ 1316, Court of Appeal**

Tuckey LJ (at pp 1164–1165; paras 19–20):

There is no doubt that a [company] director owes an equitable as well as a common law duty of care. In *Bristol and West Building Society v Mothew* [1998] Ch 1 this court was concerned to draw the distinction between such a duty and a fiduciary duty. Millett LJ explained, at pp 16–17:

'The common law and equity each developed the duty of care, but they did so independently of each other and the standard of care required is not always the same. But they influenced each other, and today the substance of the resulting obligations is more significant than their particular historic origin. In *Henderson v Merrett Syndicates Ltd* [1995] 2 AC 145, 205 Lord Browne-Wilkinson said: 'The liability of a fiduciary for the negligent transaction of his duties is not a separate head of liability but the paradigm of the general duty to act with care imposed by law on those who take it upon themselves to act for or advise others. Although the historical development of the rules of law and equity have, in the past, caused different labels to be stuck on different manifestations of the duty, in truth the duty of care imposed on bailees, carriers, trustees, directors, agents and others is the same duty: it arises from the circumstances in which the defendants were acting, not from their status or description. It is the fact that they have all assumed responsibility for the property or affairs of others which renders them liable for the careless performance of what they have undertaken to do, not the description of the trade or position which they hold.' I respectfully agree . . .'

A little later Millett LJ said, at p 17:

'Although the remedy which equity makes available for breach of the equitable duty of skill and care is equitable compensation rather than damages, this is merely the product of history and in this context is in my opinion a distinction without a difference. Equitable compensation for breach of the duty of skill and care resembles common law damages in that it is awarded by way of compensation to the plaintiff for his loss. There is no reason in principle why the common law rules of causation, remoteness of damage and measure of damages should not be applied by analogy in such a case.'

1.4 The maxims of equity

The remedial jurisdiction of equity was predicated not upon the recognition of formal entitlement, but upon the exercise of the court's discretion; and in the exercise of discretion maxims are more useful than rules.

1.4.1 Equity will not suffer a wrong without a remedy

The Latin version of this maxim suggests equity to be the healer of all ills: *nullus recedat a curia cancellariae sine remedio* (nothing yielded to the Court of Chancery will go without remedy). The reality, of course, is that equity does not concern itself with every type of wrong (see 1.3.1). However, where an activity is one with which the law is concerned, and in relation to which the law provides no sufficient remedy, equity will endeavour to supplement the shortcomings of the common law.

1.4.2 Equity follows the law

The judge in *Leech v Schweder* (1873) 9 LR Ch App 463 gave the following useful exposition of this maxim (at 475): 'I always supposed that where a right existed at law and a person only came into equity because the Court of Equity had a more convenient remedy than a court of law . . . there equity followed the law, and the person entitled to the right had no greater right in equity than at law'.

1.4.3 Equity looks to substance not form

In *Walsh v Lonsdale* (1882) 21 Ch D 9 we have already considered one of the most dramatic illustrations of this principle (see 1.3.3). Another nice illustration is provided by *Locking v Parker* (1873) 8 LR Ch App 30 where the question arose whether a real security in the form of a trust for sale of land was or was not a mortgage. The judge held that '. . . it is not for a Court of Equity to be making distinctions between forms instead of attending to the real substance and essence of the transaction. Whatever form the matter took, I am of the opinion that this was solely a mortgage transaction'.

It should not be assumed, however, that the common law is blinded by form and blind to substance. In *Street v Mountford* [1985] 1 AC 809 Lord Templeman famously refused to recognize an occupier's right in land to be a personal 'licence', even though it had been labelled a 'licence' and intended by the parties to be such. Instead he held that it was a lease, because an examination of the substantial relationship between the parties revealed that the tenant had in fact got exclusive possession of the landlord's premises. The name the parties used could not alter the substantial nature of the transaction. As Shakespeare put it in *Romeo and Juliet* (II ii): 'What's in a name? That which we call a rose by any other name would smell as sweet'. Lord Templeman preferred another gardening metaphor: 'The manufacture of a five-pronged implement for manual digging results in a fork even if the manufacturer, unfamiliar with the English language, insists that he intended to make and has made a spade'.

Nevertheless, if we take the example of a 10-year lease of land contained in a document labelled 'licence', the fact remains that the common law will only recognize the document as creating a valid legal lease if the document itself is in the *form* of a deed. It is in relation to statutory formality requirements such as these that equity is able to take a less constrained approach to fulfilling the substantial intentions of the parties. (See **Chapter 3** where we consider secret trusts at 3.3.3, and where we consider the use of constructive trusts as a means of avoiding the requirement of written formality in relation to the disposition of existing equitable interests at 3.3.1.)

1.4.4 Equity will not permit a statute to be used as an instrument of fraud

This maxim usually applies to restrain a defendant from relying in bad faith upon the absence of some statutory formality in order to defeat the claimant's legitimate claim. The leading authority is *Rochefoucauld v Boustead* [1897] 1 Ch 196, which was applied in *Bannister v Bannister* [1948] 2 All ER 133 and *Lyus v Prowsa Developments* [1982] 1 WLR 1044. See, generally, **Chapter 3** at 3.3.1.3.

A more radical, and relatively unknown possibility, is that equity might, by virtue of its *in personam* jurisdiction have power, not simply to prevent existing statutes from being used as instruments of fraud, but to restrain an improper application to Parliament for the enactment of a new private Act of Parliament. The possibility was admitted in *Re London, Chatham and Dover Railway Arrangement Act* (1869–70) 5 LR Ch App 671 although the court thought it difficult to conceive of a case in which it would be right for the court to exercise the power.

1.4.5 Equity acts in personam

One of the most useful modern applications of equity's *in personam* jurisdiction has been in relation to international freezing injunctions (formerly known as *Mareva* injunctions: *Mareva Compania Naviera SA v International Bulkcarriers SA* [1975] 2 Lloyds Rep 509; [1980] 1 All ER 2). This form of injunction is designed to prevent a defendant from dissipating assets in order to defeat a judgment of the court. The injunction is effective *in personam* against any person made a defendant to proceedings in an English court, and is not defeated by the mere fact that the assets subject to the injunction are based outside the jurisdiction of the English court (although freezing injunctions are usually used to prevent assets from being taken outside the English jurisdiction).

1.4.6 Those who come to equity must come with clean hands

In *Lee v Haley* (1869) 5 LR Ch App 155 the claimants failed when they sought an injunction to protect their trade as coal merchants. The court held that they had 'unclean hands', not because of the coal, but because they had been dishonestly selling their customers short. As the judge said (at 158): '. . . if the Plaintiffs had been systematically and knowingly carrying on a fraudulent trade, and delivering short weight [of coal], it is beyond all question that this court would not interfere to protect them in carrying on such trade'.

The maxim applies in the case of injunctions and on applications for specific performance, because the award of such remedies lies in the discretion of the court. The maxim will not be applied to prevent a claimant from bringing an action under an established equitable right (*Rowan v Dann* (1992) 64 P & CR 202).

It is crucial to realize that equity only insists on the good behaviour of those who *come to equity* seeking a remedy. It does not insist that the successful equitable claimant must continue to use his equitable interest with probity after the award. This is perhaps nowhere better illustrated than in the case of *Williams v Staite* [1979] Ch 291. The facts of that case were that the holders of an equitable right to occupy a cottage for life persistently interfered with the enjoyment by their neighbour of an adjoining cottage. The neighbour had purchased the legal titles to *both* cottages from the person against whom the bad neighbours had established their equitable interest. On account of the harassment that he had suffered, the legal owner sought to evict his bad neighbours. The judge at first instance held that the equitable rights of the bad neighbours should be revoked by reason of their conduct, and he awarded possession to the claimant. The defendants successfully appealed. Goff LJ held that, after the appropriate award has been made in satisfaction of the equity (based on estoppel, see 17.4), subsequent 'excessive user or bad behaviour towards [the legal owner] cannot bring the equity to an end or forfeit it'. Denning LJ thought that the equitable award might be revoked in 'some circumstances' (he did not specify what they might be) but held that the remedies available to the legal owner in this case would be to bring an action at common law for nuisance, trespass and so forth.

1.4.7 Those who come to equity must do equity

The 1877 edition of Story's *Commentaries on Equity Jurisprudence* states, in the context of rescission and specific performance, that:

> [T]he interference of a court of equity is a matter of mere discretion . . . And in all cases of this sort . . . the court will, in granting relief, impose such terms upon the party as it deems the real justice of the case to require . . . The maxim here is emphatically applied—he who seeks equity must do equity.

The English Court of Appeal in *O'Sullivan v Management Agency Ltd* [1985] QB 428 (see 12.2.1.2), in exercising its jurisdiction to set aside (rescind) a contract on equitable grounds, required the successful claimant to allow the other party to retain some benefits made under the contract. Their Lordships stated that, by means of the maxim *he who comes to equity must do equity*, 'the court can achieve practical justice between the parties' (*per* Dunn LJ) and 'the court will do what is practically just in the individual case' (*per* Fox LJ). For further illustrations of the maxim see *Sledmore v Dalby* (1996) 72 P & CR 196, *Cheese v Thomas* [1994] 1 WLR 129, 136 and *Vadasz v Pioneer Concrete (SA) Pty Ltd* [1995] 69 ALR 678.

1.4.8 Equity sees as done that which ought to be done

As we saw when we considered the relationship between equity and morality, equity sees as done that which ought *legally* to be done. See *Walsh v Lonsdale* (1882) 21 Ch D 9, CA, at 1.3.3. Although normally applied to private transactions, this maxim has occasionally been applied to treat a court order to transfer property as taking immediate effect in equity, so as to impose a constructive trust on the person subject to the order (*Mountney v Treharne* [2003] Ch 135, CA; *Re Flint (A Bankrupt)* [1993] Ch 319).

1.4.9 Equity imputes an intention to fulfil an obligation

Again, as we saw when we considered the relationship between equity and morality, equity only imputes an intention to fulfil a *legal* obligation. See *Re Hallett's Estate* (1880) 13 Ch D 696, CA, at 18.3.3.3.

1.4.10 *Qui prior est tempore potior est jure*: where the equities are equal the first in time prevails

This maxim is sometimes paraphrased *the first in time is the first in right*. Its use can be illustrated by taking the straightforward case of equitable mortgagees competing against each other for priority. Suppose that A grants an equitable mortgage of property to B and later grants a mortgage of the same property to C. In the usual course of events, B's mortgage will have priority over C's, in accordance with the maxim. In theory the maxim only applies if the competing equities are equal, but Kay J in *Taylor v Russell* [1890] 1 Ch 8 at 17 stated that nothing less than 'gross negligence' must be proved by a later equitable mortgagee against a prior mortgagee to give priority to a later one. Earlier authorities which appear to suggest that B might cede priority to C, if C's equity is merely *technically* superior to B's must be doubtful. See, for example, *Pease v Jackson* (1867–83) Ch App 576.

1.4.11 Where the equities are equal the law prevails

This maxim, like the previous one, operates more like a rule than a principle and operates in the context of determining priority between competing equitable claims. If we take our previous hypothetical case, where A granted an equitable mortgage to B and then another to C, the present maxim allows C to gain priority over B by the simple expedient of purchasing the legal title from A (see *Bailey v Barnes* [1894] 1 Ch 25 and *Taylor v Russell* [1893] AC 244).

One exception to this maxim is the rule in *Dearle v Hall* (1828) 3 Russ 1. According to this rule, priority between competing assignees of a *debt* is awarded to the first one to give notice to the debtor. It matters not that one of the competitors has a legal interest and the other merely an equitable one.

1.4.12 Where equity and law conflict, equity shall prevail

See *The Earl of Oxford's Case* (1615) 1 Rep Ch 1 at 1.2.1.2. This maxim is now enshrined in the Supreme Court Act 1981, s 49, which provides that:

> Every Court exercising jurisdiction in England and Wales in any civil cause or matter shall continue to administer law and equity on the basis that, wherever there is any conflict or variance between the rules of equity and the rules of common law with reference to the same matter, the rules of equity shall prevail.

It is significant that a hundred years after the Judicature Acts this section still draws a distinction between the rules of law and the rules of equity!

1.4.13 Equality is equity

For illustrations of the application of this maxim, see *IRC v Broadway Cottages Trust* [1955] Ch 20, CA, at 4.5.1.1 and *Midland Bank plc v Cooke* [1995] 4 All ER 562; [1995] 2 FLR 915, CA, at 17.3.2.

1.4.14 Delay defeats equities

The processes of law are notorious for delay. Shakespeare's Hamlet lists 'the law's delay' among the chief woes of life in his famous 'to be, or not to be' soliloquy. More than two centuries later administrative delay effectively crippled Chancery procedure. This may in part explain the requirement, enshrined in the maxim, delay defeats equities, that a person seeking an equitable remedy should not be lax in bringing their claim. In practice, however, the doctrine of laches is more often resorted to (to defeat stale claims) than is this maxim (see 15.3.4 and *The Limitation of Actions in Equity* by J Brunyate, London, 1932).

1.4.15 Equity will not assist a volunteer

See **Chapter 5** where this maxim is considered in detail.

1.4.16 There is no equity to perfect an imperfect gift

See **Chapter 5** where this maxim is considered in detail.

1.4.17 Equity abhors a vacuum in ownership

See **Chapter 5** and **Chapter 16** where this maxim is considered in detail.

CHAPTER SUMMARY

In this chapter we have seen that equity developed to prevent the unconscionable abuse of common law rights and powers, but that equity is a branch of law and not a branch of morality. True, it is assisted by principles (called maxims) and doctrines which can lead to creative results in hard cases, but it is developed where possible in accordance with precedent, just like any other branch of law in a common law system. The challenge for the student is to understand the relationship between the equity branch and the common law branch of law. Most students would like the path to understanding to be paved in simple key-points, in which case the good news is that the content of some of the chapters in this book may safely be summarized under a few key headings, and the author will attempt this at the end of chapters where appropriate. However, it would be dangerous to adopt such an approach at the end of this first chapter, in which we have encountered some of the fundamental ideas that will accompany us throughout the remainder of our study of the law of trusts. One cannot grasp the big idea of equity by holding onto a few key points any more than one can comprehend the wind by holding one's breath. Equity, like so many big ideas, must be understood as a whole, and to convey understanding of the whole it is useful to employ metaphor. But which metaphor?

We have heard it suggested that equity and the common law are streams of water that flow in the same channel in which they are now merged as one. It is submitted, however, that the image of two streams in a single channel is not a helpful one. It would be better to see the single river of the law as being composed of two parts: the river bed and the water that runs over it. The common law is the river bed, in places it is as unyielding as stone, but in those places over time it is softened by the more fluid processes of equity. Crucially, one can have a river bed without water but one cannot have a river without a river bed: equity follows the common law; it is not the other way round. Equally important is the fact that there are muddy waters which belong as much to the water of equity as to the river bed of the common law. Remedies for breach of duty of care and remedies for restitution of unjust enrichment are amongst those areas in which (in some situations) it makes little practical sense to distinguish equity from law. However, one area in which it is absolutely necessary to distinguish equity from law is the area which will form the major subject of study throughout the remainder of this book: *the trust*. In the trust, legal title (common law ownership that is, ownership by the trustee) is held apart from equitable title (beneficial ownership that is, ownership by the beneficiary). Of course the distinction between equity and law within the trust is not a particularly fluid distinction, it is a distinction which has been established over centuries, so that it is now solid and predictable to the extent that the absolute owner of an asset knows exactly what he must do in order to create a trust of that asset. In the expressly-created trust, the river has frozen so that equitable ownership and legal title are clearly distinct from one another. In the next chapter we will see that the established, institutional nature of the trust has, paradoxically, made it uniquely flexible and useful in practice.

SUMMATIVE ASSESSMENT EXERCISE

online resource centre

'Common law and equity are working in different ways towards the same ends, and it is therefore as wrong to assert the independence of one from the other as it is to assert that there is no difference between them.'

Critically discuss the above statement.

FURTHER READING

Baker, J H, 'The Court of Chancery and Equity' (Chapter 6) in *An Introduction to English Legal History* (3rd edn) (London: Butterworths, 2002).

Birks, P, *Unjust Enrichment* (2nd edn) (Oxford: Clarendon Press, 2005).

Burrows, A S, *Fusing common law and equity: remedies, restitution and reform—Hochelaga lectures 2001* (Hong Kong: Sweet & Maxwell Asia, 2002).

Cotterrell, R, *Trusting in Law: Legal and Moral Concepts of Trust* (1993) CLP 75.

Dickens, Charles, *Bleak House.*

Duggan, A J, 'Is Equity Efficient?' (1997) 113 LQR 601.

Goodhart QC, Sir William, 'Trust law for the twenty-first century' (1996) 10(2) Trust Law International 38.

Halliwell, M, *Equity & Good Conscience in A Contemporary Context* (London: Old Bailey Press, 1997); (2nd edn, 2004).

Halliwell, M, 'Equitable property rights, discretionary remedies and unclean hands' [2004] Conv 439.

Harding, A, *The Law Courts of Medieval England* (London: Allen & Unwin, 1973).

Holdsworth, W S, 'Relation of the Equity Administered by the Common Law Judges to the Equity Administered by the Chancellor' (1916) 26 Yale LJ 1.

Holmes, O, 'Early English Equity' (1885) 1 LQR 162.

Hudson, J, *The Formation of the English Common Law* (London: Longman, 1996).

Maitland, F W, 'Uses and Trusts' in *Equity: A Course of Lectures* (revsd by J Brunyate) (Cambridge, 1936).

Martin, J, 'Fusion, Fallacy and Confusion: a Comparative Study' [1994] Conv 13.

Millett, Sir Peter, 'Equity—the road ahead' (1995) 9(2) Trust Law International 35.

Pound, R, 'The Decadence of Equity' (1905) 5 Columbia L Rev 20.

Shakespeare, William, *The Merchant of Venice*, Act IV.

Simpson, A W B, 'An Introduction to the History of the Land Law' (2nd edn) (Oxford: OUP, 1986).

Tudsbery, F, 'Equity and the Common Law' (1913) 29 LQR 154.

Vinogradoff, Sir Paul, 'Reason and Conscience in Sixteenth Century Jurisprudence' (1908) 96 LQR 373.

Worthington, S, *Equity* (Oxford: Clarendon Press, 2003).

Yntema, H E, 'Equity in the Civil Law and the Common Law' (1967) 15 Am J Comp L 60.

2 Understanding trusts

OBJECTIVES

By the end of this chapter you should understand:

1 The usefulness of the trust

2 The difference between the trust and other legal concepts

3 The variety of trust types, for example, pension trusts, protective trusts

4 The role of trusts in asset protection

5 The social significance of trusts

2.1 Introduction

> If we were asked what is the greatest and most distinctive achievement performed by Englishmen in the field of jurisprudence I cannot think that we should have any better answer to give than this, namely the development from century to century of the trust idea.
>
> Maitland, The Unincorporate Body, in *Collected Papers*, vol III p 272.

If you have already studied land law you may think that you already know all there is to know about trusts. To see if you're right, attempt the following question.

? QUESTION 2.1

Which of the following do you believe will always be a feature of a trust? Tick your choices:

- the trustee holds the legal title
- the trustee is never a beneficiary of his own trust
- the trustee must discharge the purposes for which trust property is held.

You get full marks if you didn't tick any of them! While each of the propositions is true in very many cases, it is possible for a person to be a trustee of an equitable interest, to have a beneficial interest under their own trust (Trustee Act 1925, s 68(17)) and to hold property for purposes which they are not obliged to fulfil (see 7.3). You should have remembered the second point from your knowledge of land law, for where two or more persons purchase land in their joint names each of them is presumed to have an equitable ('beneficial') interest in the land and to hold their legal title subject to the equitable interests of every other co-owner. They hold the legal title as trustees for themselves.

Trusts come in all shapes and sizes. Indeed it is currently very much at issue whether we have now a coherent law of the trust, or several laws of trusts (see G Moffat, 'Pension Funds: A Fragmentation of Trust Law?' (1993) 56 MLR 471). To give yourself some idea of the breadth of activity which now falls within the law of trusts, attempt the following exercise.

EXERCISE 2.1

On a separate sheet of paper, try to list some of the uses to which trusts might be put, and the contexts in which they occur. It might assist you to consider whether or not you have personally had any contact or dealings with trusts.

Did your list contain any (or all) of the following?

(a) To provide for property to be held for the benefit of persons subject to legal disability. For example, minors are not permitted to hold the legal estate in land, but are permitted to be beneficiaries under a trust of land (see 'capacity' in **Chapter 3** at 3.2.2).

(b) To provide for property to be held for persons *in succession*, for example, 'to A for life, to A's children in remainder'.

(c) To provide for property to be held by a number of owners *concurrently* for example, co-ownership of land, see **Chapter 17**.

(d) To protect family property from the bankruptcy or extravagance of particular beneficiaries (that is, protective or 'spendthrift' trusts, see 2.3.2).

(e) To take into account possible changes in the future circumstances of beneficiaries when making a gift, instead of making an outright gift (see **Chapters 9** and **13**).

(f) To apply property for purposes, rather than for persons (for example, charitable purposes, see **Chapters 7** and **8**).

(g) To make collective investment (for example, pension funds see 2.3.3 and 14.2 and trade union funds).

(h) To enable clubs (unincorporated, non-profit associations) to receive and hold property (see **Chapter 7**).

(i) To minimize tax liability, by restructuring property ownership (see **Chapter 9**).

(j) To protect assets from creditors in the event of insolvency (see 2.3.4).

(k) To concentrate managerial power (in relation to, for example, pension funds, trade unions and clubs).

(l) To achieve privacy in dealings with property (hiding true beneficial ownership behind legal ownership), for example, secret trusts at 3.3.3.

(m) To function as trading trusts and voting trusts (these topics are outside the scope of this book, but see, for example: The Hon Mr Justice B H McPherson 'The Insolvent Trading Trust' in P D Finn 'Essays in Equity' The Law Book Company Limited, Sydney, 1985; and M A Pickering, 'Shareholders' Voting Rights and Company Control' (1965) 81 LQR 248 at 257).

2.2 Trusts: to define or describe?

Given the very wide range of functions performed by trusts, and the great variety of contexts in which they are to be found, do you think it is possible to define the trust concept?

EXERCISE 2.2

If you think you can do so at this stage, why not try to define the trust concept in your own words.

You will quickly have discovered that the definition of trusts is fraught with difficulty. To define must always mean to describe the essence of the thing, and so any definition must necessarily be either incomplete and/or circular. (As to the problem of paraphrase in legal reasoning, see H L A Hart, 'Definition and Theory in Jurisprudence' (1954) 70 LQR 37.) For what it is worth, and incomplete though it must be, this author would offer the following definition of a private trust:

> *A private trust is the legal relationship between the formal owner(s) of assets ('the trustee' or 'trustees') and the beneficial owner(s) of those assets ('the beneficiary' or 'beneficiaries'). The hallmark of the trust is that every trustee is obliged in equity to employ every incident of their formal (typically 'legal') ownership for the exclusive benefit of the beneficiaries, although a trustee might himself be one of the beneficiaries.*

The nearest we have to statutory *descriptions* of a trust (they could hardly be called *definitions*) are s 68(17) of the Trustee Act 1925 and Article 2 of the Hague Convention on the Law Applicable to Trusts and on their Recognition (the Hague Convention was incorporated into English law by the Recognition of Trusts Act 1987).

The Trustee Act 1925, s 68(17) provides that:

> 'Trust' does not include the duties incident to an estate conveyed by way of mortgage, but with this exception the expressions 'trust' and 'trustee' extend to implied and constructive trusts, and to cases where the trustee has a beneficial interest in the trust property, and to the duties incident to the office of a personal representative, and 'trustee' where the context admits, includes a personal representative, and 'new trustee' includes an additional trustee; . . .

The relevant part of the Hague Convention identifies a number of important features of expressly created trusts; but it does not attempt to define or describe the many significant trusts, such as constructive and resulting trusts, which arise in the absence of an express intention to create them:

> For the purposes of this Convention the term 'trust' refers to the legal relationship created—*inter vivos* or on death—by a person, the settlor, when assets have been placed under the control of a trustee for the benefit of a beneficiary or for a specified purpose. A trust has the following characteristics—*a* the assets constitute a separate fund and are not part of the trustee's estate; *b* title to the trust assets stands in the name of the trustee or in the name of another person on behalf of the trustee; *c* the trustee has the power and the duty, in respect of which he is accountable, to manage, employ or dispose of the assets in accordance with the terms of the trust and the special duties imposed upon him by law. The reservation by the settlor of certain rights and powers, and the fact that the trustee may himself have rights as a beneficiary, are not necessarily inconsistent with the existence of a trust.

One useful way in which trusts can be more clearly understood is to contrast and compare them with other legal concepts. This is the task of the following sections.

2.2.1 **Trusts compared with contracts**

A contract is a private relationship between the parties under which their rights and obligations are generally enforceable only against each other (*Beswick v Beswick* [1968] AC 58), whereas it is of the essence of a trust that a settlor can give property to a trustee on trust for a third party, and thereby grant the third party (the beneficiary) rights against the trustee to see that the trust is properly discharged. It is true that by virtue of the Contracts (Rights of Third Parties) Act 1999 third parties can in certain circumstances enforce their rights under a contract to which they were not a party, but they cannot enforce those rights against a person who is not a party to the contract. The beneficiary of a trust, on the other hand, can enforce his property right in the trust assets against all comers, with the exception of an innocent person who buys the trust property (that is, the formal, legal title) without notice of the trust (*Pilcher v Rawlins* (1872) 7 Ch App 259).

2.2.1.1 **Are trusts merely a special type of contract?**

Having noted the orthodox conceptual distinction between the contract and the trust, we should nevertheless be aware that many commentators have been impressed by the close relationship between the two concepts. Maitland thought it 'utterly impossible for us to frame any definition of a contract which shall not include the acts by which ninety-nine out of every hundred trusts are created' (F W Maitland, *Equity: A Course of Lectures*, 2nd edn, revised by J Brunyate (Cambridge 1936) p 111).

More recently, Professor Kevin Gray suggested that 'every gift, lease, trust and security has its origins in some arrangement of consent or assent' ('Property in Thin Air' (1991) 50(2) CLJ 252 at 302). More recently still, a leading American academic went so far as to suggest that 'the deal between settlor and trustee is functionally indistinguishable from the modern third-party-beneficiary contract. Trusts are contracts' (J H Langbein in the 'Contractarian Basis of the Law of Trusts' (1995) 105 Yale Law Journal 625 at 627).

It may well be true that every *express* trust has 'its origins in' a transaction entered into by the settlor consensually, either voluntarily or for contractual consideration. The creation of any express trust is predicated upon a finding that the settlor (the original legal owner) intended its creation (see 4.3), and therefore the consent of the settlor is always a feature of such trusts. However, many non-express trusts do not originate with the consent of the original legal owner, and some (constructive trusts being the prime example) are even created against the legal owner's true intentions (see **Chapter 16**).

If, for the sake of argument, we were to accept that all trusts *originate* in real bilateral or multilateral consensus, this would only go a little way towards illuminating the essential nature of trusts. For even where trusts are *created* consensually, even contractually, they *operate* quite differently from contracts, not least because the trust creates *property* rights whereas the rights arising under a contract are merely personal. (See 2.3.4 for consideration of the different status of contractual (personal) and trust (proprietary) claims against the estates of insolvent persons.)

In *Re Duke of Norfolk's ST* [1982] Ch 61 Fox LJ considered the contractual analysis of express trusts to be 'artificial':

> It may have some appearance of reality in relation to a trustee who, at the request of the settlor, agrees to act before the settlement is executed and approves the terms of the settlement. But very frequently executors and trustees of wills know nothing of the terms of the will until the testator is dead; sometimes in the case of corporate trustees such as banks, they have not even been asked by the testator whether they will act. It is difficult to see with whom, in such cases, the trustees are to be taken to be contracting. The appointment of a trustee by the court also gives rise to problems as to the identity of the contracting party.

To these objections to the contractarian analysis of trusts, Brightman LJ added that it gives 'little weight to the fact that a trustee, whether paid or unpaid, is under no obligation, contractual or otherwise, to provide future services to the trust' (see 'retirement' at 10.4).

? QUESTION 2.2

Do you see how the existence of infant beneficiaries undermines a strictly contractarian analysis of trusts?

Perhaps the most compelling reason for resisting the contractarian rationale of trusts is the presence of beneficiaries who are not competent to contract, such as those under a legal disability, and those as yet unborn. No amount of attention to the contract-like arrangement between the settlor and the trustees can adequately explain the presence, let alone the rights, of such beneficiaries. Without the beneficiaries there is no trust. It should not be forgotten that the beneficiary, and not the settlor, is the *cestui que trust*, and that once a trust has been established the settlor is no longer a party to it. (The phrase *cestui que trust* is Law French for 'beneficiary'. It translates literally, 'the one who trusts' and should be pronounced 'settee key trust'.)

To further support their claims, the 'contractarians' point to the historical character of the trust as a form of conveyance (see 1.2.2 where we considered the employment of the trust, and the use, as a way of avoiding feudal obligations). Again, whether this is true or not, it has limited modern significance. Equity in the form of the trust has outgrown whatever contractarian origins it may have had, just as surely as the lease has completed its historical evolution from contract to property (indeed the lease is now one of only two recognized legal estates in land: Law of Property Act 1925, s 1(1)(b)).

2.2.2 Trust compared with debt

Michael Bridge has written that '[a] debt is a monetary obligation owed by one person to another which is an item of value because it can be transferred to a third party by way of sale or security for a loan' (*Personal Property*, 2nd edn, Blackstone Press, 1996, p 4). This ability to assign a debt to a third party merits further consideration for present purposes.

At common law the assignee (new creditor) of a debt can bring proceedings against the debtor in the name of the assignor (original creditor), and if the assignor tries to resist this, he can, *in equity*, be compelled to comply (*Three Rivers District Council v Bank of England* [1996] QB 292). The fact that a debt may be assigned means that a debtor may be obliged to make payment to a person with whom he has had no dealings whatsoever. In this respect there is a passing similarity with the trust, under which the trustee must account to a beneficiary with whom he may have had no personal dealings. This, however, is the only real point of comparison between the two concepts. The crucial difference, of course, is that the creditor's right to recover a debt is always a mere right *in personam* against the debtor, albeit one that may be assigned from person to person. The beneficiary's rights under a trust include proprietary rights in the assets themselves.

Despite these differences, and in a sense by virtue of them, a number of important modern cases have acknowledged that trust and debt can co-exist in the same transaction in certain commercial contexts. The leading case is *Barclays Bank Ltd v Quistclose Investments Ltd* [1970] AC 567, see 2.3.4.2. You should recall that the House of Lords held that: (1) the monies were held by RR Ltd on trust for its shareholders, and that when that trust failed the monies were held by RR Ltd on resulting trust for QI Ltd. BB Ltd had notice of that trust and therefore held the monies on trust for QI Ltd, and (2) the fact that the transaction, had it succeeded, would have given rise to a standard common law debt owed by RR Ltd to QI Ltd did not preclude the coexistence of a trust remedy in equity. The finding of a trust in that case had been absolutely crucial to the lender's recovery of the sums loaned. This is because such a finding gave the lender a proprietary claim. Had the lender had to rely upon its personal debt claim against the borrower (RR Ltd), it would have been forced to join the long queue of RR Ltd's personal creditors.

Commenting on this case, Meagher J has said that 'whilst previously it might have been thought that debt and trust were distinct and disparate norms, it was thereafter clear that in a given case the transaction under analysis might bear a dual character' (*Re Australian Elizabethan Theatre Trust* (1991) 102 ALR 681 at 693).

2.2.3 Trusts compared with powers

A trustee is bound to discharge his trust. If the trustee fails to do so the court will intervene to ensure that the trust is fulfilled. In contrast, the court will not compel the exercise of a mere power to distribute the fund (sometimes called a power of appointment).

? QUESTION 2.3

Do you think this would still be the case if a power of appointment had been granted to a trustee?

This was considered in *Re Hay's Settlement Trusts* [1982] 1 WLR 202. It was held that a trustee does not have to exercise a mere power, and will not be compelled to do so by the court, but that a trustee must periodically consider whether or not to exercise the power. If the power is actually exercised the trustee must ensure that he acts in accordance with the terms of the power, and must consider both the range of potential beneficiaries and whether each individual appointment is appropriate. In that case the terms of the trust provided that if the trustees were to choose not to exercise their power of appointment the fund would pass to the settlor's nieces and nephews. The presence of this kind of 'gift over' or 'trust over' to other persons in default of the exercise of the power is in practice often the easiest way to distinguish between a trust and a power. In the case of a trust, where the fund *must* be distributed, there will generally be no provision for what should happen in default of distribution!

Subsequently, in *Mettoy Pension Trustees v Evans* [1990] 1 WLR 1587 a mere power in the hands of trustees was described as being a 'fiduciary power' and it was held that the court might in some circumstances intervene to ensure that the power is exercised. In that case, Warner J stepped in to give directions to the trustees of a pension fund as to the appropriate distribution of the pension fund surplus (see 2.3.3.3). In doing so, he noted that Templeman J (in *Re Manisty's Settlement* [1974] Ch 17) had expressed the view that the only right and the only remedy of an object of the power who was aggrieved by the trustees' conduct would be to apply to the court to remove the trustees and appoint others in their place (see 10.5). Warner J came very close to suggesting that *Re Manisty's* had been decided *per incuriam* on this point, but a better way to reconcile the authorities is probably to limit the *Mettoy* interpretation to pension fund trusts.

In addition to the distinction between mere powers, trust powers and mere powers held by trustees (the *Mettoy* 'fiduciary powers'), in *Re Hay's Settlement Trusts* Sir Robert Megarry V-C observed that powers of appointment can be *general* (exercisable in favour of anybody at all) or *special* (exercisable in favour of a specific class of persons, no matter how numerically large that class might be) or *hybrid/intermediate* (exercisable generally, or in favour of a specific class, but not exercisable in favour of specific named individuals or an excluded sub-class of persons).

Re Manisty's Settlement [1974] 1 Ch 17, Chancery Division

The settlement under consideration in this case gave trustees a discretionary power to apply the trust fund for the benefit of a small class of the settlor's near relations, save that any member of a smaller 'excepted class' was to be excluded from the class of beneficiaries. The trustees were also given power at their absolute discretion to declare that any person, corporation or charity (except a member of the excepted class or a trustee) should be included in the class of beneficiaries. A summons was brought to determine whether the intermediate power in this case was void for uncertainty. The power to extend the class of beneficiaries was held to be valid.

Templeman J:

> The court cannot insist upon any particular consideration being given by the trustees to the exercise of the power. If a settlor creates a power exercisable in favour of his issue, his relations and the employees of his company, the trustees may in practice for many years hold regular meetings, study the terms of the power and the other provisions of the settlement, examine the accounts

> and either decide not to exercise the power or to exercise it only in favour, for example, of the children of the settlor. . . . In my judgment it cannot be said that the trustees in those circumstances have committed a breach of trust and that they ought to have advertised the power or looked beyond the people who are most likely to be the objects of the bounty of the settlor . . .
>
> If a person within the ambit of the power is aware of its existence he can require the trustees to consider exercising the power and in particular to consider a request on his part for the power to be exercised in his favour. The trustees must consider this request, and if they decline to do so or can be proved to have omitted to do so, then the aggrieved person may apply to the court which may remove the trustees and appoint others in their place. . . .
>
> The court may also be persuaded to intervene if the trustees act 'capriciously', that is to say, act for reasons which I apprehend could be said to be irrational, perverse or irrelevant to any sensible expectation of the settlor; for example, if they chose a beneficiary by height or complexion or by the irrelevant fact that he was a resident of Greater London . . . The conduct and duties of trustees of an intermediate power, and the rights and remedies of any person who wishes the power to be exercised in his favour, are precisely similar to the conduct and duties of trustees of special powers and the rights and remedies of any person who wishes a special power to be exercised in his favour. In practice, the considerations which weigh with the trustees will be no different from the considerations which will weigh with the trustees of a wide special power.

2.2.4 Trusts compared to agency

Agents owe fiduciary duties of loyalty and good faith to their principal, and will often have some degree of managerial control over the principal's property. Crucially, however, a trustee's holding or control of the trust property is more fundamental than that of an agent, and is in the nature of entitlement to the property, albeit merely legal entitlement. Further, whereas an agency is founded upon agreement between the agent and principal, there is generally no agreement between trustee and beneficiary.

2.3 Special categories of trusts and trustees

Hopefully the preceding sections have helped to elucidate the distinction between trusts and other legal concepts with which you may already have been familiar. If only trusts were all of one sort, the study of trusts would hereafter be a relatively straightforward matter. In fact some basic conceptual and functional distinctions exist between different kinds of trust. The following sections examine categories of trusts which are not considered in depth elsewhere in this text. It should be borne in mind, however, that many other categories of trusts: constructive trusts, secret trusts, resulting trusts and express trusts, to name but a few, receive special attention in future chapters.

2.3.1 Bare trusts

A bare trust exists where a trustee holds the trust property on trust for a single beneficiary who is *sui juris* (adult and not subject to any legal disability) and absolutely entitled to the trust fund. The beneficiary under such a trust has the right to terminate the trust on giving notice to the trustee (a right established in *Saunders v Vautier*, see 9.2.1). Accordingly, the trustee of a bare trust is under no oblgation to invest them or otherwise manage them for the medium to long term, but merely to hold them until called for.

Bare trusts most frequently occur when settlement trusts come to an end. So, for example, upon the death of B in a trust 'To A to hold on trust for B for life and C in remainder', the trustee will hold the trust fund for the benefit of C under a bare trust. Bare trusts also arise in commercial contexts. So, for example, a solicitor holds a client's monies under a bare trust for the client.

2.3.2 Protective trusts

> '. . . a protective trust shows the furthest extent to which English law will permit property to be denied to creditors': *Maudsley & Burn's Trusts and Trustees* (5th edn) 1996.

The beneficiary of a *typical* protective trust has a life interest in the income of a trust fund which will determine if ever the income of the fund becomes payable to another person, for example, the beneficiaries' creditors. It follows that the most common 'determining event' will be the personal bankruptcy of the beneficiary. When the life interest determines, a discretionary trust 'springs up' under which the original beneficiary (together with certain members of his family) has a hope of being reappointed as a beneficiary by the trustees of the discretionary trust. Protective trusts are used to protect beneficiaries from financial calamity and their own folly.

Where a settlor calls his trust a 'protective trust' or uses very similar words, the terms of the trust will be presumed to be those set out in the Trustee Act 1925, s 33. That section provides that income held on trust for the principal beneficiary of a protective trust will pass to a discretionary trust in the event of the principal beneficiary committing some act (for example, an act of bankruptcy) by which his interest is forfeit. The principal beneficiary will be a potential beneficiary under the discretionary trust, together with members of his close family (or, if he has none, those persons who would have been entitled to the original trust in the event of the death of the principal beneficiary).

Where the settlor describes the trust in his own terms, those terms will be given their natural construction even if they differ from those provided by the Trustee Act, s 33. In *Re Balfour's Settlement* [1938] Ch 928, B had a life interest in the income of the settled fund until he should 'do or suffer something whereby the same or some part thereof would through his act or default or by operation or process of law or otherwise . . . become vested in or payable to some other person'. It was provided, further, that in the event of determination a discretionary trust would spring up.

In that case the trustees paid capital of the fund to B in breach of their trust, and later impounded income due to B to remedy that breach (see 15.4.5 on impounding). The question arose whether the impounding of B's income had been a determining event under the protective trust. Farwell J held that it had been. The impounding of the income had effected a forfeiture of B's life interest under the terms of the protective trust.

Consider the facts of *Re Baring's ST* [1940] Ch 737. Mrs Baring had a protected life interest under a family settlement. When she absconded abroad with the children of the family and ignored a court order to return them to England, Mr Baring obtained a court order against her property. Eventually Mrs Baring returned.

? QUESTION 2.4

Do you think that Mrs Baring had forfeited her life interest?

Morton J held that the settlor had intended that his property should be continuously available to his family, and that when the court order deprived Mrs Baring, albeit temporarily, of her interest in the income of the settlement, the settlor's intentions could only be met by forfeiting her life interest at that point. She was left with a mere hope of an interest under the discretionary trust which arose on the determination of her life interest.

Similarly, in *Gibbon* v *Mitchell* [1990] 1 WLR 1304, Mr Gibbon had a life interest under a protective trust. On the advice of his accountants and solicitors, he executed a deed purporting to surrender his life interest in favour of his children. The surrender was held to have forfeited his interest, and so his children could not take under the deed.

? QUESTION 2.5

Do you think that protective trusts should be outlawed on the basis that they defraud creditors?

In recognizing the validity of protective trusts Parliament has sought to balance the settlor's right to make provision for his family against the rights of the family's creditors. Whether the balance achieved is a fair one might be doubted. However, the law does stop short of recognizing the validity of a trust under which the settlor purports to appoint *himself* as principal beneficiary under a protective trust.

Further, the law does not recognize protective trusts which are *conditional* upon the solvency of the life beneficiary. The protective trust is only valid if it grants a *determinable* life interest. A life interest which is limited to take effect *until* bankruptcy will be valid, whereas a *condition* in a trust which purports to forfeit the life interest in the event of the bankruptcy of the life tenant will be void (*Re Leach* [1912] 2 Ch 422).

2.3.3 Pension fund trusts

In *Air Jamaica Limited v Charlton* [1999] 1 WLR 1399, the Privy Council noted that an employee pension fund can exist without a trust, but that a trust is in most cases a practical necessity:

> A pension scheme can, in theory at least, be established by contract between the employer and each employee and without using the machinery of a trust. Such a scheme would have to be very simple. It would look very like a self-employed pension policy. There would be no trust fund and no trustees. The employer would simply contract with each of his employees that, if the employee made weekly payments to the employer, the employer would pay the employee a pension on retirement or a lump sum on death. The employer would not make any contributions itself, since there would be no one to receive them.

2.3.3.1 The advantages and disadvantages of holding pension funds under a trust

The quotation in the preceding section suggests that a trust is useful because it allows employee and employer to make contributions to the same fund.

? QUESTION 2.6

The use of trusts for holding pension funds yields a number of other advantages. Can you think of any?

Trusts are a useful vehicle for pension provision because they allow the managerial control of large funds to be concentrated in the hands of a few trustees. But the great advantage in the use of a trust over most other instrumentalities (such as a corporation) is the fact that the beneficiaries under a trust have a proprietary interest in the fund. This gives them security in the event of the insolvency of the employer corporation, and allows them to leave their entitlement to another in the event of their own death.

The use of a trust also brings with it the added advantage of subjecting the pension fund manager to strict equitable obligations (see D Pollard, 'Review and disclosure of decisions by pension trustees' (1997) 11(2) TLI 42 and see *Express Newspapers Pensions Trustees Ltd v Express Newspapers Plc* [1999] PLR 9).

? QUESTION 2.7

Can you think of any disadvantages in the use of trusts for holding pension funds?

The main problems in relation to occupational pension schemes stem from the potential for fraudulent use of the (often vast) funds involved. The potential for abuse stems in turn from the fact that in the usual case half the scheme trustees will be representatives of the employer company, and the employer very often has the power to appoint new trustees. If the employees' representatives are not astute to spot a fraud on the fund (and fraud, by its very nature, is often hard to detect), the trust fund can be wrongfully employed for the employer's personal purposes. This sort of fraudulent activity lay at the root of the Maxwell scandal in the late 1980s, and prompted the *Report of The Pension Law Review Committee* chaired by Professor Roy Goode (and known as 'The Goode Report'), published in September 1993, which in turn led to the enactment of the Pensions Act 1995.

The facts of *HR and Others v JAPT* [1997] PLR 99 illustrate a simple type of fraud on a pension fund. The case typifies the dangers of having trustees who are too closely involved with the employer company. (There was a significant overlap between the management of the trust company and the management of the employer company.) The essence of the fraud was the purchase by the pension fund trust of the employer company's main business premises at a grossly inflated price. The price had been approved by independent valuers, but on the basis of fraudulent information provided by the employer company.

2.3.3.2 Are pension trusts different to other trusts?

In his article, 'Pension Funds: A Fragmentation of Trust Law' (1993) 56(4) MLR 471, Graham Moffat takes trusts of pension funds as a central case for questioning '[t]he assumption of a high degree of homogeneity in the law of trusts'. It is the assumption that Sir Robert Megarry made when he said in *Cowan v Scargill* [1985] Ch 270 at 290:

> I can see no reason for holding that different principles apply to pension fund trusts from those which apply to other trusts. Of course, there are many provisions in pension schemes which are not to be found in private trusts, and to these the general law of trusts will be subordinated. But subject to that, I think that the trusts of pension funds are subject to the same rules as other trusts.

More recent cases tend to support Moffat's view. See, for example *Imperial Group Pension Trust Ltd v Imperial Tobacco Ltd* [1991] 1 WLR 589 where Browne-Wilkinson V-C held that:

> Pension schemes are of a quite different nature to traditional trusts. The traditional trust is one under which the settlor, by way of bounty, transfers property to trustees to be administered for the beneficiaries as objects of his bounty . . . a pension scheme is quite different. Pension benefits are part of the consideration which an employee receives in return for the rendering of his services . . . contractual and trust rights can exist in parallel.

In the *Air Jamaica* case (see 2.3.3) it was stressed that the use of trusts in the pension context:

> . . . is not to say that the trust is like a traditional family trust under which a settlor voluntarily settles property for the benefit of the object of his bounty. The employee members of an occupational pension scheme are not voluntary settlors. As has been repeatedly observed, their rights are derived from their contracts of employment as well as from the trust instrument. Their pensions are earned by their services under their contracts of employment as well as by their contributions. They are often not inappropriately described as deferred pay. This does not mean, however, that they have contractual rights to their pensions. It means only that, in construing the trust instrument, regard must be had to the nature of an occupational pension and the employment relationship that forms its genesis.

2.3.4 Asset protection trusts

> He who lends money to a trading company neither wishes nor expects it to become insolvent. Its prosperous trading is the best assurance of the return of his money with interest. But against an evil day he wants the best security the company can give him consistently with its ability to trade meanwhile.
>
> Nourse LJ in *Re New Bullas Trading Ltd* [1994] BCC 36 at 37.

The 'evil day' referred to in the quote usually means the day that the borrowing company is wound up insolvent. We will consider asset protection for this purpose first, but insolvency is not the only evil from which assets might be protected.

2.3.4.1 Protecting assets from creditors

Where party A incurs a debt to party B, A will be subject to a *personal* obligation to repay the debt to B. But if A becomes insolvent before repaying the debt to B, B will have to 'join the queue' of all the creditors with personal claims against A's assets. If, however, A is a trustee (and not merely a debtor) of assets held by A for the benefit of B, the situation is very different.

In such a case B, as beneficiary of the trust, will have *proprietary* rights in those assets. B will no longer have to join the queue of A's general creditors, because the assets will be treated as having never belonged to A.

2.3.4.2 *Barclays Bank v Quistclose*

We have already considered the case of *Barclays Bank v Quistclose Investments Ltd* [1970] AC 567. Look back to 1.3.3 to remind yourself of the facts. They can be summarized diagrammatically as follows:

Before the insolvency of Rolls Razor Ltd:			After the insolvency (before payment to shareholders) of Rolls Razor Ltd:		
Q	loan 'to pay shareholders' →	RR	Q	← loan monies returned	RR
creditor		**debtor**	**beneficiary**		**trustee**

Barclays Bank v Quistclose Investments Ltd [1970] AC 567, House of Lords

Lord Wilberforce:

> The transaction, it was said, between the respondents and Rolls Razor Ltd, was one of loan, giving rise to a legal action of debt. This necessarily excluded the implication of any trusts enforceable in equity, in the respondents' favour: a transaction may attract one action or the other, it could not admit of both. . . . I should be surprised if an argument of this kind—so conceptualist in character—had ever been accepted. In truth it has plainly been rejected by the eminent judges who from 1819 onwards have permitted arrangements of this type to be enforced, and have approved them as being for the benefit of creditors and all concerned. There is surely no difficulty in recognising the co-existence in one transaction of legal and equitable rights and remedies: when the money is advanced, the lender acquires an equitable right to see that it is applied for the primary designated purpose (see *In re Rogers*, 8 Morr. 243 where both Lindley LJ and Kay LJ recognised this): when the purpose has been carried out (i.e. the debt paid) the lender has his remedy against the borrower in debt: if the primary purpose cannot be carried out, the question arises if a secondary purpose (i.e. repayment to the lender) has been agreed, expressly or by implication: if it has, the remedies of equity may be invoked to give effect to it, if it has not (and the money is intended to fall within the general fund of the debtor's assets) then there is the appropriate remedy for recovery of a loan. I can appreciate no reason why the flexible interplay of law and equity cannot let in these practical arrangements, and other variations if desired: it would be to the discredit of both systems if they could not. In the present case the intention to create a secondary trust for the benefit of the lender, to arise if the primary trust, to pay the dividend, could not be carried out, is clear and I can find no reason why the law should not give effect to it.

? QUESTION 2.8

Barclays Bank v Quistclose is a case where an equitable interest was held to co-exist with a common law contractual debt. What was the nature of the equitable interest?

Lord Wilberforce held that there was a 'primary trust' in favour of the shareholders. The trouble with that analysis is that it is unclear why the corporate insolvency should have rendered that purpose incapable of being fulfilled. If the trust was in favour of the shareholders personally, they should have been able to claim their beneficial entitlement under the trust even after the company's insolvency.

Writing extrajudicially ('The Quistclose Trust: Who can enforce it?' (1985) 101 LQR 269 at 275–6) Sir Peter Millett suggested another analysis. Namely that, apart from where the lender (A) has a private interest of its own, separate and distinct from any interest of the borrowing company (B), in seeing that the loaned sums are applied for the stated purpose: 'the purpose of the arrangements [such as those in *Quistclose*] would be fulfilled if they were treated as leaving the beneficial interest in the fund in A throughout, but subject to a power in B, revocable by A at any time, to apply the fund for the stated purpose'. In other words, the beneficial interest only leaves the lender if the borrowing company actually applies the loaned monies in favour of the beneficiaries. This 'revocable power' analysis goes some way towards providing a solution to the problem expressed by Peter Gibson J in *Carreras Ltd v Freeman Mathews Ltd* [1985] 1 Ch 207 at 223 when commenting on Lord Wilberforce's analysis: 'I do not comprehend how a trust, which on no footing could the plaintiff revoke unilaterally, and which was expressed as a trust to pay third parties and was still capable of performance, could nevertheless leave the beneficial interest in the plaintiff which had parted with the monies'.

? QUESTION 2.9

Does Lord Millett's revocable licence analysis appear in any way unorthodox?

Lord Millett's analysis is probably the best attempt to date to provide a rationale for the *Quistclose* trust (and his Lordship has recently approved it judicially at the highest level—*Twinsectra Ltd v Yardley* [2002] 2 AC 164, House of Lords). However, Lord Millett's 'revocable power' analysis is hardly compatible with Lord Wilberforce's 'primary trust' label. In another trust context, that of discretionary trusts, Lord Wilberforce went to great lengths to insist that to construe a trust (which is imperative) to be a power (which is optional) would be highly artificial (*McPhail v Doulton* [1971] AC 424, see 4.5.2.1). Nevertheless, the usual reason for insisting upon a clear distinction between powers and trusts is that a clear distinction ensures that trustees (or donees of a power) know what is expected of them. This consideration does not arise in cases like *Quistclose*, where the contractual terms of the loan arrangement leave the trustee in no doubt as to what it *ought* to do. The *Quistclose* trust only becomes significant when the trustee has already failed to do that which it ought to have done. In *Twinsectra Ltd v Yardley* [2002] 2 AC 164 Lord Millett held that the borrower is generally not obliged to *apply* the loan for the particular specified purpose (hence there is no primary trust), but rather he is obliged to *refrain from applying* the loan for any purpose other than the particular specified purpose (188, para [87]). A helpful summary of Lord Millett's analysis can be found in the recent case of *Freeman v HM Commissioners of Customs and Excise* [2005] BCC 506; [2005] EWHC 582 Ch D (Companies Ct).

The search for an orthodox legal conceptual rationale for the *Quistclose* case will probably never reach an entirely satisfactory conclusion (see, further, Rickett, 'Different Views on the

Scope of the Quistclose Analysis' (1991) 107 LQR 608; W Swadling (ed), *The Quistclose Trust: Critical Essays* (Oxford: Hart, 2004)). The brevity and content of Lord Wilberforce's speech in *Quistclose*, not to mention the insubstantial concurrence of his learned brothers, suggests a decision driven by policy rather than doctrinal legal analysis.

? QUESTION 2.10

What might have been the policy concern driving the decision in *Quistclose*?

The likely policy concern is the desire to protect lenders who make emergency loans to corporations on the brink of insolvency, for '*Quistclose* trusts are frequently beneficial in the sense of providing an injection of capital which may rescue a company in financial difficulties' (Janet Ulph, 'Equitable Proprietary Rights in Insolvency: The Ebbing Tide?' [1996] JBL 482 at 495). A rescued company is a rescued trader and a rescued employer. A failed company very often results in unemployment and consequent social ills. The only persons with personal claims against the estate of the insolvent company who are likely to be fully satisfied are the insolvency practitioners themselves.

In *Quistclose*, the broad social and commercial benefits of corporate rescue may have been to outweigh the disbenefits of granting 'emergency lenders' prior rights in the actual event of insolvency. Yet despite the supposed political desirability of the *Quistclose* trusts, the irony is that if the *Quistclose* loan had actually been applied to pay the dividend to the shareholders, the lender would at that point have lost its priority over other creditors even though the loan had not at that time been repaid. The *Quistclose* trust provides, at best, only a short-term form of security. It is perhaps this feature that more than any other explains judicial willingness to recognize '*Quistclose* trusts' despite the conceptual difficulties they raise for orthodox trust law.

2.3.4.3 Cases after *Quistclose*

Quistclose was followed in *Re EVTR Ltd, Gilbert and Another v Barber* [1987] BCLC 646, decided after the Insolvency Act 1986. There the Court of Appeal considered another claim to a proprietary interest in insolvency. EVTR Ltd was in trouble financially and B (who had just won a small fortune on his premium bonds) agreed to assist it. He deposited £60,000 with EVTR's solicitors and authorized them to release the monies 'for the sole purpose of buying new equipment'. This they did. However, EVTR went into receivership before the equipment was delivered. The receivers recovered a large part of the monies which had been paid to the equipment suppliers. The trial judge held that the sums so recovered should be held as part of the general assets of the company. B successfully appealed. The Court of Appeal held that B had paid the monies to EVTR for the specific purpose of purchasing equipment. When this purpose failed, EVTR held the monies on trust for B. Through merely contracting to purchase the equipment EVTR had not fulfilled the purpose for which the monies had been provided, the true purpose had been the acquisition of equipment, and that had failed. As Dillon LJ put it, 'I do not see why the final whistle should be blown at half time'.

QUESTION 2.11

What would have been the outcome if EVTR had acquired the equipment?

This would have left the lender with merely a personal claim under the loan agreement. However, surely his intended purpose in making the loan to a company in financial difficulties was not that the company would acquire equipment, but that he, the lender, would be repaid. In other words, it could be argued that the Court of Appeal in this case still blew the whistle at half time as far as the lender was concerned. However, it would surely be going too far to recognize the priority of the lender's claim right up until the date of repayment of the loaned monies, that is, even after all special conditions attaching to the loan had been met. *Re EVTR* represents a small step in that direction, in that it allowed the claimant to assert a proprietary claim to monies which had already been paid away to (albeit recovered from) a third party. However, if the monies had not been recovered from the third party it is certain that, as the law now stands, the claimant would not have been able to assert his proprietary claim against the general funds of the borrowing company.

So far we have been considering asset protection trusts in cases where the monies had been advanced to assist failing companies. We have already suggested that granting priority to the lender can be justified on grounds of policy and principle, because of the perceived social and commercial benefits of successful corporate rescue. In fact, asset-protection trusts have also been recognized in other circumstances.

An example is *Carreras Rothmans Ltd v Freeman Mathews Treasure Ltd* [1985] 1 Ch 207. In that case, CR, a cigarette manufacturer, had for many years employed FMT to advertise its products, for which service FMT received an annual fee. The annual fee was paid on a monthly basis. FMT eventually fell into financial difficulties and was unable to meet its own monthly debts to third party agents. Fearing that it would lose the custom of CR, FMT set up a special account into which CR would henceforth make its monthly payments and out of which FMT would finance advertising on CR's behalf. Ultimately, however, FMT went into a creditors' voluntary liquidation and the special account was frozen. CR was obliged thereafter to pay FMT's agents directly to maintain the advertising campaign. CR brought an action against FMT and its liquidators claiming a declaration that the balance of monies in the special account had been held by FMT on trust to pay for CR's advertising and, that trust having failed, the monies were now held by FMT on resulting trust for CR. It was held that the monies in the special account had never been held by FMT for its own benefit, but for a specific purpose. Accordingly, the monies were not available to FMT's general creditors, but were held by the liquidator on trust for CR. Sir Peter Millett QC, as he then was, appeared for the successful claimant.

QUESTION 2.12

In the absence of the *political* benefits of corporate rescue, can you think of any *principled* justification for allowing CR to recover its funds ahead of FMT's general creditors?

Peter Gibson J was of the opinion that 'the principle in all these cases is that equity fastens on the conscience of the person who recieves from another property transferred for a specific purpose only and not for the recipient's own purposes, so that such person will not be permitted to treat the property as his own or to use it for other than the stated purpose' (p 222).

In *Twinsectra Ltd v Yardley* [2002] 2 AC 164, Lord Millett considered a loan made by Twinsectra Limited to Mr Yardley through the agency of certain solicitors. The solicitors to whom the loan monies were paid gave an undertaking that the loan monies would be retained by them until such time as they were applied in the acquisition of property on behalf of their client. They also undertook that '[t]he loan monies will be utilised solely for the acquisition of property on behalf of our client and for no other purposes'. In the event the loan monies were not applied exclusively towards the acquisition of property and the question arose whether the solicitor had breached a trust and whether another solicitor involved in the transaction at a later stage might be liable for having dishonestly assisted in a breach of that trust. (The question of accessory liability for 'dishonest assistance' proved to be controversial, and is considered in a later chapter (see 19.6.1.4)). For present purposes it is sufficient to note that their Lordships were of the opinion that the undertaking by the recipient solicitors gave rise to a trust of the *Quistclose* variety; the terms of the undertaking corresponding to the terms of the trust.

2.3.4.4 Asset protection for reasons other than priority in insolvency

In the previous section we saw that a commercial lender might wish to use a trust as an asset protection facility to protect the loaned monies from the borrower's general creditors.

EXERCISE 2.3

Write down a brief list of any *other* reasons you can think of why an international commercial enterprise might wish to protect its assets.

For an international commercial enterprise another reason for using an asset protection trust is to protect its assets from expropriation and other political risks in particular jurisdictions (including, very often, the jurisdiction in which the head corporation in the group is itself domiciled).

For a useful overview of the sorts of risks facing international commercial enterprise, the sorts of assets at risk and the potential usefulness of the trust as a way of addressing the risks, see Harry Wiggin, *Asset Protection for Multinational Corporations* in *Commercial Aspects of Trusts and Fiduciary Obligations*, Clarendon Press, 1992, McKendrick (ed).

In the next chapter of the same book, Jeffrey Schoenblum notes at p 217 that:

> During major international conflagrations and internal political disruptions in the past, corporate and individual capital has sought refuge in the United States and, to a lesser extent, in the Caribbean Islands. The conditions that have fostered the flight of capital to these jurisdictions persist, and thus, there is a continuing demand for fail-safe mechanisms for the preservation of the assets of corporations operating around the world. The common law trust has been regarded by some as an instrumentality that is capable of assuring the protection of such capital.

Although Schoenblum went on to express a certain scepticism that the trust was actually up to the task, it must be admitted that the trust has, in this context at least, certain advantages over the usual international commercial instrumentality, the corporation.

EXERCISE 2.4

Try to think of any advantages that the trust might have over the corporation in this context.

Trusts are more private (there is no public register of trusts) and the governing law of a trust is a matter of the settlor's choice, whereas that of a corporation is determined by its domicile. Thus, by means of a trust, it is possible to create a structure under which each of the trustees, the trust fund, the settlor and the governing law are based in different jurisdictions. Asset protection of this sort works because those claiming the protected assets lose the will to litigate in the face of such complexity. (For an illustrative hypothetical example, see D McNair, 'Risk Assessment in Multi-Jurisdictional Asset Protection Structures', in *Trusts and Trustees and International Asset Management* (1996) 2(1) at p 15.)

CHAPTER SUMMARY

- We have seen that the trust is a flexible and useful legal instrument and that it is conceptually and functionally distinct from other legal concepts such as contract, agency and debt.
- The distinctiveness of the trust is seen most clearly where it is employed as a means of prioritizing the beneficiaries' claims against their trustee in the event of the trustee's insolvency. Personal claims against the trustee's personal wealth brought by the trustee's personal creditors are relegated behind the claims of trust beneficiaries to recover their *own* property from the trustee's hands.
- This proprietary dimension of trust law (the fact that the beneficiaries' interest under the trust is their property to keep or transfer, and takes priority in the event of the trustee's insolvency) combined with the high standard of care demanded of trustees, has seen the trust employed for such diverse ends as the provision of occupational pension funds and the recovery of loans in commerce.

SUMMATIVE ASSESSMENT EXERCISE

online resource centre

Of all the exploits of Equity the largest and the most important is the invention and development of the Trust. It is an 'institute' of great elasticity and generality; as elastic, as general as contract. This perhaps forms the most distinctive achievement of English lawyers.

F W Maitland, 'Uses and Trusts' in *Equity: A Course of Lectures* (revsd by J Brunyate) (Cambridge, 1936). Critically discuss this statement.

FURTHER READING

Bartlett, R T, 'When is a "Trust" not a Trust?: The National Health Service Trust' (1996) Conv 186.

Ellison, R, 'Pension fund surpluses' (1991) TLI 60.

Hayton, D, 'Pension Trusts and Traditional Trusts: Drastically Different Species of Trusts' (2005) 18 Conv 229.

Hayton, D, 'When is a trust not a trust?' (1992) 1 Journal of International Planning 3.

Langbein, J H, 'The Contractarian Basis of the Law of Trusts' (1995) 105 Yale Law Journal 625.

Langbein, J H, 'The Secret Life of the Trust as an Instrument of Commerce' (1997) 107 Yale Law Journal 165.

Mason, Sir Anthony, 'The Place of Equity and Equitable Remedies in the Contemporary Common Law World' (1994) 110 LQR 238.

Millett, Sir Peter, 'The Quistclose Trust: Who can enforce it?' (1985) 101 LQR 269.

Moffat, G, 'Pension Funds: A Fragmentation of Trust Law' (1993) 56(4) MLR 471.

Nobles, R, 'Who Owns a Pension Surplus?' (1990) 19 ILJ 204.

Nolan, R C, 'Property in a Fund' (2004) 120 LQR 108.

Rickett, C, 'Different Views on the Scope of the Quistclose Analysis' (1991) 107 LQR 608.

Sealy, L S, 'The Director as Trustee' (1967) CLJ 83.

Stevens, R, 'The Contracts (Rights of Third Parties) Act 1999' (2004) 120 LQR 292.

Swadling, W, (ed), *The Quistclose Trust: Critical Essays* (Oxford: Hart, 2004).

Warburton, J, 'Charitable Trusts—Unique' (1999) Conv 20.

3 Capacity and formality requirements

OBJECTIVES

By the end of this chapter you should be able to:

1 Advise whether a would-be settlor is legally capable of setting up a trust
2 Create a trust of any type of property in compliance with the proper formalities
3 Deal with the equitable interest under a trust in compliance with the formalities
4 Recognize the numerous trusts for which there are no formality requirements
5 Identify valid 'mutual wills' and 'secret trusts'

3.1 Introduction

In this chapter we will see that most trusts, even express trusts, can be created without any formality whatsoever. However, statute does lay down a number of requirements relating to capacity and formality in trust creation. These requirements tend to arise from special policy considerations, rather than from anything inherent in the trust per se.

3.2 Capacity

According to the Oxford English Dictionary, capacity means in this context, 'legal competency or qualification'. The two most common reasons for lack of capacity are poor mental health and minority (infancy). These are considered below. However, even so-called 'artificial' persons, such as corporations, might also lack capacity if the legal documentation according to which they are constituted restricts or excludes their powers. So, for example, the 'objects clause' in the memorandum of a limited liability company might expressly or impliedly exclude the company's power to act as a trustee.

3.2.1 Mental incapacity

Medical evidence as to the mental state of property owners may raise a presumption that they lack the mental capacity necessary to make valid dispositions of their property. Unless this presumption is rebutted by other evidence, any purported dispositions will be ineffective to transfer the beneficial interests in the property (see *Simpson v Simpson* [1992] 1 FLR 601). Sections 95 and 96 of the Mental Health Act 1983 authorize the Court of Protection to deal with the property of a person judged to be incapacitated in this way. Such dealings can be varied by the Lord Chancellor or a nominated judge in certain circumstances (s 96(3)). (Note: these sections of the 1983 Act will be repealed and replaced by new provisions to similar effect when the Mental Capacity Act 2005 comes into force (which is not expected to be before 2007).)

3.2.2 Minority (infancy)

Since 1 January 1970 a minor (infant) is any person who has not yet attained 18 years of age (known as the age of majority). Before 1970 legal minority did not come to an end until the age of 21 had been attained. Just think, if you are a student between the ages of 18 and 21 your counterpart in the 1960s would have been labelled an 'infant' by the law!

Minors lack the capacity to hold the legal estate to land, and cannot create a trust of land (Law of Property Act 1925, s 1(6)). Further, a settlement of *any* property made by an infant by instrument on or since 1 January 1970, though not void *ab initio*, is nevertheless voidable if repudiated within a reasonable time of the infant having attained majority (that is, the age of 18: see the Family Law Reform Act 1969, s 1).

3.3 Formalities

One of the maxims of equity is that *equity looks to substance not form* (see 1.4.3). It might be thought, therefore, that there are no formal prerequisites to setting up a trust. In fact, although no magic words need to be used to create a trust (one certainly does *not* have to use the word 'trust'), nevertheless the Wills Act 1837 and the Law of Property Act 1925 require certain documentary formalities to be complied with so that a proper record may be kept of dealings with property. The Inland Revenue is, of course, especially keen to ascertain who is entitled to claim the benefit of property, so that the benefit may be taxed! Indeed, you should notice as you progress through this section the remarkable proportion of cases in which the Inland Revenue appeared as claimant.

There are however, to the probable chagrin of the Inland Revenue, numerous property dealings for which *no* formality is prescribed. The most important of these are as follows.

First, a trust may be declared *inter vivos* of pure personalty (which includes money and shares but, crucially, not land) without the need to satisfy any formal requirements. A trust is said to be *inter vivos* if it is effective within the lifetime of the settlor. Such a trust should be contrasted with a *testamentary* trust (see 3.3.2).

I could, for example, declare orally, 'see this gold pen of mine, I henceforth hold it on trust for the benefit of my baby son'. Assuming the context showed that I had intended to create legal relations, these words would be sufficient to move the beneficial (equitable) ownership of the pen from me to my son. I would be a trustee of the pen for him. On account of a few words I would no longer be entitled to the use and enjoyment of the pen, even though I keep the pen in my physical possession.

Second, the formality requirements laid down in the Law of Property Act 1925, which we shall shortly be considering in depth, do not apply to the creation or operation of resulting, implied or constructive trusts (these informal trusts will be considered in greater depth in **Chapters 16** and **17**).

Third, the formality requirements laid down in the Wills Act 1837, s 9 (as amended by the Administration of Justice Act 1982, s 17), do not apply to the creation or operation of so-called 'secret trusts'.

3.3.1 *Inter vivos* transactions

Law of Property Act 1925, s 53

(1) Subject to the provisions hereinafter contained [they are contained in s. 54, below] with respect to the creation of interests in land by parol—

(a) no interest in land can be created or disposed of except by writing signed by the person creating or conveying the same, or by his agent thereunto lawfully authorised in writing, or by will, or by operation of law;

(b) a declaration of trust respecting any land or any interest therein must be manifested and proved by some writing signed by some person who is able to declare such trust or by his will;

(c) a disposition of an equitable interest or trust subsisting at the time of the disposition, must be in writing signed by the person disposing of the same, or by his agent thereunto lawfully authorised in writing or by will.

(2) This section does not affect the creation or operation of resulting, implied or constructive trusts.

EXERCISE 3.1

Consider s 53 of the Law of Property Act 1925, set out immediately above. You will see that the section describes a number of transactions and prescribes formalities which must be met for each of those transactions. On p 50 you will see two columns headed TRANSACTION and FORMALITY respectively. Simply take your pen and draw lines to join the transactions to their corresponding formality requirement(s). Then compare your choices with the solution which follows.

TRANSACTION	FORMALITY
A declaration of trust of land	1 no formality
B disposition of an equitable interest under an existing trust	2 must be proved by a document signed by the settlor (or proved by the testator's will)
C declaration of trust of a subsisting equitable interest in land	3 must be made in a document signed by the settlor or the settlor's agent (or made in the testator's will)
D transaction giving rise to a constructive trust	

Hopefully you correctly observed that a *declaration* of trust respecting any land or any interest therein must be manifested and proved by some writing signed by some person who is able to declare such trust or by his will (s 53(1)(b)). A and C should have been linked with 2.

Further, a *disposition* of an equitable interest or trust already subsisting at the time of the disposition must be in writing signed by the person disposing of the same, or by his agent thereunto lawfully authorized in writing or by will (s 53(1)(c)). **B** should have been linked with 3.

You should also have noted that the formality requirements in s 53(1) do not affect the creation or operation of resulting, implied or constructive trusts. **D** should have been linked with 1.

The words declaration and disposition have been emphasized because they are easily confused. Declaration of a trust creates the trust, and hence creates the equitable interests under the trust, whereas disposition refers to the disposition of an equitable interest under a trust which already exists. Before a trust has been declared of property, it does not make sense to describe the equitable interest under that trust as already 'subsisting'.

? QUESTION 3.1

Between 1949 and 1950 H set up six settlement trusts in favour of his grandchildren. On 1 February 1955 H transferred 18,000 £1 shares to the trustees. On 18 February H orally and irrevocably directed that the shares should be held on the trusts of the six settlements, 3,000 shares to each settlement. On 25 March the trustees made written declarations of trust in accordance with H's directions. Which transaction transferred H's equitable interest in the shares?

The facts are those of *Grey v Inland Revenue Commissioners* [1960] AC 1, a case which was heard in the House of Lords. Grey was one of the trustees of the six settlements. The instruments of 25 March, by which the trustees declared the six trusts of 3,000 shares each, were formal documents which would be taxed if they had passed any 'value'. This type of documentary tax is called stamp duty, and is charged *ad valorem* ('according to the value' passed by the instrument). The crucial question was whether the 25 March instruments had actually transferred value, or whether they had been mere formal confirmation of a substantial transfer that had already taken place, on 18 February. The Inland Revenue had assessed the 25 March instruments to *ad valorem* stamp duty. Grey had appealed.

Their Lordships held that H's oral direction of 18 February had been an attempted 'disposition' of his equitable interest in the shares, but that it had been ineffective for failing to satisfy the requirement of writing established by s 53(1)(c) of the Law of Property Act 1925. Accordingly, only the later *formal* declarations by the trustees on 25 March were effective to transfer H's equitable interest in the shares. Those formal declarations constituted 'instruments' for the purposes of the Stamp Act 1891 and had been rightly assessed to *ad valorem* stamp duty.

In *Oughtred v Inland Revenue Commissioners* [1960] AC 206, 200,000 shares in a private company were held upon trust for Mrs Oughtred for life, thereafter for her son absolutely. Mrs Oughtred also owned 72,700 shares absolutely. To avoid estate duty payable on the shares in the event of Mrs Oughtred's death, the parties determined by an oral agreement to exchange their interests. Mrs Oughtred promised to transfer the 72,700 shares to her son, and he in turn promised to transfer his remainder interest in the 200,000 shares to Mrs Oughtred. Two documents of transfer were executed at a later date. The first document recorded the transfer of legal title in the 200,000 shares from the trustees to Mrs Oughtred in consideration of the sum of 10 shillings. The second document recorded the transfer of Mrs Oughtred's 72,700 shares to her son's nominees.

The Inland Revenue claimed *ad valorem* stamp duty on the document recording the transfer of the legal title in the 200,000 shares. Mrs Oughtred argued that no value had passed by virtue of that document, the equitable interest having been transferred by the earlier oral agreement, and accordingly that there was no basis on which to charge *ad valorem* stamp duty against the document.

? QUESTION 3.2

Do you think that the Inland Revenue succeeded?

The House of Lords could not agree on the result. Two of the five law lords dissented. One of the speeches in dissent was delivered by Lord Radcliffe, who had delivered the leading speech in *Grey v IRC*.

The majority held that Mrs Oughtred did not have a beneficial interest in the 200,000 shares until the execution of the later documents. It followed, therefore, that the document relating to the transfer of the 200,000 shares was an instrument transferring value, and should be subjected to *ad valorem* stamp duty. Mrs Oughtred had argued that inasmuch as the oral agreement was an agreement of sale and purchase it gave rise in equity to a constructive trust of the remainder interest in her favour, subject only to Mrs Oughtred performing her side of the agreement to transfer the 72,700 shares to her son.

The gist of Mrs Oughtred's argument ran something like this. Because the shares in that case were shares in a *private* company they were unique (inasmuch as it could not be guaranteed that replacement shares could be obtained on the open market). It followed from the uniqueness of the shares that common law damages would not be an adequate remedy for failure to fulfil the oral agreement. Equity would therefore grant specific performance of the contract, on the basis that *equity sees as done that which ought to be done* (see 1.4.8). Accordingly, the oral agreement was binding in equity. Consequently, according to equity Mrs Oughtred was, from the date of the oral agreement, no longer the beneficial owner of the shares in her possession. The necessary conclusion was that Mrs Oughtred held those shares, not for her own benefit, but upon trust for her son, with whom the oral agreement had been made. This was not an expressly created trust, but a constructive trust. Even if the oral agreement had, strictly speaking, amounted to a 'disposition' within s 53(1)(c), nevertheless it would be valid without writing because s 53(2) disapplies s 53(1)(c) where the disposition operates by virtue of a constructive trust.

A bare majority of their Lordships rejected this submission. By analogy with the 'simple case of a contract for sale of land' they pointed out that the deed which comes after the contract and completes the sale has never been regarded as 'not stampable *ad valorem*'. It followed, on this reasoning, that the later instrument of transfer to Mrs Oughtred had transferred real value and was stampable *ad valorem* as the Inland Revenue had contended.

Lord Radcliffe, who (together with Lord Cohen) had dissented from the majority view, observed that Mrs Oughtred need never have called for the subsequent written instrument of transfer, and that she could have simply called upon the trustees of the settlement of the 200,000 shares to transfer the bare legal title to her. For Lord Radcliffe the subsequent written transfer by the son was nothing more than a transfer of the bare legal title to Mrs Oughtred, it did not transfer any equitable interest at all and should not have been assessed to *ad valorem* stamp duty.

Oughtred v Inland Revenue Commissioners [1960] AC 206, House of Lords

Viscount Radcliffe (dissenting) . . . The reasoning of the whole matter, as I see it, is as follows. On 18 June 1956, the son owned an equitable reversionary interest in the settled shares; by his oral agreement of that date he created in his mother an equitable interest in his reversion, since the subject-matter of the agreement was property of which specific performance would normally be decreed by the court. He thus became a trustee for her of that interest sub modo; having regard to subs. (2) of s. 53 of the Law of Property Act 1925, subs. (1) of that section did not operate to prevent that trusteeship arising by operation of law. On 26 June the appellant transferred to her son the shares which were the consideration for her acquisition of his equitable interest; on this transfer he became in a full sense and without more the trustee of his interest for her. She was the effective owner of all outstanding equitable interests. It was thus correct to recite in the deed of release to the trustees of the settlement, which was to wind up their trust, that the trust fund was by then held on trust for her absolutely. There was, in fact, no equity to the shares that could be asserted against her, and it was open to her, if she so wished, to let the matter rest without calling for a written assignment from her son. Given that the trustees were apprised of the making of the oral agreement and of the appellant's satisfaction of the consideration to be given by her, the trustees had no more to do than to transfer their legal title to her or as she might direct. This and no more is what they did.

Lord Jenkins: The parties to a transaction of sale and purchase may, no doubt, choose to let the matter rest in contract. But if the subject-matter of a sale is such that the full title to it can only be transferred by an instrument, then any instrument they execute by way of transfer of the property sold ranks for stamp duty purposes as a conveyance on sale, notwithstanding the constructive trust in favour of the purchaser which arose on the conclusion of the contract. . . .

? QUESTION 3.3

Do you think that *Oughtred v IRC* would have been decided differently if Mrs Oughtred had not executed the subsequent written instrument of transfer?

The Court of Appeal has now had an opportunity to consider this possibility, or something very similar to it, in *Neville v Wilson* [1996] 3 WLR 460. Neville carried on business through N Ltd. Shortly before Neville's death N Ltd acquired all the issued share capital in U Ltd; 120 shares in U Ltd being held by nominees of N Ltd, the remaining shares in U Ltd being held by N Ltd as registered owner. In 1969 N Ltd was informally liquidated by shareholder agreement, its liabilities discharged and its assets divided between the shareholders. N Ltd was later struck off the register and formally dissolved. Some years later, after profitable business and after U Ltd's assets had been reduced to cash, Neville's children (who had been shareholders in N Ltd) commenced proceedings against ex-shareholders in N Ltd to determine, *inter alia*, the beneficial ownership of the 120 shares in U Ltd held by nominees.

It was held that the informal 1969 agreement had made the shareholders in N Ltd implied or constructive trustees for each other of the assets of N Ltd, the equitable interest of each shareholder under the constructive trust being of a size proportional to his shareholding in N Ltd. Accordingly, s 53(2) of the Law of Property Act 1925 saved the 1969 agreement from being rendered ineffectual by the formality requirements contained in s 53(1). Consequently, the money representing the shares did not pass to the Crown as *bona vacantia* (ownerless property), but was divided between the shareholders as they had agreed.

The decision of the Court of Appeal in *Neville v Wilson* lends indirect support to Mrs Oughtred's sophisticated line of argument, for the oral agreement in *Neville v Wilson* was held to give rise to a constructive trust, thus taking the agreement out of the remit of s 53(1)(c). On this view Mrs Oughtred's mistake was to execute a deed of transfer subsequent to her oral agreement. Although intended by her merely to confirm that the disposition of her equitable interest had already been effected orally, it gave an apparently irresistible opportunity to the House of Lords to decide, albeit by a bare majority, that *ad valorem* stamp duty should be paid on the deed. Whether as a matter of principle Mrs Oughtred's argument should ever be permitted to succeed is another matter.

3.3.1.1 Section 53(1)(b)

Section 53(1)(b) of the Law of Property Act 1925 provides as follows:

> a declaration of trust respecting any land or any interest therein must be manifested and proved by some writing signed by some person who is able to declare such trust or by his will; . . .

It is important to appreciate that the actual declaration of trust need not be *made* in writing. The requirement is merely that the declaration be manifested and *proved* by some authorized signed writing. Indeed the written proof of the declaration could quite possibly come a long time after the declaration, it might even be contained within the will of the person who declared the trust. Without written proof of the declaration of a trust of land, the trust is not *enforceable* in court against the trustee, it is however (for what it is worth) in all other respects valid.

3.3.1.2 Section 53(1)(c)

One crucial question unites the cases of *Grey v IRC, Oughtred v IRC* and *Neville v Wilson* considered earlier. The question is this: 'What amounts to a "disposition" for the purposes of s 53(1)(c)?' It is a question of central importance because, as we have seen, 'dispositions' are ineffective unless made by writing.

EXERCISE 3.2

Place a tick next to whichever of the following you consider will amount to a 'disposition' under s 53(1)(c).

- the transfer by a beneficiary of their interest under a trust to some other person
- a direction by a beneficiary to their trustee henceforth to hold the equitable interest on trust for some other person
- a statement by a beneficiary that they hold the equitable interest to which they are entitled on trust for some other person
- in the case of a bare trust, a direction by a beneficiary to their trustee to transfer the legal estate to some other person, the intention being that the equitable interest should pass simultaneously
- the disclaimer by a beneficiary of their equitable interest under a trust.

Compare your answer with the following:

The transfer by a beneficiary of their interest under a trust to some other person/a direction by a beneficiary to their trustee henceforth to hold the equitable interest on trust for some other person

Both of these transactions qualify as 'dispositions' of subsisting equitable interests within s 53(1)(c) of the Law of Property Act 1925. In both cases the original beneficiary, having made the transfer given by the direction, drops out of the picture, their equitable interest having been disposed of. The following diagram seeks to illustrate this.

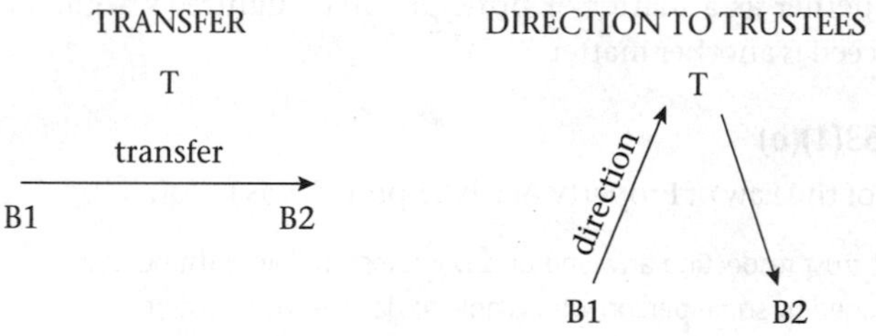

A statement by a beneficiary that they hold the equitable interest to which they are entitled on trust for some other person

The crucial question is whether this type of transaction is a declaration of trust (a subtrust, in fact), which involves the creation of an entirely novel equitable interest, or whether it is the disposition of a subsisting equitable interest.

As we have seen, s 53(1) treats 'declarations' and 'dispositions' quite differently. Generally, where a trust is declared *inter vivos* there are no formality requirements at all, only if a trust is declared of land must there be some written evidence of the declaration. In contrast, dispositions of equitable interests, whether the equitable interest is in land or some other property, must be made in writing in order to be valid.

Whether or not a statement by a beneficiary that they hold the equitable interest to which they are entitled on trust for some other person is a 'declaration' or a 'disposition' depends upon the facts of each case. If the beneficiary, having made the declaration, has no ongoing duties in relation to the equitable property, it would be nonsensical to describe the beneficiary as being a trustee of it. In such a case the equitable interest, though expressly stated to be held on trust, has in fact been disposed of outright (*Grainge v Wilberforce* (1889) 5 TLR 436). Further, for a statement of this sort to be recognized as a true declaration of trust the beneficiary must retain not only nominal duties, but duties which involve the real exercise of choice.

In the case of a bare trust, a direction by a beneficiary to their trustee to transfer the legal estate to some other person, the intention being that the equitable interest should pass simultaneously

This transaction was one of the many matters considered by the House of Lords in *Vandervell v Inland Revenue Commissioners* [1967] 2 AC 291. In 1958, Mr Vandervell, the immensely wealthy controlling director and shareholder of VP Ltd, decided to give 100,000 of his shares in the company to the Royal College of Surgeons (RCS) to found a chair in pharmacology. The shares were currently held by his bank under a bare trust for him. Accordingly, V directed the bank to transfer 100,000 shares to the RCS. It was intended that the RCS should keep the shares for a limited period only, and should relinquish them after receiving £150,000 income on the shares by way of dividends.

As to whether the direction to the bank had been void for lack of written formality, the House of Lords held that s 53(1)(c) only applied to cases where the equitable interest in property had been disposed of independently of the legal interest in that property. The object of s 53(1)(c) was to prevent hidden oral transactions in equitable interests which might defraud other parties (such as the Inland Revenue). In cases, such as the present, where the equitable owner had directed his bare trustee to deal with the legal and equitable estates simultaneously, s 53(1)(c) had no application. However, the decision in the present case ultimately went in favour of the IRC for other reasons.

Where a person entitled to a beneficial interest disclaims that interest

It was held by the Court of Appeal in *Re Paradise Motor Co Ltd* [1968] 2 All ER 625 that a disclaimer of this sort operates by way of avoidance, not by way of disposition. Consequently, the disclaimer does not need to comply with s 53(1)(c).

3.3.1.3 Lack of formality cannot be pleaded to disguise a fraud

It follows from the maxim *equity will not permit a statute to be used as an instrument of fraud* (see 1.4.4) that a party will not be permitted to perpetrate a fraud against another person by relying on that other person's failure to comply with the formality requirements laid down in s 53(1) of the Law of Property Act 1925. The *locus classicus* of this principle is the case of *Rochefoucauld v Boustead* [1897] 1 Ch 197, a case in which s 7 of the Statute of Frauds (29 Car 2, c 3), the precursor to s 53(1) of the 1925 Act, was considered in the Court of Appeal.

Lindley LJ held that 'the Statute of Frauds does not prevent proof of a fraud; and it is a fraud on the part of a person to whom land is conveyed as a trustee, and who knows it was so conveyed, to deny the trust and claim the land himself. Consequently, notwithstanding the statute, it is competent for a person claiming land conveyed to another to prove by parol [oral] evidence that it was so conveyed upon trust for the claimant'.

However, after the enactment of s 53(2) of the 1925 Act, *Rochefoucauld v Boustead* sits uneasily with the *letter* of the law. You will recall that s 53(2) disapplies s 53(1) in cases of 'resulting implied and constructive trusts'. It is arguable that, by the rule of statutory interpretation *expressio unius exclusio alterius* (express applicability to one case excludes implied applicability to another case), the wording of s 53(2) removes any possibility of an *express* trust like the one in *Rochefoucauld v Boustead* being excepted from the s 53(1) formality requirements.

3.3.2 Testamentary trusts

So far we have been considering *inter vivos* trusts, trusts which are effective within the lifetime of the settlor. Any trust which comes into effect upon the death of the person setting up the trust is said to be 'testamentary'. The person setting up such a trust is called a testator (if male) and a testatrix (if female).

To be valid a testamentary trust must comply with the formality requirements laid down in the Wills Act 1837, s 9. That section, as substituted by the Administration of Justice Act 1982, s 17, provides that:

> 9.—No will shall be valid unless—
>
> (a) it is in writing, and signed by the testator, or by some other person in his presence and by his direction; and
>
> (b) it appears that the testator intended by his signature to give effect to the will; and
>
> (c) the signature is made or acknowledged by the testator in the presence of two or more witnesses present at the same time; and
>
> (d) each witness either—
>
> (i) attests and signs the will; or
>
> (ii) acknowledges his signature, in the presence of the testator (but not necessarily in the presence of any other witness), but no form of attestation shall be necessary.

3.3.2.1 Mutual wills

The *usual* case of mutual wills occurs where a husband and wife enter into a binding agreement, intended to be irrevocable by either party acting unilaterally, that they will both draft their wills in a particular way so as to ensure that on the death of the first to die the surviving spouse will receive the property of the deceased. Frequently the wills also provide that, on the death of the last surviving spouse, certain other named persons (often their children) will receive the property. The surviving spouse may receive a life interest in the property (see *Re Green* [1951] Ch 148) or an absolute interest (see *Dufour v Pereira* (1769) Dick 419) depending upon whether the particular facts of the case show that there was to be a gift over to other persons on the death of the last surviving spouse. Of course, the device is not restricted to spouses, nor even to couples. Several people could in theory create mutual wills with one another.

? QUESTION 3.4

How can equity's recognition of the mutual wills agreement be justified where the agreement itself does not comply with the formalities of the Wills Act?

The traditional justification for equity's recognition of the agreement on which mutual wills are based is the prevention of fraud (see *Dufour v Pereira* (1769) Dick 419 at 421). It would be a fraud for the surviving party to rely on the lack of statutory formality as an excuse for reneging on the agreement, the deceased party having already performed their part of it. This rationale flows from the maxim, *equity will not permit a statute to be used as an instrument of fraud* (see 1.4.4), so from the date of the death of the first party to die, the survivor is obliged to carry out his part of the agreement. The obligation is expressed in the form of a constructive trust binding on the survivor. This use of constructive trusts to avoid the Wills Act is similar to that underlying fully secret trusts (see 3.3.3.1).

In *Re Dale* [1994] Ch 31, a husband and wife agreed that they would both draw up wills leaving their estates to their son and daughter equally. On his death the husband left his estate in accordance with the agreement. The wife, however, later drew up a new will, leaving the vast majority of the estate to her son, whom she also named as her executor. It was held that the husband and wife had entered into a binding agreement to create mutual wills, and that the son must hold his mother's estate on trust for himself and his sister equally. The most novel aspect of this decision was the acceptance that mutual wills could be created by persons who were not themselves named as beneficiaries under those wills.

Morritt J stated that:

> There is no doubt that for the doctrine to apply there must be a contract at law. It is apparent from all the cases . . . that it is necessary to establish an agreement to make and not revoke mutual wills, some understanding or arrangement being insufficient . . . it is necessary to find consideration sufficient to support a contract at law . . . It is to be assumed that the first testator and the second testator had agreed to make and not to revoke the mutual wills in question. The performance of that promise by the execution of the will by the first testator is in my judgment sufficient consideration by itself.

Contrast this approach with the *inter vivos* creation of constructive trusts of land, where the trust may be based upon mere proof of an 'understanding or arrangement'! (See 17.2.3.)

It is clear from the *dictum* of Morritt J in *Re Dale*, that for the doctrine of mutual wills to apply there must be evidence of an actual agreement to that effect. Thus even the action of executing identical wills will not, without an agreement, suffice (*Re Oldham* [1925] Ch 75).

3.3.3 Secret trusts

Secret trusts are a means by which a testator is able to bypass the formality requirements laid down in the Wills Act 1837. As Dankwerts J put it in *Re Young* (1951), 'the whole theory of the formation of a secret trust is that the Wills Act has nothing to do with the matter'. It is often said that secret trusts operate *dehors* (French: 'outside') the will. Typically, the reason for wanting secrecy arose where the testator wished to make a testamentary gift to a mistress or illegitimate child. (Note that the concept of 'illegitimacy' does not now exist, see Family Law Reform Act 1987, s 1.) This reason for creating a secret trust may or may not be largely historical today, nevertheless it is not unknown for 'modern' transactions (for example, the nomination of a beneficiary under a life insurance policy) to be argued by analogy to secret trusts (see *Gold v Hill* [1999] 1 FLR 54).

3.3.3.1 **Fully secret trusts**

This is where X *formally* leaves property to Y by his will in circumstances where Y is *informally* made aware by X during X's lifetime (and Y expressly or impliedly accepts) that Y is to hold the property as trustee for the benefit of Z. On the face of the will, Y will appear to be the beneficial owner of the property. The equitable jurisdiction to enforce a secret trust is aimed at preventing fraud on the part of the alleged trustee, as the following case illustrates.

The facts of *McCormick v Grogan* (1869) LR 4 HL 82 were that McCormick (M) left all his estate to Grogan (G) by a will in the briefest of terms. On his death bed M instructed G that his will and a letter were to be found in his desk. The letter named various intended beneficiaries and the intended gifts to them, and concluded with the words: 'I do not wish you to act strictly on the foregoing instructions, but leave it entirely to your own good judgment to do as you think I would, if living, and as the parties are deserving'. G accepted the terms of the letter. Later, one of the intended beneficiaries named in the letter (another McCormick), whom G had thought it right to exclude, sued G. The House of Lords did not doubt that in an appropriate case the terms of a secret trust could be enforced against the alleged trustee. However, it had not been shown on the facts of the present case that G should be held to any trust. The jurisdiction to enforce a secret trust is aimed at preventing equitable fraud on the part of the alleged trustee. It was held that there had been no *malus animus* (bad conscience) on G's part so the secret trust would not be enforced against him.

As has already been said, although fully secret trusts have certain testamentary characteristics they are valid, despite lack of testamentary formalities, because the trustee accepts the trust during the settlor's lifetime. They are essentially *inter vivos* and therefore operate independently of the Wills Act 1837. It is absolutely crucial, however, that the precise objects of the trust have been communicated, and the trust accepted, during the testator's lifetime. In fact, the communication of the secret trust must satisfy all three certainties required for the creation of an express trust. There must be certain *intention* to create a trust, the *subject matter* (property) of the trust must be certain, and the *objects* (beneficiaries) of the trust must be certain (see **Chapter 4**, where these certainty requirements are considered in depth). In *Re Boyes* (1884) 26 Ch D 531 there was no secret trust due to the absence of certainty of object. B had made an absolute gift to his executor by his will. The executor accepted that he was to hold the gift on trust for other persons, but the names of those persons were not communicated to the executor during B's lifetime. Only after B's death were informal letters found which detailed the intended objects of the gift. As Kay J observed, 'no case has ever yet decided that a testator can by imposing a trust upon his devisee or legatee, the objects of which he does not communicate to him, enable himself to evade the *Statute of Wills* by declaring those objects in an unattested paper found after his death'.

? QUESTION 3.5

Do you think that *Re Boyes* would have been decided differently if B had placed a sealed envelope containing detailed instructions into his executor's hand before his death?

Placing a sealed envelope containing detailed instructions in the executor's hand would have constituted constructive notice of the trusts to the executor, and the executor would be deemed to have accepted the trusts as detailed in the letter. As Lord Wright observed in *Re Keen* [1937] Ch 236 at 242: 'a ship which sails under sealed orders, is sailing under orders though the exact terms are not ascertained by the captain until later'.

In *Ottaway v Norman* [1972] Ch 698 the testator, by his will, left his bungalow to his housekeeper together with a legacy of £1,500 and half the residue of his estate. On her death the housekeeper left her property to strangers. Ottaway sued the housekeeper's executor, Norman, alleging that the housekeeper had orally agreed with the testator that she would leave various assets to Ottaway in her will. It was held that there had been an arrangement between the testator and the housekeeper under which the latter had agreed to pass on the bungalow, furnishings and fixtures to Ottaway. However, the date of the alleged agreement between the housekeeper and the testator was uncertain, and may have come after the will was drawn up.

? QUESTION 3.6

Do you think that there was a valid secret trust in this case?

Brightman J held that the testator had created a valid secret trust and that Norman now held the bungalow under a *constructive* trust for the benefit of Ottaway. The essential elements which had to be proved were:

(a) the intention of the testator to subject the housekeeper to an obligation in favour of Ottaway in relation to certain property;

(b) communication of that intention to the housekeeper; and

(c) the acceptance of that obligation by her either expressly or by acquiescence.

It was immaterial whether the informal agreement had come before or after the execution of the will. Nor was it necessary to show that the housekeeper had committed a deliberate and conscious wrong. However, his Lordship did hold that clear evidence would be needed before the court would assume that the testator had not meant what he had said in his will. The standard of proof was analogous to that required before a court would rectify a written instrument. (Contrast *Re Snowden* [1979] Ch 528, where Sir Robert Megarry V-C expressed some doubt about how far rectification was a fair analogy to secret trusts when determining the appropriate standard of proof. Apart from cases where fraud had been alleged against the trustee, he preferred to apply the ordinary civil standard of proof, that is, proof 'on the balance of probabilities'.)

Re Snowden [1979] Ch 528

Sir Robert Megarry V-C:

> The whole basis of secret trusts, as I understand it, is that they operate outside the will, changing nothing that is written in it, and allowing it to operate according to its tenor, but then fastening a trust on to the property in the hands of the recipient. It is at least possible that very different standards of proof may be appropriate for cases where the words of a formal document have to be altered and for cases where there is no such alteration but merely a question whether, when the document has been given effect to, there will be some trust of the property with which it dealt. . . . I am not sure that it is right to assume that there is a single, uniform standard of proof for all secret trusts. The proposition of Lord Westbury in *McCormick v Grogan* LR 4 HL 82, 97 with which Brightman J was pressed in *Ottaway v Norman* [1972] Ch 698 was that the jurisdiction in cases of secret trust was founded altogether on personal fraud. It is a jurisdiction by which a Court of Equity, proceeding on the ground of fraud, converts the party who has committed it into a trustee for the party who is injured by that fraud. Now, being a jurisdiction founded on personal fraud, it is incumbent on the court to see that a fraud, a malus animus, is proved by the clearest and most indisputable evidence.
>
> Of that, it is right to say that the law on the subject has not stood still since 1869, and that it is now clear that secret trusts may be established in cases where there is no possibility of fraud. *McCormick v Grogan* LR 4 HL 82 has to be read in the light both of earlier cases that were not cited, and also of subsequent cases, in particular *Blackwell v Blackwell* [1929] AC 318. It seems to me that fraud comes into the matter in two ways. First, it provides an historical explanation of the doctrine of secret trusts: the doctrine was evolved as a means of preventing fraud. That, however, does not mean that fraud is an essential ingredient for the application of the doctrine: the reason for the rule is not part of the rule itself. Second, there are some cases within the doctrine where fraud is indeed involved. There are cases where for the legatee to assert that he is a beneficial owner, free from any trust, would be a fraud on his part.

? QUESTION 3.7

Do you think that the secret trust in *Ottaway v Norman* was an express trust of land which, in accordance with the Law of Property Act 1925, s 53(1)(b) should have been unenforceable for lack of written proof?

At first sight the housekeeper had accepted an *express* trust of the testator's property, including the land, thus rendering the trust of land unenforceable for lack of writing. However, the s 53(1)(b) requirement for written proof of the trust is rather inconvenient where one is attempting to achieve secrecy! Section 53(1)(b) was not actually considered in the case. The fact that the defendant, Norman, was held to be subject to a *constructive* trust (on the ground of preventing fraud) took the trust of land into s 53(2), and thereby removed the need to comply with s 53(1)(b).

3.3.3.2 Half-secret trusts

This is where X *formally* leaves property by his will to Y *expressly* 'on trust' for another, but where Y is only *informally* made aware of the identity of that other. It will be clear on the face of the will that Y is *not* the beneficial owner of the property.

Viscount Sumner in the House of Lords in *Blackwell* v *Blackwell* [1929] AC 318 saw no relevant distinction between fully secret and half-secret trusts. 'In both cases', he observed, 'the testator's wishes are incompletely expressed in his will. Why should equity, over a mere matter of words, give effect to them in one case and frustrate them in the other?' For his Lordship the 'fraud' to be prevented was the same in both cases.

EXERCISE 3.3

Contrary to Viscount Sumner's opinion, it must be doubtful that with a half-secret trust (where the trustee is formally nominated as such) there is the risk of that fraud which the recognition of fully secret trusts seeks to prevent. Accordingly, as you read through this section try to identify another possible rationale for the recognition of half-secret trusts. A solution is given below.

Blackwell v Blackwell is itself a classic instance of a valid half-secret trust. The testator left a legacy of £12,000 to five persons by a codicil to his will, and directed them to apply the income 'for the purposes indicated by me to them', with power to apply two-thirds of the capital 'to such person or persons indicated by me to them'. The beneficiaries of the trusts (a mistress and her illegitimate son) were communicated orally by the testator to the intended trustees, with detailed instructions being given to one of the intended trustees. The intended trustees accepted the trusts before the execution of the codicil. The testator's widow challenged the validity of the half-secret trust and claimed the £12,000 for herself. The House of Lords held that the evidence of the oral arrangement was admissible and proved a valid half-secret trust in favour of the mistress and illegitimate son.

The facts of *Re Keen* [1937] Ch 236 were as follows. In advance of the execution of his will, Keen (K) handed a sealed envelope to E. The envelope contained the name of a lady to whom K had not been married. E was aware of the contents of the envelope but did not actually open it until after K's death. By a clause of his will K left £10,000 to certain friends, 'to be held upon trust and disposed of by them among such person, persons or charities as may be notified by me to them . . . during my lifetime'. This clause purported to reserve to K the power to make *future* testamentary dispositions by simply notifying the trustees during his lifetime of his intentions. Accordingly, the Court of Appeal held that the clause could not take effect, because it purported to exclude the requirement of the Wills Act 1837 that a duly executed codicil be used to amend a will.

Despite the fact that the clause was ineffective, the Court of Appeal held that the half-secret trust had to fail because the communication via the envelope had *preceded* the execution of the will and was therefore inconsistent with the reference in the clause to the *future* declaration of trusts by the testator during his lifetime. This is one of the few reported cases in which a court has consciously refused to give effect to the proved intention of the testator, and Lord Wright, the Master of the Rolls, did so with reluctance. In truth, the testator fell foul of his own choice of words. Had he expressly referred in his will to trusts which had been notified to his trusted friends in the *past* the sealed letter would probably have been admissible to prove the half-secret trust, subject only to proof of the communication and acceptance of the trust.

Re Bateman's WT [1970] 1 WLR 1463 was a similar case. There the testator directed his trustees to set aside £24,000 from his estate and to pay the income thereof 'to such persons and in such proportions as shall be stated by me in a sealed letter in my own handwriting addressed to my trustees'. The trustees received a sealed letter after the execution of the will, but before the testator's death. There was no evidence to show that the letter had been written before the execution of the will. Pennycuick V-C held that the direction to the trustees was invalid: 'once one must construe the direction as admitting of a future letter then the direction is invalid, as an attempt to dispose of the estate by a nontestamentary instrument'.

? QUESTION 3.8

Are the modern cases on half-secret trusts consistent with the statement, with which we started this topic, that 'the whole theory of the formation of a secret trust is that the Wills Act has nothing to do with the matter'?

Half-secret trusts are effective only when they can be treated as having been incorporated in the will. It follows that they must precede the execution of the will and that inconsistency with the will renders the half-secret trust invalid. In relation to half-secret trusts, the Wills Act 1837 still has something 'to do with the matter'.

CHAPTER SUMMARY

- Equity is more concerned with substance than form; hence trusts are *created* without any formality whatsoever.
- Where formality is required it is not because they are required for the creation of the trust per se, but because of other policy concerns such as the need for certainty in dealings with land and the need for certainty in testamentary dispositions.
- *Inter vivos* transactions, a summary of the formality requirements:
  - the *creation* of a trust requires no formality;
  - an expressly created trust of *land* is unenforceable without *formal evidence* of its creation;
  - the *transfer* of an equitable interest, such as an interest under a trust, must be *made* formally.
- Testamentary transactions: the Wills Act sets out strict statutory formality requirements with respect to testamentary dispositions. However, the courts have recognized a number of methods by which the testamentary formalities may be 'by-passed', these include:
  - fully secret trusts;
  - mutual wills;
  - *donationes mortis causa*.

SUMMATIVE ASSESSMENT EXERCISE

online resource centre

Explain, with reasons, the formalities (if any) that must be complied with in order to make the following actions valid and enforceable in a court of law.

(a) Bill, the freehold owner of Whitehouse, declares that he henceforth holds the legal title to Whitehouse on trust for his son, Charlton.

(b) Tony, the sole life beneficiary under a trust set up by his father, gives notice to the trustees that he disclaims his interest in favour of his son, to whom the trustees should henceforth pay all the income from the trust.

(c) Rob, who died recently, left property to Patrick by his will, having previously informed Patrick that he should secretly hold the property as trustee for the benefit of Rob's mistress.

(d) Bertie is the sole beneficial owner of a number of shares held in trust for him by a trust company wholly owned and controlled by him for the last 20 years. He now decides to instruct the company to transfer the shares to his wife.

FURTHER READING

Mental Capacity Act 2005

Bartlett, P, *Blackstone's Guide to the Mental Capacity Act 2005* (Oxford: OUP, 2005).

Green, B, 'Grey, Oughtred and Vandervell—A Contextual Reappraisal' (1984) 47 MLR 385.

Pawlowski, M, and Brown, J, 'Constituting a Secret Trust by Estoppel' (2004) Conv 388.

Rickett, C, 'Mutual wills and the law of restitution' (1989) 105 LQR 534.

4 Certainty requirements

OBJECTIVES

By the end of this chapter you should be able to:

1 Understand the three certainties that are prerequisite to the creation of an express trust: that is, certainty of intention, subject and object

2 Recognize the difference between conceptual and evidential uncertainty and the importance of that distinction

3 Appreciate the consequences where a trust fails for lack of certainty

4 Advise a settlor in drawing up a trust with sufficient certainty

4.1 Introduction

According to Lord Langdale MR in *Knight v Knight* (1840) 3 Beav 171, the courts will not acknowledge that an express trust has been created unless the 'three certainties' are shown. These are:

- a certain *intention* to create a trust (that is, words and conduct which create an imperative obligation)
- certainty as to the *subject* (property) of the trust and
- certainty as to the *object* (beneficiaries or purposes) of the trust.

The three certainties must be satisfied for the protection of the trustees. Imagine that you had been given a fund believing that it was an outright gift to you for your use and benefit. You would be in a lot of trouble if, having exhausted the fund, you were informed by a court that in fact you had been a trustee of that fund for the benefit of other persons or purposes. The requirement that the donor's intention be made certain is designed to prevent this sort of situation. The requirements of certain subject and object are similarly designed to protect the trustee, for if the trustee does not know the terms of the trust there is every chance that he or she will breach the trust and be personally liable for any loss (see **Chapter 15**).

The three certainties must also be satisfied for the benefit of the court. All trusts must be subject to control by the court, as Sir William Grant MR put it, '[t]here can be no trust over the exercise of which this court will not assume a control, for an uncontrollable power of disposition would be ownership and not trust' (*Morice v Bishop of Durham* (1804) 9 Ves 399). For a trust to be controlled by the court its object and subject must be certain.

In *Knight v Knight*, Lord Langdale MR suggested that there will be no difficulty in the application of his three certainties rule 'in simple cases'. He did acknowledge, however, that 'in the infinite variety of expressions which are employed . . . there is often the greatest difficulty in determining, whether the act desired or recommended is an act which the testator intended to be executed as a trust, or which the court ought to deem fit to be, or capable of being enforced as such'. He also stated that '[i]n the construction and execution of wills, it is undoubtedly the duty of this court to give effect to the intention of the testator whenever it can be ascertained'. To this we now turn.

4.2 A question of construction

When construing an instrument to discover whether the certainty requirements have been met, the trust must be given its natural construction.

4.2.1 Drafting background as evidence of proper construction

In *Rabin v Gerson* [1986] 1 WLR 526, the claimants took out a summons for the court's directions as to the proper construction of a charitable trust deed. During the proceedings the claimants sought to refer to the written opinions of the barristers who had originally drafted the trust deed. The opinions having being written before the drafting of the deed, the claimants hoped that they might be used as evidence of the settlor's intentions in setting up the trust. The Court of Appeal held that, as it had not been disputed that the words used in the trust deed had been the words the testator had intended to use, the deed fell to be construed according to the natural meaning of those words. Counsel's written opinions could not be admitted as evidence that the settlor had intended to achieve a specific legal effect, when such an effect did not otherwise flow from a natural reading of the deed.

Incidentally, if a court does conclude that a deed does not reflect the settlor's intentions, the court might order the deed to be rectified. See, for example, *Re Joseph Eagle 1989 Settlement* (2000) 1 WTLR 137, and compare 9.2.10.

4.2.2 The effect of precedent on construction

The general rule is that precedent should not be conclusive of the question of construction. In *Re Hamilton* (1895) 2 Ch 370, Lindley LJ determined that in each case the wording of the disposition should be construed to find its proper meaning 'and if you come to the conclusion that no trust is intended, you say so, although previous judges have said the contrary on some wills more or less similar to the one which you have to construe'.

However, if a disposition is made in terms which reproduce exactly the peculiar wording of a disposition in a previous reported case, the court may infer that the person making the disposition intended to achieve the same result as that achieved in the previous reported case.

In *Re Steele's Will Trusts* [1948] Ch 603, the testatrix left an heirloom to her son, to be held by him for his eldest son and so on 'as far as the rules of law and equity will permit', and with the request that the son should 'do all in his power by his will or otherwise to give effect to this my wish'. The phrasing of the gift exactly reproduced the wording of a disposition in a previous reported case where those words had been held to create a trust. It was held that, in choosing to adopt the precise wording used in a previous reported case, the testatrix had made clear her intention to achieve the result which was achieved in that previous case, namely a trust binding on her son. Accordingly, the wording of the present gift would take effect as a valid trust of the heirloom.

4.2.3 A pragmatic approach to construction

In theory the character of a disposition, whether it be an absolute gift or a trust, is determined from the outset on the basis of the words used by the settlor. In practice the question of construction does not come before the court at the moment that the disposition is drafted. It is generally not until quite some time later that the court is asked to declare the proper construction of the words used. This means that the court does not determine the nature of the gift in a logical vacuum, but, rather, with the full benefit of hindsight. The court knows at that point in time (far better than the settlor ever did) what the precise consequences will be of declaring the disposition to be either a trust or an absolute gift.

EXERCISE 4.1

Compare the facts of the following two cases. They were both decided at first instance and only five years apart, but the results in the cases were quite opposite. How do you account for the different decisions?

The first case is *Re The Trusts of the Abbott Fund* [1900] 2 Ch 326. A doctor in Cambridge had collected £500 from various subscribers for 'the maintenance and support' of two elderly, deaf sisters. No arrangement was made as to the disposal of any sums surplus to their needs. In the event they died leaving a surplus of £367 in the fund. The question was whether the gift had been to the old ladies 'absolutely', or subject to a trust requiring that the monies be used for no other purpose than their 'maintenance and support'. If the gift was absolute, the surplus would form part of the sisters' estates. If the gift had been made on trust, the surplus would be held under a resulting trust (see 16.2) for the contributors.

The second case is *Re Andrew's Trust* [1905] 2 Ch 48. The Bishop of Jerusalem had died and a fund was set up to finance the education of his children. When all the children had grown up and their education had been completed, there remained a surplus of monies in the fund. Again, the question was whether the gift had been to the children 'absolutely', or subject to a trust requiring that the monies be used for no other purpose than their education. If the gift was absolute, the surplus would be available to the children for whatever purpose they wished. If the gift had been made on trust, the surplus would be held under a resulting trust for the contributors.

The decision in *Re The Trusts of the Abbott Fund* was that the surplus in the account was held on a resulting trust for the subscribers to the fund in proportion to their contributions thereto. The money had never been the property, absolutely, of the ladies 'so that they should be in a position to demand a transfer of it to themselves, or so that if they became bankrupt the trustee in bankruptcy should be able to claim it' (*per* Stirling J at 330).

In contrast, it was held that the surplus in *Re Andrew's* should be divided equally between the Bishop's children. The donations were treated as an absolute gift to the children, albeit intended to be primarily for their education.

It is hard to see any justification for the different decisions in these two cases apart from the pragmatic one, namely that the donees in *Re Abbott* had died by the time the court came to consider the nature of the donation, whereas the donees in *Re Andrew's* were alive. Indeed, Kekewich J, in *Re Andrew's*, distinguished the *Abbott* case on that very basis: 'Here I am dealing with different facts, including the fact that the children are still alive.'

? QUESTION 4.1

What do you think a court would have decided in 1910 if faced with a settlement like that in *Re Andrew's* where the children had *died* before completing their education? Would the court still have concluded that the surplus should belong to the children absolutely and pass as part of their estates?

One can only guess at what the court might have decided in such a case. In the Court of Appeal in *Re Osoba* [1979] 1 WLR 247, Goff LJ eschewed any attempt to reconcile the *Abbott* case with *Re Andrew's*, accepting that: 'Both cases may well have been right on their particular facts'. In *Osoba* the testator made a bequest to his wife of the residue of his estate and of the rents from certain leasehold properties for his wife's 'maintenance' and for his daughter's 'training . . . up to University grade'. His wife died and shortly thereafter his daughter completed her university education. The testator's son claimed a share of the residue which had not been used for the daughter's education.

It was held that the gift of residue was an absolute gift to the wife and daughter equally, the expression of the purposes for which the gift was to be used being merely an indication of the testator's motive for making the gift. Further, as there had been no words of severance of the gift as between the wife and her daughter, they were deemed to hold the residue as joint tenants. Accordingly, ever since her mother's death, the daughter had held the whole of the fund absolutely for her own benefit.

EXERCISE 4.2

Read the following brief extract from the judgment of Buckley LJ in *Re Osoba*. To which factors did his Lordship attach special importance in coming to the conclusion he did?

Re Osoba **[1979] 1 WLR 247, Court of Appeal**

Buckley LJ:

> If a testator has given the whole fund, whether of capital or income, to a beneficiary, whether directly or through the medium of a trustee, he is regarded, in the absence of any contra-indication, as having manifested an intention to benefit that person to the full extent of the subject matter, notwithstanding that he may have expressly stated that the gift is made for a particular purpose, which may prove to be impossible of performance or which may not exhaust the subject matter. This is because the testator has given the whole fund; he has not given so much of the fund as will suffice or be required to achieve the purpose, nor so much of the fund as a trustee or anyone else should determine, but the whole fund. This must be reconciled with the testator's having specified the purpose for which the gift is made. This reconciliation is achieved by treating the reference to the purpose as merely a statement of the testator's motive in making the gift. Any other interpretation of the gift would frustrate the testator's expressed intention that the whole subject-matter shall be applied for the benefit of the beneficiary. These considerations have, I think, added force where the subject-matter is the testator's residue, so that any failure of the gift would result in intestacy. The specified purpose is regarded as of less significance than the dispositive act of the testator, which sets the measure of the extent to which the testator intends to benefit the beneficiary.

Did you identify the following?

(a) The testator had given the whole of the fund to the wife and daughter. This indicated that the monies were not limited to such amount as might be necessary to achieve the expressed purpose of the gift. The expressed 'purpose' was not, therefore, an imperative, overriding object of the gift, but 'merely a statement of the testator's motive in making the gift'.

(b) The gift was a gift of the residue of the testator's estate. If it failed, the result would be an intestacy, which would be most undesirable.

(c) In summary, the act of outright disposition was of greater significance than the expression of the specific purpose.

It should also be borne in mind that the words 'up to University grade' might have been nothing more than an attempt by the testator to give helpful guidance to the trustees as to the timing of the final disposition of capital in favour of the wife and daughter, although a letter of wishes outside the will would have been a less formal and therefore more appropriate means of communicating such guidance.

4.3 Certainty of intention

It may already be clear to you from the preceding section that the courts will only enforce trust obligations against B if A had clearly intended such an outcome, and A will only be held to have intended to create a trust if his words impress an imperative obligation on B.

? QUESTION 4.2

If your grandmother hands you £30 at Christmas and accompanies the disposition with the words 'get yourself a nice jumper', do you think that she has created a trust of the £30?

No, of course she hasn't. Your grandmother may have expressed her motive for making the gift, but there can be no doubt that the gift is an absolute gift. It follows that you are not a trustee of the £30 and do not have to purchase a jumper. The money is yours to do with as you wish. You may have a moral obligation to buy a jumper, but this is not enforceable against you in court (*Re Diggles* (1888) 39 Ch D 253).

There are no hard and fast rules for determining whether words of disposition have created an absolute gift or a trust. It would help if donors always used the words 'absolute' or 'trust' to express their intentions, but even that is not foolproof, for there have even been confusing cases where property has been given to persons 'absolutely in trust' (a similar case, *Comiskey v Bowring-Hanbury* [1905] AC 84, is considered at 4.3.1 below).

A disposition from A to B 'on trust for C' would be a perfectly certain trust. There is no doubt, however, that a trust can be created without using the word 'trust': as Lord O'Hagan stated in the House of Lords in *Kinloch v Secretary of State for India* (1882) 7 App Cas 619, 'there is no magic in the word "trust" '. In *Re Kayford Ltd* [1975] 1 WLR 279, Megarry J held (at 282) that 'it is well settled that a trust can be created without using the words "trust" or "confidence" or the like: the question is whether in substance a sufficient intention to create a trust has been manifested'.

It is sometimes said that precatory words will not give rise to a trust. Precatory words are words of prayer or petition (the Latin verb at the root of the word 'precatory' means 'to beg').

EXERCISE 4.3

Underline the precatory words in the following dispositions.

- I give my property to B hoping that B will look after my niece.
- I give my property to B desiring that B should distribute it amongst my cousins.
- I leave £100,000 to B, feeling confident that B will look after my uncle.
- I leave my estate to my wife, requesting that she should provide for the grandchildren.

You should have underlined the words 'hoping', 'desiring', 'feeling confident' and 'requesting'.

In the first half of the last century the courts were more willing to recognize trusts based on such precatory words. However, the attitude of the courts in the latter part of the last century hardened against trusts based on precatory words, and this remains the attitude of the courts today. Nevertheless, the test remains one of substance, to be applied on the facts of each case. Modern courts are still at liberty to recognize a trust based on precatory words if satisfied that the donor intended such a result. The courts will not determine the issue of construction on the basis of the precatory words alone, but will give the disposition its natural construction, taking the wording of the disposition as a whole.

4.3.1 Formal dispositions

Formal dispositions are usually (though not exclusively) contained within wills. What has to be done in each case is, quite literally, to construe the *will* of the testator. As Goff LJ stated in *Re Osoba* [1979] 1 WLR 247: the court should 'endeavour to ascertain his intention from the words he has used . . . in the light of such knowledge of relevant facts as we know he must have had'.

EXERCISE 4.4

Outlined below are the brief facts of three cases. In which, if any, of the cases do you think that the court held a trust to have been created?

- *Lambe v Eames* (1871) 6 Ch App 597 (CA). The testator left his entire estate to his widow 'to be at her disposal in any way she may think best, for the benefit of herself and her family'. On her death she left part of the testator's estate to an illegitimate child of one of the testator's sons.
- *Re Adams and the Kensington Vestry* (1884) 27 Ch D 394 (CA). The testator provided by his will that all his property real and personal should pass to his wife, her heirs, personal representatives and assigns, 'in full confidence that she would do what was right as to the disposal thereof between his children, either in her lifetime or by will after her decease'.
- *Comiskey v Bowring-Hanbury* [1905] AC 84 (HL). The testator left to his wife 'the whole of my real and personal estate and property absolutely in full confidence that she will make such use of it as I should have made myself and that at her death she will devise it to such one or more of my nieces as she may think fit and in default of any disposition by her thereof by her will or testament I hereby direct that all my estate and property acquired by her under this my will shall at her death be equally divided among the surviving said nieces'.

In *Lambe v Eames* it was held that there was an absolute gift to the widow, not a trust. It was accepted that similar words had in previous cases been held to create a trust, but the will fell to be construed, not according to precedent, but according to the testator's actual intention on a true construction of the will. To have found a trust in favour of the widow's family would have deprived the testator's 'illegitimate' grandchild of the gift made by the widow on her death. Compare *Re B (Child: Property Transfer)* [1999] 2 FLR 418 where a consent order transferring property from a husband to wife 'for the benefit of the child' of their marriage was held not to create a trust in favour of the child in the absence of clear words to that effect.

In *Re Adams and the Kensington Vestry* the question was, yet again, whether the disposition in the will was an absolute gift in favour of the wife or a trust in favour of her children. It was held that the words created an absolute gift in favour of the widow, unfettered by any trust. The reference to the children had been made merely to call to his widow's attention the moral obligations which had weighed upon the testator in making an absolute gift to her. His intention was merely to make express his motivation for making the gift. It was acknowledged that a testator's 'confidence' in his donee might suggest a trust in some contexts, but in the present case, on a proper construction of the whole will, no trust had been intended.

In *Comiskey v Bowring-Hanbury* it was held that, upon a true construction of the words of the will, the disposition took effect as a trust, under which the wife had a life interest. The initial part of the disposition (the gift 'absolutely in full confidence') may well have created an absolute gift if taken on its own. (The word 'confidence' is particularly ambiguous, for it can mean putting faith in another (confidence in the sense of trust) or it can mean the exact opposite, that is, putting faith in oneself.) However, the additional direction that the nieces should acquire an interest in any event, showed that the wife was not intended to acquire an absolute interest in the estate.

4.3.2 **Informal dealings**

Whether or not a disposition was intended to take effect as a trust depends primarily upon the words used, but where the words *do not appear in a formal document*, special importance is attached to the context in which the words were used.

Jones v Lock (1865) 1 Ch App 25 is a case in point. Jones, an ironmonger, returned home from conducting some business in Birmingham. When criticized by his family for failing to bring a present for his nine-month-old son, he produced a cheque in the sum of £900 made payable to himself, said, 'I give this to baby for himself' and placed the cheque in the baby's hand. He then took the cheque and said, 'I am going to put it away for him'. Six days afterwards Jones died. The cheque was found among his possessions. At issue was whether the baby was entitled to the £900. The Court of Appeal held that there had been no valid gift or declaration of trust. Accordingly, the baby was not entitled to the money. Lord Cranworth, the Lord Chancellor, accepted that an oral 'declaration of trust of personalty may be perfectly valid even where voluntary' but refused to find an intention to declare a trust in 'loose conversations of this sort'. He observed that, had the father not died, he would have been very surprised to discover that he was not able to use the £900 for his own benefit, but rather that he was bound to hold it in trust for his baby son.

Contrast the approach of Lord Cranworth with the approach of Scarman LJ in the Court of Appeal in *Paul v Constance* [1977] 1 WLR 527. Several features of the reasoning of the Court of Appeal were rather odd, indeed almost as odd as the fact that the case concerned a woman called Paul and a man called Constance!

Mrs Paul and Mr Constance lived together as man and wife. When Mr Constance received £950 in settlement of an action for personal injuries they decided to deposit the £950 in a bank account. The account was opened in the sole name of Mr Constance, so as to avoid any embarrassment in view of the fact that Mr Constance and Mrs Paul were unmarried (in fact, Mr Constance had not actually been legally divorced from his estranged wife!). Mr Constance frequently said to Mrs Paul that the money in the account 'is as much yours as mine' and that she could make withdrawals with his written authority. In fact only one withdrawal was ever made from the account, the sum withdrawn being then divided equally between them both. On the other hand, further monies were paid into the account, notably their joint winnings from playing 'bingo'. Mr Constance eventually died intestate and his executors closed the bank account, the balance being then roughly equivalent to the original deposit of £950. Mrs Paul claimed that the money in the account had been held by Mr Constance in trust for them both.

The Court of Appeal held that the words used by Mr Constance to assure Mrs Paul of her joint entitlement to the monies in the account were sufficient to constitute a declaration of trust.

The absence of the word 'trust' was not fatal to the finding of an express declaration of trust, taking into account the 'unsophisticated character of the deceased and his relationship with the plaintiff'. In coming to the conclusion that there was a trust, the Court of Appeal acknowledged that this was a 'borderline' case. In the result it was held that Mrs Paul was entitled to claim half of the money in the account. The other half went to Mr Constance's estranged wife.

? QUESTION 4.3

Do you see any problems with this decision?

Did you make the following points?

(a) According to *Jones v Lock*, the declaration of an express trust should not be recognized on the basis of 'loose conversations'. The conversations in *Paul v Constance* were of a very casual character. A recent case which illustrates that courts still find trusts in 'loose conversations' is *Gold v Hill* [1999] 1 FLR 54.

(b) If there was a declaration of trust, it is far from clear when it occurred.

(c) If there was a trust in this case it was at most an implied or constructive trust (Scarman LJ acknowledged that he was constrained by the pleadings to treat the claimant's claim, if there was to be a trust at all, as one based on an express trust).

(d) What were the terms of the so-called express trust of the money in the bank? If the terms were that the money was 'as much his as it was hers' why was she awarded only *half* of the balance? Generally the holders of a joint bank account can withdraw as much or as little of the monies in the account as they like; there is no sense in which the account is divided into half-shares. The law generally treats the holders of a domestic joint bank account as joint tenants of the balance. One important aspect of this is that when one of them dies the other owns the *whole* balance, not *half*, by '*right of survivorship*'.

For all these reasons the judgment of the Court of Appeal in *Paul v Constance* has rightly been criticized. The conclusion is inescapable that it was a highly pragmatic decision designed to achieve a rough form of justice between Mrs Paul and Mr Constance. In the absence of a trust in favour of Mrs Paul, Mr Constance would have been entitled to the balance standing in Mr Constance's account.

4.3.3 Establishing express trusts in commercial contexts

Commerce brings with it the risk of insolvency and the risk that creditors of the insolvent party will not be able to recover their money or other property from the insolvent party. If the creditor can establish a trust of the money or property that it claims, the creditor can claim as a beneficiary to be entitled ahead of the claims of the general creditors of the insolvent party to the extent of the property subject to the trust.

The facts of *Re Kayford Ltd (in liquidation)* [1975] 1 WLR 279 were as follows. K Ltd ran a mail order business, the customers of which paid either a deposit or the full price in advance. Fearing insolvency, the company sought independent advice and was advised to set up a

'Customers' Trust Deposit Account' to hold customers' monies until their goods were delivered to them. In fact, K Ltd paid customers' monies into one of its existing, dormant accounts. Only later was the name of the account changed to 'Customers' Trust Deposit Account'. Soon afterwards K Ltd went into voluntary liquidation. The liquidator raised the question whether the monies in the account belonged to the customers or to K Ltd's other creditors.

? QUESTION 4.4

What do you think *should* have been the decision in this case?

It was held that the customers were entitled to the balance of monies in the account. In the circumstances the intention to create a trust was held to have been manifestly clear, despite the failure to use a separate nominated 'trust' account from the outset. Megarry J stated (at 282A) that:

> There is no doubt about the so-called 'three certainties' of a trust. The subject-matter to be held on trust is clear, and so are the beneficial interests therein, as well as the beneficiaries. As for the requisite certainty of words, it is well settled that a trust can be created without using the words 'trust' or 'confidence' or the like: the question is whether in substance a sufficient intention to create a trust has been manifested.

His Lordship's decision was firmly based on the fact that the trust had been set up for the benefit of members of the public who had paid money in advance of receipt of goods. It was accepted that different principles might apply to trade creditors.

? QUESTION 4.5

Do you think his Lordship was right to suggest (as in effect he does) that there might be a greater element of trust involved in a case involving members of the public?

It appears that the *Re Kayford* approach need not be limited to members of the general public. In a similar case, but one where the 'subscribers' were shareholders (as opposed to customers) of the company in question, it was held that the company's promise to keep the subscribers' monies 'in a separate account' created a trust in their favour which took priority over the claims of the company's other creditors (*Re Nanwa Gold Mines Ltd* [1955] 1 WLR 1080).

? QUESTION 4.6

As a purchaser of goods and services, what implications does *Re Kayford* have for you?

As a result of *Re Kayford* it would appear to make good sense, whenever payment is made *in advance* of delivery or the rendering of services, to make payments expressly 'on trust' for the provision of those goods or services. However, in the recent case of *OT Computers Ltd (in administration) v First National Tricity Finance Ltd* [2003] EWHC 1010 (Ch) the judge doubted whether even 'equity lawyers' do this! Thankfully, in the context of purchasing a holiday, where large sums of money are paid in advance, ABTA and ATOL travel and flight agents automatically hold consumers' monies on trust to purchase their particular holiday.

Re Kayford was followed by the Court of Appeal in *Re Chelsea Cloisters Ltd (in liquidation)* (1980) 41 P & CR 98. The property management company in that case had set up a separate account in which it held tenants' deposits against damage which might occur to the rented premises or their contents. An accountant whose firm had been supervising the affairs of the company at that time, stated in evidence that the separate account had been established to prevent the tenants' monies from becoming spent as part of the company's general cashflow, and to ensure that they were available only to repay the deposits. The tenants claimed to be able to recover their deposits under a trust when the management company fell insolvent. Although Oliver LJ would have preferred independent evidence of this intention (as was provided by the independent financial advice given in *Re Kayford*) his Lordship concurred with Bridge LJ's analysis that a trust had been created in favour of the tenants.

Re Kayford and *Re Chelsea* were both followed in *Re Lewis's of Leicester Ltd* [1995] 1 BCLC 428. In *Re Lewis's* the insolvent company had traded as a department store in which floor space had been licensed to concessionaires on a 'shop within a shop' basis. These traders sold their own goods on Lewis's premises, but paid their takings into Lewis's tills, some of which were paid gross into a separate bank account in Lewis's name. One question that arose on the insolvency of Lewis's was whether the monies in the separate account could be said to have been held on trust for the concessionaires. Robert Walker J held that they had been held on trust, but that Lewis's (and hence Lewis's general creditors) had been entitled to assert its own beneficial claim to the fund to the extent of its entitlement to commission on the gross till receipts. Elsewhere in that case, his Lordship noted that 'the trust is a very versatile medium which can be and is used for a wide variety of commercial arrangements'. A suitable note on which to end this section.

4.3.4 Consequence of failure of certainty of intention

In the absence of a certain intention to create a trust, the donee takes the property beneficially (*Lassence v Tierney* (1849) 1 Mac & G 551), unless intended to take subject to a contractual or other legal obligation.

4.4 Certainty of subject matter

The lack of certainty of subject matter can take two forms. The property itself may be uncertain, in which case there will be no trust at all; or the beneficial entitlement of particular beneficiaries may be uncertain, in which case the trustees will hold the fund on resulting trust for the settlor.

4.4.1 Uncertain property

We will treat traditional and commercial trusts separately.

4.4.1.1 Traditional trusts

The leading case is *Palmer v Simmonds* (1854) 2 Drew 221. In that case a testatrix left her residuary estate to Thomas Harrison 'for his own use and benefit', and expressing her 'confidence' (or trust) in him that he would leave the bulk of her residuary estate to certain named persons if he should die without issue. Kindersley V-C asked himself 'What is the meaning then of bulk?' His conclusion was that 'what is meant is not the whole but the greater part . . . When, therefore, the testatrix uses that term, can I say that she has used a term expessing a definite, clear, certain part of her estate, or the whole of her estate? I am bound to say that she has not designated the subject as to which she express her confidence; and I am therefore of the opinion that there is no trust'.

4.4.1.2 Commercial trusts

Difficulties arise where trusts are claimed out of homogeneous bulk, that is, out of a mass of property comprising substantially identical parts (for example, a flock of sheep or a barrel of apples). So if, for example, I declare that two sheep from my flock are held by me on trust for you, the trust will be uncertain because I have not identified *which* two sheep were intended to be held on trust. A fund of money does not raise the same difficulty, because money is not specific property. Thus a trust declared of £1,000 from my account does not fail for uncertainty, even though I have not identified which bank notes are to be held on trust.

In *Re Goldcorp Exchange (in receivership)* [1995] 1 AC 74, the claimants were ordinary members of the public who had been misled into investing in non-existent gold bullion. In return for their 'investments' they were presented with certificates which allowed them to claim their bullion on giving the requisite notice to the company. On the company's insolvency, the claimants claimed, *inter alia*, to have beneficial interests under a trust in any bullion matching the contractual description. The Privy Council held that because the contracts were for 'non-allocated' bullion there was no property which could be described with sufficient certainty as being impressed with a trust. (Another important issue was whether the company had owed any fiduciary duty such as would justify impressing a trust upon the company's stocks of gold.)

A somewhat similar case is *Re London Wine Co (Shippers) Ltd (1975)* [1986] PCC 121 where customers claimed, *inter alia*, to have beneficial interests under a trust of a number of cases of wine held in a warehouse. LW Ltd was a wine merchant which ran its business on the basis that wine ordered by customers was held on trust by the company from the date of each customer's order and until delivery to the customers. However, the cases representing each order were not physically separated from the company's stocks until delivery. So, for example, if a customer had ordered 20 cases of *Chateau Lafite 1970* out of the company's bulk holding, the question to be determined was whether the subject matter was sufficiently certain for the company to be treated as trustee of that customer's order. This question was answered in the negative.

It was held that an express trust had certainly been *intended* by the company (the company's circulars referred to the customer as 'the beneficial owner' and to the company as merely having a lien, that is, the right to keep the wine until paid. It can only make sense to talk of having a lien over property in one's possession if somebody else is entitled to the property) *but* the subject matter had not been removed from the company's general stock and there was insufficient certainty of subject matter.

According to Oliver J, for there to be a valid trust of property comprised within an homogeneous whole, it must be a trust *of the whole*. Thus, if the homogeneous whole comprised 80 cases, the company could have achieved a valid trust of 20 cases by declaring a trust of 'one-quarter of the cases'. According to the judge, the company would thereby become trustee of the whole homogeneous bulk, the terms of the trust being an equitable tenancy in common between the company and the beneficiary in shares of three-quarters to one-quarter respectively. His reasoning appears to be that the subject matter of the trust is certain because 'one-quarter' is a non-specific description so can be satisfied from *any* quarter of the property. In contrast, where the subject matter of the trust is '20 cases of wine', such a specific description produces uncertainty as to *which* 20 cases were intended to form the subject matter of the trust.

Re London Wine Co (Shippers) Ltd (1975) **[1986] PCC 121**

Oliver J:

> As it seems to me, to create a trust it must be possible to ascertain with certainty not only what the interest of the beneficiary is to be but to what property it is to attach. I cannot see how, for instance, a farmer who declares himself to be a trustee of two sheep (without identifying them) can be said to have created a perfect and complete trust whatever rights he may confer by such declaration as a matter of contract. And it would seem to me to be immaterial at the time he has a flock of sheep out of which he could satisfy the interest. Of course, he could by appropriate words, declare himself to be a trustee of a specified proportion of his whole flock and thus create an equitable tenancy in common between himself and the named beneficiary, so that a proprietary interest would arise in the beneficiary in an undivided share of all the flock and its produce. But the mere declaration that a given number of animals would be held upon trust could not, I should have thought, without very clear words pointing to such an intention, result in the creation of an interest in common in the proportion which that number bears to the number of the whole at the time of the declaration. And where the mass from which the numerical interest is to take effect is not itself ascertainable at the date of the declaration such a conclusion becomes impossible.

? QUESTION 4.7

If a shareholder declared an express trust of '50 shares' in a company, do you think that such a trust would fail for uncertainty of subject matter?

The answer appears to be that the trust would not fail, provided that the shares in the company were all identical (shares can be different if, for instance, certain shares attract better voting rights than others).

Consider the decision of the Court of Appeal in *Hunter v Moss* [1994] 1 WLR 452. The defendant was the registered owner of 95 per cent of the issued share capital of a limited company. The trial judge held that the defendant had orally declared a valid trust of 50 of his shares (being five per cent of the total issued share capital of the company). The defendant applied by motion to have the judgment set aside, on the ground, *inter alia*, that there could not have been a valid declaration of trust because the subject matter of the trust was uncertain. The deputy judge dismissed the motion whereupon the defendant appealed.

The appeal was dismissed. The reason for the decision was that all the shares in the company were identical to each other, so it was quite valid to declare a trust of 50 shares without specifying which 50 shares were intended to form the subject matter of the trust. *Re London Wine Co (Shippers) Ltd* (1986) was distinguished.

? QUESTION 4.8

How can the different results in *Hunter v Moss* and *Re London Wine Co (Shipping) Ltd* be reconciled? In other words, why should cases of wine be regarded as distinct from each other while shares in a company are treated as being identical to each other?

The obvious answer, and the one which appealed to the judge in the *London Wine* case, was that, in the example of cases of wine, 'ostensibly similar or identical assets may in fact have characteristics which distinguish them from other assets in the class' ([1993] 1 WLR 934). So, for instance, certain cases may have been damaged or certain bottles been ruined.

This distinction between tangible property (such as bottles) and intangible property (such as shares) was followed, apparently with some reluctance, in *Re Harvard Securities Ltd (in liquidation)* [1998] CC 567. There the court decided that while there could not be an equitable assignment of unappropriated chattels, it was nonetheless possible to have a valid equitable assignment of unspecified shares, provided the shares are identical in type.

4.4.1.3 Where a trust fails for uncertainty of property

In such a case the trust is said to fail *ab initio* (from the very start). However, the fact that the trust attached to the gift has failed, does not mean that the gift itself must fail. Thus, in *Palmer v Simmonds* (see 4.4.1.1), the court held that upon the failure of the trust of the testatrix's residuary estate, the fund was held by her husband *absolutely* and passed under his will to those claiming under him.

4.4.2 Uncertain beneficial interests

Sometimes, even where there is no difficulty in identifying the trust assets, the subject matter of the trust may be rendered uncertain because the beneficiaries' rights in those assets are unclear.

? QUESTION 4.9

In *Boyce v Boyce* (1849) 16 Sim 476 the testator left two houses to trustees to convey one each to Maria and Charlotte. Maria was to pick 'whichever she may think proper to choose or select', the remaining house to go to Charlotte. Maria died before the testator without having made her election. Did the gift to Charlotte succeed?

No it did not. The gift to Charlotte failed for uncertainty because, in the absence of Maria's choice, it could not be said with certainty which of the houses would have been the one remaining after Maria's election had been made.

In *Re Thomson's Estate* (1879) 13 Ch D 144 the testator left realty and personalty to his wife by his will 'for the term of her natural life to be disposed of as she may think proper for her own use and benefit', providing further that, 'in the event of her decease should there be anything remaining of the said property or any part thereof', the said remainder should pass to certain named persons.

It was held that the widow took a life interest with a power to dispose of the property during her lifetime, but that the provision as to the testamentary gift of the remainder would be void for uncertainty of subject matter. The widow's *power* was incompatible with a *trust duty* in relation to the property.

EXERCISE 4.5

Compare and contrast the facts of the following two cases. Can you explain the different results?

In *Sprange v Bernard* (1789) 2 Bro CC 585 a testatrix left a legacy to her husband 'for his sole use' but went on to provide that 'at his death the remaining part of what is left that he does not want for his own wants and use' was to go to X. The Master of the Rolls held that no trust had been created. The husband was absolutely entitled to the legacy.

In *Re Last* [1958] 1 All ER 316 the testatrix, L, left all her property to her brother, directing that upon his death 'anything that is left' should pass to her late husband's grandchildren. When L's brother died intestate, and without issue or relations, the grandchildren applied to court claiming the residue of L's estate. The Treasury Solicitor argued in response that on a true construction of her will L had made an absolute gift of her property to her brother and that the Crown was therefore entitled now to the residue as *bona vacantia*. It was held that on a proper construction of the will L's brother had been entitled only to a life interest in the property and accordingly the applicants would be entitled to equal shares of the residue of L's estate. The judge was impressed by the absence of any words indicating the absolute nature of the gift to L's brother.

The decision in *Re Last* is at first sight hard to reconcile with that in *Sprange v Bernard*. However, the decision can probably be justified on the basis that the last thing the testatrix would have intended was that the property should have passed to the Crown.

Pragmatically the decision in *Re Last* may have been right. Conceptually, however, it is dubious. Karminski J can be criticized for apparently finding a trust because the words of the will did not suggest sufficient certainty of intention to make an absolute gift of the estate. The orthodox approach, as we have seen, is just the opposite. Namely, to presume an absolute gift in the absence of certainty of intention to create a trust!

? QUESTION 4.10

From everything you have already learned in this section, do you think that the gift of income in *Re Golay* [1965] 1 WLR 969 failed for uncertainty of subject matter? In that case the testator directed his executor to let a certain woman enjoy one of his flats during her lifetime 'and to receive a reasonable income from my other properties'.

The issue was obviously whether the direction to allow a 'reasonable' income was void for uncertainty. Ungoed-Thomas J held that the words 'reasonable income' invited an objective determination by either the trustees or the court. It was an objective determination which both were quite capable of carrying out. As the judge said, 'the court is constantly involved in making such objective assessments of what is reasonable'.

4.4.2.1 Where a trust fails because the beneficiary's interest is uncertain

One of the features of the cases which we have been considering is that, even where there is a certain intention to declare a trust, and even where the property is identified, the trust might still fail. See, for example, *Boyce v Boyce* (4.4.2). In such a case the property results (literally 'jumps back', see 16.2) to the settlor or his estate under a resulting trust. This is because the donee receives the property in such a case knowing that it was received in trust.

4.4.3 Uncertain subject matter may indicate uncertain intention

In *The Mussoorie Bank Ltd v Raynor* (1882) 7 App Cas 321 a testator left the whole of his estate to his widow by his will stating that he felt 'confident' that she would 'act justly to our children in dividing the same when no longer required by her'. The question was whether his widow was obliged to hold the estate on trust for their children. The Privy Council held that the precatory words, 'feeling confident' raised a doubt as to whether a trust had certainly been intended, and that the uncertainty of the subject matter cast further doubt on this intention. The widow took the estate absolutely, free from any trust. Sir Arthur Hobhouse stated that:

> There is not only difficulty in the execution of the trust because the Court does not know upon what property to lay its hands, but the uncertainty in the subject of the gift has a reflex action upon the previous words, and throws doubt upon the intention of the testator, and seems to shew that he could not possibly have intended his words of confidence, hope, or whatever they may be,—his appeal to the conscience of the first taker,—to be imperative words.

4.5 Certainty of object

The object of a trust might be to:

(a) benefit a legal person or legal persons (including corporate entities), that is, to benefit 'beneficiaries'; or

(b) advance public purposes (that is, charitable purposes—see **Chapter 8**); or

(c) advance private purposes (see **Chapter 7**).

In any case, for the trust to be valid the object must be ascertainable. This means that the object must be certain from the outset, or capable of being made certain in accordance with the maxim *certum est quod certum reddi potest* (that is certain which can be made certain). In the following sections we are mostly concerned with traditional non-commercial trusts, but it should be borne in mind that the same issues can arise in commercial contexts, thus in one recent case a company intended to set up a trust for its 'urgent suppliers', but the trust failed because that description failed to identify the objects with sufficient certainty (*OT Computers Ltd (in administration) v First National Tricity Finance Ltd* [2003] EWHC 1010 (Ch)).

4.5.1 Fixed trusts

These are trusts in which the trustees have no discretion as to the objects of the trust and no discretion as to how the trust fund is to be divided among the objects of the trust.

> **? QUESTION 4.11**
>
> Which of the following do you think are fixed trusts?
>
> - to my trustees on trust for Betty and Bill in two-third and one-third shares respectively.
> - to my trustees on trust for my employees in equal shares
> - to my trustees on trust for such of my nephews as my trustees may think fit.

Did you work out that the first two are fixed trusts? The third trust is a discretionary trust (see 4.5.2).

4.5.1.1 The class ascertainability test

For trustees to effect a division of the trust fund among a fixed class of beneficiaries in equal (or other fixed) shares, it is necessary to know how many beneficiaries there are. Taking the second example from the preceding Question, it would be necessary to know how many employees there were. If the size of the class could not be ascertained with certainty, the trustees would not know how much of the fund to give to any particular employee. Because an over-payment would be a breach of trust, the trust would become effectively unworkable.

The test for certainty of objects in a fixed trust is thus the 'class ascertainability' or 'fixed list' test. In other words, the trust will only be valid if it is possible to draw up a list containing every one of the beneficiaries. Of course, the trust does not fail for uncertainty merely because the beneficiaries on the list cannot be found. In an appropriate case the court might order that the share of the fund attributable to 'missing' beneficiaries should be distributed under a 'Benjamin Order' to those beneficiaries who have been located (see *Re Benjamin* [1902] 1 Ch 723). As an alternative to the cost and inconvenience of Benjamin Orders, courts have recommended the taking out of missing beneficiary insurance, especially where the estate is small (see *Re Evans* [1999] 2 All ER 777).

Note, however, that at one time the class ascertainability test was also applied to discretionary trusts. The reason given for applying the fixed list test to discretionary trusts (where the whole point is that the testator or settlor did *not* intend that the fund should be divided equally) was that there are circumstances when a trust might fall to be carried out by the courts, and the courts, according to the orthodox view, must effect an equal division of the fund, in keeping with the maxim *equality is equity*. Equal division obviously necessitates a complete fixed list of the members of the class of potential beneficiaries.

In *IRC v Broadway Cottages* [1955] 1 Ch 20, £80,000 was settled on trust to apply the income therefrom for the benefit of the members of a class of beneficiaries in such shares as the trustees in their absolute discretion saw fit. It was not possible to list all the members of the class at any one time but it was possible to say with certainty whether any particular claimant was or was not a member of the class. Two charities who had received monies from the trustees under the terms of the trust claimed to be exempt from income tax thereon. The Court of Appeal held that the trusts of the income were void for uncertainty of object and accordingly that the monies which the charities had received could not qualify as income for which they could claim exemption from income tax.

4.5.2 Discretionary trusts

These are trusts where the trustee 'is under a duty to select from among a class of beneficiaries those who are to receive, and the proportions in which they are to receive, income or capital of the trust property' (*per* Warner J in *Mettoy v Evans* [1990] 1 WLR 1587).

4.5.2.1 Adoption of the individual ascertainability test

As we have seen, the fixed list (class ascertainability) used to apply not only to fixed trusts but also to discretionary trusts. This caused a number of trusts to fail because a definitive list of beneficiaries could not be drawn up. However, with a discretionary trust the settlor does not want every potential beneficiary to receive a benefit, the whole point of such trusts being that the trustees should *choose* which of the potential beneficiaries should receive a benefit, and (generally) in what proportions. Thus the application of the class ascertainability test to discretionary trusts all too often defeated the settlor's dispositive intentions.

A more flexible test for certainty of object was required, one that did not require the whole of the class to be ascertained. The courts could not find the appropriate test in the law relating to trusts, but did find such a test in the law relating to powers, for a power will not fail simply because it is impossible to list all the potential objects of the power. Thereafter an artificial practice grew up under which courts would 'pretend' that a disposition was a power (when in fact it was a trust) in order to attract the more generous test of certainty of object applicable to powers.

The test of certainty for powers is to be found in the case of *Re Gestetner's Settlement* [1953] Ch 672. There the trustees had a power to distribute capital within a wide and diverse class of persons. Harman J stated that 'If . . . there be no duty to distribute, but only a duty to consider . . . there is no difficulty . . . in ascertaining whether any given postulant is a member of the specified class'. In other words, the test of certainty in relation to powers is not a class ascertainability test, but an 'individual ascertainability test'.

Re Gestetner was followed by the House of Lords in *Re Gulbenkian's Settlement* [1970] AC 508, where the settlement contained a power to appoint in favour of, *inter alia*, the settlor's son. Lord Upjohn held (at 523) that 'with respect to mere powers, while the court cannot compel the trustees to exercise their powers, yet those entitled to the fund in default must clearly be entitled to restrain the trustees from exercising it save among those within the power. So the trustees or the court must be able to say with certainty who is within and who is without the power.' Calouste Gulbenkian was one of the richest men of his generation, having amassed a fortune through oil. We, in a sense, are beneficiaries of his fortune, for it has been said that 'he left behind three enduring legacies: a vast fortune, a splendid art collection and, most fittingly of all, endless litigation over his will and the terms of his estate' (Daniel Yergin, *The Prize*, Simon & Schuster Ltd, 1991 at p 419).

In a landmark decision of the House of Lords, Lord Wilberforce brought to an end the artificial practice of construing trusts to be powers. He 'cut the Gordian knot' by simply changing the test for certainty of object in discretionary trusts.

? QUESTION 4.12

What new test did he adopt, do you think?

He adopted the test which had previously been restricted to powers. The landmark decision came in the House of Lords in *McPhail v Doulton (Re Baden's Deed Trusts No 1)* [1971] AC 424. It was, however, 'a close-run thing', their Lordships eventually recognizing the validity of the discretionary trust by a bare majority of three to two.

Mr Baden had settled a trust for the benefit of certain persons connected with a company controlled by him. The deed granted the trustees an absolute discretion to apply the net income 'to or for the benefit of any officers and employees or ex-officers or exemployees of the company or to any relatives or dependants of any such persons in such amounts at such times and on such conditions (if any) as they think fit . . .'. The first question was whether the deed had (1) granted the trustees a power of appointment among the class, or (2) subjected them to a discretionary trust. The second question, which flowed from the first, was 'is the gift void for uncertainty?' If the gift was in the form of a power, the trustees would have been able to appoint (distribute part of the fund to) any applicant of whom it could be said with certainty that they were or were not within the class of 'staff, relatives or dependants'. If, on the other hand, the gift was in the nature of a trust, the trustees would only have been able to appoint beneficiaries if every member of the class had been identified (see *IRC v Broadway Cottages* (4.5.1.1)).

It was held that the deed created a trust, not a power. However, the trust would not fail for uncertainty of object, even though it would not be possible to draw up a complete fixed list of every potential beneficiary within the class.

Lord Wilberforce rejected what he considered to be a narrow and artificial distinction between discretionary trusts and powers of appointment in the context of gifts of this sort. In his Lordship's opinion the distinction was one of 'delicate shading'. The following question is intended to illustrate just how delicate the shading can be.

QUESTION 4.13

Which of the following dispositions is a mere power and which is a trust?

- £10K to my wife to be distributed amongst my cousins as she may think fit
- £10K to my wife to be distributed amongst my cousins if she may think fit

Did you work out that the first disposition is a trust, because there must be a distribution, whereas the second disposition is a power, because distribution is not imperative? To emphasize the 'delicate shading' between discretionary trusts and powers, his Lordship described the discretionary trust in *McPhail* as being a 'trust power', which he contrasted with a 'mere power'. In the case of a trust power, if the trustees do not exercise it, the court will *require* that it is exercised 'in the manner best calculated to give effect to the settlor's or testator's intentions'. In the case of a mere power 'although the trustees may, and normally will, be under a duty to consider whether or in what way they should exercise their power, the court will not normally compel its exercise'. In the case of a mere power the court will only intervene 'if the power is exceeded or exercised capriciously' (but see now *Mettoy Pension Trustees v Evans* [1990] 1 WLR 1587 at 2.2.3, where it was held that the court may intervene to require the exercise of a 'mere power' where it is held by a trustee or other person already in a fiduciary capacity—a so-called 'fiduciary power').

EXERCISE 4.6

Examine the following brief extract from the speech of Lord Wilberforce in *McPhail v Doulton*. How did his Lordship summarize the distinction between trust powers and mere powers?

McPhail v Doulton (Re Baden's Deed Trusts No 1) **[1971] AC 424, House of Lords**

Lord Wilberforce:

It is striking how narrow and in a sense artificial is the distinction, in cases such as the present, between trusts or as the particular type of trust is called, trust powers, and powers . . .

It does not seem satisfactory that the entire validity of a disposition should depend on such delicate shading . . .

As to powers, I agree with my noble and learned friend Lord Upjohn in *Re Gulbenkian's Settlement* that although the trustees may, and normally will, be under a fiduciary duty to consider whether or in what way they should exercise their power, the court will not normally compel its exercise. It will intervene if the trustees exceed their powers, and possibly if they are proved to have exercised it capriciously. But in the case of a trust power, if the trustees do not exercise it, the court will; I respectfully adopt as to this the statement in Lord Upjohn's opinion. I would venture to amplify this by saying that the court, if called on to execute the trust power, will do so in the manner best calculated to give effect to the settlor's or testator's intentions. It may do so by appointing new trustees, or by authorising or directing representative persons of the classes of beneficiaries to prepare a scheme of distribution, or even, should the proper basis for distribution appear, by itself directing the trustees so to distribute . . . Then, as to the trustees' duty of enquiry or ascertainment, in each case the trustees ought to make such a survey of the range of objects or possible beneficiaries as will enable them to carry out their further fiduciary duty (cf *Liley v Hey*). A wider and more comprehensive range of enquiry is called for in the case of trust powers than in the case of powers.

Two final points: first, as to the question of certainty, I desire to emphasise the distinction clearly made and explained by Lord Upjohn between linguistic or semantic uncertainty [see below] . . . and the difficulty of ascertaining the existence or whereabouts of members of the class, a matter with which the court can appropriately deal on an application for directions. There may be a third case where the meaning of the words used is clear but the definition of beneficiaries is so hopelessly wide as not to form 'anything like a class' so that the trust is administratively unworkable.

His Lordship summarized the distinction between trust powers and mere powers thus: 'such distinction as there is would seem to lie in the extent of the survey which the trustee is required to carry out . . . a wider and more comprehensive range of inquiry is called for in the case of trust powers than in the case of powers'. The trustee of a discretionary trust need not have a fixed list of all the beneficiaries, but must 'survey the field' to form a reasonable view as to the number of potential beneficiaries.

It is probably because of this duty to 'survey the field' that a discretionary trust will fail if the 'class' is so large as to be 'administratively unworkable' (see below). In contrast, a mere power will not fail simply because the 'class' of potential beneficiaries is vast.

Lord Wilberforce was not convinced by the orthodox argument that a fixed list was required in order that the court might make a distribution in the event that the trust might fall to be carried out by the courts: 'Equal division is surely the last thing the settlor ever intended: equal division among all may, probably would, produce a result beneficial to none. Why suppose that the court would lend itself to a whimsical execution?' Rather, 'the court if called upon to execute the trust power, will do so in the manner best calculated to give effect to the settlor's or testator's intentions'.

In a move away from the orthodox approach, his Lordship held that the test of certainty of object which had hitherto been applied to powers (confirmed by the House of Lords in *Re Gulbenkian's Settlements* [1970] AC 508) should henceforth apply to discretionary trusts. He summarized that test, known as the 'individual ascertainability test', in the following terms: 'the trust will be valid if it can be said with certainty that any given individual is or is not a member of the class'.

His Lordship agreed with the opinion of Lord Upjohn, who had identified uncertainty of object in the context of discretionary trusts (or 'trust powers', to use Lord Wilberforce's description) to be of two types:

(a) First, 'linguistic or semantic uncertainty' (also called *conceptual uncertainty*), where the class of beneficiary is not susceptible of legal definition. An example of a conceptually certain class of beneficiaries would be 'my nephews'. An example of a conceptually uncertain class of beneficiaries would be 'my friends', for the latter is a term for which no usable definition can be agreed upon. This type of uncertainty *will* render the gift void.

(b) Secondly, *evidential uncertainty*, which is the practical difficulty of ascertaining the existence or whereabouts of beneficiaries. This type of uncertainty *will not* render the gift void.

(c) Lord Wilberforce also referred to a third case, not strictly speaking a case of uncertainty, where the meaning of the words is clear but the definition of beneficiaries is so hopelessly wide as not to form 'anything like a class' so that the trust is 'administratively unworkable'. One example of a trust that is administratively unworkable is a trust to benefit 'all the residents of greater London'. A further example of administrative unworkability is illustrated by the facts of *R v District Auditor, ex parte West Yorkshire Metropolitan County Council* [1986] RVR 24, where the council, before its abolition, purported to set up a trust 'for the benefit of any or all or some of the inhabitants of the county of West Yorkshire'.

EXERCISE 4.7

Consider *McPhail v Doulton* again. On a separate sheet of paper, list any objections you can think of to Lord Wilberforce's reasoning in *McPhail v Doulton*, and against each try to identify a possible response (perhaps taken from his Lordship's speech). Compare your list to the one below.

OBJECTION	RESPONSE
If all the trustees die, the court must administer the trust	It is nearly always possible to find new trustees
The court cannot exercise a private discretion	There are old authorities which suggest that it can
If the court exercises discretion it must do so on the basis of equal division	Equal division is the last thing that the testator wanted
The merits of the claim of every potential beneficiary must be considered	It is sufficient to make a survey of the field

4.5.2.2 Application of the individual ascertainability test

Having considered Mr Baden's deed trusts in *McPhail v Doulton*, the House of Lords remitted the case to the High Court to apply the individual ascertainability test to determine, *inter alia*, whether the trust for the class of 'relatives' must fail for uncertainty. The judgment of the High Court was appealed against. The decision of the Court of Appeal appeared as *Re Baden's Deed Trusts (No 2)* [1973] Ch 9.

Applying Lord Wilberforce's formulation of the 'individual ascertainability test', the Court of Appeal held that the term 'relatives' was conceptually certain and that the trust was valid. However, their Lordships appeared to have different conceptions of the term. Stamp LJ preferred a narrow construction, namely 'legal next-of-kin' of the employees. However, Sachs LJ took the view that even if 'relatives' was given 'a very wide meaning', that is, any persons who could 'trace legal descent from a common ancestor', there would not be conceptual uncertainty and the trust would be valid. For Sachs LJ, the problem of administrative unworkability in a class so large was automatically solved by the practical limitations on proof of relationship (in other words, family trees only ever go back so far, therefore the class would not in fact be administratively unworkable).

In *McPhail v Doulton*, Lord Wilberforce rejected any need for a fixed list of potential beneficiaries, but did he intend that a discretionary trust would be valid if a survey of the potential beneficiaries revealed that only *one* person may qualify for a benefit under the trust? Megaw LJ was alone among their Lordships in the Court of Appeal in picking up on this point, stating that '[t]o my mind, the test is satisfied if, as regards at least a *substantial number* of objects, it can be said with certainty that they fall within the trust' (emphasis added).

? QUESTION 4.14

What criticisms would you raise against the reasoning of their Lordships *in Re Baden (No 2)*?

(a) They held that the description 'relatives' was conceptually certain, even though they could not *agree* upon the meaning of the concept.

(b) If relatives is taken to mean descendants from a common ancestor, the class must be administratively unworkable as being 'nothing like a class' (it could include everyone on earth).

(c) There is nothing in Lord Wilberforce's formulation of the individual ascertainability test to suggest, as did Megaw LJ, that a discretionary trust will only be valid where there is evidence that a 'substantial number' of beneficiaries will fall within the trust.

(d) Stamp LJ took 'relatives' of X, to mean X's statutory next-of-kin even though the membership of that class cannot be certain until the death of X. Seeking to address this objection, he suggested that if X is still alive his 'next-of-kin' are 'his nearest blood relations'. These two alternative meanings of 'next-of-kin' might be said to introduce conceptual uncertainty sufficient to render void a trust for 'relatives'.

? QUESTION 4.15

Do you think that a trust for 'the members of the England soccer team that won the 1966 World Cup final' would fail for uncertainty?

At first there appears to be a conceptual difficulty. Does 'team' include all the squad members? Does it mean the eleven who started the final match? Are substitutes included? However, evidence can be admitted to show that the meaning of the word 'team', as distinguished from 'squad', is conceptually certain. Any evidential problems that might remain in relation to the actual identification of members of the class of beneficiaries can be resolved by oral evidence, newspaper reports, etc.

? QUESTION 4.16

Suppose a supporter of the Labour Party were to give money to trustees on trust to divide as they might think fit amongst the 'friends' of Tony Blair. Do *you* think that such a trust would be valid?

The trust would fail for conceptual uncertainty. Probably not one of us can come up with an acceptable definition of the word 'friend' to apply to our own social relations, it is even less certain that two or more persons could be found to agree upon a universal definition. Because no court can presume to understand what a donor meant by the term 'friend', no court will enforce trust obligations against a donee in favour of an object of that description. In *Re Barlow's Will Trusts* [1979] 1 WLR 278 (see 4.5.3.1) Browne-Wilkinson J observed that 'friend':

> has a great range of meanings; indeed, its exact meaning probably varies slightly from person to person. Some would include only those with whom they had been on intimate terms over a long period; others would include acquaintances whom they liked. Some would include people with whom their relationship was primarily one of business; others would not. Indeed, many people, if asked to draw up a complete list of their friends, would probably have some difficulty in deciding whether certain of the people they knew were really 'friends' . . .

Even if one person could be found who on *any* definition would be regarded as a 'friend of Tony Blair' the trust would fail, because, being unsure of the size of the entire class, the trustees would be unsure how much it would be appropriate to give to the one identified friend.

? QUESTION 4.17

Do you think that a trust 'for such persons as my wife considers to be my friends, in such shares as she thinks fit', would be valid?

This question is asking whether an otherwise conceptually uncertain term may be rendered certain by leaving the definition to one named person. The answer in the case of 'friends' must almost certainly be in the negative. The settlor's wife has more personal knowledge of the settlor and may be more expert at guessing the rough size of the class, but a rather more precise survey of the field is required in the case of a discretionary trust than the wife would be able to achieve by guesswork. She is no more able than a court to say with certainty whether *any* given individual is or is not within the class.

? QUESTION 4.18

What if the discretionary trust had been expressed to be for the benefit of 'Jewish children resident in Greater Manchester, any dispute as to the Jewish status of the child to be determined by the Chief Rabbi', would such a trust be valid?

The point has not arisen for decision in relation to a discretionary trust, but a similar provision in a case of a conditional gift (the beneficiary of the gift had to be of the Jewish faith and married and living with an 'approved wife', the Chief Rabbi having jurisdiction to determine whether or not the beneficiary's wife was 'approved') was held to render the condition certain and the gift valid (*Re Tuck's Settlement Trusts* [1978] Ch 49). In favour of the application of the reasoning in *Re Tuck's* to discretionary trusts it could be said that 'Jewish', unlike 'friend', has a precise meaning which the Chief Rabbi is more expert to define than is the court. Against the application of *Re Tuck's* to discretionary trusts it could be argued that the Rabbi's expert opinion can only assist with evidential uncertainty and that the term 'Jewish' can be no more conceptually certain for the Chief Rabbi than for the court.

4.5.3 Gifts subject to conditions

Having considered the different tests which apply to fixed trusts (the class ascertainability test), discretionary trusts (the individual ascertainability test) and mere powers (the individual ascertainability test), it is appropriate to consider this final category of disposition. In fact, it is a category which must be further sub-divided into *gifts subject to conditions precedent* and *gifts subject to conditions subsequent*.

4.5.3.1 Gifts subject to conditions precedent

The essence of a gift subject to a condition precedent is that the intended donee of the gift will not be entitled to the gift unless he first satisfies a particular condition.

In *Re Barlow's Will Trusts* [1979] 1 WLR 278, a testatrix died leaving a collection of paintings in her will. Having made some specific bequests she gave the remainder of the paintings to her executor on trust for sale but subject to a direction that 'any members of my family and any friends of mine who may wish to do so' should be allowed to purchase any of the paintings at far below their market values. The executor took out a summons for a declaration as to whether the gift (that is, the difference between the purchase price and the market price of the paintings) was void for uncertainty because the term 'friends' was itself uncertain. He also sought a direction as to the proper meaning of 'family' in the context of this gift.

It was held that the condition did not fail for uncertainty. If it could be said with certainty that any particular claimant qualified as a 'friend', a sale of paintings to that claimant would be valid under the terms of the will. This was because uncertainty as to whether other persons may or may not be 'friends' would have no effect upon the quantum of the gift to those persons who clearly qualified as 'friends'. The 'friends' in the instant case were taking the *whole* of the individual gift. Beneficiaries under a discretionary trust or mere power, on the other hand, do not receive the whole subject matter of the gift, but merely a *share* of the fund, hence the necessity in such a case to be able to say with certainty of *any* person at all whether or not they fall within the class of potential beneficiaries. *Re Allen* [1953] Ch 810 was followed. *Re Gulbenkian's Settlement Trusts* was distinguished.

4.5.3.2 Conditions subsequent

The essence of a gift subject to a condition subsequent is that initially the gift vests unconditionally in the donee, but will be *forfeited* if the donee subsequently breaches a condition to which the gift was subject. Such a gift can raise issues of certainty of object where the condition, as is often the case, relates to a personal attribute of the donee. So, for example, in *Re Tepper's Will Trusts* [1987] 1 All ER 970 a gift was made on condition that the donee 'shall remain within the Jewish faith and shall not marry outside the Jewish faith'. The gift was valid because the term 'Jewish faith' could be understood in certain terms from the outset (following *Clayton v Ramsden* [1943] AC 320). There was no reference to an expert arbiter of the term Jewish (as there had been in *Re Tuck's* (see 4.5.2.2)), but Scott J admitted evidence of the testator's own practice as a Jew in order to render certain what the testator had meant by the term 'Jewish'.

4.5.4 Uncertain object may indicate uncertain intention

Where the objects of the trust are uncertain, this may indicate that there was no real intention to create a trust. Consider the disposition in *Lambe v Eames* (1871) 6 Ch App 597, which, as you will recall, was a gift by a testator to his widow of his entire estate 'to be at her disposal in any way she may think best, for the benefit of herself and her family'. If the testator intended this disposition to take effect as a trust it begs the question, who are the intended beneficiaries of this trust (that is, who are 'family'?) and what interests are those beneficiaries intended to have? We have seen that courts *can* recognize such a disposition to be a valid discretionary trust for next-of-kin, but the fact that the settlor was so unclear as to the terms (in relation to the objects of the trust) might indicate, in a case where it is unclear whether a trust or an absolute gift was intended, that he did not intend to create a trust at all.

CHAPTER SUMMARY

- We have seen that there are three certainties that are prerequisite to the creation of an express trust:
  - certainty of intention—an outright gift is presumed unless a trust was clearly intended;
  - certainty of subject—which includes certainty of the assets and certainty as to the extent of the beneficiary's interest in those assets;
  - certainty of object—which may be to benefit a legal person or legal persons (including corporate entities), that is, to benefit 'beneficiaries'; or to advance public purposes (that is, charitable purposes—see **Chapter 8**); or, in special cases, to advance private purposes (see **Chapter 7**).
- When construing an instrument to discover whether the certainty requirements have been met, the words must be given a natural construction. We have seen that the courts are willing to take a fairly generous approach to construction, and will construe that to be certain which can be rendered certain on a natural construction of the words used, but that the courts cannot overcome fundamental uncertainty in the concepts used, particularly in relation to the definition of the class of objects in a discretionary trust.
- In theory the character of a disposition, whether it be an absolute gift or a trust, is determined from the outset on the basis of the words used by the settlor. In practice, however, the question of construction does not come before the court until quite some time after the disposition was drafted. This means that the court does not determine the nature of the disposition in a logical vacuum, but, rather, with

the full benefit of hindsight. Hence it is not unknown for a trust to be construed as a gift where it is practically convenient to do so.

- We have seen that the consequences of uncertainty vary according to the type of uncertainty.
  - Where the intention to create a trust is uncertain, the disposition will generally be effective as an absolute gift.
  - In the case where a trust fails for uncertainty of property the disposition is said to fail *ab initio*. Where a trust fails because the beneficiary's interest is uncertain the property will result to the settlor or his estate.
  - Where the object of the trust is uncertain there will also be a resulting trust for the settlor or his estate.

SUMMATIVE ASSESSMENT EXERCISE

online resource centre

Vincent, a renowned artist, died in 1997. His will contains the following provisions:

(a) 'to my favourite artist, Theodore van Damme, I devise my country studio and gardens on the Isle of Mull absolutely in full confidence that he will make such use of them as I should have made myself and that at his death he will leave them to the Royal Academy and in default of any disposition by him thereof by his will or testament I hereby direct that all my estate and property acquired by him under this my will shall at his death be given to the Royal Academy absolutely.'

(b) 'to my executors, my personal estate (excluding my art collection) to hold upon trust for such artists as they shall select having regard to their knowledge of my personal taste in art.'

(c) 'to my executors, the greater part of my art collection to be held by them on trust for my favourite model, Lucille Gachet, subject to any pictures which my friends may choose.'

Consider the validity of each provision, and the consequences, where relevant, of invalidity.

FURTHER READING

Hardcastle, I M, 'Administrative Unworkability—A Reassessment of an Abiding Problem' [1990] Conv 24.

Matthews, P, 'The New Trust: Obligations without Rights?' in A J Oakley (ed) *Trends in Contemporary Trust Law* (Oxford: Clarendon Press, 1996).

Worthington, S, 'Sorting Out Ownership Interests in a Bulk: Gifts, Sales and Trusts' (1999) Journal of Business Law 1.

5 The constitution of trusts

OBJECTIVES

By the end of this chapter you should be able to:

1 Distinguish between requirements of constitution and formality in relation to the creation of trusts

2 Identify a validly constituted trust

3 Apply the maxim 'equity will not assist a volunteer'

4 Explain the ways in which the common law can assist in the constitution of trusts

5 Recognize a valid *donatio mortis causa*

5.1 Introduction

In **Chapter 3** we discovered that the creation of *inter vivos* trusts of land, and the creation of testamentary trusts generally, must usually be accompanied by formal documentation. Nevertheless, in **Chapter 4** we noted that the creation of a trust does not depend upon any particular *form* of words. Whether or not an express trust was intended depends upon the *substance* of the words used, construed according to their context. In addition, there must be certainty of subject matter and certainty of object before a trust will be recognized. However, compliance with the formality and certainty requirements is not always sufficient to create an enforceable trust. Where the subject matter of the disposition is intended to pass to another person to hold as trustee, it is essential that it is passed to that person in accordance with the formal requirements for transfer of property of that type. Only when the transfer to the trustee has been completed can the trust be said to be fully constituted. And only when a trust is fully constituted is the trustee bound by it, the beneficiary entitled under it and the settlor deprived of the subject matter of it.

5.2 The distinction between requirements of formality and constitution in the creation of trusts

The distinction between requirements of formality and constitution in relation to the creation of trusts is essentially one of function.

The formality requirements laid down in s 53(1) of the Law of Property Act 1925 and s 9 of the Wills Act 1837 are designed to defeat secret fraudulent dealings and to achieve certainty through the recording of transactions. In relation to the creation of trusts they come, as it were, *ab extra* the transaction itself. Hence a declaration of trust of land may be *made* orally, but the court will not *enforce it* until the requisite formal proof has been produced. Since its inception, equity has refused to allow the shortcomings of form to defeat substantial justice, and it is well established that a person is not permitted fraudulently to rely upon the absence of statutory formality to defeat an equitable claim (see 3.3.1.3).

By way of contrast, if the requirements of valid constitution are not complied with, there is no trust at all. These requirements are a hurdle seemingly designed to prevent the casual creation of trusts. This is a sensible precaution when one considers the dramatic consequences of the typical express trust of property.

EXERCISE 5.1

On a separate sheet of paper try to list the parties who may be affected by a validly created trust and in your own words explain how they might be affected.

Did your list include the following?

- a person who creates a trust of his own property thereby *terminates* his *right to benefit from* that property (see *Re Bowden* [1936] Ch 71), except to the extent that he is identified as a beneficiary under the trust;
- the trust *confers* valuable *rights* upon persons who have not paid for them, that is, the beneficiaries;
- the trust *imposes* onerous *obligations* on persons who may not have been paid to bear them, that is, the trustees;
- in the rare case where no trustee can be found to administer the trust, the court may have to assume that function; and
- trust property does not form part of the trustee's personal estate in the event of the trustee's death or insolvency, and will therefore not be available to satisfy the trustee's personal debts to third parties.

Imagine that you declare a trust of land of which you are the sole absolute owner. You go on to produce a written memorandum of your declaration, thus complying with the formality requirement in s 53(1)(b).

If you declared yourself to be the sole trustee of the land there is nothing more that needs to be done, provided that the beneficiaries of the trust are certain. The trust is fully constituted because the legal title to the land is already in your name, therefore you already have everything you need to carry out the terms of the trust.

If, on the other hand, you declared that *other* named persons are to act as trustees, it will not be enough to have merely complied with the s 53(1)(b) formality requirement in relation to the setting up of the trust. You must, in addition, transfer the legal title in the land to the trustees so that they have everything they need in order to carry out the terms of the trust. (The legal title is needed to sell, exchange, mortgage or grant options against the legal estate.) This transfer of the legal title is said to be required for the *constitution* of an express trust. Failure to transfer the legal title to the trustees will render the trust incompletely constituted and for that reason void *ab initio*.

It is important not to confuse the requirement of valid constitution with the requirement of proper formality. It is true that where a trust of land is constituted by transfer of legal title to trustees the actual transfer must take the form of a deed (Law of Property Act 1925, s 52) but it would be a mistake to see this as a formality of trust creation. The fact is that whenever legal title to land is transferred *for whatever reason* (be it by way of sale, trust or absolute gift) the transfer must (apart from in the exceptional circumstances listed in ss 52(2) and 54 of the Law of Property Act 1925) be made by deed. The formality is a feature of transferring the particular type of property involved (that is, land), it is not a feature of the instrumentality employed (that is, trust).

5.3 Modes of constitution of trusts

It is crucially important to note that a valid will automatically constitutes any will trust incorporated within it, and that the trust thereby constituted is effective upon the death of the testator. *Inter vivos* trusts, on the other hand, must comply with one of the two modes of constitution. The first is where the settlor declares himself to be a trustee for the benefit of the beneficiaries (a declaration of self as trustee). The second is where the settlor transfers the trust property to a trustee (or trustees) for the benefit of the beneficiaries (a declaration of trust by transfer to trustees).

5.3.1 Declaration of self as trustee

In **Chapter 4**, where we considered the certainty requirements prerequisite to the creation of a valid trust, we analysed a number of cases where the settlor declared himself to be a trustee. See, for instance, *Jones v Lock* (1865) 1 Ch App 25 (4.3.2) (where Lord Cranworth accepted that an oral 'declaration of trust of personalty may be perfectly valid even where voluntary') and *Paul v Constance* [1977] 1 WLR 527 (4.3.2). The fact that the constitutional requirements in such cases are so undemanding (because there is no need to transfer the trust property) means that the certainty requirements become paramount in determining the validity of trusts in such cases. The courts have to be very sure, before holding that legal owners of property are no longer entitled to the beneficial use and enjoyment of their property, that they certainly intended to declare themselves trustees.

In this chapter we will be far more concerned with the constitution of trusts where the trust property needs to be transferred to trustees. Usually this entails the transfer of legal title to the property, but it can involve the transfer of equitable property.

5.4 Constitution by transfer of legal title to trustees

The constitutional requirements for trusts created by transfer of property to trustees vary according to the nature of the property transferred.

5.4.1 Where the trust property consists of shares

Many of the leading cases on incompletely constituted trusts and imperfect gifts have concerned trusts and gifts of shares. It is important to be aware that the general principles laid down in those cases have been applied more widely to cover trusts and gifts of other forms of property.

Shares in public companies must be transferred via the Stock Exchange. For most private companies the rule is that a transfer of shares in the company is only valid if the appropriate 'stock transfer form' is executed and delivered to the transferee (the trustee in our case) together with the share certificate, followed by the transfer of both documents by the trustee to the company. The company must then accept the transfer and register it in its books (see s 1 of the Stock Transfer Act 1963 and ss 182 and 183 of the Companies Act 1985). However, since 1996, with the introduction of the CREST system on the London Stock Exchange (see 14.1) a great deal of share dealing takes place electronically.

In the leading case, *Milroy v Lord* (1862) 4 De G F & J 264, a settlor owned shares in a bank which he purported to transfer to Lord by deed, to be held by him on trust for Milroy. The settlor later passed the share certificates to Lord. Lord was the settlor's attorney and was therefore authorized to transfer the shares to Milroy, but ultimately the transfer could only be completed by registration, at the bank, of Milroy as owner of the shares. This registration never occurred. The issue was whether Milroy could claim the shares under a trust created by the settlor.

EXERCISE 5.2

Milroy v Lord is a very important case, read the following extract thoroughly. What significant points were made about the constitution of trusts? Write down on a separate piece of paper anything that strikes you as being of particular importance. This is an exercise which will yield rich reward for the whole of this chapter.

Milroy v Lord (1862) 4 De G F & J 264

Turner LJ:

> Under the circumstances of this case, it would be difficult not to feel a strong disposition to give effect to this settlement to the fullest extent, and certainly I spared no pains to find the means of doing so, consistently with what I apprehend to be the law of the court; but, after full and anxious consideration, I find myself unable to do so. I take the law of this court to be well settled, that, in order to render a voluntary settlement valid and effectual; the settlor must have done everything which, according to the nature of the property comprised in the settlement, was necessary to be done in order to transfer the property and render the settlement binding upon him. He may of course do this by actually transferring the property to the persons for whom he intends to provide, and the provision will then be effectual, and it will be equally effectual if he transfers the property to a trustee for the purposes of the settlement, or declares that he himself holds it in trust for those purposes; and if the property be personal, the trust may, as I apprehend, be declared either in writing or by parol; but, in order to render the settlement binding, one or other of these modes must, as I understand the law of this court, be resorted to, for there is no equity in this court to perfect an imperfect gift. The cases I think go further to this extent, that if the settlement is intended to be effectuated by one of the modes to which I have referred, the court will not give effect to it by applying another of those modes. If it is intended to take effect by transfer, the court will not hold the intended transfer to operate as a declaration of trust, for then every imperfect instrument would be made effectual by being converted into a perfect trust. These are the principles by which, as I conceive, this case must be tried.

It was held on the facts of that case that no valid trust had been created. Milroy had not provided consideration for the shares, the settlement was therefore made by the settlor 'voluntarily', and Milroy was therefore a mere 'volunteer' under the settlement. Applying the maxim that *equity does not assist a volunteer*, it followed that the settlement would not be binding on the settlor (even if he had wished it to be so) unless the settlor had 'done everything which, according to the nature of the property comprised in the settlement, was necessary to be done to transfer the property'. The settlor had tried to transfer the property to Lord upon trust for Milroy, but the transfer had failed because, according to the bank's own rules, there could be no valid transfer of the shares without registration.

What is more, because the settlement was intended to take place by transfer the court would not give effect to it by finding a valid declaration of trust. It was held that if the settlor's chosen mode of disposition fails, the court will not perfect the settlement by allowing it to take effect by another of the modes.

It is clear from the leading judgment of Turner LJ that two equitable maxims underpinned these points, namely:

- *equity will not assist a volunteer*: 'in order to render a *voluntary* settlement valid and effectual, the settlor must have done everything which, according to the nature of the property comprised in the settlement, was necessary to be done in order to transfer the property and render the settlement binding upon him' (*emphasis added*); and
- *there is no equity to perfect an imperfect gift*: 'the intention was that the trust should be vested in the defendant Samuel Lord, and I think therefore that we should not be justified in

holding that by the settlement, or by any parol [oral] declaration made by the settlor, he himself became a trustee of these shares . . . by doing so we should be converting the settlement or the parol declaration to a purpose wholly different from that which was intended to be effected by it, and, as I have said, creating a perfect trust out of an imperfect transaction'.

EXERCISE 5.3

Consider the following case studies and state, in each case, whether you think that the settlor had 'done everything which, according to the nature of the property comprised in the settlement, was necessary to be done in order to transfer the property and render the settlement binding upon him'.

Case Study One

F, a resident of the United States, owned shares in an English company which he transferred by way of gift in favour of his son. By reason of wartime restrictions imposed upon the transfer of securities the English company was prohibited from registering (and refused to register) the transfer without Treasury consent. The forms necessary to obtain consent were sent to the donor to sign, which he duly did and he returned them to the company. F died, however, before consent was obtained from the Treasury.

Case Study Two

In March 1943, R transferred 10,000 shares in an unlimited company to his wife and on the same day transferred a further 10,000 shares in the same company to trustees to hold upon the terms of a settlement. The transfers were in an authorized form. In the event the transfers were not registered by the company until June 1943. R died in 1947 after which, in accordance with certain tax regulations, the Inland Revenue claimed estate duty on the shares because the gift had not been completed before April 1943.

The facts of *Case Study One* are taken from *Re Fry* [1946] Ch 312. In that case it was held that the transfer was ineffective and, consequently, that the intended gift was incomplete. The shares passed into F's residuary estate.

The facts of *Case Study Two* are from *Re Rose* [1952] Ch 499. The Court of Appeal held that R had done everything in his power to transfer his legal and equitable interest in the shares on the date of the transfer in March 1943. The factors which delayed the registration of the legal title until after April 1943 were beyond R's control. Counsel for the Inland Revenue had argued that the purported transfer must have been entirely ineffective according to *Milroy v Lord*, but the court held that *Milroy v Lord* would not invalidate a transfer in a case such as the present where the donor, after the purported transfer, would not have been permitted to assert any beneficial ownership in the shares at all. R had divested himself entirely of his equitable interest in the shares and accordingly his estate would not be liable to pay tax thereon.

Re Rose **[1952] Ch 499, Court of Appeal**

Jenkins LJ:

> . . . what was the position between the delivery of the transfers and the actual registration of the transferees as the holders of the shares? [Counsel for the Crown] has referred us to the well-known case of *Milroy v Lord*, which has been his sheet-anchor. He says that on this authority we must be forced to the conclusion that, pending registration, the transfers had no effect at all, and he arrives at that conclusion in this way: He says that these transfers, while purporting to be transfers of the property in the shares and not declarations of trust, did not transfer the property in the shares, because registration was necessary in order to get in the legal title. He says, further, that being transfers purporting to be transfers of the property in the shares and failing of their effect as such for want of registration, they could, pending registration, have no operation at all because in the case of *Milroy v Lord* it was held that a defective voluntary disposition purporting to operate as a transfer or assignment of the property in question would not be given effect to in equity as a declaration of trust. I agree with my Lord [Sir Raymond Evershed MR] that *Milroy v Lord* by no means covers the question with which we have to deal in the present case. If the deceased had in truth transferred the whole of his interest in these shares so far as he could transfer the same, including such right as he could pass to his transferee to be placed on the register in respect of the shares, the question arises, what beneficial interest had he then left? The answer can only be, in my view, that he had no beneficial interest left whatever: his only remaining interest consisted in the fact that his name still stood on the register as holder of the shares; but, having parted in fact with the whole of his beneficial interest, he could not, in my view, assert any beneficial title by virtue of his position as registered holder. In other words, in my view the effect of these transactions . . . must be that, pending registration, the deceased was in the position of a trustee of the legal title in the shares for the transferees.

After *Re Rose* the *Milroy v Lord* requirement can now be read thus: 'the settlor must have done everything *within his power* which, according to the nature of the property comprised in the settlement, was necessary to be done in order to transfer the property and render the settlement binding upon him' (italics added).

In coming to his judgment, Sir Raymond Evershed MR purported to distinguish the facts of *Milroy v Lord* from those of *Re Rose*. His Lordship did not expressly desire to relax the application of the principles in *Milroy v Lord*, but that has undoubtedly been the effect of his reasoning.

In *Re Rose* the Court of Appeal held that the settlor had successfully divested himself of his property (he had done everything in his power 'to transfer the property and render the settlement binding upon him') but, also, that the trust property had not been transferred to the intended trustees. The result is that the equitable interest in the property appears to be hanging in mid air between the date of the declaration of trust and the date when the legal title was finally registered with the company. This would all be well and good were it not for the fact that, as a matter of principle, the equitable interest in property must belong to somebody at all times. This principle is traditionally expressed in the maxim *equity abhors a vacuum in beneficial ownership*.

? QUESTION 5.1

Who, do you think, held the equitable interest in *Re Rose* between the declaration of trust and the date when the legal title was finally registered with the company?

The answer given in *Re Rose* was that the settlor, Mr Rose, held the property on trust during this period. As Sir Raymond Evershed MR stated: 'If, as I have said, the phrase "transfer the shares" is taken to be and to mean a transfer of all rights and interests in them, then I can see nothing contrary to the law in a man saying that so long as, pending registration, the legal estate remains in the donor, he was, by the necessary effect of his own deed, a trustee of the legal estate'. What type of trust this is, where the trustee has no trust obligations, it is hard to say. It is not even a bare trust properly so-called, because even if the beneficiary requested that the trust property be transferred to him, the settlor/'trustee' would be powerless to comply with the request. The best description of it might be that it is a 'nominal' trust, that is, a trust in name only.

Before proceeding to consider the transfer of other forms of property, it is important to note that the principles in *Milroy v Lord*, as interpreted in *Re Rose*, were stated in general terms and should be taken to apply to the constitution of all trusts, whatever the type of property involved, and not only to the constitution of trusts of company shares.

These general principles were applied again in *T Choithram International SA v Pagarani* [2001] 1 WLR 1, Privy Council. Thakurdas Choithram Pagarani (TCP) was a successful businessman who had been diagnosed as having terminal cancer. He executed a trust deed at his bedside to establish a foundation as an umbrella organization for a number of charities he had established during his life. Immediately after signing the deed he stated that all his wealth would now belong to the foundation (or words to that effect). TCP was a trustee of the foundation and the other trustees signed the deed the same day or shortly thereafter. Later, the directors of four companies controlled by TCP passed resolutions confirming that the companies' shares and assets would henceforth be held by the trustees of the foundation. TCP did not actually transfer any shares during his lifetime. After TCP's death the companies registered the trustees of the foundation as shareholders.

Their Lordships held that TCP had made an immediate, unconditional gift to the foundation.

? QUESTION 5.2

Do you see any problem with that decision?

At first sight there had not been a valid transfer to all the trustees, because TCP had not transferred the shares into their names. As he had not done everything he could have done, the transfer failed, and where a transfer fails equity will not constitute the transferor a trustee. However, their Lordships held that although equity will not aid a volunteer, neither would it strive officiously to defeat a gift. The words 'I give to the foundation' could have meant only one thing in the context of the case, namely 'I give to the trustees of the foundation' (for the foundation had no identity apart from its trustees). Although the words appeared to be words of outright gift, they really constituted a gift on trust. The fact that there had been no valid transfer to all the trustees was no obstacle to finding a trust on these facts, because TCP was one of the trustees and therefore all the trust property had already vested in one of the trustees. As trustee TCP's conscience was bound to give effect to the trust, and the beneficiaries of the trust could enforce it. They were not mere volunteers.

The *Choithram* decision has since been followed by the Court of Appeal in *Pennington v Waine* ([2002] 1 WLR 2075). Mrs Ada Crampton told Mr Pennington that she wished to transfer 400 shares in a private company to her nephew, Harold. She signed a share transfer form and gave it to Mr Pennington, who was a partner in the company's firm of auditors. He placed the form in a file and took no further action prior to Ada's death, apart from to write to Harold. In the letter he informed Harold that his firm had been instructed to arrange for the transfer of the 400 shares and that Harold need take no further action. Ada's will made no specific mention of the gift of 400 shares to Harold. It was held at first instance, in the absence of any evidence that the gift was intended to take effect in the future or subject to any condition precedent, that the gift of the 400 shares had taken effect *immediately* the share transfer forms had been executed, even though the form was never delivered to the intended donee or the company.

The Court of Appeal upheld that judgment, and in doing so it demonstrated generosity even greater than that which the courts had shown in *Re Rose* and *Choithram*. *Pennington* is more generous than *Re Rose* because in *Re Rose* there had actually been a transfer to the donee and all that remained to be done was to register the donee at the company, a step over which the donor had no control, and *Pennington* is more generous than *Choithram* because in *Choithram* there had at least been a notional 'transfer' from Mr Choithram in his capacity as donor to Mr Choithram in his capacity as trustee of the donee foundation. (Or, to explain the *Choithram* decision another way, it might be said—albeit not too convincingly in this author's opinion—that Mr Choithram was under a conscientious obligation, because of his status as a trustee of the donee foundation, not to assert his own claim to the subject matter of the donation at the foundation's expense.) In *Pennington* the donor had merely passed the share transfer form to her own agent. It is therefore hard to see how she could be said to have disposed outright of her beneficial interest in the shares when it remained open to her to revoke her instructions to Mr Pennington. (While it is true that her death made it impossible for her to revoke her instructions, it also removed any binding obligation on Mr Pennington to carry them out.)

EXERCISE 5.4

Read the following extract from the judgment of Arden LJ in the Court of Appeal in *Pennington v Waine* [2002] 1 WLR 2075. On what basis was the Court of Appeal able to conclude that Ada had divested herself entirely of her interest in the 400 shares?

Pennington* v *Waine **[2002] 1 WLR 2075, Court of Appeal**

Arden LJ

> The principle that, where a gift is imperfectly constituted, the court will not hold it to operate as a declaration of trust, does not prevent the court from construing it to be a trust if that interpretation is permissible as a matter of construction, which may be a benevolent construction. The same must apply to words of gift. An equity to perfect a gift would not be invoked by giving a benevolent construction to words of gift or, it follows, words which the donor used to communicate or give effect to his gift.
>
> The cases to which Counsel have referred us do not reveal any, or any consistent single policy consideration behind the rule that the court will not perfect an imperfect gift. The objectives of the rule obviously include ensuring that donors do not by acting voluntarily act unwisely in a way that they may subsequently regret. This objective is furthered by permitting donors to change their minds at any time before it becomes completely constituted. This is a paternalistic objective, which can outweigh the respect to be given to the donor's original intention as gifts are often held by the courts to be incompletely constituted despite the clearest intention of the donor to make the gift. Another valid objective would be to safeguard the position of the donor: suppose, for instance, that (contrary to the fact) it had been discovered after Ada's death that her estate was insolvent, the court would be concerned to ensure that the gift did not defeat the rights of creditors. . . . There must also be, in the interests of legal certainty, a clearly ascertainable point in time at which it can be said that the gift was completed, and this point in time must be arrived at on a principled basis.
>
> There are countervailing policy considerations which would militate in favour of holding a gift to be completely constituted. These would include effectuating, rather than frustrating, the clear and continuing intention of the donor, and preventing the donor from acting in a manner which is unconscionable. As Mr McGhee points out, both these policy considerations are evident in *Choithram* . . .
>
> There can be no comprehensive list of factors which makes it unconscionable for the donor to change his or her mind: it must depend on the court's evaluation of all the relevant considerations.

The main basis relied upon by the Court of Appeal was 'unconscionability' pure and simple. According to Arden LJ, unconscionability is a 'policy consideration' which militates in favour of holding a gift to be constituted. On the facts of the case her Ladyship held that by the time of Ada's death it would have been unconscionable of her to change her mind about making the disposition, because by that date she had 'not only told Harold about the gift and signed a form of transfer which she delivered to Mr Pennington for him to secure registration', but her agent had also 'told Harold that he need take no action. In addition Harold agreed to become a director of the Company without limit of time, which he could not do without shares being transferred to him'.

Whilst it may be broadly accurate to say that equity's notion of unconscionability promotes fundamental policy concerns, such as the prevention of the abuse of legal rights and powers, it must not be forgotten that unconscionability does not operate at the level of policy. On the contrary, it operates *in personam*, on a case-by-case or context-by-context basis. In fact, despite her Ladyship's equation of policy and unconscionability, she clearly had in mind the *in personam* nature of unconscionability when, in the very next part of her judgment, she sought to identify the specific factors which in her judgment would have made it unconscionable for the particular donor in this case to have denied the donee's beneficial interest in the 400 shares. Those factors were as follows: first, Ada made the donation of her own free will; second, she signed the share transfer form and delivered it to Mr Pennington to secure registration; third, she told Harold about the gift; fourth, Mr Pennington told Harold that he need take no further action to perfect the gift; fifth, Harold signed a form of consent to become a director without limit of time (knowing he could not become a director without shares in the company). If the first three factors, taken together or alone, were sufficient to bind Ada's conscience it would surely never be safe for a competent person voluntarily to promise to make a gift, let alone to instruct his agent to take steps preliminary to making a gift. They are not sufficient to bind Ada's conscience because it cannot be unconscionable to resile from a promise in circumstances where the promisee has suffered no detriment in reliance on it. This brings us to factors four and five. Factor four was no doubt a representation, but was it a representation on which Harold had relied to his detriment so that Ada's conscience would be affected? That must be doubtful. There was in fact nothing Harold could have done to perfect the gift in his favour, so his omission to do that which he could not have done can hardly be regarded as detrimental reliance. What then of the fifth factor? Here at last is a candidate. By accepting the directorship it is certainly arguable that Harold acted to his detriment in reliance on an expectation that he would acquire some shares in the company. However, assuming that there had been a representation plus detrimental reliance thereon, this would normally be said to raise an estoppel binding on the conscience of the representor, but their Lordships made no reference to estoppel, preferring instead to base their decision on the more general notion of unconscionability. That, with the greatest respect, will not suffice where a concept as vague as unconscionability is being applied in relation to something as dependent upon certainty as the transfer of beneficial ownership. However, if the 'unconscionability' approach survives it will no doubt come to represent a significant exception to the maxims 'equity does not assist a volunteer' and 'equity will not perfect an imperfect gift'.

5.4.2 Where trust property comprises land

The basic rule has always been that 'all conveyances of land or of any interest therein are void for the purpose of conveying or creating a legal estate unless made by deed'. This rule is now contained in the Law of Property Act 1925, s 52(1).

? QUESTION 5.3

In view of the above rule, and bearing in mind the principles in *Milroy v Lord*, do you think that the transaction detailed in the following facts (taken from the case of *Richards v Delbridge* (1874) LR 18 Eq 11) was effective?

Delbridge was the tenant of certain premises and the owner of a business which he carried on at those premises. He purported to make a gift of his lease and business to his grandson, Richards, who was an infant at the time. To give effect to the gift Delbridge endorsed and signed the following memorandum on the lease: 'This deed and all thereto belonging I give to Edward Bennetto Richards from this time forth, with all the stock-intrade.' He then delivered the deed to Richards' mother to hold for her son. Delbridge later died, making no reference to the gift in his will. At issue was whether the lease and the business should pass to Richards, by gift or trust, or whether the property should pass to other persons under the will.

It was held that the property passed under the will, there being no valid gift or declaration of trust in favour of Richards.

Richards had not given any consideration for the property and was therefore a mere 'volunteer', whom equity would not assist. Accordingly, Richards would only have been entitled to take the property if there had been evidence of a valid gift or a trust of the property. On the facts there had not been a perfect gift because there had been no formal conveyance of the legal title to Richards. There could not be a validly constituted trust imposed upon Richards' mother because there had been no conveyance of the legal title to her. Further, there could not be a validly constituted *inter vivos* trust binding on Delbridge (and binding now on his executors), because Delbridge had not expressed with sufficient certainty his intention to constitute himself a trustee by declaration of trust.

Sir George Jessel MR followed *Milroy v Lord* and refused to spell out a trust from a failed gift. The following passage from his judgment, though quite long, is worth reciting here in full. It is a very clear summary of the applicable law:

> A man may transfer his property, without valuable consideration, in one of two ways: he may do such acts as amount in law to a conveyance or assignment of the property, and thus completely divest himself of the legal ownership, in which case the person who by those acts acquires the property takes it beneficially, or on trust, as the case may be; or the legal owner of the property may, by one or other of the modes recognised as amounting to a valid declaration of trust, constitute himself a trustee and, without an actual transfer of the legal title, may so deal with the property as to deprive himself of its beneficial ownership, and declare that he will hold it from that time forward on trust for the other person. It is true he need not use the words, 'I declare myself a trustee' but he must do something which is equivalent to it, and use expressions which have that meaning; for, however anxious the court may be to carry out a man's intention, it is not at liberty to construe words otherwise than according to their proper meaning . . .

5.4.2.1 Registered land

In relation to land with registered title, in addition to the use of a deed, it is prerequisite to a valid transfer of the legal estate that the transfer of the estate be completed by the registrar entering the transferee on the register as the new proprietor (Land Registration Act 1925, s 19(1)): 'until such entry is made the transferor shall be deemed to remain the proprietor of the registered estate'. Despite this, the Court of Appeal in *Mascall v Mascall* [1985] 49 P & CR 119, applying the *Re Rose* interpretation of *Milroy v Lord*, held that a transfer of a registered estate had been effected (as far as the transferor was concerned at any rate) by the mere execution of the deed of transfer and the physical handing-over of the land certificate to the transferee. Lawton LJ observed that '[the transferor] had done everything in his power in the ordinary way of the transfer of registered property and, in the ordinary way, it was for the [transferee] to get the Land Registry to register him as the proprietor of the property'.

5.4.3 Where the trust property is an ordinary chattel

Traditionally we celebrate the anniversary of a friend's birthday by making a gift to him or her. Usually such a gift takes the form of a 'chattel', by which we mean a movable object of personal property. Examples would include books, furniture, and even animals (such as 'cattle' from which the word is derived, although nowadays they do not make ideal presents).

? QUESTION 5.4

At what point do you think that the transfer of legal title in such a gift becomes effective?

The answer is that to transfer legal title in a chattel there must be (1) physical delivery coupled with the requisite intention (that is, the intention to make an outright gift); or (2) a formally executed deed of gift. Words alone are insufficient to effect a valid transfer.

? QUESTION 5.5

If I telephone you on your birthday and say 'Happy Birthday, I've just bought a present for you. I am holding it right now and I'll bring it over later', are those words legally binding on me?

No, they are not. Despite my clear intention to make a gift to you, the gift will not be effective until I actually transfer the chattel to you. Alternatively, the gift could be effected by means of a formally executed deed of gift (although, apart from where law students are giving presents to each other, this would be rare).

In *Re Cole* [1964] 1 Ch 175, a husband bought a house in London while his wife and family were living elsewhere. Some time later his wife came to London and he took her to the house and showed her round. The wife was particularly impressed by certain chattels, namely a silk carpet and a card table. After the tour of the house the husband announced to her 'it's all yours'. Some sixteen years later the husband was declared bankrupt. In the year after the bankruptcy the wife sold the movable contents of the house. This action was brought by the trustee in bankruptcy to recover from the wife the proceeds of sale of the chattels.

? QUESTION 5.6

Do you think that there was a valid transfer of the chattels?

It was held (by the Court of Appeal in *Re Cole* [1964] 1 Ch 175) that, words of gift being in themselves insufficient to perfect a gift of chattels, the wife would have to prove some act of delivery or change of possession as would unequivocally show the husband's intention to transfer title to the wife. In the absence of evidence of such an act, legal title to the chattels must be said to have remained with the husband and to have vested in his trustee in bankruptcy. Some of their Lordships' reasoning would not, however, be well received today, as where Harman LJ held that '[i]n the ordinary case where a wife lives with her husband in a house owned and furnished by him, she has the use of the furniture by virtue of her position as wife, but that gives her no more possession of it than a servant has who uses the furniture'. The rule of law remains, however, that the possession of chattels used by both husband and wife is deemed to be with the spouse who has legal title to that chattel. Provided possession is actually delivered, the transfer will be valid if delivery is made prior to, contemporaneous with or subsequent to the words of gift. In fact, pre-existing possession by the donee, followed by words of gift, may amount to a valid gift by transfer, even though possession of the chattel actually changed hands a long time ago.

The Court of Appeal rejected the novel submission of R E Megarry QC that it is enough for the donee to be brought to the chattels, rather than the chattels to the donee, although Harman LJ did accept that if the chattels be numerous or bulky there may be 'symbolical delivery'. He gave the example of a case involving a church organ, 'where the donor put his hand upon it in the presence of the donee and accompanied his gesture with words of gift'.

In some circumstances, where the court takes a very pragmatic view, it may not even be necessary to transfer physical possession of the chattel at all. In *Jaffa v Taylor Galleries Ltd* (1990) *The Times*, 21 March, it was held that a trust of a painting had been validly constituted where the trust had been declared formally in a document (not a deed), of which the trustees each had a copy, even though the painting had not been physically transferred to the trustees. The judge commented that he 'could not conceive that a physical transfer had to take place and indeed it would be absurd so to find when one trustee was in Northern Ireland, another in England and when the third owner was the adult third plaintiff'. This very relaxed approach to the requirement of physical delivery will no doubt be restricted to cases where there is a formal document detailing the transfer and where it would be very inconvenient to require an actual change of physical possession of the chattel. Such cases will be very rare, most such gifts or trusts being effected by means of a properly executed deed of transfer as an alternative to physical delivery.

5.4.4 Where the trust property is a chose in action

A chose in action is a personal right of one person against another which can be sold, given away, subjected to a trust etc. as if it were property. Hence the name 'chose' (a thing). Common examples include patent, copyright and debt. For a less typical example see *Don King Productions Inc v Warren* [2000] Ch 291. The chose in action in that case was *the benefit of being a party to a contract to promote boxing*. The Court of Appeal held that the benefit could be held on trust, even though the contract itself could not be assigned to the partnership (due to the contract having been entered into with a third party and having by its terms been expressly rendered non-assignable).

The Law of Property Act 1925, s 136(1) provides as follows:

> Any absolute assignment by writing under hand of the assignor . . . of any debt or other legal thing in action, of which express notice has been given to the debtor . . . or other person from whom the assignor would have been entitled to claim such debt or thing in action, is effectual in law . . . to pass and transfer from the date of such notice . . . the legal right to such debt or thing in action . . .

A special rule applies to those choses of action known as bills of exchange. A bill of exchange is an unconditional order in writing requiring one person to pay money to another. To be transferred they must be endorsed in favour of the transferee (Bills of Exchange Act 1882, s 31).

5.5 Constitution by transfer where the subject of the gift or trust is an equitable interest

Where the equitable interest is an interest under a trust, the transfer of the equitable interest is not complete until the trustees of the trust have been given notice of the transfer, as the case of *Re McArdle* [1951] 1 Ch 669 illustrates. The testator, McArdle, left his residuary estate upon trust for his widow for life, remainder to his five children in equal shares. During the lifetime of the widow, one of the children, Monty, carried out improvements to a farm forming part of the testator's residuary estate. The testator's other children signed a document in these terms: 'To Monty . . . In consideration of your carrying out certain alterations and improvements to the . . . Farm . . . at present occupied by you, we the beneficiaries under the will of William Edward McArdle hereby agree that the executors . . . shall repay to you from the said estate when so distributed the sum of £488 in settlement of the amount spent on such improvements'. Accordingly, when the widow died, Monty claimed the £488. However, the other children of McArdle objected to the claim.

The questions which arose for consideration were, first, whether the signed document could take effect as a binding contract, and secondly, in the alternative, if it failed as a contract, could the document constitute an effective assignment of an equitable interest to Monty?

It was held that the document did not constitute an enforceable contract, because the works of improvement had been completed before the execution of the document and therefore the consideration for the agreement was wholly past. Nor could the document constitute a perfect gift of the equitable interest. The document had been expressed in the form of a contract for valuable consideration so it would be artificial to construe it as a valid equitable assignment (there is no equity to perfect an imperfect gift).

Regrettably, Monty had no entitlement in law or equity to receive the £488. To remedy this the beneficiaries should have authorized the executors to pay the £488. As they did not do so, they had not done everything within their power to dispose of their interest in the £488.

Lord Evershed MR made the following comment, which clearly demonstrates that equity will not interevene to assist volunteers, even if the defendant acts unconscionably: 'I am for myself sorry that the other parties have been able, as I think they have, to evade the obligation which they imposed on themselves in 1945. But that is a matter for their conscience and not for this court.'

(Note, also, the *formality* requirement that the disposition of a subsisting equitable interest be made in writing signed by the person making the disposition, or an authorized agent of that person: Law of Property Act 1925, s 53(1)(c) (see **Chapter 3** at 3.3.1.2).)

5.6 Assistance from the common law

There have been a number of cases in which people have promised to settle trusts in the future for the benefit of certain persons. If the latter have not given legal consideration for the promise, they will have no legal right to enforce the promise under the common law of contract. They will also be mere volunteers in the eyes of equity, claiming under a promise voluntarily made in their favour, and equity will not assist them. However, the following persons are not mere volunteers, and can sue at common law for performance of the promise to set up the trust (provided that they sue within the limitation period laid down by the Limitation Act 1980):

- persons who have provided money or money's worth in consideration of the promise;
- persons who are parties to a deed in which the promise was made. (Note that promises contained within a deed are called 'covenants'.) Such persons are not mere volunteers because the deed itself (or, traditionally, the seal on the deed) is deemed to satisfy the common law requirement of consideration. A person is a party to a deed when they are named in the deed and are a signatory to it. Any party to the deed can enforce the covenant against the person who made the promise (the covenantor).

Although the common law grants the right to sue in the above cases, common law damages will be inadequate where the trust relates to specific property. Ironically, then, the appropriate remedy in such a case will be the equitable remedy of specific performance of the promise. A further irony is the fact that once the trust has been constituted by one of the above common law methods, even volunteer beneficiaries under the trusts will be entitled to claim their interests under the trusts, and the settlor will not be able to stop them (*Paul v Paul* (1882) 20 Ch D 742).

Where a settlor promises an intended trustee that he will settle property on the trustee for the benefit of an intended beneficiary, it is arguable (but see 2.2.1.1) that there is a contract conferring a benefit on a third party. Since the Contracts (Rights of Third Parties) Act 1999 came into force in November 1999, the volunteer beneficiary might be tempted to try to enforce this contract under the Act (compare 5.6.2). However, any such claim is likely to fail on the ground that the contract does not confer a benefit as such, but creates a trust. It is the trust, not the contract, that confers the benefit. The volunteer's anticipated benefit under the contract would therefore be too indirect to claim under the Act.

There are, nevertheless, other circumstances in which a volunteer beneficiary can benefit, indirectly, from a contract to which they were not a party. The benefit is not the benefit under the trust (the trust is never constituted) but damages in the tort of negligence by way of compensation for loss of their expected beneficial interest. In *White v Jones* [1995] 2 AC 207, House of Lords, an award of damages in respect of pure economic loss of this type was successfully made against a solicitor who had negligently failed to amend a will in favour of certain beneficiaries. Even though the solicitor had been instructed by the testator, and had a contract with him only, it was said that the solicitor owed the beneficiaries a duty of care because he had voluntarily assumed responsibility to them. Note, however, that the duty of care is limited to cases in which the solicitor was aware of both the benefit which the testator-client had intended to confer, and the person or class of persons upon whom the benefit was to be conferred (*Gibbons v Nelsons (a Firm)* [2000] Lloyd's Rep PN 603).

5.6.1 Claims of persons within the marriage consideration

Persons within the marriage consideration include the husband and wife and the issue of the marriage. Issue will include children and even grandchildren, but not children of a previous marriage (unless their interests are 'interwoven' with those of the children of the marriage (*AG v Jacob Smith* [1895] 2 QB 341)), nor, it seems, 'illegitimate' children (despite the Family Law Reform Act 1987). The notion that children of a marriage have provided consideration is, according to Buckley J in *Re Cook's ST* [1965] Ch 902 a deliberate 'fiction'. In fact, the treatment of marriage as consideration is itself a fiction, not least because it functions as if it were common law consideration, even though strictly speaking it was a creation of the Court of Chancery.

Like all consideration, marriage consideration will be legally ineffective if given in the past in exchange for a present promise. For a marriage settlement to be truly made in consideration of marriage it must be made before the marriage takes place. One exception may be where the marriage settlement is made after the marriage but in accordance with a pre-marital (ante-nuptial) agreement to create the settlement.

The core facts of the following cases are basically the same: X executes a marriage settlement to which the trustees are parties, in which X covenants to settle any after-acquired property on trust for X, X's spouse and the issue of the marriage.

5.6.1.1 *Re Plumtre* [1910] 1 Ch 609

Plumtre and his wife executed a marriage settlement to which the trustees were also parties. In the deed the wife covenanted to settle her after-acquired property on trust for herself, her husband, their prospective children and ultimately for her next of kin. Some years later the husband made a gift to his wife of certain valuable stock. The wife sold this and reinvested the proceeds in other stock which remained registered in her sole name right up until her death. She died not having had children. After her death, letters of administration were granted to her husband and the stock was placed in his name. An action was brought by her next-of-kin, claiming to be entitled to the stock under the terms of the marriage settlement. It was held that the next-of-kin did not fall within the marriage consideration and therefore were mere volunteers. As such they were not entitled to enforce the covenant to settle. It was held that a voluntary contract (covenant) to create a trust under which the next-of-kin might get an interest must be distinguished from a declaration of trust in favour of the next-of-kin. The next-of-kin were not beneficiaries under the settlement and in the result the husband could keep the stock.

? QUESTION 5.7

Do you think that the next-of-kin in *Re Plumtre* would have had more success if there had been children of the marriage?

Probably they would have had more success. Such children would have fallen within the marriage consideration and accordingly would not have been mere volunteers. They would have been entitled to enforce the covenant to settle, with resulting benefit, not only for themselves, but also for other prospective beneficiaries such as the next-of-kin. In *Re D'Angibau* (1880) 15 Ch D 228 the Court of Appeal acknowledged the possibility that mere volunteers might benefit indirectly in this way.

5.6.1.2 *Pullan v Koe* [1913] 1 Ch 9

By a marriage settlement of 1859 a husband and wife covenanted to settle the wife's after-acquired property upon trusts for the benefit of the husband, the wife and their future children. In 1879 the wife's mother made a gift to her of £285 which the wife paid into her husband's bank account. A portion of this money was later invested in two bearer bonds which remained at the bank (gathering interest) until the husband's death in 1909. The trustees of the marriage settlement brought the present action against the husband's estate claiming that the bonds should be held for the benefit of the beneficiaries of the marriage settlement.

It was held that under the Statute of Limitations, the trustees were far too late to sue at common law for damages on the covenant. However, the husband had received the bonds with notice of the trusts of the marriage settlement and took them subject to the trusts of the marriage settlement. Accordingly, even though the trustees' legal action had been time-barred, they were able to claim the bonds in equity on behalf of the beneficiaries. While it is true that the court will not assist a volunteer, here the claimants (the trustees) were parties to the deed, and were acting on behalf of persons within the marriage consideration.

This case is further authority for the proposition that a person can covenant (or contract for valuable consideration) to settle property which is to come into existence in the future, and when it comes into existence, *equity sees as done that which ought to be done* and will insist upon the specific performance of the covenant.

> **? QUESTION 5.8**
>
> Cast your mind back to the facts of *Re Plumtre*, above. Could the principle in *Pullan v Koe* have been used by the trustees in *Re Plumtre* so as to permit the trustees to take proceedings to enforce the covenant for the benefit of the next-of-kin?

In *Re Pryce* [1917] 1 Ch 234 the trustees sought the directions of the court on this very issue, the facts of *Re Pryce* being very similar to those of *Re Plumtre*. In the event the court directed the trustees not to take steps to enforce the covenant for the benefit of the next-of-kin. The next-of-kin were not within the marriage consideration. Being mere volunteers, they had no direct means of enforcing the covenant. As they could not enforce the covenant by direct means the court refused to allow them to acquire the benefit of it by indirect means.

In *Re Kay's Settlement* [1939] Ch 329, the judge, applying *Re Pryce*, also directed the trustees not to take steps to enforce a covenant on behalf of volunteers. For clarity he also added a further direction that the trustees should not sue for damages for breach of the covenant.

5.6.2 Claims of persons who are parties to the covenant to settle

Where a person covenants to create a settlement in the future, the proposed trustees of that settlement are often joined as parties to the deed in which the covenant is contained. We have seen that this gives the trustees a legal right to enforce the covenant against the covenantor. This legal right may be time-barred under the Limitation Act, but even where it has not been time-barred the trustees should not seek to enforce the right for the benefit of mere volunteers who would be beneficiaries under the settlement. It is quite a different matter if the beneficiaries are themselves parties to the deed in which the covenant is made, as the case of *Cannon v Hartley* [1949] 1 Ch 213 illustrates. Hartley and his wife executed a deed of separation on the breakdown of their marriage. Their daughter, Cannon, was also a party to the settlement. The deed contained the following covenant to settle after-acquired property:

> If and whenever during the lifetime of the wife or the daughter the husband [Hartley] shall become entitled . . . under the will . . . of either of his parents to any money exceeding in net amount or value £1,000 he will forthwith . . . settle one half of such money or property upon trust for himself for life and for the wife for life after his death and subject thereto in trust for the daughter absolutely.

In due course Hartley became entitled to a valuable share of his mother's estate. Shortly thereafter his wife died, whereupon Hartley refused to execute a settlement in accordance with his covenant. His daughter brought this action claiming damages for breach of the covenant.

It was held that because the daughter had been a party to the deed and a direct covenantee of the covenant to settle, she was entitled to a significant award of compensatory damages at common law. Although equity will not assist a mere volunteer, in the present case the daughter did not require the assistance of equity, she was entitled, as a party to the covenant, to enforce directly her common law right to the benefits of the covenant. The problems associated with the daughter being a mere volunteer in equity simply did not arise.

5.6.3 The rule in *Strong v Bird*

In *Strong v Bird* (1874) LR 18 Eq 315, Bird borrowed the sum of £1,100 from his stepmother. She lived in his house and paid rent quarterly and so it was agreed that Bird would repay the loan by deducting £100 from each quarter's rental payment. The deduction was made on two consecutive quarter days but on the third quarter day the stepmother insisted upon paying her full rent without deduction. She continued to make full payments of rent on every quarter day until her death, four years later. Bird was appointed as his stepmother's sole executor. This action was brought by Strong, the stepmother's next-of-kin, alleging that Bird should be charged with a debt of £900, representing the unpaid portion of the loan. It was held by Sir George Jessel MR that Bird owed no debt to the stepmother's estate. His Lordship reasoned that the appointment of Bird as executor had released the debt at law, while the stepmother's continuing intention (up until her death) to make a gift of the £900 to Bird had released the debt in equity. Her continuing intention to make such a gift was amply evidenced by her making nine quarterly payments of the full rent without deduction.

The Master of the Rolls (at p 319) made it clear that Bird had not required the assistance of equity:

> . . . when a testator makes his debtor executor, and thereby releases the debt at law, he is no longer liable at law. It is said that he would be liable in this Court [i.e., Chancery]: and so he would, unless he could shew some reason for not being made liable. Then what does he shew here? Why he proves to the satisfaction of the Court a continuing intention to give, and it appears to me that there being the continuing intention to give, and there being a legal act which transferred the ownership or released the obligation—for it is the same thing—the transaction is perfected, and he does not want the aid of a Court of Equity to carry it out, or to make it complete, because it is complete already, and there is no equity against him to take the property away from him.

For the rule in *Strong v Bird* to apply it follows that two criteria must be satisfied:

1. there must be evidence of the donor's intention to make an immediate *inter vivos* gift. (If the gift is testamentary in nature it will fail for lack of formality—see **Chapter 3**.);
2. the intention to make the gift must have continued right up until the donor's death. The donor must not have treated the property as his own during the relevant period.

Re Stewart [1908] 2 Ch 251 confirms that the rule in *Strong v Bird* is not restricted to the release of a debt, but can apply to a regular gift, and that it is irrelevant that the intended donee is not a sole executor, but one of many. Neville J explained the 'double character' of the reasoning in *Strong v Bird* (at pp 254, 255):

> . . . first, that the vesting of the property in the executor at the testator's death completes the imperfect gift made in the lifetime, and, secondly, that the intention of the testator to give the beneficial interest to the executor is sufficient to countervail the equity of beneficiaries under the will, the testator having vested the legal estate in the executor.

Farwell J in *Re James* [1935] 1 Ch 449 at 451, confirmed that the donee in such a case does not call for the assistance of equity: 'equity will not aid the donee, but on the other hand if the donee gets the legal title to the property vested in him he no longer wants the assistance of equity and is entitled to rely on his legal title as against the donor or persons claiming through him'. In *Re James* the rule in *Strong v Bird* was extended to perfect a gift to an administratrix.

5.6.3.1 Extension of the rule to adminstrators?

Does the application of the rule to benefit an administrator or administratrix go too far? After all, an administrator is appointed by the court, whereas an executor is appointed by the donor personally. In *Re Gonin* [1979] Ch 16, Walton J expressed these very concerns when he observed that *Strong v Bird* had proceeded on the basis of the doctrine that at law the appointment of a person as executor effected a release of the executor's debt to the appointor, a doctrine which had never been applied to administrators: 'The appointment of an administrator . . . is not an act of the deceased but of the law. It is often a matter of pure chance which of many persons equally entitled to a grant of letters of administration finally takes them out.'

On this point Walton J is very persuasive. However, later in the same judgment his Lordship refers to the rule in *Strong v Bird* as a 'simple rule of equity'. You should not be misled by this. The donee who relies upon the rule in *Strong v Bird* is not relying upon the assistance of equity, he claims his entitlement at common law. It is true that equity recognizes this entitlement, as indeed it recognizes all legal entitlement which is unencumbered by a superior claim in equity, but only in this limited sense can the rule be seen to be a 'simple rule of equity'. Incidentally, in *Re Gonin* itself the rule in *Strong v Bird* failed to assist, because the donor gave away part of the subject matter of the gift to someone other than the claimant, thus rebutting any presumption that the donor had intended to make the donation in favour of the claimant right up until the time of his death.

5.6.3.2 Extension of the rule to trusts?

So far it is clear that the rule in *Strong v Bird* can apply to perfect an imperfect absolute gift. Whether it should also apply to constitute an incompletely constituted trust has not been conclusively decided, but it appears that it should.

Cast your mind back to the 'double character' of the reasoning in *Strong v Bird*, as delineated in *Re Stewart*. On the first line of reasoning, that the vesting of the property in the executor at the testator's death completes the imperfect gift made in the lifetime, there would appear to be no reason in principle why the rule should not be effective to transfer the legal title to trustees in the appropriate case. On the second line of reasoning, that the intention of the testator to give the beneficial interest to the executor is sufficient to defeat the equity of beneficiaries under the will, there would likewise be no difficulty in applying the rule to effect an *inter vivos* declaration of trust. The equities of the beneficiaries under that trust would take priority over the equitable claims of the beneficiaries under the will, for *the first equity in time will prevail where the equities are equal*.

As to authority, it has been suggested that in the case of *Re Ralli's Will Trusts* [1964] Ch 288 the rule in *Strong v Bird* was applied to constitute a trust. For consideration of that view see the next section.

5.6.4 The 'accidental' constitution of a trust

In *Re Ralli's Will Trusts* [1964] Ch 288, the testator, Ralli, left his residuary estate to trustees on trust for his wife for life, remainder to his daughters H and I. H, by a marriage settlement, covenanted to settle her share on trustees for the benefit of her own children and ultimately for the children of I. A clause of the marriage settlement declared that all property within the terms of the covenant should be subject to the terms of the trusts pending assignment to the trustees. H died childless. Later, a trustee who had been a party to H's marriage settlement was additionally appointed trustee under the will of Ralli. That trustee, who happened also to be I's husband, brought the present action, seeking directions as to whether H's share of her father's residuary estate should be held by him on the trusts of the marriage settlement, or under the terms of H's will. He claimed that the property should be held on the trusts of the marriage settlement. H's personal representatives claimed that H's estate should be entitled, in accordance with H's will.

EXERCISE 5.5

On a separate sheet of paper, try to represent the above facts diagrammatically. Compare your diagram with the one below.

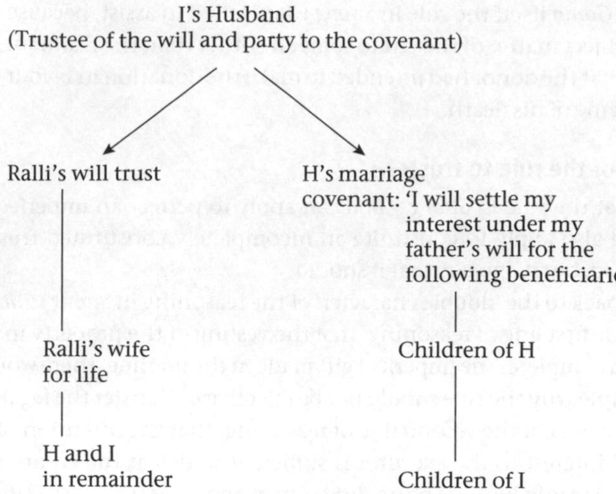

QUESTION 5.9

Bearing the preceding diagram in mind, if H has no children, if Ralli's wife is dead, and if H is dead, do you think that I's husband holds H's remainder interest for H's estate (in accordance with the will trust) or for I's children (in accordance with the marriage settlement)?

This was the question facing the court in *Re Ralli's*. It was held that the claimant (I's husband) held H's share of Ralli's estate on the trusts of the marriage settlement. Those trusts had become fully constituted when the legal title to the property had vested in the claimant in his capacity as trustee of Ralli's will trusts. The fact that the constitution had been purely fortuitous did not matter. If it had been necessary to enforce performance of the covenant, equity would not have done so at the request of the beneficiaries under the settlement, as they were mere volunteers. In the present case, however, there had been no need to invoke the assistance of equity to enforce performance of the covenant. On the contrary, it had been for the defendants to invoke equity to show that it would be 'unconscientious' for the claimant to perform the covenant. It was held not to be unconscientious for the claimant to exercise his legal authority to perform the covenant and to carry out the settlement trusts.

The above line of reasoning should strictly speaking be regarded as, if not *obiter dicta*, then as an alternative *ratio decidendi*. For Buckley J was in fact prepared to dispose of the case on the more straightforward assumption that H's remainder interest under Ralli's will was vested, not after-acquired, property at the date of execution of the marriage settlement. Accordingly, H had held that property as trustee when she was alive, because the execution of the marriage settlement had constituted a declaration of trust binding upon her pending transfer of her interest to the trustees of the settlement. That trust would now be binding upon her successors in title, that is, her personal representatives.

? QUESTION 5.10

As we noted above, it is sometimes said that *Re Ralli's WT* is a case where the rule in *Strong v Bird*, which normally applies to gifts, was applied to a trust. Do you agree with that assertion?

We saw earlier that in *Re James* the housekeeper was able, somewhat fortuitously, to claim a gift under the rule in *Strong v Bird*. *Re James* was cited with no dissent by Buckley J in *Re Ralli's WT*. However, according to Walton J in *Re Gonin* [1979] Ch 16, *Re James* was 'only used as an illustration' in *Re Ralli's*. It remains a moot point whether *Re Ralli's* is an application of the rule in *Strong v Bird*.

5.6.5 Assistance from the common law: summative exercise

Attempt the following Question by way of summary to this section. You should be able to draw upon many of the points you have learned so far.

? QUESTION 5.11

Imagine that you are a court faced with the following facts, taken from *Re Cook's Settlement Trusts* [1965] 1 Ch 902. The trustees have taken out a summons for directions as to what action they should take if the 'Rembrandt' is sold during FC's lifetime and the proceeds are then not paid to the trustees. How will you direct the trustees?

HC and his son FC executed a settlement under which it was agreed that FC's reversionary interest under a will should be exchanged for other property of equal value and that some of the new (replacement) property should be settled by FC on trust for certain named beneficiaries. That part of the new property which was not required to be so settled (primarily comprising valuable paintings) was to be held by FC for his own benefit, but FC covenanted for valuable consideration that the proceeds of the sale of any of the paintings, if sold during FC's lifetime, should be paid to the trustees of the settlement to be held by them on the trusts of the settlement. FC later made a gift of one of the paintings (a Rembrandt) to his wife and she has since expressed her intention to sell it.

Your directions to the trustees should ideally run along the following lines:

The covenant to settle the proceeds of sale of the paintings was a contract to settle after-acquired monies. These monies did not exist at the time of the covenant and might never come into existence. The beneficiaries under the settlement had not been parties to the covenant and accordingly would not be permitted to sue at common law on it. Nor had the beneficiaries provided consideration for the covenant to settle (they did not fall within marriage consideration and had not provided valuable consideration in money or money's worth). So much for the common law. In the eyes of equity, the beneficiaries were mere volunteers and equity would not assist them. The beneficiaries were not entitled to require the trustees to enforce the covenant on their behalf. Indeed, in accordance with *Re Kay's Settlement* (see 5.6.1.2), the trustees should have been directed not to enforce the covenant even if they were minded to do so.

These are essentially the same directions as those given by Buckley J in *Re Cook's Settlement Trusts*.

5.7 Assistance from Roman law

The Roman law doctrine of *donatio mortis causa* is often cited as a genuine exception to the maxim *equity will not assist a volunteer*. There is support for this view from the judgments of English courts, which tend to suggest that the doctrine is effective in English law through the use of an implied or constructive trust but in essence the doctrine is an anomalous wholesale importation of a Roman law doctrine into English law.

5.7.1 The doctrine of *donatio mortis causa*

The ancient Roman law of *donatio mortis causa* (gifts made because of death) plays a part in the modern law of England and Wales as a means by which a donee can claim a gift of certain property, where that gift has not been perfectly executed in accordance with the common law rules applicable to transfers of property of that type. The rule is almost invariably used to perfect absolute gifts, but there would appear to be no reason why it should not equally apply to perfect a trust where the gift is impressed with trust obligations (this would in any case be the inevitable result where, for example, a gift of land is made to two or more persons).

5.7.2 The Roman origins of the doctrine

Justinian, the Byzantine Roman Emperor between AD 527 and AD 565, oversaw the codification of Roman law. The result was the *Corpus Juris Civilis*, the main part of which was Justinian's *Digest*. Citation 39.6.3–6 of the *Digest* provides as follows:

> It is permissible to make a gift *mortis causa* not only on grounds of weak health, but also on grounds of impending danger of death due to enemies or robbers or the cruelty or hatred of a powerful man

> or when about to undertake a sea voyage, or to travel through dangerous places, or when one is worn out by old age, since all these circumstances represent impending danger.

As Andrew Borkowski observes in his *Textbook on Roman Law* (2nd edn) (London: Blackstone Press, 1997) at p 209:

> Such gifts were hybrid in character: they were made *inter vivos*, but did not take full effect until the contemplated death of the donor occurred. Ownership in the property normally passed to the donee on the making of the gift, but the gift was revocable before death. Automatic revocation occurred if the donee predeceased the donor, or if the latter became bankrupt.

Borkowski refers to citation 39.6.35.2 of the *Digest*, which translated reads:

> A gift *mortis causa* differs considerably from the true and absolute sort of gift which proceeds in such a way that it can in no circumstances be revoked. In that sort of case, of course, the donor wishes the recipient rather than himself to have the property. But the person who makes a gift *mortis causa* is thinking of himself and, loving life, prefers to receive rather than to give. This is why it is commonly said: 'He wishes himself rather than the recipient to have the property, but, that said, wishes the recipient rather than the heir to have it'.

(For details of the latest edition of the *Textbook on Roman Law* see further reading at the end of this chapter.)

5.7.3 The English law formulation of the doctrine: *donatio mortis causa*

The English law formulation of the doctrine is not very far removed from the Roman law conception, and has its roots firmly in that source. Consider, for example, the formulation of Lord Russell of Killowen CJ in *Cain v Moon* [1896] 2 QB 283 at 286, where he held that:

> For an effectual *donatio mortis causa* three things must combine: first, the gift or donation must have been in contemplation, though not necessarily in expectation of death; secondly, there must have been delivery to the donee of the subject matter of the gift; and thirdly, the gift must be made under such circumstances as to show that the thing is to revert to the donor in case he should recover.

It is in relation to the second of the above requirements that equity is genuinely of assistance. For where there is a formal defect in delivery of the subject matter of the gift, equity may remedy that defect in accordance with the maxim, *equity looks to substance not form*.

? QUESTION 5.12

Bearing in mind the above criteria, do you think there was a valid *donatio mortis causa* on the following set of facts?

A widow mortgaged a farm, in which she held a life interest, to her late husband's brother, A. After the widow's death he passed the deeds to the farm, apart from the mortgage deed, to the widow's executors (his nieces). It later transpired that A was dying of an incurable disease and so, in anticipation of his death, he passed a sealed envelope to his nieces which turned out to contain the mortgage deed. Some short time later A caught a chill and died of pneumonia. This action was brought by his executors, claiming that the mortgage was a subsisting security which could be enforced against the nieces.

The facts are taken from the case of *Wilkes v Allington* [1931] 2 Ch 104 where Lord Tomlin held that the mortgage could not be enforced. The otherwise imperfect gift of the mortgage to the nieces was made perfect by a valid *donatio mortis causa*, for it was clear that the gift was only to become binding on the donor's death (an intention could be implied that the property should be returned to him if he recovered). It was further held that it was not necessary for the donor to have died from the same disorder as that from which he had been suffering when contemplating death.

It was held by the Court of Appeal in the more recent case of *Sen v Headley* [1991] Ch 425 that the doctrine could apply to gifts of title to land, a point which had until that decision been in doubt. The facts were, briefly, that Mrs Sen, who had lived with a man for several years in a house owned by him, was given a set of keys as he lay on his death bed. The keys unlocked a box in which were held the deeds to the man's house. As he passed the keys to her, the dying man stated that the house was to be hers. It was held that passing possession of the deeds was sufficient to effect the *donatio*, as there had been 'a parting with dominion over the essential *indicia* of title'. The notion of ownership as 'dominion' is peculiarly Roman.

Nourse LJ noted that the orthodox equitable justification for the operation of *donatio mortis causa* in English law was that the donations are effective by means of a constructive trust, or a trust 'by operation of law', but did not feel constrained to follow any principled justification for the operation of the doctrine:

> Let it be agreed that the doctrine is anomalous, anomalies do not justify anomalous exceptions . . . to make a distinction in the case of land would be to make just such an exception. *A donatio mortis causa* of land is neither more nor less anomalous than any other. Every such gift is a circumvention of the Wills Act 1837.

5.8 Proprietary estoppel: a case of equitable assistance for volunteers?

The basic form of the doctrine of proprietary estoppel in this context is that where a volunteer has been led to rely to his detriment upon another person's representation that a disposition will be made in favour of the volunteer, the person making the representation is stopped ('estopped') from acting inconsistently with the representation.

Let us take as our first illustration the case of *Dillwyn v Llewellyn* (1862) 4 De GF & J 517. In that case there was an imperfect gift of land by a father who encouraged his son to build a house on it, at a cost to the son of £14,000. Note the following passage from the judgment of Lord Westbury LC:

> About the rules of the court there can be no controversy. A voluntary agreement will not be completed or assisted by a court of equity, in cases of mere gift. If anything be wanting to complete the

> title of the donee, a court of equity will not assist him in obtaining it; for a mere donee can have no right to claim more than he has received. But the subsequent acts of the donor may give the donee that right or ground of claim which he did not acquire from the original gift. So, if A puts B in possession of a piece of land, and tells him 'I give it to you that you may build a house on it', and B on the strength of that promise, with the knowledge of A, expends a large sum of money in building a house accordingly, I cannot doubt that the donee acquires a right from the subsequent transaction to call on the donor to perform that contract and complete the imperfect donation which was made.

It is not enough to establish merely that the person making the representation is estopped from denying that the representee has some right. The precise nature and extent of the representee's right must be established by the court. In determining the appropriate remedy, the rule is that the court should choose whatever remedy is the minimum equity to do justice in all the circumstances. The estoppel, it is said, must be 'fed'. In one recent case where the claimant gave up a tenancy to move into a castle in the expectation that he would acquire a tenancy of the castle, the court held that the minimum equity was to require the defendant to give him not less than two years' notice before eviction (*Parker v Parker* [2003] EWHC 1846 (Ch)). In *Dillwyn v Llewellyn* it was held that the minimum equity to do justice required that equity should assist the volunteer son by perfecting the imperfect gift to him of the freehold title to the land on which he had built. *Dillwyn v Llewellyn* was relied upon in *Pascoe v Turner* [1979] 1 WLR 431.

? QUESTION 5.13

Is proprietary estoppel a true exception to the maxim that *equity will not assist a volunteer* who claims under an express trust?

It is very doubtful that proprietary estoppel is a true exception to the maxim in relation to claimants under *express* trusts. Where proprietary estoppel gives rise to a trust, the trust is constructed by the court by way of remedy in satisfaction of the estoppel. It is not an express trust, but a constructive trust. (Although it is not a fully remedial constructive trust, because the proprietary estoppel arises according to institutional principles (see, generally, 17.4).)

CHAPTER SUMMARY

The figure on p120 is intended to offer a summary of the main points covered in this chapter. However, the best way to learn is to design your own chart covering the salient issues.

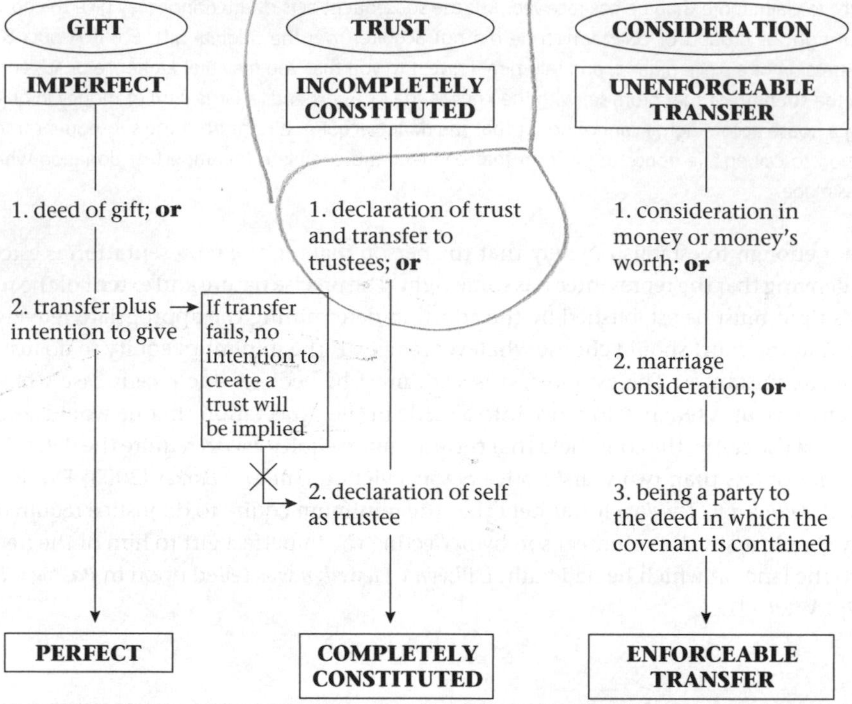

SUMMATIVE ASSESSMENT EXERCISE

online resource centre

Herbert Chance, wishing to make future provision for his adult son, entered into the following covenant in a deed to which his friends Allan Smith and Clifford Overy were the only other parties:

> I promise to settle the sum of £100,000 in cash, or assets of equivalent value, for the benefit of my son for his life, to his issue in remainder. This bounty to be held on trust by Allan Smith and Clifford Overy in accordance with the terms of the settlement annexed hereto.

Some years later Herbert fell grievously ill. As he lay on his death bed, his friend, Mr Overy, reminded Herbert of the covenant he had made. The next day, when Mr Overy came to visit, Herbert passed to him a sealed envelope. 'In there', he said 'are the share certificates for £100,000 of my shares in the family company. I want my son to have them in accordance with the terms of the settlement annexed to the covenant'. Herbert died minutes later.

Advise the son whether or not he will be able to claim any benefit under the settlement.

FURTHER READING

Baker, J H, 'Land as a donatio mortis causa' (1993) 109 LQR 19.

Barton, J L, 'Trusts and Covenants' (1975) 91 LQR 236.

Borkowski, A, *Deathbed Gifts: The Law of Donatio Mortis Causa* (Oxford: Blackstone Press, 1999).

Borkowski, A, and du Plessis, P, *Textbook on Roman Law* (3rd edn) (Oxford: OUP, 2005).

Garton, J, 'The Role of the Trust Mechanism in the rule in *Re Rose*' (2003) Conv 364.

6 Public policy limitations on the formation of trusts

OBJECTIVES

By the end of this chapter you should be able to:

1 Appreciate the dangers inherent in the recognition of trusts
2 Prevent a breach of the rules against perpetuity and accumulations
3 Detect an existing breach of those rules
4 Discern the situations in which a trust designed to shield assets from creditors will and will not be void
5 Understand a number of other public policy limitations on the formation of trusts

6.1 Introduction

In the preceding chapters we have seen that the recognition of trusts by the courts is a concession to the freedom of property owners to deal with their property as they wish. The courts tolerate trusts because of their utility to the settlor, but the courts (and Parliament) must weigh against this private utility the potential for public harm that is inherent in the recognition of trusts.

EXERCISE 6.1

On a separate sheet of paper, list any potentially harmful aspects of the creation and recognition of express trusts.

Your list may have included the following:

(a) Because trust property is subject to binding obligations as to its use, it cannot participate fully in the free market. This means that it cannot contribute as fully as other property to national economic growth. (Although the recent liberalization of trustee investment by the Trustee Act 2000 law may remove the force of this objection, see **Chapter 14**.)

(b) The fact that the wishes of the living in relation to property held by them may be defeated by the wishes of persons who have long since ceased to hold the property, and may even be dead. Should the 'dead hand' of the settlor be permitted to maintain a grip beyond the grave?

(c) Whereas the personal assets of insolvent persons will be available to their general creditors, any assets held by them in trust for another will not be available to satisfy the claims of the general creditors.

In this chapter we will be considering the way in which Parliament and the courts have sought to address some of these problems.

6.2 The rules against perpetuities

The most commonly cited justifications for the rules against perpetuities are, first, the desire to keep societal wealth in the open market, where it can assist in financial enterprise to the greater public good; and, second, the perceived need to restrict the aggrandisement, over time, of families and other private institutions. If the courts and Parliament are really concerned about such matters it is perhaps surprising that the modern corporation has been allowed to prosper as it has. (Corporations do not die and therefore property owned by corporations can potentially be excluded from the open market in perpetuity.) Nevertheless a number of rules of perpetuity have been developed in order to prevent gifts from vesting at too remote a time in the future, to prevent capital from being tied up indefinitely and to prevent income from being accumulated for too long a period.

The first rule is the rule against remoteness of vesting. It is a rule which renders void any gift to a person which may vest in that person at too remote a time in the future. To 'vest' here means to 'vest in interest', as opposed to 'vest in possession'. The difference in the two concepts can be illustrated quite simply by taking the classic trust 'to A for life and B in remainder'. In such a trust both A and B are entitled to an interest, their interests have both 'vested in interest'. However, only A can claim to be entitled to the present use and enjoyment of the trust property, B has to wait until A dies. So it is said that only A's interest has 'vested in possession'.

The second rule is the rule against inalienability of capital. It is a rule which prevents capital, which has already vested in trustees, from being tied up for too long a period of time.

The third is the rule against accumulation of income. It is designed to prevent trust income from being accumulated (added to the capital fund) for too long a time.

6.3 The rule against remoteness of vesting

This rule is concerned to prevent interests in property commencing (vesting) at too remote a time in the future, but it is not concerned with the duration of those interests after their commencement.

The modern rule against remoteness of vesting has its source in principles laid down by Heneage Finch, Lord Nottingham (Lord Chancellor between the years 1673 and 1682 and rightly called 'the father of equity'), in *The Duke of Norfolk's Case* (1681) 3 Chan Cas 1. (See A W B Simpson, *An Introduction to the History of the Land Law*, 1979, at pp 211, 212). Lord Nottingham relied, in that case, upon two earlier authorities, the principal one being *Pells v Brown* (1620) Cro Jac 590.

The judgment in *Pells v Brown*, delivered in a seamless weave of English, Latin and French, suggests that the historical motivation for the rule may not merely have been social concerns about family aggrandisement, economic stagnancy or the restrictive effect of dead men's wishes. There appears also to have been an ecclesiastical concern that to store up wealth is in some sense to deny the providence of God. As Dodridge J put it:

> quant Deus dedit terras filiis hominis, & si homes poient faire continuance de terre in lour families for ever, ceo fuit a preventer le providence de Dieu, who sets up and pulls down come a luy pleist a son pleasure, Thou fool, this night shall thy soul be taken from thee, and then what shall become of all that thou hast gathered together; mes si perpetuities serront establish ceo voilt prevent tout le power del disposition del terres per le Dieu.

The reason we still study the rule is essentially threefold. First, to ensure that we never make the mistake of breaching the rule (the effect of failure to comply with the rules against perpetuity is to render the disposition, or other direction, void). Secondly, because the rules present one of the most stimulating and demanding intellectual challenges that one can face in one's quest to understand law and the nature of legal reasoning. Thirdly, because the rules against perpetuities still impact in dramatic fashion in modern trust contexts. Take, for example, *Air Jamaica Ltd v Charlton* [1999] 1 WLR 1399, where, at first instance, a pension trust was held to be void under the rule against perpetuities with the result that the monies passed *bona vacantia* to the Crown. The Privy Council ultimately reversed this decision. Lord Millett held that the pension scheme would ordinarily be void for offending the rule against perpetuities, given that there was no applicable statutory exemption to the common law rule, but that a new settlement was created every time a new member joined the scheme. Each new settlement complied with the rules against perpetuities because every new member qualified as a 'life in being' in relation to the particular settlement. (Technical terms such as 'life in being' are explained below.) There would have been a different outcome if the pension had not been a 'defined benefits scheme'. If the rules of the scheme had allowed contributions by one member to be made available to pay out benefits to other members (who were not lives in being at the date of the settlement), the trust would have failed for perpetuity. It was, in any event, held that certain powers granting the trustees the right to change the terms of the trust were void for perpetuity, as was a power granted to widows to designate a beneficiary to receive benefits. Those powers were contingent on the *termination* of the entire pension scheme, which might have occurred more than 21 years after the death of any particular beneficiary.

Having suggested that the rule can be mastered, it must be admitted that it is currently in a most unsatisfactory state. This was acknowledged by the Law Commission in its Consultation Paper No 133, *The Law of Trusts. The Rules against Perpetuities and Excessive Accumulations*, 19 October 1993. One of the most unsatisfactory features of the present law is that there are essentially three different ways of calculating the perpetuity period applicable to a disposition.

First, a special perpetuity period (up to a maximum of 80 years) can generally be expressly provided in the instrument by which the disposition was made (Perpetuities and Accumulations Act 1964, s 1(1)).

Secondly, if no period has been specified in the instrument, the common law rules provide that the perpetuity period ends 21 years after the death of all 'lives in being' (see 6.3.1).

Thirdly, the Perpetuties and Accumulations Act 1964 provides that the perpetuity period ends 21 years after the death of all the *statutory* lives in being (a list of these persons is provided in the statute).

However, the most unsatisfactory feature of the present state of the law is that, unless an express period is specified under s 1(1), a disposition can be valid under the 1964 Act *only* if it has already been shown to be void under the common law rules. This is most inconvenient, not least because (as we shall shortly see) the 1964 Act is far more generous in recognizing the validity of dispositions than are the common law rules. In its report No 251 (1998) the Law Commission has recommended a reform which will remove the necessity of applying the common law rules before taking advantage of the modern scheme under the Act.

6.3.1 The common law rule

The common law rule against remoteness of vesting provides that where an interest is disposed of in favour of X subject to a 'contingency' (a requirement which may or may not be met) it will be void for perpetuity from the date of the disposition unless the contingency will certainly be met (thus vesting the interest in the grantee)—if it is met at all—within the 'perpetuity period'. Examples of such contingent gifts would include: 'to X upon his attaining a university degree'; to 'X upon his reaching the age of 25'; and, 'to my grandchildren', where there are no grandchildren living at the effective date of the gift. The following points need to be noted:

(a) 'Perpetuity period' for the purpose of this rule is the period ending 21 years after the death of all 'lives in being'.

(b) 'Lives in being' are persons alive (see *Re Wilmer's Trusts*) at the 'effective date' of the grant, or persons in their mother's womb at that time who are later born. However, for the purpose of the rule against remoteness of vesting 'lives in being' include only 'relevant' or 'measuring' lives in being. These descriptions usually correspond to those persons who are expressly or impliedly referred to in the instrument by which the disposition is effected. Thus the lives in being at the date of execution of an *inter vivos* gift to 'such of my grandchildren as qualify as lawyers' include not only the grandchildren, but also the settlor and any of his children who are then alive. The grandchildren were expressly referred to, the reference to the settlor and his children is implicit.

(c) The 'effective date' of a disposition varies according to whether the disposition was made *inter vivos* or by will. An *inter vivos* deed of gift or trust is effective at the date of its execution. A testamentary gift or trust is effective, not at the date of execution of the will, but at the date of the testator's/testatrix's death.

If there are no lives in being at the effective date of the disposition, the perpetuity period will be a straightforward 21 years commencing at that effective date of the disposition.

To summarize: 'no interest is good unless it must vest, if at all, not later than twenty-one years after some life in being at the creation of the interest' (Gray, *The Rule Against Perpetuities*, 4th edn, para 201).

6.3.1.1 The lack of common sense in the common law rule

At common law the rule has always been strictly applied, with the result that a gift will be declared void for perpetuity if there is the merest possibility that it might vest outside the perpetuity period, no matter how improbable the likelihood of it so doing. The common law rule against remoteness of vesting is said to be concerned with possibilities, not probabilities. The case of *Re Dawson* (1888) 39 Ch D 155 is a remarkable illustration of the lack of common sense in the common law rule.

The testator, Dawson, left all his estate to trustees upon trust to pay an annuity to his daughter, M, for her life, directing that after his daughter's death the trustees should hold the estate for those of her children, and thereafter for those of her grandchildren, who should attain 21 or (in the case of females) should marry under that age.

The lives in being at the effective date of the gift (that is, the date of Dawson's death) were M, who was then over 60 years of age, M's son and M's five daughters.

Because there was a possibility, albeit extremely remote, that M would produce more children in the future (who would not, of course, have been lives in being at Dawson's death) it followed that there was also a remote possibility that such later-born children of M might produce grandchildren of M outside the perpetuity period. It followed from this that there was also a remote possibility that certain of M's grandchildren would not satisfy the contingency until after the perpetuity period. In short, there was a remote possibility that the gift would vest outside the perpetuity period. (The perpetuity period was 21 years after the death of the last survivor of the lives in being.)

The court applied the common law rules strictly so as to hold the disposition void on the basis that it *might* not vest until too remote a time. Evidence purporting to show that at Dawson's death M had passed the age of childbearing and was, as a result, highly unlikely to produce any further children, was held to be inadmissible.

6.3.2 Class gifts

Gifts and trusts are often made to a class. An example would be a gift or trust 'to all my nephews who reach the age of 25'. A 'class' for this purpose comprises persons who 'come within a certain category or description defined by a general or collective formula, and who, if they take at all, are to take one divisible subject in certain proportionate shares' (*per* Lord Selborne LC, *Pearkes v Mosely* (1880) 5 App Cas 714 at 723). The basic common law position is that the gift or trust will be void unless *all* potential members of the class *must* satisfy the contingency within the perpetuity period. Thus if (taking the example given at the beginning of this section and assuming that the gift has become effective today) there are three nephews in being and a fourth nephew is born a year from now, none of the nephews will take under the gift. The lives in being *might* all die tomorrow, in which event the fourth nephew will not reach 25 within the remaining 21 years of the perpetuity period.

The rule in *Andrews v Partington* (1791) 3 Bro CC 401 was created to address the clear hardship of the basic common law treatment of class gifts. The rule allows a member of the class to take his share if he has already satisfied the contingency at the effective date of the gift. What is more, if members of the class are lives in being at the effective date of the gift but none has at that time already met the contingency, the rule permits the trustees to wait to see if any one of them satisfies the contingency. (If any one does, he will necessarily do so within the perpetuity period by virtue of his status as a life in being.)

The first beneficiary to meet the contingency will be given his share at that time. The size of this share is worked out by closing the class of potential beneficiaries to include all persons answering the class description (for example, 'nephew') at the date when the first member of the class satisfies the contingency (for example, reaches 25), and by effecting an equal division of the fund between the members of the closed class. Any persons answering the class description who are born after the class has been closed, and any persons who cannot possibly meet the contingency within the perpetuity period (for example, because they cannot reach the age of 25 in time), will be excluded from taking any part of the fund.

To summarize, 'where there is a bequest of an aggregate fund to children as a class, and the *share of each* child is made payable on attaining a given age, or marriage, [or, it seems any other contingency] the period of distribution is the time when the *first* child becomes entitled to receive his share, and children coming into existence after that period are excluded' (*Hawkins on Wills*, 3rd edn, 1925, p 96).

The rule was applied in *Re Clifford's Settlement Trusts* [1981] 1 Ch 63. The facts were as follows. Clifford made an *inter vivos* settlement of a fund on trustees for the benefit of his son's children 'born in Clifford's lifetime or after his death who before the expiration of the period of 21 years from the death of the survivor of Clifford and the said son shall attain the age of 25 years and the other children of the said son living at the expiration of such period'. At the date of the settlement Clifford's son was 32 and had two children of his own (aged 2½ years old and 2½ months old respectively). At the date of the hearing of this case those two children had attained 25. However, since Clifford's death the son had fathered another two children who had not yet attained 25.

The facts can be represented diagrammatically thus:

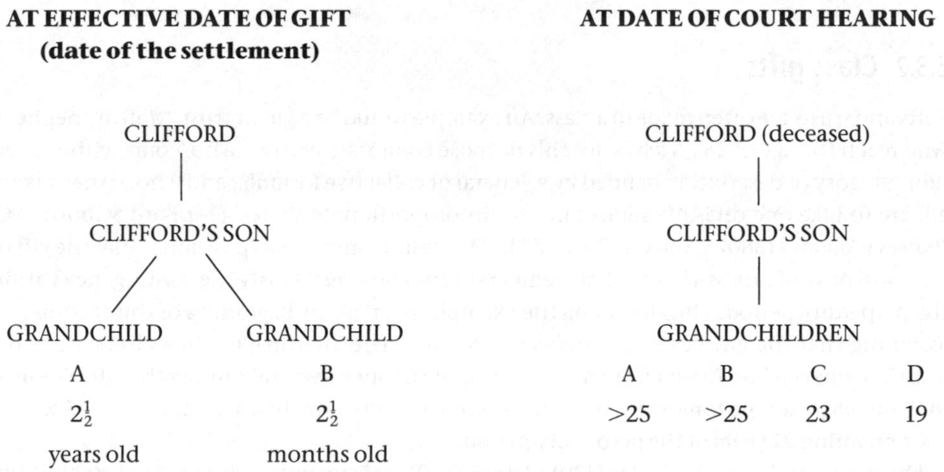

The question arising for consideration was whether A and B had each become entitled to a quarter share of the fund when they attained 25 or whether the whole class gift was void for perpetuity because further grandchildren (E, F, G etc.) might be born who might not reach 25 until some time beyond the perpetuity period prescribed by the clause (that is, 21 years after the death of Clifford's son).

? QUESTION 6.1

Apply the rule in *Andrews v Partington* to the above set of facts. Do you think the disposition was or was not valid?

Sir Robert Megarry V-C held that the rule in *Andrews v Partington* applied to save the gift of a quarter of the fund to A and B. His Lordship held that C and D would also be entitled to a quarter share upon satisfying the contingency, because they were alive when the eldest grandchild reached 25, and therefore came within the closed class. Any later born members of the class (E, F, G, etc) would be excluded from the gift.

Megarry V-C observed that:

> it is well established that the rule arises from an attempt by the court to reconcile two seemingly inconsistent directions of a settlor or testator. One is that the whole class of the children should be able to take, whenever born. The other is that a child who has reached the requisite age or satisfied the requisite condition should be able to take his share forthwith, without being forced to wait to see whether other children will be born whose claims may diminish the size of the shares to be taken.

On similar reasoning, the Law Commission in its Report No 251 (1998) concludes at paras 5.22–26 that the rule in *Andrews v Partington* is a rule designed, not to save gifts which would otherwise be void for remoteness, but to facilitate the proper administration of trusts. To illustrate this point consideration is given to the straightforward case of a testamentary gift to 'such of the children of A as shall attain the age of 21'. At the effective date of the gift (the death of the testator) we are told that A has two children, B (aged 20) and C (aged 10). B reaches 21 and demands his share of the property.

? QUESTION 6.2

If the trustees give him one-half of the property, what happens if A has future born children who later attain 21 and demand payment: do the trustees try to recover a proportionate share of the property from B and C?

No. 'Upon B reaching 21 he or she attains a vested interest and the class closing rules operate so as to exclude from the class of potential beneficiaries any future born children of A, even if they do in fact reach 21. C is the only remaining potential beneficiary under the disposition. The trustees may therefore distribute to B his or her one-half share of the property.'

Future events, such as the death of C before attaining 21, can only increase, not reduce, B's entitlement.

Paragraph 5.26 of the Law Commission's Report No 251 concludes that 'the class closing rules are rules of construction only and can be displaced by a sufficient expression of contrary intention, though this must be express'. The authority is given of *Re Tom's Settlement* [1987] 1 WLR 1021, where the draftsman of the trust expressly provided that the class should close on a particular date.

6.3.3 Age reducing provisions

Law of Property Act 1925, s 163 still applies in relation to gifts taking effect on or before 15 July 1964. That section provides that where the disposition of an interest is rendered wholly or partially void for remoteness because the vesting of the interest was made contingent upon the attainment of an age exceeding 21, that age requirement can be removed and replaced by a contingent age of 21, thus rendering the gift valid for perpetuity.

6.3.4 The problem of the unascertained spouse

Where a disposition is limited by reference to the time of death of the survivor of a person in being at the commencement of the perpetuity period and any spouse of that person, the disposition may be void at common law. The problem arises from the fact that, as a consequence of legal freedom to marry and remarry, the identity of a surviving spouse can never be ascertained until the death of the other spouse.

Consider a gift by will 'to Larry for life, with remainder to any wife of Larry who may survive him for life, with remainder to such of his brothers living at the death of the survivor'.

Larry is a bachelor, so we do not know the identity of his wife and it is possible that the wife who will survive him (if any) may not even have been conceived at the effective date of the gift. As the validity of the gift must be considered at its commencement, it follows that the common law rule will be applied on the assumption that the wife is not a life in being. The lives in being will therefore be Larry, and any of his brothers alive at the testator's death. The perpetuity period will end 21 years after the death of the last surviving life in being. It follows that the gift to the widow cannot be void for remoteness, because her interest will vest on Larry's death and will therefore vest, if it vests at all, within the perpetuity period.

The difficulty comes in relation to the gift to the brothers. Their interests are contingent upon the death of the widow, but it cannot be said for certain that the widow will die within the perpetuity period. In relation to the brothers who are lives in being there is no real problem because if they take an interest at all they *must* take it within the perpetuity period, therefore the gift to them will not fail for remoteness. The real problem arises in relation to brothers who may come into existence after the testator's death. It follows from the fact that such later born brothers will not be lives in being, and from the fact that the widow might die outside the perpetuity period, that the interests of those brothers might not vest until after the end of the perpetuity period. The gift to later born brothers will therefore be void for remoteness, and thus the gift to the entire class of 'brothers' will be void under the common law rule (unless the rule in *Andrews v Partington* helps, or Larry's parents have already died at the effective date of the gift thereby removing any possibility that later born brothers might come along).

The problem of the unascertained spouse is now solved by s 5 of the 1964 Act (see 6.3.7.8).

6.3.5 Summative chart on the common law rule of remoteness of vesting

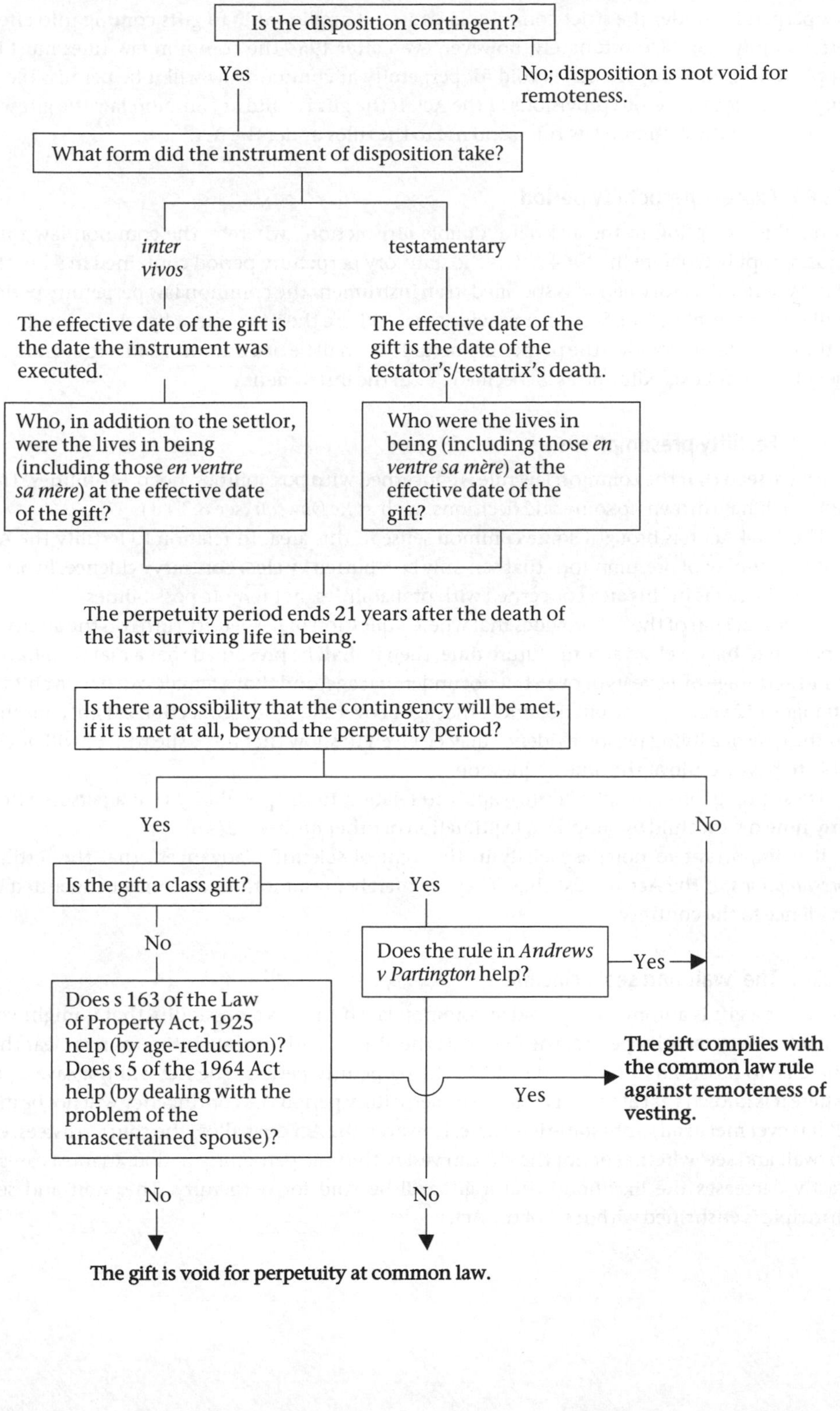

6.3.6 The Perpetuities and Accumulations Act 1964

The 1964 Act has the effect of saving a number of gifts which would otherwise have been void for perpetuity under the strict common law rules. It applies only to gifts coming into effect after 15 July 1964. Unfortunately, however, even after 1964 the common law rules must be applied first, and only if a gift is void for perpetuity at common law will it be permissible to apply the more generous provisions of the Act. If the gift is valid at common law the gift will be subject to the common law rules, and not to the rules under the Act.

6.3.6.1 Express perpetuity period

A notable exception to the awkward 'double jurisdiction', whereby the common law rules must be applied before the 1964 Act, is the statutory perpetuity period contained in s 1 of the Act. Where a statutory period is specified in an instrument the common law perpetuity period will have no application. Section 1 provides that 'Where the instrument by which any disposition is made so provides, the perpetuity period . . . shall be of a duration equal to such number of years not exceeding 80 as is specified . . . in the instrument'.

6.3.6.2 Fertility presumptions

We have seen that the common law rule is concerned with possibilities, not probabilities. This approach has thrown up some odd decisions, such as *Re Dawson* (see 6.3.1.1).

The 1964 Act has brought some common sense to this area. In relation to fertility the Act raises a number of presumptions that can only be rebutted by clear contrary evidence. In other words, the Act is in this area concerned with probabilities, not remote possibilities.

Section 2(1)(a) of the Act provides that where a question of perpetuity turns on the ability of a person to have a child at some future time, then it shall be presumed that a male can have a child at the age of 14 years or over, but not under that age, and that a female can have a child at the age of 12 years or over, but not under that age or over the age of 55. Section 2(1)(b) adds that in the case of a living person evidence may be given to show that he or she will, or will not be able to have a child at the time in question.

These provisions (except s 2(1)(b)) apply in relation to the possibility that a person will at any time have a child by adoption, legitimation or other means (s 2(4)).

It is important to note, especially in the light of scientific 'advances', that the fertility *presumptions* in the Act are just that. They are merely presumptions and may be rebutted by evidence to the contrary.

6.3.6.3 The 'wait and see' principle

Whereas a gift is automatically void at common law if there is a possibility that it might vest outside the perpetuity period, the Act treats the gift as valid until such time as it is clear that there is no possibility of it vesting within the perpetuity period. The Act will not save a gift where it is known that at the very end of the perpetuity period the contingency will not be met (if it is ever met at all) until some later date. However, the Act does allow the court, trustees, etc to 'wait and see' whether or not the gift can vest within the perpetuity period. In most cases it vastly decreases the likelihood that a gift will be void for perpetuity. The 'wait and see' principle is enshrined within s 3 of the Act.

Section 3(1) provides that where a disposition would be void on the ground that the interest disposed of might not become vested until too remote a time, the disposition shall be treated, until such time as it becomes established that the vesting must occur (if it is to occur at all) after the end of the perpetuity period, as if the disposition were not subject to the common law rule against remoteness of vesting.

Section 3(1) also provides that if the trustees dispose of the trust property during the 'wait and see' period, by way of maintenance (see 13.2), advancement (see 13.3) or otherwise, such dispositions will not be invalidated if it is later established that the interests of the beneficiaries to whom the dispositions were made cannot vest within the perpetuity period.

6.3.6.4 Calculating the wait and see period

Section 3(4) of the 1964 Act provides that where the wait and see principle applies, and where the duration of the perpetuity period has not been expressed (see 6.3), the perpetuity period shall end 21 years after the death of the last surviving statutory life in being, unless the number of statutory lives is so large as to render it impracticable to ascertain the date of the death of the survivor. The statutory lives in being are those persons listed in s 3(5) who are 'in being and ascertainable at the commencement of the perpetuity period'. Where there are no statutory lives in being the period shall be a bare 21 years.

6.3.6.5 Statutory lives in being

The persons listed in s 3(5) as statutory lives in being are as follows:

- the person by whom the disposition was made, that is, the settlor of an *inter vivos* trust
- in the case of a disposition to a class of persons, any member or potential member of the class, and their parents and grandparents
- in the case of an individual disposition to a person taking only on certain conditions being satisfied, any person who may in time satisfy all the conditions, and his parents and grandparents
- in the case of a special power of appointment in favour of a class, any member or potential member of the class
- any person on the failure or determination of whose prior interest the disposition is limited to take effect.

EXERCISE 6.2

Try to identify the statutory lives relevant to the following testamentary dispositions:

- to Mandy's first daughter to qualify as a doctor
- to Laura for life, remainder to such of my grandchildren as attain the age of 30

Give yourself full marks if you identified the following people, respectively:

- All of Mandy's daughters alive at the date of the testator's death, and their parents (including Mandy) and grandparents.
- The testator's grandchildren alive at his death (potential donees), their surviving parents and grandparents and Laura.

6.3.6.6 The class closing provisions

We noted above (see 6.3.2) that the harshness of the common law rule in relation to class gifts is mitigated to some extent by the rule in *Andrews v Partington*. However, the effect of applying that rule is nevertheless to close the class so as to exclude any persons born after the class has closed, even though such persons might actually go on to satisfy the contingency within the perpetuity period.

The class closing provisions under the 1964 Act are more generous inasmuch as they operate in combination with the wait and see principle. Section 4(4) provides that only such persons as will certainly fail to satisfy the contingency within the perpetuity period will be excluded. The trustees are accordingly permitted to wait until the end of the perpetuity period to see which members of the class have by that time satisfied the contingency. If one or more members of the class have failed to satisfy the contingency by the end of the perpetuity period, the class will be closed to exclude those members.

6.3.6.7 The age reducing provisions

We noted above that s 163 of the Law of Property Act 1925 operates to mitigate the harshness of the common law rule against remoteness of vesting in relation to gifts contingent upon achieving an age above 21 (see 6.3.3). The effect of s 163 is to replace the contingent age (for example, 30) with the age of 21, if that will save the gift from remoteness. The effect of s 4 of the 1964 Act is similar, but rather more flexible. It also reduces the contingent ages specified in gifts, but only reduces the age to whatever extent is necessary in order to save the gift. Like s 163, the 1964 Act will not reduce an age to an age below 21, but unlike s 163, the 1964 Act does not automatically reduce the age to 21. This is because the age reduction provisions in the 1964 Act operate in combination with the 'wait and see principle'. The trustees will be permitted to wait until the end of the perpetuity period and if at that time the potential beneficiary has not yet reached the contingent age, it is permissible to reduce the age requirement to whatever extent is necessary (but not below the age of 21) to save the gift.

6.3.6.8 The problem of the unascertained spouse

In 6.3.4 we considered the problem of the unascertained spouse. Section 5 of the 1964 Act solves the problem of the unascertained spouse with shameless pragmatism. That section provides, simply, that:

> [w]here a disposition is limited by reference to the time of the death of the survivor of a person in being at the commencement of the perpetuity period, and any spouse of that person, and that time has not arrived at the end of the perpetuity period, the disposition shall be treated for all purposes, where to do so would save it from being void for remoteness, as if it had instead been limited by reference to the time immediately before the end of that period.

In other words, if at common law an unascertained spouse has caused a gift to fail, the Act will save that gift.

6.4 The rule against excessive accumulation of income

Accumulation of income is not the mere retention of income for administrative purposes. It is the process of adding income to capital. As Harman LJ put it in *Re the Earl of Berkeley* [1968] Ch 744, 772: 'Accumulation to my mind involves the addition of income to capital, thus increasing the estate in favour of those entitled to capital and against the interests of those entitled to income'. The rule against excessive accumulations is currently expressed in the Law of Property Act 1925, s 164, as amended by the Perpetuities and Accumulations Act 1964, s 13. It is a rule that has a colourful history, traceable back to the case of *Thellusson v Woodford* (1798) 4 Ves Jun 227. Thellusson, it seems, had the bright idea of directing his trustees to accumulate income on a fund for the lives of all his sons, grandsons and great-grandsons living at the time of his death. On the death of the last survivor, the fund was directed to be divided between the three eldest male living descendants of his three sons. If there were no such descendants, the property was to pass to the Crown. In the event, the accumulation lasted for 70 years, but it could conceivably have gone on even longer. Nevertheless, Thellusson's direction was perfectly valid as the law then stood, and the House of Lords upheld it. Indeed, Lord Eldon pointed out that the accumulated capital was not being removed from circulation entirely, but merely locked away in land for a while. The land itself could, of course, be sold.

Nevertheless, there was an outcry against Thellusson's will. A contemporary magazine suggested that if the accumulation continued for 120 years the fund would reach £140 million. Counsel for Thellusson's widow described the will as 'morally vicious . . . politically injurious . . . and by the time, when the accumulation shall end, it will have created a fund, the revenue of which will be greater than the civil list; and will therefore give its possessor the means of disturbing the whole economy of the country' (1805) 11 Ves 112, 114. The resulting panic led to the enactment of the Accumulations Act 1800 (the so-called Thellusson Act) (see P Polden, 'Panic or Prudence? The Thellusson Act 1800 and Trusts for Accumulation' (1994) 45 NILQ 13). This Act was eventually repealed and replaced by the Law of Property Act 1925, s 164.

6.4.1 The modern rule

According to the Law of Property Act 1925, s 164 no person may settle or dispose of any property in such manner that the income thereof shall be accumulated for any longer period than one of the following:

- the life of the grantor or settlor
- a term of 21 years from the death of the grantor, settlor or testator
- the duration of the minority or respective minorities of any person or persons living or *en ventre sa mère* at the death of the grantor, settlor or testator

- the duration of the minority or respective minorities only of any person or persons who under the limitations of the instrument directing the accumulations would, for the time being, if of full age, be entitled to the income directed to be accumulated
- (added by the 1964 Act, s 13, and applicable to directions made after 15 July 1964) the period of 21 years from the date of making the disposition
- (added by the 1964 Act, s 13, and applicable to directions made after 15 July 1964) the duration of the minority or minorities of any person in being at the date of making an *inter vivos* disposition.

Any other directions to accumulate (except those within s 165, below) shall be void and the income on the property directed to be accumulated shall go to the person or persons who would have been entitled to it if the direction to accumulate had not been made.

6.4.2 An exception to the modern rule on accumulations

Section 165 of the Law of Property Act 1925 provides that where accumulations of surplus income are made during a minority under any statutory power or under the general law (see 13.2.2), the period for which such accumulations are made is not to be taken into account in determining the periods for which accumulations are permitted to be made by s 164. Therefore, according to s 165, an express trust for accumulation for any period not listed in s 164 shall not be void by reason only of accumulations having been made during a minority.

This is the major exception to s 164. There are also, if you will excuse the pun, certain minor exceptions such as accumulations to pay debts, to produce timber and so on; consideration of these is left to more specialist texts.

6.4.3 Reform of the rule

The Law Commission has recently recommended the abolition of the rule against excessive accumulation of income: Law Com 251 (1998) part X, para 10.15. However, the repeal of the rule will not be retrospective (see 6.7). The only context in which the rule will be retained is in relation to charitable trusts. The Law Commission acknowledged the risk that a settlor might direct long-term accumulations of income for the fulfilment of some charitable purpose of a grandiose kind that will not come about for many years, and that there will be no public benefit from the charity during this period. It was recommended, therefore, that 'where an instrument confers a power or duty to accumulate on trustees of property that is held in trust for charitable purposes, the direction to accumulate should cease to have effect 21 years after the first day on which the income must or may be accumulated' (para 10.21).

6.5 The rule against inalienability of capital

A gift or trust will be void for perpetuity if it has the effect of rendering capital inalienable, that is, indisposable, for a period longer than the perpetuity period. The perpetuity period here is the same as the common law period used in the rule against remoteness of vesting. However, whereas the rule against remoteness of vesting is concerned to prevent gifts from vesting in persons at too remote a time in the future, the rule against inalienability of capital is concerned to prevent trusts for non-charitable purposes from enduring until too remote a time into the future.

This rule is most often invoked where property is given to a club or other unincorporated association subject to conditions, whether imposed by the terms of the gift or the rules of the club, which restrict its use to certain purposes and prevent it from being applied for the benefit of legal persons until too remote a time. An example would be a gift of £10,000 'to the Nottingham Tennis Club to be used to replace the present clubhouse when it falls down'. This rule against perpetuity is considered in greater depth in **Chapter 7**.

It is important to note that the Perpetuities and Accumulations Act 1964 does not affect this rule (s 15(4)).

6.6 The rules against perpetuity and charities

The rule against remoteness of vesting applies to charities inasmuch as it requires that a disposition must vest in charity within the perpetuity period. However, once property has been devoted to charitable purposes, a gift over to another charity will be valid even if the gift over vests after the end of the perpetuity period. The rule against inalienability of capital has no application to capital that has been devoted to exclusively charitable purposes.

The leading case is the decision of the Court of Appeal in *Re Tyler* [1891] 3 Ch 252, a case which reads like the backdrop to one of Sir Arthur Conan Doyle's adventures of Sherlock Holmes. The testator gave a fund to the trustees of the London Missionary Society and directed them to keep his family vault at Highgate Cemetery 'in good repair, and name legible, and to rebuild when it shall require'. If the trustees failed to comply with his request the monies were directed to pass to another charity, namely the Bluecoat School, Newgate Street, London.

It was held that the condition for the maintenance and repair of the vault was valid and binding on the first charity. Further, that the gift over to the second charity on failure to comply with the condition was good. It was held that the rule against perpetuities has no application to a transfer, on a certain event, of property from one charity to another.

? QUESTION 6.3

Which rule against perpetuities might be at issue on the facts of *Re Tyler*?

The judgment refers generically to the 'rules against perpetuities' and does not distinguish one rule from another. Nevertheless, the gift to the London Missionary Society, had the society been non-charitable, would have been void for inalienability of capital, because the gift was by way of perpetual endowment (as is shown by the fact that the gift was determinable upon disrepair of the family tomb). In addition, the gift over to the Bluecoat School would have been void for remoteness of vesting. If you visit the grave of Karl Marx in Highgate Cemetery why not see if the inscription on the Tyler family tomb is still legible? The Bluecoat School in Newgate Street may be very interested to hear that you cannot read the name Tyler on any tomb in the cemetery!

Finally, it is worth noting that the rule against excessive accumulations applies to charities, but that charities appear to avoid the restrictions of the statutory rule by making extensive use of the administrative power that every trustee has to retain income on a temporary basis when it is in surfeit, in order to cover needs arising at leaner times. This is so-called 'administrative retention' (see *Re Earl of Berkeley* [1968] Ch 744).

6.7 Proposals for the reform of the rule against perpetuities

The principal reforms proposed by Law Commission Report 251, *The Law of Trusts: The Rules against Perpetuities and Excessive Accumulations* (1998) are summarized in para 1.15 of the report as follows:

> (a) The rule against perpetuities should be restricted in its application to successive estates and interests in property and to powers of appointment thereby restoring it to its original function. It would cease to apply to rights over property such as options, rights of pre-emption and future easements. The existing exclusion from the rule of some pension schemes would be widened to include virtually all such schemes.
>
> (b) There should be a single perpetuity period of 125 years and the principle of 'wait and see' should apply for this period. [Which will apply regardless of any express provision to the contrary.]
>
> (c) The rule against excessive accumulations should be abolished except in relation to charitable trusts (to which . . . special considerations apply).

Subject to certain minor exceptions, these recommendations would be prospective and not retrospective in effect. They would apply only to estates, rights and interests created after any legislation was brought into force. Because the proposed reforms are not retrospective, their effect will be to simplify the law in relation to future dispositions, but the bad news for students is that the old law will be relevant for many years to come. The Law Commission acknowledges (at para 1.20) that:

> for many years there will be different rules against perpetuity for: (1) instruments made prior to the coming into force of the 1964 Act; (2) instruments made after the coming into force of that Act but before the implementation of the reforms that we recommend in this Report; and (3) instruments made after the coming into force of the reforms that we recommend in this report.

In short, the complexity will get worse before it gets better.

6.8 Trusts created to prejudice the settlor's creditors are void

It is permissible by means of a protective trust to employ a trust to protect the trust beneficiary from his creditors (see 2.3.2) and it is permitted to create a trust which will protect the trust beneficiary from the settlor's creditors (see, for example, *Re Kayford Ltd (in liquidation)* [1975] 1 WLR 279 at 4.3.3), but it is illegal for a settlor to create a trust to protect himself from his own creditors. The leading case is the decision of the Court of Appeal in *Re Butterworth* (1882) 19 Ch D 588, where Butterworth (a baker) made a voluntary settlement of his assets in favour of his wife and children before embarking upon additional business as a grocer. ('Voluntary' means here that he received no legal consideration in return for making the settlement.) He continued in trade as a grocer for some years and then sold up. Shortly afterwards his bakery business became insolvent, his liabilities far exceeding his assets. Their Lordships held that the settlement was void as against the trustee in the liquidation (and therefore void against the creditors of Butterworth's bakery business). The settlement had clearly been executed with the intention of putting the settlor's property out of the reach of his creditors.

Re Butterworth (1882) 19 Ch D 588

Sir George Jessel MR:

> The principle of *Mackay v Douglas* LR 14 Eq 106, and that line of cases, is this, that a man is not entitled to go into a hazardous business, and immediately before doing so settle all his property voluntarily, the object being this: 'If I succeed in business, I make a fortune for myself. If I fail, I leave my creditors unpaid. They will bear the loss.' That is the very thing which the statute of Elizabeth was meant to prevent. The object of the settlor was to put his property out of the reach of his future creditors. He contemplated engaging in this new trade and he wanted to preserve his property from his future creditors. That cannot be done by a voluntary settlement. That is, to my mind, a clear and satisfactory principle.
>
> Now, as I understand the evidence in this case, the baker did very well as a baker, and probably he may not have recollected the old proverb *ne sutor ultra crepidam*. When he went into business as a grocer he was going into a business which it appears he did not understand, and it is obvious that the object was—(I am taking that as a fair inference)—to save his property for his wife and children in case the new business did not succeed. Well, that actually happened. The new business did not succeed; he lost money by it, and it probably brought him to bankruptcy.
>
> His object was, as I have said, to make himself safe against that eventuality, and, if that was his object, then I think the principle of *Mackay v Douglas* applies, and that the deed was void also under the statute of Elizabeth. But, as I have said before, it is not really necessary to decide this point, because I am clearly of opinion that the deed is void under the 91st section of the Bankruptcy Act. . . .

The principle in *Re Butterworth* is now enshrined in s 423 of the Insolvency Act 1986 (for an example of the operation of that section see *Beckenham MC Ltd v Centralex Ltd* [2004] EWHC 1287 (Ch)).

Insolvency Act 1986

423. Transactions defrauding creditors

(1) This section relates to transactions entered into at an undervalue, and a person enters into such a transaction with another person if—

(a) he makes a gift to the other person or he otherwise enters into a transaction with the other on terms that provide for him to receive no consideration;

(b) he enters into a transaction with the other in consideration of marriage; or

(c) he enters into a transaction with the other for a consideration the value of which, in money or money's worth, is significantly less than the value, in money or money's worth, of the consideration provided by himself.

(2) Where a person has entered into such a transaction, the court may, if satisfied under the next subsection, make such order as it thinks fit for—

(a) restoring the position to what it would have been if the transaction had not been entered into, and

(b) protecting the interests of persons who are victims of the transaction.

(3) In the case of a person entering into such a transaction, an order shall only be made if the court is satisfied that it was entered into by him for the purpose—

(a) of putting assets beyond the reach of a person who is making, or may at some time make, a claim against him, or

(b) of otherwise prejudicing the interests of such a person in relation to the claim which he is making or may make.

(4) In this section 'the court' means the High Court or—

(a) if the person entering into the transaction is an individual, any other court which would have jurisdiction in relation to a bankruptcy petition relating to him;

(b) if that person is a body capable of being wound up . . . any other court having jurisdiction to wind it up.

(5) In relation to a transaction at an undervalue, references here and below to a victim of the transaction are to a person who is, or is capable of being, prejudiced by it; and in the following two sections the person entering into the transaction is referred to as 'the debtor'.

6.8.1 Commercial asset-protection trusts

Look back to 2.3.4 and 4.3.3, where we considered these trusts in detail.

? QUESTION 6.4

Do commercial asset-protection trusts offend the principle laid down by Sir George Jessel MR in *Re Butterworth*?

They do not. None of the commercial asset-protection trusts considered in 2.3.4 and 4.3.3 were created with the purpose of defrauding the settlor's general creditors. Rather, the commercial asset-protection trusts were aimed at sustaining failing companies (for example, *Re EVTR*), protecting loaned monies from the general creditors of the borrower (for example, *Barclays Bank v Quistclose*), protecting mail-order consumers (for example, *Re Kayford*) and so forth.

6.8.2 Protective trusts

Look back to 2.3.2, where we considered these trusts in detail.

QUESTION 6.5

Do protective trusts offend the principle laid down by Sir George Jessel MR in *Re Butterworth*?

Although a trust set up to defraud the settlor's creditors will generally be invalid, a trust set up to protect another person from their creditors will be valid if it complies with the statutory form of 'protective trust'; see 2.3.2. Protective trusts will often defeat the interests of the spendthrift's creditors, but that to some extent is also the purpose of the insolvency legislation itself. The statutory scheme for distribution of the insolvent person's estate is designed to satisfy the creditors as far as is reasonably possible but the statutory insolvency scheme is designed also to discharge the liabilities of the insolvent person and to allow them, eventually, to have a fresh start.

6.9 Gifts subject to conditions

'A condition in a trust inciting a beneficiary to do any act prohibited by law is void'—Law Commission *Illegal Transactions: The Effect of illegality on Contracts and Trusts* Law Commission Consultation Paper No 154 para 3.1 (for further detail of this document see 16.2.1.5).

6.9.1 Conditions as to race

Refer back to *Re Barlow's* (see 4.5.3.1), where the gift had been on terms that only 'friends' should take an interest. What if the words had been 'only my black friends', or 'only my white friends'? Although the use of such words would constitute an offence against the Race Relations Act 1976 had they been attached to a job advertisement or such like, there is no legal offence under the Act if such words are used, as here, in the context of the disposal of private property. This is clear from the following case.

***Blathwayt v Baron Cawley* [1976] AC 397, House of Lords**

A large estate (valued in 1975 at £2 million) was left in 1936 on various entailed trusts, but such that any person who became entitled was to forfeit his interest if he became a Roman Catholic (or ceased to use the name and arms of Blathwayt). It was argued that with respect to the present children, the religious condition tended to restrain the carrying out of parental duties, and was therefore void on public policy grounds. It was held that the effect of the clause may have been to force the parents to choose between material and spiritual welfare for their offspring, but that this was not necessarily contrary to public policy. (In the event the House of Lords held by a 3:2 majority (Lords Wilberforce and Fraser of Tullybelton dissenting) that the clause did not apply on its construction.)

Lord Wilberforce:

> . . . Finally, as to public policy. The argument under this heading was put in two alternative ways. First, it was said that the law of England was now set against discrimination on a number of grounds including religious grounds, and appeal was made to the Race Relations Act 1968 which does not refer to religion and to the European Convention of Human Rights of 1950 which refers to freedom of religion and to enjoyment of that freedom and other freedoms without discrimination on ground of religion. My Lords. I do not doubt that conceptions of public policy should move with the times and that widely accepted treaties and statutes may point the direction in which such conceptions, as applied by the courts, ought to move. It may well be that conditions such as this are, or at least are becoming, inconsistent with standards now widely accepted. But acceptance of this does not persuade me that we are justified, particularly in relation to a will which came into effect as long ago as 1936 and which has twice been the subject of judicial consideration, in introducing for the first time a rule of law which would go far beyond the mere avoidance of discrimination on religious grounds. To do so would bring about a substantial reduction of another freedom, firmly rooted in our law, namely that of testamentary disposition. Discrimination is not the same thing as choice: it operates over a larger and less personal area, and neither by express provision nor by implication has private selection yet become a matter of public policy.

Whether the laissez-faire approach preferred by Lord Wilberforce has survived the enactment of the Human Rights Act 1998 has yet to be judicially determined (see further 9.7).

6.9.2 Conditions as to religion

In the same case, Lord Cross had this to say, in relation to *religious* discrimination:

> . . . it is true that it is widely thought nowadays that it is wrong for a government to treat some of its citizens less favourably than others because of differences in their religious beliefs; but it does not follow from that that it is against public policy for an adherent of one religion to distinguish in disposing of his property between adherents of his faith and those of another. So to hold would amount to saying that although it is in order for a man to have a mild preference for one religion as opposed to another it is disreputable for him to be convinced of the importance of holding true religious beliefs and of the fact that his religious beliefs are the true ones.

In *Blathwayt* a clause of the testator's will provided that, in the event that one of the beneficiaries under his will should 'be or become a Roman Catholic . . . the estate hereby limited to him shall cease and determine and be utterly void'. It later transpired that a life tenant had indeed become a Roman Catholic. The judge at first instance held that his estate should be forfeit, a judgment which was ultimately upheld in the House of Lords.

6.9.3 Conditions as to marriage

According to Lord Mansfield 'conditions in restraint of marriage are odious' (*Long v Dennis* (1767) 4 Burr 2052 at 2059).

Despite this sentiment, a condition will not be void which restrains the *remarriage* of a beneficiary (*Jordan v Holkham* (1753) Amb 209). Although, consistent with this, clauses which might encourage divorce or separation of husband and wife will be void. In *Re Johnson's WT* [1967] Ch 387 a clause was declared void which provided that the beneficiary would receive more income from the fund if she split up from her husband. The testator's intention had been to make greater provision in the event of such a breakdown of the marriage, it had not been his intention to promote divorce. The judge held nevertheless that the clause might operate as an incentive to divorce or separation, and that it must therefore be declared void.

Despite the fact that conditions are void which operate in restraint of marriage generally, conditions which restrain marriage to specific individuals or classes of person will be legally valid. Reported instances include conditions restraining marriage to a 'Papist' (*Duggan v Kelly* (1848) 101 Eq R 473) and to a 'Scotchman' (*Perrin v Lyon* (1807) 9 East 170).

6.10 Illegality and resulting trusts

See 16.2.1.2.

6.11 Miscellaneous public policy restrictions

6.11.1 Use of the form of a trust to conceal true ownership is prohibited

The scope of this principle is debatable. It appears to be an application of the maxim that equity looks to substance and not form, yet that maxim would normally be applied in order to recognize the existence of a trust behind formal legal title. It is applied in this context, however, in order to deny the existence of a trust, where a formal trust has been used to conceal the true ownership position. As the judge stated in *Great Western Rly Co v Turner* (1872) 8 LR Ch App 149, at 154:

> There being no bona fide reason for the creation of any trust, the terms of the trust were gone through in order to conceal the true ownership of the property. That has been held to be in truth an abuse of the forms of trust for the purpose of creating a reputation of ownership, and placing the property within the order and disposition of another with the consent of the true owner of the property.

6.11.2 Fox hunting

It is interesting to speculate whether trusts for the purpose of fox hunting have also now joined the class of illegal trusts (see 7.3.3).

6.12 Consequences of failure

Where a trust fails *ab initio* for perpetuity or public policy reasons there will be a resulting trust to the settlor. In the case of testamentary dispositions there will be a resulting trust to the residuary beneficiary of the testator's estate or to the deceased's next of kin in the event of intestacy. If there are no identifiable next-of-kin, the property will pass to the Crown as *bona vacantia*.

However, s 3(1) of the Perpetuities and Accumulations Act 1964 provides that if the trustees dispose of the trust property during the 'wait and see' period, by way of maintenance (see 13.2), advancement (see 13.3) or otherwise, such dispositions will not be invalidated if it is later established that the interests of the beneficiaries to whom the dispositions were made cannot vest within the perpetuity period.

CHAPTER SUMMARY

- Because trust property is subject to binding obligations as to its use, it cannot participate as fully in the free market as property owned absolutely. This makes it imperative to ensure that trust property returns within a reasonable time to the state of being owned absolutely. Thus:
  - A trust will be void (as infringing the rule against remoteness of vesting) if it postpones for too long a period the date at which the trust property will vest in ascertainable beneficiaries.
  - A trust will be void (as infringing the rule against inalienability of capital) if it requires capital to be tied up to provide an income for too long a period.
  - A trust will be void (as infringing the rule against accumulation of income) if it requires income to be accumulated for too long a period.
- We have seen that the rule against remoteness of vesting is very complicated. The common law rule must be applied first (see the summative chart on the common law rule of remoteness of vesting at 6.3.5). If a disposition infringes the common law rule (because there is a possibility, however unrealistic, that the gift might vest at too remote a time) it is then permitted (by the Perpetuities and Accumulations Act 1964) to wait until the end of the perpetuity period to allow the disposition the opportunity to vest in time.
- Quite apart from economic reasons for wishing a disposition to vest in an absolute owner within a reasonable time, there is also the public policy against allowing the wishes of the donors to rule over the freedoms of the living donee. Nevertheless, donors still retain the power to choose the conditions on which they dispose of their property and, controversially, conditions which in a public context would be void for racism or sexism may be permitted if they are construed to be nothing more than expressions of private choice.

- Whereas the personal assets of insolvent persons will be available to their general creditors, any assets held by them in trust for another will not be available to satisfy the claims of the general creditors. Accordingly, it is not permitted to establish a trust to protect one's own wealth from one's creditors. It is, however, permitted to establish a trust to protect one's creditors from one's insolvency and it is even permitted (by means of a protective trust) to protect another person from their creditors.

SUMMATIVE ASSESSMENT EXERCISE

online resource centre

Consider the validity of the following clauses in the will of X:

Clause One: 'I bequeath my stocks and shares to my trustees on trust for such of my grandchildren as shall attain the age of 30.'
Clause Two: 'To my son, Leonard, a life interest in the income earned from my country properties, to determine if ever the income of the fund becomes payable to another person. In the event of determination of the interest the income from the properties shall be held by my trustees on trust for such of my children and in such shares as my trustees shall in their absolute discretion think fit.'
Clause Three: 'In the event of any of the beneficiaries under this will marrying into Islam, the estate hereby limited to him or her shall cease and determine and be utterly void.'

Evidence has been produced to show that the testatrix was survived by a daughter aged 60, a son (Leonard) aged 50, a granddaughter aged 30 and two grandsons aged 25 and 23 respectively. The granddaughter wishes to convert to Islam in order to marry her Muslim boyfriend.

FURTHER READING

Davies, J D, *Presumptions and Illegality* in A J Oakley (ed) *Trends in Contemporary Trust Law* (Oxford: Clarendon Press, 1996) 33.

Enonchong, N, *Illegal Transactions* (London: LLP, 1998).

Grattan, S, *Mutual Wills and Remarriage* [1997] Conv 153.

Grattan, S, *Testamentary Conditions in Restraint of Religion* in Cooke, E, (ed) *Modern Studies in Property Law Vol I: Property 2000* (Oxford: Hart, 2001), 257–74.

Gray, J C, *The Rule Against Perpetuities* (4th edn) (Boston, Mass: Little, Brown, 1942).

Law Commission, *Illegal Transactions: The Effect of Illegality on Contracts and Trusts* Consultation Paper No 154 (1999).

Law Commission, *The Law of Trusts. The Rules against Perpetuities and Excessive Accumulations*, Consultation Paper No 133 (1993).

Law Commission, *The Law of Trusts. The Rules against Perpetuities and Excessive Accumulations* Report No 251 (1998).

Martin, J, *Fraudulent Transferors and the Public Conscience* [1992] Conv 153.

Polden, P, 'Panic or Prudence? The Thellusson Act 1800 and Trusts for Accumulation' (1994) 45 NILQ 13.

7 Purpose trusts

OBJECTIVES

By the end of this chapter you should be able to:

1. Explain the reason why trusts for private purposes are generally void
2. List the anomalous exceptions to the general rule
3. Employ the various devices for avoiding the prohibition against trusts for private purposes
4. Elucidate the special problems raised by gifts to unincorporated associations
5. Advise a donor as to the way in which they can achieve their intentions in making a gift to an unincorporated association

7.1 Introduction

One of the main reasons for disposing of property by way of a trust rather than by outright gift is to fix upon the subject matter of the gift a binding obligation as to the purposes for which it is used.

? QUESTION 7.1

We have already come across purpose trusts in previous chapters. Can you remember where?

One place where we encountered purpose trusts was in **Chapter 4** (see 4.5). There we observed that the object of an expressly created trust must be certain or capable of being rendered certain, and that the object of a trust can be a legal person (human or corporate), a public (that is, charitable) purpose or a private purpose. In this chapter we shall discover that trusts in the latter category, those for private purposes, are generally void. There are, however, a number of important exceptions to this general rule, where trusts for private purposes are valid. As, for instance, where the trust, though on one level expressed to be for a particular purpose (for example, '*to build a swimming pool* for my employees to swim in') ought actually to be construed as a trust for particular persons (for example, 'to build a swimming pool *for my employees* to swim in').

Another place where we encountered purpose trusts was in **Chapter 6** (see 6.5). There we saw that one of the main reasons why a trust for private purposes is generally void is because such trusts are often set up in the nature of a permanent endowment, thus potentially rendering the capital inalienable in perpetuity. A simple example of such a trust would be a trust 'to keep my collection of vintage cars intact and well-maintained'. Although the income from the fund will be applied in carrying out the purpose of maintaining the collection, in order to ensure that income is always available it will be necessary to keep the capital subject to the trust obligations in perpetuity.

7.2 Trusts purely for private purposes

Trusts purely for private purposes are generally void because:

(a) being in nature 'private', a trust of this sort would not be subject to the control of the courts, nor of any department of State;

(b) following on from the preceding point, in order to bring the trust within the control of the court, there must always be someone in whose favour the court can decree performance, that is, someone who will enforce the trust by, *inter alia*, bringing breaches of trust to the attention of the court. This is the so-called 'beneficiary principle' (*Leahy v AG for NSW* [1959] (see 7.5));

(c) trusts for private purposes are often required to be construed as perpetual endowments. Such endowments offend the rule against inalienability of capital (see 6.5);

(d) trusts for private purposes will fail the requirement of certainty of object if the purposes expressed are vague and indefinite, thus rendering them uncontrollable by the court. Roxburgh J made this point in *Re Astor* [1952] Ch 534, where he held that '[t]he purposes must be so defined that, if the trustees surrendered their discretion, the court could carry out the purposes declared, not a selection of them arrived at by eliminating those which are too uncertain to be carried out'. Note, however, that, a purpose will only be too uncertain where the court cannot by a reasonable construction make it certain (*certum est quod certum reddi potest*—that is certain which can be rendered certain);

(e) trusts for private purposes will fail if they are capricious (see 7.3.1.3).

Whether or not there has been an attempt to create a trust purely for private purposes is a matter of construction.

***Re Astor* [1952] Ch 534**

Non-charitable trusts were declared of substantially all the issued shares of 'The Observer Limited' for purposes including the 'maintenance . . . of good understanding . . . between nations' and 'the preservation of the independence and integrity of newspapers'. It was held that the trusts were invalid because they were not for the benefit of individuals, but for a number of non-charitable purposes which no one could enforce. The trusts would, in any event, have been void for uncertainty.

Roxburgh J:

> The question on which I am giving this reserved judgment is whether the non-charitable trusts . . . are void. Counsel for the trustees of the 1951 settlement and for the Attorney-General have submitted that they are void on two grounds: (i) that they are not trusts for the benefit of individuals; (ii) that they are void for uncertainty. Lord Parker of Waddington dealt with [the second ground] in his speech in *Bowman v Secular Society Ltd* [1917] AC 406:
>
> > A trust to be valid must be for the benefit of individuals, which this is certainly not, or must be in that class of gifts for the benefit of the public which the courts in this country recognise as charitable in the legal as opposed to the popular sense of that term.
>
> . . . if the purposes are not charitable, great difficulties . . . arise both in theory and in practice. In theory, because, having regard to the historical origins of equity, it is difficult to visualise the growth of equitable obligations which nobody can enforce, and in practice, because it is not possible to contemplate with equanimity the creation of large funds devoted to non-charitable purposes which no court and no department of State can control, or, in the case of maladministration, reform. Therefore, Lord Parker's second proposition would prima facie appear to be well founded. . . . no officer has ever been constituted to take, in the case of non-charitable purposes, the position held by the Attorney-General in connection with charitable purposes, and no case has been found in the reports in which the court has ever directly enforced a non-charitable purpose against a trustee. Indeed, where, as in the present case, the only beneficiaries are purposes and an at present unascertainable person, it is difficult to see who could initiate such proceedings. If the purposes are valid trusts, the settlors have retained no beneficial interest and could not initiate them. It was suggested that the trustees might proceed ex parte to enforce the trusts against themselves. I doubt that, but at any rate nobody could enforce the trusts against them. . . .

? QUESTION 7.2

We noted earlier that a trust might be construed as being for a beneficiary, a charitable purpose or a private purpose. Into which category do you think a bequest, to the Bishop of Durham for 'such objects of benevolence and liberality as the Bishop of Durham in his own discretion shall most approve', would fall?

This was the question for determination in the case of *Morice v Bishop of Durham* (1804) [1903–13] All ER Rep 451. Sir William Grant MR held that the words 'benevolence and liberality' were not charitable. Lord Eldon LC confirmed, on appeal, that those words could not be charitable because they were not exclusively so, with the result that the whole fund might be applied to non-charitable ends without there being a breach of the terms of the bequest (see, generally, **Chapter 8** at 8.4). Nor could the bequest be construed as a personal gift to the Bishop. The only other alternative would be to construe the bequest as a gift for purely private purposes, that is, for 'objects of benevolence and liberality'. It was held that such objects were too ill defined to come under the court's control, and that the bequest for that reason failed. Accordingly, the Bishop took the bequest on a resulting trust for the residuary beneficiaries of the testatrix's estate.

Other dispositions which have been held to be void as trusts purely for private purposes include:

1. a non-charitable trust of substantially all the issued shares of 'The Observer Limited' (the newspaper company) for purposes including the 'maintenance . . . of good understanding . . . between nations' and 'the preservation of the independence and integrity of newspapers' (*Re Astor* [1952] Ch 534);
2. amongst others, the following trusts of the income from the residuary estate of George Bernard Shaw (1856–1950): (1) to ascertain the number of persons currently using the 26-letter English alphabet; (2) to ascertain how much effort could be saved by replacing the 26-letter alphabet with a 40 letter phonetic 'British Alphabet' in which at least 14 letters are devoted to vowel-sounds. In that case, Harman J noted that 'an object cannot complain to the court, which therefore cannot control the trust' (*Re Shaw* [1957] 1 WLR 729). He approved Lord Greene in *Re Diplock* [1941] Ch 253 who had said that 'in order for a trust to be properly constituted . . . The beneficiary must be ascertained or must be ascertainable'.

It is said of Shaw that he once observed with typical haughtiness that 'England and America are two countries separated by the same language'. It is somewhat ironic that it was only by virtue of Hollywood's adaptation of his play, 'Pygmalion' (1916), into the musical film, 'My Fair Lady' (1964), that there came to be sufficient funds in his estate to bring his 'alphabet' trusts to court!

7.3 Trusts of imperfect obligation

This class of trusts is anomalous, and will not be extended (*Re Endacott* [1960] Ch 232). They are trusts for purely private (non-charitable) purposes which are valid despite the lack of any ascertainable beneficiary. They include such purposes as looking after animals and the maintenance of tombs and monuments. There is no principled reason for their exceptional status, and it may be, as Sir Arthur Underhill suggested, that they are merely concessions to human weakness or sentiment (Underhill's *Law of Trusts and Trustees*, 10th edn, p 97). In *Re Endacott* [1960] Ch 232, Harman LJ described them as 'occasions when Homer has nodded', that is, occasions where the usual logical principle of the law has lapsed. (Echoing the lament of

Horace in his treatise on the art of poetry: *indignor quandoque bonus dormitat Homerus*: I am aggrieved when sometimes even the excellent Homer falls asleep ('nods').)

They are classified as *trusts of imperfect obligation*, because even though they are valid, there is no person in a position actively to enforce the trust obligations against the trustees. The practical, if not legal, result being that the trustees are not in fact bound to apply the trust fund in furtherance of the purposes stated, unless they undertake (whether voluntarily or by order of the court) to do so. The fact that the trust might not be fulfilled has led to the suggestion that trusts of imperfect obligation will only be recognized where they appear in a will which is drafted so as to make it clear that, if the fund is not expended on the non-charitable purpose, it will fall into the residue of the deceased's estate. (See *Re Thompson* [1934] Ch 342 at 344, *Re Astor's ST* [1952] Ch 534 at 546.)

Against this suggestion it has been pointed out that the residuary legatees of a will or successors on intestacy can always apply to the court to have the residue of the deceased's estate transferred to them whenever it appears that the trustees are not going to apply the fund in furtherance of the non-charitable purposes, and that there is no reason why the subject matter of the trust of imperfect obligation should not be the residue itself (Parker & Mellows, *The Modern Law of Trusts*, 6th edn, 1994, Sweet & Maxwell, p 117).

In the following sections we shall consider the established categories of trusts of imperfect obligation.

7.3.1 The erection or maintenance of tombs or monuments

In *Re Hooper* [1932] 1 Ch 38 a testator made a bequest and declared that the income therefrom should be used for the care and upkeep of certain memorials in cemeteries and churchyards. The memorials comprised graves (including that of his son in Shotley churchyard near Ipswich), a vault and certain monuments. In addition he declared that income from the bequest should be applied to the upkeep of a tablet and a window in St Matthias' Church at Ilsham.

Maugham J held that whereas the upkeep of the tablet and window were valid as charitable purposes, the trust for the upkeep of the other memorials would take effect as a trust of imperfect obligation, and be limited to take effect for 21 years after the testator's death. (For the meaning of 'charitable purposes' see **Chapter 8**.)

7.3.1.1 Uncertainty

It was primarily because of uncertainty that the Court of Appeal refused to recognize the trust in *Re Endacott* [1960] Ch 232. There the testator left his residuary estate to his local parish council 'for the purpose of providing some useful memorial to myself'. Harman LJ refused to extend the class of 'troublesome, anomalous and aberrant cases' to include Endacott's 'unspecified and unidentified memorial'.

7.3.1.2 Perpetuity

In *Mussett v Bingle* [1876] WN 170, a testator bequeathed (1) £300 to erect a monument to his wife's first husband and (2) £200, the income from which was to be used in the upkeep of the monument. The gift of £300 was upheld but the gift of £200 failed because it offended the rule against inalienability of capital.

7.3.1.3 Capriciousness

Any trust for purposes, whether charitable or not, may fail for capriciousness. A capricious trust is one characterized by the playful whim and fancy of the settlor (the word derives ultimately from the Latin *caper*, meaning goat. A capricious settlor is one who is 'acting the goat'!). A good illustration of a capricious trust is provided by *Brown v Burdett* (1882) 21 Ch D 667. There the expressed purpose of the trust was to block up the windows and doors of a house for 20 years.

Capriciousness is perhaps raised most often as an objection in the context of trusts for the erection of tombs and monuments. Lord Kyllachy, in the Scottish case of *M'Caig v University of Glasgow* [1907] SC 231, had some strong words to say about the testamentary wishes of John Stuart M'Caig who had provided in his will that the income from his estate should be applied to the erection of 'artistic towers' in his memory. On that occasion the court disallowed his testamentary directions on the ground of capriciousness (although he somehow got his way by another route, for 'M'Caig's Tower', a useless and not particularly scenic folly, now stands imperiously above the beautiful harbour in Oban on the west coast of Scotland). Lord Kyllachy thought that it 'ought to be unlawful, to dedicate by testamentary disposition, for all time, or for a length of time, the whole income of a large estate . . . to objects of no utility . . . and which have no other purpose or use than that of perpetuating at great cost, and in an absurd manner, the idiosyncracies of an eccentric testator'. To his Lordship's mind an equally useful variation on M'Caig's trust would be a trust to 'turn the income of the estate into money, and throw the money yearly into the sea'.

7.3.2 The maintenance of specific animals

In *Re Dean* (1889) 41 Ch D 552 a testator set up a will trust for the maintenance of his horses and hounds for a period of 50 years. He declared that the trustees should not be bound to render any account of expenditure. It was held, by North J, that the trust was a valid trust of imperfect obligation. As a trust for the benefit of specific animals it could not be charitable, whereas another gift made by the testator (to the Royal Society for the Prevention of Cruelty to Animals) was held to be potentially charitable because it was a trust for the benefit of animals generally (see 8.3.6.2).

There was clearly no irony in 1889 in making simultaneous bequests for the benefit of hunting hounds and for the benefit of the RSPCA. However, the decision in *Re Dean* was in another respect highly ironic. For although North J had opined that a testator should limit his anomalous purposes to take effect within the perpetuity period, he omitted to strike down the present trust despite the fact that the trustee clearly intended the purposes to be met beyond the perpetuity period of 21 years after his death.

7.3.3 Fox hunting

The testator in *Re Thompson* [1934] Ch 342 bequeathed a legacy to a friend to be applied by him as he should in his absolute discretion think fit towards the promotion and furtherance of fox hunting. The residuary legatee, a charity, objected to the bequest (for financial rather than ethical reasons, it is supposed). Rejecting the objection of the residuary legatee, Clauson J held that this was a valid trust of imperfect obligation.

? QUESTION 7.3

Does it follow that these purpose trusts are void, now that hunting with hounds has been banned in England and Wales?

Arguably not, since the ban on hunting wild mammals with dogs which was introduced by the Hunting Act 2004 does not apply to 'exempt' hunting. Exempt hunting includes stalking vermin and flushing it out to be shot.

7.3.4 Saying private masses

In *Re Hetherington* [1990] Ch 1 the testatrix left a legacy to 'the Roman Catholic Church Bishop of Westminster for the repose of the souls of my husband and my parents and my sisters and also myself when I die', and left the residue of her estate 'to the Roman Catholic Church St Edwards Golders Green for Masses for my soul'. It was held that the gifts were for charitable purposes. However, in reaching this decision the gifts were given a benignant construction, that is, in order to validate the legacy as a gift for charitable purposes, the gift was construed to be for the purpose of saying masses in public. Had the gift been construed as a donation for the celebration of a mass in private, it would not have contained the element of public benefit necessary to charitable status, but it might nevertheless have been effective as a trust of imperfect obligation (*Bourne v Keane* [1919] AC 815, 874–5).

7.4 Devices for avoiding the rule against trusts purely for private purposes

If you wished to set up a trust to further some private purpose of your own, how do you think you would go about it? There are a number of devices that you might consider.

One possibility would be to make a gift to a charity determinable in the event of failure (not necessarily failure by the charity itself) to carry out your desired purposes (see *Re Tyler* at 6.6). In the event of determination of the gift to the charity, you should provide a gift over in favour of another charity. As long as your desired purposes are not unlawful, this device will not only fulfil your purposes, it will also enable your purposes to be carried out in perpetuity. It is essential that failure of the private purpose is described as a determining event, for it will then operate informally by way of an incentive to the first charity. If fulfilment of your private purposes is described as being a condition attaching to the gift, the gift to the charity will fail. So, for example, in *Re Dalziel* [1943] Ch 277, where a legacy was left to the governors of St Bartholomew's Hospital 'upon and subject to the condition' that the income be used to maintain a mausoleum, the gift failed to take effect as a charitable gift because charitable trusts must exist for exclusively charitable purposes (see 8.4).

7.5 Purpose trusts with indirect human beneficiaries

It is in theory always a matter of construction whether or not a disposition is held to operate as an absolute gift, a gift subject to a mere moral obligation, a gift subject to a legal condition, a trust for private purposes, a trust for public purposes, a trust for persons, or a mere power. We have already seen, however, that choosing the appropriate construction is an exercise in legal logic which appears often to be heavily influenced by pragmatic considerations (see 4.2.3). This section considers a number of cases where dispositions, which at first sight might appear to be trusts for private purposes, have in fact been construed to be dispositions in favour of the persons who would benefit from the carrying out of those purposes.

A simple example is provided by *Re Bowes* [1896] 1 Ch 507. There, the testator made a bequest of £5,000 'upon trust to expend the same in planting trees for shelter on the Wemergill estate being part of my settled estates'. The estate owners objected that this would be a very disadvantageous way of spending the money.

North J held that there was a trust to 'lay out' (apply) the £5,000, as opposed to a mere power to apply the fund. It was, however, a trust 'for the benefit of the estate, and the persons who, for the time being, are entitled to the estate', thus the expressed purpose of planting trees could be dismissed as being a mere motive for making the disposition in favour of the estate owners. The estate owners would be subject to no more than a moral obligation to use the monies to plant trees. In reaching this conclusion it appears that North J was mindful of the fact that the estate owners (the tenant for life and tenant in tail in remainder) were between them able to bring to an end the settlement of the estates, if they so wished.

? QUESTION 7.4

Consider a testamentary gift of freehold property 'upon trust for such order of nuns of the Catholic Church or the Christian Brothers as my executors and trustees shall select'. The residue to be applied to build a new convent or to update existing buildings. How would you construe such a disposition?

This disposition was considered by the Privy Council in the case of *Leahy v AG for New South Wales* [1959] AC 457. It was held that the gift of residue was saved by a particular New South Wales statute. However, the principal gift was held to be invalid as a perpetual endowment in favour of a non-charitable body. (Due to the closed nature of some of the orders the gift could not be charitable, see 8.3.5.3.) On the particular facts of *Leahy*, their Lordships refused to construe the principal gift as a gift to the members for the time being of the orders intended to take the benefit, a construction which would have saved the gift from the taint of perpetuity. However, their Lordships did accept, in principle, that in an appropriate case, where a gift is made to an association of persons 'for the general purposes of the association' those words can be disregarded and the gift can be sustained as an absolute gift to the individual members. It was in *Leahy* that Viscount Simonds gave the following exposition of the so-called 'beneficiary principle':

> A gift can be made to persons (including a corporation) but it cannot be made to a purpose or to an object; so, also, a trust may be created for the benefit of persons as *cestuis que trustent*, but not for

a purpose or object unless the purpose or object be charitable. For a purpose or object cannot sue, but, if it be charitable, the Attorney-General can sue to enforce it.

Leahy was followed by Goff J in the Chancery Division in *Re Denley's Trust Deed* [1969] 1 Ch 373. His Lordship's conclusion from *Leahy* was that 'where . . . the trust, though expressed as a purpose, is directly for the benefit of an individual or individuals . . . it is in general outside the mischief of the beneficiary principle'.

The facts of *Re Denley's* were, briefly, that land was settled on trustees for use as a sports club 'primarily' for the benefit of the employees of a company, and 'secondarily' for the benefit of such other persons (if any) as the trustees may allow to use the same. The gift was limited to take effect within 21 years of the death of certain named persons.

It was held that because of the private nexus between the potential beneficiaries of the trust and a particular company the trust was not sufficiently 'public' to be charitable. Prima facie, then, it would be void as a non-charitable purpose trust. However, though expressed to be for a purpose, the trust was indirectly for the benefit of the employees and did not fall foul of the beneficiary principle. Goff J was satisfied that, in contrast to the case of a pure purpose trust, there were persons here who would bring the matter to court if the trustees failed to meet their obligations. He preferred to confine the rule against enforcing non-charitable purpose trusts to trusts which are abstract or impersonal (see, for example, *Re Shaw* at 7.2). He did, however, acknowledge that practical difficulties might arise if some of the employees disagreed as to the purposes for which the sports club was to be used. However, this difficulty could be overcome by the court giving its approval, on an order for directions, to a scheme drawn up by the employees.

It is very important to note that this gift would have failed outright for inalienability of capital, even as a trust in favour of human beneficiaries, had it not been expressly limited to take effect within the perpetuity period.

Re Denley's Trust Deed [1969] 1 Ch 373, Chancery Division

Goff J:

[T]here may be a purpose or object trust, the carrying out of which would benefit an individual or individuals, where that benefit is so indirect or intangible or which is otherwise so framed as not to give those persons any *locus standi* to apply to the court to enforce the trust, in which case the beneficiary principle would, as it seems to me, apply to invalidate the trust, quite apart from any question of uncertainty or perpetuity. Such cases can be considered if and when they arise. The present is not, in my judgment, of that character . . .

Apart from this possible exception, in my judgment the beneficiary principle of *Re Astor*, which was approved in *Re Endacott (decd)* [1959] 3 All ER 562; see particularly by Harman LJ, is confined to purpose or object trusts which are abstract or impersonal. The objection is not that the trust is for a purpose or object *per se*, but that there is no beneficiary or *cestui que trust*. The rule is so expressed in *Lewin on Trusts* (16th edn) p.17, and in my judgment, with the possible exception which I have mentioned, rightly so. In *Re Wood, Barton* v *Chilcott* [1949] Ch 498, Harman J said:

> There has been an interesting argument on the question of perpetuity, but it seems to me, with all respect to that argument, that there is an earlier obstacle which is fatal to the validity of this

> bequest, namely, that a gift on trust must have a *cestui que trust*, and there being here no *cestui que trust* the gift must fail.
>
> Again, in *Leahy* v *A-G of New South Wales* [1959] AC 457, Viscount Simonds, delivering the judgment of the Privy Council, said:
>
> > A gift can be made to persons (including a corporation) but it cannot be made to a purpose or to an object: so, also [and these are the important words] a trust may be created for the benefit of persons as *cestuis que trust* but not for a purpose or object unless the purpose or object be charitable. For a purpose or object cannot sue, but, if it be charitable, the Attorney-General can sue to enforce it.
>
> Where, then, the trust, though expressed as a purpose, is directly for the benefit of an individual or individuals, it seems to me that it is in general outside the mischief of the beneficiary principle.

7.6 Gifts to unincorporated non-profit associations

Quite complex problems arise in construing gratuitous dispositions in favour of unincorporated, non-charitable, non-profit associations, that is, private clubs and societies. Speaking in very general terms, the law readily legislates for incorporated associations (for example, limited liability companies) and profit-oriented unincorporated associations (that is, partnerships), but it struggles to understand the essential nature of those unincorporated associations which do not exist primarily with a view to making financial profit (for example, clubs and societies).

A corporation is a legal person, so it follows that a trust for the benefit of a corporation *ipso facto* satisfies the beneficiary principle. A club, on the other hand, has no legal personality of its own, it is not a separate legal person but a mere association of individuals. The question arises, therefore, whether a gratuitous disposition in favour of a club was intended to be a gift to the individual members of the association for the time being, or a trust to further the purposes of the club or a trust to benefit present and/or future members. In fact, gratuitous dispositions in favour of non-charitable unincorporated associations can be construed in a number of different ways. They are considered in the following sections.

Trust

- as a pure purpose trust, that is, a trust for impersonal purposes; or
- on trust for the benefit of the present members of the association; or
- on trust for the benefit of the present and future members of the association.

Mandate

- as a mandate to the officers of the association to use the donation as instructed by the donor.

Power

- as the grant of a power to apply the donation for the purposes of the association.

7.6.1 Absolute gift to the members as joint tenants

Cross J described this as 'a gift to the members of the association at the relevant date [the date of the gift] as joint tenants, so that any member can sever his share and claim it whether or not he continues to be a member' (*Neville Estates v Madden* [1962] Ch 832).

If a gift is made to a club only very rarely will a sensible construction allow it to be divided among the present members in individual shares. Whether this construction will be admitted will depend in large part upon the subject matter of the gift. Where a gift of land is made to a football club it is most unlikely that the donor intended the individual members to divide the land up physically and for each member to take allotments in it. However, if an aficionado made a gift of 12 bottles of wine 'to the Barchester string quartet' there is every likelihood that the donor intended the members to take three bottles each.

In *Re Grant's WT* (see 7.6.2), Vinelott J suggested that in any case where this construction is appropriate '. . . the association is used in effect as a convenient label or definition of the class which it is intended to take: but the class being ascertained, each member takes as a joint tenant free from any contractual fetter'.

7.6.2 Absolute gifts to members subject to the contractual rules of the club

This construction was accepted *obiter* by Cross J in *Neville Estates Ltd v Madden* where it was framed as: 'a gift to the existing members not as joint tenants, but subject to their respective contractual rights and liabilities towards one another as members of the association. In such a case a member cannot sever his share. It will accrue to the other members on his death or resignation, even though such members include persons who became members after the gift took effect'. This was followed by Brightman J in *Re Recher's WT* [1972] Ch 526.

In *Re Recher's WT* a testatrix left a share of her residuary estate to 'The London and Provincial Anti-Vivisection Society'. It was conceded that the gift was not for charitable purposes and the question therefore arose whether it could be construed in some other way so as to allow the wishes of the testatrix to be fulfilled. Brightman J started from the premise that '[i]t would astonish a layman to be told that there was a difficulty in his giving a legacy to an unincorporated non-charitable society which he had or could have supported without trouble during his lifetime'. His Lordship held that the society's existing funds already formed the subject matter of a contract in accordance with which the members had bound themselves *inter se*, and that the testatrix's legacy should be construed as a gift to the present members of the society beneficially, as an accretion to the society's general funds. In short, this legacy was a gift to existing persons, not a trust for purposes. As such it did not breach the rule against inalienability of capital because if all the members agreed, they could decide to wind up the society and divide the net assets amongst themselves beneficially.

? QUESTION 7.5

The construction approved in *Re Recher's* was applied to the facts of *Re Grant's WT* [1980] 1 WLR 360. Read the following account. Can you see why the testamentary gift failed in *Re Grant's WT*?

Grant, the testator, had been financial secretary of the Chertsey Constituency Labour Party, which had since become the Chertsey and Walton Constituency Labour Party. The new constituency party was subject to rules laid down by the National Executive Committee of the Labour Party and the national annual party conference. By his will, Grant devised and bequeathed all his real and personal estate (for the benefit of the Chertsey headquarters of the new constituency party) to the committee in charge of property at the headquarters. Vinelott J held that the gift could not take effect as a gift to the current members of the new constituency party subject to their contractual rights and duties *inter se* because the members were not free, under the rules of their association, to dispose of the property in any way they thought fit. On the contrary, the rules made it plain that the decisions of the members of the local party were subject to the control of the national Labour Party. The gift must therefore fail for infringement of the rule against inalienability of capital.

If the local branch, according to its own rules, could have seceded from the national organization and dissolved itself, the gift to the local branch would not have failed for inalienability of capital (see *News Group Newspapers Ltd v SOGAT 1982* [1986] ICR 716, Court of Appeal, which concerned a local branch of a trade union). And even where there is no rule providing for dissolution, the court might accept that the members could dissolve the association by unanimous consent (see *Universe Tankships Inc of Monrovia v ITWF* [1983] 1 AC 366 (HL)).

In a recent case concerning an association called the Showmen's Guild the judge held that the primary contractual function of the association's rules was to set out the terms of the contracts between an individual member and the remaining members collectively as 'the guild'. On that basis, the judge refused to allow an individual member to sue another individual member for breach of one of the contractual rules (*Anderton and Rowland (a firm) v Rowland* (1999) *The Times*, 5 November).

7.6.3 Gift on trust for the abstract purposes of the association or club

A gift to an unincorporated association will rarely be construed in this way. An association is by definition a collection of individuals, and there is always likely to be someone in whose favour the court can decree performance and someone who will be in a position to supervise the proper discharge of the trust. In other words, there are usually ascertainable beneficiaries.

It is sometimes said that the devise in *Leahy* (see 7.5) 'upon trust for such order of nuns of the Catholic Church or the Christian Brothers as my executors and trustees shall select' failed because it was a trust purely for the abstract purposes of religious orders. In fact there is some ambiguity in Viscount Simonds's conclusion that the testator's intention was 'to create a trust not merely for the benefit of the existing members of the selected order but for its benefit as a continuing society and for the furtherance of its work'. His Lordship was not content to dismiss the devise as a pure purpose trust, but neither did he construe it to be a trust purely for present, nor indeed present and future, beneficiaries. The ambiguity did not affect the decision in that case because the devise would have failed even as a gift on trust for human beneficiaries due to the possibility that many of those beneficiaries would not be ascertainable until some time beyond the perpetuity period. When *Leahy* was followed in *Re Denley's Trust Deed* (1969) (see 7.5), Goff J preferred the view that the trust in *Leahy* had been a trust for beneficiaries, and not a trust for abstract, impersonal purposes.

7.6.4 Gifts on trust for the present members of the association or club

If a disposition can be construed to be a trust of this sort it will clearly comply with the rule against inalienability of capital, but only where the beneficiaries will certainly be able to appropriate the capital to their use and benefit within the perpetuity period. In *Re Turkington* [1937] 4 All ER 501, the trust was held to be valid on this basis because the members of the association were both trustees and beneficiaries and able to vest the capital in themselves according to the rule in *Saunders v Vautier*. However, this construction will presumably not save a gift on trust to an association of infants (for example, an association of Cub Scouts).

7.6.5 Gifts on trust for the present and future members of the association or club

Whenever a gift is made expressly 'on trust' it must be either a trust for present members only (see 7.6.4) or a trust for the present and future members of the association. No other construction would accord with a straightforward reading of the words used by the settlor or testator. However it is not necessary that the words 'on trust' be used for the disposition to be construed as a trust. As Viscount Simonds stated in the Privy Council in *Re Leahy* [1959] AC 457, at 484:

> if a gift is made to individuals, whether under their own names or in the name of their society, and the conclusion is reached that they are not intended to take beneficially, then they take as trustees. If so, it must be ascertained who are the beneficiaries. If at the death of the testator the class of beneficiaries is fixed and ascertained or ascertainable within the limit of the rule against perpetuities, all is well. If it is not so fixed and not so ascertainable the trust must fail.

Perhaps the best reported examples of dispositions which were construed to be gifts on trust for the present and future members of the association or club are those in *Re Leahy* itself (a gift on trust for certain religious orders) and *Re Denley's Trust Deed* [1969] 1 Ch 373 (a gift on trust for the employees of a company).

The trust in *Denley* succeeded because the trust had been expressly limited to take effect within 21 years. The trust in *Leahy* had not been limited in this way and would have failed had it not been saved by a particular New South Wales statute which validated the trust.

7.6.6 Mandate to officers of the association

Re Grant's WT (see 7.6.2) concerned a failed gift to a local Labour Party association. *Conservative and Unionist Central Office v Burrell* [1982] 1 WLR 522 concerned successful gifts to the central office of the Conservative Party. The Conservative and Unionist Central Office had been assessed to corporation tax on the ground that it was a 'company' within the meaning of s 526(5) of the Income and Corporation Taxes Act 1970. Included within the definition of 'company' were unincorporated associations of two or more persons bound together for common purposes (not being business purposes) by mutual undertakings and rules governing the holding and control of property. Appealing against the tax assessment the central office contended that it was not an unincorporated association within this definition.

The Court of Appeal held that donations received by the central office were not held on behalf of an unincorporated association within the 1970 Act definition. It became necessary to consider, therefore, upon what basis donations were received by the central office. It was held *per curiam* ('by the court' for the sake of clarity) that when a contributor makes a donation to the treasurer, or other officer, of the central office, that officer receives the donation as an agent and subject to a mandate that it be used for the political purposes for which it was given. The law of agency, not of trusts, is applicable. Once the donation has been mixed with the general funds under the officer's control the mandate becomes irrevocable. In other words, it is then too late for the contributor to reclaim the donation. However, the contributor has a remedy against the officials to restrain or make good a misapplication of the mixed fund except where the contributor's donation can be shown, on normal accounting principles, to have been legitimately expended before the misapplication of the mixed fund.

Vinelott J stated that 'if someone invites subscriptions on the representation that he will use the fund subscribed for a particular purpose, he undertakes to use the fund for that purpose and for no other and to keep the subscribed fund and any accretions to it . . . separate from his own property'. His Lordship did acknowledge, however, that this mandate/agency construction could not be applied to donations made by will: 'in the case of a testamentary gift there is no room for the implication of any contract between the testator and the persons who are to receive the bequest'.

7.6.7 Summative exercise

I give and devise the rest residue and remainder of my estate real and personal whatsoever and wheresoever unto my trustees upon trust to sell call in and convert into money the same with power to postpone such sale calling in and conversion and to hold the net proceeds of sale thereof and my ready money after payment thereout of my just debts and my funeral and testamentary expenses upon trust:—(a) as to one half thereof for the Hull Judeans (Maccabi) Association in memory of my late wife to be used solely in the work of constructing the new buildings for the association and or improvements to the said buildings . . .

? QUESTION 7.6

This disposition arose for consideration in the case of *Re Lipinksi* [1976] 1 Ch 235. Do you think it creates a valid trust or fails as a trust for private purposes? In coming to your conclusion it is important to be aware that the principal aim of the Hull Judeans (Maccabi) Association was 'to promote the interest, and the active participation of Anglo-Jewish youth of both sexes, in amateur sports, in all forms of cultural, and in non-political, communal activities'.

Part (a) of the trust is clearly not charitable, because it produces insufficient benefit to the general public (see **Chapter 8**). The question, therefore, was whether it was void as a pure purpose trust (it being 'solely' for the erection and maintenance of buildings in memory of the testator's wife), or whether it was a valid trust in favour of the Hull Judeans (Maccabi) Association.

Oliver J gave three alternative reasons for holding the disposition to be valid:

- first, applying *Re Denley's Trust Deed* (7.5), because there was a trust indirectly for human beneficiaries;

- secondly, applying *Re Recher's WT* (7.6.2), because the gift should be construed as an outright gift to the members of the association, subject to the rules of the association;
- thirdly, applying *Re Turkington* [1937] 4 All ER 501, because the members of the association were between them absolutely entitled to the fund, and thus able to vest the capital in themselves according to the rule in *Saunders v Vautier* (7.6.4).

EXERCISE 7.1

Not one of the reasons given for the decision in *Re Lipinski* is particularly convincing. If you were appealing against the judgment of Oliver J, what arguments would you raise against each of them? On a separate sheet of paper, attempt to draft your grounds of appeal.

- Against the judge's suggestion that *Re Denley's* should apply, it should be relatively easy to argue that the facts of *Re Lipinski* are distinguishable from those in *Re Denley's*. In *Re Denley's* the reference to building a sports ground had been construed as a mere motive for setting up the trust (applying *Re Bowes*, see 7.5). In other words, the purpose was ancillary to the ultimate human benefit. In *Re Lipinski* the trust was set up in memory of the testator's wife and was expressed to be 'solely' for the purpose of building. It is hard to dismiss such an imperative statement of purpose as an ancillary motive, the expressed purpose appears to be by its terms fundamental to the trust. Oliver J reasoned that the direction to build was not fundamental to the testator's intentions, but had been his attempt to second-guess the current needs, whatever they might be, of the ultimate human beneficiaries. A more compelling objection to the application of *Re Denley's* is that it should only apply where the trust is expressly limited to take effect during the perpetuity period. In the absence of any such provision, a trust will be void for potentially rendering the capital inalienable in perpetuity. The trust in *Re Lipinsksi* appears to fall foul of the rule against inalienability.
- The assumption underlying the judge's application of *Re Recher* to *Re Lipinski* was that an absolute gift had been made to the present members of the association. The difficulty with applying *Re Recher's* to *Re Lipinski* is that the benefiting class of persons in *Re Lipinski* are Jewish 'youth', the majority of whom would be precluded by their infancy from taking as an absolute gift that part of the residuary estate which comprised land.
- Finally, the infancy of the beneficiaries means that the rule in *Saunders v Vautier*, and therefore the reasoning in *Re Turkington*, should not have been applied in *Re Lipinksi*.

7.7 Distribution of surplus donations

When monies are given for a purpose or to an association, what happens if there are surplus funds after the purpose is fulfilled or the association dissolved? The answer depends in large part upon the way in which the original gift is construed. If the gift is construed to be a gift 'on trust' for a particular purpose, any surplus of the gift will generally be held on resulting trust for the original donor. If it was originally construed to be an absolute gift, any surplus of the gift will generally belong beneficially to the members in existence at the time of dissolution (in accordance where relevant, with the association's rules).

7.7.1 *Bona vacantia*

Where a resulting trust or contractual solution is clearly inappropriate the donation may pass to the Crown as *bona vacantia*.

EXERCISE 7.2

Look up *Cunnack v Edwards* (1896) 2 Ch 679. Why did the property in that case pass to the Crown when the society came to an end?

The society had been established to raise a fund by members' subscriptions to provide annuities for the widows of deceased members. The last member died in 1879 and the last widow died in 1892, the society having then a surplus or unexpended fund of £1,250. It was held that the widows, and not the members, were the beneficiaries of the society's funds, accordingly there would be no resulting trust of the surplus in favour of the estates of the members of the society. The surplus went instead to the Crown as *bona vacantia*. As Smith LJ stated 'as the member paid his money to the society, so he divested himself of all interest in this money for ever, with this one reservation, that if the member left a widow she was to be provided for during her widowhood'.

The *bona vacantia* solution will obviously be appropriate to a case like *Cunnack v Edwards*, where the association was utterly moribund and bereft of potential beneficiaries, but the courts will generally seek to avoid this solution. However, it will be the appropriate solution where the rules of the association do not permit a distribution according to the members' contract *inter se*, and where, in the case of a donation made on trust, a resulting trust solution is inappropriate because the donor clearly intended to part with the donation outright and for all time. This latter point, established in *Re West Sussex Constabulary's Widows, Children and Benevolent Fund Trusts* [1971] 1 Ch 1 (see 7.7.3) was confirmed *obiter* by Lord Browne-Wilkinson in the House of Lords in the *Westdeutsche* case (see 16.1 and 16.2).

7.7.2 Resulting trust

The case of *Re Gillingham Bus Disaster Fund* [1958] Ch 300 involved the distribution of surplus donations to a disaster fund. In that case Harman J stated the general principle (confirmed on appeal) that:

> where money is held on trust and the trusts declared do not exhaust the fund it will revert to the donor or settlor under what is called a resulting trust. The reasoning behind this is that the settlor or

> donor did not part with his money absolutely out and out, but only sub modo to the intent that his wishes, as declared by the declaration of trust, should be carried into effect. When, therefore, this has been done, any surplus still belongs to him.

Cunnack v Edwards was distinguished as being a case were the funds had been held subject to a contractual arrangement. Harman J was not impressed with the Crown's argument that the resulting trust solution should be avoided due to the impracticalities of identifying the anonymous donors. His Lordship was convinced that the resulting trust solution was appropriate to the named donors and saw no reason to suppose that the anonymous donor had any larger intention than the named donor as to the ultimate destination of their donation. In the event that the anonymous donors might not be found, the surplus should be held on the court's account, but should not pass as ownerless assets (*bona vacantia*) to the Crown. The preferred approach today (see 7.7.1) is to regard anonymous donations as out and out donations. The intention to make an outright disposition is said to rebut the presumption of a resulting trust (16.2.1.4).

7.7.3 Contract

In *Re West Sussex Constabulary's Widows, Children and Benevolent Fund Trusts* [1971] 1 Ch 1 a fund existed to provide for widows and orphans of deceased members of the West Sussex Constabulary, an unincorporated non-charitable non-profit association. When the constabulary amalgamated with other forces in 1968 the question arose as to how the funds should be distributed. Sources of the fund were: (1) members' subscriptions; (2) receipts from entertainments, raffles and sweepstakes; (3) collecting boxes; and (4) donations and legacies.

Goff J held that surplus of sources 1, 2 and 3 would pass to the Crown as *bona vacantia*, but that surplus of source 4 would be held on resulting trusts for the donors. He held, further, that equity would 'cut the Gordian knot' of accounting difficulties by dividing the surplus in proportion to the sources from which it had arisen. According to his Lordship, surplus of source 1 could not be the subject of a resulting trust because the members had received consideration for the payment of their subscriptions in the form of the benefits of membership. In other words, the members had already received everything they had bargained for. Surplus of source 2 could not be the subject of a resulting trust because, first, such payments had been made for consideration; and, secondly, they were not direct donations to the fund, but merely donations of net profits after payment out of prizes etc. Finally, surplus of source 3 would not be deemed subject to a resulting trust because donors to collecting boxes are presumed to have intended to part with their monies out and out.

***Re West Sussex Constabulary's Widows, Children and Benevolent (1930) Fund* [1971] 1 Ch 1**

Goff J (on the outside contributions):

> Then counsel divided the outside moneys into three categories, first, the proceeds of entertainments, raffles and sweepstakes; secondly, the proceeds of collecting-boxes; and thirdly, donations, including legacies if any, and he took particular objections to each.
>
> I agree that there cannot be any resulting trust with respect to the first category. I am not certain whether Harman J in *Re Gillingham Bus Disaster Fund* [1958] Ch 300 meant to decide otherwise.

> In stating the facts at p. 304 he referred to 'street collections and so forth'. In the further argument at p. 309 there is mention of whist drives and concerts but the judge himself did not speak of anything other than gifts. If, however, he did, I must respectfully decline to follow his judgment in that regard, for whatever may be the true position with regard to collecting-boxes, it appears to me to be impossible to apply the doctrine of resulting trust to the proceeds of entertainments and sweepstakes and such-like money-raising operations for two reasons: first, the relationship is one of contract and not of trust; the purchaser of a ticket may have the motive of aiding the cause or he may not; he may purchase a ticket merely because he wishes to attend the particular entertainment or to try for the prize, but whichever it be, he pays his money as the price of what is offered and what he receives; secondly, there is in such cases no direct contribution to the fund at all; it is only the profit, if any, which is ultimately received and there may even be none.

The *Re West Sussex* case was distinguished (rather artificially) in *Re Bucks Constabulary Widows' and Orphans' Fund Friendly Society (No 2)* [1979] 1 WLR 936, on the basis that the former case involved a simple unincorporated association, whereas the latter involved a friendly society. The facts were that the society had been established to make provision for widows and orphans of deceased members of the Bucks Constabulary. In 1968 the Bucks Constabulary was amalgamated with other constabularies to form the Thames Valley Constabulary. The rules of the society did not make provision for the distribution of surplus assets on dissolution. The trustees therefore applied to court to determine: (1) whether the surplus assets should be distributed among the persons who were members of the society at the date of its dissolution or whether they should pass to the Crown as *bona vacantia*; and (2) if the assets were to be distributed among the members whether they should be distributed in equal shares or *pro rata* the members' payment of subcriptions. Members' voluntary subscriptions had made up the majority of the fund.

Walton J held that, as there had been members in existence at the time of the dissolution, the surplus would be held for them according to a term that could be implied into the contract between the members. This would operate to the total exclusion of any claim on behalf of the Crown. As to the second issue, his Lordship held that where, as here, the contract between the members provided no other method of distribution, such funds were prima facie to be distributed amongst the surviving members in equal shares.

Walton J preferred the analysis of Brightman J in *Re Recher's WT* (see 7.6.2) to that of Goff J in *Re West Sussex*. Whereas Goff J had sought to draw a distinction between an association established for the benefit of its members and an association established for third parties or purposes, Walton J held that: 'whether the purpose for which the members of the association associate are a social club, a sporting club, to establish a widows' and orphans' fund, to obtain a separate Parliament for Cornwall, or to further the advance of alchemy. It matters not'.

7.8 When is an unincorporated association wound up?

In *Re GKN Bolts and Nuts Sports and Social Club* [1982] 1 WLR 774, Sir Robert Megarry V-C held that clubs do not automatically dissolve through mere inactivity unless the period of inactivity is such that the only reasonable inference was that the club had ceased to exist. As his Lordship put it: 'short inactivity coupled with strong circumstances, or long inactivity coupled with weaker circumstances may equally suffice. The question is whether, put together, the facts carry sufficient conviction that the society is at an end and not merely dormant.' The Vice-Chancellor (at p 860) approved Brightman J in *Re William Denby & Sons Ltd Sick and Benevolent Fund* [1971] 2 All ER 1196, who classified four categories of case in which an unregistered friendly society or benevolent fund should be regarded as having been dissolved or terminated so that its assets become distributable:

> The first three categories of dissolution or termination were (1) in accordance with the rules, (2) by agreement of all persons interested, and (3) by order of the court in the exercise of its inherent jurisdiction. The fourth category was when the substratum on which the society or fund was founded had gone, so that the society or fund no longer had any effective purpose, and the assets became distributable without any order of the court.

In *Re GKN Bolts and Nuts Sports and Social Club* itself, it was held that the club had ceased to exist, but only by virtue of the positive resolution of the members to sell the club's sports ground.

CHAPTER SUMMARY

- We have seen that trusts purely for private purposes are generally void for the following reasons:
  - being in nature 'private', a trust of this sort would not be subject to the control of the courts, nor of any department of State;
  - following on from the preceding point, in order to bring the trust within the control of the court, there must always be someone in whose favour the court can decree performance, that is, someone who will enforce the trust by, *inter alia*, bringing breaches of trust to the attention of the court. This is the so-called 'beneficiary principle'.
  - trusts for private purposes are often required to be construed as perpetual endowments. Such endowments offend the rule against inalienability of capital (see 6.5);
  - trusts for private purposes are liable to fail the requirement of certainty of object, since a purpose is never as definite as a person;
  - capriciousness.
- An exceptional class of trusts purely for private purposes, which are valid, are trusts of imperfect obligation (so-called because the trustees are not obliged to discharge them—Q: in that case are they properly described as *trusts* at all?) This class of 'trusts' is anomalous, and will not be extended (*Re Endacott* [1960] Ch 232). It includes such purposes as looking after particular individual animals, the maintenance of tombs and monuments and the saying of masses in private.
- There are ways to avoid the rule against trusts purely for private purposes.
  - One possibility is to make a gift to a charity determinable in the event of failure (not necessarily failure by the charity itself) to carry out your desired purposes (see *Re Tyler* at 6.6).
  - Another possibility is to make a gift to identifiable beneficiaries, but to express a purpose by way of motive for making the gift or by way of giving advice to the trustees.

- Another possibility is to make a gift to a company (incorporated entity).
- Another possibility is to make a gift to an unincorporated non-profit association (club/society).

- Gifts to unincorporated non-profit associations can be construed in a number of different ways.
  - Trust
    - as a pure purpose trust, that is, a trust for impersonal purposes; or
    - on trust for the benefit of the present members of the association; or
    - on trust for the benefit of the present and future members of the association.
  - Mandate
    - as a mandate to the officers of the association to use the donation as instructed by the donor.
  - Power
    - as the grant of a power to apply the donation for the purposes of the association.

SUMMATIVE ASSESSMENT EXERCISE

online resource centre

The Whitestone Sportsclub is a largely autonomous body run by a committee elected by its members (who are employees of Whitestone Ltd). It manages a sports centre on land leased to trustees of the Club for a period of 21 years and is financed by subscriptions from members. The decisions of the committee are subject to veto by the board of directors of the company but the board has only rejected one decision, a proposal last year to charge a higher subscription to senior staff. The constitution of the Club provides that on its dissolution its assets shall belong to Whitestone Ltd. By his will, Mr White (a former director of Whitestone Ltd) left £100,000 to the Club to provide a cricket ground and modest pavilion for employees. The committee have voted to use the money, not for a cricket ground, but for a football pitch.

Mr White's widow, his residuary legatee, claims the legacy.

Advise her.

FURTHER READING

Baxendale-Walker, P, *Purpose Trusts for Commercial and Private Use* (London: Butterworths, 1999).

Matthews, P, 'Gifts to Unincorporated Associations' [1995] Conv 302.

Stoljar, S J, *Groups and Entities—An Inquiry into Corporate Theory* (Sydney: Australian University Press, 1973).

Warburton, J, *Unincorporated Associations: Law and Practice* (London: Sweet & Maxwell, 1992).

8 Charitable trusts

OBJECTIVES

By the end of this chapter you should be able to:

1 Distinguish between legal and 'everyday' notions of charity

2 Identify a charitable purpose

3 Describe the advantages and disadvantages of charitable status

4 Understand what happens when a charitable purpose fails

8.1 Introduction

The law of charitable trusts is not the most complicated part of your course of studies, but what it lacks in depth it more than makes up for in breadth. The case law on the subject is encyclopaedic in volume and consequently this chapter remains overlong despite attempts at brevity. Indeed, whole texts have been devoted to this subject alone, the most notable being *Tudor on Charities*. It is an area of law that is never stagnant, and as 'superfunds' such as the 'Diana, Princess of Wales, Memorial Fund' and the 'National Lottery' continue to evidence, it is an area of law of great social significance.

8.2 Charities law in context

In the last chapter we considered trusts for private purposes. In this chapter we will be considering charitable trusts, that is, trusts for public purposes.

8.2.1 The privileges of charitable status

In 1955 the *Radcliffe Commission on Taxation* (Cmd 9474) recommended that when considering the validity of a charitable trust, the fiscal privileges attaching to such trusts should be considered separately from the general trust law privileges they enjoy. Approving this, Lord Cross has stated (in *Dingle v Turner* [1972] AC 601) that:

> [i]t is, of course, unfortunate that the recognition of any trust as a valid charitable trust should automatically attract fiscal privileges, for the question whether a trust to further some purpose is so little likely to benefit the public that it ought to be declared invalid and the question whether it is likely to confer such great benefits on the public that it should enjoy fiscal immunity are really two quite different questions. The logical solution would be to separate them and to say—as the Radcliffe Commission proposed—that only some charities should enjoy fiscal privileges.

For the purposes of the remainder of this section we will adopt the distinction between trust law and fiscal privileges.

8.2.1.1 Trust law privileges

In the last chapter we saw that trusts purely for *private* purposes are generally void because:

- a trust of this sort would not be subject to the control of the courts, nor of any department of State;
- to bring the trust within the control of the court, there must always be someone in whose favour the court can decree performance;
- trusts for private purposes must often be construed as perpetual endowments. Such endowments offend the rule against inalienability of capital (see 6.5);
- trusts for private purposes will often fail the requirement of certainty of object because the purposes expressed are vague and indefinite.

> **? QUESTION 8.1**
>
> Do you think that any of these objections apply to charitable trusts?

Charitable trusts are trusts for *public* purposes. They are not subject to the objections that are raised against *private* purpose trusts. Thus:

- although they are not public institutions, charities are subject to the constitutional protection of the Crown as *parens patriae* (acting through the Attorney-General), to the supervision of the Charity Commissioners, and to judicial control;
- it follows that charities are not subject to the beneficiary principle, the Attorney-General represents the public as the person in whose favour the court can decree performance of a charitable trust;
- charitable trusts are not subject to the rule against inalienability of capital (6.5). This is because the public policy considerations which prohibit perpetual gifts and trusts should be no bar to the public benefits which charities bring about;
- charitable trusts will not fail for uncertainty of object. Provided that the trust was intended to be applied exclusively for charitable purposes it will not fail if those purposes are, or

become, uncertain (see *cy-près* at 8.6). It may be valid even if it is impossible to discharge the trust according to its strict terms. In *Chichester Diocesan Fund and Board of Finance v Simpson* [1944] AC 341 at 348, Viscount Simon LC held that charities are an exception to the fundamental principle that the testator must by the terms of his will determine the specific destination of the property with which the will proposes to deal.

Additional privileges of charitable status include:

- the more generous approach taken by the courts to the construction of charitable trusts. In *Weir v Crum-Brown* [1908] AC 162 at 167 Lord Loreburn stated that 'there is no better rule than that a benignant construction will be placed upon charitable bequests' and in *IRC v McMullen* (8.3.4.3) Lord Hailsham of St Marylebone approved that dictum when he held that '[i]n construing trust deeds the intention of which is to set up a charitable trust, and in others too, where it can be claimed that there is ambiguity, a benignant construction should be given if possible'.
- charities must be registered, registration bringing with it a conclusive presumption of charitable status for the period of registration (Charities Act 1960, s 5).

8.2.1.2 Tax law privileges

Charitable trusts, and those who donate to them, enjoy a wide range of fiscal exemptions and privileges. They include:

- income tax: charity exempt (Income and Corporation Taxes Act 1988, s 505);
- corporation tax: charity exempt (Income and Corporation Taxes Act 1988, s 505(1)(e));
- capital gains tax: charity and donor exempt (Taxation of Chargeable Gains Act 1992, ss 256, 257);
- inheritance tax: donor exempt (Inheritance Tax Act 1984, ss 23, 76);
- stamp duty: transfers post 22 March 1982 exempt (Finance Act 1982, s 129);
- non-domestic local rates: relief of 80 per cent or more (Local Government Finance Act 1988, ss 43, 47);
- one-off donations: donor can reclaim income tax relief under the 'gift aid' scheme (Finance Act 1990, s 25(1) and (2) as amended by Finance Act 2000, s 39, subject to the Gift Aid Declaration Regulations (SI No 2074/2000)).
- covenanted donations: charities can reclaim income tax on annual covenants for more than three years (ICTA 1988, ss 660(3), 683(3)).

The extent of these privileges has prompted some to call for a costs-benefit calculus as a prerequisite to the recognition of charitable status (see, for example, Lord Cross in *Dingle v Turner* [1972] AC 601). But if such a process is to occur, might it be 'constitutionally inappropriate for the judges and Charity Commissioners to carry it out'? This is the opinion of at least one commentator (see Simon Gardner, *An Introduction to the Law of Trusts*, Clarendon Press, 1990, p 105). If it were to occur, it would undoubtedly involve a calculation of great complexity. It cannot be assumed, for instance, that gains made by the charities due to fiscal privilege are equal in value to the losses made by the Inland Revenue as a result of that privilege. To use the economists' term, it is not a 'zero-sum game'. For the fiscal privilege of charitable status may itself influence the size and frequency of donations made to the charity (at present, donors are entitled to a degree of tax relief on one-off donations of over £250 and donations covenanted to be made regularly for at least four years). The calculation is a complex one even before an attempt has been made to quantify the benefit in such abstract charitable goods as research into a cure for cancer, education in the arts and the advancement of religion.

8.2.2 The management of charities

8.2.2.1 By a corporation

Part VII of the Charities Act 1993 introduces a simplified scheme for the incorporation of charities. The increasing use of corporate status by charities should not be underestimated, but there is not the scope to consider that here. For present purposes, our attention will be confined to charitable trusts.

8.2.2.2 By trustees

The basic duties of charity trustees are the same as those of other trustees. There are, however, some additional duties peculiar to charity trustees. These include registration of the charity (most charities must be registered—see s 3 of the 1993 Act); seeking a *cy-près* scheme where the trust can no longer be discharged; avoiding needless accumulation of funds (1992 Charity Commissioners Report, p 25); keeping accounts in the form appropriate to the size of the charity (Charities Act 1993, ss 41–43); preparing an annual report (s 45). Charity trustees also have special duties in relation to the investment of the trust fund (see **Chapter 14**). If a problem should arise in the course of the administration of a charity, the trustees may, by written request, seek the advice of the Charity Commissioners (s 29).

Certain persons are disqualified from acting as trustees of charitable trusts (s 72). For example, persons who have been convicted of dishonesty offences and persons subject to an undischarged bankruptcy. The maximum punishment for acting whilst disqualified is two years' imprisonment and a fine (s 73).

8.2.2.3 By the court

As a result of the Charities Act 1993 the role of the courts in deciding whether or not a body is charitable has been largely transferred to the Charity Commissioners. The court remains the forum of ultimate appeal. The court's jurisdiction to establish a scheme for the administration of a charity (matters such as the appointment of trustees, extending powers of investment, etc) is concurrent with that of the Charity Commissioners (as to which, see s 17 of the 1993 Act).

8.2.2.4 By the Charity Commissioners

The Charity Commissioners supervise the compulsory registration and administration of most charitable trusts and have the power to institute *ad hoc* inquiries with regard to any charity (Charities Act 1993, s 8). They are civil servants (one Chief Commissioner and two others) appointed by the Home Secretary, to whom they submit an annual report. They in turn appoint the Official Custodian for Charities (a corporation sole) in whom charity trustees may vest trust property, thereby avoiding the need to transfer land and securities on the appointment of new trustees.

In *Neville Estates Ltd v Madden* [1962] Ch 832, the trustees of a synagogue attempted to resist the claim of Neville Estates to specific performance of a contract for the sale of land owned by a synagogue. The trustees of the synagogue claimed, with success, that the synagogue existed for charitable purposes and that the consent of the Charity Commissioners would be required before sale could proceed. The law is now contained in s 36 of the 1993 Act. The main requirement of s 36 is that charity trustees should obtain and act upon a report from a qualified surveyor before dealing with charity land by way of disposition, lease or security.

8.3 The legal definition of charity

Lord Macnaghten said this of the word 'charity':

> Of all the words in the English language bearing a popular as well as a legal signification I am not sure that there is one which more unmistakably has a technical meaning in the strictest sense of the term, that is a meaning clear and distinct, peculiar to the law as understood and administered in this country, and not depending upon or coterminous with the popular or vulgar use of the word.
>
> (*Commissioners for Special Purpose of the Income Tax v Pemsel* [1891] AC 531.)

And Lord Porter opined that:

> 'charity' and 'charitable' are technical words in English law and must be so construed unless it can be seen from the wording of the will as a whole that they are used in some other than their technical sense.
>
> (*Chichester Diocesan Fund and Board of Finance v Simpson* [1944] AC 341, at 363.)

EXERCISE 8.1

On a separate sheet of paper, attempt to draw up your own definition of charity, and in doing so try to define charity as you would have understood the word before you commenced your legal studies. As part of the process, consider which of the following pursuits you would regard as being charitable, place a tick next to your choices, and review them at the end of the chapter:

- campaigning to end the Gulf War
- seeking a ban on vivisection
- the provision of sporting facilities to the Royal Navy
- faith healing
- giving cash to a destitute nephew
- the provision of a sanctuary for wild animals
- the exhibition of watercolours by a little known artist.

8.3.1 Statutory definitions

Existing statutory definitions of charity are utterly circular and provide no real definition at all. Thus, s 96(1) of the Charities Act 1993 provides that: 'In this Act, except in so far as the context otherwise requires "charity" means any institution, corporate or not, which is established for *charitable purposes* and is subject to the control of the High Court in the exercise of the court's jurisdiction with respect to charities' (emphasis added). Section 97(1) adds little when it informs us that ' "charitable purposes" means purposes which are exclusively charitable *according to the law of England and Wales*' (emphasis added). But what does the law of England and Wales say on the matter? The only other statutory clue is s 38(4) of the Charities Act 1960, which provides that: 'Any reference in any enactment or document to a charity within the meaning, purview and interpretation of the Charitable Uses Act 1601 or of the preamble to it, shall be construed as a reference to a charity within the meaning which the word bears as a legal term according to the law of England and Wales'.

The Act of 1601, the so-called 'Statute of Elizabeth I', remains the only statutory guidance available to the courts and the Charity Commissioners when determining the charitable status of a trust. The irony is that the statute itself was not at all concerned with the definition of charity. Nevertheless, the preamble to the statute contained a list of contemporary charitable uses 'so varied and comprehensive that it became the practice of the court [of Chancery] to refer to it as a sort of index or chart' (Lord Macnaghten, *Income Tax Commissioners v Pemsel* [1891] AC 531, 581).

Statute of Charitable Uses (1601) 43 Eliz I, c 4

Preamble

Whereas Lands, Tenements, Rents, Annuities, Profits, Hereditaments, Goods, Chattels, Money and Stocks of Money, have been heretofore given, limited, appointed and assigned, as well as by the Queen's most excellent Majesty, and her most noble Progenitors, as by sundry other well disposed persons; some for Relief of aged, impotent and poor People, some for the Maintenance of sick and maimed Soldiers and Mariners, Schools of Learning, Free Schools, and Scholars in Universities, some for the Repair of Bridges, Ports, Havens, Causeways, Churches, Sea-Banks and Highways, some for the Education and Preferment of Orphans, some for or towards Relief, Stock or Maintenance for Houses of Correction, some for the Marriages of Poor Maids, some for Supportation, Aid and Help of young Tradesmen, Handicraftsmen and Persons decayed, and others for the Relief or Redemption of Prisoners or Captives, and for Aid or Ease of any poor Inhabitants concerning Payments of Fifteens [a tax on moveable property], setting out of Soldiers and other Taxes; which Lands, Tenements, Rents, Annuities, Profits, Hereditaments, Goods, Chattels, Money and Stocks of Money, nevertheless have not been employed according to charitable Intent of the givers and Founders thereof, by reason of Frauds, Breaches of Trust, and Negligence in those that should pay, deliver and employ the same: For Redress and Remedy whereof, Be it enacted. . . .

Morice v Bishop of Durham **(1804) 9 Ves 399, Court of Appeal**

A bequest was made to the Bishop upon trust for 'such objects of benevolence and liberality as the Bishop of Durham in his own discretion shall most approve'.
Sir William Grant MR:

> Is this a trust for charity? Do purposes of liberality and benevolence mean the same as objects of charity? That word in its widest sense denotes all the good affections men ought to have towards each other; in its most restricted and common sense relief of the poor. In neither of these senses is it employed in this court. Here its signification is derived chiefly from the statute 43 Eliz., c. 4 [relating to charitable gifts]. Those purposes are considered charitable which that statute enumerates or which by analogies are deemed within its spirit and intendment, and to some such purpose every bequest to charity generally shall be applied. But, it is clear, liberality and benevolence can find numberless objects not included in that statute in the largest construction of it. The use of the word 'charitable' seems to have been purposely avoided in this will in order to leave the bishop the most unrestrained discretion. Supporting the uncertainty of the trust no objection to its validity, could it be contended to be an abuse of the trust to employ this fund upon objects which all mankind would allow to be objects of liberality and benevolence though not to be said, in the language of this court, to be objects also of charity? But what rule of construction could it be said that all objects of liberality and benevolence are excluded which do not fall within the statute of Elizabeth? The question is not whether he may not apply it upon purposes strictly charitable, but whether he is bound so to apply it? I am not aware of any case in which the bequest has been held charitable where the testator has not either used that word to denote his general purpose or specified some particular purpose, which this court has determined to be charitable in its nature.

All this talk of the 'spirit of the preamble' will understandably lead you to think that the legal definition of charity floats cloud-like above the judge's head. In fact, to decide whether or not a particular enterprise is charitable is an invidious task, and the judges have generally preferred to avoid it by means of rules and precedent (see Gardner, *An Introduction to the Law of Trusts*, Clarendon Press, 1990 at pp 105–6). This brings us to the next section.

8.3.2 The four heads of charity

In *Commissioners for Special Purpose of the Income Tax v Pemsel* [1891] AC 531 Lord Macnaghten held that 'charity' in its legal sense comes under four principal heads:

- trusts for the relief of poverty
- trusts for the advancement of education
- trusts for the advancement of religion and
- trusts for other purposes beneficial to the community, not falling under any of the preceding heads.

On the question whether a trust 'for the general purposes of maintaining, supporting and advancing the missionary establishments among heathen nations of the protestant Episcopal Church, commonly known as the Moravian church' was or was not for 'charitable purposes', the House of Lords held that it was not charitable as that purpose did not fall within any of the four heads. (For the reason why this trust was not for the advancement of religion, see 8.3.5.3.)

? QUESTION 8.2

In *Scottish Burial Reform and Cremation Society Ltd v Glasgow Corporation* [1968] AC 138 the appellant was a non-profit making company incorporated to promote cremation, which service it had carried out in Glasgow for many years. It provided opportunities for religious observance but had not been incorporated on any religious basis. Do you think that the business of the company fell within any of Lord Macnaghten's four heads of charity?

The House of Lords held that the objects of the company were for the benefit of the community and fell within the fourth of Lord Macnaghten's heads of charity. However, Lord Wilberforce asserted that the 'four heads' were a classification of convenience and not necessarily a comprehensive set of charitable classes, that Lord Macnaghten's words should not be given the force of statute and that the law of charity is a continually evolving subject. His Lordship, however, with these qualifications, approved of Lord Macnaghten's categorization. He accepted that decisions by courts as to the scope of the preamble of 1601 had superseded attention to the wording of the preamble itself.

In the same case (at p. 153), Lord Upjohn urged caution in the recognition of new charities:

> the authorities show that the 'spirit and intendement' of the preamble to the Statute of Elizabeth have been stretched almost to breaking point. In the nineteenth and early twentieth centuries this was often due to a desire on the part of the courts to save the intentions of the settlor or testator from failure from some technical rule of law. Now that it is used so frequently to avoid the common man's liability to rates or taxes, this generous trend of the law may one day require reconsideration.

In a similarly cautious vein, Lord Simonds in *Gilmour v Coats* [1949] AC 426 (as followed by Cross J in *Neville Estates Ltd v Madden* [1962] Ch 832 at 853) warned (at 449) that in enlarging the compass of charity 'it is dangerous to reason by analogy from one head of charity to another'.

EXERCISE 8.2

On a separate sheet of paper quickly try to define the following concepts in your own words:
• Poverty • Education • Art • Sport • Religion • Impotent • Political

The presence of some of the words in the list might surprise you. Trying to define them might perplex you. Nevertheless, it has been the task of the courts down the years to attach useful meaning to some of these concepts and terms. As you work through this chapter reflect upon how the judicial approach differs from yours.

8.3.3 The first head: relief of poverty

8.3.3.1 The meaning of poverty

Does 'the relief of poverty' equate to 'the meeting of a material need'?

In *Re Gwyon* [1930] 1 Ch 255, the testator directed that the residue of his estate should be applied by his executor to establish the 'Gwyon's Boys Clothing Foundation'; a foundation to provide 'knickers' (a sort of trouser) for boys between the ages of 10 and 15 in a certain district. The boys could replace their old pair for a new pair, provided that the words 'Gwyon's Present' were still legible on the waistband of the old pair. The claim that the gift was a valid charitable trust for the relief of poverty failed. None of the conditions of the gift necessarily imported poverty. Eve J noted that the trustees would have no power to refuse a boy his gift on the ground merely that the boy was materially affluent. (In fact a closer examination of the conditions attaching to the gift reveals that the gift was anything but charitable. According to its terms, no boy was eligible who was already receiving support from a charity or the local parish and no 'black boy' was eligible!)

Does the 'relief of poverty' equate to 'the relief of the destitute'?

The *Oxford English Dictionary* defines 'destitute' in this sense as 'without the very necessaries of life or means of bare subsistence, in absolute want'. The attitude of the courts has always been that the destitute are always poor, but that the poor are not always destitute. In *Re Gardom* [1914] 1 Ch 662 at 668, Eve J held that 'there are degrees of poverty less acute than abject poverty or destitution, but poverty nevertheless'. In *Re Gardom* a trust for 'ladies of limited means' was held to be charitable, as was a trust for 'distressed gentlefolk' in *Re Young* [1951] Ch 344. The relative nature of 'poverty' was made explicit by the Court of Appeal in *Re Coulthurst* [1951] Ch 622.

The testator, Coulthurst, directed that the income from his estate should be applied by his trustees 'to or for the benefit of such . . . of the . . . widows and orphaned children of deceased officers and deceased ex-officers' of a bank 'as the bank shall in its absolute discretion consider by reason of his, her or their financial circumstances to be most deserving of such assistance . . .'. This was held to be a valid charitable trust intended to benefit the poor, in accordance with the meaning of the preamble to the Act of 1601. The fact that the beneficiaries were chosen by reference to their employment with a particular bank did not defeat the charitable nature of a gift for the relief of poverty.

Evershed MR held that 'poverty does not mean destitution; it is a word of wide and somewhat indefinite import; it may not unfairly be paraphrased for present purposes as meaning persons who have to 'go short in the ordinary acceptation of that term, due regard being had to their status in life, and so forth'.

Are the 'working classes' poor?

It has long been accepted by the courts that 'the poor need not necessarily be poor of the class known as the working class, and many of the working class . . . are not poor' (*per* Lord Wrenbury in *Re Sutton* [1901] 2 Ch 640, 646). Nevertheless, the question still came up for consideration in *Re Sanders' Will Trusts* [1954] Ch 265. There the testator had directed his trustees, by a codicil to his will, to 'apply one equal third part of my residuary trust fund in . . . providing dwellings for the working classes and their families resident in the area of Pembroke Dock, Pembrokeshire, Wales, or within a radius of five miles therefrom (with preference to actual dockworkers and their families employed at the said docks)'. Harman J held that the words 'working class' did not indicate a gift to the poor: 'These are not old persons; they are not widows, they are merely men working in the docks and their families, and, therefore, I cannot infer any element of poverty here'.

? QUESTION 8.3

What if a testator provided that his residuary estate should be held upon trust to pay the capital and income to a local authority in a needy part of Cyprus 'on condition that the same shall be used for the purposes only of the construction of or as a contribution towards the cost of the construction of a working men's hostel'.

This disposition arose for consideration in *Re Niyazi's Will Trusts* [1978] 1 WLR 910. Megarry V-C held that this was a valid charitable trust for the relief of poverty. The judge described the case as 'desperately near the borderline', but concluded that only poor persons would be likely to live in a hostel. The word 'hostel', he said, was very different from the word 'dwelling' as used in *Re Sanders' WT* (see above), the former suggested a poor inhabitant, the latter was appropriate to any house. The judge also took into account (1) the depressed nature of the area in which the hostel had been directed to be built, and (2) the fact that the relatively modest size of the fund made it unlikely that a 'grandiose building' would be erected.

8.3.3.2 The public benefit requirement under the first head

The usual rule is that a charitable trust must confer a public benefit. In other words, the trust must (1) confer a tangible benefit, and (2) confer it on the public at large or upon a sufficient section of the public. However, the usual rule does not apply to charitable trusts for the relief of poverty. Whilst it has never been doubted that such trusts confer a tangible benefit, it has never been a requirement that such trusts should confer that benefit upon the general public. Trusts for the relief of poverty will be charitable even if they benefit a class of persons who are identified by reference to a particular person or employer (such as the bank in *Re Coulthurst*, above). Having said that, a trust to relieve the poverty of named or identified individuals will not be charitable.

In *Re Scarisbrick* [1951] Ch 622 a testatrix left one-half of her residuary estate upon ultimate trusts for such of the relations of her son and daughters as the survivor of her son and daughters shall deem to be 'in needy circumstances'. The Court of Appeal held that the disposition was a valid charitable trust for the relief of poverty because the gift was for a class of poor persons. The fact that the survivor of the sons and daughters had the power to elect beneficiaries did not alter this conclusion, that power having been included merely to avoid disputes.

Re Scarisbrick was approved by the House of Lords in *Dingle v Turner* [1972] AC 601. There the testator gave his residuary estate to trustees upon trust for his wife for her life and thereafter to place £10,000 on trust 'to apply the income thereof in paying pensions to poor employees of E Dingle & Co. Ltd' who were old or disabled. It was held that the terms of the will created a valid charitable trust for the relief of poverty, despite the personal nexus between the beneficiaries and the named company. In the case of trusts for the relief of 'poverty' the distinction between a public charitable trust and a private non-charitable trust depended upon whether, on a true construction of the gift, it was for the relief of poverty amongst a particular description of poor people or was merely a gift to particular poor persons.

Trusts for the benefit of 'poor relations' had been accepted as charitable for more than 200 years when the House of Lords heard *Dingle v Turner*, but trusts for 'poor employees' had only been recognized since around 1900 (*Re Gosling* (1900) 48 WR 300). It was suggested in argument that the poor relations cases were an established anomaly and should not be disturbed, but that trusts for poor employees should not be afforded the same respect. The House of Lords rejected this suggestion, as it would lead to 'illogical' distinctions between different types of poverty.

The report of *Dingle v Turner* records, at p 610, that in 1972 it was estimated that nearly £100,000,000 was held on trust for poor employees, poor members of associations or professional groups, and a mere £68,000 on poor relations trusts. The annual income from these trusts was, respectively, £4,690,000 and £3,400.

A classic instance of a trust for poor relations is provided by *Re Cohen* [1973] 1 WLR 415. There the testatrix gave part of her residuary estate to trustees upon trust to apply the same in their absolute discretion 'for or towards the maintenance and benefit of any relatives of mine whom my trustees shall consider to be in special need'. Templeman J held that the instant case was indistinguishable from *Re Scarisbrick*, and had therefore created a valid charitable trust for the relief of poverty amongst a class.

In 1976, the Goodman Committee recommended that gifts to relatives or to employees of the donor for the relief of poverty should no longer be regarded as charitable. (National Council of Social Service, *Charity Law and Voluntary Organizations: Report of the Goodman Committee*, Bedford Square Press, London.) This view has clearly won little support in the courts, for *Re Scarisbrick* is applied today with more dramatic results than ever. In *Re Segelman* [1996] 2 WLR 173 the court recognized the charitable status of a trust for the 'poor and needy' of a class comprising at the time of the hearing a mere 26 people related to the testator, a multi-millionaire. These 26 were for the most part 'comfortably off' (although the court accepted that they might need financial assistance to 'overcome an unforeseen crisis'). Chadwick J held that, although this case very nearly infringed the rule that relief should not be restricted to named individuals, it was saved by the inclusion within the class of after-born issue of the 26 identified beneficiaries, thereby raising the possibility of quite substantial numbers of additional beneficiaries, who might themselves be, or become, poor.

? QUESTION 8.4

Can you imagine a trust for a class of poor relations that will not be charitable?

After *Re Segelman* it is not easy to imagine such a case. Presumably the entire class of potential beneficiaries would have to be very small indeed, for example, a trust 'for such of my brothers as fall on hard times'.

8.3.4 The second head: the advancement of education

Amongst the catalogue of charitable uses appearing in the preamble to the Statute of Elizabeth reference is made to Schools of Learning and Scholars in Universities. In fact the class of educational charitable trusts now includes museums, nursery schools, scholarly societies, trusts for industrial and technical training, and trusts for the promotion of the arts.

> **? QUESTION 8.5**
>
> Can you think of any educational charities of which you are a beneficiary?

If you are a student at a university in the UK your institution will have charitable status (even private universities have charitable status). As a law student there is at least one further educational charity of which you are a beneficiary—the Incorporated Council of Law Reporting for England and Wales (see *Incorporated Council of Law Reporting for England and Wales v AG* [1972] Ch 73). The principal object of the society is 'the preparation and publication . . . at a moderate price, and under gratuitous professional control, of Reports of Judicial Decisions of the Superior and Appellate Courts in England'. These reports are used to draw judicial attention to the current state of the law. The society's profits are not distributed to its members, but are applied to the further pursuit of its objects. The society applied for registration as a charity under the Charities Act 1960 and this case came to court after the Charity Commissioners refused registration. The Court of Appeal held that the purposes of the council were exclusively charitable.

Their Lordships were unanimous in their opinion that the trust would fall within the fourth head of charity, that of 'purposes beneficial to the community' (see 8.3.6). The suggestion that the law reports were merely a tool of the lawyer's trade was sharply dismissed as being as untenable as the suggestion that charitable trusts for the development of medicinal drugs exist only to promote the medical profession. Sachs LJ referred once again to the disjunction between the popular and the legal meaning of the word 'charity' (see 8.3) stating that 'it is . . . necessary to eliminate from one's mind a natural allergy, stemming simply from the popular meaning of "charity," to the idea that law reporting might prove to be a charitable activity'.

What is more important for present purposes is that two of their Lordships held the primary purpose of the society to be the advancement of education: 'The practising lawyer and the judge must both be lifelong students in the field of scholarship for the study of which The Law Reports provide essential material'. In reaching this conclusion they echoed the words of the Rt Hon Edmund Burke who in 1816 opined that 'to put an end to reports, is to put an end to the law of England'. Buckley LJ held (at p 102) that '[f]or the present purpose the second head should be regarded as extending to the improvement of a useful branch of human knowledge and its public dissemination'.

? QUESTION 8.6

Suppose that a society had been established having as its objects 'the study and dissemination of ethical principles' and 'the cultivation of a rational religious sentiment'. Do you think that such a society would be charitable under this head?

These are the facts of *Barralet v Attorney-General* [1980] 3 All ER 918 in which the objects of the South Place Ethical Society were scrutinised. Those objects being 'the study and dissemination of ethical principles' and the 'cultivation of a rational religious sentiment'. The society contended that its objects were charitable as being for the advancement of religion, for the advancement of education or for other purposes beneficial to the community. It was held that the whole of the society's objects were charitable as being for the advancement of education, for a 'rational' sentiment could be cultivated only through education. The 'dissemination' through the society's lectures, concerts and monthly publications satisfied the public benefit requirement.

8.3.4.1 Educative value of research

George Bernard Shaw's trust for research into a new English alphabet failed as a charitable trust for the advancement of education (see 7.2). The judge held that 'if the object be merely the increase of knowledge, that is not in itself a charitable object unless it be combined with teaching or education'. Perhaps the judge had in mind the words of St Paul: 'knowledge puffeth up, but charity edifieth'. Shaw's trust was a trust for private purposes and therefore failed (see 7.2).

In contrast, the testamentary gift in *Re Hopkins* [1965] Ch 669 was held to be charitable because of the importance of the research that was being carried out. The testatrix had left a third of her residuary estate to the Francis Bacon Society, to be 'applied towards finding the Bacon–Shakespeare manuscripts and in the event of the same having been discovered by the date of my death then for the general purposes of the work and propaganda of the society'. The society, which was a registered charity under the Charities Act 1960, existed primarily to study the evidence for Francis Bacon's authorship of plays commonly ascribed to William Shakespeare. It was held that for a gift for research to be charitable it must be combined with teaching or education, albeit the education of the researchers themselves. Wilberforce J held that it did not matter that the charitable purposes might not fall neatly into any one only of the four heads of charity. He considered the possibility that the research might fall within the general head of charities 'beneficial to the community', and stressed that 'benefits' need not be material and would include intellectual or artistic benefits.

The Amnesty International organization set up a trust to administer those of its purposes which were considered to be charitable. Its aims included the release and humane treatment of prisoners of conscience, research into the observance of human rights and the dissemination of the results of such research. It applied to the Charity Commissioners for registration of the trust as a charity under s 4 of the Charities Act 1960. Registration was refused. (See *McGovern v Attorney-General* [1982] 1 Ch 321.) On appeal to the High Court, Slade J confirmed the Commissioners' decision. The major part of the trust purposes was of a political, and therefore non-charitable, nature (see 8.3.8). However, had the provisions as to research stood alone they would have been charitable. The subject matter of the research was 'capable of adding usefully to the store of human knowledge'. His Lordship noted that human rights has become an accepted academic discipline, and stated that it should be benignly presumed that the trustees would not implement the research in a political manner.

8.3.4.2 Educative value of art

When Lord Greene MR held the Royal Choral Society to be a charitable society, he opined that 'the education of artistic taste is one of the most important things in the development of a civilised human being' (*Royal Choral Society v IRC* [1943] 2 All ER 101, 104). If by 'artistic taste' the Master of the Rolls was referring to 'critical appreciation', there can be little doubt that the cultivation of critical appreciation is as educational in the field of art as it is in the field of science or law. However, if by 'artistic taste' the Master of the Rolls meant 'artistic *good* taste' the concept becomes a highly subjective one and hardly the proper subject matter for determination by a court.

EXERCISE 8.3

Read the extract from *Re Pinion* [1965] Ch 85 set out next. How did the courts resolve the problem of having to make a subjective value judgment on the merits of the art in that case? (The answer follows after the discussion of *Re Delius* [1957] 1 Ch 299, below.)

Re Pinion [1965] Ch 85, Court of Appeal

The testator left his freehold studio, together with his paintings and some antique furniture, silver, china etc to be offered to the National Trust to be kept together as a collection. The income from his residuary estate was left to be used for the maintenance of the collection. In the event that the National Trust might decline the gift, his executors were directed to keep the collection as a museum. The Court of Appeal held that this was not a valid trust for the advancement of education.

Harman LJ:

> For myself a reading of the will leads me rather to the view that the testator's object was not to educate anyone, . . . there is a strong body of evidence here that as a means of education this collection is worthless. The testator's own paintings, of which there are over fifty, are said by competent persons to be in an academic style and 'atrociously bad' and the other pictures without exception to be worthless. . . . Indeed one of the experts expresses his surprise that so voracious a collector should not by hazard have picked up even one meritorious object. The most that a skilful cross-examination extracted from the expert witnesses was that there were a dozen chairs which might perhaps be acceptable to a minor provincial museum and perhaps another dozen not altogether worthless, but two dozen chairs do not make a museum and they must, to accord with the will, be exhibited stifled by a large number of absolutely worthless pictures and objects.
>
> It was said that this is a matter of taste, and *de gustibus non est disputandum* [tr: an opinion cannot be disputed], but here I agree with the judge that there is an accepted canon of taste on which the court must rely, for it has itself no judicial knowledge of such matters, and the unanimous verdict of the experts is as I have stated. The learned judge with great hesitation concluded that there was that scintilla of merit which was sufficient to save the rest. I find myself on the other side of the line. I can conceive of no useful object to be served in foisting on the public this mass of junk. It has neither public utility nor educative value. I would hold that the testator's project ought not to be carried into effect and that his next-of-kin is entitled to the residue of his estate.

In *Re Delius*, the widow of Frederick Delius, the composer, left her residuary estate to trustees upon trust to apply the income therefrom 'for or towards the advancement . . . of the musical works of my late husband under conditions in which the making of profit is not the object to be attained . . . by means of the recording upon the gramophone or other instrument for the mechanical reproduction of music of those works . . . the publication and issue of a uniform edition of the whole body of the works . . . and . . . the performance in public of the works'. Roxburgh J held that the trusts were valid charitable trusts for the advancement of education. The court did not have to make a value judgment in this case because counsel on both sides were unanimous in their view that the standard of Delius's work was very high. The judge did not consider what he might have decided had the works been of an 'inadequate composer', he mused that 'perhaps I should have no option but to give effect even to such a trust'. Although, later in his judgment he did state, *obiter*, that 'if it is charitable to promote music in general it must be charitable to promote music of a particular composer, presupposing . . . that the composer is one whose music is worth appreciating'!

The fact that the trust would incidentally enhance the reputation of Delius and bring pleasure to listeners were not reasons for denying the charitable nature of the trust. It was, however, crucial to the success of the case that the residuary legatee was held to have no possibility of profiting personally from the trusts.

In *Re Pinion* the court was able to avoid the need to form a purely subjective value judgment on the merits of the art by the admission of expert evidence. In that case the experts concluded that the collection had no value as a means of education.

8.3.4.3 **Educative value of sport**

Is the pursuit of sport a charitable object in itself? Certainly there is no express reference to sport in the preamble to the Statute of Elizabeth I. The word 'sport' is derived from the word disport, which is itself derived from the french *porter*, 'to carry'. Literally, sport is that which carries one off, that which acts as a diversion from work and the mundane, so when for amusement we read about 'sport' on the back pages of our daily newspapers and watch it on our televisions, it is we, and not the professionals whom we observe, who are the ones engaged in sport! Clearly the professional pursuit of 'sport' for personal profit will not be charitable. Indeed George Orwell once famously wrote that 'serious sport has nothing to do with fair play. It is bound up with hatred, jealousy, boastfulness, and disregard of all the rules' (*Shooting an Elephant* (1950)). But might there be a public benefit in the promotion of sport for leisure, health and to promote ideals of teamwork and fair play?

The courts have in general been reluctant to acknowledge sport to be a charitable object in itself, but have been willing to support it where it is being pursued in an educational context. In *Re Dupree's Deed Trusts* [1945] Ch 16 the issue was the charitable status of a gift of £5,000 for the promotion of an annual chess tournament for boys and young men under 21 resident in the City of Portsmouth. Vaisey J accepted that chess is something more than a game, that it is an historic institution which encourages foresight, concentration, memory and ingenuity. He did acknowledge, however, that recognizing this trust as a charitable trust for the advancement of education 'may be a little near the line' and could put the courts on a 'slippery slope. If chess, why not draughts: if draughts, why not bezique and so on, through to bridge, whist, and, by another route, stamp collecting and the acquisition of birds' eggs?' In recognizing the charitable status of the present gift the judge was ultimately swayed by the fact that one trustee was the chairman of the Portsmouth Education Committee and another the headmaster of Portsmouth Grammar School.

The scholastic context of sport was also conclusive in *Inland Revenue Commissioners v McMullen* [1981] AC 1. Under consideration was the FA Youth Trust, created by the Football Association in 1972. The objects of the trust were 'to organise or provide or assist in the organisation and provision of facilities which will enable and encourage pupils of schools and universities in any part of the United Kingdom to play Association Football or other games or sports and thereby to assist in ensuring that due attention is given to the physical education and development of such pupils as well as to the development and occupation of their minds'. The Charity Commissioners agreed to register the trust as a charity. The Crown appealed against the registration.

It was held in the House of Lords that on the proper construction of the objects of the trust the word 'thereby' showed that the purpose of the trust was not merely to organize the playing of sport, but to promote physical education. Regard being had to the need for a balanced education and the fact that the benefits were limited to students, this was a valid charitable trust for the advancement of education. A majority of their Lordships held that a benign construction should be given to ambiguity in the wording of a purportedly charitable trust. The possibility that the trust might be charitable under the Recreational Charities Act 1958 was left open (see 8.3.7).

? QUESTION 8.7

Can you think of any non-scholastic contexts in which the provision of sports facilities is likely to be charitable?

In *Re Gray* [1925] Ch 362, an endowment for 'the promotion of sport (including in that term only shooting fishing cricket football and polo)' was held to be charitable because the proposed beneficiaries were soldiers, it being charitable to promote the well-being of the army (perhaps in the spirit of 'setting out of soldiers' as that term is used in the preamble to the Statute of Elizabeth). It is also charitable to promote the well-being of the police force (*IRC v City of Glasgow Police Athletic Association* [1953] AC 380) and the fire service (*Re Wokingham Fire Brigade Trusts* [1951] Ch 373).

8.3.4.4 The public benefit requirement in educational trusts

The key case is the decision of the House of Lords in *Oppenheim v Tobacco Securities Trust Co Ltd* [1951] AC 297. In that case a settlement directed trustees to apply the income from the trust fund 'in providing for . . . the education of children of employees or former employees of the British-American Tobacco Co. Ltd . . . or any of its subsidiary or allied companies in such manner . . . as the acting trustees shall in their absolute discretion . . . think fit'. The employees referred to numbered over 110,000. The issue was whether the class of potential beneficiaries constituted a sufficient section of the general public. It was held by the majority that, despite the huge number of potential beneficiaries, they were identified by the personal nexus between them and the employer company. Accordingly, the trust did not satisfy the requirement that it produce a benefit to a sufficient section of the community. The words 'section of the' community have no special meaning, but they indicate, first, that the possible beneficiaries must not be numerically negligible, and secondly, that they must not be distinguishable from other members of the public by reason of a relationship to a particular individual.

> **? QUESTION 8.8**
>
> Would a trust to establish a school in a small mining village be charitable if the education it provided was limited to children of employees of the mining company?

According to the majority in *Oppenheim* it would not. Against this Lord Cross of Chelsea had this to say in *Dingle v Turner* [1972] AC 601:

> That reasoning—based on the distinction between personal and impersonal relationships—has never seemed to me very satisfactory and I have always—if I may say so—felt the force of the criticism to which my noble and learned friend Lord MacDermott subjected it in his dissenting speech in the *Oppenheim* case. For my part I would prefer to approach the problem on far broader lines . . . with the bare contrast between 'public' and 'private' . . . One might say that . . . the employees in such concerns as ICI or GEC are just as much 'sections of the public' as the residents in some geographical area.

8.3.4.5 Preferences

Imagine that you are the Charity Commissioners. You have received an application to register a charitable trust in the following terms:

> for the promotion and furtherance of commercial education of persons of either sex who are British born subjects who are desirous of educating themselves or obtaining tuition for a higher commercial career, but whose means are insufficient or will not allow of their obtaining such education or tuition at their own expense; in selecting beneficiaries it is my wish that *the charity trustees shall give a preference* to any employees of J. Co. Ltd or any members of the families of such employees; failing a sufficient number of beneficiaries under such description then the persons eligible shall be any persons of British birth as the charity trustees may select. Provided that the total income to be available for benefiting the preferred beneficiaries shall not in any one year be more than seventy-five per cent of the total available income for such year.

> **? QUESTION 8.9**
>
> Would you grant the application?

The facts set out on p 183 replicate almost exactly the trust that was considered in *Re Koettgen* [1954] Ch 252. Surprising as it may seem, Upjohn J held that the trust was a charitable one, despite the preference. His Lordship held that the primary class of beneficiaries was sufficiently large to satisfy the public benefit requirement for educational trusts and that the direction to prefer could not affect the validity of the primary trust given that it was not certain that the preferred class would exhaust 75 per cent of the fund in any year. However, if the direction to 'prefer' a class is made in absolute, imperative terms, so as to elevate the preferred class to the status of primary class of beneficiaries, the trust will only be charitable if the preferred class is itself large enough to constitute a sufficient section of the public. A trust for the education of 'deserving youths of the Islamic faith', which directed the trustees to grant an absolute priority to the settlor's family, failed as a charitable trust (*Caffoor v Commissioners of Income Tax* [1961] AC 584 (PC)).

QUESTION 8.10

Crucial to the decision in *Re Koettgen* was the fact that it could not be said that the trustees would actually apply a full 75 per cent of the income in favour of the preferred class in any given year. Would it still be a charitable trust if the trustees did in fact exercise their power to favour the preferred class in this way?

This is what occurred in *Inland Revenue Commissioners Ltd v Educational Grants Association Ltd* [1967] Ch 123. In that case the Inland Revenue Commissioners successfully challenged an educational association which had very close links with a commercial company (the principal donor to the association). Evidence showed that 76 to 85 per cent of the association's income had been applied to educate the children of persons connected with the commercial company. Despite this, the association had claimed a tax refund from the Inland Revenue. The Inland Revenue refused the refund, claiming that the association had failed to apply its funds to exclusively charitable ends. Pennycuick J criticized and distinguished *Re Koettgen* and decided in favour of the IRC. The Court of Appeal upheld his judgment, but without airing any opinion of *Re Koettgen*. The present status of *Re Koettgen* is therefore somewhat uncertain. The Charity Commissioners have followed *Re Koettgen* and registered similar trusts on a few occasions, but the Annual Report of the Charity Commissioners warned (in their 1978 report) that the 'application of too large a proportion of the income would constitute an application for noncharitable purposes'.

8.3.5 The third head: the advancement of religion

8.3.5.1 Churches and churchyards

The preamble to the Statute of Elizabeth 1601 lists amongst charitable uses the 'Repair of Bridges, Ports, Havens, Causeways, Churches'. Inspired by this, the courts have recognized as charitable, trusts for the maintenance of a churchyard (*Re Douglas* [1905] 1 Ch 279) and for the erection, to the memory of the testatrix and her relations, of a stained glass window in a parish church (*Re King* [1923] 1 Ch 243).

? QUESTION 8.11

Do you think that a trust for the maintenance of a particular tomb or grave would be charitable?

You should recall from *Re Hooper* [1932] 1 Ch 38 (see 7.3.1) that where a testator declared a trust for the care and upkeep of certain tombs in cemeteries and churchyards (including that of his son) and for the upkeep of a tablet and a window in a church, the judge held that whereas the upkeep of the tablet and window were valid as charitable purposes, the trust for the upkeep of the individual tombs would take effect as a trust of imperfect obligation. This meant that the trustees would not be obliged to discharge the trust for the maintenance of the individual tombs, and that the trust would in any event be limited to take effect for only 21 years after the testator's death.

8.3.5.2 What is religion?

George Bernard Shaw, whom we encountered under the previous head of charity was a confirmed agnostic. In the preface to Volume 2 of *Plays Pleasant and Unpleasant* (1898) he opined that 'there is only one religion, though there are a hundred versions of it'. Absent the cynicism, the courts have taken a similarly liberal approach to the recognition of religion.

EXERCISE 8.4

Before progressing, remind yourself of the definition of religion which you wrote down on a piece of paper at the beginning of this chapter. Now see how closely it resembles the approach taken by the courts.

In *Thornton v Howe* [1862] 31 Beav 14, the court considered a gift of land which had been made to assist in the promotion and publication of the 'sacred writings of the late Joanna Southcote'. She had claimed that she was with child by the Holy Spirit and would give birth to a Second Messiah. Romilly MR described her as 'a foolish ignorant woman' but nevertheless held that the gift was a charitable gift for the advancement of religion. The Master of the Rolls stated that 'the Court of Chancery makes no distinction between one religion and another . . . [or] one sect and another . . . [unless] the tenets of a particular sect inculcate doctrines adverse to the very foundations of all religions and . . . subversive of all morality . . . If the tendency were not immoral and although this Court might consider the opinions sought to be propagated foolish or even devoid of foundation' the trust would nevertheless be charitable. If the decision seems a surprising one, its context should be borne in mind. As a charitable gift of land, it failed under the Statute of Mortmain (now repealed) and passed to the donor's heir.

Thornton v Howe was followed in *Re Watson* [1973] 1 WLR 1472. There the testatrix left her estate 'for the continuance of the work of God as it has been maintained by Mr. HG Hobbs and myself since 1942 by God's enabling . . . in propagating the truth as given in the Holy Bible . . .'. Hobbs (a retired builder) predeceased the testatrix but had written a number of religious tracts during his lifetime. His publications were regarded by experts as being unlikely to extend the knowledge of the Christian religion, but quite likely to confirm, in the group who had produced the publications, their own religious opinions. The trust was held to be a valid charitable trust for the advancement of religion.

It is clear from these judgments that all religions are regarded equally by the courts. It is also obvious that the courts regard any religion as better than none (if they did not, it would be difficult to justify their charitable status on public benefit grounds), indeed Cross J said as much in *Neville Estates v Madden* [1962] Ch 832 (8.3.5.3). What is not entirely clear is what belief systems count as 'religions'.

? EXERCISE 8.5

Place a tick against whichever of the following practices and beliefs you would regard as being for the advancement of religion. They are all taken from decided cases, discussion of which will follow:

- ancestor worship
- promotion of agnostic (not atheistic) ethics
- faith healing.

Is ancestor worship a religious practice?

In *Yeap Cheah Neo v Ong Chen Neo* (1875) LR 6 PC 381 the Judicial Committee of the Privy Council held that it is not, giving two main reasons. First, worship of human ancestors did not involve the worship of a deity and could not, therefore, be described as a religion. Secondly, on the terms of the particular trust there was no assurance that the worship would produce a sufficient public benefit (see *Gilmour v Coats* [1949] AC 426 (8.3.5.3)).

Does an agnostic (not atheistic) 'ethical society' exist for the advancement of religion?

In *Barralet v Attorney-General (Re South Place Ethical Society)* (see 8.3.4 above) Dillon J held that it does not. It was stated that 'religion' is concerned with mankind's relations with God or gods, whereas ethics is concerned with relations between humans only. Without belief in a supernatural entity, faith could not properly be described as religious, no matter how sincerely held. The view held in America that a religion is any belief occupying in the life of the possessor a place parallel to that occupied by belief in God prompted the judge to remark that 'parallels, by definition, never meet'. The judge suggested, further, that worship of God or gods was essential to religion, and worship in that sense had no place between humans, and accordingly no place in a humanist ethical system of belief.

Is faith healing a religious practice?

In *Funnell v Stewart (Re Le Cren Clarke)* [1996] 1 WLR 288 it was held that faith healing could be charitable under either the category of advancement of religion or other purposes beneficial to the community. The private religious services of the group were ancillary to their work for the public benefit, and many of their services were open to the public.

8.3.5.3 The public benefit requirement in trusts for the advancement of religion

In *Gilmour v Coats* [1949] AC 426 (discussed in *Neville Estates v Madden* [1962] Ch 832) £500 was settled upon trust for the purposes of the Carmelite Priory, a community of strictly cloistered nuns. The nuns devoted themselves to prayer, meditation, fasting, penance and self-sanctification. They conducted private religious services, but were not engaged in any good works outside of the convent.

? QUESTION 8.12

Do you think that the nuns' activities were for the benefit of the community?

Your answer to this will probably depend upon whether you believe in the power of prayer! The House of Lords held that the trust for the purposes of the cloistered community did not satisfy the public benefit. Accordingly this was not a valid charitable trust for the advancement of religion. The potential for religious edification of others through the example set by the nuns was said to be too vague. Nor did their Lordships accept the argument, made by analogy to educational trusts, that the public benefit requirement had been met through the fact that membership of the community was potentially open to any woman in the whole world. Lord Simonds made the following general observation: 'the law of charity . . . has been built up not logically but empirically . . . To argue by a method of syllogism or analogy from the category of education to that of religion ignores the historical processes of law'.

Gilmour v Coats was distinguished in *Neville Estates Ltd v Madden* [1962] Ch 832.

***Neville Estates Ltd v Madden* [1962] Ch 832**

The company claimed specific performance of a contract for the sale of land owned by a synagogue. The trustees of the synagogue claimed that the synagogue existed for charitable purposes and that the consent of the Charity Commissioners would be required before sale could proceed. It was held that the synagogue's purposes were charitable. The decision of the House of Lords in *Gilmour v Coats* [1949] AC 426 (in which a gift to an order of cloistered nuns failed) was distinguished.

Cross J:

> . . . the trust with which I am concerned resembles that in *Gilmour v Coats* [1949] AC 426 in this, that the persons immediately benefited by it are not a section of the public but the members of a private body. All persons of the Jewish faith living in or about Catford might well constitute a section of the public, but the members for the time being of the Catford Synagogue are no more a section of the public than the members for the time being of a Carmelite priory. The two cases, however, differ from one another in that the members of the Catford Synagogue spend their lives in the world, whereas the members of a Carmelite priory live secluded from the world. If once one refuses to pay any regard—as the courts refused to pay any regard—to

the influence which these nuns living in seclusion might have on the outside world, then it must follow that no public benefit is involved in a trust to support a Carmelite priory. As Lord Greene MR, said in the Court of Appeal: 'Having regard to the way in which the lives of the members were spent, the benefit was a purely private one'. But the court is, I think, entitled to assume that some benefit accrues to the public from the attendance at places of worship of persons who live in this world and mix with their fellow citizens. As between different religions the law stands neutral, but it assumes that any religion is at least likely to be better than none.

But then it is said—and it is this part of the argument that has caused me the greatest difficulty: But this is a case of self help. Suppose that a body of persons, being dissatisfied with the facilities for the education of small children provided in their district, form an association for the education of the children of members . . .

I feel the force of this analogy; but, as Lord Simonds pointed out in *Gilmour v Coats*, it is dangerous to reason by analogy from one head of charity to another. . . .

? QUESTION 8.13

Do you think that proselytization is charitable?

In the *Pemsel* case (see 8.3.2) Lord Bramwell asked 'What of a trust for the conversion of the Jews? Is that a charitable purpose? If so, what of a trust for their reconversion?' He concluded that this was not a charitable purpose. Lord Herschell in the same case observed, somewhat cynically, that 'You may desire to convert the richest people, and very often do . . . A religious object is not necessarily a charitable object'.

8.3.6 The fourth head: other purposes beneficial to the community

Not every trust purpose which is beneficial to the community will fall within this fourth head and thereby qualify as a charitable purpose. Every purpose within this head must still fall within the 'spirit and intendment' of the preamble to the Statute of Elizabeth I (*per* Sir William Grant MR in *Morice v Bishop of Durham* (1804) 9 Ves 399, 405). Russell LJ in the *Council of Law Reporting v AG* [1972] Ch 73 at 88 described this as 'a line of retreat . . . in case [the courts] are faced with a purpose (for example, a political purpose) which could not have been within the contemplation of the Statute even if the then legislators had been endowed with the gift of foresight into the circumstances of later centuries'.

In later centuries it has indeed become clear that not all that is beneficial to the public is charitable. In 1976 the Goodman Committee (see 8.3.3) stated (at para 27) that 'many things which are far removed from charity may benefit the community. For instance, a highly successful commercial venture, generating exports and providing massive employment is of immense benefit to the community but it is not charitable.' Lord Macnaghten in *Pemsel* stated, in similar vein, that 'A layman would probably be amused if he were told that a gift to the

Chancellor of the Exchequer for the benefit of the nation was a charity'. His Lordship went on to give 'support for a lifeboat' as an example of something which would fall within the fourth category.

Could it be that those activities recognized by the courts to be for the public benefit are activities which the State would have to finance were they not supported from private funds? Take for example, the provision of cremation services (see *Scottish Burial Reform and Cremation Society Ltd v Glasgow Corporation* at 8.3.2; private hospitals (see 8.3.6.3), and 'retraining and assistance to the unemployed' (*IRC v Oldham Training and Enterprise Council* [1996] STC 1218).

8.3.6.1 Trusts for the aged or impotent

The preamble to the Statute of Elizabeth I 1601 refers to the relief of 'the aged, the impotent and poor'. In *Pemsel* Lord Macnaghten read this phrase disjunctively when he isolated the relief of poverty within the first of his four heads of charity. Trusts for the relief of the aged and impotent will come within Lord Macnaghten's fourth head of charity. It has been suggested, however, that a trust for the aged and impotent which excludes the poor may not be charitable (*Re MacDuff* [1896] 2 Ch 446). For example, a trust for the relief of aged millionaires would not be charitable.

Although the meaning of 'aged' is relatively unproblematic, the word 'impotent' has never been defined by an English court. *The Oxford English Dictionary* defines it in this sense as 'Physically weak; without bodily strength; unable to use one's limbs; helpless, decrepit'. *Tudor on Charities* (8th edn, 1995) suggests that this definition is 'sufficiently wide to cover not only those suffering from permanent disability, whether of body or mind, but those temporarily incapacitated by injury or illness, or in need of rest, and young children incapable of protecting themselves from the consequences of cruelty or neglect'. However wide the meaning of the word may be today, in 1601 it seems to have been associated with disability of limbs. In 1603, R Johnson referred in *Kingdom & Commonwealth* (at p 184) to 'Those onely who are impotent in their limbs'. And in Shakespeare's *Othello*, written around the same time, Desdemona berates Iago's reasoning for its 'most lame and impotent conclusion!' (Act II Scene i).

> **? QUESTION** 8.14
>
> Which of the next two cases do you think were held to be charitable under the fourth head?

Re Mead's Trust Deed [1961] 1 WLR 1244: the National Society of Operative Printers and Assistants, a trade union, executed a deed of trust for the provision of a convalescent home for its aged and ill members. No means test was used to select residents of the home.

Joseph Rowntree Memorial Trust Housing Association Ltd v Attorney-General [1983] 2 WLR 284: a charitable housing association desired to build individual dwellings for sale to elderly people on long leases in consideration of a capital payment. On the tenant's death the lease would be assigned to the tenant's spouse or a family member, provided that person was also elderly. Failing such an assignment the lease would revert to the association who would pay to the tenant's estate 70 per cent of the then current market value of the lease. The Charity

Commissioners objected to the scheme on the grounds *inter alia* that it operated by way of contract, benefited private individuals rather than a charitable class and could produce a financial profit for those individuals.

In *Re Mead's Trust Deed* Cross J held that the trust was not exclusively for the relief of poverty. Accordingly it was necessary for the trust to benefit a sufficient section of the community. Residents of the home were restricted to members of the society, accordingly the trust could not take effect as a valid charitable trust. Oppenheim J followed.

In the *Joseph Rowntree* case it was held that the scheme was a valid charitable scheme for the relief of the aged notwithstanding the objections of the Charity Commissioners.

8.3.6.2 Trusts for animals

? QUESTION 8.15

Suppose that I leave a bequest to my faithful dog, Fido. Would the bequest be charitable? If so, why? If not, what will happen to the bequest?

Trusts for specific animals must be distinguished from trusts for animals generally. A trust for animals *generally* may be charitable: examples include a trust to establish a home for lost dogs (*Re Douglas* (1887) 35 Ch D 472) and a trust for animal welfare (*Re Wedgwood* [1915] 1 Ch 113). However, your bequest to your faithful dog, Fido will not be charitable. It might nevertheless take effect as a private purpose trust of imperfect obligation (see, for example, *Re Dean* at 7.3.2).

The reason for recognizing the charitable status of trusts for the benefit of animals generally was said by Swinfen-Eady LJ in *Re Wedgwood* [1915] 1 Ch 113 (at 122) to be that the trust would 'tend to promote and encourage kindness towards [animals], and to ameliorate the condition of the brute creation, and thus to stimulate humane and generous sentiments in man towards the lower animals, and by this means to promote feelings of humanity and thus elevate the human race'.

A trust to provide an animal sanctuary where wild animals could thrive without the intrusion of people failed because it did not appear to prevent cruelty to animals or in any other way provide an elevating lesson to mankind, on the contrary, the wild animals would be free to molest each other (*Re Grove-Grady* [1929] 1 Ch 557). It may be that the Court of Appeal also harboured an objection to the fact that all the officials of the society had to be anti-vivisectionists and opponents of all blood sports (including angling).

? QUESTION 8.16

Do you think that an anti-vivisection society should have charitable status under this head of charity?

This was the issue before the House of Lords in *National Anti-Vivisection Society v IRC* [1948] AC 31. The society had claimed to be exempt from income tax as being 'a body of persons established for charitable purposes only'. It was held that the society was not charitable because it failed the overriding test of charitable status, that is, whether the purposes of the organization existed for the public benefit. It was held that, on balance, the object of the society was detrimental to the public benefit (Lord Porter dissenting). Further, a prime object of the society was political, namely, to secure the repeal of the Cruelty to Animals Act 1876 and to see it replaced by an enactment absolutely prohibiting vivisection. The court could not award charitable status to a trust for a political purpose (see 8.3.8).

The front page of the *Daily Telegraph*, 7 February 1998 carried the following headline: 'RSPCA drops animal rights after threat to charity status'. In the article the reporter noted that the RSPCA had withdrawn a key policy statement declaring support for 'animal rights' following warnings from the Charity Commissioners that it breached the society's charitable status. The response of one member of the society's ruling council was to accuse the commission of acting 'as an official Government censor in suppressing the expression of religious and ethical opinion'. Do you agree?

When the Charities Bill 2004 (see 8.5.1) eventually becomes law it will confirm that 'the advancement of animal welfare' is presumed to be for the public benefit, but we can expect the presumption of this particular public benefit to continue to clash fiercely with the courts' (and the Charity Commission's) refusal to recognize charities established to change the law of the land.

? QUESTION 8.17

One borderline case is the Wolf Trust, which seeks to promote the reintroduction of wolves into the Highlands of Scotland which at present is generally prohibited under the Wildlife and Countryside Act 1981, s 14(1) (it may be licensed by the Secretary of State for Scotland). Is such a trust charitable, as being for the public benefit? Does it infringe the prohibition on charities established for political objects?

The Decision of the Charity Commissioners for England and Wales On the Application for Registration of the Wolf Trust (30 January 2003) was to refuse to register the Wolf Trust as a charity pursuant to s 3 of the Charities Act 1993. It was held that the Wolf Trust was not established for exclusively charitable purposes in that its primary purpose was 'to promote the reintroduction of the wolf into Scotland as an end in itself', and further, that such a purpose 'could not be charitable as it was designed to influence the opinion of the public and the decisions of the relevant Government authorities and neither the Court nor the Commission could determine whether such a purpose was for the benefit of the public'.

8.3.6.3 Trusts for private hospitals

In *Resch's Will Trusts* [1969] 1 AC 514, the testator left his residuary estate (then valued at around eight million Australian dollars) to trustees upon trust to pay two-thirds of the income 'to the Sisters of Charity for a period of 200 years so long as they shall conduct the

St Vincent's Private Hospital'. The hospital did not seek to make a commercial profit, but its charges for treatment, while not necessarily excluding the poor, were not low. The Privy Council held that it was a valid charitable trust for purposes beneficial to the community. The requisite public benefit had been satisfied because evidence showed that the public needed accommodation and treatment of the type provided by the hospital. A gift for the purposes of a hospital is *prima facie* a good charitable gift, but the presumption could be rebutted if evidence showed that the hospital was carried on commercially for the benefit of private individuals.

8.3.7 Recreational trusts

> The Englishman never enjoys himself except for a noble purpose. He does not play cricket because it is a good game, but because it makes good citizens. He does not love motor races for their own sake, but for the advantages they bring to the engineering firms of his country. And it is common knowledge that the devoted persons who conduct and regularly attend horse-races do not do so because they like it, but for the benefit of the breed of the English horse.
>
> —Plush J in *R v Leather* (A P Herbert, *Uncommon Law* (1942), p 195)

We observed earlier (at 8.3.4.3) that sport is probably not charitable in itself (the point was left open by the House of Lords in *IRC v McMullen* [1981] AC 1, but has in any event been fairly well settled since *Re Nottage* [1895] 2 Ch 649). Sport seems to be afforded charitable status only where it promotes some other charitable end, such as education in schools and universities, or the promotion of the armed forces (but see 8.5 on reform). The status of recreational charities generally was also in some doubt until the enactment of the Recreational Charities Act 1958.

The Act was a response to the decision of the House of Lords in *Inland Revenue Commissioners v Baddeley* [1955] AC 572. In that case, land, including a mission church, lecture room and store, was given to trustees on trust to permit the leaders of the mission to promote thereon 'the religious, social and physical well-being of persons resident in the county boroughs of West Ham and Leyton . . . by the provision of facilities for religious services and instruction and for the social and physical training and recreation of such aforementioned persons who for the time being are in the opinion [of the leaders of the mission] members of or likely to become members of the Methodist Church'.

The House of Lords held that the trust was not for the relief of poverty, for 'relief' implied the meeting of a need or quasi-necessity, such as the provision of a dwelling. Nor could the trust be charitable as being for a purpose beneficial to the community. The trust did not benefit a sufficient section of the public because the beneficiaries had been selected not only by reference to a particular geographical area, but by the further condition that they share a particular creed. Further, promotion of 'religious, social and physical well-being' was too wide a statement of the trust's objects, and accordingly the trust would be void for potentially including non-charitable purposes.

The Recreational Charities Act 1958 recognizes as charitable the provision of (or assistance in the provision of) facilities for recreation or other leisure time occupation if the facilities are provided in the interests of social welfare. This requirement can be established by one of two routes:

Route one	Route two
The provision of facilities for persons in need due to youth, age, infirmity or disablement, poverty or social and economic circumstances: s 1(2)(b)(i)	The provision of facilities available to the members or female members of the public at large: s 1(2)(b)(ii)
With the object of improving the conditions of life for the persons for whom the facilities are primarily intended: s 1(2)(a)	With the object of improving the conditions of life for the persons for whom the facilities are primarily intended: s 1(2)(a)
And for the public benefit: s 1(1)	And for the public benefit: s 1(1)

Recreational Charities Act 1958

1. General provision as to recreational and similar trusts, etc.

(1) Subject to the provisions of this Act, it shall be and be deemed always to have been charitable to provide, or assist in the provision of, facilities for recreation or other leisure-time occupation, if the facilities are provided in the interests of social welfare:

Provided that nothing in this section shall be taken to derogate from the principle that a trust or institution to be charitable must be for the public benefit.

(2) The requirement of the foregoing subsection that the facilities are provided in the interests of social welfare shall not be treated as satisfied unless—

(a) the facilities are provided with the object of improving the conditions of life for the persons for whom the facilities are primarily intended; and

(b) either—

(i) those persons have need of such facilities as aforesaid by reason of their youth, age, infirmity or disablement, poverty or social and economic circumstances; or

(ii) the facilities are to be available to the members or female members of the public at large.

(3) Subject to the said requirement, subsection (1) of this section applies in particular to the provision of facilities at village halls, community centres and women's institutes, and to the provision and maintenance of grounds and buildings to be used for purposes of recreation or leisure-time occupation, and extends to the provision of facilities for those purposes by the organising of any activity.

? QUESTION 8.18

Do you think that the trust in *IRC v Baddeley* would be charitable under the provisions of the 1958 Act?

The trust in *Baddeley* might have been valid under route one, to the extent that it provided facilities for persons in need due to their youth, were it not for the inclusion of other, potentially non-charitable objects.

In Re Guild [1992] 2 AC 310, a testator left the residue of his estate for a sports centre in North Berwick and 'similar' purposes 'in connection with sport'. The IRC claimed that the gift was liable to capital transfer tax. The executor appealed, claiming that the gift was for charitable purposes and therefore exempt from the tax. The House of Lords held that, on a proper construction of s 1(2)(a) of the Recreational Charities Act 1958, a gift for the provision of recreational facilities could be charitable notwithstanding the fact that the intended beneficiaries were not in a position of social disadvantage and did not suffer from any particular deprivation. Accordingly, the gift in the present case was a charitable one, the facilities having been provided in the interests of social welfare. In construing the second part of the gift, 'or some similar purpose in connection with sport', it should be presumed that the testator had intended those other purposes to share the aspects of social welfare provision and public benefit which had been present in the first part of the gift. Such a benignant construction should be applied to deeds whose wording was ambiguous and susceptible to two constructions, one of which would render the trust void, the other of which would render it a valid charitable trust.

8.3.7.1 Reform

The Charities Bill 2004 contains special provisions concerning recreational charities, including a new (substitute) s 1(2) which provides that basic conditions must be met in order to satisfy the requirement in subs (1) that the facilities are provided in the interests of social welfare. Those basic conditions are that the facilities are provided with the object of improving the conditions of life for the persons for whom the facilities are primarily intended (s 1(2A)(a)); and that either those persons have need of the facilities by reason of their youth, age, infirmity or disability, poverty, or social and economic circumstances (s 1(2A)(b)(i)), or the facilities are to be available to members of the public at large or to male, or to female, members of the public at large (s 1(2A)(b)(ii)). Incidentally, it also provides for the repeal of s 2 of the 1958 Act (miners' welfare trusts) and removes the charitable status of 'a registered sports club established for charitable purposes' (being a sports club for the time being registered under Sch 18 to the Finance Act 2002).

8.3.8 Trusts for political purposes

In *Bowman v Secular Society Ltd* [1917] AC 406, Lord Parker stated that '. . . a trust for the attainment of political objects has always been held invalid, not because it is illegal . . . but because the court has no means of judging whether a proposed change in the law will or will not be for the public benefit . . .'. The prime reason for refusing charitable status to trusts for political purposes is that courts, whose role it is to enforce the law of Parliament, cannot sanction organizations whose role it is to change the law of Parliament (see *National Anti-Vivisection Society v IRC* [1948] AC 31).

For these reasons Amnesty International was denied charitable status in *McGovern v Attorney-General* [1982] 1 Ch 321. Slade J held that a trust for the relief of human suffering was capable of being charitable, but not where a direct and main object of the trust was to secure such relief through attempting to change the laws of a foreign country. Such a trust would be a trust for a political purpose and as such would not be capable of being a valid charitable trust. The judge stated that an English court has 'no adequate means of judging whether a proposed change in the law of a foreign country will or will not be for the public benefit' of the foreign community. The judge also pointed out the risk of prejudicing relations between the United Kingdom and foreign states if English courts passed judgment on foreign regimes. The judge did acknowledge, however, that if the main objects of a charitable trust are non-political it will not cease to be charitable if the trustees have the power to use political means to achieve those non-political ends.

In its response to the decision in that case, the Charity Commissioners gave, amongst others, the following guidelines to charity trustees:

> To avoid doubt being cast on the claim of the institution to be a charity, its governing instrument should not include power to exert political pressure except in a way that is ancillary to a charitable purpose . . . In general, what is ancillary is that which furthers the work of the institution, not something that will procure the performance of similar work by, for example, the Government of the day. (Paragraph 54(ii).)
>
> Charities, whether they operate in this country or overseas, must avoid . . . seeking to eliminate social, economic, political or other injustice. (Paragraph 54 (vii).)

References are to the Annual Report of the Charity Commissioners for 1981.

More recently, the Charity Commissioners issued a circular summarizing the law in relation to charities and politics (Political Activities and Campaigning by Charities, July 1995 (Leaflet CC 9)). The Commissioners drew a fundamental distinction between political purposes and political activities. A charitable organization may be involved in the latter, but can never be established to achieve the former. They point out that 'any political activity undertaken by trustees must be in furtherance of, and ancillary to, the charity's stated objects and within its powers' (para 8). At para 9 they provide the following guidance:

> To be ancillary, activities must serve and be subordinate to the charity's purposes. They cannot, therefore, be undertaken as an end in themselves and must not be allowed to dominate the activities which the charity undertakes to carry out its charitable purposes directly. The trustees must be able to show that there is a reasonable expectation that the activities will further the purposes of the charity, and so benefit its beneficiaries to an extent justified by the resources devoted to those activities.

It is also clear that the courts will not recognize the charitable status of a political trust merely because it is masquerading as a trust for education or some other charitable purpose. See, for example, *Re Hopkinson* [1949] 1 Ch 346, where the testator gave his residuary estate to four well-known members of the Labour Party:

> as trustees of the educational fund hereinafter mentioned . . . for the advancement of adult education with particular reference to the following purpose (but in no way limiting their general discretion in applying the fund for adult education), that is to say, the education of men and women of all classes on the lines of the Labour Party's memorandum headed 'A note on Education in the Labour party'.

(It is clear that trusts for the promotion of one political party (*Bonar Law Memorial Trust v IRC* (1933) 49 TLR 220) and trusts for the promotion of a particular political doctrine (*Re Bushnell* [1975] 1 WLR 1596) are not charitable.)

Contrast *Re Hopkinson* with *Re Koeppler* [1986] Ch 423. The testator, Koeppler, came to England from Germany in 1933. After World War II he ran conferences, known collectively as the 'Wilton Park' project, for politicians, academics, civil servants, industrialists and journalists. By his will he left a large part of his estate to 'Wilton Park' for 'as long as Wilton Park remains a British contribution to the formation of an informed international public opinion and to the promotion of greater cooperation in Europe and the West in general . . .'. The will provided that, in the event of Wilton Park ceasing to exist, there should be a gift over to a named Oxford college. The Wilton Park conferences were private, unofficial and not intended to follow any party political line. In fact, the law had never acknowledged Wilton Park to be an entity, rather it was a sort of movement or body of thought. Accordingly the gift was bound to fail outright unless it could be shown to be a gift for a charitable purpose. The judge at first instance decided that the gift must fail for vagueness of purpose. The Attorney-General appealed.

The Court of Appeal held that because Wilton Park was not a legal entity Koeppler's gift must have been intended to be for *purposes* of one sort or another. Those purposes must be taken to be the purposes of the Wilton Park project, namely for the advancement of education through the provision of conferences. It followed that this was a valid charitable gift for the advancement of education. The persons attending the conferences would benefit themselves and pass on the benefits of their education to the general public. So far as the conferences touched upon political matters they were merely genuine attempts objectively to ascertain and disseminate truth. The trust was entitled to a 'benignant construction'. In other words, it should be assumed that the trustees would act in accordance with their duties, and would not use the funds to propagate tendentious political opinions.

8.3.8.1 Student unions

In *Webb v O'Doherty* [1991] *The Times*, 11 February a student union, being an educational charity, was not permitted to make donations to a national student campaign to stop the Gulf War. Following Scott J in *AG v Ross* [1986] 1 WLR 252, Hoffmann J held that discussion of political issues was undoubtedly included within the union's charitable educational purposes, but:

> There is . . . a clear distinction between the discussion of political matters, or the acquisition of information which may have a political content, and a campaign on a political issue. There is no doubt that campaigning, in the sense of seeking to influence public opinion on political matters, is not a charitable activity. It is, of course, something which students are, like the rest of the population, perfectly at liberty to do in their private capacities, but it is not a proper object of the expenditure of charitable money.

8.4 The exclusivity requirement

The basic rule is that the purposes of a charitable trust must be exclusively charitable. In the following sections we will consider what 'exclusively' means in this context.

8.4.1 Purposes ancillary to, incidental to, or *de minimis* in comparison with, the charitable purposes

In *Re Coxen* [1948] Ch 747, the testator gave the residue of his estate, some £200,000, to the Court of Aldermen of the City of London upon trust to: (1) spend £100 towards an annual dinner for the aldermen upon their meeting together upon the business of his trust; (2) pay one guinea to each alderman who attended the whole of a committee meeting in connection with the trust; (3) to apply the remainder for the benefit of certain medical charities.

? QUESTION 8.19

Do you think that this was a valid charitable trust?

All the trusts were valid charitable trusts. It was held that the provisions in favour of the aldermen personally were made to ensure the better administration of the main charitable trusts. In any event, even if those provisions had not themselves been charitable, the sums involved were so insignificant in comparison with that part of the fund devoted to the medical charities that the provisions for the benefit of the aldermen personally could be seen as merely ancillary to the principal trust and would take effect on that basis. In cases where the non-charitable allocation was so significant as not to be 'ancillary' the whole trust must fail, unless the non-charitable part could be precisely quantified in which case only that part would fail.

8.4.2 Non-charitable purposes compounded with charitable purposes

In *Re Best* [1904] 2 Ch 354, a bequest of residue was made to such 'charitable and benevolent institutions' as the trustees shall in their discretion determine. The gift was construed to be exclusively charitable. The use of the conjunction 'and' meant that there was no possibility of an institution benefiting which was benevolent but not charitable.

8.4.3 Non-charitable purposes severable from the charitable purposes as a matter of construction

In *Salusbury v Denton* (1857) 3 K & J 529, a testator left a fund to his widow for life and directed that after her death she should leave a part of the fund to certain charities and the remainder to his relatives. The widow died having failed to make the relevant appointments. The Vice-Chancellor, Sir W Page-Wood held that the wording of the trust permitted a severance of the non-charitable from the charitable objects, because the will clearly bound the trustees to apply an unspecified moiety (part) of the estate to charity. In accordance with the maxim *equality is equity* the court applied half of the fund towards the charitable purposes and the other half to the testator's relatives.

8.4.4 Validation under the Charitable Trusts (Validation) Act 1954

A trust provision which could properly be construed as being for exclusively charitable purposes, but which could nevertheless be used for non-charitable purposes, is validated as a charitable trust by s 1 of this Act. However, the Act only applies where the trust provision is contained in an instrument which took effect before 16 December 1952. The effect of the Act on a relevant trust provision is to render it exclusively charitable for the period before the commencement of the Act. For the period after the commencement of the Act any relevant trust provision will be construed as valid only to the extent that it authorized the use of trust property for charitable purposes.

8.4.5 Where non-charitable purposes are alternatives to the charitable purposes

If on a proper construction of the gift it is clear that the non-charitable purposes are alternatives to the charitable purposes, the trust will not be a valid charitable trust. In *Chichester Diocesan Fund and Board of Finance (Incorporated) v Simpson* [1944] AC 341 Caleb Diplock left the residue of his estate on trust 'for such charitable institution or institutions or other charitable or benevolent object or objects as his executors might in their absolute discretion select'. The residue was distributed amongst several charities. After the distribution the testator's statutory next-of-kin claimed that the residuary gift was not a valid charitable bequest because the words 'charitable or benevolent' had rendered the gift uncertain.

The House of Lords held that, upon a true construction of the clause, the conjunction 'or' indicated that 'benevolent' was intended to be an alternative to 'charitable', rather than merely descriptive of it. 'Or' was used in this disposition as it is used in the phrase 'House of Commons or House of Lords' and not as it is used in the phrase 'House of Lords or Upper Chamber'. Accordingly, the gift was void for uncertainty. Though it was surely never as uncertain as Lord Porter's 'explanation' of the law, to quote: 'the word "charitable" to be exegetical of "benevolent", should follow and not precede it. The wording should be "benevolent" or "charitable" meaning "benevolent, i.e., charitable" not charitable or benevolent meaning charitable, i.e., benevolent'.

The decision in that case meant, of course, that the statutory next-of-kin had to try and recover the misapplied property—for that stage of the court proceedings see *Re Diplock* [1948] 1 Ch 465 (18.3.3.3). It may be true to say that if Viscount Simon had held the gift to be charitable, English law would have been denied, in the form of *Re Diplock*, the leading case in the modern law of tracing and restitution.

8.5 The reform of the law of charity

The majority of this chapter has been devoted to the technical legal definition of charity. In *Chichester Diocesan Fund v Simpson* [1944] AC 341 at 353 Lord Wright said: 'I am convinced that the time has come when modern minds imbued with modern ideas should attempt to achieve a clear, workable, and comprehensive definition of what is meant by charitable and its cognate terms, such as benevolent, philanthropic, and the like. This is a task for the legislature.' It is also the task that you were set at the beginning of this chapter. The legislature has so far failed to come up with any usable definition—perhaps you have done better.

EXERCISE 8.6

Review the definition of charity that you wrote down at the beginning of this chapter and look again at the items you ticked in Exercise 8.1. Do you still agree with your choices? How far does the legal concept of charity differ from your own?

8.5.1 The Charities Bill 2004 (the new Charities Act)

The government published a Charities Bill in May 2004 but a lack of parliamentary time meant that the Bill did not become law before the 2005 general election, and it is unlikely to become law before the end of 2005 at the earliest. At the time of writing the most recent development was a formal reading in the House of Lords on 19 November 2005. (To keep track of the Bill's progress see http://bills.ais.co.uk/AC.asp and look out for updates on the OUP Online Resource Centre for this book.) The explanatory notes accompanying the Bill explain that the Bill arose out of a review ('Private Action, Public Benefit') carried out by the Prime Minister's Strategy Unit in September 2002 and the subsequent publication by the government in July 2003 of the document 'Charities and Not-for-Profits: a Modern Legal Framework'. In short, there has recently been much ado in the reform of charity law, but as yet it has been much ado for nothing, and a critical examination of the Charities Bill 2004 suggests that it might be much ado about nothing so far as the definition of charities is concerned. Certainly, the Bill does not offer a statutory definition of charity. Instead it provides a consolidated schedule of charitable objects which does not expand the list of charitable objects much beyond those already recognized by the courts and Charity Commissioners.

The Bill has 77 clauses and nine Schedules and is divided into four Parts. Part 1 deals with the definition of a charity and of charitable purposes, which is our main concern here. Nevertheless, a brief summary of the other parts of the Bill is worthwhile (for links to the full text of the Bill, and explanatory notes, see the Online Resource Centre).

Part 2 deals with the regulation of charities and is divided into 11 Chapters. These cover the objectives, functions and constitution of the Charity Commission, which is established by the Bill as the regulatory body for charities (Chapter 1); the creation of The Charity Appeal Tribunal to hear appeals against some types of decision made by the Charity Commission (Chapter 2); the registration of charities, including more rigorous arrangements for the regulation of 'exempt charities', being charities which, by virtue of the Charities Act 1993, are currently neither registered nor regulated by the Charity Commission (Chapter 3); changes to the rules governing the occasions when charity property will be applied '*cy-près*', and the schemes by which it will be applied (Chapter 4, see 8.6 below); the assistance and supervision of charities by the court and the Charity Commission, including the grant of power to the Commission to give advice and guidance to charity trustees and in an appropriate case to direct charity trustees to take certain actions, even as to the application of charity property, and where appropriate in the course of statutory investigations, conferring power on the Commission to enter premises and take possession of information and documents; there is even power to suspend or remove trustees (Chapter 5); the audit and examination of the accounts of unincorporated charities and the duties of auditors and examiners of those charities (Chapter 6); relaxation of the rule restricting amendments to the memorandum of charitable companies and the audit and examination of their accounts (Chapter 7); the creation of Charitable Incorporated Organizations, a new legal form for charities (Chapter 8); changes to the rules on the remuneration of charity trustees, and the relief of trustees from personal liability for breach of trust or duty and the possibility of waiver of trustees' disqualification (Chapter 9); changes to the rules under which small unincorporated charities may transfer their property to other charities, replace their current charitable purposes with new ones, or modify their constitutional powers or procedures (Chapter 10); the spending of capital endowment funds by charities, and the registration of mergers between charities (Chapter 11).

Part 3 contains three chapters covering, respectively, public charitable collections, fund raising and the power of the Secretary of State (or the National Assembly for Wales) to give financial assistance to charitable, benevolent or philanthropic institutions by way of grants or loans.

Part 4 contains final provisions covering the usual statutory material of consequential amendments, repeals and transitional provisions, interpretation, short title and commencement.

8.5.1.1 Part 1 of the Charities Bill 2004

Part 1 of the Charities Bill concerns the meaning of Charity and Charitable Purposes. 'Charity' is defined (in clause 1(a)) as any institution which is 'established for charitable purposes only'. Charitable purposes are defined in clause 2(1) as being purposes which fall within subclause 2(2) and are for the 'public benefit'. It is 'not to be presumed that a purpose of a particular description is for the public benefit' (clause 3(2)) and the Charity Commission is required to issue guidance (periodically reviewed and revised if necessary) as to the meaning of public benefit (clause 4).

EXERCISE 8.7

Read subclause 2(2) to subclause 2(5) of the Bill (set out next) and underline or highlight the sections which you consider to be significant changes to the current law. For the full text of the bill, see the weblinks in the Online Resource Centre accompanying this book.

(2) A purpose falls within this subsection if it falls within any of the following descriptions of purposes—

(a) the prevention or relief of poverty;

(b) the advancement of education;

(c) the advancement of religion;

(d) the advancement of health or the saving of lives;

(e) the advancement of citizenship or community development;

(f) the advancement of the arts, culture, heritage or science;

(g) the advancement of amateur sport;

(h) the advancement of human rights, conflict resolution or reconciliation or the promotion of religious or racial harmony or equality and diversity;

(i) the advancement of environmental protection or improvement;

(j) the relief of those in need by reason of youth, age, ill-health, disability, financial hardship or other disadvantage;

(k) the advancement of animal welfare;

(l) any other purposes within subsection (4).

(3) In subsection (2)—

(a) in paragraph (c) 'religion' includes—

(i) a religion which involves belief in more than one god; and

(ii) a religion which does not involve belief in a god;

(b) in paragraph (d) 'the advancement of health' includes the prevention or relief of sickness, disease or human suffering;

(c) paragraph (e) includes—

(i) rural or urban regeneration, and

(ii) the promotion of civic responsibility, volunteering, the voluntary sector or the effectiveness or efficiency of charities;

(d) in paragraph (g) 'sport' means sport which involves physical skill and exertion; and

(e) paragraph (j) includes relief given by the provision of accommodation or care to the persons mentioned in that paragraph.

(4) The purposes within this subsection (see subsection (2)(l)) are—

(a) any purposes not within paragraphs (a) to (k) of subsection (2) but recognised as charitable purposes under existing charity law or by virtue of section 1 of the Recreational Charities Act 1958 (c. 17);

(b) any purposes that may reasonably be regarded as analogous to, or within the spirit of, any purposes falling within any of those paragraphs or paragraph (a) above; and

(c) any purposes that may reasonably be regarded as analogous to, or within the spirit of, any purposes which have been recognised under charity law as falling within paragraph (b) above or this paragraph.

(5) Where any of the terms used in any of paragraphs (a) to (k) of subsection (2), or in subsection (3), has a particular meaning under charity law, the term is to be taken as having the same meaning where it appears in that provision.

Arguably the most novel provision in Part 1 of the Bill is clause 2(3) which, *inter alia,* extends the definition of religion to religions not involving belief in God (thereby removing any doubt that Buddhism is a religion for charitable purposes, whilst at the same time raising the hope of religious status for purely humanist belief systems). It also excludes chess and such like from the new charitable category 'amateur sport', since such games do not involve physical skill and exertion. Presumably darts and snooker are excluded for the same reason. Even static rifle and pistol shooting, which are sports with Olympic status, might struggle to meet the requirement of physical exertion.

8.6 *Cy-près*

Where a private trust fails, the property usually results to the settlor or testator's estate (see 16.2.2.1). However, where money has been successfully dedicated to charity, rarely will it result to the settlor or testator's estate in this way. For where a charitable trust cannot be carried out, or is fulfilled leaving a surplus of charitable funds, the doctrine of *cy-près* may enable an application of the funds to charitable purposes of a type 'as near as possible to' those intended by the settlor. (*Cy-près* means 'as near' in Law French.)

Property can only be applied *cy-près* at the direction of the court or the Charity Commissioners, the trustees having a duty under s 13(5) of the Charities Act 1993 to make the appropriate application to court wherever circumstances deem it necessary.

Different considerations apply to the operation of the doctrine according to whether or not the gift fails *ab initio* or at some later date.

8.6.1 Initial failure

Where a gift fails from the outset the *cy-près* doctrine will only save the gift where the donor, in making the gift, had a *general* or *paramount* charitable intent. The question to be asked is: did the donor desire a charitable outcome by whatever means, or was the means specified essential to the donor's intention in making the charitable gift? If the donor's intention is restricted to making a gift for a particular purpose (albeit a charitable purpose) in a particular way, the gift will fail and the subject matter of the gift will result to the donor.

? QUESTION 8.20

In each of the following cases there was an initial failure of the gift. In which of the cases do you think the donor has displayed a general charitable intention in making the gift?

Case 1

A testator left £5,000 'to the rector for the time being of St Thomas' Seminary for the education of priests in the diocese of Westminster'. Reference was made in the gift to the choice of particular candidates. At the date of the will the seminary still existed, but it had ceased to exist at the date of the testator's death (that is, at the effective date of the gift).

Case 2

A testator left money to pay the salary of a school master. He was to teach at a specified school according to a syllabus of the testator's design. In the event the school was never built.

Case 3

A testatrix settled the net residue of her estate on the Royal College of Surgeons as trustee for the charitable purposes of the college. Conditions attaching to the gift excluded women, Jews and Roman Catholics from partaking of a studentship funded by the gift. The college threatened to disclaim the trusteeship unless those conditions were removed from the gift.

Case 4

A testatrix left £200 to the Wisbech Peace Society, Cambridge and £300 to the Peace Society of Belfast. The former had ceased to exist before the date of the testatrix's death, while the latter had never existed at all.

Case 5

A testatrix left gifts to the National Radium Commission, an unincorporated association, and to the National Council for Maternity and Child Welfare, an incorporated company.

How do your conclusions compare with the following?

Case 1

In *Re Rymer* [1895] 1 Ch 19, on the question whether the £5,000 could be applied *cy-près* it was held, instead, that the gift lapsed and resulted to the testator's residuary estate. Chitty J held that this was a gift for the particular seminary, and not a general gift for the education of the priests in the diocese of Westminster. It was plain from the language used, which referred to the saying of masses and the choice of candidates, that the choice of the seminary was not mere 'machinery' for the carrying out of a general charitable intent, but went to the very substance of the testator's gift.

Case 2

In *Re Wilson* [1913] 1 Ch 314, it was held that there was an initial failure but that the doctrine of *cy-près* would not apply to save the gift because the fine details of the testator's gift were not consistent with a general charitable intent.

Case 3

In *Re Lysaght* [1966] 1 Ch 191, the court removed the conditions, stating that the gift would otherwise fail. The court was able to find (perhaps artificially) a general charitable intention by making these 'peripheral' alterations to the donor's expressed intentions.

Case 4

In *Re Harwood* [1936] Ch 285, it was held that the gift of £200 to the Wisbech Peace Society failed and would not be applied *cy-près* as the testatrix had lacked a general charitable intention in making that gift. As regards the gift of £300, it was held that the testatrix had shown a general charitable intention to benefit any society connected with Belfast which existed for the promotion of peace. The gift of £300 was applied *cy-près*.

Case 5

In *Re Finger's WT* [1972] 1 Ch 286, it was held that the gift to the former institution was valid as a trust for general charitable purposes, whereas the gift to the company was *prima facie* void as being for a particular legal person which had ceased to exist (see *Re Harwood* above). However, Goff J thought the present case to be a special one and distinguished *Re Harwood* on the basis that here the major part of the estate, including the residue, had been specifically devoted to charitable purposes. Accordingly, the gift to the corporation was validated by the operation of the *cy-près* doctrine.

? QUESTION 8.21

Do you think that there was an initial failure of the following gift?

A testatrix left £200 to 'Mrs Bailey's Charity, Rotherhithe'. The charity, founded in 1756 for the benefit of poor widows of Rotherhithe, had, by the date of the gift, been amalgamated in 1905 with other charities in the area of Rotherhithe (see *Re Faraker* [1912] 2 Ch 488).

In this case the Court of Appeal held that the amalgamated charities would be entitled to the legacy. However there had been no initial failure, and this was not a case for the application of the doctrine of *cy-près*. The amalgamated charities were entitled to receive the legacy because the original charity continued to exist in a slightly modified form.

8.6.2 The modern law of *cy-près*

Prior to the Charities Act of 1960 the *cy-près* doctrine would only be applied where the charitable objects of the trust were *impossible* or *impracticable* to fulfil. Section 13 of the 1960 Act relaxed these limitations on the application of *cy-près*. That law is now consolidated in s 13 of the Charities Act 1993. Before proceeding it is absolutely crucial to note that s 13 does not affect the need to show a general or paramount charitable intent before the doctrine of *cy-près* will apply in cases of initial failure (s 13(2)) (see 8.6.1). This was confirmed by the Court of Appeal in *Varsani v Jesani* [1999] Ch 219.

? EXERCISE 8.8

Examine the Charities Act 1993, s 13, set out next. In what circumstances will the doctrine of *cy-près* apply today?

Charities Act 1993, s 13

(1) Subject to subsection (2) below, the circumstances in which the original purposes of a charitable gift can be altered to allow the property given or part of it to be applied cy près shall be as follows—
 (a) where the original purposes, in whole or in part—
  (i) have been as far as may be fulfilled; or
  (ii) cannot be carried out, or not according to the directions and to the spirit of the gift; or
 (b) where the original purposes provide a use for part only of the property available by virtue of the gift; or
 (c) where the property available by virtue of the gift and other property applicable for similar purposes can be more effectively used in conjunction, and to that end can suitably, regard being had to the spirit of the gift, be made applicable to common purposes; or
 (d) where the original purposes were laid down by reference to an area which then was but has since ceased to be a unit for some other purpose, or by reference to a class of persons or to an area which has for any reason since ceased to be suitable, regard being had to the spirit of the gift, or to be practical in administering the gift; or
 (e) where the original purposes, in whole or in part, have, since they were laid down,—
  (i) been adequately provided for by other means; or
  (ii) ceased, as being useless or harmful to the community or for other reasons, to be in law charitable; or
  (iii) ceased in any other way to provide a suitable and effective method of using the property available by virtue of the gift, regard being had to the spirit of the gift.

(2) Subsection (1) above shall not affect the conditions which must be satisfied in order that property given for charitable purposes may be applied cy-près except in so far as those conditions require a failure of the original purposes.

(3) [. . .]

(4) [. . .]

(5) It is hereby declared that a trust for charitable purposes places a trustee under a duty, where the case permits and requires the property or some part of it to be applied cy-près, to secure its effective use for charity by taking steps to enable it to be so applied.

The circumstances in which the original purposes of a charitable gift can be altered to allow the property given or part of it to be applied *cy-près* are as follows:

1. *Impossibility*: where the original purposes, in whole or in part, have been as far as may be fulfilled (s 13(1)(a)(i)) or cannot be carried out, or cannot be carried out in accordance with the letter and spirit of the gift (s 13(1)(a)(ii)).
2. *Surplus property*: where the original purposes provide a use for part only of the property available by virtue of the gift (s 13(1)(b)).
3. *Common investment*: where the property available by virtue of the gift and other property applicable for similar purposes can be more effectively used in conjunction for common purposes, regard being had to the spirit of the gift (s 13(1)(c)).
4. *Unsuitability or impracticality of benefiting persons or area*: where the original purposes were laid down by reference to a class of persons or to an area which has for any reason ceased to be suitable (regard being had to the spirit of the gift) or to be practical (s 13(1)(d)).
5. *Unsuitability and ineffectiveness*: where the original purposes, in whole or in part, have, since they were laid down, been adequately provided for by other means (s 13(1)(e)(i)) or ceased, as being useless or harmful to the community or for other reasons, to be in law charitable (s 13(1)(e)(ii)) or ceased in any other way to provide a suitable and effective method of using the property available by virtue of the gift, regard being had to the spirit of the gift (s 13(1)(e)(iii)).

The Charity Commissioners referred to some of the uses to which s 13(1)(e) had been put in para 43 of their Annual Report for 1970:

> we have made schemes for a number of charities established for the repair of roads and bridges, substituting for those purposes other general purposes for the benefit of local inhabitants which could include, for instance, the promotion of the arts, the provision of seats and shelters, the preservation of old buildings, or the improvement of local amenities.

8.6.3 Subsequent failure

In *National Anti-Vivisection Society v IRC* Lord Simonds stated *obiter* that the concept of what is charitable may change from age to age, and that a trust which was once held to be charitable might one day cease to be so, in which case the trust fund should be applied *cy-près*.

The crucial point to grasp is that in cases of subsequent impossibility the property can be applied *cy-près* without the need to show a general or paramount charitable intention.

In *Re King* [1923] 1 Ch 243 the testatrix left the residue of her estate to provide for the erection, to the memory of the testatrix and her relations, of a stained glass window in a parish church. This was held to be a valid charitable trust of the whole fund, so that any surplus remaining after the erection of the stained glass window should be applied *cy-près*, with the consent of the Attorney-General, towards the provision of a further stained glass window or windows in the same church. Romer J stated (at p 246): 'in the case of a legacy to a charitable institution that exists at the death of the testator, but ceases to exist after his death and before the legacy is paid over, the legacy is applied *cy-près*, even in the absence of a general charitable intention: see *Re Slevin* [1891] 2 Ch 236'. This example brings us to our next topic.

8.6.4 The disposal of surplus donations

Prior to the Charities Act 1960 *cy-près* would only apply to cases of this type where the donors had shown a general or paramount charitable intent, the practical (or impractical) consequence of this being that all other surplus donations resulted to the donors, many of whom (being anonymous) could not be found. In response to this unsatisfactory state of affairs, s 14 of the Charities Act 1993 provided that surplus monies donated to collecting boxes, raffles, entertainments and so on, may be applied *cy-près* without having to obtain the donors' consent. As regards other donations, the trustees must advertise and take steps to find the donors and, if they are found, return the donation to them or obtain in writing a waiver of the donors' claims to the donation.

8.6.5 Reform of *cy-près*

The Charities Bill 2004 (see 8.5.1 above) contains provisions for the reform of *cy-près*. Clause 15 of the Bill substitutes the new phrase 'appropriate considerations' for the phrase 'spirit of the gift' currently appearing in s 13 of the 1993 Act. The 'appropriate considerations' are defined in the Bill as the spirit of the gift concerned *and*, significantly, 'the social and economic circumstances prevailing at the time of the proposed alteration of the original purposes'. Clause 16 of the Bill extends to the Commission the courts' 1993 Act power to apply *cy-près* gifts by unknown or disclaiming donors.

Clause 17 of the Bill makes amendments to s 14 of the 1993 Act in relation to the application *cy-près* of gifts made in response to certain solicitations, and clauses 18 and 19 of the Bill make further minor amendments to the operation of *cy-près* schemes under s 14 of the 1993 Act. Those reforms lie outside the scope of the present text, but their full text can be accessed via the web-links in the Online Resource Centre accompanying this book.

CHAPTER SUMMARY

- We have distinguished the legal notion of charity from the common notion that charity connotes altruism and benevolence. We have seen that a purpose is only charitable in law when it is directly beneficial to the public or (being a trust for the relief of poverty) is indirectly beneficial to the public. A charitable purpose must also fall within the spirit of the purposes listed in the preamble to the Charitable Uses Act 1601, the main examples have been grouped under four heads:
  - trusts for the relief of poverty
  - trusts for the advancement of education
  - trusts for the advancement of religion and
  - trusts for other purposes beneficial to the community, not falling under any of the preceding heads.
- When the Charities Act 2004 becomes law, charitable purposes will be grouped under many more heads:
  - the prevention or relief of poverty

  - the advancement of education
  - the advancement of religion (including a religion which involves belief in more than one god and a religion which does not involve belief in a god)
  - the advancement of health or the saving of lives (including the prevention or relief of sickness, disease or human suffering)
  - the advancement of citizenship or community development (including rural or urban regeneration and the promotion of civic responsibility, volunteering, the voluntary sector or the effectiveness or efficiency of charities)
  - the advancement of the arts, culture, heritage or science
  - the advancement of amateur sport involving physical skill and exertion
  - the advancement of human rights, conflict resolution or reconciliation or the promotion of religious or racial harmony or equality and diversity
  - the advancement of environmental protection or improvement in the relief of those in need by reason of youth, age, ill-health, disability, financial hardship or other disadvantage (including relief given by the provision of accommodation or care to such persons)
  - the advancement of animal welfare
  - any additional purpose recognized as charitable under the existing charity law or by virtue of section 1 of the Recreational Charities Act 1958
  - any purposes that may reasonably be regarded as analogous to, or within the spirit of, any of the purposes listed above.
- The fact that charitable trusts are beneficial to the public explains the many privileges they enjoy. These include:
  - exemption from the requirement that a trust must have an ascertainable object
  - exemption from the beneficiary principle (that is, the usual requirement that a trust must have a beneficiary interested in enforcing the trust)
  - exemption from the rule against inalienability of capital (6.5)
  - a wide range of fiscal (tax) exemptions and privileges.
- Where a charitable trust cannot be carried out, or is fulfilled leaving a surplus of charitable funds, the doctrine of *cy-près* may enable an application of the funds to charitable purposes of a type 'as near as possible to' those intended by the settlor. We have seen that different considerations apply to the operation of the doctrine according to whether or not the gift fails *ab initio* or at some later date.

In this chapter we have been considering trusts for charitable purposes. The word *purpose* immediately puts one in mind of motive and intentions. In fact, charities are defined at law primarily according to the outcomes they yield, in terms of public benefit, rather than the motives of the founder. We have seen that mere goodwill (benevolence) is not a charitable purpose in law. Only where the outcomes cannot be achieved, or having been achieved, yield a surplus of funds, is the matter determined by direct reference to the intentions of the founder of the charity. This is achieved by means of the doctrine of *cy-près*.

SUMMATIVE ASSESSMENT EXERCISE

online resource centre

Reginald died recently. Consider which of the following provisions in his will might be a valid charitable legacy.

(a) £100,000 to my trustees on trust to provide temporary shelter for Old Etonians who have fallen on hard times. Preference to be given to my old class mates.
(b) £10,000 to my trustees to support research into the likely consequences for political and public life of a legal ban on the Society of Free and Accepted Masons.
(c) £5,000 to my trustees to promote the playing of card games by deprived youth as an alternative to watching television.
(d) £5,000 to my psychotherapist, Doctor F Rreud, to buy a new couch for the greater comfort of his many grateful patients.

FURTHER READING

Cabinet Office Strategy Unit, 'Private Action, Public Benefit: A Review of Charities and the Wider Not-For-Profit Sector' http:// www.strategy-unit.gov.uk/2002/charity/report/index.htm.

Charity Commission, Decision of the Charity Commissioners for England & Wales: Application for Registration as a Charity by the Church of Scientology (England and Wales) 17 Nov 1999.

Edge, P, 'Charitable Status for the Advancement of Religion: An Abolitionist's View' (1995–6) 3 Charity Law and Practice Review 29–35.

Hill, M, 'Judicial Approaches to Religious Disputes' in R O'Dair and A Lewis (eds) *Current Legal Issues: Law and Religion* (Oxford: OUP, 2001) 409.

Keeton, G W, *Modern Law of Charities*, (4th edn) (Chichester: Barry Rose, 1992).

Law Commission, 'Charities: A Framework for the Future' Cm 694 (1989).

Luxton, P, *The Law of Charities* (Oxford: OUP, 2001).

National Council for Voluntary Organizations, 'For the public benefit?: A Consultation Document on Charity Law Reform' (2001).

Radcliffe Commission on Taxation Cmnd 9474 (1955).

Report of the Goodman Committee, *Charity Law and Voluntary Organizations* (1976).

Warburton, J, and Morris, D, *Tudor on Charities*, (8th edn) (London: Sweet & Maxwell, 1995).

Warburton, J, 'Charitable Trusts—Unique' (1999) Conv 20.

Watt, G, 'Giving unto Caesar: Rationality, Reciprocity and Legal Recognition of Religion' in R O'Dair and A Lewis (eds) *Current Legal Issues: Law and Religion*, (Oxford: OUP, 2001) 45.

9 Variation of trusts

OBJECTIVES

By the end of this chapter you should be able to:

1 Explain the possible reasons for varying the terms of a trust

2 Detail the numerous modes of varying trusts

3 Distinguish administrative variations from variations in beneficial interests

4 Manage an application to the court for a variation under the Variation of Trusts Act 1958

5 Advise as to when a variation will be for the benefit of the beneficiaries

6 Judge the extent to which courts take the settlor's intentions into account when considering a variation

9.1 Introduction

> A court will not re-write a trust.
>
> *Re Downshire Settled Estates* [1953] Ch 218 at 248, *per* Lord Evershed MR

This quote demonstrates what Professor Harris called the court's general 'fidelity' to the settlor's intentions. Nevertheless, the fact cannot be escaped (as Professor Harris demonstrated in his book *Variation of Trusts* (1975)) that the court must weigh in the balance the equitable property rights of the persons beneficially entitled under the trust against the wishes of the person who set up the trust in the first place. The latter may, of course, be already dead.

In most reported cases the motive for seeking a variation is to achieve a financial benefit for the beneficiaries, and in the majority of these cases the financial benefit is a fiscal one. Tax laws change every year. If the terms and structures of trusts were fixed once and for all by the settlor, trusts would be 'sitting ducks' for the guns of the Inland Revenue. The court's power to vary trusts is a valuable means of dodging the shot!

To the extent that variation of trusts can be seen to be a tax-avoidance measure we must question the assumption that variation necessarily conflicts with the settlor's intentions. In most trusts the settlor would surely wish their trust to adapt positively to changes in fiscal regulation.

To the extent that the court's jurisdiction to vary trusts is a tax-avoidance facility, it is a facility which reduces the amount of revenue available to the Treasury. It might be asked whether the jurisdiction to vary trusts is giving the average taxpayer value for their money. How many of them will ever need to vary a trust? There is nothing illegal in arranging one's affairs so as to avoid attracting a tax liability (although it is illegal to evade a tax liability once it has arisen), but even though tax avoidance is not illegal, is it something that the courts should actively assist in? The courts have turned a blind eye to this question and have been content to make the best interests of the beneficiary their 'moral' imperative. This contrasts sharply with the courts' insistence upon a guarantee of public benefit prior to any grant of fiscal privilege through the recognition of a trust's charitable status.

However, not every variation is made to achieve tax advantages. Sometimes there is undoubtedly a public interest in the variation of a trust, as where a settlor has included a clause in the trust which requires or invites racial or religious prejudice. We shall consider some cases in this category later.

9.2 Modes of varying trusts

We will discover in the following sections that some variations involve a variation of the beneficial interests under the trust, whereas others involve a variation in the way in which the trust is administered.

9.2.1 The rule in *Saunders v Vautier*

According to the rule in *Saunders v Vautier* (1841) 10 LJ Ch 354 an adult beneficiary who is solely entitled to the trust property may deal with his equitable interest as he wishes. The trustee will hold the trust property on what is called a 'bare trust' for the sole beneficiary. Beyond this and perhaps more remarkable, is the aspect of the rule which applies where there are several beneficiaries. If they are all *sui juris* (adult and of sound mind) and together absolutely entitled to the trust property, they may unanimously agree to terminate the trust and may demand that the trust property be handed over to them. There are, however, some limitations on the application of the rule designed to protect trustee discretions. The rule was considered in detail in *Stephenson (Inspector of Taxes) v Barclays Bank Trust Co Ltd* [1975] 1 All ER 625. There Walton J stated some 'elementary principles' of the application of the rule: (1) where persons, being *sui juris*, between them hold the entirety of the beneficial interest under a trust, they can direct the trustees as to how to deal with the trust property; (2) but they cannot thereby override the existing trusts and at the same time keep them in existence; (3) so, for instance, they cannot require the current trustees to make particular investments; (4) nor can they deny the trustees' basic right to be indemnified out of the trust fund for any expenses incurred by them in carrying out the trust.

In *Saunders v Vautier* itself the testator left property on trust for Vautier with a direction that interest should be accumulated until he reached 25. On reaching 25, he was to become entitled to claim the capital and all the accumulated income. When Vautier reached the age of majority (21 in those days) he claimed the whole of the fund.

? QUESTION 9.1

Can you explain why Vautier's action succeeded?

The then Master of the Rolls and the then Vice-Chancellor decided that Vautier's interest had vested absolutely upon his attaining majority, and he was entitled to claim the property now, notwithstanding the settlor's obvious intention that Vautier's enjoyment of the property should be postponed until he reached the age of 25.

This is an extreme instance of the variation of a trust, and it is in many ways the conceptual precedent for the Variation of Trusts Act 1958 (see 9.3). Having said that, the rule in *Saunders v Vautier* is concerned more with revocation than with variation. *Saunders v Vautier* is *not* authority for allowing the adult beneficiaries to instruct the trustees to act as they are told. So, under the rule, the beneficiaries are not permitted to direct the trustees to make investments chosen by the beneficiaries. Either the beneficiaries keep the old trusts 'on foot', in which case they must not interfere with the trustees' management of the trust, or the beneficiaries must bring the old trust to an end and divide the trust property between them, or resettle it on new trusts. It is the latter possibility that illustrates how the rule in *Saunders v Vautier* might be utilized to effect a genuine variation of a trust, as opposed to a mere revocation of it. A genuine variation might also be achieved if the beneficiaries being *sui juris* and between them absolutely entitled to the fund wish to vary the terms of the trust and the trustees agree to act on the trusts in their varied form.

9.2.2 Trustee Act 1925, s 57

Trustee Act 1925

57. Power of court to authorise dealings with trust property

(1) Where in the management or administration of any property vested in trustees, any sale, lease, mortgage, surrender, release, or other disposition, or any purchase, investment, acquisition, expenditure, or other transaction, is in the opinion of the court expedient, but the same cannot be effected by reason of the absence of any power for that purpose vested in the trustees by the trust instrument, if any, or by law, the court may by order confer upon the trustees, either generally or in any particular instance, the necessary power for the purpose, on such terms, and subject to such provisions and conditions, if any, as the court may think fit and may direct in what manner any money authorised to be expended, and the costs of any transaction, are to be paid or borne as between capital and income.

(2) The court may, from time to time, rescind or vary any order made under this section, or may make any new or further order.

(3) An application to the court under this section may be made by the trustees, or by any of them, or by any person beneficially interested under the trust.

(4) This section does not apply to trustees of a settlement for the purposes of the Settled Land Act 1925.

EXERCISE 9.1

Imagine a trust under which 10 beneficiaries are entitled to an equal share in the fund. Could the Trustee Act 1925, s 57 be used to vary the trust so as to permit an arrangement which (to achieve a tax saving for every beneficiary) would remove the requirement of equal division?

No, it could not. Section 57 permits variations in the way that the trust is managed, it does not authorize the remoulding of the beneficial interests under the trust. In the words of the section, it allows the court to authorize the trustees to carry out any transaction 'in the management or administration' of the trust property where such transaction is 'expedient'. It was suggested in *Re Downshire SE* [1952] 2 All ER 603 that the section would permit 'specific dealings' with the trust property, which the court might not otherwise be authorized to permit under its inherent jurisdiction (see 9.2.5). So, for example, variation of investment powers should normally be sought under this section (*Anker-Petersen v Anker-Petersen* (1991) 16 LS Gaz 32).

According to *Re Mair* [1935] Ch 562, s 57 operates by inserting an 'overriding power' in the trust instrument so as to permit the trustees to act in accordance with the variation ordered by the court. It might, therefore, be useful in relation to trusts of land where the settlor has removed the trustees' powers of disposition under s 8(1) of the Trusts of Land etc. Act 1996. (See G Watt, 'Escaping Section 8(1) Provisions in "New Style" Trusts of Land' [1997] 61 Conv 263.)

9.2.3 Trustee Act 1925, s 53

Under this section the trust may be varied for the maintenance, education or benefit of an infant beneficiary. The variation is effected by making a conveyance on sale of the beneficiary's interest. The capital proceeds of the sale and income made thereon are then 'applied' for the maintenance of the infant. This power is most useful where the beneficiary has an interest only in capital under the trust, and in other situations where the trustees will not have the usual power to maintain the beneficiary (see **Chapter 13**).

9.2.4 Variation of Trusts Act 1958

This is discussed at 9.3.

9.2.5 Variation under the court's inherent jurisdiction

The court has always had an inherent jurisdiction to vary the manner in which a trust is administered, although the courts prefer that such variations be sought under s 57 wherever appropriate. This inherent jurisdiction of the courts is limited to cases of 'salvage' and 'emergency'. What do these terms mean?

'Salvage' cases almost exclusively involve infants. In such cases the administration of the trust may be varied in the interests of the infant beneficiary, but only in situations of absolute necessity. An example might be where one part of the property is mortgaged to raise monies to prevent another part of the property from becoming valueless—as where Greenacre is mortgaged to prevent Green Mansion from falling down.

Trusts may be varied in situations of 'emergency' without having to show that the variation is absolutely necessary. 'Emergency' refers to situations which the settlor had not foreseen. A variation under this heading can therefore be made entirely in keeping with the settlor's presumed intention for the trust.

EXERCISE 9.2

Read the case of *Re New* [1901] 2 Ch 534, set out next. This case has been described as the 'high watermark' of this jurisdiction. Why was it necessary to resort to the court's inherent jurisdiction in that case? Why was the case called the 'high watermark'?

Re New [1901] 2 Ch 534, Chancery Division

The trustees wished to approve a proposal to reorganise a limited company in which the trust owned shares, but they had no power to do so. The beneficiaries could not approve the reorganisation because they were not all *sui juris*, but the reorganisation would certainly have been to their benefit. Accordingly the trustees applied to the court for a variation under the court's inherent jurisdiction. It was held that the court could approve the variation under its inherent jurisdiction to alter the administration of a trust in cases of 'emergency', where circumstances have arisen which the settlor of the trust had not foreseen and had not made provision for. Such variations would be approved only where the variation was desirable in the best interests of the beneficiaries.

Romer LJ:

> As a rule, the Court has no jurisdiction to give, and will not give, its sanction to the performance by trustees of acts with reference to the trust estate which are not, on the face of the instrument creating the trust, authorised by its terms. The cases of *In re Crawshay WN* (1888) 246, decided by North J, and *In re Morrison* [1901] 1 Ch 701, decided by Buckley J, are instances where the Court was asked to sanction steps to be taken by trustees which it thought unjustifiable, and which it declared it had no jurisdiction to authorise. But in the management of a trust estate, and especially where that estate consists of a business or shares in a mercantile company, it not infrequently happens that some peculiar state of circumstances arises for which provision is not expressly made by the trust instrument, and which renders it most desirable, and it may be even essential, for the benefit of the estate and in the interest of all the cestuis que trust, that certain acts should be done by the trustees which in ordinary circumstances they would have no power to do. In a case of this kind, which may reasonably be supposed to be one not foreseen or anticipated by the author of the trust, where the trustees are embarrassed by the emergency that has arisen and the duty cast upon them to do what is best for the estate, and the consent of all the beneficiaries cannot be obtained by reason of some of them not being sui juris or in existence, then it may be right for the Court, and the Court in a proper case would have jurisdiction, to sanction on behalf of all concerned such acts on behalf of the trustees as we have above referred to . . .
>
> Of course, the jurisdiction is one to be exercised with great caution, and the Court will take care not to strain its powers. It is impossible, and no attempt ought to be made, to state or define all the circumstances under which, or the extent to which, the Court will exercise the jurisdiction; but it need scarcely be said that the Court will not be justified in sanctioning every act desired by trustees and beneficiaries merely because it may appear beneficial to the estate; and certainly the Court will not be disposed to sanction transactions of a speculative or risky character. But each case brought before the Court must be considered and dealt with according to its special circumstances.

The case was referred to as the high watermark because there were suggestions in the judgment that the court could vary the administration of the trust under its inherent jurisdiction in cases where the variation would be desirable, even if it was not in fact essential. However, Romer LJ did state that the court will not be justified in sanctioning every act desired by the trustees and beneficiaries 'merely because it may appear beneficial to the estate'.

9.2.6 Compromise of disputes—a dubious jurisdiction to 'vary' trusts

It is a truism to say that courts have an inherent jurisdiction to compromise disputes. If a dispute arises as to the proper construction to be given to the words of a trust instrument, it goes without saying that the courts are the most expert arbiters of it. In the past, beneficiaries would seek to vary the terms of their trusts by recourse to the court's inherent jurisdiction to resolve disputes in relation to the meaning of trusts. This procedure became a popular way to effect a variation of the beneficial interests under the trust, in relation to variations which could otherwise be achieved only by bringing the trust to an end under the rule in *Saunders v Vautier*. However, the courts began to consider cases where there was no real dispute at all. The 'disputing' parties would agree a 'compromise' in terms favourable to the beneficiaries, and the court would sanction the sham compromise by court order. This practice continued until it was brought to an end by the House of Lords in the case of *Chapman v Chapman* [1954] AC 429 (Lord Cohen dissenting) after which it was decided that the courts would be able to vary trusts under this jurisdiction only in cases of genuine dispute.

Chapman v Chapman was reported in 1954, and it is no coincidence that Parliament enacted the Variation of Trusts Act in 1958. After *Chapman v Chapman* the Law Reform Committee noted that the House of Lords had deprived the courts of a very flexible and, as they saw it, necessary jurisdiction to vary trusts. It approved Lord Cohen's view that a compromise did involve a genuine variation. The Variation of Trusts Act 1958 was passed in response to the recommendations of the Law Reform Committee.

9.2.7 Matrimonial jurisdiction

Section 24 of the Matrimonial Causes Act 1973 grants to the courts a wide power to vary the beneficial interests under trusts to achieve a fair distribution of property upon the pronouncement of a decree of divorce or nullity of marriage. In this context tax avoidance will not be a factor in determining the exercise of the court's discretion (*Thomson v Thomson and Whitmee* [1956] P 384).

9.2.8 Mental Health Act jurisdiction

Section 96(3) of the Mental Health Act 1983 grants the Court of Protection the jurisdiction to place into trusts the property of a person of unsound mind. These trusts can be varied later if there is a significant change of circumstances, for example, if the patient ceases to be of unsound mind.

9.2.9 Inherent jurisdiction to maintain

Even where a trust orders that income should be accumulated, which would normally be taken as evidence of the settlor's intention to exclude the statutory power to maintain beneficiaries out of that income, the court has an inherent jurisdiction to maintain beneficiaries where there are no other monies out of which they could be maintained (see *Re Walker* [1901] 1 Ch 879).

The statutory power of maintenance is restricted to infant beneficiaries (see **Chapter 13**) but the court's inherent jurisdiction to maintain is not so limited. Nor is this jurisdiction restricted to cases of absolute necessity or emergency. The assumption is that the settlor would not have intended that the beneficiaries should want for life's basic necessities.

9.2.10 Rectification of wills

According to the Administration of Justice Act 1982, s 20(1), if a court is satisfied that a will is so expressed that it fails to carry out the testator's intentions, in consequence of a clerical error or a failure to understand his instructions, it may order that the will may be rectified so as to carry out his intentions. The meaning of 'clerical error' was considered in *Re Segelman (deceased)* [1996] 2 WLR 173. The error in question was solicitor's failure to remove an inconsistency between the drafting of a will and a schedule to it. The test applied by Chadwick J was whether or not the solicitor had 'applied his mind to the significance and effect of the words used. If he had not it will be clerical error. If he had, the will must stand'. Chadwick J held that the solicitor had committed an error through mere inadvertence, and the will should therefore be rectified.

9.3 Variation of Trusts Act 1958

The Variation of Trusts Act 1958 permits the remoulding of beneficial interests under trusts as well as permitting incidental changes to the administration of the trust. Section 57 of the Trustee Act 1925 (9.2.2) is restricted to variations in the management of the trust, and such variations do not depend upon the consent of the beneficiaries. The Variation of Trusts Act 1958, on the other hand, has, as its theoretical basis, the consent of the beneficiaries. Variations will not be approved under the Act unless all the beneficiaries have consented to the variation. If all the beneficiaries are *sui juris* and between them absolutely entitled to the trust fund they can take advantage of the rule in *Saunders v Vautier* (see 9.2.1). Other beneficiaries such as infants and the unborn cannot take advantage of that rule. The essence of the 1958 Act is that it authorizes the Chancery Division of the High Court to approve, on behalf of beneficiaries in these (and certain other) categories, an arrangement varying or revoking all or any of the trust. The consents of beneficiaries who do not fall within the relevant categories must be given by them personally (that is, cannot be given by the court) if the proposed arrangement is to go ahead.

You should note that the Act merely authorizes the court to approve the arrangement, the court is never obliged to vary a trust under the Act. In the words of s 1, the 'court may *if it thinks fit* by order approve . . . any arrangement (by whomsoever proposed, and whether or not there is any other person beneficially interested who is capable of assenting thereto) varying or revoking all or any of the trusts, or enlarging the powers of the trustees of managing or administering any of the property subject to the trusts' (emphasis added).

Variation of Trusts Act 1958

1. Jurisdiction of courts to vary trusts

(1) Where property, whether real or personal, is held on trusts arising, whether before or after the passing of this Act, under any will, settlement or other disposition, the court may if it thinks fit by order approve on behalf of—

(a) any person having, directly or indirectly, an interest, whether vested or contingent, under the trusts who by reason of infancy or other incapacity is incapable of assenting, or

(b) any person (whether ascertained or not) who may become entitled, directly or indirectly, to an interest under the trusts as being at a future date or on the happening of a future event a person of any specified description or a member of any specified class of persons, so however that this paragraph shall not include any person who would be of that description, or a member of that class, as the case may be, if the said date had fallen or the said event had happened at the date of the application to the court, or

(c) any person unborn, or

(d) any person in respect of any discretionary interest of his under protective trusts where the interest of the principal beneficiary has not failed or determined, any arrangement (by whomsoever proposed, and whether or not there is any other person beneficially interested who is capable of assenting thereto) varying or revoking all or any of the trusts, or enlarging the powers of the trustees of managing or administering any of the property subject to the trusts:

Provided that except by virtue of paragraph (d) of this subsection the court shall not approve an arrangement on behalf of any person unless the carrying out thereof would be for the benefit of that person.

The reference in s 1 to powers of 'administering' trust property does not supersede Trustee Act 1925, s 57. Where all that is being requested is an administrative variation an order should still be sought by making an application under s 57.

For judicial consideration of the ideological underpinning of the 1958 Act see *Goulding v James* [1997] 2 All ER 239 (9.6).

9.3.1 Applications under the Act—who should be the parties?

Section 1 states that the court has authority to approve an arrangement 'by whomsoever proposed'. In fact, applications should be made by adult beneficiaries under the trust. According to *Re Druce's ST* [1962] 1 WLR 363 the trustees should not make the application themselves unless, first, they believe that the variation would be for the benefit of the beneficiaries and, secondly, that there is no adult beneficiary willing to make the application for a variation. In fact, far from being claimants under the application, the trustees should be joined as defendants, for it is they who have the fiduciary duty to protect the interests of all the beneficiaries under the trust and they who should raise objections if the proposed variation appears to benefit some but not all of the beneficiaries. If the beneficiaries are not unanimous in making the application the non-claimant beneficiaries should be joined as additional defendants. The settlor should be joined as a defendant where variation of an *inter vivos* trust is proposed and the settlor is still alive. The form of the application is an originating summons exhibiting a draft scheme of arrangement.

9.3.2 How does the variation occur?

Megarry J stated in *Re Holt's Settlement* [1969] 1 Ch 100 that:

> Any variation owes its authority not to anything in the initial settlement but to the statute and the consent of the adults coming, as it were, *ab extra*. This certainly seems to be so in any case not within the Act where a variation or resettlement is made under the doctrine of *Saunders v Vautier*... by all the adults joining together, and I cannot see any real difference in principle in a case where the court exercises its jurisdiction on behalf of the infants under the Act of 1958.

On the further question, whether the variation involved a disposition of equitable interests by the beneficiaries who had consented to the variation, the learned judge decided that it did. However, he yielded reluctantly to counsel's submission that this disposition should be treated as an exception to the Law of Property Act 1925, s 53(1)(c) and need not be formalized by signed writing. Thus, the beneficiaries were saved from a liability to stamp duty which then attached to dispositions of equitable interests by signed writing. This appears to be yet another instance of the courts granting the beneficiaries a fiscal advantage in this area. Megarry J was persuaded to recognize this exception to s 53(1)(c) because it accorded with the practice which had been accepted by the Inland Revenue and by the courts for many years 'in some thousands of cases'.

9.3.3 Consents given by the court

We have seen that a variation under the Act will be approved only if all the beneficiaries give their consent to it. We have also noted that the court may itself consent on behalf of certain beneficiaries, but that all other beneficiaries must give their own consent.

EXERCISE 9.3

As a preliminary exercise read s 1 of the Variation of Trusts Act 1958 set out above. You will note that the court consents on behalf of four different classes of person, defined in paras (a), (b), (c) and (d), respectively, of s 1(1). Try to summarize each of the class definitions as succinctly as you can. Having formulated your own definitions, see how they compare to the explanations given in the following sections.

9.3.3.1 Persons under legal disability (s 1(1)(a))

This class includes minors (infants) and any other persons who are incapable of assenting to the arrangement varying the trusts. Included in this category would be persons of unsound mind and persons suffering from a severe (and relevant) physical disability.

? QUESTION 9.2

As you will already be aware a minor is defined as being any person under the age of 18. Can there be any justification for allowing the courts to give consent on behalf of a 17-year-old?

It may seem rather surprising that the consent of persons aged, say, 16 and 17 should be treated in the same manner as the consent of persons of unsound mind. However, in practice the court will take into account the expressed wishes of persons approaching majority, although their lack of actual consent is, at the end of the day, not a conclusive consideration. An arrangement will be approved if the court believes that it is in the interest of the infant beneficiary, even if the infant does not share that view. If the infant is still under parental influence there is the very real possibility that the parents would try to influence the exercise of their child's consent in order to achieve their own ends. By giving the court the power to consent on the infant's behalf this potential abuse is prevented to some degree.

9.3.3.2 Persons with mere expectations (s 1(1)(b))

This class of persons on whose behalf the court may give consent is by far the most difficult to comprehend. However, a series of cases has helped to isolate those persons who do and those persons who do not fall within this class. Section 1(1)(b) is transcribed below with certain key words highlighted. These key words have received particular attention in those cases where the courts have considered s 1(1)(b).

According to s 1(1)(b) the court may, if it thinks fit, approve a variation on behalf of:

> any person (whether ascertained or not) who *may* become entitled, *directly or indirectly*, to an interest under the trusts as being at a future date or on the happening of *a future event* a person of any specified description or *a member of any specified class of persons, so however* that this paragraph shall not include any person who *would be* of that description or a *member of that class*, as the case may be, if the said date had fallen or the *said event had happened at the date of the application to the court* (emphasis added).

Re Suffert's Settlement [1960] 3 All ER 561 demonstrates the operation of the section. Miss Suffert was a 61-year-old spinster, who had no children and her only ascertainable relations were three adult first cousins. The court held that it could give its consent on behalf of any persons unascertained as they would fall within s 1(1)(b) and it could consent on behalf of any persons unborn as they would fall within s 1(1)(c). The stumbling block was the consent of the three cousins. One of them had expressly joined Miss Suffert in making the application to the court, but that still left two adult cousins who had not given their consent to the arrangement. Could the court consent on their behalf? In other words, did those two cousins fall within s 1(1)(b)?

Under the terms of the original trusts if Miss Suffert died without issue, and in default of her having exercised a power of appointment to other persons, the fund would pass in trust to her statutory next-of-kin. The three cousins were her statutory next-of-kin. Let us, then, apply the wording of s 1(1)(b) to the case, as did the court.

First, were the cousins persons who 'may become entitled . . . as being . . . on the happening of a future event . . . member[s] of any specified class of persons'? Yes they were. They could be ('may be') the next-of-kin ('specified class of persons') on Miss Suffert's death ('a future event'). Because 'next-of-kin' is a class of persons the constitution of which can change continually it is possible to say only that the cousins 'may be' next-of-kin.

So, the cousins also fall within s 1(1)(b) and is the court able to consent on their behalf? Not necessarily. We should be careful not to jump to a premature conclusion. There is more to s 1(1)(b).

Secondly, we must take into account the important proviso to s 1(1)(b). This is the part of the paragraph which begins with the words 'so however'. It goes on to say that s 1(1)(b) does not include 'any person who *would be* . . . a member of that class . . . if the . . . said event had happened *at the date of the application to the court*'.

> **? QUESTION** 9.3
>
> Do the cousins fall within this exception to s 1(1)(b)?

Yes they do. If the said event (Miss Suffert's death) had happened 'at the date of the application to the court' (taken to be the date of the court hearing) the cousins would be immediately entitled as next-of-kin to an interest under the trust. In effect, on account of the proviso, the court asks itself at the date of the court hearing of the application, 'What would be the cousins' entitlement if Miss Suffert died today?' By asking itself this question the court is able to ignore the theoretical possibility that the class of 'next-of-kin' might change at sometime in the future. In the case of *Re Suffert's Settlement* the court decided that if Miss Suffert had died on the date of the court hearing the cousins would then have had a definite entitlement as her next-of-kin. They would therefore have fallen within the proviso to s 1(1)(b) and the court accordingly refused to consent to the arrangement on their behalf. No matter that the court may have been of the view that the cousins would have willingly consented to the application; the cousins had to be sought out and their own consent procured before the court would approve the arrangement.

The reasoning in *Re Suffert's Settlement* was followed in the case of *Re Moncrieff's ST* [1962] 3 All ER 838 which was reported a year later. The facts of this case are reproduced below in diagrammatic form, along with those of *Re Suffert's Settlement*. The decision in *Re Moncrieff's ST* was different because of a subtle difference in the facts of the two cases. In *Re Moncrieff's ST* the primary beneficiary, Mrs Joan Parkin, applied to court for an order approving of an arrangement to vary the trusts under which she was entitled. Mrs Parkin had an adopted son, Alan. If she survived Alan, her next-of-kin would be the four infant grandchildren of her maternal aunt.

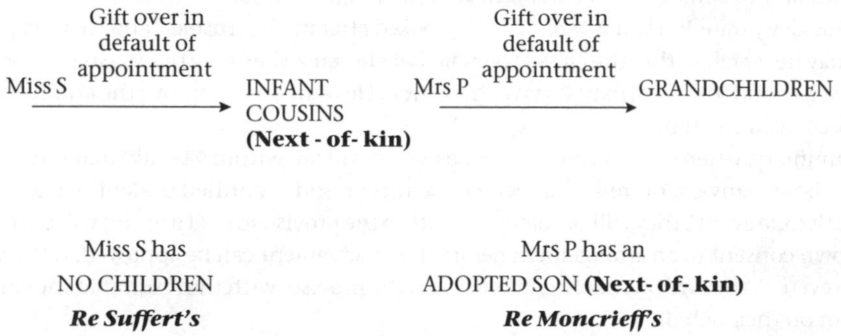

? QUESTION 9.4

Do you think the application in *Re Moncrieff's ST* succeeded?

The judge in *Re Moncrieff's ST* was able to provide the consent of Alan because he was still an infant and therefore fell within s 1(1)(a) of the Act. However, the consent of the four infant grandchildren could not be provided in the same way. Section 1(1)(a) could not apply to them because that section applies only to persons 'having' an interest under the trust. Because the class of 'next-of-kin' can change continually it would be possible to say only that the infant grandchildren 'may' have an interest under the trust. Because s 1(1)(a) did not apply to them the crucial question in the case was whether they fell within s 1(1)(b). Let us try to answer that question.

First, were the cousins persons who 'may become entitled . . . as being . . . on the happening of a future event . . . member[s] of any specified class of persons'? Yes they were. They could be ('may be') the next-of-kin ('specified class of persons') on the death of Mrs Joan Parkin ('a future event').

However, as we already know, this is not the end of the story. Secondly, we must take into account the important proviso to s 1(1)(b), which states that s 1(1)(b) does not include 'any person who *would be* . . . a member of that class . . . if the . . . said event had happened *at the date of the application to the court*'.

? QUESTION 9.5

Would the four infant grandchildren have been 'next-of-kin' if Mrs Parkin had died on the date of the application to the court?

The answer is, of course, no. Alan, Mrs Parkin's adopted son, would have been her statutory next-of-kin if she had died at the date of the application to the court. The infant grandchildren did not fall within the proviso to s 1(1)(b) and so their own consent was not required before approval could be given for the arrangement varying the trusts. The court in *Re Moncreiff's ST* was itself able to consent on behalf of the four infant grandchildren.

As Buckley J stated: 'Their interests can be looked after by the trustees, and they are persons who may never fall within the class of beneficiaries because they may predecease the settlor or the first respondent [Alan] may survive the settlor'. He went on to approve the arrangement as proposed by Mrs Parkin.

In summary, when considering whether a person will fall within s 1(1)(b) it might be useful to ask, 'how many events must happen before this person is entitled under the trust?' If the answer is 'one event', they will probably fall within the proviso to s 1(1)(b) and will have to give their own consent to an arrangement before the arrangement can be approved. If the answer is 'two events', they will probably not fall within the proviso, with the result that the court can consent on their behalf.

EXERCISE 9.4

Read the extract from the case of *Knocker v Youle* [1986] 2 All ER 914, set out next. What importance was attached to the phrase 'may become entitled', as it appears in s 1(1)(b)?

Knocker v Youle [1986] 2 All ER 914, Ch D

Under the original terms of the settlement in question, the primary beneficiary, the settlor's daughter, had a life interest in income under the trust. The remainder of the fund would pass to persons appointed by the primary beneficiary in her will. If she made no appointment the remainder interest would pass to the following persons or classes of person in the following strict order:

- the settlor's son; or if he were dead to
- the settlor's sisters; or if they were dead to
- their issue at the age of 21.

The settlor's daughter and son applied to court for an order approving a variation of the trusts. The settlor's sisters had all died. The question arose whether the sisters' issue had to give their consent to the arrangement, or whether the court was able to consent on their behalf under s. 1(1)(b). The court concluded that the sisters' issue were not persons who 'may' be entitled upon the happening of a certain event etc. They must give their own consent to the arrangement. Although their interests were very remote and contingent, they nevertheless had more than a mere expectation that they would acquire an interest under the trusts; they had an interest directly conferred by the settlement.

Warner J:

> What counsel invited me to do was in effect to interpret the word 'interest' in s. 1(1) loosely, as a layman might, so as not to include an interest that was remote. I was referred to two authorities: *Re Moncrieff's Settlement Trusts* [1962] 3 All ER 838 and the earlier case of *Re Suffert's Settlement, Suffert v Martyn-Linnington* [1960] 3 All ER 561. In both those cases, however, the class in question was a class of prospective next of kin, and, of course it is trite law that the prospective or presumptive next of kin of a living person do not have an interest. They have only a spes successionis, a hope of succeeding, and quite certainly they are the typical category of persons who fall within s. 1(1)(b). Another familiar example of a person falling within that provision is a potential future spouse. It seems to me, however, that a person who has an actual interest directly conferred on him or her by a settlement, albeit a remote interest, cannot properly be described as one who 'may become' entitled to an interest . . .
>
> Otherwise, the words 'whether vested or contingent' in section 1(1)(a) would be out of place . . . the distinction between an expectation and an interest is one which I do not think that I am entitled to blur.

Warner J went on to state that even if the applicants had been able to argue a way around the importance that he had attached to the word 'may', the sisters' issue would still have been required to give their own consent to the arrangement because they would have been in the same position as the cousins in *Re Suffert's Settlement*, being persons within the proviso to s 1(1)(b).

9.3.3.3 The spectral spouse

Suppose an unmarried primary beneficiary applies to the court for an order approving an arrangement varying or revoking the trusts under which they are presently entitled. A potential future spouse whom they might marry could fall within the ambit of s 1(1)(b). This potential future spouse has been given the eerie title of 'spectral spouse'. In the case of *Re Steed's WT* [1960] 1 Ch 407 which is discussed below (see 9.6) the court refused to consent to a proposed arrangement on behalf of the spectral spouse because it was thought that the proposed arrangement would not be for his benefit. This was despite the fact that the primary beneficiary was aged 53, had never married, and did not consider it at all likely that she would ever marry. The Master of the Rolls took a more romantic view, observing that 'many have said that before and subsequent events have proved them wrong'.

9.3.3.4 The unborn (s 1(1)(c))

The court may consent to an arrangement on behalf of any person unborn. This class is not restricted to persons in the womb. It would include 'the children of X', even if X were an avowed celibate (presumably by extension of the reasoning that 'many have said that before and subsequent events have proved them wrong' (see 9.3.3.3)). It is uncertain whether the presumptions of fertility and infertility established by the Perpetuities and Accumulations Act 1964 (see 6.3.7.2) would apply by analogy to this context. Consider, for example, a trust 'to Ms A for life and to her issue in remainder in equal shares absolutely'. If Ms A is a childless octogenarian who makes an application to court for the revocation of the trust under which she holds her life interest, would the court be required to consent on behalf of her non-existent issue before approving the arrangement? Would her 'potential' issue be 'unborn' within s 1(1)(c)? The fertility presumptions in the 1964 Act would respond with a resounding 'no'! In any event, fertility presumptions are nothing new to the administration of estates. Traditionally the court has been happy to distribute estates on the basis that a woman will pass her child-bearing age in her mid to late fifties.

As a final note in this section it is worth being aware of the Vice Chancellor's Practice Direction of 27 July 1976. By that direction the long-established Chancery Division practice of requiring counsel's opinion upon the compromise of proceedings in which an infant is interested, was extended to the variation of trusts under the 1958 Act. According to the Direction, 'such a written opinion is helpful, and in complicated cases it is usually essential to the understanding of the *guardian ad litem* and the trustees, and to the consideration by the court of the merits and the fiscal consequences of the arrangement'.

This Practice Direction has application to all cases 'where any infants or unborn beneficiaries will be affected by an arrangement' under the Act. It will therefore guide the court's decision whether or not to provide the consents of persons falling within s 1(1)(a) and (c).

9.3.3.5 Protective trusts (s 1(1)(d))

Where there is a protective trust the court may provide the consent of any person who would have an interest under a discretionary trust springing up on the determination of the life interest. To make any sense of this section it is necessary first of all to have a basic acquaintance with the concept of a protective trust.

EXERCISE 9.5

Refer back to 2.3.2 where we considered the nature of 'protective trusts'. Can you identify the persons in the following scenario who would fall within s 1(1)(d)?

S has settled a trust upon trustees for P for life and R in remainder. By the terms of the trust P's interest will determine in the event of P being declared bankrupt. Upon the determination of P's interest the trust fund will be held by the trustees upon a new trust, with the duty to distribute the fund as they, in their absolute discretion, think fit, amongst a range of potential beneficiaries. P is one of those potential beneficiaries; others include Q and R, P's brothers.

No doubt you have worked out that P, Q and R are all technically within s 1(1)(d) and their consents will not be required to an arrangement varying or revoking all or any of the trusts. In practice P is an exception to this, because as well as falling within s 1(1)(d), P is also the primary beneficiary under the protective trust and in this capacity, always assuming that P's interest has not yet determined, P's own consent will be needed before the court will approve of the arrangement.

9.3.4 The benefit requirement

Where the court provides the consent of any person under s 1(1)(a), (b) or (c) it may not approve the arrangement varying the trusts unless the carrying out thereof would be for the benefit of that person. Section 1(1)(d) is expressly excluded from this benefit requirement. The consent of a person falling within para (d) may be given even if the arrangement would not be for their benefit (see *Re Turner's WT* [1960] 1 Ch 122).

EXERCISE 9.6

Re-read s 1 of the Variation of Trusts Act 1958 (set out in 9.3 above). Is 'benefit' defined anywhere?

The Act gives no indication as to what may constitute a 'benefit', nor how benefit and detriment are to be weighed, but the cases provide some guidance.

9.3.4.1 Financial benefits

In the great majority of cases, the benefit provided by the Act is a tax-planning advantage, and so, ultimately, a financial one. In *Re Duke of Norfolk's WT* (1966) *The Times*, 23 March, the beneficiaries saved £550,000 in taxes because of the variation.

This case illustrates how the jurisdiction to vary trusts under the Act appears to serve the financially more privileged members of society, at the 'expense' of the ordinary taxpayer. Of course, persons benefiting from variations in cases like *Re Norfolk's WT* would no doubt argue that they are extraordinary taxpayers attempting merely to retain ownership of their own property and that ordinary taxpayers would be well-advised to do the same wherever possible. Less controversial, one assumes, would be a variation designed to shield from taxation a damages award held in trust to maintain a person who had been seriously injured in a road traffic accident.

9.3.4.2 Social and moral benefits

In *Re Holt's Settlement* [1969] 1 Ch 100, Megarry J held that benefit is 'not confined to financial benefit, but may extend to social or moral benefit'. Hence in *Re Weston's Settlements* [1969] 1 Ch 223 the Court of Appeal refused to approve of an arrangement which would have provided a tax-planning advantage, and thus a financial benefit, to the beneficiaries. The applicant in the case, Mr Stanley Weston, applied for an order approving an arrangement under which the trust would be exported to Jersey from England. Because Jersey is a 'tax haven' the trust would stand to save £163,000 in capital gains tax if the trust could be exported. However, the family had been resident in Jersey for only three months and it was highly likely that they would not stay there after the exportation of the trust. Lord Denning MR laid emphasis on the moral and social benefits of being brought up in England which, for him, outweighed the financial benefits that tax avoidance would bring: 'There are many things in life more worthwhile than money. One of these things is to be brought up in this our England which is still "the envy of less happier lands" '.

It might surprise us that Jersey was deemed to fall within the class of less happy lands! In fact, Lord Denning had other reasons for reaching the conclusion he did. He seemed impressed by the need for stability in a young beneficiary's life: 'Are they to be wanderers over the face of the earth, moving from this country to that, according to where they can best avoid tax? I cannot believe that to be right. Children are like trees: they grow stronger with firm roots.'

The benefits of stability, coupled with the perceived benefits of an English upbringing, were deemed to be more important in this case than the financial proceeds of a tax-avoidance scheme. However, Lord Denning did not doubt that tax avoidance was a quite proper use of the courts' jurisdiction to vary trusts: 'the exodus of this family to Jersey is done to avoid British taxation. Having made great wealth here, they want to quit without paying the taxes and duties which are imposed on those who stay. So be it. If it really be for the benefit of the children, let it be done'.

9.3.4.3 Benefit by deferral

In *Re Holt's Settlement* it was seen to be a benefit to the beneficiaries to defer the vesting of the gift until they were reasonably advanced in a career and settled in life. This involved a deferral of the contingent age from 21 to 30. Megarry J stated that he did not require evidence of special immaturity or irresponsibility. In *Re T's Settlement* [1963] 3 All ER 759 it was likewise seen to be a benefit to the beneficiary to defer the vesting of a gift until she was more mature and responsible thereby protecting her from creditors, exploitation and her own folly.

9.3.4.4 The benefit of familial harmony

In some cases applicants for a variation have sought to set the benefit of familial harmony against the reduced financial benefits which would flow from the new arrangement. They have had varying degrees of success.

In *Re Tinker's Settlement* a fund was held on trust for the settlor's son and daughter in equal shares. The daughter's share was contingent upon her attaining the age of 30, failing which it would pass to her issue or to her brother if she died without issue. The brother's share was given upon a similar contingency but with no gift over to his issue should he fail to attain the age of 30; instead his share would pass to his sister. This crucial difference between the two gifts was quite reasonably presumed to have resulted from an inadvertent omission in the drafting of the settlement. By applying to court for an order approving an arrangement varying the trusts it was hoped to rectify the error so as to allow the brother's children to take if he died before the age of 30. The application failed and approval was refused. The court had to be satisfied that the new arrangement would be for the benefit of unborn beneficiaries within s 1(1)(c) of the Variation of Trusts Act 1958. The daughter's unborn children could not possibly benefit financially from the arrangement, as they had a financial advantage over their unborn cousins under the original settlement. The variation would remove that advantage. Russell J was not persuaded that the advantage of familial harmony would outweigh the financial advantage. There are even suggestions in Russell J's judgment that only financial benefits would be a valid consideration, but we have seen that this cannot be correct after *Re Weston's* and *Re Holt's Settlement*.

By way of contrast to *Re Tinker's Settlement* we will now turn to *Re Remnant's ST* [1970] 1 Ch 560, where the testator left a fund ultimately upon trust to the issue of his two daughters. However, he provided that any child who, on the death of its mother, was 'practising Roman Catholicism' (which included being married to a Roman Catholic) should forfeit any interest. The forfeited share was directed to be passed to the issue of the other sister. One of the daughters had become a Roman Catholic, and it was likely that her children would forfeit their interests under the terms of the will. Both daughters disliked the forfeiture clause and they applied, within less than two years of their father's death, for a variation of the trusts which would cut out the forfeiture clauses. Additionally, the new arrangement, if approved, would accelerate the interests of the sisters' children in £10,000 of the fund which would be set aside for that purpose.

Pennycuick J took into account the fact that the forfeiture clause might 'operate as a deterrent to each of the . . . children in the selection of a husband when the time comes' and 'might well cause very serious dissension between the families of the two sisters'. These considerations, together with the fact that each of the sisters' issue had an accelerated financial entitlement, persuaded the judge to approve the arrangement. As he said, 'I have not found this an easy point, but I think that I am entitled to take a broad view of what is meant by "benefit", and so taking it, I think this arrangement can fairly be said to be for their benefit'.

So, are we able to explain the different decisions in *Re Tinker's Settlement* and *Re Remnant's ST*? It has been suggested that the distinction lies in the fact that in *Re Remnant's ST* both sides of the family could benefit from the freedom to marry without financial penalty which the new arrangement secured.

There may be a better distinction. *Re Tinker's Settlement* involved the granting of a beneficial interest to a beneficiary who would have had nothing under the original settlement. On the other hand, the variation in *Re Remnant's ST* did not give any beneficiary anything that they did not already have, but simply removed a forfeiture provision which could have stripped them of their entitlement and accelerated their entitlement to part of the fund. *Re Tinker's Settlement* involved the creation of an equitable entitlement, *Re Remnant's ST* involved the protection of an existing equitable entitlement. The judge in *Re Remnant's ST* acknowledged that the new arrangement 'defeats the settlor's intention', but that had to be set against the fact that 'forfeiture provisions are undesirable in themselves'.

9.3.4.5 Risks of detriment?

What if the arrangement which has been put forward for approval would, in the normal course of events, be for the benefit of all the beneficiaries, but carries a risk that certain potential beneficiaries might in certain possible circumstances suffer a detriment rather than a benefit? How much weight should be attached to the potential that such a beneficiary might someday suffer the detriment? The question is of particular relevance when the court comes to consider whether the arrangement would be for the benefit of unborn beneficiaries under s 1(1)(c). In *Re Cohen's Will Trusts* [1959] 1 WLR 865 Danckwerts J held that in exercising the jurisdiction under the Act the court must, on behalf of those persons for whom it was approving the arrangement, take the sort of risk which an adult would be prepared to take on their own behalf. In the similarly named case of *Re Cohen's Settlement Trusts* [1965] 1 WLR 1229 approval for an arrangement was refused because the prospects for one unborn person under the arrangement would have been hopeless whatever events might actually have happened to pass.

? QUESTION 9.6

You should already be acquainted with the case of *Re Holt's Settlement* in which Megarry J followed *Re Cohen's WT*. On what basis was the decision in *Re Cohen's ST* distinguished there?

In *Re Holt's Settlement* there was a risk that one of the unborn beneficiaries would receive no interest under the trust if their mother died during or shortly after childbirth. However, this risk had to be balanced against the possibility that the mother might survive for a reasonable, or indeed substantial, period after the birth, whereupon the infant would undoubtedly receive a benefit under the new arrangement. In *Re Holt's Settlement* Megarry J concluded that the risk was one which an adult would be prepared to take in order to secure the benefit. Accordingly, he gave approval for the new arrangement.

There is authority to show, however, that if the proposed arrangement involves risks as to whether or not a financial benefit would accrue to a beneficiary, the court will require that the trustees take out insurance against that risk, even at the expense of that beneficiary's income (*Re Robinson* [1976] 3 All ER 61). If the insurance premiums would involve an excessive drain on the income, insurance would not be required. The arrangement taken as a whole must, after all, be for the benefit of the beneficiary.

The hypothesis that an adult would have taken the sort of risk that the court took on behalf of the unborn beneficiary in *Re Holt's Settlement* involves the court in mental gymnastics. The court in *Re CL* [1968] 1 All ER 1104 carried out a similar exercise. There the court provided the consent of a mentally unsound beneficiary, under s 1(1)(a), on the basis that the beneficiary would have given their own consent had they been in a position to do so. This was despite the fact that the new arrangement resulted in the removal of the beneficiary's interest under the trust. Cotterell (1971) 34 MLR 98 has observed in relation to this case that 'it is hard to avoid the conclusion that benefit and the measure of it is simply what the court says it is'. Certainly the lack of a statutory definition of 'benefit' seems to provide wide scope for judicial intervention.

9.4 Resettlement or variation?

The Act, as we have seen, permits the court to approve any arrangement 'varying or revoking all or any of the trusts . . .'. However, does there come a point at which a trust has been so varied that it cannot be said to be a variant of the original trust at all, but is, in truth, a wholly different settlement? Does the Variation of Trusts Act 1958 permit resettlements or must arrangements be genuine variations?

We have already considered (at 9.1.3.3) the case of *Re T's Settlement* [1963] 3 All ER 759. You should recall that in that case a mother wished to avoid the effect of her immature and irresponsible daughter becoming entitled to the capital at the age of 21. She applied for an order approving an arrangement under which her daughter's share would be transferred to a new trust under which the fund would be held on a protective trust for the daughter's life, with remainder to her issue. Approval for the arrangement was refused. Wilberforce J stated that where the arrangement 'is in truth a complete new settlement' it will not be approved. But read on!

In *Re Ball's Settlement* [1968] 1 WLR 899, Megarry J laid down a test for distinguishing resettlements which would be void, from variations which would be valid. Megarry J's test has been referred to as the 'substratum test'. He said, 'if an arrangement, while leaving the substratum, effectuates the purpose of the original trust by other means, it may still be possible to regard the arrangement as merely varying the original trusts, even though the means employed are wholly different and even though the form is completely changed'.

This analysis is in accordance with the general maxim that 'equity looks to substance, not form'. In *Re Ball's Settlement* the settlor's life interest was removed, and so the form of the trust had undoubtedly changed but the remaining trusts were held to be 'still in essence trusts of half of the fund for each of the two named sons and their families'. However, it must be queried whether the removal of a life interest is merely a change of form. It does appear to be a fairly substantial alteration. Indeed, the whole distinction between extensive variation and total resettlements looks like a rather artificial one. A J Oakley (Parker and Mellows, *The Modern Law of Trusts*, 6th edn, London: Sweet & Maxwell, 1994, p 553) suggests that 'a pedantic distinction has grown up between "variation" and "resettlement" for which there appears to be no sanction in the words of the Act, nor any practical justification'. The distinction looks especially weak after the judgment of the Court of Appeal in *Goulding v James* [1997] 2 All ER 239 (see 9.6).

9.5 Exporting the trust

This is a form of varying a trust which involves the wholesale removal of the administration of a trust to a foreign jurisdiction. We have considered some of the factors which a court will take into account when considering whether an export will be for the benefit of the beneficiaries (see *Re Weston's Settlements* at 9.3.4.2). In this section it is intended to show that if there is a benefit to the beneficiaries in exporting the trust, for example smoother administration, without any outweighing disadvantages, the court will generally give its approval. (We will consider the appointment of foreign trustees at 10.2.2.2.)

In *Re Seale's Marriage Settlement* [1961] 3 WLR 262, the beneficiaries under the original settlement had emigrated to Canada a number of years before the date on which their application was heard. They had taken Canadian citizenship and intended to live there permanently. This case was clearly different from *Re Weston's* where the children were at risk of being uprooted during crucial developing years. Further, the financial advantage of exporting the trust in *Re Seale's Marriage Settlement* was primarily the saving that would be made on administration costs. The primary aim of the export was not to secure a short-term tax advantage.

In *Re Windeatt's WT* [1969] 2 All ER 324, the contrast with *Re Weston's* is even more dramatic as both cases involved applications for an export to Jersey. The judge in *Re Windeatt's* did not take Lord Denning's view that Jersey was 'a less happy land' than 'this our England'. In fact, the export of the trust to Jersey was permitted. Again the facts were quite different from those in *Re Weston's* because here the family had lived in Jersey for 19 years and were clearly settled there.

9.6 The settlor's intentions

In *Re Remnant's ST* (see 9.3.4.4) the judge held that defeat of the testator's intentions was a 'serious but by no means conclusive consideration'. It is certainly true that cases in which the courts have insisted upon the paramountcy of the settlor's expressed intentions are rare (a good example of such a case is *Re Steed's WT* [1960] 1 Ch 407).

? QUESTION 9.7

How serious a consideration was the settlor's intent in *Goulding v James* [1997] 2 All ER 239?

***Goulding v James* [1997] 2 All ER 239, Court of Appeal**

The testatrix, Mrs Froud, made a will in 1992 whereby she directed that her estate was to be divided into two parts to be given to her daughter June and June's husband, Kenneth. She further provided that their interest was to pass to their son, Marcus, contingent upon his attaining the age of 40 if either June or Kenneth predeceased the testatrix. This will was revoked in 1994 and replaced with a new will which created a trust under which June had a life interest in possession of the residuary estate subject to which Marcus was to take absolutely provided he reached the age of 40. The new will further provided that if Marcus failed to attain the age of 40 or died before June, then Marcus's children would take the estate absolutely. After the death of the testatrix, June and Marcus applied to court for a variation of the trust contained in the will under s. 1(1)(c) of the Variation of Trusts Act 1958. The variation sought was for 45 per cent of the estate to be held for June, 45 per cent for Marcus and the remaining 10 per cent for Marcus's children. Laddie J at first instance declined to approve the arrangement as it was contrary to the testatrix's wishes.

Mummery LJ:

> The effect of Megarry J's observation in [*Re Holt's Settlement, Wilson v Holt* [1968] 1 All ER 470 at 479, *Re Ball's Settlement Trusts* [1968] 2 All ER 438 at 442 and *Spens v IRC, Hunt v IRC* [1970] 3 All ER 294 at 301] is this. First, what varies the trust is not the court, but the agreement or consensus of the beneficiaries. Secondly, there is no real difference in principle in the rearrangement of the trusts between the case where the court is exercising its jurisdiction on behalf of the specified class under the 1958 Act and the case where the resettlement is made by virtue of the doctrine in *Saunders v Vautier* (1841) 4 Beav 115 and by all the adult beneficiaries joining together. Thirdly, the court is merely contributing on behalf of infants and unborn and unascertained persons the binding assents to the arrangement which they, unlike an adult beneficiary, cannot give. The 1958 Act has thus been viewed by the courts as a statutory extension of the consent principle embodied in the rule in *Saunders v Vautier*. The principle recognises the rights of beneficiaries, who are *sui juris* and together absolutely entitled to the trust property, to exercise their proprietary rights to overbear and defeat the intention of a testator or settlor to subject property to the continuing trusts, powers and limitations of a will or trust instrument.

The answer is, not a great deal! The Court of Appeal held that in deciding whether or not to grant the approval under that section, its only concern was to ensure that the arrangement was 'beneficial' to those for whom its consent was sought. The purpose of the section was merely to enable a *Saunders v Vautier* type of arrangement to take place where it would otherwise be precluded because there were beneficiaries who could not give their consent. The court approved the arrangement.

CHAPTER SUMMARY

- We have seen that the allocation of beneficial interests under trusts can be varied, even in spite of the settlor's intentions. Where all the potential beneficiaries are adult and between them absolutely entitled to the trust fund they can bring the trust to an end and re-allocate their beneficial interests as they wish under the rule in *Saunders v Vautier*. Where the beneficiaries are not competent to consent on their own behalf, the court can in certain circumstances consent on their behalf to an arrangement varying the trusts under the Variation of Trusts Act 1958.
- The wide power of courts to vary beneficial interests under trusts produces dilemmas.
  - One is the difficulty in weighing the settlor's intentions against the interests of the persons entitled to the fund. The courts appear to have resolved this dilemma in favour of the beneficiaries. Another dilemma, to which you must come to your own conclusion, is one which we anticipated in the introduction: the need to balance the interest of the general taxpayer against the provision of a tax-avoidance facility for beneficiaries.
  - There is also the dilemma of whether or not to remove potentially offensive and divisive forfeiture clauses in trusts. At present there is no law to prevent the inclusion of such clauses in private trusts. It remains to be seen what effect the Human Rights Act 1998 will have upon this state of affairs. Will courts, as public authorities subject to the Act, be required to exercise their discretion so as to remove such clauses in every case in which such a variation is proposed? That is doubtful. Rather, it may be that some undesirable incidents of private dispositive freedom will remain so long as the

State retains (under Article 1 of the First Protocol of the European Convention on Human Rights) the authority to organize its system of property law as a coherent whole, with private dispositive choice as its informing ideal.

- A variation of the trustee's administrative power which does not impact upon the allocation of the beneficial interests under the trusts, should be sought under the Trustee Act 1925, s 57.

SUMMATIVE ASSESSMENT EXERCISE

online resource centre

By his will Abdul provided that £500,000 should be held on trust for his wife, Fatima, for life, with remainder to such of their children as should attain the age of 21 absolutely. Abdul died in 1985 leaving two sons, Bashir and Dan, aged seven and five respectively. The trustees of the fund are experienced businessmen, and due to their efforts the fund is now worth £700,000.

Fatima feels that the income from the fund is more than sufficient to meet her needs, and wishes to surrender her interest in one half of the income of the fund in favour of Bashir and Dan. Additionally, she is worried about the effect of inherited wealth on Bashir and Dan, and would like to postpone their interests until they are 35 years old. In the meantime she would like the income on their respective shares to be accumulated until they attain 30 or die.

Fatima wishes to settle in Guernsey where she has friends. Bashir and Dan attend Harrchester School in England and it is proposed that they should complete their education in England. Fatima believes that the trust could be administered more easily in Guernsey, but the trustees do not agree.

Advise Fatima.

FURTHER READING

Harris, J W, *Variation of Trusts* (London: Sweet & Maxwell, 1975).

Law Reform Committee's Sixth Report *Court's Power to Sanction Variation of Trusts* (1957) Cmnd 310 para 13.

10 Trustee appointments

OBJECTIVES

By the end of this chapter, you should be able to:

1 Apply the principle that a trust does not fail for want of a trustee

2 Identify the persons able to appoint trustees and the persons able to act as trustees

3 Organize the matters to which a trustee should attend upon appointment

4 Advise a trustee how to may disclaim the trust

5 Identify the modes by which a trustee might retire, or be removed, from the trust

10.1 Introduction

The maximum number of trustees permitted in a private trust of land is four (in charitable trusts and trusts of pure personalty there may be many more). In the case of land at least two trustees are required in order to make a valid sale (unless the sole trustee is a trust corporation). In any case where there are two or more trustees they will hold the legal title as joint tenants and upon the death of any of them the legal title remains vested in the surviving trustees by 'right of survivorship'. But what happens when a trustee (perhaps the last, or only, trustee) dies or for some other reason ceases to act? It is said that 'a trust does not fail for want of a trustee', but who is able to appoint new trustees, and who should be appointed? Let us find some answers.

10.2 Appointment of the trustee

10.2.1 Who can appoint a trustee?

EXERCISE 10.1

Familiarize yourself with the following extracts from the Trustee Act 1925, s 36, and the Trusts of Land and Appointment of Trustees Act 1996, ss 19–20. These sections are crucial to the law on the appointment of trustees.

Trustee Act 1925

36. Power of appointing new or additional trustees

(1) Where a trustee, either original or substituted, and whether appointed by a court or otherwise, is dead, or remains out of the United Kingdom for more than twelve months, or desires to be discharged from all or any of the trusts or powers reposed in or conferred on him, or refuses or is unfit to act therein, or is incapable of acting therein, or is an infant, then, subject to the restrictions imposed by this Act on the number of trustees,—

(a) the person or persons nominated for the purpose of appointing new trustees by the instrument, if any, creating the trust; or

(b) if there is no such person, or no such person able and willing to act, then the surviving or continuing trustees for the time being, or the personal representatives of the last surviving or continuing trustee;

may, by writing, appoint one or more other persons (whether or not being the persons exercising the power) to be a trustee or trustees in the place of the trustee so deceased, remaining out of the United Kingdom, desiring to be discharged, refusing, or being unfit or being incapable, or being an infant, as aforesaid.

(2) Where a trustee has been removed under a power contained in the instrument creating the trust, a new trustee or new trustees may be appointed in the place of the trustee who is removed, as if he were dead, or, in the case of a corporation, as if the corporation desired to be discharged from the trust, and the provisions of this section shall apply accordingly, but subject to the restrictions imposed by this Act on the number of trustees.

(3) . . .

(4) The power of appointment given by subsection (1) of this section or any similar previous enactment to the personal representatives of a last surviving or continuing trustee shall be and shall be deemed always to have been exercisable by the executors for the time being (whether original or by representation) of such surviving or continuing trustee who have proved the will of their testator or by the administrators for the time being of such trustee without the concurrence of any executor who has renounced or has not proved.

(5) . . .

(6) Where a sole trustee, other than a trust corporation, is or has been originally appointed to act in a trust, or where, in the case of any trust, there are not more than three trustees (none of them being a trust corporation) either original or substituted and whether appointed by the court or otherwise, then and in any such case—

(a) the person or persons nominated for the purpose of appointing new trustees by the instrument, if any, creating the trust; or

(b) if there is no such person, or no such person able and willing to act, then the trustee or trustees for the time being;

may, by writing appoint another person or other persons to be an additional trustee or additional trustees, but it shall not be obligatory to appoint any additional trustee, unless the instrument, if any, creating the trust, or any statutory enactment provides to the contrary, nor shall the number of trustees be increased beyond four by virtue of any such appointment.

(7) Every new trustee appointed under this section as well before as after all the trust property becomes by law, or by assurance, or otherwise, vested in him, shall have the same powers, authorities, and discretions, and may in all respects act as if he had been originally appointed a trustee by the instrument, if any, creating the trust.

(8) The provisions of this section relating to a trustee who is dead include the case of a person nominated trustee in a will but dying before the testator, and those relative to a continuing trustee include a refusing or retiring trustee, if willing to act in the execution of the provisions of this section.

(9) Where a trustee is incapable, by reason of mental disorder within the meaning of the Mental Health Act 1983, of exercising his functions as trustee and is also entitled in possession to some beneficial interest in the trust property, no appointment of a new trustee in his place shall be made by virtue of paragraph (b) of subsection (1) of this section unless leave to make the appointment has been given by the authority having jurisdiction under Part VII of the Mental Health Act 1983.

You will see from s 36(1) that one or more new trustees may be appointed, in writing, whenever an existing trustee dies, remains abroad for more than a year, retires, refuses to act, is unfit to act, is incapable of acting or is an infant. The person empowered to make the appointment is the person named in the trust deed to carry out that particular function. Only if nobody is so named is the power to appoint given to the existing trustees or, if they have all died, to the personal representatives of the last trustee to have died. In fact, when a sole trustee dies that trustee's personal representatives will become the trustees for the time being if they accept the trusts (Administration of Estates Act 1925, s 1(2)) but they can be ousted by the appointment of other trustees by a person nominated in the trust instrument to appoint trustees.

Since 1 January 1997 ss 19 and 20 of the Trusts of Land etc. Act 1996 apply where there is no person nominated under the trust instrument to appoint new trustees to allow the beneficiaries to appoint new trustees in certain circumstances (see 10.2.1.2).

Trusts of Land and Appointment of Trustees Act 1996

19. Appointment and retirement of trustee at instance of beneficiaries

(1) This section applies in the case of a trust where—

(a) there is no person nominated for the purpose of appointing new trustees by the instrument, if any, creating the trust, and

(b) the beneficiaries under the trust are of full age and capacity and (taken together) are absolutely entitled to the property subject to the trust.

(2) The beneficiaries may give a direction or directions of either or both of the following descriptions—

(a) a written direction to a trustee or trustees to retire from the trust, and

(b) a written direction to the trustees or trustee for the time being (or, if there are none, to the personal representative of the last person who was a trustee) to appoint by writing to be a trustee or trustees the person or persons specified in the direction.

(3) Where—

(a) a trustee has been given a direction under subsection (2)(a),

(b) reasonable arrangements have been made for the protection of any rights of his in connection with the trust,

(c) after he has retired there will be either a trust corporation or at least two persons to act as trustees to perform the trust, and

(d) either another person is to be appointed to be a new trustee on his retirement (whether in compliance with a direction under subsection (2)(b) or otherwise) or the continuing trustees by deed consent to his retirement, he shall make a deed declaring his retirement and shall be deemed to have retired and be discharged from the trust.

(4) Where a trustee retires under subsection (3) he and the continuing trustees (together with any new trustee) shall (subject to any arrangements for the protection of his rights) do anything necessary to vest the trust property in the continuing trustees (or the continuing and new trustees).

(5) This section has effect subject to the restrictions imposed by the Trustee Act 1925 on the number of trustees.

Trusts of Land and Appointment of Trustees Act 1996

20. Appointment of substitute for incapable trustee

(1) This section applies where—

(a) a trustee is incapable by reason of mental disorder of exercising his functions as trustee,

(b) there is no person who is both entitled and willing and able to appoint a trustee in place of him under section 36(1) of the Trustee Act 1925, and

(c) the beneficiaries under the trust are of full age and capacity and (taken together) are absolutely entitled to the property subject to the trust.

(2) The beneficiaries may give to—

(a) a receiver of the trustee,

(b) an attorney acting for him under the authority of a power of attorney created by an instrument which is registered under section 6 of the Enduring Powers of Attorney Act 1985, or

(c) a person authorised for the purpose by the authority having jurisdiction under Part VII of the Mental Health Act 1983,

a written direction to appoint by writing the person or persons specified in the direction to be a trustee or trustees in place of the incapable trustee.

10.2.1.1 **Person nominated**

Occasionally a settlor or testator will include in the trust instrument a clause nominating a person able to appoint replacement or additional trustees although such clauses are usually found only in large institutional trusts such as pension fund trusts and charitable trusts. However, if the clause says something like: 'I nominate X as the person able to appoint trustees in the event of the death of any of the current trustees', the obvious question arises, did the settlor intend X to be treated as the person referred to in s 36(1) as having the power to appoint trustees in the numerous circumstances listed in s 36(1), or is X limited to making appointments only in the event of the death of the current trustees? Following *Re Wheeler* [1896] 1 Ch 315, and the judgment of Kekewich J, the answer is that X's power is limited to the event expressly mentioned in the trust instrument and does not extend to all the events listed in s 36(1).

Let us now consider another problem with nominated appointors.

? QUESTION 10.1

Andrew is named in a trust deed as the person able to appoint new trustees. The settlor originally appointed three trustees. Do you think Andrew should appoint himself as the fourth trustee? Read s 36(6) and think carefully.

Andrew is permitted to appoint some other person to the fourth post but he should not appoint himself. There is a very good reason for this. The settlor clearly knew of Andrew's existence and availability, but nevertheless decided not to appoint him as the fourth trustee (*Re Power's Settlement Trusts* [1951] 1 Ch 1074).

An infant (any person under the age of 18) cannot act as a trustee. However, you may be surprised to discover that an infant can be nominated to exercise the power of appointing new trustees. Nevertheless, an appointment made by an infant is liable to be set aside if the appointment is prejudicial to the infant or could affect his interest under the trust or is in some other way imprudent. See *Re Parsons* [1940] 1 Ch 973.

10.2.1.2 **The beneficiaries**

Sections 19 and 20 of the Trusts of Land etc. Act 1996 apply since 1 January 1997. Section 19 applies where all the beneficiaries under the trust are of full age and capacity and are together absolutely entitled to the trust property. Section 19(2)(b) provides that, apart from where there is a person nominated under the trust instrument to appoint new trustees (see 10.2.1.1), the beneficiaries may in writing direct the existing trustees (or, if there are none, the personal representatives of the last surviving trustee), to appoint by writing such person or persons as may specified in the direction to be a trustee or trustees.

Section 20 is also notable in that it provides that where a trustee is incapable of acting by reason of a mental disorder, the beneficiaries (if they are of full age and capacity and together absolutely entitled to the trust property) may in writing direct the receiver or attorney of the trustee, to appoint by writing such person or persons as may be specified in the direction to be a trustee or trustees. Section 20 applies only where there is no person entitled, able and willing to make the appointment under s 36(1).

10.2.1.3 The court

EXERCISE 10.2

Read the Trustee Act 1925, s 41. According to this section when will the court appoint new trustees?

41. Power of court to appoint new trustees

(1) The court may, whenever it is expedient to appoint a new trustee or new trustees, and it is found inexpedient, difficult or impracticable so to do without the assistance of the court, make an order appointing a new trustee or new trustees either in substitution for or in addition to any existing trustee or trustees, or although there is no existing trustee. . . .

(4) Nothing in this section gives power to appoint an executor or administrator.

You should note that this section does not say that the court can appoint a trustee whenever it is expedient to do so. It says that the court will appoint a new trustee whenever it is expedient to appoint a new trustee *and* inexpedient, difficult or impractical to do so without the court's assistance. In one case (*Re May's Will Trusts* [1941] Ch 109) where a trustee was trapped in territory occupied by the Germans during World War II, the court would not certify that the persons empowered by s 36 to appoint trustees were, within the wording of s 36, able to appoint a new trustee in these circumstances. It was therefore inexpedient to appoint without the court's assistance and so the court made the appointment. In another case the person empowered by s 36 to appoint new trustees had become incapable through age and infirmity of being able to exercise the power and the court intervened to appoint new trustees (*Re Lemann's Trusts* (1883) 22 Ch D 633).

A trustee appointed by the court may act in every respect just as if they were one of the original trustees (Trustee Act 1925, s 43).

10.2.2 Who can be appointed as trustees?

Nowadays it is quite common for professional trustees to be appointed, such as a solicitor or trust corporation. However, the factors which we are about to consider, though of general application, are perhaps of most relevance to the appointment of private persons as trustees.

10.2.2.1 Persons unfit, incapable or unwilling to act

It would be quite wrong to attempt to appoint persons who are bankrupt, who have convictions for offences involving dishonesty or who are otherwise unfit for the office of trustee. Nor should persons be appointed who are incapable of acting by reason of mental disorder, ill health or some other relevant disability. (Note: when the new Mental Capacity Act 2005 becomes law (probably in 2007) the phrase 'incapable of' which appears in s 41 will be replaced by 'lacks capacity to' (Sch 6, s 3(3)).)

10.2.2.2 Persons resident abroad

In *Re Whitehead's WT* [1971] 1 WLR 833, Pennycuick V-C said that, 'apart from exceptional circumstances, it is not proper to make such an appointment . . . The most obvious exceptional circumstances are those in which the beneficiaries have settled permanently in some country outside the United Kingdom and what is proposed to be done is to appoint new trustees in that country'. More recently, in *Richard v The Hon A B Mackay*, 14 March 1987 (unreported) Millett J suggested that 'the language of Sir John Pennycuick, which is narrowly drawn, is too restrictive for the circumstances of the present day if, at least, it is intended to lay down any rule of practice'. In that case, Millett J approved the trustees' request for a declaration that transfer of part of the trust fund to new trustees in Bermuda would be valid. In coming to this decision his Lordship placed some weight on the fact that the trustees had already decided that the export of the fund would be for the benefit of the beneficiaries, and were merely seeking the court's approval of that course. His Lordship suggested that where the court is being asked to exercise an original discretion of its own (for example, under s 41 of the Trustee Act 1925 or under the Variation of Trusts Act 1958 (see 9.3)) the applicants must make out a positive case to show that the scheme gives the beneficiaries more than a mere tax advantage.

10.2.2.3 Factors which the court considers

EXERCISE 10.3

Read the following extract from *Re Tempest* (1866) LR 1 Ch App 485 and underline the factors which guide the exercise of the court's discretion when appointing new trustees. What other factors do you think should influence appointments by the court?

***Re Tempest* (1866) LR 1 Ch App 485, Court of Appeal**

The will of Sir C R Tempest, Bart appointed Stonor and Fleming as trustees of certain real estates. A codicil to the will appointed Stonor, Fleming and Lord Camoys as trustees of certain charitable trusts. Stonor predeceased the testator. Fleming and one Arthur Tempest, the testator's uncle, were empowered by the will to appoint new trustees of the real estates, but they could not agree upon a replacement trustee. Most of the beneficiaries concurred with Arthur Tempest's choice, but Fleming opposed it on the ground that the proposed trustee was connected with a branch of the family with whom the testator had not been on friendly terms. The surviving trustees of the charitable trusts were, on the other hand, able to agree to a replacement trustee of those trusts. It was held that the trustee proposed by Arthur Tempest should not be appointed to the trusts.

Sir G J Turner LJ:

> The following rules and principles may, I think, safely be laid down as applying to all cases of appointments by the Court of new trustees.
>
> First, the Court will have regard to the wishes of the persons by whom the trust has been created, if expressed in the instrument creating the trust, or clearly to be collected from it . . .

> Another rule which may, I think, safely be laid down is this—that the Court will not appoint a person to be trustee with a view to the interest of some of the persons interested under the trust, in opposition either to the wishes of the testator or to the interests of others of the *cestuis que trusts*. I think so for this reason, that it is of the essence of the duty of every trustee to hold an even hand between the parties interested under the trust. Every trustee is in duty bound to look to the interests of all, and not of any particular member or class of members of his *cestuis que trusts*.
>
> A third rule which, I think, may safely be laid down, is, that the Court in appointing a trustee will have regard to the question, whether his appointment will promote or impede the execution of the trust, for the very purpose of the appointment is that the trust may be better carried into execution. . . .
>
> . . . but, on the other hand, if the continuing or surviving trustee refuses to act with a trustee who may be proposed to be appointed . . . I think it would be going too far to say that the Court ought, on that ground alone, to refuse to appoint the proposed trustee; for this would, as suggested in the argument, be to give the continuing or surviving trustee a veto upon the appointment of the new trustee. In such a case, I think it must be the duty of the Court to inquire and ascertain whether the objection of the surviving or continuing trustee is well founded or not, and to act or refuse to act upon it accordingly. If the surviving or continuing trustee has improperly refused to act with the proposed trustee, it might be a ground for removing him from the trust.

In addition to the guidance in *Re Tempest*, the court will never appoint a person to be a sole trustee of a valuable fund (*per* Bennet J in *Re Parsons* [1940] 1 Ch 973) and the court inclines against appointing a beneficiary or a beneficiary's spouse to be a trustee (*Re Kemp's Settled Estate* (1883) 24 Ch D 485, CA).

10.2.3 Actions of the trustee upon appointment

In the game of cricket the person who has just come in to bat is generally more vulnerable than the person who is comfortable and has already scored a few runs. The same may be true of trustees. A new trustee is vulnerable and more likely than an established trustee to commit an honest breach of trust. A new trustee should make careful enquiries as to the nature of the trust and must be sure to carry out their initial duties diligently and without unreasonable delay.

10.2.3.1 Ascertaining the terms of the trust

The first action that a trustee must carry out upon accepting an appointment is to check that they have been validly appointed. They should acquaint themselves with the trust instrument and other trust documentation.

EXERCISE 10.4

List the sorts of things a trustee might try to ascertain from the trust instrument and other trust documentation. Compare your list with the following.

From an examination of the documents the trustee will discover the identity of the beneficiaries and the extent of their equitable entitlements. Further, memoranda on the trust instrument will inform the trustee whether the beneficiaries have sold or otherwise dealt with their interests under the trust. (The beneficiaries must inform the trustees, by notice, of dealings with their equitable interest.) The trustee will also discover the nature of the trust property. This raises issues which are dealt with in the next section.

10.2.3.2 Transfer of trust property

The legal title to the trust property must be transferred into the names of the new and continuing trustees. Where a new trustee is appointed by deed the legal title to most forms of land, chattels and choses in action will vest automatically in the names of the new and continuing trustees as joint tenants. This is in accordance with s 40 of the Trustee Act 1925. Although in the case of registered land the register must be amended to reflect the new proprietorship (Land Registration Act 1925, s 47). However, apart from some technical exceptions (as to which you may wish to read the section in detail) s 40 is not effective to transfer mortgages, land held under leases, or stocks and shares. If the subject matter of the trust consists of any property of this kind it is the duty of the trustees actively to 'get it in'. See *Re Brogden* (1888) 38 Ch D 546.

10.2.3.3 Duty to act on suspicions

This duty makes the new trustee sound like a private detective. In fact, it is not like that at all. The new trustee is under no obligation to search for suspicious circumstances. The duty is simply to take action to recover the trust fund if, having acquainted himself with the trust, it appears that the previous trustees have committed a breach of trust which has resulted in a depletion of the fund. If the new trustee fails to act upon a suspicion, that failure to act might in itself constitute a breach of trust unless the new trustee reasonably considers that taking action would be fruitless.

10.3 Disclaimer of the trust

10.3.1 The general law

A person appointed as trustee of an express trust may decide to decline the appointment, in which event they should do so by a disclaimer, usually in the form of a deed. But if the trustee acts in performance of the trust it will then be too late to disclaim.

10.3.2 No partial disclaimer

In *Re Lord and Fullerton's Contract* [1896] 1 Ch 228, the question arose whether a trustee of real and personal property, some existing in England and some abroad, could disclaim the trust except as to the property abroad. The Court of Appeal decided against partial disclaimer in any circumstances. Lindley LJ did not think that a trustee could 'accept the office as to some part of the estate and not accept it as to the rest'. One reason for this decision was the undesirable consequences of partial disclaimer for a purchaser from the trustee who would be uncertain as to the trustee's power to sell particular property.

10.3.3 Trust void because of disclaimer

In certain limited situations a trust will fail because the potential 'trustee' disclaims the trusteeship.

? QUESTION 10.2

Is there a conflict here with the principle that a trust does not fail for want of a trustee?

There appears to be a conflict at first sight, but it can be resolved. In those rare situations where disclaimer causes a trust to fail it is because the trust is treated as never having come into being. It is said to have been void *ab initio*. The rule that a trust does not fail for want of a trustee only applies to existing trusts and so it has no application to trusts which are made void by disclaimer.

10.3.3.1 Trusts which require specific trustees

It is prerequisite to the existence of some trusts that only a specific, named trustee shall hold the office. As Buckley J said in *Re Lysaght* [1966] 1 Ch 191, 'If it is of the essence of a trust that the trustees selected by the settlor and no one else shall act as the trustees of it and if those trustees cannot or will not undertake the office, the trust must fail'.

10.3.3.2 *Inter vivos* trusts disclaimed before constitution

You should recall from 5.4 that, apart from cases where a settlor declares himself to be a trustee, an *inter vivos* trust is not fully constituted until the trust property has been transferred to the trustees. (A will trust, on the other hand, is perfectly constituted by the death of the testator.) It should follow, that an *inter vivos* trust is void *ab initio* if the trustees disclaim the trust before the trust property is transferred to them. On the basis of this analysis one jurist (P Matthews [1981] Conv 141) has argued that the decision in *Mallott v Wilson* [1903] 2 Ch 494 was wrong. In that case the trustee disclaimed the trust 'as soon as he heard of it' and the trust property was never transferred to the trustee. Despite this the judge decided that the trust was not void *ab initio*, but valid until the disclaimer.

10.4 Retirement from the trust

10.4.1 General

In *Re Chetwynd's Settlement* [1902] 1 Ch 692, Farwell J stated that 'No trustee accepts the responsibility for the term of his natural life, or for more than a reasonable period'. It is important to note, however, that a trustee cannot retire on a whim and in some circumstances their retirement will not be valid unless a new trustee is appointed in their place.

10.4.2 Modes of retirement

Trustees may retire whenever the trust instrument entitles them to do so and, as a last resort, whenever the court approves an application for retirement. Apart from these instances the Trustee Act 1925 details two modes of retirement.

10.4.2.1 Retirement under Trustee Act 1925, s 36

You will recall that this section provides, *inter alia*, for the appointment of a new trustee, or trustees, 'in the place of' a trustee 'desiring to be discharged'. The crucial point to note is that a retirement purported to be carried out in pursuance of this section will only be valid to discharge the trustee if at least one new trustee has been appointed in their place. Subject to the trust instrument providing to the contrary, s 36 does not authorize the appointment of a sole trustee, not being a trust corporation, where the trustee, when appointed, would not be able to give valid receipts for all capital money arising under the trust (Trustee Act 1925, s 37). In practice this means that where the only trustee of the trust retires, he must be replaced by two trustees or a trust corporation (*see Adam & Co International Trustees Ltd v Theodore Goddard (a firm)* (2000) 97(13) LSG 44).

10.4.2.2 Retirement under Trustee Act 1925, s 39

The essential difference between s 39 and s 36 is that s 39 permits retirement of a trustee without the appointment of a replacement trustee.

EXERCISE 10.5

Read s 39, set out next, and underline the conditions which must be satisfied before a trustee may retire under this section.

Trustee Act 1925

39. Retirement of trustee without a new appointment

(1) Where a trustee is desirous of being discharged from the trust, and after his discharge there will be either a trust corporation or at least two individuals to act as trustees to perform the trust, then, if such trustee as aforesaid by deed declares that he is desirous of being discharged from the trust, and if his co-trustees and such other person, if any, as is empowered to appoint trustees, by deed consent to the discharge of the trustee, and to the vesting in the co-trustees alone of the trust property, the trustee desirous of being discharged shall be deemed to have retired from the trust, and shall, by the deed, be discharged there from under this Act, without any new trustee being appointed in his place.

(2) Any assurance or thing requisite for vesting the trust property in the continuing trustees alone shall be executed or done.

The conditions are as follows:

- the trustee must retire by deed
- the trustee must obtain the consent of the other trustees and any person who is empowered to appoint new trustees
- such consent must be given by deed and must approve of the retirement and of the vesting of the trust property in the remaining trustees alone
- the retirement will only be valid if two trustees remain or a trust corporation remains after the retirement.

If any one of these conditions is not met the retirement will not be effective to discharge the trustee from their obligations under the trust.

10.4.2.3 Retirement under Trusts of Land etc. Act 1996, s 19

As was indicated earlier (10.2.1.2) the Trusts of Land etc. Act 1996, s 19 applies where all the beneficiaries under the trust are *sui juris* and together absolutely entitled, unless there is someone nominated under the trust instrument to appoint new trustees. In relation to retirement, s 19(2)(a) provides that the beneficiaries may in writing direct a trustee to retire from the trust. Before the retiring trustee declares his retirement (which he must do by deed), arrangements must be made to ensure that the trustee's rights in connection with the trust have been protected and to ensure that upon retirement at least two trustees (or a trust corporation) will remain. Further, if no other trustee is to be appointed in the place of the retiring trustee, the continuing trustees must consent to the retirement by deed.

10.4.3 Liability after retirement

A trustee continues to be liable for breaches of trust which occur after they have attempted to retire if their 'retirement' was technically defective, but what if the retirement was technically valid? The general rule here is that a trustee will only be liable for breaches of trust which occurred when they were a trustee.

EXERCISE 10.6

According to *Head v Gould* (see next) in what exceptional circumstance might a trustee be liable even after retirement?

Head v Gould **[1898] 2 Ch 250, Ch D**

Kekewich J:

> It is the duty of trustees to protect the funds entrusted to their care, and to distribute those funds themselves or hand them over to their successors intact, that is, properly invested and without diminution, according to the terms of the mandate contained in the instrument of trust. This duty is imposed on them as long as they remain trustees and must be their guide in every act done

> by them as trustees. On retiring from the trust and passing on the trust estate to their successors—and this whether they appoint those successors or merely assign the property to the nominees of those who have the power of appointment—they are acting as trustees, and it is equally incumbent on them in this ultimate act of office to fulfil the duty imposed on them as at any other time. If therefore they neglect that duty and part with the property without due regard to it, they remain liable and will be held by the Court responsible for the consequences properly traceable to that neglect. This explanation will, I think, be found consistent with all judicial utterances on the subject, and haply aid to make them consistent with themselves. . . .

According to this case, a trustee will be liable if he retires with a negligent disregard for the future well-being of the fund.

10.5 Removal of trustees

10.5.1 General

In certain circumstances trustees may be removed from office against their will. Removal is effected by persons nominated for that task by the terms of the trust instrument, or (in the absence of a nominee) by persons authorized under s 36 of the Trustee Act 1925, or under s 19 of the Trusts of Land etc. Act 1996 (see 10.4.2.3), or by the court. The court may carry out such removal under its inherent jurisdiction or when appointing substitute trustees under the Trustee Act 1925, s 41. Where the trustees are removed under a power contained in the trust instrument they can be replaced under s 36 as if they had died.

10.5.2 Removal under Trustee Act 1925, s 36(1)

The grounds for removal include absence abroad for more than a year, refusal to act, unfitness to act and incapacity. The persons empowered by s 36 to appoint new trustees are similarly the persons empowered to remove the current trustees (see 10.2.1).

10.5.3 Removal under the court's inherent jurisdiction

In the case of *Letterstedt v Broers* (1884) 9 App Cas 371, Lord Blackburn said that 'In exercising so delicate a jurisdiction as that of removing trustees, their Lordships do not venture to lay down any general rule beyond the very broad principle . . . that their main guide must be the welfare of the beneficiaries'. In *Re Wrightson* [1908] 1 Ch 798 Warrington J expanded upon this by adding that trustees will be removed if the court thinks that the trust property is endangered by their continuing in office. While courts look at the circumstances of each case separately, the cases do provide limited guidelines. Thus it has been held that a trustee will not be removed simply because he has interests in conflict with the trust, provided the trust can function properly without his ever having to choose between the trust and his private interests (*Public Trustee v Cooper* [2001] WTLR 901) and it has been held that the occasional error by a trustee is not of itself a ground for removal (*Isaac v Isaac* [2005] EWHC 435 (Ch) Ch D para 73). The following sections set out further points of general guidance.

10.5.3.1 Hostility between trustees and beneficiaries

In *Letterstedt*, Lord Blackburn said that hostility of this sort was 'not of itself a reason for the removal of the trustees' but should not be disregarded. In that case several factors, including the hostility between the trustees and the beneficiaries, had the cumulative effect of leading to the removal of the trustees.

10.5.3.2 Trustees' dishonesty

In *Letterstedt*, Lord Blackburn approved the removal of trustees whose acts or omissions 'show a want of honesty, or a want of proper capacity to execute the duties, or a want of reasonable fidelity'. In *Re Wrightson* Warrington J approved this approach, saying that it was ancillary to the court's principal duty to see that the trusts are properly performed.

10.5.3.3 The expense of removal

There are indications in *Re Wrightson* that the court is sometimes reluctant to remove trustees because of the administrative expense to the trust fund of doing so. This may mean that courts will be more reluctant to remove trustees from trusts with smaller funds.

10.5.4 Removal under Trustee Act 1925, s 41

In *Re Lemann's Trust* (1883) 22 Ch D 633, an aged trustee was removed because, 'through old age and consequent bodily and mental infirmity' she was incapable of executing any documents. In *Re Henderson* [1940] Ch 764 a trustee was removed because she initially stated her wish to retire from the trust but at a later date insisted that she would not retire unless certain conditions were met. In *Re Tempest* (1866) LR 1 Ch App 485 it was stated that, if an existing trustee unreasonably refuses to cooperate with a new trustee whom the court has appointed, this might be a ground for removing the *existing* trustee from office.

10.6 What if nobody is willing to act as trustee?

Simon Gardner in his *Introduction to the Law of Trusts*, Clarendon Press, 1990, observes (at p 165) that 'human goodwill and the profit motive between them can be relied upon to produce a supply of people *prima facie* willing to be trustees'. This finds support in a survey carried out by C Bell in 1988 of 'a group of solicitors in Lancashire and Cumbria who do trust work on a regular basis':

C. Bell, 'Some reflections on choosing trustees', *Trust Law & Practice*, January 1988

Non-professional trustees

The solicitors' survey showed that despite the onerous nature of the office of trustee, getting suitable private individuals to agree to become trustees is not a major problem. Friendship for the settlor/testator or a sense of duty arising from the fact that the settlor/testator is a relative are the main reasons for private individuals agreeing to act as trustees. However, knowledge of the beneficiaries and a desire to help them was also highlighted in the solicitors' survey as a factor. It is interesting to note that private individuals who agree to act as trustees usually regard it as an honour and not a chore.

Clearly a non-professional trustee must be trustworthy. However, the solicitors' survey revealed that he ought also to have some or all of the following attributes: (i) a genuine interest in the objects of the trust; (ii) financial acumen and preferably with some business experience; (iii) sound judgment; (iv) common sense; and (v) strength of character to deal with difficult beneficiaries. The message from the survey was that it helps if a non-professional trustee is 'street wise'.

In the opinion of the solicitors questioned, very few private individuals who become trustees have a clear conception of the duties and responsibilities of trusteeship prior to their appointment. However, it seems that most of them do have some general appreciation of what is involved before becoming trustees.

Most trusts of any size are handled either solely by professional trustees or (more usually) by a mixture of professional and non-professional trustees. Although the latter combination generally works well in practice some problems clearly do arise. Sometimes non-professional trustees may have difficulty in understanding the niceties of trust law and fail to appreciate requirements, the reasons for which are obvious to professional trustees. Further in relation to the operation of discretionary powers, non-professional trustees may not infrequently try to 'bend' the rules for well-meaning reasons. Finally, there can be some disagreement between non-professional and professional trustees over investment/sale policies. Sometimes, non-professional trustees may be reluctant to follow a professional recommendation as to investment which the professional trustees are prepared to accept. . . .

But what if no willing person can be found to carry out the trust? The maxim states that no trust will fail for want of a trustee. If nobody can be found who is willing to accept the appointment, the court will in certain circumstances appoint the Public Trustee or a judicial trustee to discharge the trust. As a last resort, the court can even act as trustee itself on an *ad hoc* basis. As Lord Eldon LC acknowledged long ago in *Morice v Bishop of Durham* (1805) 10 Ves 539: 'As it is a maxim, that the execution of a trust shall be under the control of the court . . . if the trustee dies, the court itself can execute the trust'.

Judicial trustees are appointed where the ordinary trustees of the trust have failed in their administration of the trust. Their appointment under the Judicial Trustees Act 1896 is designed to avoid the expense of the court itself discharging the administrative obligations of the trustee. They have all the powers of ordinary trustees, but, as officers of the court, they also have ready access to the court's directions as to administration of the trust. The remuneration of a Judicial Trustee must be justified, reasonable and proportionate and is generally limited to 15 per cent of the capital value of the trust property (Judicial Trustees Rules 1983, r 11(1)(a), see Practice Direction [2003] All ER (D) 93 (Jul)).

The office of Public Trustee was established by s 1 of the Public Trustee Act 1906. The role of the Public Trustee is to administer trusts (typically private, non-business trusts), no matter how small, for whom no other trustee can be found. Although the court will take into account the wishes of the settlor when choosing new trustees, the settlor cannot exclude appointment of the Public Trustee in an appropriate case (*Re Duxbury's Settlement Trusts* [1995] 1 WLR 425).

It is in the office of the Public Trustee that the maxim *a trust will never fail for want of a trustee* finds its fullest expression.

CHAPTER SUMMARY

- We have seen that a trust does not fail for want of a trustee. According to the Trustee Act 1925, s 36(1) one or more new trustees may be appointed, in writing, whenever an existing trustee dies, remains abroad for more than a year, retires, refuses to act, is unfit to act, is incapable of acting or is an infant.
- We have identified the persons able to appoint trustees and the persons able to act as trustees:
  - The person empowered to make the appointment is the person named in the trust deed to carry out that particular function.
  - Only if nobody is so named is the power to appoint given to the existing trustees or, if they have all died, to the personal representatives of the last trustee to have died.
  - When a sole trustee dies that trustee's personal representatives will become the trustees for the time being if they accept the trusts (Administration of Estates Act 1925, s 1(2)) but they can be ousted by the appointment of other trustees by a person nominated in the trust instrument to appoint trustees.
- We have identified the matters to which a trustee should attend upon taking up an appointment, including:
  - Ascertaining the terms of the trust
  - 'Getting in' the trust property
  - Acting on suspicions, bringing a claim against current and former trustees if necessary.
- We can advise a trustee as to how they may disclaim the trust:
  - A person appointed as trustee of an express trust may decide to decline the appointment, in which event they should do so by a disclaimer, usually in the form of a deed. But if the trustee acts in performance of the trust it will then be too late to disclaim.
  - In *Re Lord and Fullerton's Contract* [1896] 1 Ch 228, the question arose whether a trustee of real and personal property, some existing in England and some abroad, could disclaim the trust except as to the property abroad. The Court of Appeal decided against partial disclaimer in any circumstances.
  - In certain limited situations a trust will fail because the potential 'trustee' disclaims the trusteeship:
    - trusts which require specific trustees
    - *inter vivos* trusts disclaimed before constitution.
- We know the methods by which a trustee might retire, or be removed, from the trust:
  - Retirement under Trustee Act 1925, s 36—this section provides, *inter alia*, for the appointment of a new trustee, or trustees, 'in the place of' a trustee 'desiring to be discharged'.
  - Retirement under Trustee Act 1925, s 39—the essential difference between s 39 and s 36 is that s 39 permits retirement of a trustee without the appointment of a replacement trustee.
  - Removal under Trustee Act 1925, s 36(1)—the grounds for removal include absence abroad for more than a year, refusal to act, unfitness to act and incapacity. The persons empowered by s 36 to appoint new trustees are similarly the persons empowered to remove the current trustees.

- Where the facts which constitute the grounds for removal are not disputed, the court may remove trustees under s 41 of the Trustee Act 1925 when appointing one or more replacement trustees under that section. In any other case the court may remove a trustee under its inherent jurisdiction.
- Removal under the court's inherent jurisdiction. Possible grounds include:
  - hostility between trustees and beneficiaries
  - trustees' dishonesty.

SUMMATIVE ASSESSMENT EXERCISE

online resource centre

The following scenario has been devised to raise several of the matters considered in this chapter.

Sarah settled an *inter vivos* trust. The deed appointed Tom, Tracy, Tim, Terry and Tarquin to be trustees and Albert, who was then 17, to be the person able to appoint new trustees. The trust property consisted of two freehold houses, directed to be held upon trust for certain infant beneficiaries as joint tenants in equity. Immediately upon hearing of the trust the named trustees executed a 'Deed of Disclaimer'. Without delay Albert told a friend, Tabitha, that she could be a trustee and sometime afterwards he appointed himself as a trustee. A short while later Tabitha expressed a desire to be discharged from the trust. Albert agreed to release her.

Who are the current trustees, if any, of the trust?

FURTHER READING

Bell, C, 'Some reflections on choosing trustees', *Trust Law & Practice*, January 1988.

Kirkland, K, 'Recruiting, Selecting and Inducing Charity Trustees' (2002) 4 Private Client Business 253.

Matthews, P, 'The Constitution of Disclaimed Trusts *Inter Vivos*' [1981] Conv 141.

11 The nature of trusteeship

OBJECTIVES

By the end of this chapter, you should be able to:

1 Advise a trustee as to how to meet their fiduciary obligations to the trust

2 Define the standard of care which trustees must exercise in service of the trust

3 Brief a trustee on the discretionary nature of their decision-making powers

4 Explain the requirement that trustees must act unanimously

11.1 Introduction

In this chapter we shall analyse the general nature of trusteeship (what it means to be a trustee on a day-to-day basis) and in the next chapter we shall see how this is expressed in terms of a number of specific duties (for example, the duty to act without payment).

> **? QUESTION 11.1**
>
> What do you think the terms 'trustee' and '*cestui que trust*' mean? What do the definitions tell you about trusteeship?

'Trustee' means 'one who is trusted', and '*cestui que trust*' literally means 'the one who trusts'. Although nowadays we invariably refer to the *cestuis que trust* as the 'beneficiaries', the message is still clear: the trustee must act in the interests of the beneficiaries and not out of self-interest. This does not mean that a trustee must obey the wishes of the beneficiaries. The trustee must serve the beneficiaries, but within their larger obligation to serve the trust in accordance with the terms of the trust instrument and the general law. The trustees must, it is said, discharge the trust that is placed in them, for in one sense the settlor is 'the one who trusts'.

Trustees might be held personally liable to the beneficiaries for breaches of their trust whether arising out of their acts or omissions. In particular you should be aware that trustees can breach their trust by inactivity. Trustees must act, but they must act carefully. (We consider the standard of care at 11.3.) Trustees must also act loyally—we consider that duty next.

11.2 Fiduciary office

We have already noted that the trustee's relationship to the beneficiary of the trust is a fiduciary one.

? QUESTION 11.2

Can you think of other relationships which the law generally regards to be fiduciary?

You might have chosen the relationship between:

- an agent and their principal (for example, solicitor and client)
- a director and their company
- partner and co-partner.

The first party to each of these relationships is in some sense in a position of trust and certain consequences flow from this. For example, a solicitor is not permitted to place their own money and clients' money in the same bank account. Likewise, a company director 'on appointment to that office, assumes the duties of a trustee in relation to the company's property' (*per* Chadwick LJ in *JJ Harrison (Properties) Ltd v Harrison* [2002] 1 BCLC 162). It is important to appreciate, however, that not every duty of a person in a fiduciary office is necessarily a fiduciary duty (*New Zealand Netherlands Society v Kuys* [1973] 1 WLR 1126 (PC) *per* Lord Wilberforce at 1130).

Who is and who is not a fiduciary is a question which has taxed the minds of leading judges and academics for many years. For a flavour of the difficulties involved see Professor Paul Finn's chapter, 'Fiduciary Law', in *Commercial Aspects of Trusts and Fiduciary Obligations*, McKendrick (ed), 1992, OUP. Professor Finn's illuminating work was at the forefront of the thinking of Millett LJ in *Bristol and West Building Society v Mothew* [1998] Ch 1, where he said (at p 18):

> A fiduciary is someone who has undertaken to act for or on behalf of another in a particular matter in circumstances which give rise to a relationship of trust and confidence. The distinguishing obligation of a fiduciary is the obligation of loyalty. The principal is entitled to the single-minded loyalty of his fiduciary. This core liability has several facets. A fiduciary must act in good faith: he must not make a profit out of his trust; he must not place himself in a position where his duty and his interest may conflict; he may not act for his own benefit or the benefit of a third person without the informed consent of his principal. This is not intended to be an exhaustive list, but it is sufficient to indicate the nature of fiduciary obligations. They are the defining characteristics of the fiduciary. As Dr Finn

pointed out in his classic work *Fiduciary Obligations* (1977) p. 2, he is not subject to fiduciary obligations because he is a fiduciary; it is because he is subject to them that he is a fiduciary.

The trustee-beneficiary relationship is the fiduciary relationship *par excellence*. Transactions carried out by the trustee will be scrutinized. As the Privy Council stated in *Williams v Scott* [1900] AC 499: 'the burden of proof that the transaction is a righteous one rests upon the trustee'. But, what is more, the law will not permit trustees so much as to put themselves in a position where there might be (a) a conflict between their duty to the trust and their self-interest or (b) a conflict between their duty to the trust and their duty to others.

It may be legitimate to suggest a distinction between two basic forms of breach of fiduciary duty. The first, 'positional' breach, occurs when the fiduciary puts himself in a position of potential conflict of interest and duty. The second, 'transactional' breach, occurs when the potential conflict is actualized by some transaction, for example, the purchase of trust property off the trust (see self-dealing at 11.2.1.1). In *Bristol and West BS v Mothew* (above) Millett LJ (now Lord Millett) stated that a fiduciary must take special care to avoid, not only *potential* conflict, but what his Lordship described as a position of 'actual conflict'. This, in his Lordship's words, is a position where he 'cannot fulfil his obligations to one principal without failing in his obligations to the other . . . if he does, he may have no alternative but to cease to act for at least one and preferably both'. In such a case the inevitability of the transactional breach creates a positional breach, even where the fiduciary finds himself in the position of conflict through no fault of his own.

11.2.1 Conflict of interest and duty

Under this general heading we will include, for present purposes, cases of conflict between the trustees' duty to the trust and their duty to others *and* cases where the conflict is between the trustees' duty to the trust and their self-interest.

EXERCISE 11.1

Read the following extract from the decision of the Court of Appeal in *Sargeant and Another v National Westminster Bank plc and Another* (1990) 61 P & CR 518. In that case the trustees were in a position of potential conflict between their self-interest and their duties to the beneficiaries, but they were not in breach of trust. Why?

Sargeant and Another v National Westminster Bank plc and Another (1990) 61 P & CR 518, Court of Appeal

A testator let a number of farms to his children which they worked as a partnership. He then appointed his children to be executors and trustees under his will. When one of the children (Charles) died the surviving children exercised an option to purchase the deceased child's share of the partnership. Later they revealed plans to purchase the freehold of one of the farms of which they were tenants, and to sell the other freeholds. The administrators of the estate of the deceased child objected to these plans and argued that the surviving children would be in breach of their trust were they to sell, to themselves, the trust-owned freeholds of which they were trustees and under which they were tenants. The trustees sought a declaration that they would be entitled to sell the freeholds. This declaration was granted. The administrators appealed.

Nourse LJ:

> What then happened on the death of Charles? He necessarily ceased to be a trustee of the will. His estate retained his beneficial interest in the farms, subject to the tenancies. The arrangements between the children might have been such that his estate retained his interest in the tenancies as well. No doubt for a short period it did. But under the provisions of the partnership deed, to which Charles himself had been a party, the trustees acquired his share in the partnership, including his share in the tenancies. Thenceforth each of the trustees continued to have the rights of a tenant and a beneficiary. But Charles' estate only had the rights of a beneficiary.
>
> It cannot be doubted that the trustees have ever since been in a position where their interests as tenants may conflict with their duties as trustees to the estate of Charles. But the conclusive objection to the application of the absolute rule on which Mr Romer relies is that it is not they who have put themselves in that position. They have been put there mainly by the testator's grant of the tenancies and by the provisions of his will and partly by contractual arrangements to which Charles himself was a party and of which his representatives cannot complain. The administrators cannot therefore complain of the trustees' continued assertion of their rights as tenants.

If the trustees had put themselves in the position of potential conflict of interest and duty that would indeed have constituted a breach of trust. However, the trustees in *Sargeant* were not liable because it was the testator who had placed the trustees in the position of conflict. In the absence of evidence that the trustees had failed, or would fail, to discharge their duty to the beneficiaries there was no breach of trust. The trustees were able to exercise their pre-existing right, as tenants, to purchase the trust-owned freeholds from themselves. There had been no 'positional' breach of trust, and provided that the trustees obtained the best price reasonably obtainable for these freeholds (subject to the tenancies) there would be no 'transactional' breach of trust.

In *Re Mulholland's WT* [1949] 1 All ER 460, Wynn-Parry J stated that 'the existence of the fiduciary relationship creates an inability in the trustee to contract in regard to the trust property [but] does not touch the position arising where the contract in question has been brought into existence before the fiduciary relationship'. *Mulholland* was not referred to in *Sargeant* but the consequence of these cases when read together seems to be that, to some degree at least, the beneficiaries must take the trustees as they find them, despite the existence of prior, potentially conflicting, interests.

EXERCISE 11.2

Read the following extract from the judgment of Millett LJ (as he then was) in the Court of Appeal in *Bristol and West Building Society v Mothew*. In what circumstances is a trust beneficiary (or the 'beneficiary' of a fiduciary duty) entitled to complain of conflict of interest even though the conflict pre-existed the trust or was otherwise authorized?

***Bristol and West Building Society v Mothew* [1998] Ch 1**

Millett LJ:

> Even if a fiduciary is properly acting for two principals with potentially conflicting interests he must act in good faith in the interests of each and must not act with the intention of furthering the interests of one principal to the prejudice of those of the other (see Finn p. 48). I shall call this 'the duty of good faith'. But it goes further than this. He must not allow the performance of his obligations to one principal to be influenced by his relationship with the other. He must serve each as faithfully and loyally as if he were his only principal. Conduct which is in breach of this duty need not be dishonest but it must be intentional. An unconscious omission which happens to benefit one principal at the expense of the other does not constitute a breach of fiduciary duty, though it may constitute a breach of the duty of skill and care. This is because the principle which is in play is that the fiduciary must not be inhibited by the existence of his other employment from serving the interests of his principal as faithfully and effectively as if he were the only employer. I shall call this 'the no inhibition principle'. Unless the fiduciary is inhibited or believes (whether rightly or wrongly) that he is inhibited in the performance of his duties to one principal by reason of his employment by the other, his failure to act is not attributable to the double employment. Finally, the fiduciary must take care not to find himself in a position where there is an *actual* conflict of duty so that he cannot fulfil his obligations to one principal without failing in his obligations to the other: see *Moody v Cox* [1917] 2 Ch 71 and *Commonwealth Bank of Australia v Smith* (1991) 102 ALR 453. If he does, he may have no alternative but to cease to act for at least one and preferably both. The fact that he cannot fulfil his obligations to one principal without being in breach of his obligations to the other will not absolve him from liability. I shall call this 'the actual conflict rule'. . . .

We have already observed that, as a general rule, the inquiry according to which one determines whether there is a conflict of interest is to ask 'not what was done, but what *might* be done' (*per* Viscount Dunedin in *Wright v Morgan* [1926] AC 788 (emphasis added)). A number of cases have been decided as exceptions to this general rule. One is *Holder v Holder* [1968] Ch 353 where Harman LJ held in favour of a trustee having acknowledged that 'there must never be a conflict of duty and interest but in fact there *was none* here' (emphasis added). A more recent exception appears from the case of *Re Drexel Burnham Lambert UK Pension Plan* [1995] 1 WLR 32. Here a scheme to distribute surplus assets in a pension fund was approved, even though it had been proposed by trustees who were beneficiaries under the scheme. Lindsay J recognized that there were many exceptions to the general rule and that the trustees in this case had doubtless been selected as persons able to exercise their discretion properly.

11.2.1.1 The self-dealing rule and fair-dealing rule

Chapter 12 examines the specific duties of trustees arising from the general nature of trusteeship. However, it is convenient to mention here the self-dealing and fair-dealing rules, the principal rationale of which is that trustees must not let their duty and interest conflict.

EXERCISE 11.3

Analyse the passage from *Re Thompson's Settlement* [1985] 2 All ER 720 set out next. Try to define in your own words the distinction between self-dealing and fair-dealing.

***Re Thompson's Settlement* [1985] 2 All ER 720**

Vinelott J:

> It is clear that the self-dealing rule is an application of the wider principle that a man must not put himself in a position where duty and interest conflict or where his duty to one conflicts with his duty to another: see in particular the opinion of Lord Dunedin in *Wright v Morgan* [1926] AC 788 which I have cited. The principle is applied stringently in cases where a trustee concurs in a transaction which cannot be carried into effect without his concurrence and who also has an interest in or owes a fiduciary duty to another in relation to the same transaction. The transaction cannot stand if challenged by a beneficiary because in the absence of an express provision in the trust instrument the beneficiaries are entitled to require that the trustees act unanimously and that each brings to bear a mind unclouded by any contrary interest or duty in deciding whether it is in the interest of the beneficiaries that the trustees concur in it.
>
> The same principle also applies, but less stringently, in a case within the fair-dealing rule, such as the purchase by a trustee of a beneficiary's beneficial interest. There, there are genuinely two parties to the transaction and it will be allowed to stand if freely entered into and if the trustee took no advantage from his position or from any knowledge acquired from it.
>
> In the instant case the concurrence of the trustees of the grandchildren's settlement was required if the leases were to be assigned to or new tenancies created in favour of the new company and the partnership. The beneficiaries were entitled to ask that the trustees should give unprejudiced consideration to the question whether they should refuse to concur in the assignments in the expectation that a surrender of the leases might be negotiated from the old company and the estates sold or let on the open market. . . .

In *Re Thompson's*, Vinelott J followed the authority of *Tito v Waddell (No 2)* [1977] 3 All ER 129 in which he had appeared as counsel and had successfully advanced the orthodox view that the self-dealing and fair-dealing rules were different rules and not merely separate limbs of the same rule. The self-dealing rule is that 'if a trustee sells the trust property to himself the sale is voidable by any beneficiary *ex debito justitiae*, however fair the transaction'. The fair-dealing rule, on the other hand, is that 'if a trustee purchases the beneficial interest of any of his beneficiaries, the transaction is not voidable *ex debito justitiae* but can be set aside by the beneficiary unless the trustee can show that he has taken no advantage of his position and has made full disclosure to the beneficiary, and that the transaction is fair and honest'. (*Ex debito justitiae* means, literally, 'out of a debt to justice'.)

In *Re Thompson's*, Vinelott J stated that the principle that a trustee must not put himself in a position where his duty and interest may conflict applies less stringently in a case of fair-dealing, as compared with a case of self-dealing, because the former can involve a genuine contract between two independent parties.

11.2.1.2 The effect of retirement

In *Re Boles* [1902] 1 Ch 244 the purchase of trust property by the trustee 12 years after his retirement was held not to infringe the rule that trustees must not put themselves in a position where their interest and duty might conflict. According to Buckley J a retired trustee can purchase trust property if 'there is nothing to show that at the time of retirement there was any idea of a sale'. This will be hard to prove unless a very long period of time has gone by (although a span of 12 years is unlikely to be required in the majority of cases). The court will certainly regard with suspicion a purchase of trust property occurring shortly after retirement. In any event, do not forget that the burden is on the trustee to show that the transaction is a 'righteous' one.

11.3 Trustees' standard of care

We have already observed that trustees must *act* in service of the trust, they cannot stand idly by. It follows that they should act carefully, but just how careful must they be?

The answer to that question is clearer since the Trustee Act 2000 came into force on 1 February 2001.

11.3.1 The law before the Trustee Act 2000

Before the Act it was sometimes hard to identify the standard of care appropriate to particular trustees in particular circumstances. It was fairly clear that the standard of care varied according to whether the trustees were amateur or professional and according to whether or not they were remunerated. However, it was difficult to discern from the cases the relative weight attached by the courts to the factors of 'professionalism' and 'remuneration'. Whilst it was apparently of some significance that trustees were remunerated (for example, *Bartlett v Barclays Bank (No 1)* [1980] 1 All ER 139; *Re Waterman's WT* [1952] 2 All ER 1054), others did not consider remuneration in itself to be a factor that should lead to a higher standard of care (*Jobson v Palmer* [1893] 1 Ch 71). Those cases in which the standard was raised on account of trustees' professed expertise usually involved trust corporations so it was no easy task to determine how a human trustee professing particular expertise should be judged.

Absent any special factors such as remuneration and professionalism and the standard of care generally applied to trustees in the performance of their duties is the standard of the ordinary prudent person of business. Jessel MR in *Speight v Gaunt* (1883) 22 Ch D 727 expressed that duty thus:

> a trustee ought to conduct the business of the trust in the same manner that an ordinary prudent man of business would conduct his own.

In the Court of Appeal in *Re Whiteley* (1886) Ch D 347 (later approved in the House of Lords) Lindley LJ enlarged upon the *Speight* test:

> The duty of the trustee is to take such care as an ordinary prudent man of business would take if he were minded to make an investment for the benefit of *other people* for whom he felt morally obliged to provide. That is the kind of business the ordinary prudent man is supposed to be engaged in (emphasis added).

QUESTION 11.3

Do you think that such a high standard of care is fair? (You might want to list the arguments for and against it.)

At first sight it does not seem fair, but courts often have the invidious task of trying to establish where loss to the trust should fall as between the honest trustee in breach and the innocent beneficiary. Why should they not prefer the innocent beneficiary, as long as the office of trustee is not be made so onerous that honest people will be reluctant to undertake it?

Perhaps the strongest argument *in favour* of a high standard of care is that the trustees have undertaken their office voluntarily and the beneficiaries rely upon them. This argument is all the more compelling where the trustee is a paid professional. As Harman J put it in *Re Waterman's WT* [1952] 2 All ER 1054: 'I do not forget that a paid trustee is expected to exercise a higher standard of diligence and knowledge than an unpaid trustee, and that a bank which advertises itself largely in the public press as taking charge of administration is under a special duty' (followed in *Bartlett v Barclays Bank (No 1)* [1980] 1 All ER 139). Conversely, in one case the court appears to have been persuaded, by the fact that the particular trustee was an unpaid non-professional ('a missionary ignorant of business affairs' is how he was described), to judge that trustee by a subjective standard of care. That case was *Re Vickery* [1931] 1 Ch 572. The facts were similar to those in *Speight v Gaunt* (1883) 22 Ch D 727, in that the loss was caused to the trust fund by a third party who had been appointed as an agent by the trustee. Both cases were similar in their result, the court deciding that the loss caused by the third party should fall upon the trust fund and not upon the trustees personally, but whereas in *Speight* an objective standard was applied, in *Re Vickery* the trustee was held not have breached his trust because he had not been *subjectively* conscious of any wrongdoing. The reasoning in *Re Vickery* has been much criticized because it appears to protect 'honest fools', but even its most determined critic (G H Jones (1959) 22 MLR 388) admits that 'in the result' the case may have been correctly decided. The authors of *Parker and Mellows* (6th edn) also express the view that the result in the case was arguably 'desirable', despite the fact that it was 'technically incorrect'.

EXERCISE 11.4

Read the following brief quotation from 'The Trustee's Duty of Skill and Care' [1973] 37 Conv 48. For which types of trustees does the author recommend a subjective standard of care?

Dennis R Paling, 'The Trustee's Duty of Skill and Care' [1973] 37 Conv 48

The traditional view stated by Underhill and by the editors of subsequent editions of his text-book up to and including the tenth edition was that the same standard should be demanded of a trustee whether he acts gratuitously or receives payment. Romer J in *Jobson v Palmer* [1893] 1 Ch 71 expressed the same view. He thus held that a paid trustee, who had selected a servant with the same degree of prudence as an ordinary man of business would exercise in his own affairs, was not liable when the servant stole trust property.

But it is preferable to distinguish between the standards imposed upon paid and unpaid trustees, because the status of paid and unpaid trustees is different. The paid trustee is frequently a banker or actuary who advertises for business and has no personal relationship with the settlor. The unpaid trustee is frequently a personal friend of the settlor . . . if the standard of skill and care expected of an unpaid trustee is that of an ordinary prudent man in the conduct of his own affairs, the higher standard to be imposed upon a paid trustee must be oppressively high. This may make the trustee excessively cautious, and because he chooses the safest investments the income produced will often be relatively less. Moreover, unless the court is prepared to examine the adequacy of the payment, it may enable the settlor to impose the higher standard of liability by making a token payment.

The distinction between paid and unpaid trustees could however be retained and these unfortunate consequences could be avoided if the standard of skill and care demanded of an unpaid trustee were to be that which he is accustomed to exercise with regard to his own private affairs, whilst the standard of skill and care demanded of a paid trustee was henceforth that which the ordinary prudent man would exercise in the management of his own affairs if he were regardful of the pecuniary interests in the future of those having claims upon him. . . .

Dr Paling suggested a subjective standard of care for unremunerated trustees precisely because they are, typically, also amateurs. He contrasts them with the usual paid trustee who is 'frequently a banker or actuary who advertises his services for business and has no personal relationship with the settlor'.

11.3.2 The law after the Trustee Act 2000

The new standard of care, as set out in s 1 of the Trustee Act 2000, is as follows:

1.—(1) Whenever the duty under this subsection applies to a trustee, he must exercise such care and skill as is reasonable in the circumstances, having regard in particular—

(a) to any special knowledge or experience that he has or holds himself out as having, and

(b) if he acts as trustee in the course of a business or profession, to any special knowledge or experience that it is reasonable to expect of a person acting in the course of that kind of business or profession.

(2) In this Act the duty under subsection (1) is called 'the duty of care'.

According to Schedule 1 of the Act the duty of care applies to a trustee (a) when exercising the general power of investment or a power of investment conferred on him by the trust instrument and (b) when carrying out statutory duties relating to the exercise of a power of investment or to the review of investments.

According to the notes accompanying the Act, the duty applies to trustees not only 'when carrying out their functions under the Act' but also when carrying out 'equivalent functions under the trust instrument'. The notes add that 'the phrase "duty of care" signifies a duty to take care to avoid causing injury or loss'. The duty is intended to take effect in addition to such fundamental duties of trustees as acting in the best interests of the beneficiaries and complying with the terms of the trust *but* 'will exclude any common law duty of care which might otherwise have applied'. The Act is not intended to alter the orthodox rule of trust law which prohibits beneficiaries from suing their trustees for negligence at common law. If one were suspicious that the reason for this was because the statutory duty of care is merely a version of the common law duty of care in negligence applied to a trust (equitable) context, the notes accompanying the Act seek to allay those suspicions. They provide (at note 12) that:

> In relation to the investment of trust funds the new duty makes statutorily explicit the present common law duty which measures the behaviour of the trustees against that expected of the ordinary prudent man of business.

The statutory duty of care is intended to enact, and not to discredit, the standard of care which was formerly set out in such cases as *Speight v Gaunt* and *Re Whiteley*. The standard remains a high one, akin to the care that might be expected from a prudent family provider. However, the new duty of care resolves the uncertainties of the old cases. There can now be no doubt that *Re Vickery* is bad law, that trustees should never be judged according to their own subjective *opinions* as to what constitutes prudent behaviour. Having said that, the statutory 'duty of care', whilst objective, is nevertheless one which is variable according to the subjective *characteristics* of the trustee. Factors which might lead to a stricter standard would include the trustee's experience and expertise (professed or real). Hence, according to note 13 of the explanatory notes accompanying the Act:

> in relation to the purchase of stocks and shares, a higher standard may be expected of a trustee who is an investment banker, specialising in equities, than of a trustee who is a beekeeper, particularly if the investment banker is acting as a trustee in the course of his or her investment banking business.

According to s 1(1) the appropriate level of the new standard of care is to be determined according to whatever is reasonable 'in the circumstances'. It could be raised (for example, if the trustee professed a relevant expertise) or perhaps even lowered (for example, in the case of a trainee professional). The circumstances appearing in paras 1(1)(a) and (b) (set out at the start of this section) will be of particular relevance to the determination of the appropriate standard. Other circumstances which might be taken into account include the nature, composition and purposes of the trust.

It is notable that s 1(1) makes no express reference to remuneration, which may be because the 2000 Act introduces a presumption that all professional trustees will be remunerated (see 12.2). Yet despite this omission one imagines that an especially high level of remuneration would be a factor in favour of raising the standard of care required of a trustee, although equally one expects that the courts will wish to avoid as far as possible passing judgment on the highly subjective and sensitive question of what constitutes normal remuneration. It should be noted that, even if remuneration is not relevant to the identification of the appropriate standard of care, it will be relevant to determining whether a trustee ought to be relieved of liability for a breach of trust. A paid trustee is less likely to be relieved of liability under the Trustee Act 1925, s 61 than an unpaid trustee (see 15.4.4).

Schedule I to the Act lists the circumstances in which the statutory duty of care will apply (Trustee Act 2000, s 2). They include the exercise of general investment powers, 'however conferred' (Sch I, para 1, see **Chapter 14**); the exercise of any power, 'however conferred', to acquire land (Sch I, para 2, see **Chapter 14**); the appointment of agents, nominees and custodians (Sch I, para 3) and the insurance of trust property (Sch I, para 5). But '[t]he duty of care does not apply to powers conferred by a trust instrument if or in so far as it appears from the trust instrument that the duty is not meant to apply' (Sch I, para 7).

11.3.3 Exemption clauses

Having seen that the general law applies a high standard to certain professional trustees it may come as a surprise to discover that in practice professional trustees are often subject to a lower standard than their amateur and unpaid counterparts. This is because professional trustees are more likely than other trustees to insist upon the inclusion in the trust instrument of carefully drafted exemption clauses designed to limit their liability. Such clauses are construed strictly *contra proferentem*. In other words, if there is any ambiguity in their meaning, they will be construed against the trustee who is seeking to rely upon the clause. In *Bogg v Raper* (1998) *The Times*, 22 April, Millett LJ held that settlements should be fairly construed without any presumption in favour of one party or the other, but if there remained a doubt whether the matter complained of came within the scope of the exemption clause it must be regarded as falling outside it. See, also, *Wight v Olswang (No 1)* [1999] *The Times*, 18 May, where a settlement contained two exemption clauses, a general one protecting all trustees, and one which specifically did not apply to paid trustees. The Court of Appeal held that the paid trustees could not even rely upon the general clause.

EXERCISE 11.5

Attempt to draft an exemption clause for a trustee who wishes to secure immunity from breaches of trust. After reading the remainder of this paragraph, and the extract from the judgment of Millett LJ (as he then was) in *Armitage v Nurse*, you should re-examine your draft clause and decide whether or not it is valid.

The crucial question, as the preceding Exercise suggests, is whether such clauses are effective, or should be effective, to exclude a trustee's liability for breach of trust in every case. For example, should the trustee be immune from liability for errors of judgement which amount to gross negligence? What about immunity for deliberate wrongdoing?

An answer was provided in *Rae v Meek* (1889) 14 App Cas 558, a decision of the House of Lords under Scottish law. There Lord Herschell approved the view that 'such a clause is ineffectual to protect a trustee against the consequences of *culpa lata*, or gross negligence on his part, or of any conduct which is inconsistent with bona fides'.

The decision in *Rae v Meek* to fix liability upon the honest trustee on the basis of culpable negligence sits somewhat uneasily with the decision of the Court of Appeal in *Armitage v Nurse* [1997] 2 All ER 705. There a clause in a trust instrument purported to excuse the trustees from all liability apart from that which might arise from their own actual fraud. Millett LJ held that the clause was effective to exclude liability no matter how indolent, imprudent, lacking in diligence, negligent or wilful the trustees may have been, so long as they had not acted dishonestly. It was held that the clause was not void for repugnancy or contrary to public policy. The beneficiaries in *Armitage* did not allege dishonesty, therefore the trustees were not liable for any breach of trust. Millett LJ accepted that there was an irreducible core of obligations owed by trustees to beneficiaries and enforceable by them, namely, obligations of honesty and good faith, but his Lordship did not accept that those core obligations include duties of skill, care, prudence and diligence. In *Bristol and West v Mothew* [1997] 1 Ch 1 at 17 his Lordship drew a similar distinction between breach of fiduciary duty (that is, breach of the fiduciary duties of loyalty, honesty and good faith) and the obligation to use proper skill and care in the discharge of his duties.

Armitage v Nurse [1997] 3 WLR 1046, Court of Appeal

By a settlement made on 11 October 1984 the plaintiff, who was then aged 17, became entitled in remainder to settled agricultural land of which her mother was tenant for life. Her portion was to be held on certain trusts until she reached the age of 40. Clause 15 of the settlement provided that no trustee should be liable for any loss or damage to the plaintiff's fund or the income thereof at any time or from any case unless it was caused by his own actual fraud. It was held by Millett LJ that there was 'no question of the clause being repugnant to the trust'.

Millett LJ:

> I accept the submission made on behalf of [the plaintiff] that there is an irreducible core of obligations owed by the trustees to the beneficiaries and enforceable by them which is fundamental to the concept of a trust. If the beneficiaries have no rights enforceable against the trustees there are no trusts. But I do not accept the further submission that these core obligations include the duties of skill and care, prudence and diligence. The duty of the trustees to perform the trusts honestly and in good faith for the benefit of the beneficiaries is the minimum necessary to give substance to the trusts, but in my opinion it is sufficient. As Mr Hill pertinently pointed out in his able argument, a trustee who relied on the presence of a trustee exemption clause to justify what he proposed to do would thereby lose its protection: he would be acting recklessly in the proper sense of the term. . . .
>
> The submission that it is contrary to public policy to exclude the liability of a trustee for gross negligence is not supported by any English or Scottish authority. . . .
>
> At the same time, it must be acknowledged that the view is widely held that these clauses have gone too far, and that trustees who charge for their services and who, as professional men, would not dream of excluding liability for ordinary professional negligence should not be able to rely on a trustee exemption clause excluding liability for gross negligence. Jersey introduced a law in 1989 which denies effect to a trustee exemption clause which purports to absolve a trustee from liability for his own 'fraud, wilful misconduct or gross negligence.' The subject is presently under consideration in this country by the Trust Law Committee under the chairmanship of Sir John Vinelott. If clauses such as clause 15 of the settlement are to be denied effect, then in my opinion this should be done by Parliament, which will have the advantage of wide consultation with interested bodies and the advice of the Trust Law Committee. . . .

The meaning of dishonesty was considered in *Walker v Stones* (2000) *Independent*, 27 July, CA. The judge at first instance had held ((2000) 1 WTLR 79) that the deliberate commission of a breach of trust was dishonest only where the trustee committing that breach acted in the knowledge that it was contrary to the interests of the beneficiary or was recklessly indifferent thereto. A trustee's conduct in breach of trust could not be categorized as dishonest where he acted in a genuine, if misguided, belief that his actions were for the benefit of the beneficiary. The Court of Appeal disagreed. Allowing the appeal, it was held that an individual could act dishonestly, in the ordinary sense of the word, even where they genuinely believed their actions to be morally justified.

11.3.3.1 Reform of the law relating to trustee exemption clauses

The Law Commission has provisionally proposed that legislation should be introduced to prohibit reliance by professional trustees (trust corporations and other trustees acting in a professional capacity) on exemption clauses which purport to exclude liability for breach of trust arising from negligence (*Trustee Exemption Clauses*, Consultation Paper No 171, 2 December 2002).

11.4 Trustee decision-making

Trustees must necessarily make various decisions in discharging their duties under the trust.

EXERCISE 11.6

On the basis of what you have already learned about trustees draw up a list of the sort of issues you think trustees have to make decisions on.

You will be able to add many items to your list by the end of this book. Trustees must, for example, decide whom to appoint as new trustees should the need arise, how to invest the trust fund, and we have already seen that in 'discretionary trusts' they must appoint the beneficiaries of the trust and decide how to divide the trust fund amongst them. Although trustees are obliged to exercise their own discretion, they are permitted to ask the court to confirm any proposed course of action. The court will give its guidance by way of an order for directions or declaratory relief.

11.4.1 The exercise of discretion

Trustees' discretions are classified as being either 'dispositive' or 'administrative'. According to the orthodox view, dispositive discretions relate to the disposition of the trust property and administrative discretions relate to the management of the trust. Examples of 'dispositive discretions' include the distribution of income and capital under discretionary trusts (see 4.5.2) whereas the class of 'administrative discretions' includes the trustees' choice as to how best to invest the trust property (see **Chapter 14**). The detail of these specific examples is to be found in other chapters and our aim here is to attempt to distil from the cases general principles which should inform the exercise by trustees of their discretions. In particular, trustees should be aware of the degree to which their decisions will be subject to review by the courts.

The first thing to note is that where the trustees have a power and the trust instrument gives them the discretion to exercise it or not, the new duty of care (Trustee Act 2000, s 1) governs the manner of the exercise of that power should the trustee choose to exercise it. However, the notes to the Act make it clear that the duty of care 'will not apply to a decision by the trustees as to whether to exercise that discretionary power in the first place'.

Gisborne v Gisborne (1877) 2 App Cas 300 was a case involving a dispositive discretion. A will trust granted the trustees an absolute discretion and 'uncontrollable authority' over a fund. Lord Cairns, the Lord Chancellor, stated that:

> Larger words than these, it appears to me, it would be impossible to introduce into a will. The trustees are not merely to have a discretion, but they are to have 'uncontrollable', that is, 'uncontrolled', authority. Their discretion and authority, always supposing that there is no *mala fides* with regard to its exercise, is to be without check or control from any superior tribunal.

For the Lord Chancellor 'the question . . . must really come back to the construction of the will'.

The trustees in *Re Locker's Settlement* [1977] 1 WLR 1323 had an 'absolute and uncontrolled' dispositive discretion, according to the terms of the settlement. Goulding J, following *Gisborne v Gisborne*, acknowledged that this prevented interference by the court in a *bona fide* exercise of that discretion but held that it did not prevent the court's intervention in a case where the trustees had totally failed to act. However, if the trustees, as in *Re Locker's ST*, wished to exercise their discretion late the court would normally encourage them to do so, as Goulding J acknowledged:

> A tardy distribution at the discretion of the trustees is . . . nearer to . . . what the settlor intended, than tardy distribution by the trustees at the discretion of someone else.

In *Re Locker's ST* the beneficiaries' best interests required that the court did intervene to exercise the discretion.

These cases illustrate the court's general reluctance to interfere in the exercise of trust discretions. They should be contrasted with the case of *Re Roper's Trust* (1879) 9 Ch D 272 where the testator's will required the trustees to pay income to his niece, Fanny Keech, for her to hold upon trust for her children and 'to be by her applied for their benefit at her discretion'. Fry J said, 'I think that Fanny Keech has not exercised a sound discretion, and that where the court finds such to be the case, though the income is by the words of the will left to the discretion of a given person, the court has power to control that discretion and to deal with the income'. It is notable that in *Re Roper's Trust* the discretion had not been expressly described in the trust instrument as being 'absolute' or 'uncontrolled' and it must be doubted that Fry J would have set aside the exercise of a trustee's discretion in the face of such wording.

It is one thing for the court to set aside the exercise of a discretion because it does not approve of the result (as in *Re Roper's Trust*); it is another thing to set aside a decision on the ground that the mode of its exercise was fundamentally flawed. A trustee's purported exercise of discretion, whether qualified as 'uncontrollable' or not, will be liable to be set aside if there has been no real exercise of discretion at all. To this we now turn.

***Sieff v Fox* [2005] EWHC 1312 (Ch D)**

Lloyd LJ (sitting as a judge of the Chancery Division) (para 38):

There are several different categories of case where an exercise by trustees of a discretionary power may be held to be invalid.

i) There may be a formal or procedural defect, such as the failure to use the stipulated form of document, for example a document under hand instead of a deed, or to obtain a necessary prior consent. (In some such cases, and for the benefit of some interested persons, equity may relieve against such a formal or procedural defect.)

ii) The power may have been exercised in a way which it does not authorise, for example with an unauthorised delegation, or by the inclusion of beneficiaries who are not objects of the power.

iii) The exercise may infringe some rule of the general law, such as the rule against perpetuities.

iv) The trustees may have exercised the power for an improper purpose, in cases known as fraud on the power. *Cloutte v Storey* [1911] 1 Ch 18, among the cases cited to me, is an example of this, where the power was exercised in favour of one of the objects, but under a private arrangement whereby he passed the benefit back to his parents, who had made the appointment. Another example, in a different context, was *Hillsdown Holdings plc v Pensions Ombudsman* [1997] 1 All ER 862. I take it that references, for example in *Gisborne v Gisborne*, cited above (and in *Re Hastings-Bass* [see 11.4.1.1 below] to good faith are to be understood in this context, so that an exercise which is not in good faith is, or at any rate includes, a case where the exercise is a fraud on the power.

v) The trustees may have been unaware that they had any discretion to exercise: see *Turner v Turner* [1984] Ch 100, an extreme and highly unusual case on the facts, which has been described as equitable *non est factum*.

iv) To these categories, of which the first four are clear and well-established, the rule or principle in *Re Hastings-Bass* is said to add a further class of case . . .

11.4.1.1 The rule in Re Hastings-Bass

Warner J in *Mettoy Pension Trustees Ltd v Evans and Others* [1990] 1 WLR 1587 interprets *Re Hastings-Bass* [1975] Ch 25 as establishing a rule that three questions must be asked by the courts when reviewing the exercise by trustees of their discretions. The questions are: (1) what were the trustees under a duty to consider?; (2) did they fail to consider it?; and (3) if so, what would they have done if they had considered it? The last of these questions is absolutely crucial. As Warner J observed, under the rule in *Re Hastings-Bass* before a court will set aside the trustees' exercise of their discretion 'it must be clear that the trustees would not have done what in fact they did' had they taken the proper issues into consideration. In fact, he went so far as to state that 'It is not enough to show that the trustees would have realised that what they were doing was to some extent unsatisfactory'.

The case of *Re Hastings-Bass* involved the exercise by trustees of the power of advancement, which is granted (in the absence of contrary intention in the trust instrument) to all trustees by s 32 of the Trustee Act 1925 (see **Chapter 13** for the details of this power). For present purposes it is sufficient to be aware that the power of advancement is a power to apply trust capital in favour of the trust beneficiaries at a time other than the date their interests would ordinarily have vested in possession. The Court of Appeal in *Re Hastings-Bass* refused to interfere with the trustees' decision to advance monies by means of a subsettlement which they had not appreciated would be void for perpetuity. Buckley LJ asked: 'In these circumstances, can it be said that the trustees have never exercised their discretion under s. 32?' He concluded: 'There is no reason to suppose that, in the light of their understanding or advice as to the law, they failed to ask themselves the right questions or to arrive in good faith at a reasonable conclusion'. His Lordship decided that so long as the end result was beneficial to the advancee, as it was in this case, it could properly be described as an 'advancement' within s 32. The fact that the trustees had not been aware of the true legal situation when making their decision was not held against them, because even if they had taken the proper issues into consideration they would still have been justified in acting as they did.

It will not always be clear which matters the trustees are under a duty to consider in exercising their discretion. What if a clause in a trust instrument conferring a decision-making power is open to more than one possible construction? Here, the trustee must beware. As A Kiralfy stated in 'A Limitation on the Discretionary Powers of Trustees' (1953) 17 Conv (NS) 285:

> The court cannot exercise a personal discretion connected with a trustee's personality or experience . . . but, if there are well-established canons of construction, on which the trustee cannot be so well informed as the court, the court will not permit an usurpation by the trustee, even under the terms of the trust, of jurisdiction to construe a trust document.

Re Hastings-Bass and *Mettoy Pension Trustees Ltd* were cases involving the exercise of dispositive discretions. The courts may be more ready to intervene to control the exercise of administrative discretions. A case involving the review of a fiduciary's exercise of an administrative discretion was *Bishop v Bonham* [1988] 1 WLR 742. Although the fiduciary had been authorized to exercise their discretion 'as they think fit', Slade LJ held that:

> the natural construction of words authorising a person to carry out such a transaction in such a manner and upon such terms and for such consideration as you think fit is as authorising that person to carry out the transaction in such manner (and so on) as he thinks fit, within the limits of the duty of reasonable care imposed by the general law—no more, no less.

Perhaps the most significant administrative discretion that trustees have to exercise is that which relates to their choice of investments (see, generally, **Chapter 14**). Investment is not a mere transaction, some policy choices must be made, but the discretion is basically administrative (although it could be argued that the duty to invest fairly as between beneficiaries with successive interests, because it is not necessarily a duty to invest equally (see 12.4.1), invites an element of dispositive discretion). It follows from the administrative nature of the investment discretion that even where an express investment clause authorises trustees to invest 'as they think fit' this does not exempt the trustee from the duty to invest with prudence according to the standard of care imposed by the general law.

Because the investment discretion is basically administrative, it is submitted that it would be wrong to apply the rule in *Hastings-Bass* to the discretion that is exercised in the choice of investments. If the rule in *Hastings-Bass* were applied to investment decisions the court might have to relieve even a professional corporate trustee of liability for investment decisions made imprudently and on incorrect assumptions, merely because the choice it had imprudently made was one which a prudent, correctly advised trustee, might also have made. This, the author submits, is precisely the error that occurred in the reasoning of the Court of Appeal in *Nestle v National Westminster Bank* (see 14.3.4).

11.4.1.2 The demise of the rule in *Hastings-Bass*?

Recently the Court of Appeal has tightened the *Hastings-Bass* rule in the context of pension trusts. In pension trusts the beneficiaries are not mere volunteers; they have paid contributions into the fund. Consequently the trustees owe them a special duty in exercising their discretions. So decisions by trustees of pension funds will be set aside if they 'might' have reached a different decision had they exercised a proper discretion (see *Amp (UK) Ltd plc v Barker*, [2001] Pens LR 77, following *Stannard v Fisons Pensions Trust Ltd* [1991] PLR 225). There have even been initial suggestions that the rule in *Hastings-Bass* might be tightened in non-pension contexts because 'It cannot be right, whenever trustees do something which they later regret and think they ought not to have done, they can say they never did it in the first place' (Park J in *Breadner v Granville-Grossman* [2000] 4 All ER 705 at 722—in this case a deed of appointment was set aside because the trustees had given no thought to the capital gains tax implications of their decision). See also, *Abacus Trust Co (Isle of Man) v Barr* [2003] Ch 409.

11.4.1.3 The exercise of discretion by the court

In very exceptional cases the court will actually exercise a discretion for the trustee, if the trustee encounters a particular problem in its exercise. The case of *Mettoy Pension Trustees v Evans* [1991] 2 All ER 513 is an example of this. There, as you may recall (see 2.3.3.3) the liquidator of an insolvent company had to exercise a discretion as to the proper destination of a pension fund surplus. However, the liquidator had conflicting fiduciary obligations: on the one hand to safeguard the interest of the company (the liquidator was trustee of the insolvent company's estate and affairs); on the other to exercise the fiduciary power to allocate the surplus fairly as between the company and the employees entitled to the pension fund. Faced with this dilemma, Warner J intervened to exercise the fiduciary power on behalf of the liquidator. For another instance of a court exercising a trust discretion, see the Privy Council in *Marley v Mutual Security Merchant Bank & Trust Co Ltd* [1991] 3 All ER 198. In that case it was stressed that the court will only be able to exercise the discretion if it is in possession of all the necessary information.

11.4.2 Reasons for decisions

Trustees need not give reasons for their decisions (*Re Londonderry's Settlement* [1965] Ch 918). In *Re Beloved Wilkes' Charity* (1851) 3 Mac & Cr 440 the Lord Chancellor suggested that trustees would be 'most prudent and judicious' simply to state 'that they have met and considered and come to a conclusion'.

In *Re Londonderry's Settlement* the Court of Appeal held that even though the beneficiaries of the trust might have a proprietary interest in the trust documentation, the trustees would not have to disclose trust documentation containing reasons for their decisions. *Re Londonderry's* was followed in *Wilson v Law Debenture Trust Corp plc* [1995] 2 All ER 337. Wilson (W) had contributed to the pension scheme of his former corporate employer. When the company was sold to CMP, another corporation, W became a member of CMP's pension scheme. The defendant was the trustee of CMP's scheme. By the terms of CMP's scheme the defendant trustee had a discretion to transfer into the new scheme such part of the assets of the original pension scheme as the trustee determined to be appropriate having taken actuarial advice. In the event the trustee transferred only a small part of the original pension fund into the new scheme. W issued a summons seeking disclosure of the trustee's reasons for exercising its discretion in the way it did. Rattee J dismissed the summons, holding that where a discretion is entrusted to a trustee by the trust instrument, the trustee is not required to give reasons for the exercise of the discretion. In the absence of disclosure of evidence that the trustee had acted improperly, whether from an improper motive, or through infringement of the rule in *Re Hastings-Bass*, the court would not interfere with the exercise of the trustee's discretion. (For pensions generally, see 2.3.3.)

11.4.3 Unanimity

Trustees must act unanimously in exercising any of their powers under a trust, including their decision-making. There can be 'sleeping partners' in business ventures who take no active role in the management of the business, but there is no such thing as a 'sleeping trustee'. All the trustees must be unanimous in the exercise of their discretions. There are, however, some exceptions to this rule. The Charities Act 1993 provides, for example, that in small trusts a two-thirds majority of the trustees is competent to pass resolutions authorizing the transfer of the entirety of the trust property to other charities (s 74) and the expenditure of trust capital as well as income (s 75). Furthermore, it is quite usual for the trust instruments of charitable trusts and pension fund trusts to reserve the exercise of administrative discretions to a core group of managing trustees.

CHAPTER SUMMARY

- In this chapter we have seen that a trustee owes a fiduciary duty to the beneficiaries of the trust as part of a broader duty to serve the trust. Trustees must never put themselves in a position where their duties to the trust might conflict with their self-interest or their duty to others.
- A trustee should conduct the business of the trust in the same manner as an ordinary prudent man of business would conduct his own. However, this standard might be raised or lowered according to the characteristics of the particular trustee, so trust corporations and professional trustees will be judged according to higher standards. In Chapter 12 we will note that such trustees are presumed to be entitled to remuneration.
- In this chapter we considered that the level of remuneration might be a factor relevant to the identification of the standard of care to which such trustees should be subject. However, even if remuneration is not relevant to the identification of the appropriate standard of care, it will be relevant to determining whether a trustee ought to be relieved of liability for a breach of trust. A paid trustee is less likely to be relieved of liability under Trustee Act 1925, s 61 than an unpaid trustee (see 15.4.4).

- We have seen, however, that the practical significance of this may be limited, since in practice most corporate and professional trustees insist upon the inclusion in the trust deed of exculpatory clauses. Such clauses are capable of excluding liability for all breaches of trust, apart from those tainted by the trustee's dishonesty.
- According to the notes which accompany the Trustee Act 2000 it is intended that the new standard of care will act as a safeguard for beneficiaries sufficient to off-set the increased risks which will attend the wider powers of investment and delegation introduced by the Act. The new standard of care may prove to be a weak safeguard in practice due to the widespread use by professional trustees of exculpatory clauses.
- Finally, in this chapter we examined the factors which a trustee should consider in exercising a trust discretion. We noted that courts are reluctant to review the exercise of trustee discretions (especially dispositive discretions) unless the trustee has acted fraudulently, capriciously or has failed to exercise a proper discretion in accordance with the rule in *Re Hastings-Bass*.

SUMMATIVE ASSESSMENT EXERCISE

online resource centre

Albert settled a trust on Beryl and Charlie as trustees for certain beneficiaries. The fund consisted of freehold properties of which Beryl and Charlie were tenants, and cash. The trust instrument granted the trustees the power to invest in such investments as they in their absolute discretion and uncontrolled authority should think fit. The trust instrument also included a charging clause which permitted the trustees to be handsomely remunerated out of the fund. In the event, the trustees invested trust monies in shares in Y Co, a company with which they had no connection. Some time later the trustees purchased the freehold properties at market value by exercising options to purchase which they had been granted at the commencement of their leases. They also bought the shares in Y Co from the trust for what was a very fair and even generous price, believing that the price of those shares was about to rise. In the event those shares did increase in value, but only very slightly. The trustees made fresh investments of the trust fund in Z Co, whose trading record they had taken no steps to investigate. The value of the shares in that company have now plummeted dramatically.

Advise the trustees, who are concerned that the beneficiaries might have grounds to take action against them for breach of their trust.

FURTHER READING

Trustee Act 2000, explanatory notes

Herbert, M, 'Attacking Trustee Decisions—Grounds for Complaint' (2005) 4 Private Client Business 219.

Hilliard, J, 'Limiting *Re Hastings-Bass*' (2004) Conv 208.

Kiralfy, A, 'A Limitation on the Discretionary Powers of Trustees' (1953) 17 Conv (NS) 285.

Walker, R, 'The Limits of the Principle in *Re Hastings-Bass*' (2002) 4 Private Client Business 226.

FURTHER READING

12 Trustees' duties

OBJECTIVES

By the end of this chapter you should be able to:

1 Advise a potential trustee as to the consequences of accepting office

2 Define the extent of the duty to act gratuitously and the rule that a trustee must not profit from the trust

3 Explain the extent of the duty to provide personal service to the trust

4 Identify a breach of the duty to act impartially and the duty to keep trust accounts

12.1 Introduction

Chapter 11 considered the general fiduciary nature of the office of trustee. This chapter analyses some specific duties to which trustees are subject.

Breach of trustees' duties can result in personal liability for the trustee concerned (**Chapter 15** considers the consequences of breach of trust). Indeed, as a general rule the trustees have all the duties and burdens, while the beneficiaries have all the rights and benefits. So, why would anybody agree to be a trustee? As we progress through this chapter we will see that the courts are involved in an ongoing attempt to balance the strict enforcement of the trustees' duties with the need to ensure that there are always persons willing to act as trustees. In carrying out this balancing act the courts have as their ultimate goal the best administration of the trust in the interest of the beneficiaries. We will also see that the Trustee Act 2000 has made trusteeship more attractive to trust corporations and professional trustees than it used to be. The Act grants them improved powers of delegation and raises a presumption in favour of their remuneration, but without prejudice to the potential of trust instruments to make even more generous provision by express terms.

12.2 Trustee profits

The first point to make is that the law distinguishes trustees' profits from their expenses. 'A trustee is entitled to be reimbursed from the trust funds, or may pay out of the trust funds, expenses properly incurred by him when acting on behalf of the trust', Trustee Act 2000, s 31(1), replacing the provision to like effect in the Trustee Act 1925, s 30(2)). Where the expenses (and this includes ongoing contractual liability) have not been incurred 'properly' there is no indemnity and the trustee will be personally liable to any third party to whom he owes a debt or other contractual obligation. (The fact that the third party has no direct claim against the trust fund in such a case is a problem under consideration by the Law Commission for England and Wales as part of its project on *The Rights of Creditors Against Trustees and Trust Funds*.)

The courts' approach to trustees' expenses should be contrasted with their approach to trustees' profits. The general rule is that trustees must not profit from their trust, and, according to Lord Herschell in *Bray v Ford* [1896] AC 44, this rule is an 'inflexible' one. (Although his Lordship did allow for trustees to be make a profit where the trust instrument so provides.)

Now, according to Part V of the Trustee Act 2000, certain types of trustee (broadly speaking 'professional' trustees) are presumed to be entitled to remuneration unless the trust instrument provides to the contrary. Trustees who do not have the benefit of this statutory right to remuneration (broadly speaking 'non-professional' trustees) are still subject to the old rule as expressed by Russell J in *Williams v Barton* [1927] 2 Ch 9: '[o]n the same principle [that a trustee may not profit from their trust] a trustee has no right to charge for his time and trouble'. If 'non-professional' trustees desire remuneration or improved remuneration in respect of the services they provide to the trust, they will have to apply to the court for it (see 12.2.2).

In circumstances other than remuneration the rule remains strict. It is no defence that the profit was made without loss to the trust (see *Keech v Sandford* at 12.2.1.4), nor that the transaction which yielded the profit to the fiduciary also yielded a profit for the trust (see *Boardman v Phipps* [1966] 3 All ER 827 (HL) at 12.2.1.2). The Court of Appeal has suggested, obiter, that it might be time to relax the rule in 'harsh circumstances' (*Murad v Al-Saraj* [2005] EWCA Civ 959 (para 82)).

12.2.1 The Trustee Act 2000

The Trustee Act 2000 has removed the rule against remuneration, except in the case of lay (non-professional) trustees. Part V of the Act (being ss 28–33 of the Act) is the relevant part, and it applies regardless of when the trust was created.

Section 29 provides that, apart from in the case of charitable trusts, and subject to contrary provision in the trust instrument, a trust corporation is entitled to receive reasonable remuneration out of the trust fund for services provided to the trust (s 29(1)), and a trustee acting in a professional capacity (for example, a solicitor) is similarly entitled, provided that the trustee receiving the remuneration is not a sole trustee and provided also that every other trustee has agreed to the remuneration in writing (s 29(2)). It does not matter that a lay trustee would be capable of providing the services charged for (s 29(4)).

Section 28(2) confirms that where the trust instrument provides for the remuneration of a trust corporation, or a trustee acting in a professional capacity, the trustee will be entitled to that remuneration even when it is claimed in relation to services which a lay trustee could have provided. However, this right only applies to a 'non-trust corporation' trustee of a charitable trust if there are other trustees, and only then 'to the extent that a majority of the other trustees have agreed that it should apply to him' (s 28(3)).

'Reasonable remuneration' means such remuneration as is reasonable in the circumstances for the provision of the services. Expressly included are reasonable banking charges levied by trustees who are authorized institutions (typically, banks) under the Banking Act 1987.

For the purpose of Part V of the Act a trustee 'acts in a professional capacity' if he acts in the course of a profession or business which consists of or includes the provision of services connected with trust administration or management. A person 'acts as a lay trustee' if he is not a trust corporation and does not act in a professional capacity.

However, the general right to remuneration provided by s 29 will not apply in every case. Section 29(5) excludes it in any case where there is express provision regarding remuneration in other legislation or in the trust instrument itself. (Presumably it matters not whether the provision approves remuneration or excludes it.) The benefit of s 28(2) is also subject to 'inconsistent provision' in the trust instrument (s 28(1)). All of this means that the right to remuneration will still turn, in the majority of cases, upon a question of construction of the clauses appearing in trust instruments. That question is essentially twofold. First, does the instrument provide for remuneration directly (that is, by way of a 'charging clause')? Second, does it provide for remuneration indirectly (for example, by permitting the trustee to hold a remunerated post in a trust-owned company)? When the general rule (that is, the default position according to general law) was against trustee remuneration, the courts were not slow to find that a trust instrument had indirectly authorized remuneration. Now that the default position for professional trustees is in favour of remuneration it will be interesting to see if the courts will be as quick to treat the indirect provision of remuneration by trust instruments as a sufficient basis for excluding the s 29 general right to remuneration. However, one thing is fairly clear—the construction of trust instruments remains of paramount importance, not only to lay trustees, for whom the Trustee Act 2000 has provided no general right to remuneration, but to professional trustees and trust corporations also.

12.2.2 The trust instrument

Jenkins J in *Re Llewellin's WT* [1949] 1 Ch 225 allowed a clause in a trust instrument its 'ordinary construction' even though this meant that the trustees would be able to appoint themselves to be directors of a company whose shares they held on trust. As directors they would be empowered to award themselves remuneration at a level they themselves could fix. The result appears to be a very real conflict between the interests of the director-trustees and the beneficiaries and a breach of the rule that a trustee must not profit from their trust. However, it was held that on the 'ordinary construction' of the trust instrument such remuneration had obviously been authorised by the testator, and the 'inflexible' rule had not been breached.

Fox LJ in the Court of Appeal in *Re Duke of Norfolk's ST* [1981] 3 All ER 220 said, 'If it be the law, as I think it clearly is, that the court has inherent jurisdiction on the appointment of a trustee to authorise payment of remuneration to him, is there any reason why the court should not have jurisdiction to increase the remuneration already allowed by the trust instrument?' He concluded that the court did have an inherent jurisdiction to increase remuneration.

? QUESTION 12.1

According to *Re Duke of Norfolk's ST* does the court have jurisdiction to award remuneration where the trust instrument does not award *any*?

Fox LJ suggested, *obiter*, that the court would have jurisdiction to award remuneration where the trust did not award any at all, 'if it was in the interests of the beneficiaries and if the trustee felt unable gratuitously to devote his time to trust affairs'.

? QUESTION 12.2

Towards the end of his judgment Fox LJ, whilst accepting that the office of trustee is essentially gratuitous, states that there is another, to some extent conflicting, consideration which the court must take into account. What is it?

Fox LJ's second 'factor' is the beneficiaries' interest in seeing that the trusts are well administered: 'If . . . the court concludes . . . that it would be in the interests of the beneficiaries to increase the remuneration, then the court may properly do so'. Keith Hodkinson ((1982) 46 Conv 231) has written approvingly of the Court of Appeal's decision to overturn the judgment of Walton J at first instance:

> One can . . . see with some force [the] view that as a matter of policy the court should not exercise its jurisdiction to bail out professional trustees who have made a bad bargain. But given that a trustee may retire and that there is no means of compelling him to continue in office, the fact must be faced that there will often be a stark choice between increasing remuneration of a skilled trustee familiar with the trust property and being forced to look for new trustees who may well not undertake the office without the inducement of higher fees.

Let us summarize the situation so far:

- the proper construction of the terms of the trust instrument *prima facie* determines whether or not trustees are entitled to remuneration
- if the trust instrument is silent, the general position (except in the case of trustees to whom to s 29 applies) is that trustees must act gratuitously
- the courts have an inherent jurisdiction to grant or to increase prospective (future) remuneration if it is in the interests of the beneficiaries on the facts of the particular case.

? QUESTION 12.3

Consider the clause: 'I direct that my executor and trustee "EC" shall be the solicitor to my trust property and shall be allowed all professional and other charges for his time and trouble notwithstanding his being such executor and trustee'. Does this clause allow 'EC' to charge for business he *could* have carried out in his private capacity, as opposed to in his professional capacity, even though it was business a solicitor would have charged an ordinary client for?

In *Re Chalinder and Herrington* [1907] 1 Ch D 58 it was held that, according to the strict construction of the clause, the trustee could not charge for this business. *Re Chalinder* illustrated how the courts construe remuneration clauses and other terms of trust instruments '*contra proferentem*', that is, against the trustee who is seeking to rely on them. *Re Chalinder* has now been superseded by s 28(2) of the Trustee Act 2000 (see 12.2.1 above). This section would allow EC to charge for the services outlined in the preceding Question, but on condition that the majority of the other trustees agree that he should be paid for such services.

12.2.3 *Quantum meruit*

We have seen that a lay trustee may not be remunerated out of the trust fund unless remuneration is permitted by the trust instrument or is in the interests of the beneficiaries as furthering the good administration of the trust. Having said that, this section considers cases where the courts seem to approve the remuneration of trustees more on account of their exemplary past performance, than on account of the future good administration of the trust. The trustee or fiduciary may be awarded remuneration by way of *quantum meruit*, which literally means 'sums deserved'. It is often very hard to see how such awards can be made in the interests of the beneficiaries of the particular trust. Although one might argue that potential beneficiaries everywhere will derive an indirect benefit, in the form of willing trustees, from the fact that the courts are seen to treat trustees fairly. Nevertheless, it is in the case of an award by way of *quantum meruit* that the inflexible rule seems to bend almost to breaking point.

In *Boardman v Phipps* [1966] 3 All ER 827 a bare majority of the House of Lords held that a solicitor, who had used information gained from his fiduciary role in relation to a trust (of which he was not in fact a trustee), had to account for all profits he had made for himself by virtue of his fiduciary position. This was despite the fact that his activity had also resulted in substantial benefits for the trust and had been carried out openly and honestly. However, whilst deciding that the fiduciary had breached the inflexible rule, their Lordships held that he should be paid for the work he had done to the great profit of the trust, and 'that payment should be on a liberal scale' (for more detail, see 16.4.1).

In *O'Sullivan and Another v Management Agency and Music Ltd and Others* [1985] 3 All ER 351, a case where a musician's agent was held to have profited from a position of undue influence over an inexperienced pop star ('Gilbert O'Sullivan'), the recording contracts were set aside and the agent was ordered to account for all profits made on them. However, Dunn LJ stated that 'in taking the account the defendants are entitled to an allowance . . . for reasonable remuneration, *including a profit element*, for all work done in promoting and exploiting O'Sullivan and his compositions' (emphasis added). He stated that 'although equity looks at the advantage gained by the wrongdoer rather than the loss to the victim, the cases show that in assessing the advantage gained the court will look at the whole situation in the round'. He approved the defendants' counsel's submission that the maxim *he who seeks equity must do equity* should be applied (see 1.4.7). Mr O'Sullivan had sought the assistance of equity to recover monies from the agency, and he would have to allow the agency reasonable remuneration for its work. It should also be emphasized, of course, that the judgment did not go so far as to approve 'profit sharing' as such (*O'Sullivan* was applied to very similar facts in *Badfinger Music v Evans* (2001) 2 WTLR 1).

The maxim, *he who seeks equity must do equity* was applied again in *Re Berkeley Applegate Ltd* [1989] Ch 32. There Edward Nugee QC stated that:

> The authorities establish, in my judgment, a general principle that where a person seeks to enforce a claim to an equitable interest in property, the court has a discretion to require as a condition of giving effect to that equitable interest that an allowance be made for costs incurred *and skill and labour expended* in connection with the administration of the property. (Emphasis added).

The orthodox view is that the fiduciaries have all the obligations and their principals have all the rights, but modern applications of the maxim *he who seeks equity must do equity* represent a pragmatic shift away from this orthodox position. Decisions such as *O'Sullivan* and *Re Berkeley* suggest that equity will not recognize the principal's claim without ensuring that the fiduciary is also dealt with equitably, even if this does involve allowing him to profit from his trust. In *O'Sullivan* the claimant was seeking the exercise of equitable *discretion* in his favour. The maxim will not apply where a beneficiary of an orthodox trust is bringing a claim against their trustee on the basis of an equitable *entitlement*. However, in such cases the courts have attempted to achieve justice between the parties on another basis, that of 'unjust enrichment'. Thus, in *Foster v Spencer* [1996] 2 All ER 672, the judge made an award of remuneration to trustees for their past services to the trust. Refusal of the award, he said, would 'result in the beneficiaries being unjustly enriched at the expense of the trustees'. However, unless one assumes that the trustees had a pre-existing right to remuneration it is hard to see in what way the receipt of the trustees' services can constitute an enrichment of the beneficiaries, still less how it can be said to have been gained unjustly, and still less how it can be said to have been gained at the trustees' expense. On the contrary, if regarded as an incident of the beneficiaries' equitable entitlement, any 'windfall' there might have been must have been entirely 'just' enrichment. See *Foskett v McKeown* (18.3.3.4) where, albeit on very different facts, the House of Lords rejected a submission that a windfall received by beneficiaries had enriched them unjustly. More recently, in *Crown Dilmun v Sutton* [2004] 1 BCLC 468, Chancery Division, Peter Smith J did not rule out the possibility that the fiduciary's liability to account may be reduced where it would otherwise unjustly enrich his principal, but noted that in this area, 'the law favours conferring benefits on the wronged even though that is at the expense of the wrongdoer' and stressed that where the fiduciary has acted dishonestly there can be no question of reducing his liability to account.

In *Paul v Preston*, 12 December 1996 (unreported) Robert Walker J approved Walton J in *Re Duke of Norfolk*, who had doubted that remuneration should be awarded where the trustees' claim comes a long time after the date of their appointment. Robert Walker J distinguished *Foster v Spencer*, where the trustees (of a cricket club) had been awarded past remuneration a very long time after their appointment, on the 'unusual facts' of that case (there were no funds against which to claim remuneration until the sale of the cricket field some time after the trustees' appointment).

It is important to note that, a *quantum meruit* award will be restricted to those cases where it cannot have the effect of encouraging trustees or fiduciaries in any way to 'put themselves in a position where their interests conflict with their duties as trustees', *per* Lord Goff in *Guinness plc v Saunders* [1990] 2 AC 663, HL.

12.2.4 The causal connection

The inflexible rule is that a person in a fiduciary position is not entitled to make an unauthorized profit 'by virtue' of that position. There is no rule preventing a fiduciary from obtaining a profit by other means where there could be no possible conflict with the interests of the beneficiaries. In *Boardman v Phipps* [1967] 2 AC 46 (where, you will recall, a solicitor made a personal profit on shares in a private company by virtue of information gained in his fiduciary capacity) Lord Cohen stated that 'had the company been a public company and had the appellants bought the shares on the market, they would not, I think, have been accountable'. It was the fact that the profit had been made by virtue of the fiduciary office that gave rise to liability in *Boardman v Phipps*. *Boardman v Phipps* followed *Regal (Hastings) Ltd v Gulliver* [1967] 2 AC 143 where Viscount Sankey had reached a similar conclusion:

> In the result I am of the opinion that the directors standing in a fiduciary relationship to Regal in regard to the exercise of their powers as directors, and having obtained these shares *by reason and only by reason* of the fact that they were directors of Regal and in the course of the execution of that office, are accountable for the profits which they have made out of them.

The preceding *dicta* are hard to reconcile with the judgment of Morritt LJ in the Court of Appeal in *United Pan-Europe Communications NV v Deutsche Bank AG* [2000] 2 BCLC 461, where his Lordship said:

> If there is a fiduciary duty of loyalty and if the conduct complained of falls within the scope of that fiduciary duty . . . then I see no justification for any further requirement that the profit shall have been obtained by the fiduciary 'by virtue of his position'.

The implication of this judgment is that a solicitor such as Mr Boardman should sometimes be disqualified from purchasing shares even if they are quoted on the public stock exchange, and that directors such as those in *Regal* should sometimes be accountable for profits made on shares even if they might have been acquired independently of their fiduciary position. (In *United Pan-Europe* itself, the defendant had received documents from the claimant in confidence and, on the basis of information contained within the documents, had proceeded to purchase shares in competition with the claimant.) However, Morritt LJ does not remove considerations of causation entirely. He still requires that the conduct complained of must 'fall within the scope of' the fiduciary duty. There must, in other words, be a basic factual connection between the particular gains and the defendant's lack of authority to retain such gains. His Lordship's point is that the duty to account should arise directly when profits are made in breach of fiduciary duty without any additional requirement to prove that such profits arise from a fiduciary position as such. Read in this way, his Lordship's *dictum* can be seen as an inevitable next step in the movement (started by Millett LJ in the *Mothew* case) to describing remedies against fiduciaries in terms of the fiduciary's duty as opposed to the fiduciary's 'status' or 'relationship' or 'position'. Since a fiduciary duty can arise independently of any traditional category of fiduciary position (solicitor, agent, director, etc) it follows that there is no need to prove that an unauthorised profit was made by virtue of a fiduciary position in order to establish a fiduciary duty to account for it. In fact, the explanation for Morritt LJ's *dictum* may be even more straightforward than this. It is arguably nothing more than a restatement of the principle that the burden of proof in fiduciary transactions rests heavily upon the fiduciary. If this analysis of his Lordship's *dictum* is correct it is significant in at least two respects. First, it explains why the claimant is under no obligation to prove causation as an element of his cause of action. Second, it leaves open the possibility that the defendant will be able to raise the absence of basic factual causation as a defence.

An approach similar to that adopted in the *United Pan-Europe* case was adopted by the court in *Crown Dilmun v Sutton* [2004] 1 BCLC 468. The case concerned an action against a former employee of the claimant company. The claimant was successful in preventing the defendant from taking the benefit on his own account of a business opportunity which he had acquired in the course of his employment and had declined to pursue on the company's account. It was no defence for the defendant to show that he could have acquired the information independently of his fiduciary position. Peter Smith J held that 'Whether or not the information is confidential, if the opportunity that arises by reason of the acquisition of the information puts the fiduciary in a position of conflict, he cannot take that opportunity' [para 187]. The disputed business opportunity in this case concerned the commercial development of Craven Cottage, the home ground of Fulham FC (see the website of the Fulham Supporters' Trust http://www.backtothecottage.co.uk/frp_timeline.htm).

12.2.5 Is the rule against fiduciary profits too strict?

In *Keech v Sandford* (1726) Sel Cas Ch 61, a trustee had taken advantage of an opportunity to renew a lease in circumstances where the landlord had made it clear that he would not have permitted the beneficiary to enjoy the same privilege. The trustee's gain could in no way have been to the detriment of the trust, although it was gained by virtue of the trustee's fiduciary office. Lord King LC said: 'This may seem harsh that the trustee is the only person of all mankind who might not have the lease; but it is very proper that the rule should be strictly pursued, and not in the least relaxed'.

Lord Upjohn attempted, but failed, to relax the rule in his dissenting speech in *Boardman v Phipps* [1967] 2 AC 46. He preferred to restrict the trustee's liability to cases where there was 'a real and sensible possibility of conflict'. Professor Peter Birks has objected that in cases like *Boardman v Phipps* the strict rule produces 'windfalls to rather sharp plaintiffs at the expense of honest and industrious defendants' (*Butterworth Lecture* 1990, p 55 at 97).

Whatever the arguments may be in relation to fiduciaries like the solicitor in *Boardman v Phipps*, in the case of trustees of express trusts there are arguably good reasons for maintaining a strict presumption of gratuitous service. First, the settlor is always free to make express provision for remuneration in the trust instrument. Second, the trustee is always entitled to refuse to accept the terms of a trust if they do not provide for remuneration. Third, if trustees were automatically entitled to remuneration out of the trust fund (which might involve them paying cheques to themselves) the opportunity for fraud would surely increase. Fourth, even if there was no such obvious fraud, the risk that fee-paying work might be generated unnecessarily would surely increase. Fifth, retaining gratuitous service in small family trusts might ensure the continued appointment of trustees who are close family members or friends, who might be expected to work more conscientiously on behalf of the trust than a 'hired hand'. It is arguable that insufficient weight was attached to considerations such as these when the Law Commission made the recommendations which now appear in Part V of the Trustee Act 2000.

12.3 The duty of personal service

The classic statement of this duty is the maxim '*delegatus non potest delegare*'—the person to whom responsibility has been delegated may not delegate that responsibility to another. In other words, a trustee must provide personal service to the trust. In fact, the maxim cannot be strictly applied in the modern world, where a trustee will often need to delegate specialist functions to expert agents. In the seminal text, *Farwell on Powers* (3rd edn, 1916), the learned authors asserted that strictly speaking the rule only ever prohibited the delegation of trustees' *fiduciary* powers, and does not prohibit the delegation by them of 'powers to do acts merely ministerial' (p 498). In relation to the delegation of fiduciary powers and duties, the position was summarized by Viscount Radcliffe in the House of Lords in *Pilkington v IRC* [1964] AC 612: 'The law is not that a trustee cannot delegate: it is that trustees cannot delegate unless they have authority to do so'. In the following sections we shall be considering the sources and extent of trustees' authority to delegate. We shall also consider the standard of care which trustees must exercise in appointing and supervising their agents.

12.3.1 Authority to delegate

As in the case of remuneration, one must look first to the trust instrument. The trust instrument can enlarge upon the trustee's powers of delegation as authorized by the general law, but it can also restrict or exclude them (Trustee Act 2000, s 26(b)). Subject to what is said in the trust instrument, one should then turn to consider the trustee's authority to delegate as provided by the general law. Such authority is to be found in a number of statutes and statutory provisions. It should also be borne in mind that the court has the power, on an application under s 57 of the Trustee Act 1925, to vary the powers of delegation authorised by a particular trust (see 9.2.2).

12.3.1.1 Statutory authority

The major statutory provisions regarding the delegation of trustees' functions are now to be found in Part IV of the Trustee Act 2000 (ss 11–27).

According to Part IV of the Trustee Act 2000 a trustee function is delegable unless it appears in the list of *non-delegable* functions set out in s 11(2). In the case of charitable trusts, however, a trustee function is non-delegable unless it appears on the list of *delegable* functions set out in s 11(3).

? QUESTION 12.4

Having read s 11 of the Trustee Act 2000, place the following trustee functions under two columns headed respectively 'delegable function' and 'non-delegable function':

- the appointment of a trustee to a non-charitable trust
- the purchase of shares by a stockbroker on the trustees' instructions
- implementing an advertising campaign on behalf of a charity
- appointing persons to benefit from a discretionary trust
- deciding to pay tax out of trust capital
- appointing a person to appoint agents to assist with trust administration.

Subject to any express provision to the contrary appearing in the trust instrument itself, only functions (b) and (c) are delegable. Section 11(2) provides that in the case of non-charitable trusts, all functions are delegable apart from the distribution of trust assets (for example, under a discretionary trust), the choice between income or capital as the source of a payment (such as payment of tax due) and the appointment of a trustee, agent, nominee or custodian. Section 11(3) provides that in the case of a charitable trust the only delegable functions are those which involve the carrying out (administration) of decisions the trustees have made, for example, investing trust assets and managing trust-owned land. Also, most forms of fund-raising activity can be delegated, and any other function can be delegated if the Secretary of State makes an order authorizing the delegation.

The Trustee Act 2000 repeals the Trustee Act 1925, s 23. Section 23(1) permitted trustees to appoint an agent 'to transact any business or do any act required to be transacted or done in the execution of the trust'. Section 25(1) of the 1925 Act, according to which a trustee was permitted to delegate by power of attorney 'for a period not exceeding twelve months the execution or exercise of all or any of the trusts, powers and discretions vested in him as trustee either alone or jointly with any other person or persons', has been replaced by a new s 25(1) (by s 5 of the Trustee Delegation Act 1999). The new s 25(1) introduces more procedural safeguards into this potentially very risky form of delegation. The safeguards include such things as giving notice to the other trustees that a trustee has appointed a person to act as his attorney, and requiring the actual appointment of the attorney to be made by means of a standard form. However, delegation under this section is not attractive, not least because trustees remain liable for the acts and defaults of their delegate as if they were the trustees' own acts and defaults (Trustee Delegation Act 1999, s 5(7) which reproduces the wording of, and repeals, Trustee Act 1925, s 25(5)).

12.3.1.2 Restrictions as to the terms of an agency

Section 14 of the 2000 Act provides that trustees may authorize agents to act on such terms as they may determine, even in regard to remuneration. However, unless the trust instrument otherwise provides (see s 26(b)), there are certain terms which trustees are not permitted to include 'unless it is reasonably necessary for them to do so' (s 14(2)). The terms in question are those which would permit agents to appoint substitutes (s 14(3)(a)), restrict the agent's liability (s 14(3)(b)) or permit the agent to act in circumstances capable of giving rise to a conflict of interest (s 14(3)(c)). There is obviously good sense in restricting terms of this kind, but regrettably one suspects that trustees will not struggle to satisfy the requirement of 'reasonable necessity' with regard to their use. The spectre of well-paid sub-agents with limited liability in positions of conflict will send shivers down the spines of beneficiaries everywhere.

12.3.1.3 Special restrictions on the delegation of asset management

Trustees are not permitted to authorize an agent to exercise asset management functions except by an agreement evidenced in writing in which the agent agrees to comply with a 'policy statement' which the trustees are obliged to provide as a guide to the exercise of asset management functions in the best interests of the trust (Trustee Act 2000, s 15(1)). The agent must agree to be bound by any revisions of the policy statement made under s 22 of the Act (s 15(2)(b)(ii)). The policy statement (and presumably any revisions of it) must be in writing or evidenced in writing (s 15(4)).

According to s 15(5) 'asset management functions' are those functions which relate to the investment of assets subject to the trust (s 15(5)(a)), the acquisition of property which is to be subject to the trust (s 15(5)(b)) and the management of property subject to the trust, including the creation or disposition of interests in such property (s 15(5)(c)).

12.3.2 Choice of agent

12.3.2.1 Trustees must choose prudently

In *Fry v Tapson* (1884) 28 Ch D 268, Kay J said: 'I am most reluctant to visit trustees acting *bona fide* with the consequences of a want of due caution, but . . . they most incautiously employed the mortgagor's agent . . . although he was a London surveyor, and it was most important to obtain the opinion of some experienced local surveyor'. The principle laid down in this case is still good law, namely that a trustee (even an honest one) will be liable for losses caused to the fund by an agent who was appointed to perform a task outside that agent's field of expertise. According to s 23(1)(a) of the Trustee Act 2000, trustees may be liable if they fail to exercise the standard of care set out in s 1(1) of the Act (see 11.3.2) when appointing agents, nominees and custodians.

12.3.2.2 Persons who may be appointed

Subject to what was said in 12.3.2.1, trustees may even appoint one or more of their own number to act as agents to the trust (Trustee Act 2000, s 12(1)) but no two (or more) agents may be appointed to exercise a function unless they are to exercise it jointly (s 12(2)). Beneficiaries may not be appointed to act as agents to the trust, even if they are also trustees (s 12(3)).

12.3.3 Supervision of agents

12.3.3.1 Trustees must supervise prudently

According to the Trustee Act 2000, s 23(1)(b), even where a trustee has validly appointed an agent, the trustee will still be subject to the standard of care as laid down in s 1(1) of the 2000 Act.

Consider *Re Lucking's WT* [1968] 1 WLR 866, where the claimant was one of the beneficiaries under a will trust. L, the son of the testatrix, was the sole trustee of the trust and a beneficiary under it. Part of the trust property was a majority holding in a private company. To secure the profitable running of the company, L appointed D to be a director. Over time, a practice was established whereby D sent blank cheques to L to be signed (two signatures were needed to authorize drawings on the company's account) to cover D's expenses. It became apparent to L that D was making withdrawals for his own ends but L took no action to prevent this, and continued to sign D's blank cheques. The company's gross profits had increased under D's management, but so had its overdraft. D's personal indebtedness to the company eventually reached such a level that he was dismissed from his directorship. He was declared bankrupt whilst still owing £15,890 to the company. It was held that L had failed adequately to supervise D's financial activities. He should have exercised the care of an ordinary prudent man of business. This would have meant ensuring that he had been represented on the board of the company. Having failed to do so he was liable to the other beneficiaries for the devaluation in the shares owned by the trust. Nowadays, L would be liable under s 23(1)(b) of the Trustee Act 2000.

Law Commission Report No 260 (1999), *Trustees' Powers and Duties* recommended that trustees should, so long as delegation continues, keep under review the arrangements relating to it and the manner in which those arrangements are implemented (para 4.10). This recommendation is enacted in ss 21–23 of the Trustee Act 2000. These sections also provide that trustees must, where appropriate, exercise any power of intervention they have to protect the trust (s 22(1)(c)).

Trustees must also keep under review any policy statement made (for the purposes of s 15 of the Act, see 12.3.1.3) in relation to delegated asset management functions.

12.3.3.2 Restrictions on the exercise of delegated functions

Given that trustees must supervise their agents it makes sense that they should be aware of the restrictions to which the agents are subject in the exercise of the delegated functions. The trust instrument may impose certain restrictions, such as requiring that an agent must report to the trustees at given intervals. However, even if there are no restrictions apparent from the trust instrument, s 13 of the Trustee Act 2000 makes it clear that agents do not have a totally free hand with regard to the manner in which they exercise the functions delegated to them. That, however, is the only thing that is very clear about s 13. The section is set out in rather convoluted fashion, but the gist of it is that agents are subject to any restrictions specific to the particular function that they are carrying out. So, for example, if a person is authorized to *invest* on behalf of the trust, they are subject to statutory restrictions relating to *investment*, such as those appearing in s 4 of the 2000 Act (see **Chapter 14**).

Under s 11 of the 2000 Act a person authorized 'to exercise any function relating to land subject to the trust' is not required to consult competent adult beneficiaries and give effect to their wishes. Other delegates exercising functions relating to trusts of land are so required (unless the general interests of the trust suggest otherwise—s 11(1) of the Trusts of Land and Appointment of Trustees Act 1996), and the trustees may not authorize such delegates to carry out their delegated functions on terms which would prevent them from complying with that duty.

12.3.4 Appointment of nominees and custodians

Sections 16–20 of the 2000 Act relate to the appointment of nominees and custodians to trusts other than trusts already having custodian trustees (the latter include charitable trusts where the assets are vested in the official custodian for charities). A nominee is a person in whose name trust assets are vested. A custodian is a person who 'undertakes the safe custody of the assets or of any documents or records concerning the assets' (s 17(2)).

According to s 16, the appointment of a nominee must be in writing or evidenced in writing and may relate to such assets as the trustees may determine. The section authorizes trustees to take such steps as are necessary to vest the relevant assets in the nominee. Likewise, the appointment of a custodian must be in writing or evidenced in writing (s 17).

Unless the trust instrument (or legislation) provides to the contrary, the appointment of a custodian is a *requirement* whenever the trust holds 'bearer securities' (securities payable to the bearer) (s 18).

A person cannot be appointed to act as nominee or custodian unless one of the following conditions are satisfied. They are (a) the person's business includes acting as a nominee or custodian, (b) 'the person is a body corporate controlled by the trustees' (to be determined in accordance with s 840 of the Income and Corporation Taxes Act 1988) or (c) the person is a body corporate recognized under s 9 of the Administration of Justice Act 1985. (Trustee Act 2000, s 19.)

Subject to the above, trustees may appoint one of their number to act as a nominee or custodian, or two (or more) of their number to act jointly in that capacity, and may appoint the same person(s) to be nominee(s), custodian(s) and agent(s). However, nominees and custodians are subject to the same restrictions as those we considered at 12.3.1.2 in relation to agents (Trustee Act 2000, s 20). Sections 21–23, concerning the supervision, review and intervention of agents (see 12.3.3.1), also apply to nominees and custodians.

Section 23 is most significant because it provides that a trustee will not be liable for the defaults of any agent, nominee or custodian unless he failed to meet the requisite standard of care (see 11.3) in appointing the delegate or supervising the delegate as required by s 22. Similarly, the trustee is not liable for the defaults of any person acting as substitute for an agent, nominee or custodian, unless the trustee failed to meet the requisite standard of care (11.3) in giving the agent, nominee or custodian the power to appoint a substitute, or in supervising the performance of the agent, nominee or custodian in relation to the substitute.

12.3.5 Summative exercise

This following Question is intended to test a number of aspects of the law relating to the delegation of trustees' functions. Assume in each of the situations described that the trust instrument makes no reference to the trustees' powers of delegation, so that the general law applies.

? QUESTION 12.5

Against each of the following transactions place a cross if the trustees have breached their trust and a tick if there has been a valid delegation:

(a) A two-thirds majority of the trustees of a small charitable trust appointed Mr Brownfield, an expert valuer, to carry out the conveyance of trust-owned land to another charity.

(b) The trustees placed trust-owned land in the name of a nominee with a view to sale, but with the direction that the nominee must not consult any of the beneficiaries of the trust at any time. The beneficiaries are all adult and competent.

(c) The trustees appointed an expert tax solicitor to choose whether a payment to the Inland Revenue of tax due from the trust should be made out of trust income or capital.

(d) The trustees appointed a leading firm of solicitors to evict squatters from trust-owned land, but having paid sums on account to cover the solicitors' fees, the trustees took no further steps to ensure that the squatters had been evicted. In the event the squatters completed 12 years of adverse possession and have now been registered as proprietors of the fee simple estate.

(e) The trustees of a charitable trust appoint a stockbroker to decide upon an ethical investment policy that would be both financially profitable and in accordance with the charities' aims.

The trustees breached their trust in every case! In (a) because, even if the two-thirds majority were entitled to pass a resolution to sell the land, the agent was not qualified to discharge that delegated function, an estate agent or solicitor should have been appointed (see 12.3.2.1). In (b) because, apart from a person authorized (under s 11 of the 2000 Act) 'to exercise any function relating to land subject to the trust' delegates are required to consult competent adult beneficiaries and give effect to their wishes and the trustees may not authorize such delegates to carry out their delegated functions on terms which would prevent them from complying with that duty. In (c) because this was a non-delegable function. A solicitor can be appointed to advise on such a matter, but not to make the choice (see Trustee Act 2000, s 11(2)). In (d) because the trustees must exercise prudence, not only in relation to the appointment of the trustees, but in relation to their supervision also (see 12.3.3). In (e) because this was a non-delegable function. A stockbroker can be appointed to advise on such a matter, but not to decide upon the investment policy (see Trustee Act 2000, s 11(3)).

12.4 Miscellaneous duties

We have focused on the duty to act gratuitously and the duty to provide personal service, and the correlating rules that trustees may not profit from their trust and must not delegate their trust. This section briefly considers some of the other duties to which trustees are subject in the execution of their office.

12.4.1 The duty to act impartially

Where a trust instrument gives a trustee the power to choose between persons with competing claims on the fund (for example, in a discretionary trust, see 4.5.2) that dispositive discretion will almost inevitably mean that, in the appointment of beneficiaries, some persons will be preferred to others, and as between beneficiaries some will get more than others (see 2.3.3.3). However, even in such a case, the trustee must not be swayed by a subjective personal preference for one beneficiary or class of beneficiaries. Similarly, in a traditional settlement trust (for example, to A for life, to B in remainder), where A and B have *competing* claims to the fund (the traditional view is that A wants more income and B wants more capital—but see 14.2.1, 14.2.3.2), the trustee's duty is to consider fairly their competing claims and to exercise its administrative investment discretion even-handedly. Fairness, however, need not import 'equality' (*per* Hoffmann J in *Nestle v National Westminster Bank plc* (1996) 10 TLI 112 at 115).

? QUESTION 12.6

Suppose that Terry has just been appointed trustee of the residue of a will trust under which Libby is the life beneficiary and Ronnie the remainderman. Upon his appointment Terry discovered the whole of the fund to be invested in crates of fine pink champagne. Is there a potential breach of the duty to act impartially?

The crates of champagne are wasting assets, their value decreases the more the champagne is consumed, with the possibility that the investment may be worthless before Ronnie's interest vests in possession. In contrast, Libby, during her life would have been in receipt of the benefits of the consumption of the champagne.

In such a case the trustee may be obliged to sell the champagne and re-invest in property which will more fairly meet the beneficiaries' respective claims (*Howe* v *Earl of Dartmouth* (1802) 7 Ves 137—note that the rule in this case applies only to residuary estates of personalty). The case law even lays down rules to guide trustees as to how to apportion investments properly between capital and income. Those rules are outside the scope of this book and are, in any event, usually excluded by the express terms of trust instruments. What is more, it must be doubtful that such technical, restrictive rules on the trustees' powers of investment can survive the coming into force of the general investment power provided by the Trustee Act 2000 (see 14.2.1). Indeed in July 2004 The Law Commission published a consultation paper on *Capital and Income in Trusts: Classification and Apportionment* (cp 175) in which it provisionally proposes that there ought to be imposed on trustees a new flexible statutory duty to balance the interests of income and capital beneficiaries, which will be presumed to apply even in relation to original investments (http://www.lawcom.gov.uk/files/cp175.pdf). The consultation paper expresses the view that there 'should not be a statutory list of factors relevant to a proper balance between the competing interests of income and capital beneficiaries' because a proper balance is already achieved by trustees using their 'common sense' [para 5.26]. The paper recommends that 'settlors should in principle be free to exclude (or modify) the duty to balance, but only by doing so expressly, or by necessary implication, in the terms of the trust' [para 5.29].

The main proposal of the consultation paper with regard to the duty to achieve a fair balance of investments between income and capital beneficiaries is the suggestion that statute should supply trustees with a new administrative power to allocate investment gains to income or capital at their discretion. A more radical alternative which has been proposed in Canada is to allocate a fair percentage of the total investment yield (regardless of whether it arises as income or capital gain) to the various classes of beneficiary and to abandon the traditional assumption that life beneficiaries are entitled to income and remainder beneficiaries to capital. The consultation paper suggests that this radical 'percentage trust' alternative will not be appropriate in English law so long as the UK tax system continues its significant reliance on the distinction between income and capital gains. It is for reasons of taxation (and because of general problems of subjectivity and uncertainty) that the paper also proposes that trustees should not be permitted to refer to personal circumstances of individual beneficiaries when deciding upon a fair allocation of investment gains to different classes of beneficiary.

12.4.2 The duty to keep accounts and to give information

Trustees have a duty to keep a diary-like record of the administration of the trust for production to new trustees (*Tiger v Barclays Bank Ltd* [1951] 2 KB 556 (CA)). The traditional view has been that this record, together with the trust accounts and other trust documentation, belong, in equity, to the beneficiaries, and that the beneficiaries are therefore *prima facie* entitled to inspect them upon request. However, in a recent decision of the Privy Council it was held that trust beneficiaries are not entitled to disclosure of trust documents, but that disclosure may be ordered on a case-by-case basis as part of the courts' inherent jurisdiction to ensure the proper administration of trusts (*Schmidt v Rosewood Trust Ltd* [2003] 2 WLR 1442). The approach advanced by the Privy Council is in practice preferable to an approach that presumes beneficiaries to have a right to disclosure. The later approach inevitably conflicts with the fact that trustees are under no duty to disclose reasons for their decisions on trust matters (see 11.4.2).

? QUESTION 12.7

If it is assumed that beneficiaries have a right to inspect trust documents, how might that right be reconciled with the right of the trustees to keep secret their reasons for making decisions in trust matters?

In *Re Londonderry's Settlement* [1964] 3 All ER 855 Harman LJ decided that 'if necessary' the principle that trustees are not required to disclose reasons for their decisions should override the ordinary rule that beneficiaries are entitled to inspect trust documents. His Lordship acknowledged that it is very difficult to resolve the dilemma in a way 'which will not cut down the rights of the beneficiaries too much'. In the same case Salmon LJ reached the same conclusion by another route. He concluded, albeit tentatively, that if any part of a document contains information which the beneficiaries are not entitled to know, such a document should not be regarded as being a trust document.

A professional trustee may in certain circumstances raise professional privilege as a defence to a summons to disclose trust documents. To displace this professional privilege, the beneficiaries must make out a *prima facie* case of fraud (*O'Rourke v Darbishire* [1920] AC 581 (HL)).

CHAPTER SUMMARY

- The law relating to the duties of trusteeship has undergone a sea-change as a result of the Trustee Act 2000.
  - Perhaps the most significant aspect of this change that we have considered in this chapter is that which relates to the delegation of trustees' functions. According to the 'summary' to Law Commission Report No 260, the reform of trustee delegation was intended to facilitate the liberalization of trustee investment (see **Chapter 14**), for 'to leave the law on trustee delegation in its (pre-Trustee Act 2000) state would detract from the benefits to be gained from giving trustees wider powers of investment'. The reforms may not have a significant impact in cases where trust deeds are drawn up by professionals, but the Law Commission envisaged that they would have an impact where trusts arise in 'home-made' wills. Trusts arising in this way will sometimes include no remuneration clause in favour of the trustees, and are unlikely to permit delegation of investment decisions and the appointment of nominees and custodians, and will almost certainly fail to allow investment in the full range of modern financial products.

- The Law Commission assumed that these features of home-made trusts are all bad, presumably because the real purchasing power of an under-managed fund will be eroded over time by inflation. However, we are not living in times of high inflation. The times we live in are, rather, times of high risk associated with investments. There is risk associated with the available investment types (witness the burst of the so-called 'dot.com. bubble'), and there is risk associated with the supervision of those who invest on our behalf (consider, for example, the Barings/Leeson fiasco, where expert bankers were not competent to supervise the highly complex investment activities of their own employee). The choice has always been between the over-cautious approach of trustees who are unpaid friends of the testator and placing trust assets in the name of remote experts subject to minimal restrictions on freedom of investment. Prior to the 2000 Act settlors were presumed to favour the former. After the Act they are presumed to favour the latter.
- The only real compensation for this new world of risk is that s 34 of the 2000 Act (replacing s 19 of the Trustee Act 1925) provides that a trustee may insure any property which is subject to the trust against risks of loss or damage due to any event, and may pay the premiums out of the trust funds. However, even taking into account the fact that, in bare trusts, premiums may be reduced if the beneficiary or beneficiaries direct that certain property should not be insured, the increase in premiums in 'home-made' trusts might turn out to be as high as the inflationary losses that would have been incurred under the old scheme.

SUMMATIVE ASSESSMENT EXERCISE

online resource centre

Trudy has been appointed trustee. The trust deed contains the following clause: 'The trustees shall be entitled to all professional charges incurred in the execution of the trust and shall be entitled to delegate all or any of their duties in accordance with the general law.'

Trudy has accepted the trust, even though she is a total amateur and rather ignorant of business affairs. She purchases a large quantity of office equipment and stationery to facilitate the smooth running of her tasks but still finds that the job is too complicated. After putting in several months of work in service of the trust she eventually enlists the assistance of a friend who, having run his own betting office for many years, is more at ease with commercial matters. She transfers the trust fund into the friend's bank account with the instruction that he should invest it wisely for the benefit of the trust. In fact the friend 'invests' the money on Lucky Laddie, the favourite to win a greyhound race. Lucky Laddie loses the race and the trust fund is lost.

Is Trudy liable for breach of her trust, and why? If she is liable, will she be required to reinstate the full value of the fund, or can she claim remuneration and/or expenses?

FURTHER READING

Austin, R P, 'Moulding the Content of Fiduciary Duties' in A J Oakley (ed) *Trends in Contemporary Trusts Law* (Oxford: Clarendon Press, 1996) 153.

Birks, P, 'The content of fiduciary obligation' (2002) 16(1) Tru LI 34.

Conaglen, M, 'The Nature and Function of Fiduciary Loyalty' (2005) 121 LQR 452.

Finn, P, 'Fiduciary Law and the Modern Commercial World' in McKendrick (ed) *Commercial Aspects of Trusts and Fiduciary Obligations* (Oxford: OUP, 1992).

Finn, P, *Fiduciary Obligations* (Sydney: Law Book Co, 1977).

Finn, P, 'The Fiduciary Principle' in Youdan, T G (ed) *Equity, Fiduciaries and Trusts* (Toronto: Carswell, 1989).

Griffiths, G Ll H, 'Antipodean Revelations? The Beneficiary's Right To Information After *Rosewood*' (2005) Conv 93.

Jones, G H, 'Delegation by Trustees: A Reappraisal' (1959) 22 MLR 388.

Jones, G H, 'Unjust Enrichment and the Fiduciary's Duty of Loyalty' (1968) 84 LQR 477.

Law Commission, *Fiduciary Duties and Regulatory Rules* Consultation Paper No 124 (1992).

Law Commission, *Trustees' Powers and Duties* Report No 260.

Law Commission, *Trustees' Powers and Duties* Consultation Paper No 146.

Reynolds, F M B, 'Solicitors and Conflicts of Duties' [1991] 107 LQR 536.

Sealy, L S, 'Fiduciary Obligations, Forty Years On' (1995) 9 JCL 37.

Simpson, E, 'Conflicts in Breach of Trust' in P Birks and A Pretto (eds) *Breach of Trust* (Oxford: Hart, 2002) 75–94.

13 Maintenance and advancement

OBJECTIVES

By the end of this chapter you should be able to:

1 Advise a settlor as to the extent of the statutory powers of maintenance and advancement

2 Advise a settlor how to exclude or modify the statutory powers by the express terms of the settlement

3 Identify a valid exercise of the powers of maintenance and advancement

13.1 Introduction

Take a typical trust, 'To A for life, to B in remainder'. The settlor has expressed an intention as regards the extent of the beneficial entitlements under the trust. The two beneficiaries are to have vested interests. A will have an interest vested in possession now and B's entitlement will be vested 'in interest' until A's death, when it will vest in possession.

But does the settlor's intention end there? Suppose that A is an infant so not yet absolutely entitled to the income of the trust, and is currently in urgent need of financial assistance. Or suppose that B desperately requires capital during A's lifetime. Surely it is natural to presume that the settlor's general motivation for setting up the trust in the first place will extend to providing for the beneficiaries in these circumstances.

It has long been the practice to insert clauses in trusts to deal with the situations outlined above and Parliament confirmed this practice in the Trustee Act 1925. The Act implies into every trust a power in the hands of the trustees to make payments out of the trust income for the maintenance of infant beneficiaries (s 31) and a power to make payments out of trust capital for the advancement and benefit of infant and adult beneficiaries (s 32). However, these provisions can be excluded or modified by the express terms of the trust instrument.

13.2 Maintenance

Section 31 of the Trustee Act 1925 provides that trustees may 'at their sole discretion' apply the whole or any part of the income of the trust property for 'the maintenance, education or benefit' of an infant beneficiary. (An 'infant' is any person under the age of 18—Family Law Reform Act 1969, s 1.)

The power is crucial because unmarried infant beneficiaries, unlike married infant beneficiaries, cannot give a valid receipt for income (Law of Property Act 1925, s 21). This means that, even where the infant's interest has vested 'in possession' the trustees cannot safely pay income to the infant. If they do so, the beneficiary could demand the money again upon attaining majority.

EXERCISE 13.1

Read s 31(1) of the Trustee Act 1925, set out next. Although the power is exercised in the trustees' 'sole discretion', there are numerous factors which the trustee must take into account. Read through s 31(1) and make a rough list of these factors before moving on.

Trustee Act 1925, s 31

(1) Where any property is held by trustees in trust for any person . . . then, subject to any prior interests or charges affecting the property—

(i) during the infancy of any such person, if his interest so long continues, the trustees may, at their sole discretion, pay to his parent or guardian, if any, or otherwise apply for or towards his maintenance, education or benefit, the whole or such part, if any, of the income of that property as may, in all the circumstances, be reasonable . . .

(ii) if such person on attaining the age of [18 years] has not a vested interest in such income, the trustees shall thenceforth pay the income of that property and of any accretion thereto under subsection (2) of this section to him, until he either attains a vested interest therein or dies, or until failure of his interest:

Provided that [in deciding whether or not to maintain an infant] the trustees shall have regard to the age of the infant and his requirements and generally to the circumstances of the case, and in particular to what other income, if any, is applicable for the same purposes . . .

Your list might contain the following:

(a) The trustees' power to maintain is subject to the rights of persons with prior interests. So, if the trust provides for A for life and for B in remainder the income should not be applied to maintain B, because A is absolutely entitled to all the income on the fund.

(b) When income is applied to maintain an infant beneficiary the income should not actually be paid to the infant. Payment should be made to the infant's parent or guardian or paid directly to address the particular financial need. So, for example, if the payment of income is intended to pay for the infant's school fees, the trustees should make the payment to the child's guardian or to the school direct.

(c) The maintenance payment must be reasonable in all the circumstances. In determining what is reasonable the trustees must have regard to the 'age of the infant and his requirements and generally to the circumstances of the case, and in particular to what other income, if any, is applicable for the same purposes'.

(d) If the trustees know that more than one fund is available to meet a particular financial need, the trustees should not meet the particular need entirely out of the income from their trust fund. Contribution from the trust income should be made *pro rata*. Accordingly if the other available funds are together twice as large as the trust fund the trustees should pay out only half as much as those other funds towards the beneficiary's school fees. If it is not practicable to make a proportional contribution, the trustees may meet the school fees entirely out of their trust income. This might be necessary where, for example, the other available funds have already been totally used up or allocated to other purposes.

13.2.1 Gifts carrying intermediate income

Section 31(3) states that the power of maintenance contained in s 31(1) will not apply to every interest under a trust:

> This section applies in the case of a contingent interest only if the limitation or trust carries the intermediate income of the property, but it applies to a future or contingent legacy by the parent of, or a person standing *in loco parentis* to, the legatee.

We shall consider contingent legacies below (13.2.1.2). First we shall scrutinize other forms of gift to discover which carry the 'intermediate income'. 'Intermediate', here, refers to the period between the effective date of the gift and the date that the beneficiary's interest vests in possession.

13.2.1.1 Testamentary gifts

The Law of Property Act 1925, s 175 applies to devises and bequests in post-1925 wills.

The Law of Property Act 1925

175. Contingent and future testamentary gifts to carry the intermediate income

(1) A contingent or future specific devise or bequest of property, whether real or personal, and a contingent residuary devise of freehold land, and a specific or residuary devise of freehold land to trustees upon trust for persons whose interests are contingent or executory shall, subject to the statutory provisions relating to accumulations, carry the intermediate income of that property from the death of the testator, except so far as such income, or any part thereof, may be otherwise expressly disposed of.

(2) This section applies only to wills coming into operation after the commencement of this Act.

Before examining the section a reminder of a few definitions may be helpful.

A devise is a gift of realty made by will and a bequest is a gift of personalty made by will. The section does not cover legacies, which are gifts of cash made by will. Devises, bequests and legacies may be specific or residual. If T leaves Blackacre (freehold property) to S and the rest of his realty to R, S is said to have a specific devise and R is said to have been given a residuary devise. Do not forget that leases are classed as personalty, even though they are interests in land.

Finally, it is worth being reminded of the distinction between a contingent and a deferred (or 'future' gift). A contingent gift is one which might never take effect, for example, 'To A when she qualifies as a doctor'. A deferred gift is one which will take effect at some time in the future, the gift is vested 'in interest' now, but actual beneficial enjoyment of the property (the vesting 'in possession') is deferred, for example, 'To A when X dies'. X will certainly die at some point and A will take the gift 'in possession' at that date. If A has already died by the date that A's interest vests in possession, A's beneficial interest will pass to those entitled under A's will or, if there is no will, to those entitled under the intestacy rules.

With these definitions in mind you should be able to carry out the following Exercise.

EXERCISE 13.2

Read s 175 of the Law of Property Act 1925, set out above. According to this section which of the following testamentary gifts *to A* will carry the intermediate income?

(a) '£1,000 to B, Whiteacre (leasehold) to A at 25, residue to C';

(b) 'Greenacre (freehold) to A on 1 January 2000';

(c) 'Greenacre (freehold) to B, the rest of my freehold property to A upon his attaining 21 or graduating from university, whichever is the earlier'.

The answers are as follows:

(a) This is a contingent specific bequest of personalty. It does carry the intermediate income, as would a contingent specific devise of realty.

(b) This is a deferred ('future') specific devise of realty. It carries the intermediate income. A deferred ('future') specific bequest of personalty also carries the intermediate income.

(c) This is a contingent residuary devise of freehold land. It also carries the intermediate income.

The wording of s 175 omits several types of gift. One important omission is the 'pecuniary legacy', which is dealt with in 13.2.1.3. Certain other gifts not included in s 175 are considered in the next section.

13.2.1.2 Some gifts not included in s 175

Immediate vested gifts

As has already been indicated, 'immediate' vested gifts of any property, whether made by will or *inter vivos*, will carry the income arising on the property unless there is a contrary intention in the trust instrument.

An example of an immediate vested gift to A would be a clause in a will or an *inter vivos* settlement stating: 'I instruct my trustees to hold everything I own for the benefit of A and B in equal shares absolutely'.

Inter vivos contingent gift

Section 175 only applies to *testamentary* dispositions. Generally, *inter vivos* contingent gifts will carry the intermediate income.

An example of an *inter vivos* contingent gift would be a settlement on trustees, effective during the lifetime of the settlor, under which the beneficiary would be entitled to the trust fund upon graduating from law school.

Contingent residuary bequests of personalty

Such gifts carry the intermediate income not otherwise disposed of. *Re Adams* [1893] 1 Ch 329 concerned a bequest of residue to such of a class of children who shall attain 21 or, being daughters, marry. North J asked 'How does the matter stand as to the income?' and concluded 'I think it is fallacious to say that they take an interest in the income, *qua* income of the capital they have an interest in. But it is undisposed of income, and as such becomes part of the residue . . . the income belongs contingently to the children, in the same way as the capital belongs contingently to them'. In other words, undisposed income results to the residue of the testator's estate, so contingent residual bequests carry the intermediate income by default.

Deferred residuary bequests of personalty

According to Jenkins J in *Re Oliver* [1947] 2 All ER 162, the general rule is that 'a gift expressly limited to take effect on a future date does not carry the intermediate income'. Deferred residuary bequests follow this general rule and do not carry the intermediate income. An example of such a gift to A would be the following clause in a will: 'I leave my car to B and the residue of my personal estate to A on B's death or on 1 January 2010, whichever is the later'.

Deferred residuary devises

In *Re McGeorge* [1963] Ch 544, Cross J accepted the general rule that an expressly deferred gift will not carry the intermediate income, interpreting s 175 of the Law of Property Act 1925 as providing that because the income had not been otherwise disposed of, the devise would carry the intermediate income. Whether or not that was a correct construction of the section, he went on to hold that the mere fact that the gift technically carried the intermediate income would not lead him to hold that the beneficiary should be maintained out of that income. He held that to maintain the infant would defeat the testator's intention, for to do so would establish her as the only beneficiary entitled to the income, effectively granting her an interest in possession in the income on the devise during the lifetime of the testator's wife. To permit the interest in the income from the land to vest in possession now would be inconsistent with the testator's expressed intention to defer the vesting in possession of the interest in the land itself.

Deferred-contingent bequests of residuary personalty

An example of such a gift, to A, would be a gift of 'My Rolls-Royce to B and the rest of my personalty to A'.

In *Re Geering* [1964] 3 All ER 1043, it was held that a deferred-contingent residuary bequest does not carry the intermediate income. In this case, as in *Re McGeorge* [1963] Ch 544, Cross J drew a clear distinction between contingent gifts which are immediate and contingent gifts which are deferred: 'The very fact that a testator defers a gift of residue to a future date is itself *prima facie* an indication that he does not intend the legatee to have the income of residue accruing before that date'.

Deferred-contingent devises of residuary realty

An example of such a gift, to A, would be a gift of Greenacre (freehold) to B, with a gift of the rest of the testator's realty to A on 1 January 2000 upon condition that A had married by that date. If A marries he will be entitled to the residuary realty, but will have to wait until the year 2000 for the gift to vest in possession. Due to the omission of this category of gift from the wording of s 175 it is debatable whether it will or will not carry the intermediate income. No case has been decided on the point. There are, however, good reasons to suppose that it will not.

First, one of the prime aims of the 1925 legislation, and of the Law of Property Act in particular, was to assimilate as far as possible the legal treatment of real property to the legal treatment of personal property, in order to make land easier to sell. Section 175 was drafted with this very aim in mind (according to Cross J in *Re McGeorge* [1963] Ch 544). As there is authority to show that deferred-contingent gifts of residuary personalty do not carry the intermediate income (*Re Geering*) it would surely be inconsistent to permit deferred-contingent gifts of residuary realty to carry the intermediate income.

Secondly, it is quite clear from the wording of s 175 that vested deferred devises of residuary realty do not carry the intermediate income and this has been confirmed in numerous cases since (see, for example, *Re McGeorge*). If vested forms of the gift do not carry the intermediate income there can be no sensible reason for supposing that contingent forms of the gifts will, or should.

Contingent pecuniary legacies

This important class of gifts is dealt with in the next section.

13.2.1.3 Contingent pecuniary legacy

The general rule, established not long after s 175 came into being, is that such a gift will not carry the intermediate income (*Re Raine* [1929] 1 Ch 716). This was because s 175 refers only to 'bequests' and 'devises'. However, there are exceptions to the general rule (see B S Ker, 'Trustees' Powers of Maintenance' (1953) 17 Conv 273).

The main exceptions are as follows:

(a) A contingent (or, indeed, a deferred) pecuniary legacy will carry the intermediate income if the testator was the parent of, or was a person standing *in loco parentis* to, the legatee (see s 31(3)). This exception is based on the presumed intention of the testator and can be rebutted by evidence that the testator has provided another fund out of which the infant is to be maintained. It is sometimes suggested that this exception will not apply if the contingency attached to the pecuniary legacy is the attaining of an age greater than the age of majority (now 18). The reasoning goes, once again, to the presumed intention of the testator: the testator, in choosing the higher contingency age, clearly did not intend his gift to meet the beneficiary's needs as an infant. The courts will not presume that the testator intended the contingent pecuniary legacy to carry the intermediate income for the purpose of maintaining the infant beneficiary.

(b) Even where the testator was not a parent or person *in loco parentis* the contingent pecuniary legacy will carry the intermediate income if the testator has shown an intention to maintain the beneficiary. For instance, in *Re Churchill* [1909] 2 Ch 431 the testatrix empowered her trustees to apply 'the share to which any beneficiary . . . may be contingently entitled in or towards the advancement in life or otherwise for the benefit of such beneficiary'. This clause was construed as authorizing maintenance of an infant beneficiary (the beneficiary was entitled to a pecuniary legacy upon his attaining 21).

(c) Finally, the case of *Re Medlock* (1886) 54 LT 828 is authority for another exception to the general rule. In this case it was held that a contingent pecuniary legacy would carry the intermediate income if the testator had separated the legacy from the rest of his estate. In *Re Medlock* the legacy was held by trustees on separate trusts.

13.2.1.4 Conceptual rationale

? QUESTION 13.1

From our study of gifts which do and gifts which do not carry the intermediate income, can you suggest a possible conceptual rationale which could give principled justification for the distinctions which are drawn in the statutes and cases?

The underlying rationale, which we keep coming back to, is the presumed intention of the person who made the gift. The only contingent gift which does not automatically carry the intermediate income is the pecuniary legacy, it is an exception that is hard to justify. Easier to rationalize is the general rule that deferred gifts do not carry intermediate income. A deferred gift, unlike a contingent gift, has been deliberately put back in time. The only deferred gift that does carry the intermediate income is a gift of a specific item of property.

13.2.1.5 Summative chart

Does the gift carry the 'Intermediate Income'?

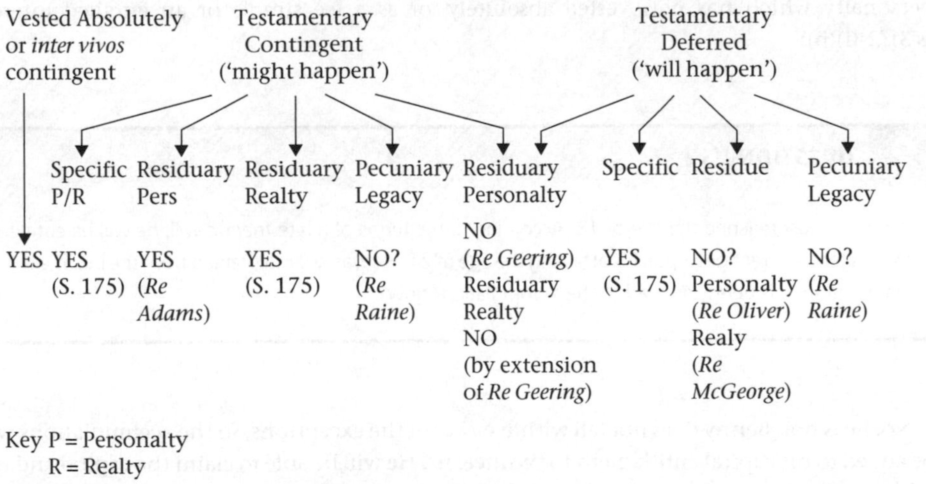

Note: All 'yes' answers are subject to express contrary intention apparent from the terms of the trust, (LPA 1925 s 69(2)).

13.2.2 During infancy

The trustees do not have a *duty* to maintain if the gift carries the intermediate income: they have a *power* to do so. Accordingly it may be that in certain cases the intermediate income is not applied to maintain the beneficiary, perhaps because the beneficiary has no financial needs, or because those needs are being fully met from other sources (for example, parents).

What happens to the unapplied income in these circumstances? According to the Trustee Act 1925, s 31(2) this 'residue' of the income should be accumulated annually 'in the way of compound interest' (to understand how compound interest is calculated see 15.2.3). These accumulations may be applied in future years to maintain the infant beneficiary.

If a beneficiary dies during infancy the accumulations on that beneficiary's share are added to the capital of the trust as a whole, and not just to that beneficiary's share. The accumulations will not, therefore, devolve on the estate of the deceased infant. This is so even though the infant had a vested interest in the income during their life (*Re Delamere's ST* [1984] 1 WLR 813).

13.2.3 Attaining majority

When the infant beneficiary attains majority (reaches the age of 18), or marries under that age, the trustees must add the accumulations to the main capital from which the accumulated income arose. There are two exceptions to this rule. When either of those exceptions applies the trustees will not add the accumulations to the main capital, but will hold them on trust for the beneficiary absolutely, so that the accumulations may be paid to the beneficiary and the beneficiary's receipt will discharge the trustee.

The exceptions are to be found in the Trustee Act 1925, s 31(2). The first covers cases where the beneficiary already had a vested interest in the income *before* they attained majority (or earlier marriage). The second exception is where the beneficiary's contingent interest in the income vests *at the date* that they attain majority (or earlier marriage). For the latter exception to operate it is crucial that the beneficiary's interest had been a contingent interest in realty or personalty which has now vested absolutely, or as a fee simple or an entailed interest (s 31(2)(i)(b)).

? QUESTION 13.2

Benny has just reached the age of 18. According to the terms of a late friend's will, he will be entitled to 'Whiteacre' (freehold) upon his attaining the age of 21. He was not maintained from the income during his infancy. Is Benny entitled to the accumulations now?

No, he is not. Benny does not fall within either of the exceptions, so the accumulations will be added to his capital entitlement to 'Whiteacre'. He will be able to claim the capital and the accumulations when he reaches the age of 21.

What if Benny needs (or wants) financial assistance now that he is 18? He cannot be maintained because he is not an infant (unless there is an express provision for maintenance of adult beneficiaries in the will the court will not maintain adult beneficiaries under its inherent jurisdiction) and the trustees are unable to pay him the accumulations made during his infancy. Is Benny entitled to anything now? Section 31(1)(ii) of the Trustee Act 1925 reflects what would probably have been the testator's intention for such a situation. It provides that beneficiaries in Benny's position will be absolutely entitled *now* to the income which is currently being earned on the combined fund of capital and accumulations.

13.2.4 **Class gifts**

If there is a gift to a class contingent upon its members attaining the age of 21, or some other age, the class will close provisionally (for the purpose of maintenance) when the first person attains that age (the class will include all members living at the date the class closed). The trustees may then maintain that beneficiary out of the income attributable to their notional share. If a new beneficiary is born later the class is re-closed, again on a provisional basis, and a fresh allocation of notional shares made. This re-allocation occurs every time a member of the class attains the contingent age or a new member is born.

13.2.5 **Tax considerations**

During the minority of a beneficiary to whom the power of maintenance applies the trust is charged income tax on all income. If the beneficiary receives the accumulations upon attaining majority the accumulations will be treated as capital and therefore inheritance tax will be charged on all capital above a fixed-value threshold (currently £263,000). If the beneficiary is not entitled to the accumulations upon attaining majority they will be entitled to the income under s 31(1)(ii) and they will have to pay income tax on it. The level at which the beneficiary will pay income tax depends upon the level of their total income from this and other sources.

These fiscal considerations will influence the exercise of a trustee's discretion whether or not to maintain the infant beneficiary.

However, if the trust satisfies the criteria for an 'accumulation and maintenance trust' under the Inheritance Tax Act 1984, s 71 the beneficiary will not have to pay inheritance tax upon attaining an interest in possession or becoming absolutely entitled to the trust property.

13.2.5.1 **Reform of taxation of trusts**

In the 2004 Budget the Chancellor announced that, with effect from April 2005, there would be a new tax regime for trusts for the most vulnerable (backdated to 6 April 2004), a £500 basic rate band applying to the income of all trusts otherwise chargeable at the rate applicable to trusts and harmonized trust definitions and tests for income tax and CGT purposes. In August 2004 the Inland Revenue published a consultation document, *Modernising the Tax System For Trusts* which is intended to deliver a modernised tax system consistent with the following principles:

- The tax system should be as simple and easy to understand as possible.
- Compliance with tax obligations should be straightforward.

- Where a beneficiary receives income or benefits from a trust they should where possible be taxed as if they have received them direct.
- Where a settlor retains an interest in a trust they should be treated as if they still owned the assets.
- Where the income or assets cannot readily be identified with settlors or beneficiaries, tax should be levied on the trustees.
- Trustees with low income and no gains should not have to complete Self Assessment tax returns every year.
- Trusts set up to protect the vulnerable should receive special treatment.
- Anti-avoidance legislation is appropriate for those who use trusts to avoid tax.

13.2.6 Perpetuities

Look back to the rule against excessive accumulations (6.4) and attempt the following Question.

> **? QUESTION 13.3**
>
> Tina left certain shares to Belinda in her will, and directed that dividends on the shares should be accumulated until Belinda reached the age of 25. At the date of Tina's death Belinda was aged five. Is the gift void for excessive accumulation? Would the answer be any different if Belinda had been two at the date of Tina's death?

If Belinda was five, the answer is that the gift is not void for perpetuity, this is because the accumulation will come to an end within 21 years of the testator's death. If Belinda was two, the result would be different. The direction to accumulate would infringe the rule against excessive accumulations. Having said that, the gift as a whole will not be void for perpetuity. Only the accumulations made beyond the authorised period will be disallowed. The whole gift would only be void for perpetuity if the direction to accumulate might extend the period of accumulation beyond the common law 'perpetuity period'.

13.3 Advancement

The Trustee Act 1925, s 32 provides that trustees may apply capital money for the advancement or benefit of a beneficiary, regardless of whether that beneficiary is an infant or an adult. The power has no application to Settled Land Act settlements.

Trustee Act 1925

32. Power of advancement

(1) Trustees may at any time or times pay or apply any capital money subject to a trust, for the advancement or benefit, in such manner as they may, in their absolute discretion, think fit, of any person entitled to the capital of the trust property or of any share thereof, whether absolutely or contingently on his attaining any specified age or on the occurrence of any other event, or subject to a gift over on his death under any specified age or on the occurrence of any other event, and whether in possession or in remainder or reversion, and such payment or application may be made notwithstanding that the interest of such person is liable to be defeated by the exercise of a power of appointment or revocation, or to be diminished by the increase of the class to which he belongs:

Provided that—

(a) the money so paid or applied for the advancement or benefit of any person shall not exceed altogether in amount one-half of the presumptive or vested share or interest of that person in the trust property; and

(b) if that person is or becomes absolutely and indefeasibly entitled to a share in the trust property the money so paid or applied shall be brought into account as part of such share; and

(c) no such payment or application shall be made so as to prejudice any person entitled to any prior life or other interest, whether vested or contingent, in the money paid or applied unless such person is in existence and of full age and consents in writing to such payment or application.

(2) This section applies only where the trust property consists of money or securities or of property held upon trust for sale calling in and conversion, and such money or securities, or the proceeds of such sale calling in and conversion are not by statute or in equity considered as land, or applicable as capital money for the purposes of the Settled Land Act 1925.

(3) This section does not apply to trusts constituted or created before the commencement of this Act.

13.3.1 Capital money

Although s 32 states that maintenance must be made out of capital *money* it has been held that trustees may apply capital *assets* for the advancement of the beneficiary. This happened in *Re Collard's Will Trusts* [1961] 1 All ER 821. The capital asset in that case was a farm to which the beneficiary was entitled under a will. Buckley J observed that the trustees would have the power to advance £20,000 in capital monies to the beneficiary and then to sell the farm to the beneficiary at that price. The judge concluded, therefore, that the farm could be given to the beneficiary directly. R E Megarry described this as the 'healthy realism' of equity (1961) 77 LQR 161 at 163.

13.3.2 The meaning of 'advancement'

EXERCISE 13.3

Read the short section of Viscount Radcliffe's speech in *Pilkington v IRC* [1964] AC 612 (below). How does his Lordship define 'advancement', and what examples does he give of payments which would be for the 'advancement' of the beneficiary?

***Pilkington* v *IRC* [1964] AC 612**

Viscount Radcliffe:

> The word 'advancement' itself meant in this context the establishment in life of the beneficiary who was the object of the power or at any rate some step that would contribute to the furtherance of his establishment. Thus it was found in such phrases as 'preferment or advancement' (*Lowther v Bentinck* (1874) LR 19 Eq 166), 'business, profession, or employment or . . . advancement or 'preferment in the world' (*Roper-Curzon v Roper-Curzon* (1871) LR 11 Eq 452) and 'placing out or advancement in life' (*In re Breeds' Will* (1875) 1 ChD 226). Typical instances of expenditure for such purposes under the social conditions of the nineteenth century were an apprenticeship or the purchase of a commission in the army or of an interest in business. In the case of a girl there could be advancement on marriage (*Lloyd v Cocker* (1860) 27 Beav. 645). Advancement had, however, to some extent a limited range of meaning, since it was thought to convey the idea of some step in life of permanent significance, and accordingly, to prevent uncertainties about the permitted range of objects for which moneys could be raised and made available, such words as 'or otherwise for his or her benefit' were often added to the word 'advancement.' It was always recognised that these added words were 'large words' (see Jessel MR in *In re Breeds' Will*) and indeed in another case (*Lowther v Bentinck*) the same judge spoke of preferment and advancement as being 'both large words' but of 'benefit' as being the 'largest of all'. So, too, Kay J in *In re Brittlebank* (1881) 30 WR 99. Recent judges have spoken in the same terms—see Farwell J in *In re Halsted's Will Trusts* [1937] 2 All ER 570 and Danckwerts J in *In re Moxon's Will Trusts* [1958] 1 WLR 165. This wide construction of the range of the power, which evidently did not stand upon niceties of distinction provided that the proposed application could fairly be regarded as for the benefit of the beneficiary who was the object of the power, must have been carried into the statutory power created by s. 32, since it adopts without qualification the accustomed wording 'for the advancement or benefit in such manner as they may in their absolute discretion think fit.'

His Lordship defines 'advancement' as 'the establishment in life of the beneficiary who was the object of the power or at any rate some step that would contribute to the furtherance of his establishment'. It is a common semantic error to think of advancements as payments 'in advance', in the sense of 'early' payment. It is true that payments of capital under s 32 are often made early, in anticipation of the beneficiary's interest vesting in possession, but the technical meaning of 'advancement' in this context is 'getting on in life'.

The historical examples given by his Lordship are payment to support an apprenticeship, to purchase a commission in the army or an interest in a business or to provide a dowry on the marriage of a female. Later in his speech he gives the further examples of paying off the beneficiary's debts or setting up the beneficiary's spouse in business. More modern examples have included the purchase of a house for the beneficiary to live in and to use as a doctor's surgery and enabling a beneficiary to purchase shares in a family company for which he worked. In *Pilkington v IRC* itself, applying capital monies to reduce the tax liability of the beneficiary was considered to be a valid advancement.

Additionally, there are suggestions in some of the cases that 'advancement', historically at least, is understood to take place in the 'early period' of the beneficiary's life. It is a process for 'getting them started'.

13.3.3 The meaning of benefit

Traditionally, the power to make a payment for the advancement of a beneficiary had to be exercised so as to contribute a major step in the furtherance of the beneficiary. Section 32, however, provides that capital money may be applied for the advancement or 'benefit' of the beneficiary. Benefit has a much wider meaning than advancement. *Re Clore's ST* [1966] 1 WLR 955 illustrates just how broad the concept of benefit can be. The beneficiary's father had established a charitable foundation to which the beneficiary felt morally obliged to contribute. It would be more tax efficient for the donation to be made by the trustees out of the trust capital than out of the beneficiary's private funds. At one level, then, the benefit was nothing more remarkable than the receipt of a tax saving, but at another level the benefit to the beneficiary was being relieved of a moral obligation in the most tax efficient way.

? QUESTION 13.4

Betty's beneficial interest under a trust is contingent upon her attaining the age of 25. The trustees are proposing to apply capital monies for her advancement by resettling her beneficial interest on new trusts under which her interest will vest when she reaches the age of 30. Could this possibly be for her benefit?

These facts are similar to the facts of *Re T's Settlement Trusts* [1963] 3 All ER 759, which were considered in **Chapter 9** on variation of trusts. In that case it was held that a postponement of the beneficiary's entitlement could be for their benefit where the evidence suggests that the beneficiary is immature, reckless or a spendthrift. Similar reasoning might be applied in the context of making an advancement.

13.3.3.1 Incidental beneficiaries

We have already seen that it will be a valid exercise of the power in s 32 to apply capital monies to pay off the beneficiary's debts and, in another case, to set the beneficiary's spouse up in business. In these cases it is clear that the beneficiary's creditors and spouse are benefiting from the exercise of the trustees' power. This, however, does not make the exercise of the power invalid. As Viscount Radcliffe stated in *Pilkington v IRC* [1964] AC 612: 'It is no objection to the exercise of the power that other persons benefit incidentally from the exercise of the power.' Miss Pilkington was the object of the power of advancement. The trustees had proposed to advance her by resettling capital monies for her benefit. Her children would have received nothing under the original trust, but under the resettlement they would benefit if she died under the age of 30 leaving surviving issue. The children were the 'incidental beneficiaries'.

13.3.4 The provisos to s 32

Section 32 lists various conditions governing the exercise by the trustees of the power of advancement.

13.3.4.1 Section 32(1)(a)

This section provides that the money paid for the advancement or benefit of the beneficiary 'shall not exceed altogether in amount one-half of the presumptive or vested share or interest of that person in the trust property'. This proviso is without prejudice to the settlor's right to include a more generous power of advancement in the trust instrument. The settlor could, if they wished, incorporate a clause permitting the trustees to apply the whole of the beneficiary's interest by way of advancement.

Certain aspects of this proviso need to be considered in more detail. First, what is meant by a 'presumptive' share? This can be answered by way of an example. If we take a typical gift 'to A at the age of 25', if A is presently only 15 years old it is clear that he does not yet have a vested interest. (He might never reach the age of 25.) He does however have a presumptive interest in the subject matter of the gift. A may be advanced out of half the value of the property even though he has not yet met the contingency.

? QUESTION 13.5

A gift has been made by way of trust for A and B in equal shares upon their graduating from university. The trust fund is valued at £100,000. What is the maximum payment by way of advancement that can be made, today, to A? (Assume that A has not previously received monies from the fund.)

The answer is that A can receive up to £25,000. A's presumptive share is currently valued at £50,000. The trustees may apply up to half the value of that presumptive share, that is, £25,000.

The good news for A is that he will not have to repay the £25,000 to the trust if, in the event, he fails to satisfy the contingency.

EXERCISE 13.4

After A received £25,000, the remaining £75,000 worth of trust property increased in value and is now estimated to be worth £300,000. B now requests a payment of £100,000 by way of advancement and A requests a further £25,000. Advise the trustees.

The trustees will not be able to advance B in the sum of £100,000. B's presumptive share is half of the sum of £300,000 and £25,000, that is, £162,500. (A's presumptive share, incidentally, is £162,500 less £25,000, that is, £137,500.) It follows that the trustees may only apply up to half of £162,500 for B's advancement, that is, a maximum of £81,250. The trustees will not be permitted to pay any further sums to A. According to *Re Marquess of Abergavenny's Estate Act Trusts* [1981] 2 All ER 643 a beneficiary will be unable to claim further payments by way of advancement if the trustees have already used the power to the full in respect of that beneficiary.

Does this appear to you to create an unfair result? Suppose that A and B both become absolutely entitled to the capital today. A will receive £137,500 and B will receive £162,500. However, A will no doubt have put the £25,000 he has already received to profitable use. That £25,000, if it has done as well as the rest of the fund (that is, increased threefold since the date the power of advancement was exercised), will today be worth £75,000. In real terms it may be that A will receive a total benefit of £212,500 (£137,500 plus £75,000), compared with B's £162,000. The Law Commission has expressed some concern in relation to this possibility, and has recommended that when the beneficiaries become absolutely entitled to the capital, any beneficiary who received capital early by way of advancement should account, not for the nominal cash value of the capital at the date of the advancement, but for its value *as a proportion of the fund at the date of the advancement.* (See Law Commission, 23rd Report, paras 4.43–4.47.)

In fact the s 32(1)(a) limitation may not be as strict and inflexible as previously thought. A recent first instance decision in the Chancery Division of the High Court has held that the court has power under the Variation of Trusts Act 1958 (see **Chapter 9**) to approve an arrangement removing or relaxing the s 32(1)(a) limitation. In *CD (a minor) v O* [2004] All ER (D) 413 the one-half limit was exceeded in favour of a child (indeed it was held that the child's entire presumptive share could be used) in order to pay her school fees. This decision seems a somewhat radical departure from the statutory rule restricting advancement to one-half of a beneficiary's presumptive share, but the judge was understandably fortified by the fact that the beneficiary in this case was solely entitled to the fund and would (but for her age) have been entitled to bring the trust to an end.

13.3.4.2 Section 32(1)(b)

This section provides that if a beneficiary becomes absolutely and indefeasibly entitled to a share in the trust property the money they have already received by way of advancement must be brought into account as part of their share. This process is called 'hotchpot'. It can be illustrated by way of the following activity.

? QUESTION 13.6

A and B are the beneficiaries of a trust under which they will become entitled to an equal share of the fund upon their attaining the age of 21. The trustees paid £10,000 to A to finance A's time as a student at university. A is 21 today, and the fund is today valued at £100,000. How much is A entitled to?

A is entitled to £45,000. The whole fund is £110,000, of which A's share is £55,000 but A must bring into 'hotch-pot' the £10,000 that has already been received.

13.3.4.3 **Section 32(1)(c)**

According to this section the trustees will not be permitted to make a payment by way of advancement if to do so would prejudice any person with a prior interest in the fund, unless the person with the prior interest gives their consent in writing to the advancement.

If a trust provides for A for life and for B in remainder, the trustees will not be permitted to apply any capital money for the advancement or benefit of B unless A has given consent in writing, because A has a definite interest in income earned on the capital of the trust. If A had been the potential object of a discretionary trust his consent would not be required, because such a beneficiary has merely a 'hope' that he will receive an interest in the trust (see *Re Beckett's Settlement* [1940] Ch 279).

The written consent of a person with a prior interest will still be required despite a clause in the trust instrument dispensing with the requirement. This is a rare instance of the settlor being unable to oust the provisions of the general law by the express terms of the trust instrument. The case which decided the point, *Henley v Wardell* (1988) *The Times*, 29 January, involved a clause in a will which purported to remove the requirement for consent. The caption to *The Times Law Report* carried a witty summary of the decision: 'Will Power Doesn't Override Consent'.

13.3.5 Advancement by resettlement

There is nothing wrong in principle with making an advancement by way of resettlement, but such an exercise of the power is fraught with risks. The resettlement may be invalid if it is not made for the benefit of the advancee, if it is void for perpetuity or if it involves the unauthorized delegation of a basic discretion. We have considered the 'benefit' factor above (13.3.3) and the rule against perpetuities has been considered at length in **Chapter 6**. The factor which requires further attention here is the risk that the resettlement will involve the delegation of a basic discretion.

In *Pilkington v IRC* [1964] AC 612, Viscount Radcliffe stated that 'the law is not that a trustee may not delegate; it is that trustees may not delegate unless they have authority to do so' (see 12.3). Upjohn J in *Re Wills* [1959] Ch 1, stated that 'unless upon its proper construction the power of advancement permits delegation of powers and discretion, a settlement created in exercise of the power of advancement cannot in general delegate any powers or discretion, at any rate in relation to beneficial interests'. The final reference to discretions involving beneficial interests suggests that the learned judge had the so-called 'dispositive discretions' in mind (see 11.4.1).

13.3.6 Exercise of discretion

What are the factors which should be taken into account when exercising the discretion to make an advancement? Some relevant factors are considered in the following sections.

13.3.6.1 **Benefit**

The most important question that the trustees should ask themselves when considering an exercise of their power under s 32, is 'will the application of capital monies be for the benefit of the beneficiary?' As Dankwerts J stated in *Re Moxon's WT* [1958] 1 All ER 386: ' "Benefit" is the widest possible word one could have and . . . it must include a payment direct to the beneficiary; but that does not absolve the trustees from making up their minds whether the payment in the particular manner which they contemplate is for the benefit of the beneficiary'. What will and will not constitute 'benefit' has been discussed above (13.3.3).

13.3.6.2 Trustees as incidental beneficiaries

What if one of the *trustees* exercising the power of advancement stands to profit from the exercise of that power? In *Molyneux* v *Fletcher* [1898] 1 QBD 648 the trust instrument granted the trustees the power to make payments for the 'advancement in life' of the beneficiary. It was held to be an invalid exercise of the trustees' discretion to pay monies to the beneficiary with the knowledge that the sums would be used by the beneficiary's spouse to repay a debt due to one of the trustees.

13.3.6.3 The fiduciary aspect

The power to make an advancement is a fiduciary power. Therefore the trustees must weigh, against the benefit to the advancee, the interests of other persons entitled under the trust (*Re Pauling's Settlement Trusts* [1963] 3 All ER 1). They must also ensure that the capital monies paid to the advancee are used by the advancee for the use intended by the trustees. As Wilmer LJ stated in *Re Pauling's ST* in the Court of Appeal: 'They [the trustees] cannot . . . prescribe a particular purpose, and then raise and pay the money over to the advancee leaving him or her entirely free, legally and morally, to apply it for that purpose or to spend it in any way he or she chooses, without any responsibility on the trustees even to inquire as to its application'. The trustees (a bank) in *Re Pauling's* had been advised by counsel that they could pay trust monies over to the adult advancees, and what they did with them thereafter was their concern. Clearly, the Court of Appeal came to a different view.

As stated, the power of advancement is a fiduciary power, the trustees cannot simply pay over the capital monies and then wash their hands of the affair. They have a duty to make enquiries as to how the monies are actually spent. If the monies are not used for the prescribed purpose, and the trustees receive notice of this fact, they will be under a duty not to make further advances in the future without first satisfying themselves that the money will be properly applied.

13.4 Contrary intention

The statutory powers of maintenance and advancement apply only in so far as a contrary intention is not expressed in the trust instrument (Trustee Act 1925, s 69(2)). In the case of *IRC v Bernstein* [1961] 1 Ch 399 the settlor had directed that the income on his trusts should be accumulated during his lifetime and this was held to be evidence of an intention to exclude the statutory power to make an advancement of capital monies. The court found that the settlor had clearly intended that capital should not be distributed until his death. The direction to accumulate would, of course, be evidence of an intention to exclude the power of maintenance also.

In *Re Ransome* [1957] 1 All ER 690 a similar direction to accumulate income was held to amount to an intention to exclude the trustees' duty to pay income on accumulations under s 31(1)(ii) (see 13.2.3 above). This was in spite of the fact that the direction to accumulate was held to be void for perpetuity. The beneficiary in this case got the worst of both worlds! They did not receive the accumulations which the settlor had intended should be made for their benefit, but neither did they receive the income released when the direction to accumulate was declared void. *Re Ransome* looks like a case where the settlor's 'true' intentions for the beneficiary have been denied because of the strict application of the settlor's presumed 'contrary intention' under s 69(2). (See J G Riddall's imaginative article, '*Re Ransome* Revisited or "First The Good News" ' (1979) 43 Conv 423.)

13.4.1 Express powers of maintenance and advancement

Before this chapter concludes, it is worth reiterating that the statutory powers of maintenance and advancement may be extended, or otherwise varied, by express provision in the trust instrument. We have considered a number of instances throughout this chapter. See, for example, 13.2.1.3 and 13.3.4.1.

13.4.2 The court's inherent jurisdiction

Even where a trust instrument excludes the statutory powers of maintenance and advancement, and does not contain any such provisions of its own, the court retains an inherent jurisdiction to maintain infant beneficiaries out of income and capital and to advance infant beneficiaries out of capital.

CHAPTER SUMMARY

- We have seen in this chapter that the law reads between the lines of a gift. The settlor or testator has a general intention to benefit the beneficiary, that much is obvious from the fact that they have made a gift at all. The statutory powers of maintenance and advancement are an acknowledgement that the intentions of most 'gift-makers' will go beyond the express terms of the gift.
  - Thus, where a gift of antique furniture is made to an infant, it is natural to assume that the trustees will have power to sell the furniture and maintain the beneficiary out of the interest on the proceeds of sale. Few 'gift-makers', if asked, would want the infant's education or health to suffer by insisting upon the retention of an old table and some chairs.
- In any case, we have seen that if a settlor or testator objects to the statutory powers of maintenance and advancement they have the power to exclude them by the express terms of their gift. Conversely, if they feel that the statutory powers are not extensive enough, the 'gift-makers' are at liberty to make more generous provision of their own.

SUMMATIVE ASSESSMENT EXERCISE

online resource centre

Wilhelm, who died in 1996, left the residue of his estate in trust for his grandchildren, Betty and Andrew, at the age of 25, in equal shares absolutely. The trustees have invested the fund and accumulated all the income on it. The capital value of the fund is now £20,000.

Betty is 19 years old; Andrew is 12.

The trustees have received the following requests:

First, they have been asked to transfer £4,000 into a trust fund set up by the children's uncle in 1995 under which the fund trustees may, in their sole discretion, pay income or capital to any of his nephews or nieces who are students at university, and any capital remaining after a period of 21 years will be divided equally between all his nephews and nieces. At present the fund is valued at £6,000 and Betty is the only eligible beneficiary.

Secondly, Andrew's parents have asked the trustees to pay all the income of the fund to them for 10 years to enable them to meet the initial running costs of a riding school which they propose to establish at their home. Andrew is interested in riding and supports the proposal.

Advise whether the trustees may comply with these requests.

FURTHER READING

Ker, B S, 'Trustees' Powers of Maintenance' (1953) 17 Conv 273.

Riddall, J G, '*Re Ransome* Revisited or "First The Good News" ' (1979) 43 Conv 423.

14 Investment

OBJECTIVES

By the end of this chapter you should be able to:

1 Advise a trustee as to the types of investment permitted by the general law

2 Identify a breach of the duty to invest with appropriate care

3 Explain the significance to trustee investments of modern portfolio theory

4 Assess the impact of the Trustee Act 2000 upon trustee investments

14.1 Introduction

Previously the general law would not allow trustees to participate in the market as if they were absolute owners of the fund. That could only be achieved by the terms of the trust instrument or, in an exceptional case, by a special order of the court enlarging the trustees' investment powers. Now, as a result of Part II of the Trustee Act 2000 every trustee 'may make any kind of investment that he could make if he were absolutely entitled to the assets of the trust' (Trustee Act 2000, s 3(1)). This power 'will enable trustees to hold investments jointly or in common with other persons' (note 20, accompanying the Act). In fact, the only type of investment which still requires express authorization in the trust instrument is investment in interests in land other than mortgages (s 3(3)), and freeholds and leaseholds (s 8).

Note, however, that the provisions of Part II of the Act do not apply to occupational pension schemes and authorized unit trusts, or to certain schemes under the Charities Act 1993. These special forms of trust are subject to their own statutory rules (which, in the case of pension trustees, grant investment powers as wide as those provided by the 2000 Act. See the Pensions Act 1995, s 34(1)). For 'normal' trustees the Trustee Act 2000 repeals the old scheme for investment laid down by the Trustee Investments Act 1961. It did this because (as the notes to the 2000 Act put it):

> [T]he law governing the powers and duties of trustees, particularly the relevant provisions of the Trustee Act 1925 and the Trustee Investments Act 1961, has not kept pace with the evolving social and economic role which trusts now fulfil. This discrepancy has been brought into sharp focus by the

> fundamental changes in the conduct of investment business during the last ten years such as the introduction of the CREST system on the London Stock Exchange. The situation is now so serious that the view is widely held that it is very difficult for such trustees acting under the terms of trust instruments which make no specific provisions as to investment powers, to satisfy their paramount duty to act in the best interests of the beneficiaries of the trust. (Note 6.)

If you were wondering what 'the CREST system on the London Stock Exchange' is, the authors of *The Penguin Dictionary of Economics* (Bannock, Baxter and Davis, 1998) define it as an:

> Electronic share settlement system introduced to the UK Stock Exchange in 1996. By recording title to shares electronically it will reduce the cost of the traditional system of share certificates sent through the post. Title will be recorded through nominee companies set up by stockbrokers and others. However, shareholders may continue to hold paper certificates if they wish.

14.2 The meaning of 'investment'

Before s 3 of the Trustee Act 2000 introduced 'the general power of investment', an investment, to be valid, had to be of an authorized type and had to be an appropriate investment of that type. Now (with the exception of some minor interests in land) there are no unauthorized *types* of investment. The crucial question becomes whether the type of investment chosen was appropriate to the trust in the light of the 'standard investment criteria' (s 4(2)). We will consider these criteria below at 14.2.4 but a preliminary issue needs to be addressed at this point. It stems from the fact that s 3 authorizes any kind of 'investment'. The question is whether 'investment' is a term that is apt to describe some purchases, assets and financial products, but not others. The simple answer to that question is 'yes'. It stretches the language too far to describe such things as insurance cover, lottery tickets and personal services as 'investments'. An investment is something that is acquired in the expectation that it will produce profit in the form of direct financial returns. The acquisition of insurance cover is not intended to produce a financial return (all being well); the payment of agents, custodians, nominees and delegates of every kind is sometimes intended to produce financial returns, but only indirectly; and we would not describe the acquisition of a lottery ticket as an investment, because there is no realistic expectation of any return. These examples would suggest that it is not particularly difficult to identify forms of financial outlay which do *not* qualify as investments, but courts have sometimes found it hard to identify the boundary between investments and non-investments.

14.2.1 The historical need for income production

Before the 2000 Act, the law identified the boundary between investments and non-investments by holding that an acquisition made on behalf of a trust would only qualify as an 'investment' if it produced direct financial benefits in the form of income. As Buckley J put it in *Re Peczenik's Settlement* [1964] 1 WLR 720: 'property which is acquired merely for use and enjoyment is not an investment'. In a similar vein, Jenkins J held (in *Re Power* [1947] Ch 572) that an investment must produce income of a financial nature and that the appreciation of benefits-in-kind is not sufficient:

> there is a distinction between purchasing freehold property for the income one is going to get from it and purchasing freehold property for the sake of occupying it.

The requirement that a trust investment must be income-producing arises from the strict distinction that has traditionally been drawn between the entitlements of life beneficiaries and remainder beneficiaries under settlement trusts. It was always assumed that life beneficiaries are interested only in income and that remainder beneficiaries are interested only in capital, therefore both could be satisfied by the deposit of monies in bank accounts or by the purchase of assets such as gilts and bonds, which are income-producing but have more or less stable capital values.

14.2.2 A new approach: capital gains as investment returns

In *Cowan v Scargill* [1985] Ch 270, 287 Megarry V-C acknowledged that the return on an investment can include capital appreciation, but he was reluctant to acknowledge that an investment need not produce income. His Lordship stated that the trustees' investment power: 'must be exercised so as to yield the best return for the beneficiaries, judged in relation to the risks of the investment in question; and the prospects of the yield of income and capital appreciation, both have to be considered in judging the return from the investment'. Nicholls V-C seemed to accept that income production and capital growth can be alternative bases for assessing the success of an investment. In *Harries v Church Commissioners* [1992] 1 WLR 1241, 1246 his Lordship stated that:

> *prima facie* the purposes of the trust will be best served by the trustees seeking to obtain therefrom the maximum return, whether by way of income or capital growth, which is consistent with commercial prudence.

? QUESTION 14.1

Can it be said that 'investment' under the new 'general investment power' (Trustee Act 2000, s 3) should now be taken to include financial outlay which is expected to realise returns in the form of capital growth alone?

There is nothing expressly to that effect anywhere in Part II of the Trustee Act 2000, but the 'general investment power' in s 3 implies that 'investment' should now be given the meaning that an absolute owner would attach to the word. An absolute owner will generally be far less concerned than trust beneficiaries to ensure that an investment maintains a balance between income and capital returns. This is borne out by consideration of one of the most common forms of investments made by absolute owners: houses. A house is acquired for its day-to-day usefulness, but also because of its investment potential. For most owners the anticipated investment returns will not take the form of income, but long-term capital growth.

The explanatory notes which accompany the Act also suggest that capital growth will be just as acceptable a form of return as income production (note 22, see 14.2.3.2). However, the suggestion is made (note 23) that one factor relevant to determining the suitability of a particular investment is 'the need to produce an appropriate balance between income and capital growth'. What is appropriate will depend upon the 'needs of the trust'. Presumably, unless the trust is of the traditional sort where the beneficiaries are assumed to have competing interests in income and capital, there will be no need to balance income and capital growth at all.

14.2.3 Modern portfolio theory

According to Hoffmann J in *Nestle v National Westminster Bank plc* (1988) (reported in (1996) 10 TLI 112):

> Modern trustees acting within their investment powers are entitled to be judged by the standards of current portfolio theory which emphasises the risk level of the entire portfolio rather than the risk attaching to each investment in isolation.

Viewed in isolation any investment in shares in a private company will look prohibitively risky. Investment in any particular share will expose the fund to specific risks, such as the failure of the company in question and the collapse of the share price. The major insight offered by modern portfolio theory is that such specific risks can be reduced through diversification. Crudely, the investor is able to off-set the risk that stock in X Co will decrease, against the chance that stock in Y Co will increase. To come close to eliminating such specific risk entirely the investor would need to invest in every available equity in proportion to the size of the company, holding the shares of just a few different companies will off-set the greater part of the risk. Nevertheless, there remains the problem of the market in shares as a whole suffering loss, perhaps in the form of a 'stock market crash'. This 'systemic' or 'non-diversifiable' risk remains a real one, as evidenced by the recent collapse in the market for shares in high-technology industries.

Prior to the Trustee Act 2000 there were a number of obstacles to modern portfolio theory woven into the fabric of the English law of trusts. The Trustee Act removes them all, either directly or indirectly. The explanatory notes which accompany the Act expressly state that the 'standard investment criteria' (suitability and diversity) are intended to accord with modern portfolio theory (note 25).

14.2.3.1 Obstacle one: a restrictive range of investment options

The Trustee Act 2000 removes this obstacle by repealing the Trustee Investments Act 1961. The preamble to the 1961 Act introduced it as 'an Act to make fresh provision with respect to investment by trustees'. In 1961 its provisions were indeed 'fresh'. The general law had previously restricted trustees' investments to a limited class of ultra-secure investments such as stocks issued or guaranteed by the British government. The Act broadened the range of investments permitted under the general law considerably by permitting investment in companies listed on the London Stock Exchange. However, even such companies had to be very secure. According to Part IV of the First Schedule to the 1961 Act, they had to have a paid-up capital of £1 million and had to have declared a dividend on all shares in each of the last five years. Furthermore, trustees were only permitted to invest in fully paid-up shares in these secure public limited companies. £1 million is not as significant a restriction in the year 2001 as it was in 1961, but the other conditions would still be very restrictive had they not been repealed. They would, for instance, prohibit the purchase by trustees of shares in newly privatized utilities and demutualized building societies. What is more, according to s 2 of the Trustee Investments Act 1961 a maximum of 50 per cent of the fund could be devoted to such investments, and the other 50 per cent had to be devoted to ultra secure investments (although the greater profitability of shares tended over time, along with other factors, to reduce the proportion of the fund held in ultra-secure investments). Not until 1996 was the 50-50 rule modified to allow three-quarters of the fund to be devoted to investment in shares in quoted companies and other 'risky' investments (SI 1996 No 845). The Trustee Act 2000 has now removed such restrictions entirely.

14.2.3.2 **Obstacle two: the rule that trust investments must yield an income**

This rule unduly limits the range of possible trust investments, and reduces the possibility for investment in a balanced portfolio. (See E M David, 'Principal and Income—Obsolete Concepts', Penn Bar Association Quarterly 1972, Vol 43, p 247). We have already considered the possible impact of the 2000 Act on this rule (see 14.2.1). The explanatory notes which accompany the Act anticipate that the general power of investment will permit trustees to invest assets with a view to income *or* capital return (note 22).

14.2.3.3 **Obstacle three: the standard of care**

Prior to the Trustee Act 2000 the standard of care expected of trustees in relation to the exercise of their investment powers did not allow them to make risky or speculative investments, but the Trustee Act 2000 now authorizes trustees to invest as if they were absolute beneficial owners of the fund, and it is consistent with this that they should be permitted to select a portfolio that is prudent overall, even if it includes some individual investments of a more or less speculative nature. The modern equities (shares) market is said to be 'efficient' in the sense that new information relating to shares is immediately reflected in current share prices. This means that investors have little hope of finding undervalued shares, and consequently the only way to increase returns is to increase risk. What is needed, is to produce a portfolio in which the risks inherent in investment X are hedged against risks inherent in investment Y. In this modern investment environment trustees will still be judged by an objective standard of prudence, but prudence should be assessed in relation to the choice and management of the portfolio (which includes appropriate recourse to proper expert advice), and should not be presumed automatically to exclude 'risky investments' per se. (See, generally, Bevis Longstreth, *Modern Investment Management and the Prudent Man Rule*, OUP, 1986 and 14.2.3.)

14.2.3.4 **Obstacle four: the 'anti-netting' rule**

This is the rule that insists that trustees may not set-off gains made in one breach of trust (for example, investment in a speculative investment) against losses made in another breach of trust (see generally, 15.4.1). The Trustee Act 2000 does not abolish that rule as such, but there will be no breach of trust under the 2000 Act unless the trustee is imprudent in the choice of portfolio. Individual investments will not be judged in isolation.

14.2.4 The standard investment criteria

According to s 4(1) of the 2000 Act:

> In exercising any power of investment . . . a trustee must have regard to the standard investment criteria.

The standard investment criteria require that investments should be suitable and diversified. The suitability and diversity of the investments must be subjected to periodic review and proper advice should be taken in deciding whether or not to vary the portfolio as a result of the review.

Trustee Act 2000

Part II Investment

S.3 General power of investment

(1) Subject to the provisions of this Part, a trustee may make any kind of investment that he could make if he were absolutely entitled to the assets of the trust.

(2) In this Act the power under subsection (1) is called 'the general power of investment'.

(3) The general power of investment does not permit a trustee to make investments in land other than in loans secured on land (but see also section 8).

[subsections (4), (5) and (6) have been omitted due to limits of space]

S.4 Standard Investment Criteria

(1) In exercising any power of investment, whether arising under this Part or otherwise, a trustee must have regard to the standard investment criteria.

(2) A trustee must from time to time review the investments of the trust and consider whether, having regard to the standard investment criteria, they should be varied.

(3) The standard investment criteria, in relation to a trust, are—

(a) the suitability to the trust of investments of the same kind as any particular investment proposed to be made or retained and of that particular investment as an investment of that kind, and

(b) the need for diversification of investments of the trust, in so far as is appropriate to the circumstances of the trust.

S.5 Advice

(1) Before exercising any power of investment, whether arising under this Part or otherwise, a trustee must (unless the exception applies) obtain and consider proper advice about the way in which, having regard to the standard investment criteria, the power should be exercised.

(2) When reviewing the investments of the trust, a trustee must (unless the exception applies) obtain and consider proper advice about whether, having regard to the standard investment criteria, the investments should be varied.

(3) The exception is that a trustee need not obtain such advice if he reasonably concludes that in all the circumstances it is unnecessary or inappropriate to do so.

(4) Proper advice is the advice of a person who is reasonably believed by the trustee to be qualified to give it by his ability in and practical experience of financial and other matters relating to the proposed investment.

The provision as to periodic reviews enacts the previous wisdom of the judges: 'a trustee with a power of investment must undertake periodic reviews of the investments held by the trust': *Nestle v National Westminster Bank plc (No 2)* [1993] 1 WLR 1260, 1282G, *per* Leggatt LJ. However, in *Nestle* itself the bank escaped liability despite a deplorable failure to review the trustee investments. The Court of Appeal held that the claimant had failed to prove that the bank's omission to carry out periodic reviews had caused a loss to her (see 14.3.4). It is notoriously difficult to establish that a loss has been caused by omissions, especially in the investment context, and one imagines that the mere statutory enactment of the requirement to conduct reviews will do nothing to assist claimants to prove such loss.

14.2.4.1 Suitability and diversity of investments

The standard investment criteria, which require that investments should be suitable and diverse, are not new. Section 6(1) of the Trustee Investments Act 1961 provided that:

> In the exercise of his powers of investment a trustee will have regard—
>
> - to the need for diversification of investments of the trust, in so far as is appropriate to the circumstances of the trust
> - to the suitability to the trust of investments of the description of investment proposed and of the investment proposed as an investment of that description.

Now, according to s 4(3)(a) of the Trustee Act 2000, trustees are required, when investing the trust fund, to consider the suitability to the trust of investments of the type proposed (the trustee must ask, for example, '*in general*, are private company shares suitable for the trust?'). And they must also consider the suitability to the trust of the *particular* investment as an investment of that kind (the trustee must ask, for example, 'are these *particular* private company shares, suitable to the trust?').

Prior to the 2000 Act the suitability of a particular investment was judged in isolation, according to the strict investment standard of prudence. The standard investment criteria have not changed in any material way, but the liberalization of the duty of care should now permit trustees to invest, as a private investor would, in accordance with modern portfolio theory (see 14.2.3). It is likely that courts will from now on judge the *suitability* of particular investments in the light of the overall portfolio of investments. Having said that, factors such as the size and risk of the investment and the need to produce an appropriate balance between income and capital growth (see 12.4.1), and even 'ethical considerations' (see 14.3.1) will be relevant in judging whether the portfolio is a suitable one (these factors are suggested by note 23 of the explanatory notes accompanying the Act).

Like the old Trustee Investments Act 1961, the Trustee Act 2000, s 6(1)(a) provides that trustees should have regard to 'the need for diversification of investments of the trust, in so far as is appropriate to the circumstances of the trust' (s 4(3)(b)).

? QUESTION 14.2

What do you think is meant by the circumstances of the trust?

In *Cowan v Scargill*, Megarry V-C stated that:

> the reference to 'circumstances of the trust' plainly includes matters such as the size of the trust funds: the degree of diversification that is practicable and desirable for a large fund may plainly be impracticable or undesirable (or both) in the case of a small fund.

The requirement that investments should be diversified is based on the idea that it would be imprudent to place all the eggs in the same basket. However, in the case of small trusts it might be most prudent, as one analyst once put it, to put all the eggs in one basket and to take special care of the basket. There are transaction costs involved in building a portfolio and in smaller trusts these might off-set the risk-spreading benefits of diversification.

Another 'circumstance of the trust' which might be relevant is the presence of successive interests under the trust for example, a life interest followed by an interest in remainder. In these circumstances the trustees' duty to act fairly between the beneficiaries may necessitate a certain degree of diversification so as to include investments the capital value of which is likely to be maintained for the benefit of the remainderman.

***Nestle v National Westminster Bank Plc* (1996) 10(4) TLI 11, Chancery Division**

Hoffmann J: . . .

> The preservation of the monetary value of the capital requires no skill or luck. The trustees can discharge their duties, as they often did until 1961, by investing the whole fund in gilt-edged securities. Preservation of real values can be no more than an aspiration which some trustees may have the good fortune to achieve. Plainly they must have regard to the interests of those entitled in the future to capital and such regard will require them to take into consideration the potential effects of inflation, but a rule that real capital values must be maintained would be unfair to both income beneficiaries and trustees.
>
> . . . the trustee must act fairly in making investment decisions which may have different consequences for different classes of beneficiaries. There are two reasons why I prefer this formulation to the traditional image of holding the scales equally between tenant for life and remainderman. The first is that the image of the scales suggests a weighing of known quantities whereas investment decisions are concerned with predictions of the future. Investments will carry current expectations of their future income yield and capital appreciation and these expectations will be reflected in their current market price, but there is always a greater or lesser risk that the outcome will deviate from those expectations. A judgment on the fairness of the choices made by the trustees must have regard to these imponderables. The second reason is that the image of the scales suggests a more mechanistic process than I believe the law requires. The trustees have in my judgment a wide discretion. They are for example entitled to take into account the income needs of the tenant for life or the fact that the tenant for life was a person known to the settlor and a primary object of the trust whereas the remainderman is a remoter relative or a stranger. Of course these cannot be allowed to become the overriding considerations but the concept of fairness between classes of beneficiaries does not require them to be excluded. It would be an inhuman law which required trustees to adhere to some mechanical rule for preserving the real value of the capital when the tenant for life was the testator's widow who had fallen upon hard times and the remainderman was young and well off.

14.2.4.2 Periodic review

The Trustee Act 2000, s 4(2) provides that '[a] trustee must from time to time review the investments of the trust and consider whether, having regard to the standard investment criteria, they should be varied'.

14.2.5 The need to take proper advice

In relation to the exercise of any power of investment and the carrying out of a periodic review of investments, trustees must 'obtain and consider proper advice about whether, having regard to the standard investment criteria, the power should be exercised' or 'the investments... varied' (s 5(1) and (2)). Obviously 'obtain and consider' (which was also the wording of the old Trustee Investments Act 1961, s 6) does not mean 'follow', but trustees depart from expert advice at their peril. In *Cowan v Scargill*, Megarry V-C stated that the duty to take advice was part of a trustee's general duty of care, and this has now been put on a statutory footing by the Trustee Act 2000. Accordingly, a trustee who imprudently fails to follow proper advice risks liability for breach of trust.

Section 5(4) defines 'proper advice' as 'the advice of a person who is reasonably believed by the trustee to be qualified by his ability in and practical experience of financial and other matters relating to the proposed investment'. There is no requirement that the advice be given or confirmed in writing, but 'to do so will no doubt be regarded as best practice in many circumstances, and may be necessary for trustees to show compliance with the general duty of care in section 1' (note 28, accompanying the Act). If one of the trustees is qualified to give advice the trustees are together entitled to rely on the advice of the 'expert' trustee.

There is, however, an important exception to the duty to obtain and consider advice. According to s 5(4) 'a trustee need not obtain such advice if he reasonably concludes that in all the circumstances it is unnecessary or inappropriate to do so'. However, unless trustees have a personal expertise upon which they are confident to rely, it is hard to imagine their being prepared to risk investment without considering proper advice.

? QUESTION 14.3

Can you imagine any other case in which it would be reasonable for a trustee to conclude that it would not be appropriate to seek advice?

The explanatory notes accompanying the Act suggest that if the proposed investment is *small*, the cost of obtaining advice might be disproportionate to the benefit to be gained from doing so, in such a case it would therefore be reasonable not to seek the advice (note 26).

Arguably, the move to portfolio-based investment has made it necessary to take advice even in relation to investment in bank accounts and ultra-secure bonds and gilt-edged securities. Ultimately, the propriety of the trustees' decision whether or not to obtain and consider advice will be judged, as will be their decision whether or not to follow proper advice, according to the general standard of prudence required of trustees by s 1 of the 2000 Act.

14.2.6 Particular types of investment

There may now be very few types of investment which are prohibited by the general law, but certain types of investment still call for special consideration.

14.2.6.1 **Investment in land**

We have seen that 'the general power of investment does not permit a trustee to make investments in land other than in loans secured on land' (that is, mortgages), but a very significant exception appears in s 8 of the Trustee Act 2000. That section provides that a trustee may acquire 'freehold or leasehold land in the United Kingdom'. . . 'as an investment'. . . 'for occupation by a beneficiary' or 'for any other reason'.

Previously, investment in freehold land was not permitted unless expressly authorized by the trust instrument, but that state of affairs has now been reversed. The power to invest in legal estates is general (apart from in cases of settled land and university land), but the trust instrument can exclude or restrict that power (Trustee Act 2000, s 9).

14.2.6.2 **Investments on personal security**

In *Khoo Tek Keon v Ch'ng Joo Tuan Neoh* [1934] AC 529, Lord Russell of Killowen stated that 'loans on no security beyond the liability of the borrower to repay . . . are not investments'. Buckley J in *Re Peczenik's Settlement* also doubted investments 'merely upon personal security' although there is authority to show that a trustee will be permitted to 'invest' on personal security if the trust expressly and precisely authorizes such an investment (in *Re Laing's Settlement* [1899] 1 Ch 593 the instrument authorized investment 'upon such personal credit without security as the trustees . . . think fit'). If Lord Russell was correct, investments on personal security are not really investments at all, and they will therefore remain unauthorized despite the general investment power provided by the Trustee Act 2000. However, a better approach under the 2000 Act may be to allow this type of investment, but to presume that such investments will not satisfy the standard investment criterion of 'suitability' unless specifically authorized by the trust instrument.

14.2.6.3 **Investment in limited companies**

The bank in *Bartlett and Others v Barclays Bank Trust Co Ltd (No 1)* [1980] Ch 515 had breached its trust because it had failed adequately to supervise one of the trust investments, namely a limited company in which the trust had a 99.8 per cent shareholding. Brightman J said this about the trustees' duty to supervise investment in a limited company:

> What the prudent man of business will *not* do is to content himself with the receipt of such information on the affairs of the company as a shareholder ordinarily receives at annual general meetings. Since he has the power to do so, he will go further and see that he has sufficient information to enable him to make a responsible decision from time to time either to let matters proceed as they are proceeding, or to intervene if he is dissatisfied.

His Lordship pointed to a number of 'convenient' methods of securing 'sufficient' information. These included the appointment of a director or nominee to the board of directors who would act on behalf of the trust, or even 'receipt of the copies of the agenda and minutes of board meetings if regularly held'. His Lordship did not wish to lay down a general rule and stated that the prudent approach would vary according to the facts of each case.

14.2.6.4 **Mortgages**

According to the Trustee Act 1925, s 8 a trustee should take expert advice as to the value of land which is to be security for a loan. If a trustee, acting on that advice, advances a loan which does not exceed two-thirds of the expert's valuation, the trustee will not be liable if the land is subsequently shown to be inadequate security. According to s 8, the trustee in the preceding Question is liable for a breach of trust in making an improper investment. However, according to the Trustee Act 1925, s 9 a loan of £180,000 would be treated as a proper investment (being two-thirds of £270,000), and the trustee will be liable to make good only the £20,000 difference between the proper loan and the improper loan, plus interest.

Note that trustees do not have to abide by the value restrictions laid down in s 8, but it is prudent that they do so. They will be liable for loss arising out of their failure to abide by the valuation guidelines, as such failure will be treated as *prima facie* evidence of imprudence (*Palmer v Emerson* [1911] 1 Ch 758).

Note that ss 8 and 9 only affect loans and investments made before the coming into force of the Trustee Act 2000.

14.3 Investment policy

In general, a trustee is required to invest with a view to achieving the maximum financial return consistent with prudence. However, this requirement has been considered in a number of cases where trustees have wanted to invest in accordance with policies which do not have financial considerations as their only goal.

In *Cowan v Scargill* [1985] 1 Ch 270 one half of the management committee of the National Coal Board's pension fund trust sued the other half, which comprised Mr Arthur Scargill and four other officials of the National Union of Mineworkers (NUM). The complaint was that the NUM trustees had refused to invest the pension fund in certain overseas industries. The NUM trustees objected to the fact that the overseas industries were competitors of the British mining industry. They defended their refusal to invest as being in the beneficiaries' best interests. The beneficiaries were, of course, retired British mineworkers.

? QUESTION 14.4

Read the following extract from *Cowan and Others v Scargill*. Were the NUM trustees in breach of trust in refusing to invest in the overseas industries?

***Cowan v Scargill* [1985] 1 Ch 270, Chancery Division**

Sir Robert Megarry V-C:

> In considering what investments to make trustees must put on one side their own personal views. Trustees may have strongly held social or political views. They may be firmly opposed to any investment in South Africa or other countries, or they may object to any form of investment in companies concerned with alcohol, tobacco, armaments or many other things. In the conduct of their own affairs, of course, they are free to abstain from making any such investments. Yet under a trust, if investments of this type would be more beneficial to the beneficiaries than other

> investments, the trustees must not refrain from making the investments by reason of the views that they hold.
>
> . . . I should say that I am not asserting that the benefit of the beneficiaries which a trustee must make his paramount concern inevitably and solely means their financial benefit, even if the only object of the trust is to provide financial benefits. Thus if the only actual or potential beneficiaries of a trust are all adults with very strict views on moral and social matters, condemning all forms of alcohol, tobacco and popular entertainment, as well as armaments, I can well understand that it might not be for the 'benefit' of such beneficiaries to know that they are obtaining rather larger financial returns under the trust by reason of investments in those activities than they would have received if the trustees had invested the trust funds in other investments. The beneficiaries might well consider that it was far better to receive less than to receive more money from what they consider to be evil and tainted sources. 'Benefit' is a word with a very wide meaning . . . But I would emphasise that such cases are likely to be very rare, and in any case I think that under a trust for the provision of financial benefits the burden would rest, and rest heavy, on him who asserts that it is for the benefit of the beneficiaries as a whole to receive less by reason of the exclusion of some of the possibly more profitable forms of investment. Plainly the present case is not one of this rare type of case.

Yes they were. Sir Robert Megarry V-C also went on to held that:

> In considering what investments to make trustees must put on one side their own personal interests and views . . . [and] . . . the broad economic arguments of the defendants provide no justification for the restrictions that they wish to impose. Any possible benefits from imposing the restrictions under the scheme . . . are far too speculative and remote.

The political arguments of the NUM trustees were disallowed, and the financial benefits they hoped to secure for retired British miners (by preventing investment in overseas competitors to the British coal trade) were held to be too indirect.

A pension fund trust has as its purpose the provision of financial benefits to the pensioners, so it is not surprising that the NUM trustees were required to invest with a view to obtaining the best financial returns to the exclusion of other considerations, but what if the trust had existed to achieve other purposes? This question brings us to the next section.

14.3.1 Ethical investment

The explanatory notes which accompany the Trustee Act 2000 suggest that the appropriateness of a proposed investment is to be judged partly according to ethical considerations (note 23). This is very encouraging, but there is no such reference in the Act itself, and it may prove as difficult as ever to persuade judges that trustees should, in certain cases, be permitted to prefer ethical considerations over financial considerations in some cases.

In *Cowan v Scargill* [1985] 1 Ch 270, the Vice-Chancellor had acknowledged that 'benefit is a word with a very wide meaning, and there are circumstances in which arrangements which work to the financial disadvantage of the beneficiary may yet be for his "benefit" '. However, his Lordship emphasized that such cases would be very rare and that the onus would rest heavily upon the trustee to show that non-financial benefits were a valid investment criterion in the particular case. It is assumed, however, that ethical considerations will be permissible to determine a choice between two investments of equal financial merit. (In support of that view see Lord Nicholls of Birkenhead, 'Trustees and their broader community: where duty, morality and ethics converge' (1995) 9(3) TLI.)

EXERCISE 14.1

Look at the extract from *Cowan v Scargill* again. List some of the situations which the Vice-Chancellor acknowledged might justify investment with a view to non-financial benefits. Try to think of some examples yourself and add them to the list.

The Vice-Chancellor gives, amongst others, the examples of trusts in which all the beneficiaries have strong views against tobacco and alcohol. He acknowledges that such beneficiaries might prefer to receive smaller financial returns from investments which avoid the industries to which they strongly object. Applying this, the trustees of a cancer research trust will not be in breach of their investment duties for refusing to invest in the tobacco industry, for example.

An important limitation on the Vice-Chancellor's concession to allow investments with non-financial benefits is that the actual or potential beneficiaries must all be adults who share the same strict views. Problems arise where the beneficiaries of a trust are likely to have differing views on particular investments, some objecting to them, others approving of them. What should happen here?

In *Harries and Others v The Church Commissioners for England and Another* [1992] 1 WLR 1241 the Bishop of Oxford, Richard Harries, sought a declaration from the court requiring the Church Commissioners to invest according to Christian ethics. The Church Commissioners are trustees of a charitable trust, and the Bishop of Oxford was himself one of the trustees.

***Harries and Others v The Church Commissioners for England and Another* [1992] 1 WLR 1241**

Sir Donald Davidson V-C:

> In most cases the best interests of the charity require that the trustees' choice of investments should be made solely on the basis of well-established criteria, having taken expert advice where appropriate and having due regard to such matters as the need to diversify, the need to balance income against capital growth, and the need to balance risk against return.
>
> In a minority of cases the position will not be so straightforward. There will be some cases, I suspect comparatively rare, when the objects of the charity are such that investments of a particular type would conflict with the aims of the charity. Much-cited examples are those of cancer research companies and tobacco shares, trustees of temperance charities and brewery and distillery shares, and trustees of charities of the Society of Friends and shares in companies engaged in production of armaments. If, as would be likely in those examples, trustees were satisfied that investing in a company engaged in a particular type of business would conflict with the very objects their charity is seeking to achieve, they should not so invest... [however, it] is not easy to think of an instance where in practice the exclusion for this reason of one or more companies or

sectors from the whole range of investments open to trustees would be likely to leave them without an adequately wide range of investments from which to choose a properly diversified portfolio.

There will also be some cases, again I suspect comparatively rare, when trustees' holdings of particular investments might hamper a charity's work either by making potential recipients of aid unwilling to be helped because of the source of the charity's money, or by alienating some of those who support the charity financially. In these cases the trustees will need to balance the difficulties they would encounter, or likely financial loss they would sustain, if they were to hold the investments against the risk of financial detriment if those investments were excluded from their portfolio. The greater the risk of financial detriment, the more certain the trustees should be of countervailing disadvantages to the charity before they incur that risk. Another circumstance where trustees would be entitled, or even required, to take into account non-financial criteria would be where the trust deed so provides.

QUESTION 14.5

The Bishop failed to obtain the declaration. What do you think might have been the court's reasons for refusing it?

First, the court noted that it was not possible to say with any certainty that all the beneficiaries would agree with the Bishop's investment policy. Sir Donald Davidson V-C stated that 'different minds within the Church of England, applying the highest moral standards, will reach different conclusions' as to the merits of a particular investment. It must be acknowledged that in an institution as large and inclusive as the Church of England opinions will vary on a range of ethical issues. If the beneficiaries do not have a completely unanimous approach to a particular ethical issue, a trustee should be wary of investing along those ethical lines. The court may take the view, as they did in *Cowan v Scargill*, that the trustees were simply putting their own ethical opinions before the interests of the beneficiaries.

Second, the court in *Harries* noted that the Church Commissioners' existing investment policy already excluded investment in 13 per cent (by value) of listed UK companies, and they were concerned to note that the Bishop's proposals would have excluded a further 24 per cent of that important investment market. (See 14.3.3 in relation to diversification.)

On the particular facts of *Harries* the court rejected the argument that potential donors to the charity would be discouraged from making donations unless the Church Commissioners' current investment policy were extended. However, the court did acknowledge that where there is a real risk of financial detriment due to reduced donations this should be taken into account, and weighed against the financial benefits of retaining ethically 'unsound' investments. In a similar vein it was acknowledged that it might be possible to argue that a particular ethical investment policy should be pursued if otherwise potential donees of the charitable fund would refuse to accept donations.

? QUESTION 14.6

Do you agree with the Vice-Chancellor's conclusions in *Harries*? How might they be criticized?

Richard Nobles, in 'Charities and Ethical Investment' (1992) 56 Conv 115, forcefully makes the point that charity trustees are permitted to give away trust property to meet the charitable purposes of the trust, and so logically they should be permitted a wider discretion to invest with a view to meeting the charitable purposes.

The following Question incorporates several of the points covered in this section. Take some time to try to identify all the issues.

? QUESTION 14.7

Certain of the trustees of a charitable trust 'for the promotion of health education and compassion through vegetarianism' wish to invest in a highly profitable British public limited company, one subsidiary business of which is to export live veal calves. Two of the trustees object to such an investment. Advise them.

Your advice should take into account the following points:

(a) The burden on the objecting trustees to justify a restriction on the investment options is a heavy one. The other trustees are not proposing to invest in the veal trade *per se*, but to invest in a large British company with a subsidiary interest in the veal trade. Trustees must not exclude too large a section of top UK-listed companies. A factor which will have an important bearing on your advice is whether the trustees already pursue an ethical investment policy, and the restrictions which the current policy places on the investment market.

(b) It is not clear that the potential beneficiaries of the 'health education' would object to the export of live calves. When the potential beneficiaries cannot be presumed to be unanimous in their ethical views the trustees may be in breach of trust if they prefer a less profitable/more ethical investment over a more profitable/less ethical investment.

(c) A more pertinent consideration for charity trustees than the last one, may be whether the proposed investment would accord with the charitable purposes of the trust. How the trustees answer this question will depend upon the range of charitable purposes and the degree to which a proposed investment conflicts with those charitable purposes.

(d) This might be a case in which potential patrons of the charity will refuse to make donations if the charity invests, albeit indirectly, in the export of live veal calves. This would probably be the strongest ground on which to object to the proposed investment.

(e) A quite radical (and risky) piece of advice would simply be to encourage the trustees to prefer ethical investments (without, of course, advising them to volunteer the fact that they have done so) in the secure knowledge that it is notoriously difficult to prove that a 'less ethical' investment would in fact have been more profitable (see 14.3.4).

14.3.2 The trust instrument

It should not be forgotten that the application of the general law may be excluded or modified by the express terms of the trust instrument. Even the general investment power introduced by the Trustee Act 2000 is subject to any other provision appearing in the trust instrument (s 6(1)(b)), provided the trust instrument was not made before 3 August 1961 (s 7(2)). In the same vein, the trust instrument can authorize preference for ethical benefits over financial ones. As Sir Donald Nicholls V-C acknowledged in *Harries*, 'trustees would be entitled, or even required, to take into account non-financial criteria . . . where the trust deed so provides'. *Re Harari's ST* [1949] 1 All ER 430 confirms that clauses in trust instruments should be given their plain meaning.

? QUESTION 14.8

What if the settlor of a trust executed on the 10 April 1997 included the clause: 'My trustees' powers of investment are those currently permitted by the general law'. Are the trustees of that trust restricted to the general law as at 10 April 1997, or can they take advantage of the wider investment powers introduced by the 2000 Act?

The answer is that, according to the Trustee Act 2000, s 7(3)(a), the trustees would be able to take advantage of the new general power of investment. The explanatory note for this provision explains that it 'ensures that an intention of a settlor to provide ample powers of investment is not frustrated by this liberalisation of the general law'.

? QUESTION 14.9

What if the settlor of a trust executed on 10 April 1997 included the clause: 'My trustees are permitted to invest in nothing other than government bonds'. Are the trustees of that trust bound by that restriction, or can they take advantage of the wider investment powers introduced by the 2000 Act?

This question is taken from the explanatory notes to the 2000 Act. The answer is that a clause of this nature, because it was created after 2 August 1961, is effective to exclude the general power provided by the 2000 Act.

? QUESTION 14.10

What if the settlor of a trust executed on 10 April 1997 included the clause: 'My trustees are permitted to invest in shares quoted on the London Stock Exchange, but not in shares of X plc'. Can the trustees take advantage of the general investment power provided by the 2000 Act?

A version of this example appears in the explanatory notes to the Act. The answer is that the trustees would have the benefit of the general power of investment, but subject to the prohibition against investment in X plc (Trustee Act 2000, s 6(1)).

14.3.3 Extension of investment powers

Prior to the Trustee Act 2000, despite widespread use of express investment clauses, many trusts were still subject to restrictive powers of investment. Consequently, trustees sometimes sought the courts' approval for an extension to these powers. Such extensions were authorized by the Trustee Investments Act 1961, s 15. The approach of the courts to requests for extensions evolved dramatically during the years after the 1961 Act. In 1961 Cross J stated that 'the powers given by the Act must, I think, be taken to be *prima facie* sufficient and ought only to be extended if, on the particular facts, a special case for extending them can be made out' (*Re Kolb's WT* [1962] 1 Ch 531). (The fact that all the beneficiaries in this case were *sui juris* and could have agreed between them to confer wider powers on the trustees seems also to have influenced the judge's decision). The principle in *Re Kolb's WT* was followed in 1983 in *Mason v Farbrother* [1983] 2 All ER 1078, but in that case the trustees' application for an extension was granted. Blackett-Ord V-C noted that *Re Kolb's WT* permitted extensions if 'special circumstances' could be shown in the particular case. The 'special circumstances' were 'inflation since 1961' and also the fact that the trust was not 'a private or family trust but a pension fund with perhaps something of a public element in it'. But are these circumstances truly 'special' at all? Later in the same year Sir Robert Megarry V-C in *Trustees of the British Museum v Attorney-General* [1984] 1 All ER 337 said:

> I would hesitate to describe inflation since 1961 as amounting to 'special circumstances'; it is, unhappily, a very general circumstance. With all respect, I can see little virtue (judicial comity and humility apart) in seeking to preserve the rule [in *Re Kolb's WT*] and yet establishing universal special circumstances which will engulf the rule.

Megarry V-C held that 'the principle laid down in the line of cases started by *Re Kolb's WT*' should no longer be followed because conditions had changed greatly since 1961. In future, each application for an extension of the trustees' investment powers should be judged on its own merits, 'without being constrained by the provisions of the 1961 Act'.

In *Steel v Wellcome Custodian Trustees Ltd* [1988] 1 WLR 167, the trustees sought an extension of their powers to permit them to invest as if they were beneficial owners of the fund. They succeeded because:

(a) Investment practice had changed in the last 20 years. For example, inflation had caused a general move away from long-term investment in fixed-interest securities and into equities and property ('equities' here is the investor's term for shares).

(b) The fund was very large, suggesting a greater need for a diverse portfolio of investments and investment flexibility.

(c) The trustees would be in receipt of specialist advice from a number of professional fund managers.

Ironically, the stock market crashed shortly after this wide extension had been granted.

The Trustee Act 2000 now authorizes all trustees to invest as if they were absolute beneficial owners of the trust fund. It might be thought that there will no longer be any need to apply to court for an extension of investment powers. For the most part that is true, but it should not be forgotten that the Trustee Act 2000 still excludes certain types of investment in land, and there may be a question mark over investments on merely personal security. If trustees ever thought it desirable to make investments of that sort, they would be obliged (in the absence of express authorization in the trust instrument or the unanimous consent of the beneficiaries) to apply to court for an extension to their investment powers. Any such application would probably be brought under s 57 of the Trustee Act 1925 (s 15 of the Trustee Act 1961 having been repealed).

14.3.4 Over-cautious investment?

In *Nestle v National Westminster Bank Plc* [1993] 1 WLR 1260, far from seeking wider investment powers, the trustees were cautious to the point of 'incompetence or idleness' (*per* Staughton LJ). When the claimant (the remainder beneficiary) became absolutely entitled to the trust fund in 1986 the fund was valued at £270,000. She claimed that with proper investment it should have been worth nearly £2 million. The fund was initially (in 1922) valued at £53,963, which in real terms would be equivalent to about £1 million in 1986.

The Court of Appeal held that the claimant had to prove a loss, and although it was conceded that loss *could* include making a gain less than that which would have been made by prudent investment, Staughton LJ found that there was no proof that a prudent trustee would *in fact* have acted differently from the bank. This was despite the finding that the bank had misconstrued the terms of the trust and had mistakenly believed that it could invest only within the provisions of the Trustee Investments Act 1961. Leggatt LJ stated that:

> it does not follow from the fact that a wider power of investment was available to the bank than it realised, that it would have been exercised or that, if it had been, the exercise of it would have produced a result more beneficial . . . than was actually produced. Loss cannot be presumed, if none would necessarily have resulted.

Nestle v National Westminster Bank Plc [1993] 1 WLR 1260, Court of Appeal

Leggatt LJ:

> A breach of duty will not be actionable, and therefore will be immaterial, if it does not cause loss. In this context I would endorse the concession of Mr Nugee for the bank that 'loss' will be incurred by a trust fund when it makes a gain less than would have been made by a prudent businessman. A claimant will therefore fail who cannot prove a loss in this sense caused by breach of duty. So here in order to make a case for an inquiry, the plaintiff must show that loss was caused by breach of duty on the part of the bank. . . . it does not follow from the fact that a wider power of investment was available to the bank than it realised either that it would have been exercised or that, if it had been, the exercise of it would have produced a result more beneficial to the bank than actually was produced. Loss cannot be presumed, if none would necessarily have resulted. Until it was proved that there was a loss, no attempt could be made to assess the amount of it . . .
>
> No testator, in the light of this example, would choose this bank for the effective management of his investment. But the bank's engagement was as a trustee; and as such, it is to be judged not so much by success as by absence of proven default. The importance of preservation of a trust

> fund will always outweigh success in its advancement. Inevitably, a trustee in the bank's position wears a complacent air, because the virtue of safety will in practice put a premium on inactivity. Until the 1950s active management of the portfolio might have been seen as speculative, and even in these days such dealing would have to be notably successful before the expense would be justified. The very process of attempting to achieve a balance, or (if that be old-fashioned) fairness, as between the interests of life-tenants and those of a remainderman inevitably means that each can complain of being less well served than he or she ought to have been. But by the undemanding standard of prudence the bank is not shown to have committed any breach of trust resulting in loss.

Gerard McCormack has observed ('Liability of trustees for negligent investment decisions', *Professional Negligence* (1997) 13(2), 45) that:

> Some people might see it as remarkable that the bank incurred no liability notwithstanding the fact that they plainly misconstrued the scope of their investment powers especially since the trustee was a paid professional who supposedly owes higher duties of care.

As was suggested at 11.4.1.1, the decision in *Nestle* appears to have been an erroneous application of *Hasting-Bass*-type reasoning to a form of discretion to which that type of reasoning is inappropriate. This analysis would explain why the court felt constrained to deny the claimant's claim on the basis that the investment choices the bank had made were such that a prudent, correctly advised trustee, *might* also have made. The better approach, it is submitted, is not to ask the three questions in *Re Hastings-Bass*, but to ask the questions suggested by Brightman J in *Bartlett v Barclays Bank Trust Co Ltd* [1980] 1 All ER 139:

> (1) what was the duty of the bank . . . ? (2) was the bank in breach of duty in any and if so what respect? (3) if so, did that breach of duty cause the loss which was suffered by the trust estate? (4) if so, to what extent is the bank liable to make good that loss?

If these questions had been asked in *Nestle* it must be doubted that the bank would have escaped liability. (1) The bank in *Nestle* had a duty to acquaint itself with its investment powers, and to review the appropriateness of its investments periodically. (2) The bank was clearly in breach of that duty. (3) In *Nestle* their Lordships held that no loss had necessarily been caused. What, it might be asked, does necessarily have to do with it? The causal inquiry should be a straightforward question of fact, informed by the best available evidence (from share indices, etc) and designed to establish how the shares would probably (not necessarily) have behaved if the trustee had retained them instead of selling them because it thought it had no authority to keep them. (4) The trustee in *Nestle* should have been liable on the civil standard of proof (the balance of probabilities) to the full extent of the loss it had probably caused, subject only to the possibility of defences and relief (see **Chapter 15** and G Watt and M Stauch, 'Is there Liability for Imprudent Trustee Investment?' (1998) 62 Conv 352).

The approach taken by the court in the New Zealand case of *Re Mulligan* (deceased) [1998] 1 NZLR 481 is to be preferred. (The court distinguished *Nestle*.) In *Re Mulligan* the testator died in 1949 leaving his widow a substantial legacy and a life interest in a farm. The widow was one of the trustees of the estate. The farm was sold in 1965 and the estate invested in fixed-interest securities until the widow died in 1990. The other trustee had, between 1965 and 1990, tried to persuade the widow to invest in shares to counter inflation but she adamantly refused to do so.

That trustee (a trust corporation) was held to be in breach of trust because it had appreciated the corrosive effect of inflation on the estate capital (which was held to be reliable evidence of the standard of prudence in the industry at the time), but had nevertheless deferred to the widow's wishes.

The court in *Re Mulligan* should be commended for its (successful) attempt to identify objective contemporary *indicia* of trustee prudence against which to measure the prudence of the defendant trust corporation. However, the English courts still appear reluctant to take that course, preferring instead to relieve a trustee of liability where there is a possibility that one prudent trustee (somewhere out there) might have acted as the defendant trustee did, even in the face of evidence that the particular defendant trustee probably failed to discharge his duties prudently. The problem with the one prudent trustee approach is that it puts an almost impossible burden on the claimant to prove, as the judges put it, that 'no prudent trustee' would have acted in the way the particular defendant trustee acted.

The 'no prudent trustee' test was again considered by the Court of Appeal in the case of *Wight v Olswang (No 2)* [2001] CP Rep 54. There Mummery LJ appeared to approve the test in principle, in the context of a decision to sell or retain investments, but by concluding that the test had no application to the facts of *Wight*, his Lordship did at least invite judges to consider more limited application of the test in future.

In *Wight v Olswang*, the defendant was a solicitor in private practice who was appointed as a new trustee of a trust, the principal assets of which were about 228,000 ordinary shares in 'Aegis', a plc. The defendant solicitor had started acting on behalf of Aegis just before he accepted the trusteeship. The claims arose out of (a) the defendant's refusal to consider a bid for all the shares in May 1991 because he was at that time 'in possession of price sensitive information' and did not wish to commit an offence under ss 2 and 3 of the Companies Securities (Insider Dealing) Act 1985 (this was despite the fact that in May 1991 the shares could have been sold for 210p each and expert brokers had advised in favour of the sale); and (b) his failure to implement an agreement between the trustees to sell one-half of the shares in September 1991, when the shares could have been sold for 215p each. That agreement had been entered into because the trustees realized that 'the trust was overexposed by currently being invested solely in Aegis'. In the end, the bulk of the shares were sold between April 1992 and November 1996 at prices varying from 104p to 18p a share.

It was claimed that the defendant was in breach of a fiduciary duty and/or breach of a duty to take reasonable care when considering whether to accept appointment as a trustee, and, in particular, that he had failed to mention the risk posed by the 1985 Act of his being prevented from performing his duties and exercising his powers as a trustee. It was further claimed that he had failed adequately to consider s 7 of the 1985 Act, according to which he would have been presumed to have acted with propriety for the purpose of the 1985 Act, had he relied on the brokers' advice.

The claimants contended that if the defendant had taken the proper matters into consideration, he would have considered the offer made in May 1991, and would have accepted it. The claimants claimed that the defendant should compensate for the difference between the actual value of the trust fund and the value the trust fund would have had, if all the remaining shares had been sold on about 7 May for 210p a share and the proceeds invested. It was further claimed that the defendant had also failed to take any or any sufficient steps to implement the resolution of the trustees on 13 September to sell half the remaining shares. As a result, the value of the trust fund was less than it would have been had the decision been implemented.

At first instance the judge held that the claims failed for two reasons. First, because the claimants had to plead and prove that 'no reasonable trustee', exercising the ordinary prudence that he would exercise in managing his own affairs, could have done other than sell the shares in May 1991 and September 1991. Second, because, as a matter of causation, any breach of duty by Mr Olswang in May 1991 was 'overtaken by events' and was 'effectively abrogated by what happened in September 1991'. As the judge put it, the failure to sell in September 'was causative of the claimants' loss'. However, although the judge dismissed the claim at the summary stage on the basis that the claimants had no real prospect of success, he did not do so on the basis that the trustees would not have decided to sell in May in any event. He thought that there was a real case for arguing that the trustees would have decided to sell in May 1991 if the defendant 'had put his mind to it'.

The Court of Appeal allowed the appeal against the judge's summary dismissal. Mummery LJ disagreed with the judge's assumption that 'failing to sell the shares', 'the decision not to sell the shares' and 'the decision to retain the shares' constituted the relevant breach of trust. His Lordship observed that '[t]he retention of the shares was the consequence of the alleged breach of trust, rather than itself constituting the breach of trust'. The breach was the defendant's placing himself 'in an untenable position for a trustee' (what Lord Millett has described as a position of 'actual conflict', see 11.2) and then simply refusing to consider the bid at all:

> [T]he essence of the claim is that the trustees had in fact decided to sell the shares (presumably because it was in the interests of the beneficiaries to do so), and then failed to carry out that decision. The beneficiaries are at least entitled to an explanation as to why the decision to sell half the shares was not implemented and, in the absence of a satisfactory explanation, to invite the court to infer that there was a dereliction of duty amounting to a breach of trust. In brief, the judge mistakenly treated the claims as based on a decision by the trustees not to sell shares or a decision to retain them. That was the basis on which he applied the 'no reasonable trustee' test to the pleading and the proof of the claims against Mr Olswang. That test is not applicable to the main case which is actually pleaded, namely that Mr Olswang refused to consider a bid for the shares.

CHAPTER SUMMARY

- The Trustee Act 2000 has introduced a new general power of investment, but the exercise of this power is still subject to the trustees' usual duty of care or prudence. It is also required that trustees should have regard to the standard investment criteria and from time to time review the investments of the trust and consider whether, having regard to the standard investment criteria, they should be varied. The standard investment criteria are:
  - the suitability to the trust of investments of the same kind as any particular investment proposed to be made or retained and of that particular investment as an investment of that kind, and
  - the need for diversification of investments of the trust, in so far as is appropriate to the circumstances of the trust.
- In *Nestle v National Westminster Bank Plc* [1993] 1 WLR 1260, Leggatt LJ stated that 'the importance of preservation of a trust fund will always outweigh success in its advancement'. The bias of the law is

towards caution, or prudence. If the motto of the private investor is 'speculate to accumulate', the motto of the trustee investor is 'select to protect'.

- The prudence of the trustees' choice will from now on be judged according to whether an investment is suitable to the portfolio as a whole, in accordance with modern portfolio theory. Individual investments will not be judged in isolation.
- Whereas it may be straightforward enough to prove that the trust has suffered a loss on account of an unauthorized or imprudent *exercise* of investment powers, the *Nestle* case shows that it is an altogether more difficult task to establish that an imprudent *omission* to exercise investment powers or sell investments has caused a loss to the fund.

SUMMATIVE ASSESSMENT EXERCISE

online resource centre

Steve and Jane are trustees of a £300,000 cash fund for the benefit of their sister Joanne for her life, remainder to her sons Mark and Peter. Joanne is a widow and her only source of income is the trust.

The trust instrument, dated 1 March 1993, states that the trustees are 'subject to the default powers of investment for the time being permitted by the general law'.

Steve and Jane propose to purchase freehold premises for Joanne to live in. The freehold is valued at £50,000. They also propose to put aside £10,000 for investment in Chelsea porcelain figurines, because Jane collects these, and the remainder is to be put in a bank account.

Advise Steve and Jane as to the validity of the proposed investments.

FURTHER READING

American Law Institute, The, *Restatement of the Law of Trusts* (3rd edn): *The Prudent Investor Rule* (St Paul, Minnesota: American Law Publishers, 1992).

Dale, H P, and Gwinell, M, 'Time for Change: Charity Investment and Modern Portfolio Theory' (1995) Charity Law and Practice Review 3(2).

David, E M, 'Principal and Income—Obsolete Concepts' (1972) 43 Penn Bar Association Quarterly 247.

Docking, P, and Pittaway, I, *Social Investment by English Pension Funds: Can it Be Done?* (1990) Trust Law and Practice 25.

Ford, E, *Trustee investment and modern portfolio theory* (1996) 10(4) TLI 102.

H M Treasury, *Investment Powers of Trustees: A consultation document*, May 1996.

Law Commission, *Trustees' powers and duties* Report No 260 (1999).

Longstreth, B, *Modern Investment Management and the Prudent Man Rule* (Oxford, New York: OUP, 1986) 133.

McCormack, G, 'Liability of trustees for negligent investment decisions' (1997) 13(2) Professional Negligence 45.

Morris, D, 'Charity Investment in the UK: Some Contemporary Issues for the 1990s' [1995] 3 Web JCLI.

Lord Nicholls of Birkenhead, 'Trustees and their broader community: where duty, morality and ethics converge' (1995) 9(3) TLI 71.

Nobles, R, 'Charities and Ethical Investment' (1992) 56 Conv 115.

Watt, G, and Stauch, M, 'Is there Liability for Imprudent Trustee Investment?' (1998) 62 Conv 352.

15 Breach of trust: defences and relief

OBJECTIVES

By the end of this chapter you should be able to:

1 Advise beneficiaries as to the remedies available against trustees for breaches of trust

2 Brief trustees as to the range of possible defences to a breach of trust

3 Advise trustees as to the possibility of obtaining relief from liability for a breach of trust

15.1 Introduction

In previous chapters we have considered numerous ways in which a trustee might breach their trust. Attempt the following activity, by way of revision.

EXERCISE 15.1

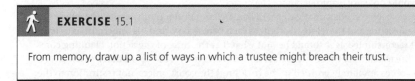

From memory, draw up a list of ways in which a trustee might breach their trust.

Your list might contain, amongst others, the following breaches of trust:

- making an unauthorized investment
- making an improper payment to a beneficiary in purported exercise of the power of advancement; self-dealing
- competing with the interests of the trust
- failing to 'get in' trust property upon appointment to the office of trustee.

The above examples are by no means exhaustive. No doubt the full list would be a very depressing read for a trustee! Not only is the range of possible breaches very broad, the consequences of certain breaches of trust can be devastating for the trustee.

This chapter considers the extent to which a trustee will be liable for a breach of trust. Even where a breach has occurred, trustees may be able to raise a defence to some or all of their liability against some or all of the beneficiaries. In addition, even if trustees are unable to raise a defence the court may relieve them of some or all of their liability.

15.2 Beneficiaries' remedies

The basic right of a beneficiary is to have the trust duly administered in accordance with the provisions of the trust instrument, if any, and the general law (*per* Lord Browne-Wilkinson in *Target Holdings Ltd v Redferns* [1996] AC 421 at 434).

Target Holdings Ltd v Redferns **[1996] AC 421; [1995] 3 All ER 785**

Lord Browne-Wilkinson:

> The equitable rules of compensation for breach of trust have been largely developed in relation to such traditional trusts, where the only way in which all the beneficiaries' rights can be protected is to restore to the trust fund what ought to be there. In such a case the basic rule is that a trustee in breach of trust must restore or pay to the trust estate either the assets which have been lost to the estate by reason of the breach or compensation for such loss. Courts of Equity did not award damages but, acting in personam, ordered the defaulting trustee to restore the trust estate . . . If specific restitution of the trust property is not possible, then the liability of the trustee is to pay sufficient compensation to the trust estate to put it back to what it would have been had the breach not been committed . . . Even if the immediate cause of the loss is the dishonesty or failure of a third party, the trustee is liable to make good that loss to the trust estate if, but for the breach, such loss would not have occurred . . . Thus the common law rules of remoteness of damage and causation do not apply. However, there does have to be some causal connection between the breach of trust and the loss to the trust estate for which compensation is recoverable, viz the fact that the loss would not have occurred but for the breach . . .
>
> Hitherto I have been considering the rights of beneficiaries under traditional trusts where the trusts are still subsisting and therefore the right of each beneficiary, and his only right, is to have the trust fund reconstituted as it should be. But what if at the time of the action claiming compensation for breach of trust those trusts have come to an end? . . . in the ordinary case where a beneficiary becomes absolutely entitled to the trust fund the court orders, not restitution to the trust estate, but the payment of compensation directly to the beneficiary. The measure of such compensation is the same, ie the difference between what the beneficiary has in fact received and the amount he would have received but for the breach of trust. . . .

Certain breaches of trust can be remedied by the acts of the trustees. So, for example, if they have failed to 'get in' trust property, they can get it in late. In such a case the court can order that the appropriate remedial action be taken. In many situations, however, the breach will not be susceptible of such straightforward rectification, examples include the situation where an unauthorized investment has been made and the investment has proved worthless, resulting in a loss to the fund, and the situation where a trustee has obtained an unauthorized personal profit by virtue of their fiduciary position. It is the trustees' liability to compensate for financial losses caused to the trust and their duty to disgorge unauthorized benefits that will be our main concern in this chapter. The first step in determining trustee liability will usually be for the beneficiary to seek the remedy of account: this is a procedure and a remedy. It involves the production of the trust's financial accounts and requires the trustee to give an account of his dealings with the trust property. (For a further analysis of the remedy of account see Robert Chambers, 'Liability', in *Breach of Trust*, Birks & Pretto (eds), Hart Publishing Ltd, Oxford, 2002, at p 1). It requires the trustee to account personally to the trust for any trust property or money which, according to the procedure, is or ought to be in the trustee's possession or under his control. An account is in essence a package of the following more basic remedies:

- compensation for loss caused to the trust
- an account of monies due to the trust
- specific restitution of property due to the trust.

In some cases an account will not be appropriate (especially where the trust is a bare trust arising in a commercial context) and the three basic remedies should be considered separately. This is not to say that a beneficiary may not seek more than one of these remedies at the same time. So, for example, if a trustee has misappropriated property belonging to the trust he will be liable to make immediate restitution to the trust fund of the specific property. If that property has been, let us say, destroyed, the trustee will be liable to compensate the trust for the loss of that property. Further, suppose that the trustee has been paid to destroy the trust property, he would be liable to account to the trust fund for the unauthorized profit he had made. Where the remedies available to the claimant are inconsistent, the claimant must at some stage elect between them, as the next section explains.

15.2.1 Election between inconsistent remedies

Where a claimant has the right to claim for both compensation and an account of profits, the claimant has to elect which remedy he wishes to pursue, so affirmed the Judicial Committee of the Privy Council in *Tang Man Sit (Decd) (Personal Representative) v Capacious Investments Ltd* [1996] 1 All ER 193). Their Lordships held that the claimant company's action for an account of profits was incompatible with its action for an award of compensation for loss. The two remedies were alternative, not cumulative.

The facts of the case were briefly that Tang, the owner of land, was party to a joint venture for the building of houses on the land. He agreed to assign some of the houses to the claimant after completion of the building works. No assignment was made. Instead, Tang let out the houses as homes for the elderly without the claimant's knowledge or approval. The presence of the tenants in the flats produced rents but it reduced the letting value of the flats, their presence therefore produced a gain and caused a loss. Accordingly, the claimant sought, on the one hand, an account of unauthorized profits and compensation for breach of trust, and, on the other hand, damages for loss of use and occupation and diminution of the value of the property due to wrongful use and occupation. Lord Nicholls held that the two sides of the claimant's claim were mutually exclusive, and that the claimant would have to elect between the two remedies, the basic rule being that election between remedies must be made before judgment is finally entered against the defendant. His Lordship cited, with approval, Lord

Wilberforce in *Johnson v Agnew* [1979] 2 WLR 487 who had held that 'Election, though the subject of much learning and refinement, is in the end a doctrine based on simple considerations of common sense and equity'.

QUESTION 15.1

Applying *your* common sense, can you see why the actions for compensation and an account are inconsistent with each other when claimed in respect of the same breach?

Lord Nicholls described this as the 'classic example' of alternative, inconsistent remedies. The reason they are incompatible, he explained, is because: 'the former is measured by the wrongdoer's gain, the latter by the injured party's loss'. You might be thinking that the wrongdoer's gain will be the same as the injured party's loss. In fact, one can think of many cases where this will not be so.

EXERCISE 15.2

Try to think of a fact situation in which you, the beneficiary of a trust, would rather bring an action against your trustee for compensation than for an account of profits.

The obvious example is where the trustee has destroyed or dissipated the trust property and any profits made from it. There is no point seeking an action for an account in such circumstances. However, there are more sophisticated examples. Suppose that I am the beneficiary of a trust in which the trust property is a rare matching pair of Chippendale chairs. If my trustee sells one of them for cash he will gain, let us say, £2,000. I, on the other hand will have lost more than £2,000 because there is added value in holding a pair of matching antiques. Each chair might be worth only £2,000 as a single piece, but a pair might be worth £5,000. Let us take another example. Suppose that I am the beneficiary of a controlling interest in a private company (the trust owns 80 per cent of the shares in the company and I am the sole beneficiary of the trust). If my trustee sells half the shares and misappropriates the profits to himself, his gain will not be as large as my loss. I have lost more than a mere 40 per cent of the shares in the company, I have also lost control of the company.

EXERCISE 15.3

Try to think of a fact situation in which you, the beneficiary of a trust, would bring an action against your trustee for an account of profits rather than an action for compensation.

It may be that the trustee has misappropriated the trust fund to his own use, but has put it to work and produced a vast profit from it. In such a case you will not be content to recover merely that which you have lost, you will want to recover that which the wrongdoer has gained. (Sometimes even innocent fiduciaries find themselves on the wrong end of such an action, see *Boardman v Phipps* at 16.4.1.2.)

We nowadays hold it to be self-evident that compensation and an account for profits are incompatible, hence the need to elect between them. However, this view was until fairly recently one upon which there was academic debate. The late Professor Stoljar argued that where the defendant makes a profit this is a profit that the claimant could have made so it is a profit made at the defendant's expense. The account for profit becomes a form of compensation for loss. (S Stoljar, 'Restitutionary Relief for Breach of Contract' (1989) 2 JCL 1.) One problem with that view is that it will not always be the case that the claimant could have made the profit. Indeed, sometimes it would have been practically impossible for the claimant to have made the profit (see, for example, *Keech v Sandford* at 16.4.1.1).

15.2.2 Comparison with common law remedies

Brightman J in *Bartlett v Barclays Bank (No 1)* [1980] Ch 515 stated that 'the obligation of a trustee who is held liable for a breach of trust is fundamentally different from the obligation of a contractual or tortious wrongdoer'.

Broadly speaking, the aim of contractual damages is to put the injured party in the position that they would have been in had the contract been properly performed, while the aim of tortious damages is to place the injured party, as near as possible, in the position that they were in before they suffered the tortious wrong. In both cases the remedies focus upon the personal circumstances of the injured party; damages are awarded because 'damage' has been suffered. As a general rule, it is incorrect to refer to an equitable award of 'damages', although Brightman J in *Bartlett v Barclays Bank Trust Co Ltd* [1980] 2 All ER 94 at 96 stated that in reality compensation for breach of trust is 'not readily distinguishable from damages except with the aid of a powerful legal microscope'. In situations where the trust fund has suffered a loss due to the breach of trust, the trustee's obligations are similar, but not identical to, those of the contractual or tortious wrongdoer. If specific restitution of the trust property is not possible, then the liability of the trustee is to pay sufficient compensation to the trust estate to put it back to what it would have been had the breach not been committed. However, in determining the proper level of the equitable award the courts prefer to risk over-compensating beneficiaries than to risk the possibility that a trustee might profit from their wrong. Rather than focusing exclusively upon the personal circumstances of the injured party, which is the focus of a common law award of damages, the focus in an award for breach of trust is to a greater extent upon the wrongdoer.

This peculiar focus of an equitable award influences the answers that a court will give to the following questions, when considering the appropriate level of the award:

- how much capital must be repaid to the trust?
- is interest payable, and if so, how much?
- must the trustee who has paid tax on the sums claimed by the beneficiaries pay the full amount or only the amount net of tax?

The following sections attempt to answer these questions.

15.2.3 Capital repayment

15.2.3.1 In an award of compensation

Compensation is an equitable monetary remedy to recover for loss caused by the defendant. It seeks to restore to the claimant that which has been lost through the breach of trust. The level of compensation should be equivalent to the claimant's actual loss, assessed at the date of the court hearing with the full benefit of hindsight. It was held in *Re Dawson* [1966] 2 NSWR 211 that equitable compensation 'is not limited to common law principles governing remoteness of damage', but at least one recent UK case suggests a growing judicial acceptance of common law reasoning (or language). In *Nationwide Building Society v Various Solicitors (No 3)* [1999] PNLR 606, Blackburne J held that the conduct of the person to whom a fiduciary duty was owed could be relevant and that there may come a point, following the breach of fiduciary duty, where the loss would be 'too remote' to be said to flow from the breach. However, his Lordship declined to reduce the solicitors' liability to take account of the lenders' contributory fault, despite New Zealand authority which supports such an approach.

Day v Mead [1987] 2 NZLR 443, New Zealand Court of Appeal

Sir Robin Cooke, President:

> Whether or not there are reported cases in which compensation for breach of a fiduciary obligation has been assessed on the footing that the plaintiff should accept some share of the responsibility, there appears to be no solid reason for denying jurisdiction to follow that obviously just course, especially now that law and equity have mingled or are interacting.

EXERCISE 15.4

Read the extract from *Target Holdings v Redferns* (15.2 above). In your own words, briefly state why the trustee was not liable to compensate the beneficiary in that case.

There was no liability to compensate the beneficiary in that case, because on a common sense reading of the facts the trustee's breach had not caused the beneficiary's loss. The beneficiary would have suffered to the same degree even if there had not been a breach.

The facts of *Target* were as follows. The defendants were a firm of solicitors acting on behalf of a mortgagor (an established client) and a mortgagee on the creation of a mortgage. The defendants held the loan monies on trust for the mortgagee but paid them over to the mortgagor before the mortgage had been completed. This was in breach of trust. The mortgagee sued the firm of solicitors. In their defence the solicitors argued that they had only committed a technical breach of trust and that the claimant had not suffered any loss because the solicitors had acquired the mortgages to which the claimants were entitled. It was held in the Court of Appeal that when the trustees (solicitors) paid away the trust monies to a stranger they came under an immediate duty to reinstate the trust fund, and that an inquiry into whether the breach of trust actually caused loss to the trust fund was unnecessary, the causal connection being obvious.

The House of Lords reversed this, holding that a common sense view of causation should be applied, with the full benefit of hindsight. Applying this test the defendants were not liable, because the claimant would have suffered the same loss without the defendant's breach of trust. (See, generally, D Capper, 'Compensation for Breach of Trusts' (1997) 61 Conv 14.)

This approach to causation was applied in *Swindle v Harrison* [1997] 4 All ER 705 where Evans LJ stated the aim of compensation to be to put the claimant in the position he would have been in now had wrong not been committed (p 714). In this case the solicitors' firm knew that one of their clients would probably fail to raise certain finance she needed in order to purchase an hotel. The solicitors took advantage of this knowledge by arranging to lend her the money from the partnership account. They made a secret profit on this loan. In the event the hotel proved to be a financial failure. When the solicitors sought to recover their loan she brought a counter-claim for compensation for the losses she had suffered through the failure of the hotel. She claimed that she would not have proceeded with the purchase if the solicitors had made full disclosure of all the information they had in relation to the hotel. Evans LJ dismissed this claim: 'Since she would have accepted the loan and completed the purchase, even if full disclosure had been made to her, she would have lost the value of the equity in her home in any event' (p 718). She had failed to prove that her loss had been caused, on any common sense view, by the solicitors' breach of fiduciary duty. This is one case in which the claimant should have elected to seek an account of profits. Note, however, that if the solicitors had known that the hotel was going to be a financial failure, and failing to disclose the facts known to them had advised and induced their client to proceed with the purchase, they would have been liable to compensate her in full, by analogy to the common law tort of deceit (*Nationwide Building Society v Various Solicitors (No 3)* [1999] PNLR 606.

? QUESTION 15.2

What was the nature of the trust, and of the breach of trust, in *Target Holdings v Redferns* [1996] AC 421? Would the decision have been different in the case of a more traditional trust, where, for example, trustees are appointed to hold a fund on trust for A for life and B in remainder?

The trust in *Target Holdings v Redferns* was a bare trust which had arisen in a commercial setting. Lord Browne-Wilkinson indicated that the level of capital repayment in a traditional trust (of the generic type 'to A for life and B in remainder') should be assessed on a different basis—at least where the life beneficiary is still alive. (When the life beneficiary dies the settlement comes to an end and the trust between trustee and remainder beneficiary should then be treated as a bare trust of the *Target Holdings* type, see, for example, *Hulbert v Avens* (2003) WTLR 387.)

With a bare trust or fiduciary relationship in a commercial context the commercial losses of the claimant can be compensated by analogy to a common law award of damages, but in a traditional trust compensation to individual beneficiaries is generally impracticable. What is needed there is compensation to the trust fund in which the beneficiaries collectively have interests. Accordingly, in determining the proper level of capital compensation in a traditional trust, courts may be prepared to risk over-compensation to particular beneficiaries in order to ensure that the trust fund as a whole is adequately compensated.

Target provides a very clear and helpful rule of causation to be applied when attempting to fix the appropriate level of an award of equitable compensation for loss. However, it is no panacea. It is a rule that only applies to bare trusts (or settlement trusts that have come to an end), and it does not answer the more basic question: *what is loss? Target* informs us that loss is to be calculated at the date of judgment, but does loss correspond to (a) the difference between the original nominal value of the investments and the gain any prudent trustee would have made (see *Nestle*), or (b) the difference between the original nominal value and the current market value if there had been no breach (see *Bartlett*)?

15.2.3.2 In an account of profits

A trustee is not permitted to profit from his trust; consequently, the rule is that a trustee must reinstate the original capital and account for all profits made on it.

15.2.3.3 In an action for specific restitution

Occasionally, the beneficiaries will wish to recover specific trust property which trustees have misappropriated. So, for example, in *Re Massingberd's Settlement* (1890) 63 LT 296, CA, the trustees had sold an authorized investment and had invested the proceeds in breach of trust, in an unauthorized investment. The beneficiaries were entitled to recover the proceeds of sale of the authorized investment but took the alternative option to recover the original investments *in specie* because their value had now increased beyond the level of the original sale proceeds.

Note, however, that in *Re Bell's Indenture* [1980] 1 WLR 1217, Vinelott J held that the decision in *Re Massingberd's* (that the date for valuing assets sold in breach of trust was the date of issue of the writ) was reached *per incuriam* and the correct date should be the date of judgment (which is, of course, in line with *Target*).

15.2.4 Interest on the judgment

By virtue of s 3(1) of the Law Reform (Miscellaneous Provisions) Act 1934 only simple interest may be awarded on common law damages. Equity, on the other hand, allows an award of compound interest where a person has improperly profited from their fiduciary position (see *Wallersteiner v Moir (No 2)* [1975] 1 QB 373). Simple interest would be charged merely on the capital 'owed' by the trustee whereas compound interest is charged not only on the capital, but also on the interest accumulated to date. It is usual to calculate the simple interest owing at the end of the first year. That figure is added to the main capital 'debt' and compound interest is thereafter charged annually on the combined fund of capital plus interest.

The object of awarding compound interest on an account of profits is to ensure that the defendant is not permitted to retain any profits he might have made on misappropriated funds. The award of compound interest is intended to prevent unjust enrichment at the expense of the trust. Compound interest should not be awarded as a punishment.

In *Westdeutsche Landesbank Girozentrale v Islington London Borough Council* [1996] 2 WLR 802 the parties had entered a 10-year interest swap agreement based on a notional sum of £25 million. (Under such an agreement one party pays a fixed rate of interest on the sum, the other party pays a variable rate of interest on the sum.) Ancillary to the agreement the bank paid £2.5 million to the council. The council paid 'interest' to the bank under the interest swap agreement. Subsequently it was established (in another case) that interest swap agreements were *ultra vires* the authority of councils. The council in the instant case therefore made no further payments under the agreement. The bank brought this action to recover the balance of the £2.5 million, plus interest. The judge at first instance awarded judgment to the bank for the principal sum plus compound interest. The Court of Appeal dismissed the council's appeal. It brought a further appeal against the award of compound interest.

It was held that in the absence of fraud (or the possibility that a fiduciary might have misapplied property so as to give rise to a personal profit) equity would not award compound interest. The recipient of monies under a contract subsequently rendered void for mistake or as being *ultra vires* did not hold those moneys on a resulting trust (see 16.2). As the council was not a trustee or other fiduciary of the monies, the proper award was of simple interest only. It has since been confirmed that the court does not have jurisdiction to award compound interest against a fiduciary on damages for deceit unless the deceit relates to the use of a fund held by the fiduciary, since the purpose of the award of compound interest is to ensure the defendant does not profit from his breach (*Black v Davies* [2004] EWHC 1464 QB). When the same case went to appeal it was indicated that the essentially contractual nature of the council's rights (in *Westdeutsche*) might have barred the award of compound interest even if the claimant had been able to establish fiduciary liability alongside liability in contract (*Black v Davies* [2005] EWCA Civ 531 Court of Appeal (Civ Div)).

We have seen that the type of interest awarded is in the discretion of the court, and the same is true of the rate of interest. Thus in *Wallersteiner v Moir (No 2)* the interest was fixed at one per cent above the minimum bank-lending rate. In *West v West* [2003] All ER (D) 17 (Jun) it was fixed (in order adequately to compensate the beneficiaries for their losses caused by a breach of trust) at one per cent over the special account rate. In *Bartlett v Barclays Bank (No 1)* [1980] Ch 515 it was fixed at the rate from time to time allowed on the court's short-term investment account.

15.2.5 Is liability net of tax?

When trustees reinstate the trust 'net of tax' this means that they have reduced their repayment to the trust by the amount of tax that the trust has been relieved from having to pay by reason of the breach of trust. The trustees may, for instance, have already paid tax on their improper profits during the time that those profits had been in their hands. This was the situation in *O'Sullivan v MAM Ltd* [1985] QB 428. In that case the fiduciary was given credit for the tax which it had already paid on the improper profits, and which it would be unable to reclaim from the Inland Revenue. Clearly there could be no question of the fiduciary profiting from this reduction in its liability to account.

The result in *Bartlett v Barclays Trust (No 2)* [1980] Ch 515 was less generous. There the defendant trustee contended that by reason of its breach the sums repayable to the claimant beneficiaries would not, or may not, have been taxable in their hands, whereas they would probably have been taxable had the breach not occurred. The defendant claimed that compensation should not exceed the amount which the claimant would have been left with after taxation. Rejecting that submission, Brightman LJ stated that 'the tax liability of individual beneficiaries . . . do not enter into the picture because they arise not at the point of restitution to the trust estate but at the point of distribution of capital or income out of the trust estate. These are different stages . . .'. The judge accepted the fact that this may place a heavier burden on fiduciary wrongdoers as compared with contractual or tortious wrongdoers.

? QUESTION 15.3

Brightman LJ was considering a traditional type of trust in that case. Do you think that he would have come to the same conclusion if he had been considering a bare trust in a commercial context?

Probably not. After *Target Holdings v Redferns* [1996] AC 421 the tax liabilities of 'individual beneficiaries' would be considered. In such a case the courts can be expected to take a common sense view of the extent of trustees' liability, taking all the facts into account, with the benefit of hindsight.

15.3 Defences

15.3.1 Limitation Act 1980

15.3.1.1 The general time limit

According to s 21(3) of the Act 'an action by a beneficiary to recover trust property or in respect of any breach of trust . . . shall not be brought after the expiration of six years from the date on which the right of action accrued'.

The right of action may accrue to different beneficiaries at different times. Consider a typical trust under which A has a life interest and B will take in remainder. A's interest is vested in possession, but B's interest is currently vested in interest only. B's interest will not vest in possession until A's death. If the trustees commit a breach of trust during the currency of A's life interest (that is, during A's life) A will have six years within which to bring an action for breach of trust. However, time does not begin to run against B until B's interest falls into possession on A's death.

? QUESTION 15.4

Lindsey, an adult beneficiary, has a life interest under a trust of which Roger is remainderman. Eleven years ago the trustees of the settlement had placed the trust fund in unauthorized investments. Lindsey died four years ago, having never got around to suing the trustees for their breach. Advise Roger who now wishes to sue.

Even though the breach of trust occurred 11 years ago, Roger has only been able to sue for the last four years. He is still able to bring an action against the trustees, as long as he does so within two years.

15.3.1.2 Disability

If the person to whom a right of action has accrued was under a disability at the date when the right accrued, they may bring their action within six years from the date that they ceased to be under the disability (Limitation Act 1980, s 28). This applies even if they cease to be under the disability by reason of their death—in which case their personal representatives may bring the action on behalf of their estate.

Infants and persons of unsound mind are treated as being under a disability for the purposes of the Act.

> **? QUESTION 15.5**
>
> Laura, an adult beneficiary, has a life interest under a trust of which Richard is remainderman. Sixteen years ago the trustees of the settlement placed the trust fund in unauthorized investments. Laura died nine years ago, never having got around to suing the trustees for their breach. Advise Richard, aged 20, who now wishes to sue.

Even though the breach of trust occurred 16 years ago, and Richard's interest vested in possession seven years ago, he has only been absolutely entitled and able to sue for the last two years—before then he had been an infant. He is therefore still able to bring an action against the trustees, as long as he does so within four years.

15.3.1.3 Concealment

If any fact relevant to the right of action against the trustee has been deliberately concealed by the defendant, the period of limitation will not begin to run until the claimant becomes aware of the concealment (Limitation Act 1980, s 32(1)). The words 'deliberately concealed' received a rather creative interpretation in *Liverpool Roman Catholic Archdiocese Trustees Inc v Goldberg* (2000) *The Times*, 18 July, where the judge held that 'concealment' need not be a deliberate concealment of a fact, but could be a deliberate breach of duty of a sort which was not likely to be discovered for some time. The words 'by the defendant' also require further consideration, as the case of *Thorne v Heard* [1895] AC 495 illustrates.

The claimant's action was time-barred in *Thorne v Heard* because, even though the claimant's cause of action had been concealed, the defendant had not been responsible for the concealment. The defendant in that case was the first mortgagee of a property. The claimants were second mortgagees of the property. The property had been sold and the solicitor employed by the first mortgagee paid off the first mortgage from the proceeds of sale of the property. The solicitor should also have accounted to the second mortgagee. Instead, he kept that part of the proceeds of sale to himself but kept paying off the second mortgage in his dual capacity as solicitor to the mortgagor. The second mortgagee had a right of action against the first mortgagee because the agent of the first mortgagee (the solicitor) had failed to hand over the proceeds of sale, but this right of action had been concealed by the solicitor's actions.

Because of the solicitor's continued repayments of the second mortgage the second mortgagee had had no reason to think that anything was amiss. By the time they realized the true state of affairs they were too late to bring an action against the first mortgagee. They could not rely upon s 32 to achieve an extension of time because their right of action had been concealed by the solicitor, and not by the defendant.

15.3.2 Situations to which the act does not apply

The Limitation Act 1980 has no application where a beneficiary brings an action for a fraudulent breach of trust, nor where the trustee still holds trust property in breach of trust. Certain crucial sections of the Act will not apply to an action brought by the Attorney-General against the trustees of a charitable trust.

15.3.2.1 Fraud

Section 21(1)(a) states that no period of limitation prescribed by the Act shall apply to an action brought by a beneficiary 'in respect of any fraud or fraudulent breach of trust to which the trustee was a party or privy'. Fraud includes 'dishonesty' for this purpose, as where a trustee dishonestly conceals the fact that he has a personal interest in a transaction carried out on behalf of the trust (*Gwembe Valley Development Company Ltd v Koshy* [2003] EWCA Civ 1478). This subsection removes the statutory six-year time limit on actions brought by beneficiaries not only against trustees, but also against third parties who were parties to the breach and certain third parties who have received trust property (see **Chapters 18** and **19**).

15.3.2.2 Still holding property

Section 21(1)(b) states that no period of limitation under the Act shall apply to actions 'to recover from the trustee trust property or the proceeds of trust property in the possession of the trustee, or previously received by the trustee and converted to his use'. In *Wassell v Leggatt* [1896] 1 Ch 554 a husband who held his wife's property as a trustee was unable to use the Limitation Act as a defence to her action due to his continuing breach of trust in failing to account to her for property that was still in his hands. As Romer J said, 'He was her trustee at first, and never ceased to be her trustee'. In a sense, therefore, a fresh duty to account arose each day and a corresponding cause of action accrued to the beneficiary on a daily basis. The Limitation Act could have no sensible application to this sort of situation, hence its express exclusion by s 21(1)(b).

Contrast *Re Howlett* [1949] 2 All ER 490 where the property was 'notional'. It did not really exist. The father (trustee) was liable to account to his son (beneficiary) for an 'occupation rent' which the father should have been paying by virtue of his occupation of freehold trust property belonging, in equity, to his son. The trustee had been occupying the premises for his own benefit, and because he could not be permitted to profit from his position he was deemed to owe rent to the trust. Accordingly, the son's action for breach of trust would not be barred by the Act because the trustees still had trust property (notional rent) in his possession.

Although s 21(1)(b) excludes the Limitation Act as a defence, s 21(2) places a limit on trustees' liability for actions brought under s 21(1)(b): a claim brought after the limitation period has expired, against a trustee who is also a beneficiary under the trust, is limited to property in *excess* of that trustee's proper share under the trust.

In *Martin v Myers* [2004] EWHC 1947 (Chancery) the issue was whether a surviving cohabitee who remained in the home she had shared with her deceased partner had become a constructive trustee for their children (who were entitled on her partner's intestacy) so as to be barred from relying on the Limitation Act 1980 to claim title to the house by long possession. It was held that the surviving cohabitee never became a constructive trustee for her children because her conscience was never affected by knowledge of any entitlement her children might have in the house.

15.3.2.3 Breaches of mere fiduciary duty/'nominal' trust

In *Paragon Finance plc v D B Thakerar & Co (a firm)* [1999] 1 All ER 400, Court of Appeal, Millett LJ referred to a case in which a defendant was 'entitled to pay receipts into his own account, mix them with his own money, use them for his own cash flow, deduct his own commission, and account for the balance to the plaintiff only at the end of the year'. His Lordship held that such a defendant will not be a constructive trustee in the event of failure to account, even if he is in a fiduciary relationship (for example, a solicitor/client) with the person to whom he must account. As his Lordship stated:

> It is fundamental to the existence of a trust that the trustee is bound to keep the trust property separate from his own and apply it exclusively for the benefit of his beneficiary. Any right on the part of the defendant to mix the money which he received with his own and use it for his own cash flow would be inconsistent with the existence of a trust. So would a liability to account annually, for a trustee is obliged to account to his beneficiary and pay over the trust property on demand. The fact that the defendant was a fiduciary was irrelevant if he had no fiduciary or trust obligations in regard to the money. If this was the position, then the defendant was a fiduciary and subject to an equitable duty to account, but he was not a constructive trustee.

Of course the significance of this decision for present purposes is that a trustee who is still holding trust property cannot claim the time-bar defence under the Limitation Act 1980, whereas a time limit of six years would apply in the case of a mere fiduciary duty to account.

His Lordship's judgment will reward close study, not least for its academically rigorous survey of the law relating to constructive trusts. In the course of that discussion his Lordship noted that where equity has traditionally held defendants 'liable to account as constructive trustee' in cases of knowing receipt or dishonest assistance (see **Chapter 19**) (even though such persons are not in fact trustees at all and there is usually no possibility of a proprietary remedy against them) such 'nominal' trustees will not fall within the Limitation Act 1980, s 21(1)(b) (*Paragon* was followed on this point in *UCB Home Loans Corporation Ltd v Carr* [2001] 1 Lloyd's Rep 754).

15.3.2.4 Charitable trusts

In *Attorney-General v Cocke* [1988] Ch 414 Harman J held that the Limitation Act could be no bar to an action for an account brought by the Attorney-General against the trustees of a charitable trust, because the only possible 'beneficiary' of a charitable trust, to whom a cause of action could accrue, would be 'the public at large'. Accordingly, as it could not sensibly be said in such a case that an action had accrued, the action could not be said to have been barred by the Limitation Act 1980.

15.3.3 Time-bars by analogy to the Act

According to *Knox v Gye* (1872) 5 App Cas 656, 674 where equity exercises a concurrent jurisdiction (giving the same or corresponding relief) as the common law, the exercise of such equitable jurisdiction will be time-barred by analogy to the time-bar under the Act in relation to the comparable common law jurisdiction. In *Coulthard v Disco Mix Club Ltd* [1999] 2 All ER 457, an equitable claim based on breaches of fiduciary duty by way of deliberate and dishonest under-accounting, arising from the same facts as a common law fraud, were held to be subject to the Limitation Act 'by analogy'.

The Limitation Act 1980, s 36(1) states that the time limits under the Act may be 'applied by the court by analogy', to bar equitable relief of a sort which would have been time-barred under the Act in comparable legal proceedings.

15.3.4 *Laches*

The doctrine of *laches* bars an action by reason of the 'staleness' of the claim. (The word *laches* has its root in the Latin *laxus*, meaning 'loose'. Even in everyday speech we might describe as 'lax' a person who acts in a tardy manner.) But this defence can be resorted to only in situations where the Act does not apply either expressly or by analogy. According to Lindley LJ in *Re Sharpe* [1892] 1 Ch 154, 'A defence based on the staleness of demand renders it necessary to consider the time which has elapsed and the balance of justice or injustice in affording or refusing relief'. The modern approach to the doctrine of laches does not entail slavish adherence to formulae derived from earlier cases. Each case is decided on its facts applying a broad approach directed to ascertaining whether, in all the circumstances it would be unconscionable for a party to be permitted to exercise his beneficial right (*Frawley v Neill* [2000] C P Rep 20, Court of Appeal; followed in *Patel v Shah* [2005] EWCA Civ 157, Court of Appeal). However, as well as seeking justice between the parties, the courts are also conscious of the public interest in seeing an end to litigation (G Watt, 'Laches Estoppel and Election' in *Breach of Trust*, Birks & Pretto (eds) Hart Publishing Ltd, Oxford, 2002, at p 353).

The following *dictum* of Lord Camden in *Smith v Clay* (1767) Ambl 645, 3 Bro CC 639 n, expounds the relationship between laches and 'time-bars by analogy' (see 15.3.3).

> A Court of Equity, which is never active in relief against conscience or public convenience, has always refused its aid to stale demands, where the party has slept upon his right and acquiesced for a great length of time . . . But, as the Court has no legislative authority, it could not properly define the time bar by a positive rule to an hour, a minute or a year; it was governed by circumstances. But so often as Parliament had limited the time of actions and remedies to a certain period in legal proceedings, the Court of Chancery adopted that rule and applied [it] to similar cases in equity. For when the legislature had fixed the time at law it would have been preposterous for equity (which by its own proper authority always maintained a limitation) to countenance laches beyond the period that law had been confined to by Parliament.

In *Burdick v Garrick* (1870) LR 5 Ch App 233, it was stated (at p 243) that: '. . . where the duty of persons is to receive property, and to hold it for another, and to keep it until it is called for, they cannot discharge themselves from that trust by appealing to the lapse of time'. It is surprising therefore, that laches *can* apply as a defence in a case of fraud. The position in equity on this matter was set out as long ago as *Bulli Coal Mining v Osborne* [1899] AC 351 at p 363: 'It has always been a principle of equity that no length of time is a bar to relief in a case of fraud, in the absence of laches on the part of the person defrauded'.

15.3.5 Beneficiary's instigation of or consent to the breach

It will be a defence to show that a beneficiary has instigated or consented to a breach of trust, but the trustee may raise this defence only to the particular beneficiary who requested or instigated the breach, and only then if the beneficiary was *sui juris* and not subject to any undue influence. The claims of other beneficiaries will not be prejudiced.

A beneficiary can only be said to have instigated or consented to a breach of trust if they have knowledge of all the facts constituting the breach of trust. However, it is not necessary for the trustee to show that the beneficiary was aware that these facts amounted to a breach of trust to raise a successful defence.

Somerset v Earl Poullett **[1894] 1 Ch D 231, Court of Appeal**

Trustees of a settlement committed an innocent breach of trust when they invested in an under-secured mortgage. One of the beneficiaries had consented in writing to investing by way of mortgage, the question therefore arose whether the trustees should for that reason be indemnified by the beneficiaries for the consequences of their breach. It was held that the trustees would be liable in full.

Lindley LJ:

> If a *cestui que trust* instigates, requests, or consents in writing to an investment not in terms authorised by the power of investment, he clearly falls within the section; and in such a case his ignorance or forgetfulness of the terms of the power would not, I think, protect him—at all events, not unless he could give some good reason why it should, e.g., that it was caused by the trustee. But if all that a *cestui que trust* does is to instigate, request, or consent in writing to an investment which is authorised by the terms of the power, the case is, I think, very different. He has a right to expect that the trustees will act with proper care in making the investment, and if they do not they cannot throw the consequences on him unless they can show that he instigated, requested, or consented in writing to their non-performance of their duty in this respect.

A beneficiary who has instigated or consented to the breach of trust may have to relieve the trustees from liability in actions taken by the other beneficiaries (see the discussion on impounding below at 15.4.5).

15.3.6 Beneficiary's acquiescence in breach

If the breach has already occurred a beneficiary might release the trustee from liability by either a formal release or by acquiescing in the breach by words or conduct. As for instigation or consent, acquiescence must be fully informed and the beneficiary must be *sui juris*. In *Holder v Holder* [1968] 1 All ER 665 a trustee bought trust property in a manner which was voidable at the instance of the beneficiary. The beneficiary did not take advantage of his right to avoid the sale but was held not to have acquiesced because they had not been aware of their right to avoid the sale.

The Court of Appeal in *Holder v Holder* approved the following *dictum* of Wilberforce J in *Re Pauling's ST* [1963] 3 All ER 1:

> The court has to consider all the circumstances in which the concurrence of the cestui que trust was given with a view to seeing whether it is fair and equitable that, having given his concurrence, he should afterwards turn around and sue the trustees: that, subject to this, it is not necessary that he should know that what he is concurring in is a breach of trust, provided that he fully understands what he is concurring in, and that it is not necessary that he should himself have directly benefited by the breach of trust.

15.4 Relief from liability

If trustees are unable to raise a defence to a breach of trust, or if the defence can only be raised against some of the beneficiaries, trustees may nevertheless be relieved from all or some of their liability.

15.4.1 Set-off

The general rule is that if a trustee makes a gain in one breach of trust he cannot set-off that gain against a loss arising out of another breach of trust. However, in the modern commercial environment, investments are often made on a 'portfolio' basis. A number of apparently separate investments may be treated as part and parcel of a single transaction.

? QUESTION 15.6

In *Bartlett v Barclays Trust (No 1)* [1980] 1 All ER 139 a property development company, which was almost wholly owned by the trust corporation (the bank), made a loss on one speculative property investment and made a gain on another. What was the result of that case? Did the result infringe the general rule against set-off of one breach against another?

The court treated both investments, the successful investment in Guildford and the failed investment in London, as part of the same wrongful course of conduct. Gains made in Guildford were set-off against the losses made in London. However, the result in the case did not infringe the general rule against set-off between breaches of trust, because both investment transactions could easily be seen as forming part of the same breach of trust, that is, the same failure to supervise the trust-owned company. It is interesting to speculate whether the set-off would have been permitted if the trustee, and not the trust-owned company, had entered into the two transactions.

15.4.2 Contribution

A trustee who is liable for a breach of trust may recover a contribution from any other person (usually another trustee) who is liable for the same damage.

Trustees are, of course, liable only for their own defaults; they will not be held vicariously liable for breaches committed by their co-trustees. The trustees will, in theory, be jointly and severally liable only for breaches to which they have together been parties. In practice however, even if only one of the trustees commits a breach of trust, the other trustees will often be liable for failing to prevent the breach. This was the situation in *Bahin v Hughes* (1886) 31 Ch D 390. In that case a trustee was unable to escape liability merely by showing that they had taken a passive role in the execution of the trust. It was held that they had been in a position to supervise the activities of their co-trustees and to prevent the breach. This liability for omissions goes beyond that which is found in the law of torts.

In *Bahin v Hughes* the trustees were held to be equally liable, despite their relative wrongdoing. However, if a breach of trust occurred after 1978, the Civil Liability (Contribution) Act 1978 applies. Under this Act the court may apportion liability between trustees who are 'jointly and severally liable' for the same breach of trust, according to whatever is 'just and equitable'. Apportionment is effected by requiring one trustee to make a financial contribution to another trustee in reduction of the latter's liability to the trust.

15.4.3 Indemnity

A trustee who is liable to the beneficiaries for a breach of trust may claim an indemnity from a co-trustee, if that co-trustee:

- is a solicitor-trustee whose controlling influence over the other trustees resulted in the breach (see 15.4.3.2) or
- committed the breach fraudulently or
- exclusively benefited from the breach.

15.4.3.1 The trustee-beneficiary

Where a trustee who has exclusively benefited from a breach of trust is also a beneficiary under the trust, he will be liable to indemnify his co-trustees up to the extent of his beneficial interest under the trust. This is because a beneficiary cannot complain of a breach to which they were a party. The judge in *Chillingworth v Chambers* [1896] 1 Ch 685 described this as the co-trustee's 'lien'.

As a general rule defaulting trustees cannot claim any beneficial entitlement in a trust estate until they have made good their default, as they are deemed to have received their share already.

This rule did not apply in *Re Towndrow* [1911] 1 Ch 662 because the trustee was entitled only to a specific legacy under the trust whereas his breach had caused a loss to the residue of the testator's estate. Because the legacy and the residue were held upon distinct trusts the trustee beneficiary was not liable to indemnify out of the legacy.

15.4.3.2 Trustees with controlling influence

In *Re Partington* (1887) 57 LT 654, a solicitor-trustee had a controlling influence over the other trustee, the testator's widow. The widow made an unauthorized investment in breach of trust. The court held that the solicitor-trustee had misled the widow into making the investment. He would therefore have to indemnify the widow against her liability to the trust. However, it will not be presumed that a solicitor has a controlling influence (*Head v Gould* (1898) 2 Ch 250).

15.4.4 Trustee Act 1925, s 61

Under this section the courts may relieve a trustee who has acted honestly and reasonably and ought fairly to be excused. As long as these three requirements are met the award of relief is in the discretion of the court, and consequently appellate courts have shown some reluctance to overturn the decisions of judges at first instance (see *Marsden v Regan* [1954] 1 WLR 423).

Before awarding relief under this section, all three requirements must be met. The honesty requirement is straightforward enough, the other two require further analysis.

15.4.4.1 'Reasonably'

Section 61 of the Trustee Act 1925 seems to introduce a tort-like test of reasonableness by the back door. An 'imprudent' trustee will be liable for a breach of trust, but the same trustee, if he has acted reasonably (and the other conditions of s 61 are satisfied) might be relieved from some or all of their liability. (See A M Kenny, 'The Reasonable Trustee' (1982) 126 SJ 631.)

There are numerous reported cases in which trustees have sought to rely upon s 61 or its statutory precursors. While they have almost invariably satisfied the honesty requirement, many of them have failed to show that they have acted reasonably. For example, relief was refused in *Re Pauling's ST* [1963] 3 All ER 1 because the trustee bank had deliberately put itself into a position where its self-interest might conflict with its duty to the trust. Clearly, the bank had not acted reasonably.

15.4.4.2 'Ought fairly to be excused'

In *Marsden v Regan* [1954] 1 WLR 423, the claimant complained that the defendant executrix had paid off all the business creditors of a trust-owned business before the business had eventually been wound up, but had not paid him. Given that the claimant had been the landlord of the premises from which the business had been run, the claimant argued that it would not be fair to relieve the defendant of her liability to account to him. It is interesting that the claimant had relied upon evidence of the defendant's treatment of others as a basis for showing that the defendant should not be relieved from her particular liability to him.

The judge at first instance decided that the defendant had acted honestly and reasonably and ought fairly to be excused. In the Court of Appeal Denning LJ doubted that the defendant ought fairly to be excused, but he felt that it would not be proper to interfere in the fully informed exercise of the judge's discretion at first instance.

In the same case Evershed MR made it clear that it will not be sufficient, by itself, for a trustee seeking relief from liability to say, 'I acted throughout on solicitor's advice'.

15.4.5 Impounding the beneficiary's interest

The court has the power to impound a beneficiary's interest under the trust in certain circumstances. That impounded interest can then be used, in whole or in part, to relieve a trustee from their liability to the other trustees.

15.4.5.1 Impounding under the court's inherent jurisdiction

Under its inherent jurisdiction the court can impound if the beneficiary:

- instigated or requested the breach with the intention of obtaining a personal benefit or
- consented to the breach and actually benefited from it.

15.4.5.2 Impounding under s 62

Under this section the court can impound if the beneficiary:

- instigated or requested the breach or
- consented in writing to the breach.

15.5 Exemption from liability

We have considered trustees' exemption clauses in some detail in the context of trustees' standard of care. We have seen the extent to which the appropriate standard might be reduced by an exemption clause excluding or limiting trustees' liability for breaches of trust. As an end-note to this chapter it is worth clarifying that a trustee will be able to raise an absolute defence to a beneficiary's claim if by the express terms of the trust the trustee has no duty to that beneficiary. Where the trust excludes a duty there can be no question of liability arising if that duty has not been executed, or if it has been executed without appropriate care.

As was stated in *Hayim v Citibank* [1987] 1 AC 730:

> It is of course unusual for a testator to relieve the trustee of his will of any responsibility or duty in respect of the trust property, but a testator may do as he pleases.

In that case, a particular clause of the will had relieved the trustee of any 'responsibility or duty' to the beneficiaries with respect to certain property owned by the trust. It appears to follow from this decision that, whereas a trustee may not disclaim a trust in part (by accepting the trust as regards some property and disclaiming the trust as regards other property (see 10.3.2)) a similar 'partial trusteeship' may be achieved by virtue of the express terms of the trust.

CHAPTER SUMMARY

- The liability of trustees for breach of trust can be extensive. They may even be liable where they have acted reasonably, although their reasonableness is one of the factors relevant to whether or not the court will relieve them from their liability.
- The basic duty of a trustee is to account for the assets entrusted to him. The trustee will be liable to make up any shortfall by compensating the fund ('accounting to the fund', may be a better description), but only where the fund is still being managed for the benefit of several beneficiaries. Where there is only one beneficiary, the trustee will be required to compensate that beneficiary directly by the payment of damages (called 'equitable compensation' to distinguish it from common law damages). The trustee might also be required to make specific restitution of particular assets (for example an heirloom) which ought to have been retained in the fund and was wrongfully misapplied.
- Beyond the basic duty to account for losses, the trustee must also account for unauthorized gains, and on top of any liability there may be additional liability to pay interest (which in the case of a breach of fiduciary duty or fraud may be compound interest).
- On the positive side for the trustee, there are a number of defences he can turn to. They include:
  - Time bar under the Limitation Act 1980 (but this does not apply to cases of fraudulent breaches of trust and cases where the trustee is still holding the trust property)
  - Time-bars by analogy to the Act (time limits under the Act may be 'applied by the court by analogy', to bar equitable relief of a sort which would have been time-barred under the Act in comparable legal proceedings)
  - *Laches*

    - Beneficiary's instigation of or consent to the breach.
- A trustee in breach might also seek to be relieved of some or all of his liability, in an appropriate case this can be achieved by any of the following methods:
    - Contribution from other (more blameworthy) trustees
    - Indemnity from a co-trustee, if that co-trustee:
        - is a solicitor-trustee whose controlling influence over the other trustees resulted in the breach (see 15.4.3.2) or
        - committed the breach fraudulently or
        - exclusively benefited
    - Impounding the interest of any beneficiary who instigated or consented to the breach.

Often, the choice is stark: either the courts visit the trustee with liability or they allow the loss to remain with the beneficiaries. Where the choice is between an honest and reasonable, but imprudent, trustee on the one hand, and wholly innocent beneficiaries on the other, the trustee will never win.

SUMMATIVE ASSESSMENT EXERCISE

online resource centre

Theresa died in 1993. In her will she settled a trust of £20,000 cash on trustees for the benefit of her nephew Bill and her niece Barbara, 'in equal shares upon their attaining the age of 21'. At the date of Theresa's death Bill was 14 and Barbara was 15. Theresa had also made a gift in her will of £10,000 to another nephew, Barry. The trustees are Tricia, Tracy and Barry. Tricia is a solicitor.

In 1996 Tricia urged Tracy and Barry to join her in investing in a private limited company which, she said, promised to be a very profitable investment. She explained to the trustees that although the investment was 'technically unauthorized' (the trust instrument prohibited investment in private companies) it was very secure. In the event the trustees went ahead with the investment in the company, having first obtained the consent of Bill and Barbara, who had been told that the investment was a 'secure one'.

Shortly after making the investment the shares rose in value and yielded large dividends to the trust, but later they fell in value and today they are practically worthless.

It is now April 2003 and Bill and Barbara have issued proceedings against the trustees.

Advise the trustees as to the possible extent of their liability to the trust and any defences which might be open to them.

FURTHER READING

Birks, P, and Pretto, A, (eds), *Breach of Trust* (Oxford: Hart Publishing, 2002).

Brunyate, J, *The Limitation of Actions in Equity* (London, 1932).

Capper, D, 'Compensation for Breach of Trusts' (1997) 61 Conv 14.

Conaglen, MD J, 'Equitable Compensation for Breach of Fiduciary Dealing Rules' (2003) 119 LQR 246.

Elliott, S, and Edelman, J, '*Target Holdings* Considered in Australia' (2003) 119 LQR 545.

Hayton, D, 'The Irreducable Core Content of Trusteeship' in A J Oakley (ed), *Trends in Contemporary Trust Law* (Oxford: Clarendon Press, 1996) 47.

Oakley, A J, 'The Liberalising Nature of Remedies for Breach of Trust' in A J Oakley (ed) *Trends in Contemporary Trusts Law* (Oxford: Clarendon Press, 1996) 217.

Paling, D R, 'The Trustee's Duty of Skill and Care' [1973] 37 Conv 48.

16 Resulting and constructive trusts

OBJECTIVES

By the end of this chapter you should be able to:

1 Distinguish resulting trusts from constructive trusts

2 Apply the law of resulting trusts to the many contexts in which they occur

3 Appreciate the essential nature of constructive trusts

4 Compare constructive trusts with fiduciary liability to account

5 Understand the range of situations in which constructive trusts are to be found

16.1 Introduction

Until this point we have been largely concerned with the creation and operation of express trusts. Such trusts are characterized by the settlor's expressed intention to create a trust, whether or not the word 'trust' is actually used. This chapter considers the creation and operation of trusts which are not based on any express intention. We will see that resulting trusts arise in accordance with the presumed intention of the settlor or donor. In relation to constructive trusts, the trust is enforced against the personal wishes of the constructive trustee. As Lord Browne-Wilkinson stated in *Westdeutsche Landesbank Girozentrale v Islington LBC* [1996] 2 WLR 802 at 828–9: 'A resulting trust is not imposed by law against the intentions of the trustee (as a constructive trust) but gives effect to his presumed intention'.

The Law of Property Act 1925, s 53(2) provides that 'the creation or operation of resulting, implied or constructive trusts' is not subject to any written formality. This is a particularly important provision in relation to the creation of trusts of land, as we shall witness in the next chapter.

In *Westdeutsche Landesbank Girozentrale v Islington LBC* [1996] 2 WLR 802 at 828–9 Lord Browne-Wilkinson described the basic features of trusts in the following terms:

(a) Equity operates on the conscience of the owner of the legal interest. In the case of a trust, the conscience of the legal owner requires him to carry out the purposes for which the property was vested in him (express or implied trust) or which the law imposes on him by reason of his unconscionable conduct (constructive trust).

(b) Since the equitable jurisdiction to enforce trusts depends upon the conscience of the holder of the legal interest being affected, he cannot be a trustee of the property if and so long as he is ignorant of the facts alleged to affect his conscience.

(c) To establish a trust there must be identifiable trust property. The only apparent exception to this rule is a constructive trust imposed upon a person who dishonestly assists in a breach of trust who may come under fiduciary duties even if he does not receive identifiable trust property (see 19.6).

(d) Once a trust is established . . . the beneficiary has, in equity, a proprietary interest in the trust property, which proprietary interest will be enforceable in equity against any subsequent holder of the property (whether the original property or substituted property into which it can be traced) other than a purchaser for value of the legal interest without notice (see 18.3.3).

Lord Browne-Wilkinson went on to say that 'These propositions are fundamental to the law of trusts and I would have thought uncontroversial'. By the end of this chapter we might not agree with that broad assertion.

16.2 Resulting trusts

If you are a ballet aficionado you will be familiar with all sorts of *sauts*, which are balletic leaps of various types. If the circus is your preferred entertainment, you will be familiar with the *somersaults* of the trapeze artist. Both words have their root in the Latin *saltus*, meaning 'a jump'. The *resulting* in 'resulting trust' has the same derivation. Resulting trusts are jumping trusts. Whereas an express trust is a form of disposition under which the beneficial interest in the trust assets *leaves* the settlor, a resulting trust describes the trust under which, in certain circumstances, the beneficial interest is said to *jump back to* the settlor.

The etymology can be highly informative. Take the simple case where A delivers an asset to a stranger, B, in circumstances where B gives nothing in return and there is no available evidence of A's intentions in making the transfer. We cannot tell to whom the asset belongs. Equity is said to 'abhor' such a vacuum in beneficial ownership and therefore presumes that the asset, although held by B, has 'jumped back' to A under a resulting trust. Until the asset is transferred back to A, B will remain legal owner by virtue of his possession, but A will be the owner of the benefit in equity. Now imagine the simple case where A delivers an asset to B, to be held on trust by B for a specific purpose. If that trust fails for some reason, perhaps because the purpose has become impossible to perform, who, in equity, will own the asset? Again, equity sees a resulting trust as the solution to the vacuum in beneficial ownership, and regards B as a trustee for A.

The current starting point for any attempt to classify resulting trusts must be the speech of Lord Browne-Wilkinson in *Westdeutsche Landesbank Girozentrale v Islington London Borough Council* [1996] 2 WLR 802. The case concerned a dispute over the type of interest (compound or simple) appropriate to a restitutionary award (see 15.2.4). His Lordship's comments on resulting trusts may strictly speaking be *obiter dicta*, and it would be simple enough to distinguish *Westdeutsche* in future cases, but his Lordship has deliberately attempted to consolidate the law in this area, and his analysis will doubtless be accorded great respect in the House of Lords and inferior courts.

EXERCISE 16.1

Consider the following extract from his Lordship's speech. He classified all resulting trusts as falling within one of two main categories. What were they?

Westdeutsche Landesbank Girozentrale v Islington LBC **[1996] 2 WLR 802, House of Lords**

Lord Browne-Wilkinson:

> Under existing law a resulting trust arises in two sets of circumstances: (A) where A makes a voluntary payment to B or pays (wholly or in part) for the purchase of property which is vested either in B alone or in the joint names of A and B, there is a presumption that A did not intend to make a gift to B: the money or property is held on trust for A (if he is the sole provider of the money) or in the case of a joint purchase by A and B in shares proportionate to their contributions. It is important to stress that this is only a presumption, which presumption is easily rebutted either by the counter-presumption of advancement or by direct evidence of A's intention to make an outright transfer: see Underhill and Hayton, Law of Trusts and Trustees, pp. 317 et seq. *Vandervell v Inland Revenue Commissioners* [1967] 2 AC 291, 312 et seq.; *In re Vandervell's Trusts (No. 2)* [1974] Ch 269, 288 et seq. (B) Where A transfers property to B on express trusts, but the trusts declared do not exhaust the whole beneficial interest: ibid. and *Quistclose Investment Ltd v Rolls Razor Ltd (In Liquidation)* [1970] AC 567. Both types of resulting trust are traditionally regarded as examples of trusts giving effect to the common intention of the parties. A resulting trust is not imposed by law against the intentions of the trustee (as is a constructive trust) but gives effect to his presumed intention. Megarry J in *In re Vandervell's Trusts (No. 2)* suggests that a resulting trust of type (B) does not depend on intention but operates automatically. I am not convinced that this is right. If the settlor has expressly, or by necessary implication, abandoned any beneficial interest in the trust property, there is in my view no resulting trust: the undisposed-of equitable interest vests in the Crown as bona vacantia: see *In re West Sussex Constabulary's Widows, Children and Benevolent (1930) Fund Trusts* [1971] Ch 1....

His Lordship held that resulting trusts arise in two sets of circumstances, which he labelled (A) and (B) and described as follows:

> (A) where A makes a voluntary payment to B or pays (wholly or in part) for the purchase of property which is vested either in B alone or in the joint names of A and B, there is a presumption that A did not intend to make a gift to B: the money or property is held on trust for A (if he is the sole provider of the money) or in the case of a joint purchase by A and B in shares proportionate to their contributions...
>
> (B) Where A transfers property on express trusts, but the trusts declared do not exhaust the whole of the beneficial interest.

We will now turn to consider each of Lord Browne-Wilkinson's categories in turn, under their orthodox denomination 'presumed resulting trusts', and will consider whether, contrary to his Lordship's view, there exists an additional category of 'automatic resulting trusts'. However, before proceeding, it is important to note that resulting trusts will only be presumed where the settlor has made no express provision to the contrary. The settlor's intentions cannot be *presumed* to be one thing, when he has *expressly* intended another. As Harman J stated in *Re Cochrane's Settlement Trusts* [1955] 1 All ER 222: 'A resulting trust is the last resort to which the law has recourse when the draftsman has made a blunder or failed to dispose of that which he has set out to dispose of...'.

16.2.1 Presumed resulting trusts on a voluntary conveyance or payment

This is Lord Browne-Wilkinson's category (A). Under this category a resulting trust is presumed to arise where property is transferred for no consideration to another person in circumstances in which the objects of the trust are uncertain (for an example see *IRC v Broadway Cottages* [1950] 1 Ch 20 at 4.5.1.1). This presumption of the resulting trust is theoretically based upon the presumed intentions of the transferor.

According to *Dyer v Dyer* (1788) 2 Cox Eq Cas 92 this category of resulting trust will apply whether the trust property is real or personal. An interesting contemporary example of the latter appears from the case of *Abrahams v Trustee in Bankruptcy of Abrahams* [1999] BPIR 637. A wife paid £1.00 each week into a National Lottery syndicate under the name of the husband, from whom she had separated. The syndicate won. The court held that the right to winnings had the character of a property right, and that this right, though in the husband's name, was presumed to be the wife's under a resulting trust because she had contributed the winning £1.00.

Some of the best examples of resulting trusts within this category are to be found in the purchase of land. Those cases will be considered in **Chapter 17**. This chapter confines itself, in the main, to resulting trusts of personalty; in relation to which one of the leading cases is *Fowkes v Pascoe* (1875) 10 Ch App 343 (which is discussed in the next section).

16.2.1.1 Rebutting the presumption of a resulting trust

The presumption of a resulting trust is not a strong one. Indeed, it 'is rebutted by evidence of *any* intention inconsistent with such a trust', *per* Lord Browne-Wilkinson in *Westdeutsche* (emphasis added). His Lordship approved the analysis put forward by William Swadling in 'A New Role for Resulting Trusts', 16 Legal Studies 110 and rejected that put forward by Professor Peter Birks in *Equity and Contemporary Legal Developments*, S Goldstein (ed), Oxford 1992. The conclusion of Mr Swadling's paper was that:

> it boils down to a debate as to the types of evidence which will rebut the presumption of resulting trust in the case of a gratuitous transfer outside any relationship of advancement (see 16.2.1.6). For Professor Birks, only one type of evidence will do, *viz*, evidence of a positive intention to give. My argument has been that the presumed intention resulting trust which arises in the case of a gratuitous transfer is a presumption of actual intent and therefore *any* evidence that the parties intended something other than a transfer on trust will suffice. Evidence of a mistaken intent to give will therefore rebut the presumption of a resulting trust...

? QUESTION 16.1

Can you think of any examples of an actual intention in the transferor that would be inconsistent with the presumption of a resulting trust?

One possibility is that the transferor might have intended to make an outright gift, another is that a loan might have been intended.

Vajpeyi v Yusaf [2003] All ER (D) 128 (Sep), (Approved judgment) is a recent case in which the claimant, who had given the defendant money to buy a house, failed in her claim to recover the house under a resulting trust. The court held that the money had been given as a loan and the defendant's obligation to the claimant was completely discharged by repayment of the loan.

In *Fowkes v Pascoe* (1875) 10 Ch App 343, Mrs B purchased certain stock in the joint names of herself and P, the son of her daughter-in-law. On the same day she purchased more of the same stock in the joint names of herself and a lady companion. Mrs B's will left the residue of her estate to the daughter-in-law for life, thereafter for P and his sister equally. The Court of Appeal held that the presumption of a resulting trust had been rebutted by evidence that a gift had been intended. Mellish LJ could think of no other reason why Mrs B, who already owned £5,000 worth of the stock in her own name, should invest £250 in the joint names of herself and P on the same day as investing £250 in the joint names of herself and her companion. The facts were not consistent with an intention to subject the stock to a trust. Contrast the outcome in that case with the outcome in *Re Vinogradoff* [1935] WN 68. There Mrs V placed £800 worth of stock into the joint names of herself and her granddaughter. On the question whether the property belonged to the granddaughter after Mrs V's death, it was held that it did not. The presumption of resulting trust applied and so the stock belonged to Mrs V's estate.

? QUESTION 16.2

The most common situation in which property is transferred is where it is transferred under a contractual obligation. Having bought your morning paper you cannot return in the evening to reclaim the purchase monies under a resulting trust. It is not that the presumption of a resulting trust is rebutted, rather that it does not even arise in the first place. Why does not it arise?

The answer is that the presumption of a resulting trust within Lord Browne-Wilkinson's category (A) will only arise in the case of a voluntary transfer, that is, a transfer made for no consideration. A legal contract is, by definition, made for consideration.

16.2.1.2 Illegality and the presumption of a resulting trust

Where a claim to an interest under a resulting trust is based on an illegal transaction the resulting trust will not be allowed. It is sometimes said that this is because illegality rebuts the presumption of a resulting trust. In fact, it has got nothing to do with the settlor's presumed intentions. Rather, it is a case of public policy preventing the assertion of a right obtained by illegal means.

Note, however, that even where there has been illegality, a right under a resulting trust may be asserted if no reliance is placed upon the illegality. (This is the so-called 'reliance principle'.) In *Tinsley v Milligan* [1993] 3 All ER 65, Milligan deliberately left her name off the legal title to land owned by her partner, Tinsley, so as not to prejudice her claim to social security (in itself an illegal concealment of ownership). She was nevertheless able to claim an interest in the land under a resulting trust. Her interest under the trust arose according to a legal presumption and so she did not need to rely upon the illegal transaction in order to assert her claim. Arguably this case allowed Milligan to have her cake and eat it, in that she was able to conceal her legal ownership for social security purposes, but to assert it as against her partner for purposes of private property. Nevertheless justice would not have been served by denying her claim, as this would have merely led to the unjust enrichment of Tinsley at Milligan's expense. *Tinsley v Milligan* has been followed in a number of recent cases, for example *Lowson v Coombes* [1999] 3 WLR 720. In that case a married man bought a house with his mistress but conveyed it into her sole name to illegally prevent his wife from claiming his share under matrimonial proceedings. He was entitled to a declaration that the mistress held his half share on resulting trust for him. In seeking the declaration he did not need to place reliance upon the illegality of the conveyance to the mistress.

Similarly, in *Tribe v Tribe* [1995] 4 All ER 236 (CA), a father transferred to his son shares in a company controlled by the father at a time when the company's creditors were pressing for satisfaction of their debts. The transfer had been effected for a nominal consideration, which meant that if it had been relied upon in the event of the father's bankruptcy, it would have been illegal as an attempt to defraud the father's creditors (see 6.8.1). Nevertheless, after the creditors had settled their claim, the father was able to reclaim the shares from his son under a presumed resulting trust. The resulting trust did not fail for illegality because it had risen from a legal presumption and the father had not needed to rely upon the illegality in order to assert his claim. This approach should be contrasted with the approach in *Collier v Collier* [2002] BPIR 1057, where a father failed in his attempt to recover a freehold from his daughter. To defraud his creditors the father had granted his daughter a lease with an option to purchase the freehold. She exercised that option and sought to take possession of the freehold from her father. The judge held that although the daughter knew that she had not received the property by way of gift, but on trust, the trust was unenforceable because it had been established for an illegal purpose.

The Law Commission has recommended that the rather mechanical 'reliance principle' should be abandoned and replaced with a judicial discretion to decide when illegality should rebut the application of general trust principles. This discretion would be structured to take into account the seriousness of the illegality, the knowledge and intention of the party claiming relief, whether denying the claim would deter illegality and promote public policy concerns and whether denying the claim would be proportionate to the illegality involved. (*Illegal Transactions: The Effect of Illegality on Contracts and Trusts*, Law Commission Consultation Paper No 154 1999). This recommendation has not yet become law, and is unlikely to become law in the near future. The Law Commission's website notes that a 'strong minority' of respondents felt that the proposed structured discretion 'would introduce even greater uncertainties into the law'. The Law Commission is now looking at methods by which the law could be improved without statutory intervention.

16.2.1.3 The presumption of advancement

Where a voluntary conveyance is made to the wife, fiancée or child of the transferor, or where the transferor is *in loco parentis* ('in the position of parent') to the transferee, there is a presumption that the transferor has made a gift for the advancement of the transferee. This presumption rebuts the presumption of a resulting trust. However, the presumption of advancement can itself be rebutted if there is evidence that the transferor did not in fact intend to make a gift to the volunteer transferee, provided that the evidence is of a type that the court may take into account.

In *Gascoigne v Gascoigne* [1918] 1 KB 223, Mr G purchased a leasehold in the name of his wife, with a view to protecting the lease from his creditors. Mrs G claimed the property to be her own, on the basis of the presumption of advancement. Mr G brought the present action against her to recover the property. It was held that Mr G could not rely upon evidence of his own fraud to rebut the presumption of advancement. The maxim *ex turpi causa non oritur actio* ('no action may be founded upon a wrong') was applied.

Nowadays the presumption of advancement is relatively easy to rebut. The decision of the Court of Appeal in *McGrath v Wallis* [1995] 2 FLR 114 is a good illustration of this. The facts were, briefly, that a father bought a house subject to a mortgage, but placed both the house and the mortgage in the name of the son. Nourse LJ held that the presumption of advancement had been rebutted by evidence (that the son was unemployed and could not have bought a house in his own name) which showed that the father had not intended to make an outright gift to the son, but to make provision only until the son could afford to purchase a house in his own right. See, also, *Sekhon v Alissa* [1989] 2 FLR 94. However, in *Collier v Collier* [2002] BPIR 1057, a father failed in his attempt to recover a freehold from his daughter. To defraud his creditors the father had granted his daughter a lease with an option to purchase the freehold. She exercised that option and sought to take possession of the freehold from her father. The judge held that although the daughter knew that she had not received the property by way of gift, but on trust, the trust was unenforceable because it had been established for an illegal purpose. See also *Lavelle v Lavelle* [2004] EWCA Civ 223, Court of Appeal, where the presumption of advancement from father to daughter was rebutted by evidence that the transfer of land into the daughter's name had been made with the intention of avoiding inheritance tax. (*Lavelle* was followed in *Kyriakides v Pippas* [2004] EWHC 646.)

16.2.2 Presumed resulting trusts where express trusts do not exhaust the whole of the beneficial interest

16.2.2.1 General

The simplest example is where A settles property 'on trust for B for life', but makes no provision as to what should be the destination of the capital fund on the death of B. Equity abhors a vacuum in beneficial ownership, so insists that somebody must be entitled to the fund at all times. Accordingly, equity presumes that a resulting trust had been intended, and that the capital jumps back (results) to A (or A's estate if A has died) upon the death of B.

Examples of this category of trust can be found in less traditional contexts. Indeed, Lord Browne-Wilkinson places the *Quistclose* trust (see 2.3.4.2) in this category.

16.2.2.2 Automatic resulting trusts

Suppose that A intends to give away all his beneficial interest in a piece of property and thinks he has done so, but by some mistake or accident or failure to comply with the requirements of the law, he has failed to do so. There is a debate as to whether a resulting trust arises in such a case.

Consider the detail of the cases in the *Vandervell* saga, as set out in the following sections.

***Vandervell v Inland Revenue Commissioners* [1967] 2 AC 291**

In 1958, Vandervell (V), the controlling director and shareholder of VP Ltd, decided to give 100,000 shares in VP Ltd to the Royal College of Surgeons (RCS) to found a chair in pharmacology. The shares were currently held by V's bank under a bare trust for V. Accordingly, V directed the bank to transfer 100,000 shares to the RCS. It was intended that the RCS should keep the shares for a limited period only, and should relinquish them after receiving £150,000 income on the shares by way of dividends. To ensure that the Royal College did not keep the shares forever, the College, upon receipt of the shares, executed an option in favour of a trustee company set up by V. The terms of the option provided that the College must transfer the shares to the trustee company upon the future receipt of a payment of £5,000 from the trustee company. By 1961 the College had received over £150,000 in dividends from the shares and so the trustee company exercised the option to repurchase the shares for £5,000. The present action was brought by the Inland Revenue Commissioners to recover tax from V which had been assessed on the dividends for the period between 1958 and 1961. The question therefore arose whether V had owned the shares during the period in which the dividends were declared. The Revenue argued that V, in directing the bank to transfer the shares to the College, had purported to dispose of his equitable interest in the shares but had failed to do so because the disposition had not been made in writing (LPA 1925, s 53(1)(c)).

The House of Lords held that s 53(1)(c) did not apply to these facts. However, the decision in the present case ultimately went in favour of the Revenue for other reasons. Three out of the five Lords of Appeal in Ordinary held that the option had been held by the trustee company upon unspecified trusts. In accordance with the maxim *equity abhors a vacuum in beneficial ownership*, the option could not be permitted merely to remain 'in the air'. Their Lordships held that the benefit of the option must have been held by the trustee company under a resulting trust for V. In failing to specify trusts of the option, V had failed to divest himself of his equitable interest in the option. It followed that he had also failed fully to divest himself of his equitable interest in the shares which were the subject of the option. As a result, V was liable to pay tax on the dividends declared on the shares.

***Re Vandervell's Trusts (No 2)* [1974] 1 All ER 47**

As a result of the Inland Revenue's claim against him personally, V executed a deed in 1965 under which he transferred to his trustee company all or any right, title or interest which he might have in the option (see *Vandervell v IRC*), to be held by it on trust for V's children according to the terms of an existing settlement. V died in 1967. His executors brought the present action against the trustee company, claiming that V had owned the shares for the period between 1961 and 1965. The Inland Revenue was joined to the action and sought to recover tax from V's estate for the period between 1961 (when the option was exercised) and 1965 (when V executed the deed divesting himself entirely of his equitable interest). The trustee company claimed that the shares should be treated as belonging to the children's settlement.

Megarry J identified two main issues in this stage of the *Vandervell* saga. First, to determine whether the defendant trustee company had taken the option beneficially or on trust. Second, what those trusts were. Having decided that the trustee company held the option on trust, his Lordship then asked: 'was the option held on a resulting trust or other trust for Mr Vandervell, or was it held on the trusts of the children's settlement?'

Megarry J concluded that a resulting trust in favour of Mr Vandervell had arisen automatically:

> I cannot see how an intention not to get the shares back can negative a resulting trust if in the event he made no effective disposition of his beneficial interest in them and the operation of equity brought them back to him in ways never considered by him. Whatever may be the position under a presumed resulting trust, I do not see how the donor's intention not to have the beneficial interest can prevail where the resulting trust is automatic.

Re Vandervell's Trusts (No 2) [1974] 3 All ER 205 (Court of Appeal)

It was held, on appeal from Megarry J, that as a result of the exercise of the option by the trustee company in 1961, the trustee company thereafter held the shares on the trusts of the children's settlement. This was because it had been the intention of V and the trustee company that the shares should be thereafter held for the benefit of the children's settlement, and the £5,000 used to exercise the option had actually been taken from the fund of the children's settlement. It followed that, after the exercise of the option, the shares did not form part of V's estate and his estate could not be taxed for the period 1961 to 1965. Lord Denning MR stated that when the option was exercised the 'gap in the beneficial ownership' came to an end. The resulting trust under which the shares had previously been held for the benefit of V ceased to exist upon the exercise of the option and the registration of the shares in the name of the trustee company. Applying *Milroy v Lord* (see 5.4.1), V and the trustee company had, after the exercise of the option, 'done everything which needed to be done to make the settlement of these shares binding upon them'.

Lord Denning MR stated, further, that even if V had retained an equitable interest in the shares after the exercise of the option he would have been estopped from asserting his entitlement to those shares as against his children. He could not claim to own the shares after having done everything possible to give them away to the trustees of the children's settlement.

? QUESTION 16.3

Can you see any inconsistency between the judgment of Lord Denning MR and the speeches of their Lordships in *Vandervell v IRC*?

There are arguably several points of inconsistency. For example, Lord Denning MR held that in 1961 V intended, and did indeed divest himself, of his equitable interest in the shares, despite the fact that V apparently did not realize until much later that he might have any equitable interest in the shares. (He waited until 1965 to disclaim his beneficial interest in them.)

The most significant of the *Vandervell* cases as regards 'automatic' resulting trusts is *Re Vandervell (No 2)* [1974] 3 All ER 205. In that case, as you will recall, Megarry J held that 'the option was granted to the defendant company on trust, but that no effective trusts were ever established and so the defendant company held the option on a resulting trust for Mr. Vandervell'. As to the type of resulting trust, Megarry J concluded that the resulting trust was automatic, rather than presumed: 'Whatever may be the position under a presumed resulting trust, I do not see how the donor's intention not to have the beneficial interest can prevail where the resulting trust is automatic'. His Lordship was of the view that 'there are branches of the law of resulting trusts where the proof of an intention carries one a very little distance'.

Megarry J's view can claim some support from Lord Upjohn in *Vandervell v IRC* [1967] 1 All ER 1, who held that:

> If A intends to give away all his beneficial interest in a piece of property and thinks he has done so but by some mistake or accident or failure to comply with the requirements of the law, he has failed to do so, either wholly or partially, there will, by operation of law, be a resulting trust for him of the beneficial interest of which he had failed effectually to dispose.

However, in *Westdeutsche* Lord Browne-Wilkinson observed that:

> Megarry J in *In re Vandervell's Trusts (No. 2)* suggests that a resulting trust of type (B) does not depend on intention but operates automatically. I am not convinced that this is right. If the settlor has expressly, or by necessary implication, abandoned any beneficial interest in the trust property, there is in my view no resulting trust.

? QUESTION 16.4

What was Lord Browne-Wilkinson's preferred solution to any case where the donor had clearly intended to part outright with property and that intention had failed in some unforeseen way? (See the extract appearing earlier in this chapter.)

His Lordship held that the undisposed-of equitable interest in such a case vests in the Crown as *bona vacantia* (ownerless property). In support of this view he cited *In re West Sussex Constabulary's Widows, Children and Benevolent (1930) Fund Trusts* [1971] Ch 1 (see 7.7.3). This analysis has a greater conceptual appeal than Megarry J's distinction between automatic and resulting trusts, but is surely apt to create injustice in some cases. Why, it might be asked, should the Crown receive a windfall, where, for instance, the vacuum in beneficial ownership arose because of the settlor's reasonable mistake in his understanding of the legal effect of a particular disposition?

? QUESTION 16.5

Do you see any possible conflict between Lord Browne-Wilkinson's statement: 'If the settlor has expressly, or by necessary implication, abandoned any beneficial interest in the trust property, there is in my view no resulting trust' and his 'uncontroversial' fundamental propositions of trust law? (For which, see 16.1 above.)

One of Lord Browne-Wilkinson's fundamental propositions was that '[i]n the case of a trust, the conscience of the legal owner requires him to carry out the purposes for which the property was vested in him'. Here 'the legal owner' must be a reference to the trustee, rather than the settlor, for the trustee is the one who has had property 'vested in him'. This suggests, in apparent contradiction to Lord Browne-Wilkinson's analysis of *Vandervell*, that where a resulting trust arises (whether because of failure of the trust or a surplus of funds) it is the trustee's state of mind (and not that of the settlor) that is relevant to determination of the ultimate destination of the funds. Yet, to add further confusion, Lord Browne-Wilkinson, immediately after outlining his two categories of resulting trust, suggested that '[b]oth types of resulting trust are traditionally regarded as examples of trusts giving effect to the *common* intention of the parties' (emphasis added).

It is submitted that the correct analysis is that the trustee's conscience will be affected by his knowledge of the purposes for which the settlor vested the property in him, and that this is the only extent to which the settlor's intentions are relevant once the trust has been established. It follows that, only if the trustee knew that the settlor wished to part with the property outright will the trustee be justified in surrendering the property to the Crown as *bona vacantia*. In other cases one can see the force in Megarry J's opinion that the funds should be returned to the settlor.

An example is *Re Gillingham Bus Disaster* [1958] 1 All ER 37. The facts of *Re Gillingham Bus Disaster* were tragic. A bus careered into a column of Royal Marine cadets, who were marching along a road in Gillingham, Kent. Twenty-four were killed and others were injured. A memorial fund was set up for the purpose of meeting funeral expenses, caring for the disabled, and for other worthy causes. It was held that the surplus should be held on resulting trust for the donors. Harman J held that:

> This doctrine does not rest... on any evidence of the state of mind of the settlor, for in the vast majority of cases no doubt he does not expect to see his money back; he has created a trust which, as far as he can see, will absorb the whole of it. The resulting trust arises where that expectation is, for some unforeseen reason, cheated of fruition, and is an inference of law based on after-knowledge of the event.

The problem with Megarry J's distinction between presumed and automatic trusts is that it is hard to justify analytically, and even harder to apply in practice. To say that the resulting trust arises automatically is to make an assertion without any conceptual foundation, it explains merely that such a trust does not arise according to the settlor's presumed intention, it does *not* explain, for example, why, when a settlor clearly intended to make an outright disposition of his property, the surplus does not pass 'automatically' to the Crown as *bona vacantia*. On the other hand, the problem with Lord Browne-Wilkinson's analysis is that it provides no solution to a case like *Vandervell v IRC*, where Vandervell clearly did not intend to retain the benefit of the shares, but even more clearly did not intend that they should pass to the Crown as *bona vacantia*.

A new approach is needed to the destination of surpluses when express trusts fail or are fulfilled early. Lord Browne-Wilkinson's taxonomy is conceptually rigorous, but has the potential to produce an unjust windfall for the Crown. Megarry J's analysis tends to produce practical justice in most cases, but can operate in the face of a sensible view of the parties' intentions, and has no real conceptual underpinning.

One alternative would be to remove Megarry J's automatic trust from the category of resulting trust, and to regard it as *sui juris*. This would have the merit of removing the conflict with

Lord Browne-Wilkinson's taxonomy. However, it would not solve the more fundamental question: 'on what conceptual basis can one justify the recognition of such a trust?' Perhaps, like Harman J (*Re Gillingham*, above) we will be forced to recognize that the court's response is pragmatic, not dogmatic.

The controversy received fresh impetus in the recent Privy Council case of *Air Jamaica v Charlton* (see 2.3.3). There Lord Millett held that:

> Like a constructive trust, a resulting trust arises by operation of law, though unlike a constructive trust it gives effect to intention. But it arises whether or not the transferor intended to retain a beneficial interest—he almost always does not—since it responds to the absence of any intention on his part to pass a beneficial interest to the recipient. It may arise even when the transferor positively wished to part with the beneficial interest.

Charles Harpum, commenting on the *Air Jamaica* case has suggested that Lord Millett's analysis might herald a swing of the pendulum back in favour of Megarry J's 'automatic resulting trust' (Harpum (2000) Conv 170). If Lord Millett's analysis is correct, says Harpum, it is doubtful that a resulting trust arising where *express* trusts do not exhaust the whole of the beneficial interest can ever be rebutted. That which cannot be rebutted should not be described as 'presumed', hence Megarry's preference for describing such trusts as 'automatic'.

Of course the best (perhaps the only satisfactory) remedy to the problem of automatic resulting trusts lies in prevention rather than cure. An appropriately worded trust ought to leave no doubt as to the settlor's intentions in the event of failure of his primary intention. A clearly worded trust would prevent a vacancy from arising in the beneficial ownership of the fund or any part of it, and pre-empt the fund from passing *bona vacantia* to the Crown. Such a prophylactic approach would have assisted in all the reported category (B) cases, for example, *Quistclose* (see 2.3.4.2). But in many cases, practically speaking, it is simply never going to happen (see, for example, the collection box donations in *Re Gillingham*).

16.3 Constructive trusts

You will recall that Lord Browne-Wilkinson in *Westdeutsche* characterized constructive trusts as trusts imposed against the legal owner of the trust assets on account of the legal owner's unconscionability. We will take this to be the hallmark of true constructive trusts, but it must be admitted that in some of the situations said to give rise to a 'constructive trust', the trust appears to have been at the very least intended by the settlor and willingly accepted by the trustee (see for example, secret trusts, 3.3.3).

The judgment of Millett LJ in *Paragon Finance plc v D B Thakerar & Co (a firm)* [1999] 1 All ER 400 takes this into account. Having stated that a constructive trust arises by operation of law whenever the circumstances are such that it would be unconscionable for the owner of property (usually but not necessarily the legal estate) to assert his own beneficial interest in the property and deny the beneficial interest of another, his Lordship proceeded to identify two classes of constructive trust:

> In the first class of case . . . the constructive trustee really is a trustee. He does not receive the trust property in his own right but by a transaction by which both parties intend to create a trust from the

> outset and which is not impugned by the plaintiff. His possession of the property is coloured from the first by the trust and confidence by means of which he obtained it, and his subsequent appropriation of the property to his own use is a breach of that trust... The second class of case is different. It arises when the defendant is implicated in a fraud. Equity has always given relief against fraud by making any person sufficiently implicated in the fraud accountable in equity. In such a case he is traditionally though I think unfortunately described as a constructive trustee and said to be 'liable to account as constructive trustee'. Such a person is not in fact a trustee at all, even though he may be liable to account as if he were. He never assumes the position of a trustee, and if he receives the trust property at all it is adversely to the plaintiff by an unlawful transaction which is impugned by the plaintiff. In such a case the expressions 'constructive trust' and 'constructive trustee' are misleading, for there is no trust and usually no possibility of a proprietary remedy; they are 'nothing more than a formula for equitable relief': *Selangor United Rubber Estates Ltd v Cradock (No 3)* [1968] 2 All ER 1073 (see **Chapter 19**).

Millett LJ's analysis is a welcome diversion from the ongoing judicial and academic inquiry into whether beneficial interests under constructive trusts are *created* by the courts (remedially) or merely *recognized* by the courts (as equitable rights arising institutionally—that is, predictably—from particular fact situations). The conflict between the 'remedial' and 'institutional' approach to constructive trusts is considered next.

16.3.1 Constructive trust: property-based or free-standing remedy?

> The court does not give relief because a constructive trust has been created; but the court gives relief because otherwise the defendant would be unjustly enriched; and because the court gives this relief it declares that the defendant is chargeable as a constructive trustee.
>
> Professor A W Scott in (1955) 71 LQR 39 at 41.

16.3.1.1 The English approach

In the preceding quote, Professor Scott was describing the situation in the USA. English law does not as yet recognize a remedial constructive trust on the basis of unjust enrichment. There have, however, been indications that the courts may be moving in that direction. Lord Browne-Wilkinson in *Westdeutsche* (see 16.3) stated that:

> The court may by way of remedy impose a constructive trust on a defendant who knowingly retains the property of which the plaintiff has been unjustly deprived. Since the remedy can be tailored to the circumstances of the particular case, innocent third parties would not be prejudiced and restitutionary defences, such as change of position, are capable of being given effect.

(As to the change of position defence, see 18.2.2.) His Lordship concluded, however, that whether English law should adopt this remedy would have to be decided in a future case when the point was directly in issue.

It seems clear from the above *dictum* that even when English courts eventually recognize a constructive trust on the basis of unjust enrichment, it will only be where the enrichment of the defendant had been at the claimant's expense (so-called 'subtractive unjust enrichment'). In *Halifax Building Society v Thomas* [1995] 4 All ER 673, a mortgagee, after its loan had been fully repaid, claimed the surplus proceeds of sale of the mortgagor's property. The claim was brought on the basis of a constructive trust arising because the mortgage loan had been obtained by fraud. The Court of Appeal rejected the mortgagee's claim because the fraudulent borrower had not been unjustly enriched at the mortgagee's expense.

In the light of *Westdeutsche* and *Halifax v Thomas* it may only be a matter of time before English courts remedy substractive unjust enrichment by means of a constructive trust. However, at present, English law does not go this far, and only recognizes constructive trusts where they are asserted to vindicate a pre-existing proprietary right.

In *Re Sharpe (a bankrupt)* [1980] 1 WLR 219, Browne-Wilkinson J (as he then was) recognized the claimant's constructive trust interest, but refused to regard the imposition of a constructive trust as a mere remedy which the court could impose to address injustice: '... it cannot be that the interest in property arises for the first time when the court declares it to exist. The right must have arisen at the time of the transaction in order for the plaintiff to have any right the breach of which can be remedied'.

EXERCISE 16.2

Read the extract from *Re Sharpe* below. Do you agree that the claimant in that case had a pre-existing proprietary right, or do you think that this was a case of remedial constructive trust in all but name?

Mr S, Mrs S and the claimant, Mrs Johnson (an elderly aunt), lived together in leasehold premises which were held in the name of Mr S. The claimant had contributed the majority of the purchase price of the lease. In providing the money, she had been told that she would be permitted to reside in the premises for as long as she wished. Upon Mr S being declared bankrupt, the trustee in bankruptcy took out a summons for possession of the premises. The court dismissed the summons. His Lordship held that the claimant did not have an interest in the land under a resulting trust because she had given her money by way of loan. The terms of the loan gave her a mere contractual right to reside in the premises until the loan had been repaid, and such a right would not bind the trustee in bankruptcy.

Re Sharpe **(a bankrupt) [1980] 1 WLR 219, Chancery Division**

Browne-Wilkinson J:

Even if it be right to say that the courts can impose a constructive trust as a remedy in certain cases—which to my mind is a novel concept in English law—in order to provide a remedy the court must first find a right which has been infringed... in cases such as this, it cannot be that the interest in property arises for the first time when the court declares it to exist. The right must have arisen at the time of the transaction in order for the plaintiff to have any right the breach of which can be remedied.

Accordingly, if I am right in holding that as between the debtor and Mrs Johnson she had an irrevocable licence to remain in the property, authority compels me to hold that that gave her an interest in the property before the bankruptcy and the trustee takes the property subject to that interest. In my judgment the mere intervention of the bankruptcy by itself cannot alter

> Mrs Johnson's property interest. If she is to be deprived of her interest as against the trustee in bankruptcy, it must be because of some conduct of hers which precludes her from enforcing her rights, that is to say, the ordinary principles of acquiescence and laches which apply to all beneficiaries seeking to enforce their rights apply to this case.
>
> [his Lordship held that Mrs Johnson had not acquiesced in the breach, see, generally, 15.3.6.]
>
> Accordingly, I hold that Mrs Johnson is entitled as against the trustee in bankruptcy to remain in the property until she is repaid the sums she advanced. I reach this conclusion with some hesitation since I find the present state of the law very confused and difficult to fit in with established equitable principles. I express the hope that in the near future the whole question can receive full consideration in the Court of Appeal, so that, in order to do justice to the many thousands of people who never come into court at all but who wish to know with certainty what their proprietary rights are, the extent to which these irrevocable licences bind third parties may be defined with certainty. Doing justice to the litigant who actually appears in the court by the invention of new principles of law ought not to involve injustice to the other persons who are not litigants before the court but whose rights are fundamentally affected by the new principles.

There are echoes of the *Re Sharpe* approach in *Chase Manhattan Bank NA v Israel–British Bank (London) Ltd* [1981] Ch 105. This was another case, on a larger scale, in which the claimant needed to establish a proprietary claim to recover its funds from the estate of an insolvent defendant. The claimant had mistakenly made two payments of $2 million to the defendant bank, when it had only intended to make one. Goulding J held that the claimant bank could trace its property in equity into the hands of the defendant bank, and that the defendant would be a constructive trustee of those funds until it made restitution to the claimant. In reaching this judgment his Lordship emphasized the need to show a pre-existing proprietary right in the fund: 'a person who pays money to another under a factual mistake retains an equitable property in it and the conscience of that other is subjected to a fiduciary duty to respect his proprietary right'.

Sir Peter Millett, writing extra-judically, has affirmed the restrictive approach to recognizing constructive trusts: 'there is neither room nor need for the remedial constructive trust. In my view it is a counsel of despair which too readily concedes the impossibility of propounding a general rationale for the availability of proprietary remedies' (1995) 9 TLI 35 at 40. Professor Andrew Burrows (*The Law of Restitution* (1993) at 37) has suggested that, 'even if one puts to one side the difficulty in describing the constructive trust as a remedy, there is an immediate obstacle to justifying it, within a restitutionary framework, in a case of unjust enrichment by subtraction in a case like *Chase Manhattan*'. One difficulty pointed out by Professor Burrows is that straightforward restitution would insist upon the return of $2 million plus interest, whereas a constructive trust solution would entitle the claimant to $2 million plus any profits made by the trustee through the use of that $2 million, plus interest on the total. (The remedial constructive trust was once again dismissed by the Court of Appeal in *Re Polly Peck International plc (No 4)* [1998] 3 All ER 812.)

16.3.1.2 **Commonwealth approaches**

Having considered the approach taken in the United States, as summarized by Professor Scott (16.3.1), let us make the short journey north to Canada. In that jurisdiction the constructive trust has been used widely as a remedial device for the reversal of unjust enrichment (see

Simon Gardner, 'Rethinking Family Property' (1993) 109 LQR 263 at 269–274). The leading case is *Pettkus v Becker* (1980) 117 DLR (3d) 257. The facts were that Miss Becker had worked for 14 years on a honey farm owned by her cohabitee, Mr Pettkus. The Supreme Court of Canada, led by Dixon J, granted her a half-share in Mr Pettkus's property under a constructive trust in order to remedy his unjust enrichment at her expense. According to the judge, this 'unjust enrichment' arises where there is 'an enrichment, a corresponding deprivation and absence of any juristic reason for the enrichment'. As Gardner points out in his article, the first and third elements are problematic. The first because, apart from to the extent that it has yielded an obvious financial benefit, the defendant can simply deny that he has been enriched by the claimant's services. The third, because it is never easy to show that an enrichment has been unjustly received when it was consensually conferred. Untroubled by this Dixon J held that:

> where one person in a relationship tantamount to spousal prejudices herself in the reasonable expectation of receiving an interest in property and the other person in the relationship freely accepts benefits conferred by the first person in circumstances where he knows or ought to have known of that reasonable expectation, it would be unjust to allow the recipient of the benefit to retain it.

In Australia constructive trusts have been granted to remedy the 'unconscionability' of the legal owner, a concept even more nebulous than 'unjust enrichment'. This modern trend has its origins in the judgment of Deane J in *Muschinski v Dodds* (1985) 160 CLR 583. In that case Mrs Muschinski met the entire purchase price of property which had been purchased in the joint names of Mrs Muschinski and Mr Dodds, with whom she had embarked upon a commercial joint venture. She did so in the expectation that he would pay half the cost in due course. He never did, and so the court imposed a constructive trust on his half share of the property to repay her contributions to the extent that they exceeded his. Deane J held (at p 451) that 'the constructive trust can properly be described as a remedial institution which equity imposes regardless of actual or presumed intention . . . to preclude the retention or assertion of beneficial ownership of property to the extent that such retention or assertion would be contrary to equitable principle', or, as he later stated, 'to the extent that it would be unconscionable' (p 455).

The constructive trust in *Muschinski* is a free-standing remedy. It is not based on the vindication of any pre-existing proprietary right. On the contrary, it operates from the date of the court order granting it. This was confirmed in the leading Australian case, *Baumgartner v Baumgartner* (1987) 164 CLR 137 in which Deane J appeared again, but this time with Wilson J and Mason CJ in the High Court of Australia.

The facts of *Baumgartner* were typical of the sorts of cases which will form the focus of the next chapter. The Baumgartners, an unmarried couple, had both contributed to a house which had been purchased in the man's name alone. Their Lordships held that the woman was entitled to a share in the house under a constructive trust, and that the size of that share should be roughly equivalent to the value of her contributions. The judgment of the majority of the High Court in *Baumgartner* was that:

> [his] assertion, after the relationship had failed, that the . . . property, which was financed in part through the pooled funds, is his sole property, is his property beneficially, to the exclusion of any interest at all on [her part], amounts to unconscionable conduct, which attracts the intervention of equity and the imposition of a constructive trust . . .

Simon Gardner has observed (*op cit* at 275) that the judgment 'gives no very definite account of the parameters of unconscionability. It implicitly rejects the idea of resting the doctrine merely on idiosyncratic notions of what is fair and just, but then invokes these very notions'. Weight is added to this criticism by the definition provided by Deane J in *Commonwealth v Verwayen* (1990) 170 CLR 394, 441: ' "Unconscionable" should be understood in the sense of referring to what one party "ought not in conscience, as between [the parties] be allowed to do" '.

In a rather different constructive trust context (see 19.6) Lord Nicholls has stated that: 'unconscionable is not a word in everyday use by non-lawyers. If it is to be used... it is essential to be clear on what, in this context, unconscionable means.' (*Royal Brunei v Tan* [1995] 3 WLR 64, Privy Council.)

Lord Nicholls is a forward thinking judge, but his conservatism in this respect is representative of the English House of Lords in recent cases (see also *Lloyds Bank plc v Rosset* [1991] 1 AC 107 (17.2.4)). The fear of the English courts is no doubt that the elevation of 'unconscionability' to the status of free-standing cause of action will not herald a positive movement 'from an era of strict law to one which gives greater emphasis to equity and natural law' (Mason CJ (1994) 110 LQR 238, 259), but will be retrograde. It might put back the clock of English jurisprudence to the days when equitable intervention was based on the bare notion of fraud. One does not have to go back too far (relative, that is, to the long history of equity) to discover aberrant cases such as *Chattock v Muller* (1878) 8 Ch 177). And, of course, one could go back still further; to the days when equity was said to vary according to the length of the Chancellor's foot (see 1.2.1.1).

? QUESTION 16.6

Despite this criticism, can you imagine that there would be any advantage in granting constructive trusts as a free-standing equitable remedy, rather than as a means of vindicating pre-existing proprietary rights?

The great advantage of a true remedial constructive trust is that it would not be awarded if to do so would be inequitable in all the circumstances. This means that remedial constructive trusts would not be awarded if to do so would prejudice the interests of innocent third parties. This is of particular relevance where the defendant is insolvent, because in such circumstances the award of a constructive trust in favour of the claimant would, because it is a proprietary award, reduce the fund available to satisfy the defendants' general creditors. As Mummery LJ observed in *Re Polly Peck International plc (No 2)* [1998] 3 All ER 812: 'The insolvency road is blocked off to remedial constructive trusts, at least when judge driven in a vehicle of discretion'. In this respect the great disadvantage of the institutional constructive trust is that it is designed to vindicate a pre-existing proprietary right. The court is left, in theory at least, with no discretion as to whether or not to award the remedy, no discretion as to the nature of the remedy, and only a limited discretion as to its quantum. Because the claimant's institutional constructive trust will take priority in the event of the defendant's insolvency, the potential prejudice to the defendant's innocent third party creditors is obvious.

16.3.2 The obligations of a constructive trustee

> It is a mistake to suppose that in every situation in which a constructive trust arises the legal owner is necessarily subject to all the fiduciary obligations and disabilities of an express trustee.
>
> *Per* Millett J in *Lonrho plc v Fayed (No 2)* [1992] 4 All ER 961.

The facts of *Lonrho* were as follows. The claimant, a large shareholder in ACo, had given an undertaking to the Secretary of State for Trade and Industry that it would not acquire more than 30 per cent of the shares in ACo. It sold its shares in ACo to BCo, thereby hoping to be released from its undertaking, to enable a future take-over of ACo. However, having received the shares in Aco, BCo went on to acquire more than 50 per cent of the shares in ACo. The claimant *was* subsequently released from its undertaking, but by then it was too late to acquire a majority shareholding in ACo. The claimant claimed *inter alia* that BCo held the shares in ACo on trust for the claimant because they had been acquired by the fraud of BCo.

Millett J held that a contract obtained by fraudulent misrepresentation is voidable, not void, even in equity. The representee (the claimant) may elect to avoid it, but until he does so no fiduciary relationship arises and the representor (BCo) cannot be a constructive trustee of the property transferred pursuant to the contract. In the present case there was no constructive trust because the claimant had demonstrated only that the majority shareholding in ACo might have been acquired by fraud, it had not shown that it would be unconscionable for its interest to be denied.

It follows from the fact that many constructive trustees do not know that they are trustees until the court determines that they are, that they are not subject to the full rigours of the general law in relation to express trusts. They do not, for example, have to invest the trust fund prudently within the terms of the Trustee Investment Act 1961.

16.4 Types of constructive trusts

The following catalogue of situations in which constructive trusts have been recognized illustrates how diverse are the circumstances in which the constructive trust has been employed, and how difficult it is to establish any underlying unifying concept that can be applied with theoretical rigour to new cases.

16.4.1 Constructive trustee of unauthorized profits

For more general consideration of the principle that fiduciaries must not profit from their position without authorization, see 12.2.

At this juncture the author's intention is a limited one. Namely, to distinguish the proprietary claim against a constructive trustee of unauthorized profits from the personal claim against a fiduciary for an account of unauthorized profits. When one considers that a fiduciary often *is a trustee* to his principal of whatever property he holds in his fiduciary capacity, the distinction may appear to be a somewhat slight one. Whether the conceptual distinction is or is not artificial we will consider in a moment, but what cannot be doubted are the potentially serious practical implications of the distinction, especially in the context of the defendant's insolvency. If a mere fiduciary becomes insolvent the claim of the principal against the fiduciary's estate will rank with other unsecured personal claims against the fiduciary. If, on the other hand, a trustee becomes insolvent, the claim of the beneficiary ranks ahead of the claims of general creditors.

It is for this reason that it is frequently objected that constructive trusts disturb the normal priority of claims in insolvency, and should not readily be recognized in insolvent contexts. A J Oakley objects to constructive trusts in commerce because general trade creditors cannot discover them in the usual course of their business (AJ Oakley (1995) 54(2) CLJ 377 at 381). He is right, of course. But, as we have seen, the same is true of many express trusts in commercial contexts (see 2.3.4). In any case, the courts continue to apply the presumption that a secret commission received in breach of fiduciary duty is held by the fiduciary on constructive trust. A recent example is *Daraydan Holdings Ltd v Solland Interiors Ltd* [2004] EWHC 622 (Ch).

16.4.1.1 **Claims against a constructive trustee of unauthorized profits**

The reports provide numerous examples of cases in which successful claims have been brought to recover unauthorized profits on the basis of a constructive trust. In some of these cases, the defendant was an express trustee to start with, in others the defendant was a mere fiduciary at the outset.

An example of the former situation is provided by the case of *Keech v Sandford* (1726) Sel Cas Ch 61. There the trustee held a lease in trust for an infant beneficiary. The landlord was unwilling to renew the lease for the benefit of the trust, but did renew it in favour of the trustee personally. King LC adjudged that the trustee held the renewed lease, and any profits made from it, on constructive trust in favour of the infant beneficiary: '[t]his may seem hard, that the trustee is the only person of all mankind who might not have the lease; but it is very proper that rule should be strictly pursued'. The Lord Chancellor was confirmed in his judgment by the 'very obvious' risk that unscrupulous trustees might take advantage of their position, if the legal rule were in any way relaxed. *Keech v Sandford* has been extended to the case where a fiduciary purchases the freehold reversion of his principal's lease (*Protheroe v Protheroe* [1968] 1 WLR 519 and *Thompson's Trustee v Heaton* [1974] 1 WLR 605).

An example of the latter situation appears from *AG for Hong Kong v Reid* [1994] 1 All ER 1, where the Privy Council held that whenever a fiduciary receives property of his principal in breach of his fiduciary duty, he is a constructive trustee of it, and of any traceable profit from and proceeds of it (as to tracing see **Chapter 18**). Mr Reid was acting Director of Public Prosecutions in Hong Kong. In breach of his fiduciary duty to the Crown he received substantial bribes in consideration of which he obstructed the prosecution of certain criminals. The Crown was able to trace the bribe monies through to three freehold properties in New Zealand, and to assert a restitutionary claim to them under a constructive trust. Mr Reid failed in his assertion that the Crown should be limited to its claim against him personally, and that the personal claim should be limited to the value of the initial bribe. Lord Templeman held: 'Equity considers as done that which ought to be done. As soon as the bribe was received, whether in cash or in kind, the false fiduciary held the bribe on a constructive trust for the person injured'.

16.4.1.2 Claims against a fiduciary for an account of unauthorized profits

Let us consider *Boardman v Phipps* [1967] 2 AC 46. Boardman, the solicitor to a trust, attended the AGM of a company in which the trust had a substantial shareholding. Unhappy with the state of the company he (together with one of the beneficiaries under the trust) decided to launch a personal take-over bid for those shares in the company which were not already trust-owned. Insider-knowledge of the company gained in his capacity as solicitor to the trust enabled the solicitor to make the take-over bid. Boardman wrote to the beneficiaries outlining his plans to take a personal interest in the company, giving them an opportunity to raise any objections they might have to his so doing. No objectors having come forward, Boardman proceeded with the take-over. In the event the take-over was very successful and the value of all the shares in the company increased in value. The trust had profited from the take-over, and so had the solicitor. So, was everybody happy? Not quite.

The present action was brought by Phipps, a beneficiary under the trust, for an account of profits made by Boardman in his fiduciary capacity as solicitor to the trust. The trial judge found as a fact that Phipps had not been fully informed by Boardman as to the precise nature of his plans. A bare majority of their Lordships (Viscount Dilhorne and Lord Upjohn dissenting) held that Boardman had placed himself in a fiduciary position in relation to the trust and would be accountable for the profits that he had made on information obtained in his fiduciary capacity. However, it was held that he had acted honestly and openly throughout and because his actions had yielded profits for the trust he was awarded generous remuneration as reward for his work and skill (see 12.2.1.2).

? QUESTION 16.7

Do you think that Boardman's insider information might fall within the legal definition of property?

The majority of their Lordships rejected this suggestion. Lord Cohen stated that information was 'not property in the strictest sense of that word'. However Lord Guest and Lord Hodson regarded the information obtained by Boardman to be property of the trust and held him liable to account as a constructive trustee for profits he had made thereon.

(It is interesting to note that even where information is the subject of a fiduciary obligation, the confidential nature of the information might not last for ever. In *AG v Blake* [1996] 3 All ER 903, the Attorney-General sought to recover the profits made on the publication of memoirs by a person who had sworn to the Official Secrets Act. The claim failed as the information disclosed in the memoirs was no longer confidential.)

Returning to *Boardman v Phipps*, it was suggested that Boardman should be treated as a constructive trustee 'by reason of the fiduciary position in which [he] stood' (applying the *dictum* of Lord Selborne in *Barnes v Addy* [1874] 9 Ch App 244 (see **Chapter 19**)).

In response to this, Professor Birks has suggested ((1988) LMCLQ 128) that the use of constructive trust language was as inappropriate to the facts of *Boardman v Phipps* as it was to the facts of *Barnes v Addy*. For Birks, *Boardman v Phipps* was a case which should have been disposed of as a straightforward personal claim against the principal, and that in essence, despite the occasional unconvincing reference to constructive trusteeship, this is how the case was disposed of. It is true that the House of Lords made no order requiring that the defendants should transfer the shares to the claimant. Against this Professor Andrew Burrows points out that a declaration that the defendant held the shares on constructive trust was made at first instance, and (that judgment having been upheld) 'it must follow that the plaintiffs would have been entitled to proprietary remedies, affording priority, had the defendants been insolvent' (*The Law of Restitution* (1993), p 413).

16.4.1.3 Can a distinction between the fiduciary account and the constructive trust be justified?

In view of the extra benefits attached to a proprietary remedy in the event of the defendant's insolvency it has been argued that such remedies should only be awarded in favour of claimants who can show that a pre-existing proprietary right has been prejudiced, hence the debate in *Boardman* as to whether the information was itself 'property'. This would be in keeping with the orthodox English law conception of the constructive trust as an institution which vindicates a pre-existing proprietary right.

However, in his commentary on *Boardman v Phipps* ((1968) 84 LQR 472) Professor Gareth Jones suggested an interesting 'culpability' basis for determining the appropriate remedy, namely that the:

> principal should be allowed a proprietary claim only if the court considers it appropriate that he should be granted the additional benefits which naturally flow from such a grant. The honest fiduciary who is deemed to have breached his duty of loyalty but who has not been unjustly enriched and whose principal has suffered no loss should only be liable to account for his profits. On the other hand a fiduciary who is dishonest or who has otherwise manifestly disregarded his principal's interest should be held to be a constructive trustee of the benefits obtained at his principal's expense.

? QUESTION 16.8

Suppose that a sergeant in the British Army had been bribed to accompany civilian lorries through security checkpoints in Egypt in order to assist the transport of contraband goods. In the light of what you have learned so far, do you think that these facts would give rise to a constructive trust or mere personal liability to account?

These facts are taken from *Reading v Attorney-General* [1951] AC 507. It was held that Sgt Reading owed a fiduciary obligation to the Crown not to use his position against the interests of the Crown and that he had to account for any profits made through a breach of those obligations. The fact that a fiduciary relationship was acknowledged at all was, on these facts, fairly exceptional in itself (in the Court of Appeal Asquith LJ acknowledged that he was applying a very 'loose' concept of fiduciary ([1949] 2 KB 232)). The fact is that the Crown needed some legal basis on which it could require Reading to disgorge his ill-gotten gains (£19,000 was found in his possession).

? QUESTION 16.9

If the defendant had been insolvent would the award of a constructive trust have been justified?

According to Professor Gareth Jones's dishonesty-based analysis (above) it presumably would be. However, against this it can surely be argued that because the Crown had not lost any property due to Reading's breach of his duty, it would be quite unjust to allow the Crown to recover the £19,000 to the prejudice of Reading's personal creditors. This very objection was considered by the Privy Council in *AG for Hong Kong v Reid* (see 16.4.1.1) where Lord Templeman, having decided that the 'false fiduciary' held the proceeds of his bribe on constructive trust for the Crown, acknowledged, that 'the unsecured creditors of the false fiduciary will be deprived of their right to share in the proceeds... [b]ut the unsecured creditors cannot be in a better position than their debtor'. Whilst this is a rigorous application of equity's *in personam* jurisdiction as between the parties to the case, it has the undesirable side-effect of causing prejudice to innocent third parties.

This potential injustice to third parties may be an inevitable product of the English law conception of the constructive trust as an institution which vindicates an existing property right. It could, however, be avoided if the grant of a proprietary remedy were restricted to cases where the fiduciary's profit had been made by means of wrongful use of his principal's property. A bribe is in no sense derived from funds previously owned by the Crown.

? QUESTION 16.10

Did the defendant in *Reading v AG* use his principal's property to make his wrongful gain?

The answer, at a basic level, is 'yes he did'. Reading had used a British Army uniform, the Crown's property, to make his wrongful gain. Whether this is a sufficient proprietary base to justify the imposition of a constructive trust is a nice point, but ultimately something of a red herring. The gains had not been made because of the uniform, but because of Reading's position. This case is not comparable to the situation where wrongful gains have been made through the misapplication of the principal's cash, shares, etc. If the uniform had truly been the effective cause of the wrongful gain, the smugglers could have saved themselves a great deal of money by simply acquiring a British Army uniform or manufacturing a replica.

16.4.2 Constructive trust to prevent fraudulent or unconscionable assertion of legal rights in land

More general examples of this will be considered in the next chapter. Here, we will focus on the issues raised by the peculiar case of *Lyus v Prowsa Developments* [1982] 1 WLR 1044.

Mr and Mrs Lyus contracted to purchase a house from property developers who in fact became insolvent before the house could be built. Unfortunately, Mr and Mrs Lyus had not placed a notice of their estate contract against the developers' registered title to the land. The Lyus' bank was under no obligation to build the house, and instead sold the vacant plot to the defendants, but expressly subject to the Lyus' contract to have a house built. Dillon J held that the Lyus' contract was itself a property right (an estate contract) and that the defendants took subject to it. This was despite the fact that, according to the Land Registration Act 1925, the defendants had taken the land free from any unprotected estate contracts (ss 20(1) and 59(6)). Because they had expressly agreed to take the land subject to the estate contract, the contract would be enforced against them. Dillon J held that a constructive trust had arisen when the defendants purchased the land, to prevent the defendants from unconscionably or fraudulently denying their promise and relying upon their rights under the Land Registration Act 1925.

Charles Harpum, lately the Law Commissioner for property and trusts, has suggested ([1983] CLJ 54) that:

> The *Lyus* constructive trust looks to be 'remedial' rather than 'substantive' and as such without much precedent in English law, which has tended to treat constructive trusts as part of the law of property, preferring to develop the remedial possibilities of estoppel instead (see 17.5). It remains to be seen whether the *Lyus* constructive trust is a one-case mutant or the progenitor of a new species.

In the years since *Lyus* there has been no further evidence of a new species of constructive trust. *Lyus* sits uneasily with the decision of the House of Lords in *Midland Bank v Green* [1981] AC 513, another unregistered land case. It established very firmly that an unregistered estate contract would not bind a *bona fide* purchaser of the legal estate, even if the purchaser actually knew of the existence of the estate contract. However, it is arguable that *Green* can be distinguished because, unlike the defendant in *Lyus*, the purchaser in *Green* did not take expressly subject to the estate contract.

The real objection to the anomalous case of *Lyus v Prowsa* is not that it proceeded from an unorthodox application of equitable principles, but rather that the equitable reasoning was employed to the unorthodox end of thwarting the policy of purchaser-protection which underlies the 1925 scheme of legislation.

16.4.3 Vendor-purchaser trust

Suppose that A is the absolute legal owner of a parcel of land which he intends to sell to B. Some time later A and B enter into a valid legal contract for the sale of the land from A to B. Finally A and B execute a legal deed under which the land is conveyed at law from A to B, thus completing the sale.

? QUESTION 16.11

We know that A was the owner at the beginning, and that B is the owner at the end. But who was the owner from the creation of the contract until the execution of the deed?

The answer is that A and B were both owners during that period. A was the legal owner at law because a deed is necessary to transfer legal ownership (Law of Property Act 1925, s 52) and one had not been executed. B was the owner in equity because equity regards A's contractual promise as binding on A's conscience from the moment the promise is made in legally binding form (as to the form, see Law of Property (Miscellaneous Provisions) Act 1989, s 2), in accordance with the maxim *equity sees as done that which ought to be done* (see *Walsh v Lonsdale* at 1.3.3). From the moment of contract, A is said to hold his legal title on trust for B.

Because the trust arises against the intentions of the vendor it is said to be a constructive trust. However, it is somewhat misleading to describe the vendor-purchaser trust as a constructive trust. For one thing, its existence depends upon a formal contract, whereas most constructive trusts do not depend upon any written formality. For another, the constructive trust is co-existent with the award of specific performance, a remedy which in theory the court awards in its discretion (although normally it is awarded as a matter of course). This lends this 'constructive trust' an unorthodox remedial flavour. As we have seen, the orthodox view is that constructive trusts are awarded to vindicate pre-existing proprietary rights. M P Thompson has contended that '[w]hile it is too late to argue against the view that some sort of trust arises, it is contended that it is misleading to describe it as a constructive trust and that it is better to regard it as *sui generis*' ('Must a Purchaser buy a Charred Ruin?' (1984) 48 Conv 43).

16.4.4 Mutual wills

See 3.3.2.1 where mutual wills are considered in detail.

16.4.5 The equitable liability of strangers as constructive trustees

This topic forms the subject matter of **Chapter 19**.

16.4.6 Secret trusts

See 3.3.3, where secret trusts are considered in detail.

16.4.7 'New model' constructive trusts

This is the appellation attached to a remedial form of constructive trust developed by Lord Denning MR in the 1970s as an attempt to achieve a just distribution of property between cohabitees.

See 17.2.5.1 where this approach is considered in more detail.

16.4.8 Commercial agreement constructive trusts

This is not a traditional category of constructive trust, but it is included to illustrate the flexibility of the constructive trust and the potential relevance of the constructive trust to the solution of commercial problems. You might recall from a previous chapter that we have already considered a case where a constructive trust was employed to give effect to an agreement between the shareholders of a company relating to the distribution of the company's assets on its winding up (*Neville v Wilson*, see 3.3.1). The case of *Banner Homes Group plc v Luff Developments Ltd (No 1)* [2000] Ch 372 provides a similar illustration of the commercial utility of the constructive trust, this time in relation to agreement to acquire site by joint venture.

Luff agreed in principle with Banner that they would create a new joint venture company to purchase a commercial site. They agreed to take equal shares in the new company. On that understanding, Luff purchased S Ltd (a new company) for use in the joint venture. Later, Luff began to have doubts about the proposed joint venture and started looking for a new partner. It did not tell Banner, fearing that Banner might put in an independent bid for the commercial site. Banner continued to act on the footing that the joint venture would proceed, always anticipating that Banner and Luff would enter into a formal agreement setting out the terms of the joint venture. S Ltd eventually acquired the site with funds provided by Luff, and only then did Luff inform Banner that the proposed joint venture would not be going ahead.

Banner contended, *inter alia*, that it was entitled to half the shares in S Ltd under a constructive trust. At first instance, the judge rejected this contention. He held that equity could not transform the agreement, which was implicitly qualified by the right of either side to withdraw, into a binding arrangement. He also held that Banner had suffered no detriment, inasmuch as he refused to accept that Banner might have made an independent bid for the land if it had been aware of Luff's intention to abandon the proposed joint venture.

The Court of Appeal overturned that judgment. It was held that an equity arose because it would have been inequitable to allow Luff to claim, outright, a site which it had acquired in furtherance of the non-contractual, pre-acquisition understanding that it would be held for the joint benefit of Luff and Banner. The Court would have held otherwise if Luff had informed Banner soon enough to avoid advantage to Luff and detriment to Banner. Their Lordships held that in many cases the advantage/detriment would be found, as in this case, in the undertaking of the non-acquiring party (Banner in this case) not to make an independent bid for the site. Their Lordships did stress, however, that it was not necessary that there should be both an advantage and a detriment, although the two would normally go hand in hand. The advantage to Luff in the instant case was not merely the knowledge that Banner would not make an independent bid, but the comfort of knowing that Banner would support Luff in acquiring a site which Luff had originally been wary of purchasing at its sole risk. (*Pallant v Morgan* [1952] 2 All ER 951 was applied.)

Perhaps the most controversial aspect of this decision is that Luff's 'conscience' was held to be bound in equity by Banner's detrimental reliance on the parties' informal understanding. It is hard to see how Banner's lost opportunity to make an independent bid can be described as a detriment without evidence being pleaded to suggest that Banner would probably have made such an independent bid in the absence of the understanding with Luff.

In *Cox v Jones* [2004] EWHC 1486 (Ch), (Transcript) Mann J applied *Pallant v Morgan* (*Banner v Luff*) reasoning to the acrimonious (and litigious) break-up of two barristers (Mr Jones and Miss Cox) who were formerly engaged to be married. The main dispute related to ownership of certain assets, including a flat bought as an investment in the name of Mr Jones. The judge held that Miss Cox should be recognized as the beneficial owner of the flat because there was a clear arrangement before the acquisition that Mr Jones would hold as trustee and not beneficially and that in the absence of the agreement there would have been no purchase at all. Crucially, Mann J held that Miss Cox had suffered a detriment 'in that she did not pursue her own attempts to acquire the property herself in her sole name' even though 'it was not conclusively proved that those attempts would have been successful'.

CHAPTER SUMMARY

- This chapter has considered the creation and operation of two special types of trusts which are not based on any express intention.
- We have seen that resulting trusts arise *in accordance* with the presumed intention of the settlor. Where an attempt is made by the owner of an asset to dispose of the beneficial ownership of the asset, the benefit will return to the donor under a resulting trust whenever the attempt is for any reason unsuccessful, unless it is clear that the owner intended to abandon the entirety of his interest in the asset.
- Whereas a resulting trust is enforced to fulfil the intentions of the true owner, a constructive trust is enforced to prevent the claim of a false owner. Sir Robert Megarry once observed that, '"Constructive"' is, of course, an unhappy word in the law... "Constructive" seems to mean "It isn't, but has to be treated as if it were", and the less of this there is in the law, the better' ('Historical Development' *in Special Lectures of the Law Society of Upper Canada 1990* (*Fiduciary Duties* (1991) 1 at 5)). However, we have seen that all law is an attempt to achieve a balance between general regulation through formality and certainty, and justice in the individual case. Constructive trusts lie on the latter side of the balance, and it may be that the more of this there is in the law, the better. It is still the case, however, that the English constructive trust is not remedial. Rather, it vindicates pre-existing beneficial entitlement. Hence the glossary to this book defines the 'constructive trust' as a 'trust imposed by the court on the legal owner of an asset to prevent that person asserting beneficial ownership of the asset in bad conscience to the prejudice of the true beneficial owner'.

SUMMATIVE ASSESSMENT EXERCISE

online resource centre

In his book, *Property and Justice* (Clarendon Press, Oxford, 1996), Professor J W Harris observed that the strict rule that a fiduciary must account for unauthorized profit 'confers the windfall constituted by the fiduciary's profit, not on the community, but on his principal', with the result that the principal is entitled to claim it in preference to the fiduciary's creditors. Professor Harris asks: 'Why should the principal take a windfall in priority to those to whom the fiduciary owes purchased obligations?'

Outline the reasons why English law takes this approach, and state why, in your opinion, this is (or is not) the correct approach for the law to take.

FURTHER READING

Birks, P, 'Restitution and Resulting Trusts' in Goldstein (ed) *Equity: Contemporary Legal Developments* (Jerusalem: Hebrew University of Jerusalem, 1992).

Browne-Wilkinson, Sir Nicolas, 'Constructive trusts and unjust enrichment' (1996) 10(4) Tru LI 98–101.

Chambers, R, *Resulting Trusts* (Oxford: Clarendon Press, 1997).

Davies, J D, 'Presumptions and Illegality' in A J Oakley (ed) *Trends in Contemporary Trust Law* (Oxford: Clarendon Press, 1996) 33.

Elias, G, *Explaining Constructive Trusts* (Oxford: Clarendon Press, 1990).

Hopkins, N, 'The *Pallant v Morgan* "Equity"?' [2002] Conv 35.

Ing, N D, *Bona Vacantia* (2nd edn) (London: Butterworths, 2000).

Law Commission, *Illegal Transactions: The Effect of Illegality on Contracts and Trusts* Consultation Paper No 154 (1999).

Martin, J, 'Fraudulent Transferors and the Public Conscience' [1992] Conv 153.

McFarlane, B, 'Constructive Trusts Arising on a Receipt of Property *Sub Conditione*' (2004) 120 LQR 667.

Millett, Sir Peter, 'Remedies: The Error in *Lister v Stubbs*' in P Birks (ed), *The Frontiers of Liability* (Oxford: OUP, 1994) vol I, p 51.

Oakley, A J, *Constructive Trusts* (London: Sweet & Maxwell, 1997).

Sherwin, E, 'Constructive Trusts in Bankruptcy' (1989) U Ill L Rev 297.

Swadling, W, 'A new role for resulting trusts?' 16 Legal Studies 133.

Waters, D W M, *Constructive Trusts* (London: The Athlone Press, 1964).

17 Informal trusts of land

OBJECTIVES

By the end of this chapter you should be able to:

1 Appreciate the special social issues addressed by the recognition of informal trusts of land

2 Understand when an informal trust of land is a resulting trust and when it is a constructive trust

3 Identify and quantify interests under constructive trusts of land

4 Grasp the relationship between proprietary estoppel and informal trusts

17.1 Introduction

In **Chapter 3** we discovered that the declaration of an express trust of land, or of any interest therein, need not be made in writing, but must be evidenced in writing. To be precise, such a trust must be 'manifested and proved by some writing signed by some person who is able to declare such trust or by his will' (Law of Property Act 1925, s 53(1)(b)). In this chapter we will be focusing on the exceptions to this requirement made possible by s 53(2) of the Law of Property Act 1925, which provides that the formality requirements laid down in s 53(1) shall not affect 'the creation or operation of resulting, implied or constructive trusts'.

Chapter 16 introduced resulting and constructive trusts. In this chapter we will have the opportunity to apply our learning on those subjects to trusts of land, and in particular to the trusts which arise, if any, where A (who claims an interest in land owned by B) commences cohabitation with B (the legal owner of land). Usually A is a woman and B a man, but the law draws no such distinction. In highlighting the fact that there may not be any trust consequences at all, one must bear in mind that where property is purchased in the name of a sole legal owner that person will *prima facie* be the sole beneficial owner as well.

The social circumstances giving rise to the legal problem are commonplace. While it is increasingly likely that cohabitees, married or unmarried, will vest the legal title to their home in their joint names (not least because institutional lenders nearly always require it when advancing a loan secured by mortgage), it is still often the case that legal title to their residence will be vested in the name of one of them only. Where (in the case of married cohabitees) only one spouse has a legal entitlement to occupy the matrimonial home, the Family Law Act 1996, s 30 grants occupation rights to the non-owning spouse. It takes effect as a charge against the proprietary interest of the non-owning spouse and must be registered if it is to take priority to the rights of third party purchasers and mortgagees. The 1996 Act also empowers the court to make occupation orders in relation to married cohabitees in limited circumstances (ss 33–35).

Even where legal title is vested jointly in the names of A and B, it does not follow that the equitable situation is necessarily one of joint tenancy or even of tenancy in common in equal shares. The maxim that equity follows the law 'may be a starting point but it is easily displaced' (*McKenzie v McKenzie* [2003] EWHC 601 (Ch); *Goodman v Gallant* [1986] 2 WLR 236, 246). The law of England does not recognize any doctrine of communal ownership, in accordance with which it could be assumed that A and B in living together had agreed to share all their property equally. On the contrary, cohabitation continues to be a fertile source of property disputes, and chief amongst them are claims to a beneficial interest, or a larger beneficial interest, in the joint residence. Of course, such disputes are not limited to the cohabitees themselves. Very often the respective rights of the cohabitees only fall to be determined by the courts when a mortgagee, having sought to enforce its security against the joint residence, has been repelled by the proprietary claims of a cohabitee of whom it had been unaware.

The reason why family property is such a fertile source of dispute is because cohabitation is legally disorganized. Unlike business partners, familial cohabitees do not deal with each other at arm's length. If they did, any disputes as to proprietary entitlement could be prevented by the simple expedient of a purchase or transfer of the legal title in their joint names, accompanied by an express declaration of trust (evidenced in writing, ideally in the form of an express trust deed) stating that they are to hold as joint tenants in equity, or specifying their respective shares as equitable tenants in common.

Where the property dispute arises between *married* parties in the context of proceedings for divorce or judicial separation, the court has wide powers to apportion proprietary entitlement according to what is fair in all the circumstances (see Matrimonial Causes Act 1973, s 24). In *Hammond v Mitchell* [1991] 1 WLR 1127 at 1129, Waite J summarized the particular property law difficulties facing unmarried cohabitees when their relationship breaks down. Of the couple in that case ('a married man of 40 separated from his wife' and 'a Bunny Girl employed at a high salary by the Playboy Club in Mayfair') his Lordship observed:

> Had they been married, the issue of ownership would scarcely have been relevant, because the law these days when dealing with the financial consequences of divorce adopts a forward-looking perspective in which questions of ownership yield to the higher demands of . . . the needs of each, the first consideration given to the welfare of children. Since the couple did not marry, none of that flexibility is available to them, except a limited power to direct capital provision for their children. In general, their financial rights have to be worked out according to their strict entitlements in equity, a process which is anything but forward-looking and involves, on the contrary, a painfully detailed retrospect.

His Lordship paints a bleak scene (made all the more so by statistics which show that non-marital cohabitation is on the increase—see (1990) 20 FLR 442). And after his promotion to the Court of Appeal, he added one or two more clouds to the scene when he opined, at the beginning of his judgment in *Midland Bank plc v Cooke* [1995] 4 All ER 562, that 'the rights of married occupiers can be equally problematic... when the claims of third parties such as creditors or mortgagees become involved'. Thus the Civil Partnership Act 2004, which recently confers marriage-like property rights on civil partnerships (defined as registered relationships between two people 'of the same sex') does not confer a regime of perfectly protected property rights.

***Midland Bank plc v Cooke* [1995] 4 All ER 562, Court of Appeal**

Waite LJ:

> Equity has traditionally been a system which matches established principle to the demands of social change. The mass diffusion of home ownership has been one of the most striking social changes of our own time. The present case is typical of hundreds, perhaps even thousands, of others. When people, especially young people, agree to share their lives in joint homes they do so on a basis of mutual trust and in the expectation that their relationship will endure. Despite the efforts that have been made by many responsible bodies to counsel prospective co-habitants as to the risks of taking shared interests in property without legal advice, it is unrealistic to expect that advice to be followed on a universal scale. For a couple embarking on a serious relationship, discussion of the terms to apply at parting is almost a contradiction of the shared hopes that have brought them together. There will inevitably be numerous couples, married or unmarried, who have no discussion about ownership and who, perhaps advisedly, make no agreement about it. It would be anomalous, against that background, to create a range of home-buyers who were beyond the pale of equity's assistance in formulating a fair presumed basis for the sharing of beneficial title, simply because they had been honest enough to admit that they never gave ownership a thought or reached any agreement about it.

Let us now turn to the law according to which the respective financial rights of the cohabitees, married or unmarried, 'have to be worked out according to their strict entitlements in equity'.

17.2 Problems in defining the trust

In *Drake v Whipp* [1996] 1 FLR 826 Peter Gibson LJ called for clearer use of terminology in cases where one cohabitee asserts a beneficial ownership claim against property vested in the name of another cohabitee. He rejected the suggestion that the distinction between resulting and constructive trusts is a purely semantic one. He pointed out that resulting trusts operate according to the presumed intention of the contributing party, in the absence of rebutting evidence of actual intention, whereas constructive trusts operate according to the common intention of both parties, whether actual or inferred.

? QUESTION 17.1

Which type of informal trust do you think is most suitable to a residential cohabitation situation?

The answer, as we shall discover by the end of the chapter, is that a resulting trust is the best analysis in some cases, but that a constructive trust is the best analysis in others. We shall also discover that a trust will not be the best solution in every case. The doctrine of proprietary estoppel (see 17.4) may have an important role to play.

17.2.1 Resulting trusts

Remind yourself of the two broad categories of resulting trusts identified by Lord Browne-Wilkinson in *Westdeutsche Landesbank Girozentrale v Islington LBC* [1996] 2 WLR 802 (see 16.1).

? QUESTION 17.2

Which category will have particular relevance, do you think, to the context of residential cohabitation?

The first of Lord Browne-Wilkinson's categories (his category (A)), appears to be the most relevant for present purposes. Resulting trusts within the first category are those arising:

> where A makes a voluntary payment to B or pays (wholly or in part) for the purchase of property which is vested either in B alone or in the joint names of A and B, there is a presumption that A did not intend to make a gift to B: the money or property is held on trust for A (if he is the sole provider of the money) or in the case of a joint purchase by A and B in shares proportionate to their contributions.

Applying this *dictum* to the characters A and B in our cohabitation scenario, it appears that A (who claims an interest in land owned by B) might be able to establish an interest under a resulting trust by paying (wholly or in part) for the purchase of the land which is vested in B's name alone. Lord Browne-Wilkinson explains his reasoning: 'there is a presumption that A did not intend to make a gift to B' and that B's conscience is so affected that B cannot deny his position of trust in relation to A, always supposing that B was aware of the relevant facts giving rise to the trust. It is important to appreciate that the resulting trust arising where B acquires property in the name of A, arises at the moment of purchase and not later, hence it is sometimes referred to as a purchase money resulting trust (*Curley v Parkes* [2004] EWCA Civ 1515, Court of Appeal).

Note, incidentally, that the Court of Appeal has confirmed that placing property in the joint names of A and B does not of itself amount to an express declaration of trust (*Springette v Defoe* [1992] 2 FCR 561).

17.2.1.1 Section 60(3) of the Law of Property Act 1925

This section provides that on 'a voluntary conveyance a resulting trust for the grantor shall not be implied merely by reason that the property is not expressed to be conveyed for the use or benefit of the grantee'. Does this mean that the presumption of a resulting trust in Lord Browne-Wilkinson's category (A) does not apply to land? His Lordship has said himself that this is 'arguable' (*Tinsley v Milligan* [1993] 3 All ER 65), and Russell LJ has suggested that it is 'debatable' (*Hodgson v Marks* [1971] Ch 892). However, the statute describes s 60 as a section concerning the 'abolition of technicalities in regard to conveyances and deeds', so it could also be argued that s 60(3) is merely a word-saving provision that is not intended to alter the law in any substantive way; its purpose being simply to save the grantor the trouble of stating expressly that his conveyance is intended to be for the benefit of the grantee. In *Lohia v Lohia*, 7 July 2000 (unreported) Judge Nicholas Strauss QC considered the arguments on both sides and concluded that the subsection has removed the presumption of a resulting trust on the voluntary conveyance of land, but does not deny the possibility that a resulting trust may be implied in the case of a voluntary conveyance, provided such implied resulting trust is not to be based 'merely' upon the absence of express words confirming that the grantee is to take beneficially.

17.2.2 Constructive trusts

The facts of the leading House of Lords case, *Lloyds Bank v Rosset* [1991] 1 AC 107, are fairly typical. Mr Rosset had received a loan to buy a derelict house on the understanding that the house should be in his name alone. Mrs Rosset did a limited amount of work towards the renovation of the house, in particular she helped with the interior decorations. However, the vast bulk of the work was carried out by contractors employed and paid for by the husband. Following matrimonial problems, the husband left home, leaving his wife and children in the premises. The loan which the husband had taken out was not, in the event, repaid. Consequently, the bank brought proceedings for possession. The husband raised no defence to that action, but the wife did resist. She claimed to have a beneficial interest in the house under a trust. The House of Lords held that, to succeed, Mrs Rosset would have to show that there had been some 'agreement' (evidenced by express discussions between herself and her husband) that they were to share the property beneficially in equity. In the absence of evidence of such an agreement, a trust would not arise in her favour unless she had made direct contributions to the purchase price or mortgage repayments. P Clarke, 'The Family Home: Intention and Agreement' [1992] Family Law 72, 73 suggested that Lord Bridge's analysis in this case is 'showing signs, it appears, of becoming the new orthodoxy'.

EXERCISE 17.1

Read the extract from the speech of Lord Bridge of Harwich in *Lloyds Bank v Rosset* [1991] 1 AC 107 reproduced below. What does his Lordship say about resulting trusts?

Lloyds Bank v Rosset **[1991] 1 AC 107, House of Lords**

Lord Bridge of Harwich:

> The first and fundamental question which must always be resolved is whether, independently of any inference to be drawn from the conduct of the parties in the course of sharing the house as their home and managing their joint affairs, there has at any time prior to acquisition, or exceptionally at some later date, been any agreement, arrangement or understanding reached between them that the property is to be shared beneficially. The finding of an agreement or arrangement

> to share in this sense can only, I think, be based on evidence of express discussions between the partners, however imperfectly remembered and however imprecise their terms may have been. Once a finding to this effect is made it will only be necessary for the partner asserting a claim to a beneficial interest against the partner entitled to the legal estate to show that he or she acted to his or her detriment or significantly altered his or her position in reliance on the agreement in order to give rise to a constructive trust or a proprietary estoppel.
>
> In sharp contrast with this situation is the very different one where there is no evidence to support a finding of an agreement or arrangement to share, however reasonable it might have been for the parties to reach such an arrangement if they had applied their minds to the question, and where the court must rely entirely on the conduct of the parties both as the basis from which to infer a common intention to share the property beneficially and as the conduct relied on to give rise to a constructive trust. In this situation direct contributions to the purchase price by the partner who is not the legal owner, whether initially or by payment of mortgage instalments, will readily justify the inference necessary to the creation of a constructive trust. But, as I read the authorities, it is at least extremely doubtful whether anything less will do.
>
> The leading cases in your Lordships' House are *Pettitt v Pettitt* [1970] AC 777 and *Gissing v Gissing* [1971] AC 866. Both demonstrate situations in the second category to which I have referred and their Lordships discuss at great length the difficulties to which these situations give rise.

The key part of Lord Bridge's speech is the distinction he draws between two very different bases on which A might successfully claim a beneficial interest against the legal owner, B. Lord Bridge had very little to say about purchase money resulting trusts (that is, those within Lord Browne-Wilkinson's category (A)). Instead, Lord Bridge seemed content to use constructive trusts (and maybe proprietary estoppel) to satisfy the beneficial ownership claims of non-owning cohabitees.

It is important to note that although the payment of mortgage instalments is presumed to give rise to an interest, this will only be the case where the mortgage was an acquisition mortgage. Thus in *McKenzie v McKenzie* [2003] EWHC 601 (Ch), where Mr McKenzie senior re-mortgaged his land, his son, who helped pay off the instalments, failed to acquire a beneficial share in it.

17.2.3 Express agreement plus detrimental reliance

In **Chapter 4** we noted that the courts are, in theory, reluctant to hold that an express trust has been created on the basis of 'loose conversations' (see *Jones v Lock* at 4.3.2). Cases where the courts have recognized express trusts on the basis of such conversations are exceptional (see, for example, *Paul v Constance* at 4.3.2). It might come as something of a surprise to discover that Lord Bridge is prepared to recognize a constructive trust on the basis of 'any agreement, arrangement or understanding . . . that the property is to be shared beneficially . . . based on evidence of express discussions between the partners, however imperfectly remembered and however imprecise their terms may have been'.

? QUESTION 17.3

Do you think Lord Bridge is being over-generous?

The criteria laid down by Lord Bridge for the recognition of trusts of this sort are not particularly stringent and the danger is that they will encourage the fanciful recollection of discussions that never in fact existed. However, the potential for injustice to a bank, such as Lloyds, may not be statistically significant. Even where there has been an agreement between the cohabitees, it will only bind the bank where the agreement was concluded before the bank took the mortgage. And before taking the mortgage the bank, like any purchaser, should have carried out a prudent search for evidence of any such pre-existing agreement by making an inquiry into the rights of all occupiers of the land.

In short, Lord Bridge's first basis for a constructive trust appears to have the twin merits of conceptual clarity and practical utility. However, before we ascribe the status and force of statute to this 'new orthodoxy', we should look at the defining ingredients more closely.

17.2.3.1 'Express'

In *Springette v Defoe* [1992] 2 FCR 561, Court of Appeal, Dillon LJ confirmed that '[i]t is not enough to establish a common intention which is sufficient to found an implied or constructive trust of land that each of them happened at the same time to have been thinking on the same lines in his or her uncommunicated thoughts'.

In *Grant v Edwards* [1986] Ch 638, the defendant explained that if he were to place the claimant's name on the legal title, it would prejudice matrimonial proceedings pending between her and her estranged husband. In *Eves v Eves* [1975] 1 WLR 1338 the defendant told the claimant that the only reason why the property was to be acquired in his name alone was because she was under 21 and that, but for her age, he would have had the house put into their joint names. Lord Bridge (in *Rosset*) held that *Grant v Edwards* and *Eves v Eves* were cases decided on the basis of an express agreement plus detrimental reliance thereon.

The case of *Grant v Edwards* is particularly intriguing because in that case the only expressed intention was the defendant's intention not to give the claimant any interest in the property. To get from these words to an understanding that the claimant should have an interest in the property could only have been achieved by inferring that those words had an actual meaning contrary to their apparent meaning. As Nourse LJ put it, in *Grant v Edwards*: 'these facts raise a clear inference that there was an understanding . . . otherwise no excuse for not putting her name onto the title would have been needed'.

Simon Gardner has criticized this type of reasoning. He says, '[i]f I give an excuse for rejecting an invitation to what I expect to be dull party, it does not mean that I thereby agree to come: on the contrary, it means that I do not agree to come, but for one reason or another I find it hard to say outright'. ('Rethinking Family Property' (1993) 109 LQR 263 at 265.)

The case of *Rowe v Prance* [1999] 2 FLR 787 illustrates how different can be the law's response to trusts of personal property. On facts otherwise reminiscent of *Grant v Edwards*, the cohabitees bought a boat to live on. The man paid for it but frequently stated that the boat belonged to them both. His explanation ('excuse') for not registering the woman as joint owner was that she did not possess 'a relevant certificate'. The court held that he had constituted himself an express trustee of the boat for himself and the woman in equal shares. Surely *Grant v Edwards* would likewise have been disposed of as a case of express trust had it not been for the fomality requirements in relation to express trusts of land (see 3.2).

17.2.3.2 'Agreement'

Lord Bridge described it as an 'agreement, arrangement or understanding reached between them that the property is to be shared beneficially'. Lord Diplock in *Gissing v Gissing* [1971] AC 866 called it a 'transaction between the trustee and the *cestui que trust*'. For the agreement, arrangement or understanding to found a constructive trust it must be an agreement, arrangement or understanding that the non-legal owner should get a beneficial interest in the land. In a recent case a husband and wife contributed their common fund of money to the purchase of a house for the husband's mother. When the husband's mother died the wife (then divorced) sought to claim a share in the house. She failed because, although the husband and wife would together have been entitled to a beneficial interest in the house, it was perfectly consistent with the nature of their joint venture for the husband to get the entire beneficial ownership of his mother's house and for the wife merely to get the use of the house (*Buggs v Buggs* [2003] EWHC 1538 (Ch)). However, it is not necessary that the agreement should contain a consensus as to the size of the parties' respective shares under the trust (*per* Peter Gibson LJ in *Drake v Whipp* [1996] 1 FLR 826). Nor is it necessary for there to have been an actual subjective agreement, as cases like *Grant v Edwards* and *Eves v Eves* show.

The date of the agreement will usually be prior to or concurrent with the financial outlay of the claimant, but Fox LJ in *Burns v Burns* held that, even where 'initially, there was no intention that the claimant should have any interest in the property, circumstances may subsequently arise from which the intention to confer an equitable interest upon the claimant may arise (for example, the discharge of a mortgage or the effecting of capital improvements to the house at his or her expense)'. Lord Bridge in *Rosset* also accepted that the agreement between the parties need not be established prior to acquisition, but may occur 'exceptionally at some later date'.

The discovery of an agreement between the parties can appear to be somewhat convenient. It may also be value-laden. Simon Gardner (*op cit*) has described the law regarding the discovery of a common understanding as being 'very far from neutral'. He continues:

> Its basic proclivity is towards finding an understanding and so a trust, because its approach is not very literal: the necessary understanding can be inferred on the basis of quite remotely extrinsic material. But this proclivity extends only to cases where the woman's input has been essentially financial; otherwise, she is left unaided.

It only takes one more small step for the cynic to ask why agreement should create trusts at all! It is, after all, rather unorthodox to make consensus prerequisite to the creation of a trust. Trusts are generally created in accordance with the unilateral intentions of one party and constructive trusts are typically imposed by courts against the intentions of the legal owner.

? QUESTION 17.4

Why have the courts deemed it necessary to prove a common understanding to establish a constructive trust?

The answer is, of course, that proof of agreement is proof that B's conscience is affected, and it is because B's conscience is affected by A's claim that B is made a constructive trustee for the benefit of A.

17.2.3.3 'Detrimental reliance'

In *Grant v Edwards* [1986] Ch 638, Browne-Wilkinson V-C approved the decision in *Midland v Dobson* [1986] 1 FLR 171 that 'mere common intention is not by itself enough: the claimant has also to prove that she has acted to her detriment in the reasonable belief by so acting she was acquiring a beneficial interest'.

> **? QUESTION 17.5**
>
> Imagine that you are a woman who has lived for 15 years with the legal owner of your quasi-matrimonial home. You have borne him two children and given up a promising career to bring them up, on the express understanding that you would have a half beneficial share in the house. Can you see any difficulties you might face in showing that you have relied to your detriment upon your common understanding?

There are two main obstacles. The first is showing that you have suffered any detriment at all as a consequence of the arrangement. On one (deliberately overstated) view you have been liberated from the need to work, you have benefited from the joys of children and you have lived rent-free for 15 years in someone else's house. The second obstacle you will face, assuming you can show that you have suffered a detriment, is to prove that the detriment was suffered as a result of (that is, was causally connected to) the arrangement.

In *Grant v Edwards* the Vice-Chancellor was alert to these obstacles when he held that 'setting up house together, having a baby and making payments to general housekeeping expenses . . . may all be referable to the mutual love and affection of the parties and not specifically referable to the claimant's belief that she has an interest in the house'. However, in granting the claimant a half interest in the house in that case their Lordships decided that Mrs Grant had acted to her detriment. In so holding, Nourse LJ described detrimental reliance as 'conduct on which the woman could not reasonably be expected to embark unless she was to have an interest in the home'.

17.2.4 Direct financial contributions

This is Lord Bridge's second basis for acknowledging a cohabitation constructive trust. It exists in stark contrast to the first basis (that is, express agreement plus detrimental reliance) because it proceeds on the assumption that there is no evidence of any express agreement whatsoever. In other words, in establishing a constructive trust on the second basis the court must infer a common intention on the basis of the conduct of the parties and nothing more.

QUESTION 17.6

Imagine that you are a woman who has lived for 15 years with the legal owner of your quasi-matrimonial home. You have borne him two children and you gave up work to bring them up. There was no express agreement of any sort in relation to your ownership of the house. Do you think that an agreement should be inferred from your conduct?

No doubt you think that it should, and yet the courts have been happy to explain such behaviour on other grounds ('mutual love and affection', etc). In *Rosset* Lord Bridge held that:

> direct contributions to the purchase price by the partner who is not the legal owner, whether initially or by payment of mortgage instalments, will readily justify the inference necessary to the creation of a constructive trust. But, as I read the authorities, it is at least extremely doubtful whether anything less will do.

Lord Bridge cited *Grant v Edwards* as a case in which the woman's conduct would not have been sufficient to create a constructive trust in her favour. (Mrs Grant contributed to general household expenses, provided housekeeping and brought up the children.)

17.2.4.1 Direct financial contributions to purchase price

It is uncontroversial that direct financial contributions to the purchase price of the land, whether made initially (by way of deposit at the contract stage or money provided on completion of the purchase) or subsequently by payment of mortgage instalments, will 'readily justify the inference necessary to the creation of a constructive trust' (Lord Bridge in *Rosset*).

17.2.4.2 Subsequent expenditure on improving the land

Improvements are not a contribution to purchase, so it is not clear that they will be a sufficient basis on which to recognize a constructive trust within Lord Bridge's analysis. It may be that they should be dealt with by proprietary estoppel where the legal owner acquiesces in the non-owner's expenditure (see 17.4).

In the case of married couples, s 37 of the Matrimonial Proceedings and Property Act 1970 applies. That section provides that where a spouse makes a substantial contribution in money or money's worth to the improvement of property in which either or both have a beneficial interest, the spouse will get a share or enlarged share in the property unless there is any express or implied agreement to the contrary. The share will be that which has been agreed or, in the absence of agreement, whatever would be fair. (This provision applies to engaged couples by virtue of the Law Reform (Miscellaneous Provisions) Act 1970, s 2(1).) Lord Denning MR was also of the view that s 37 was declaratory of the previous law, and should therefore extend to cover engaged couples (*Davis v Vale* [1971] 2 All ER 1021), although there is little other support for this view.

The fact that an interest under s 37 is subject to contrary agreement caused the claim in *Thomas v Fuller-Brown* [1988] FLR 237 to fail. The improvements in that case had been very substantial, but the court held that they had been made in return for rent-free accommodation, rather than for any interest in the house itself.

EXERCISE 17.2

Write down one or two typical ways in which land is improved by financial expenditure.

You might have written down any number of things, including landscaping a garden, building an extension, adding a conservatory. Lesser activities, such as repainting the outside of a house, will probably not be substantial enough. An activity such as having new double glazing fitted would be on the borderline, depending upon the expense involved. Further, whether expenditure is 'substantial' or not ought logically to depend upon the level of the expenditure relative to the value of the property that has been improved.

So, apart from the case of married and engaged couples, it remains controversial whether subsequent improvements to property will suffice to raise the inference of an agreement thereby to acquire a beneficial interest in the property. However, where there is evidence of a special agreement that calculation of the parties' respective beneficial shares should be left until such time as the property ceased to be theirs, substantial improvements carried out by the parties will be relevant to the quantification of their interests (*Passee v Passee* [1988] 1 FLR 263, Court of Appeal). As to quantification generally, see 17.3.

17.2.5 Indirect financial contributions

Lord Bridge, in *Rosset*, thought it extremely doubtful that such contributions would suffice to raise the inference of a common understanding to grant a beneficial interest.

QUESTION 17.7

Can you think of any form of expenditure that might qualify as an indirect financial contribution?

The classic example is where one partner pays the mortgage instalments and the other pays the household bills, in circumstances in which neither partner could afford to do both without the assistance of the other.

EXERCISE 17.3

Consider the following extract from *Gissing v Gissing* [1971] AC 866. What did Lord Diplock have to say about indirect financial contributions?

Gissing v Gissing [1971] AC 866, House of Lords

Lord Diplock:

> It may be no more than a matter of convenience which spouse pays particular household accounts, particularly when both are earning, and if the wife goes out to work and devotes part of her earnings or uses her private income to meet joint expenses of the household which would otherwise be met by the husband, so as to enable him to pay the mortgage instalments out of his moneys, this would be consistent with and might be corroborative of an original common intention that she should share in the beneficial interest in the matrimonial home and that her payments of other household expenses were intended by both spouses to be treated as including a contribution by the wife to the purchase price of the matrimonial home . . .
>
> Where in any of the circumstances described above contributions, direct or indirect, have been made to the mortgage instalments by the spouse into whose name the matrimonial home has not been conveyed, and the court can infer from their conduct a common intention that the contributing spouse should be entitled to *some* beneficial interest in the matrimonial home, what effect is to be given to that intention if there is no evidence that they in fact reached any express agreement as to what the respective share of each spouse should be?
>
> . . . In such a case the court must first do its best to discover from the conduct of the spouses whether any inference can reasonably be drawn as to the probable common understanding about the amount of the share of the contributing spouse on which each must have acted in doing what each did, even though that understanding was never expressly stated by one spouse to the other or even consciously formulated in words by either of them independently. It is only if no such inference can be drawn that the court is driven to apply as a rule of law, and not as an inference of fact, the maxim 'equality is equity', and to hold that the beneficial interest belongs to the spouses in equal shares.

Lord Denning MR in *Falconer v Falconer* [1970] 3 All ER 449 confirmed the then orthodox view (it might now have been supplanted by Lord Bridge's 'new orthodoxy') that indirect financial contributions referable to the purchase price will suffice to raise the inference necessary to establish a constructive trust. There he suggested that contributions: 'may be indirect as where both go out to work and one pays the housekeeping and the other the mortgage instalments . . . so long as there is a *substantial financial contribution* towards the family expenses it raises the inference of a trust' (emphasis added). As we shall see in the next section, Lord Denning did not confine himself to this orthodox approach in every case that came before him.

17.2.5.1 Lord Denning's 'new-model' constructive trust

In the light of doubt that has been cast upon indirect financial contributions by *Rosset*, one would have thought it virtually impossible to infer the requisite common intention from indirect non-financial contributions. English law's refusal to acknowledge community of property certainly stands like an impassable wall before development in this direction. It would take a highly unorthodox judge with an instinctive desire for *ad hoc* justice to climb that wall, break it up or attempt to walk around it (whatever may be the correct metaphor). In Lord Denning MR England had such a judge.

In *Hussey v Palmer* [1972] 3 All ER 744 Lord Denning held that the cohabitation constructive trust '. . . is a trust imposed by the law whenever justice and good conscience require it. It is a liberal process, founded on large principles of equity, to be applied in cases where the defendant cannot conscientiously keep the property for himself alone but ought to allow another to have the property or a share in it'.

In *Cooke v Head* [1972] 2 All ER 38 the house was in the name of the man, and he paid the deposit, but the woman contributed to mortgage repayments and helped physically to demolish old buildings (the court held that she 'did quite an unusual amount of work for a woman'). She was held to have a one-third interest in the property, her work having been taken into account. Had only her direct financial contribution been taken into account, she would have been entitled to only one-twelth of the value of the property under the constructive trust.

It is clear from these decisions, and the facts of *Cooke v Head* in particular, that Lord Denning's 'new-model' constructive trust represented a radical innovation in the law. For a few years at least, English law inferred the common intention necessary to establish a constructive trust on the basis of indirect non-financial contributions. The only higher 'authority' for this approach is the following *dictum* taken from the speech of Lord Diplock in *Gissing*:

> A resulting, implied or constructive trust—and it is unneccessary for present purposes to distinguish between these three classes of trusts—is created whenever the trustee has so conducted himself that it would be inequitable to deny the *cestui que trust* a beneficial interest in the land acquired. And he will be held so to have conducted himself if by his words or conduct he has induced the *cestui que trust* to act to his own detriment in the belief that by so acting he was acquiring a beneficial interest in the land.

Lord Denning MR relied upon this *dictum* when formulating his 'new-model' constructive trust in *Eves v Eves* [1975] 3 All ER 768. The woman in that case had moved in with a married man, took his name, but never married him. The reason he gave for leaving her name off the title deeds was the fact that she was under the age of 21. She did not make a financial contribution but she did housework and gardening and looked after him and their children. Lord Denning held that 'a few years ago . . . equity would not have helped her. But things have altered now. Equity is not past the age of child bearing. One of her latest progeny is a constructive trust of a new model. Lord Diplock brought it into the world and we have nourished it'.

EXERCISE 17.4

Remind yourself of the content of Lord Diplock's speech in *Gissing v Gissing*. Is it entirely consistent with Lord Denning's new formulation?

It would appear not. As we have already noted, Lord Diplock made it fairly clear that direct or indirect contributions must be financial. He refers repeatedly to contributions 'to the mortgage instalments'. Certainly he provides no example of a situation in which non-financial contributions might suffice.

The reasoning underlying Lord Denning's new model was not followed by the differently constituted Court of Appeal in *Burns v Burns* [1984] 1 All ER 244. Their Lordships' judgments in *Burns v Burns* displayed a return to *Gissing v Gissing* orthodoxy. While Fox LJ accepted that the 'basis of such a claim . . . is that it would be inequitable for the holder of the legal estate to deny the claimant's right to a beneficial interest', his Lordship went on to say that, in the absence of either an express declaration of trust, an express agreement to share or a direct financial contribution, it is necessary to infer that the parties had the requisite common intention:

> In determining whether such common intention exists it is, normally, the intention of the parties when the property was purchased that is important . . . it seems to me that at the time of the acquisition of the house nothing occurred between the parties to raise an equity which would prevent the defendant denying the plaintiff's claim. She provided no money for the purchase; she assumed no liability in respect of the mortgage; there was no understanding or arrangement that the plaintiff would go out to work to assist with the family finances; the defendant did nothing to lead her to change her position in the belief that she would have an interest in the house. It is true that she contemplated living with the defendant in the house and, no doubt, that she would do housekeeping and look after the children. But those facts do not carry with them any implication of a common intention that the plaintiff should have any interest in the house.

The Court of Appeal in *Burns v Burns* [1984] Ch 317 confirmed that indirect financial contributions will suffice if 'referable to the acquisition of property'. *Burns v Burns* was strongly endorsed by the House of Lords in *Winkworth v Edward Baron Development* [1987] 1 All ER 114.

The move away from Lord Denning's liberal approach is now pretty much complete. In *Springette v Defoe* in 1992 Dillon LJ stated that 'the court does not, as yet, sit under a palm tree to exercise a general discretion to do what the man in the street, on a general overview of the case, might regard as fair'. Having said that, Lord Denning did much to develop another broad equitable concept, that of proprietary estoppel. His judgments in relation to that concept continue to exert great influence (see 17.4).

? QUESTION 17.8

As a man or woman in the street, do you think that the orthodox rules on 'qualifying contributions' are fair, or apt to create injustice?

Simon Gardner in *An Introduction to the Law of Trusts*, Clarendon Press (1990) suggests, at p 238, that 'the position of the law regarding the discovery of a common understanding—and so of the constructive trust itself—is very far from neutral'. He argues that there are two major concerns to counter the social imbalance against women in respect of ownership of family assets. The first is based on the idea of the family as a communal entity: 'The argument is that it is adventitious that the man undertakes the income-generating work which enables him to acquire assets, while she undertakes domestic functions; both roles are equally essential to the success of the family as a whole'. The second is based on an unjust enrichment which should be addressed: in that where the woman is earning money herself, 'her earnings are . . . more likely to be spent on fungibles (food, clothes, etc), which are wasting assets at best, while the man's go, in particular, to buying the house, with its capital appreciation'. Gardner submits that the law's orthodox 'referability rules' redress the second kind of imbalance, but not the first. This, he submits, means that help is withheld where it is most needed. (See, further, Simon Gardner, 'Rethinking Family Property' (1993) 109 LQR 263.)

17.3 Quantification of the interest under the trust

Arguably it is in relation to the quantification of A's entitlement that the need to distinguish between resulting and constructive trusts is most important. In *Drake v Whipp* [1996] 1 FLR 826 the Court of Appeal stressed the importance of distinguishing between resulting and constructive trusts. In this case A and B purchased property which was conveyed into B's name alone. A had contributed 40 per cent of the original cost and a small proportion of the extensive conversion work subsequently undertaken on the property. The Court of Appeal held that she was entitled to a one-third share under a constructive trust. Under a resulting trust A would have been entitled only to one-fifth of the value of the converted house.

The correct date at which to quantify A's interest in the property of which B is legal owner is the date when A's interest is realised, in other words, the date when the joint residence is sold, or when B buys out A's interest.

17.3.1 Resulting trust

As the judgment in *Drake v Whipp* illustrates, the quantification of the parties' respective beneficial entitlements under a resulting trust is determined by the extent of their respective financial contributions. It is a fairly mechanical calculus. Whatever each party puts in will 'jump back' to them under the resulting trust.

Springette v Defoe [1992] 2 FCR 561 was described by Dillon LJ, who sat in the case, as 'yet another . . . in which it falls to the court to decide the proportions of the beneficial interests of a man and a woman, who are not married to each other, in the proceeds of sale of a house which they have acquired in their joint names for the purpose of living together in it'. The reason the issue fell for determination by the court was because there had been no express declaration of the trusts upon which the property was to be held. It was also found as a matter of fact that the parties had not entered into any discussions relating to their respective shares in the property.

Having referred to *Rosset*, Dillon LJ stated that '[s]ince . . . it is clear in the present case that there never was any discussion between the parties about what their respective beneficial interests were to be, they cannot, in my judgment, have had in any relevant sense any common intention to the beneficial ownership . . . The presumption of a resulting trust is not displaced'.

Steyn LJ made the same point very succinctly: '[g]iven that no actual common intention to share the property in equal beneficial shares was established, one is driven back to the equitable principle that the shares are presumed to be in proportion to the contributions'. On that basis, the court calculated Miss Springette's share to be 75 per cent and Mr Defoe's share to be 25 per cent. In arriving at such neat proportions it is clear that the court was prepared to approximate the figures somewhat in order to produce an outcome that could be applied in practice without involving unnecessary accounting complexity.

17.3.2 Constructive trust

The quantification of interests under constructive trusts is first to be determined according to any express agreement made between the parties as to their respective shares. (Or it may be that the parties are not to have shares at all, but have expressly agreed to hold the land as joint tenants in equity (see *Goodman v Gallant* [1986] 2 WLR 236).) Only where there is no such express agreement as to shares will the court quantify the parties' entitlements according to whatever shares the parties can be assumed to have intended. It goes without saying, of course, that this exercise will be necessary in any case where the common intention that A should acquire any beneficial interest at all in land legally owned by B was itself inferred rather than expressed.

In *Midland Bank plc v Cooke and Another* [1995] 4 All ER 562 Waite LJ held that after A has successfully asserted an equitable interest in B's land under a constructive trust, the duty of the judge (in the absence of express evidence of intention) is to determine what proportions the parties must be assumed to have intended for their beneficial ownership. His Lordship held that if there was express agreement as to the parties' respective shares under the trust this concludes the question of quantification. However, his Lordship also stated that 'positive evidence that the parties neither discussed nor intended any agreement as to the proportions of their beneficial interest does not preclude the court, on general equitable principles, from inferring one'. ('Infer' has the same etymological root as 'ferry' and means to 'carry in', so his Lordship is saying that the court can carry into the facts a common understanding between the parties in order to make sense of the parties' conduct and express words). The parties are (in his Lordship's words) entitled to 'equity's assistance in formulating a fair presumed basis for the sharing of the beneficial title' in a case where the parties 'had been honest enough to admit they never gave ownership a thought'.

If agreement is inferred from words or conduct the parties' respective shares will be in whatever proportions the parties can be inferred to have agreed. Only if no agreement as to quantum can be inferred will it be presumed that they were to share equally. (Lord Diplock in *Gissing* noted, in relation to quantification, that if an inference of *fact* is not possible, the court is driven to apply as a rule of *law* the maxim 'equality is equity'.)

? QUESTION 17.9

Imagine that you are a woman who has lived for 15 years with the legal owner of your quasi-matrimonial home. There was no express agreement of any sort in relation to your ownership of the house. You contributed half the initial deposit, but since then you have not been working and have not contributed a penny to the mortgage instalments. However, you have given birth to, and raised, two children and carried out the vast majority of all housework, cooking, shopping and gardening. What should be the extent of your equitable interest in the house?

From your direct financial contribution it can be inferred that at the date of purchase you were to have some beneficial interest in the house. All that remains is to quantify the extent of your interest. In relation to which, there is surely every reason to infer a common understanding that you were to have a half-share in the house. In *Midland Bank plc v Cooke* Waite LJ summarized the task of quantification thus:

> . . . the duty of the judge is to undertake a survey of the whole course of dealing between the parties relevant to their ownership and occupation of the property and their sharing of its burdens

> and advantages. That scrutiny will not confine itself to the limited range of acts of direct contribution of the sort that are needed to found a beneficial interest in the first place. It will take into consideration all conduct which throws light on the question what shares were intended. Only if that search proves inconclusive does the court fall back on the maxim that 'equality is equity'.

The reference in the above *dictum* to 'the whole course of dealing . . . relevant to their ownership *and occupation* of the property' (emphasis added) is particularly significant. It represents a departure from the more narrow approach enshrined in the judgment of the Court of Appeal in *Burns v Burns* [1984] Ch 317, where May LJ held (at 344) that:

> Where . . . the house is bought with the aid of a mortgage, then the court has to assess each party's respective contributions in a broad sense; nevertheless, the court is only entitled to look at the financial contributions, or their real and substantial equivalent, to the acquisition of the house; that the husband may spend his weekends redecorating or laying a patio is neither here nor there, nor is the fact that the woman has spent so much of her time looking after the house, doing the cooking and bringing up the family.

In *Oxley v Hiscock* [2004] EWCA Civ 546, an unmarried couple disputed the extent of their respective entitlements in their shared home, legal title to which was registered in the man's sole name. It was agreed that there had been no express agreement as to their respective shares and the man therefore contended that resulting trust principles should apply, which would give the woman about a one-fifth share based on her contribution to the initial acquisition of the home. At first instance Her Honour Judge Hallon held that in the absence of express agreement the presumption 'equality is equity' should apply, and awarded each party a half-share in the house. The Court of Appeal allowed the appeal. It was held (applying *Midland Bank v Cooke*) that a fair division of the proceeds of sale 'having regard to the whole course of dealing between them in relation to the property' was 60 per cent to H and 40 per cent to O. This approximated an assessment of the parties' total contribution to the current value of the home (being a £60,700 contribution by the man and a £36,300 contribution by the woman). In *Stack v Dowden* [2005] EWCA Civ 857 the Court of Appeal confirmed that this approach to quantification of beneficial shares should also be adopted where legal title to the property is registered in the parties' joint names, although the fact that it has been registered in joint names should be taken into account when having regard 'to the whole course of dealing between them in relation to the property'.

Stack v Dowden [2005] EWCA Civ 857, Court of Appeal (paras 25–26)

Chadwick LJ:

> In *Oxley v Hiscock* I referred ([at] paragraphs [68] and [69]) to the two distinct questions which arise in cases where property had been purchased in the sole name of one of two cohabitees. The first question is whether there was evidence from which to infer a common intention, communicated by each to the other, that each should have a beneficial share in the property. As I have said, in a case (as the present) where the property has been transferred into the joint names of cohabitees, the answer to that question is unlikely to present any difficulty. It can usually be taken for granted that each was intended to have some beneficial interest in the property. Why else was the property transferred into their joint names? But an affirmative answer to the first question

> leads to the second question: 'what is the extent of the parties' respective beneficial interests in the property?'. It was in relation to that question that I said this ([at] paragraph [69]):
>
> 'Again, in many such cases, the answer will be provided by evidence of what they said and did at the time of the acquisition. But, in a case where there is no evidence of any discussion between them as to the amount of the share which each was to have—and even in a case where the evidence is that there was no discussion on that point—the question still requires an answer. It must now be accepted that (at least in this Court and below) the answer is that each is entitled to that share which the court considers fair having regard to the whole course of dealing between them in relation to the property. And, in that context, "the whole course of dealing between them in relation to the property" includes the arrangements which they make from time to time in order to meet the outgoings (mortgage contributions, council tax and utilities, repairs, insurance and housekeeping) which have to be met if they are to live in the property as their home.'
>
> I remain of that view.

17.4 Proprietary estoppel

Judges frequently use the term 'proprietary estoppel' as if it were interchangeable with the term 'constructive trust'. Indeed a clear example of the practice can be found in the seminal speech of Lord Bridge in *Lloyds Bank plc v Rosset*. Another clear example appeared a year later, in *Hammond v Mitchell* [1991] 1 WLR 1127 at 1137B, where Waite J used the terms 'proprietary estoppel' and 'constructive trust' interchangeably without any apparent unease. For a more recent example see *Van Laethem v Brooker* [2005] EWHC 1478 (Ch) Ch D. In this section we shall attempt to determine the meaning of the former term, and its proper relationship to the latter. We will discover that they are not synonymous.

At the start of this chapter, we observed that the formality requirements for the creation of trusts do not affect the creation or operation of resulting, implied or constructive trusts (Law of Property Act 1925, s 53(2)). It is now worth noting that the requirement of writing in relation to *contracts* for the sale of land (Law of Property (Miscellaneous Provisions) Act 1989, s 2) is similar, in that it has no effect upon 'the creation or operation of resulting, implied or constructive trusts' (s 2(5)), which means to say that a failure of contractual formality does not preclude a finding of an informal trust.

There is no mention in those statutory sections of the concept of proprietary estoppel. This is surprising in view of the courts' treatment of the term on a par with the constructive trust, and even more surprising given that the Law Commission Report which preceded the enactment of the 1989 Act suggested (at para 5.4) that proprietary estoppel could be used by the courts to prevent a legal owner from being unjustly enriched where, for example 'a person genuinely believes he has a contract to buy a piece of land and does work on it, to the knowledge of the owner'. In *Yaxley v Gotts* [1999] Ch 162, the Court of Appeal confirmed that the social policy of simplifying conveyancing by means of formal contracts for the sale of land did not necessitate that unconscionable conduct be allowed to prevail. Their Lordships held that the 'constructive trust' exception to the requirement of contractual formality (s 2(5) of the Law of Property (Miscellaneous Provisions) Act 1989) could be taken to embrace any cases of proprietary estoppel which might equally well have been categorized as a case of constructive trust.

The most obvious role for proprietary estoppel is to remedy those cases, not covered by purchase money resulting and constructive trusts, where after the purchase A expends money or labour improving B's property in a way that cannot be shown to be referable to the mortgage instalments or otherwise referable to the purchase price.

17.4.1 The origins of proprietary estoppel

As early as *Wilmot v Barber* (1880) 15 Ch D 96 an attempt was made to lay down the defining ingredients, or '*probanda*', of proprietary estoppel. These *probanda* were reiterated in *Matharu v Matharu* (1994) 68 P & CR 93, at 102, by Roch LJ as being that:

- [A] has made a mistake as to his or her legal rights
- [A] has expended some money or done some act on the faith of that mistaken belief
- [B] must know of the existence of his legal right which is inconsistent with the equity, if it exists
- [B] must know of the other person's mistaken belief as to his or her rights
- [B] must have encouraged [A] in his or her expenditure of money or in doing the other acts on which [A] relies, either directly or by abstaining from asserting his legal right.

Oliver J in *Taylors Fashions Ltd v Liverpool Victoria Trustees Co Ltd* [1982] 1 QB 133, at 154 preferred a 'broad test of whether in the circumstances the conduct complained of is unconscionable without the necessity of forcing those incumbrances into a Procrustean bed constructed from some unalterable criteria'. This more relaxed approach would no doubt have commended itself to Lord Denning MR. In *Crabb v Arun District Council* [1976] Ch 179 Lord Denning MR said:

> The basis of this proprietary estoppel . . . is the interposition of equity. Equity comes in, true to form, to mitigate the rigours of the strict law. The early cases did not speak of it as 'estoppel' they spoke of it as 'raising an equity'. If I may expand what Lord Cairns LC said in *Hughes v Metropolitan Railway Co.* (1877) 2 App Cas 439, 448: 'it is the first principle upon which all courts of equity proceed', that it will prevent a person from insisting on his strict legal rights—whether arising under a contract, or on his title deeds, or by statute—when it would be inequitable for him to do so having regard to the dealings which have taken place between the parties.

The 'dealings' relevant to establishing an estoppel are now taken to be:

- a representation made, or assurance given, by the owner of land (A) to another person B
- to the effect that B would acquire some interest in A's land
- upon which assurance B has quite reasonably relied by act or omission
- in such a way that it would be detrimental to B (and therefore unconscionable of A) if A were subsequently to resile from his representation or assurance and assert his ownership of the land unencumbered by any rights claimed by B.

These elements of estoppel are not to be regarded as entirely distinct from one another. They are frequently compounded or amalgamated on particular sets of facts; the nature of the assurance will often be bound up in the reasonableness of the reliance and the nature of the reliance will often be inseparable from the detriment. This point was forcefully made by Robert Walker

LJ in *Gillett v Holt* [2001] Ch 210, where his Lordship emphasized that 'detriment', is 'not a narrow or technical concept':

> The detriment need not consist of the expenditure of money or other quantifiable financial detriment, so long as it is something substantial. The requirement must be approached as part of a broad enquiry as to whether repudiation of an assurance is or is not unconscionable in all the circumstances. (at p 232)

The facts of *Gillett v Holt* read like a Dickensian novel. (A similar case to *Gillett v Holt* is *Murphy v Burrows* [2004] EWHC 1900 (Ch), involving facts which the judge actually described as 'Dickensian'). Mr Gillett was 12 years old when Mr Holt (then a 38-year-old gentleman farmer) took him under his wing. Mr Gillett left school at the age of 16 at Mr Holt's suggestion and began a long career working on Mr Holt's farm. Mr Gillett's wife and children became in due course a surrogate family to Mr Holt (who had no immediate family of his own), a fact confirmed by Mr Holt's frequent assurances (often in public) that Mr Gillett would one day inherit the farm. However, the relationship between the men eventually cooled and ultimately broke down entirely. Mr Holt wrote Mr Gillett out of his will and Mr Gillett commenced action seeking to establish an interest in the farm under proprietary estoppel, on the basis of Mr Holt's assurances and Mr Gillett's detrimental reliance upon them. The judge at first instance held that Mr Holt's representation could not be considered irrevocable and that in any event Mr Gillett had suffered no detriment in reliance upon them. The Court of Appeal rejected any need to show that the assurance was irrevocable and held that, despite the obvious material benefits of Mr Holt's patronage, it would be detrimental to deny him an interest in the farm because he had forgone the opportunity to educate himself and make alternative provision for his retirement and old age. A most interesting feature is the detriment Mr Gillett was held to have suffered when Mr Holt paid the private school fees of Mr Gillett's eldest son. How is that detrimental one might ask? The answer is that Mr Gillett had another son whom he then felt obliged to educate privately at his own expense!

Gillett v Holt was followed by the Court of Appeal in *Lloyd v Dugdale* [2001] EWCA Civ 1754, where their Lordships confirmed that if the person to whom an assurance is given forsook an opportunity he can be said to have suffered a detriment. So if X declines to take up an advantageous lease of Blueacre because he has been assured a lease of Redacre, the person (Y) giving the assurance may be estopped (assuming he is the owner of Redacre) from denying X's right to a lease of Redacre. Of course it is quite obvious that the positive expenditure of time and effort, even if it involves relatively little financial outlay, will also qualify as detriment for the purpose of establishing an estoppel (see, for example, *Cobbe v Yeomans Row Management Ltd* [2005] EWHC 266 (Ch) Ch D where the claimant successfully went through the process of applying for planning permission to develop land, and the defendant was estopped from taking the entire benefit of the increased value of the land).

Gillett v Holt was also followed in *Century (UK) Limited SA v Clibbery* [2004] EWHC 1870 (Ch), (Transcript). If *Gillett v Holt* belongs in a novel by Charles Dickens, the facts of *Century (UK) Limited SA v Clibbery* would be at home in a novel by Jilly Cooper: a Panamanian company owned and controlled by a racehorse trainer (Mr Allan) sought to recover possession of a substantial eight-bedroomed house in Newmarket from the mother of one of Mr Allan's mistresses. The defendant claimed to have made several hours of video recordings (of horse races) for Mr Allan and carried out other secretarial work and work about the house, as if she were his personal assistant. She claimed that this was in reliance on an expectation that she would be entitled to some interest in the house. The company succeeded in gaining repossession and damages for unpaid rent during the four years in which the defendant had resisted the claim to repossession. Blackburne J noted the argument that 'by living at The Gables Mrs Clibbery lost the opportunity of making other arrangements for her accommodation when she reached retirement age' but held that 'apart from a weekly pension of £175, Mrs Clibbery was unwilling to indicate what further resources she had access to' so that '[o]n the evidence it was quite impossible to assess to what extent (if at all) she had made a sacrifice of this kind'.

Inwards v Baker [1965] 1 All ER 446 is a classic illustration of the facts giving rise to the proprietary estoppel. Baker junior was keen to build himself a bungalow, but he could not afford the price of a vacant site. His father had some spare land. Baker senior said to his son, 'Why don't you build the bungalow on my land and make it a bit bigger?' Baker junior did exactly that, and made the bungalow his permanent home. Baker senior retained legal ownership of the fee simple to the land, and so the house also became Baker senior's property as a matter of law. All was well while both senior and junior were alive, but when senior died his will (made long before the bungalow was built) left the land in question not to Baker junior, but to Inwards. Inwards brought proceedings to recover possession of the bungalow.

The Court of Appeal held that Baker junior [A] had acquired, in equity, a right to occupy the land for life, and that this right was in principle binding against third parties who had notice of the equitable right. Lord Denning MR held that:

> if the owner of land [B] requests another [A], or indeed allows another, to expend money on the land under an expectation created or encouraged by [B] that he will be able to remain there, that raises an equity in [A] such as to entitle him to stay . . . and [quoting *Plimmer's case* (1884) 9 App Cas 699 (PC)] . . . the equity arising from the expenditure on land need not fail 'merely on the ground that the interest to be secured has not been expressly indicated' . . . the court must look at the circumstances in each case to decide in what way the equity can be satisfied.

Dankwerts LJ, concurring with the conclusion of the Master of the Rolls, went on to state that:

> It is not necessary, I think, to imply a promise. It seems to me that this is one of the cases of an equity created by estoppel, or equitable estoppel, as it is sometimes called, by which the person who has made the expenditure is induced by the expectation of obtaining protection, and equity protects him so that an injustice may not be perpetrated.

It is notable that neither Lord Denning MR nor Dankwerts LJ actually defined or named A's equitable interest. In the years following *Inwards v Baker* many judges and commentators assumed, quite understandably, that Baker junior's right was a particular equitable right called a proprietary estoppel. On first reading Dankwerts LJ appears to suggest as much. Upon closer examination, however, it seems that his Lordship was not describing Baker junior's equitable interest as an 'equitable estoppel', but merely stating that his equitable interest had been created by 'equitable estoppel'. The problem with *Inwards v Baker* is that there was never any need to specify the nature of the son's equity because the son never asserted a right but merely defended Inwards's claim. He used his estoppel as a shield, not a sword, so the Court of Appeal was able to satisfy the estoppel by the award of a nebulous, innominate equity. If Inwards had been a purchaser rather than the beneficiary of a will the court might have felt constrained to be more specific about the nature of the son's equitable right.

In *Dodsworth v Dodsworth* (1973) 228 EG 1115, the Court of Appeal was of the opinion that Baker junior had been awarded a life interest, which would have had the knock-on effect of constituting Baker junior a life tenant under a strict settlement trust in accordance with s 1 of the Settled Land Act 1925. (Since the commencement of the Trusts of Land etc. Act 1996 on 1 January 1997 no new strict settlements can be created, and the award of a life interest would today take effect under a new-style 'trust of land'.) However, as the next Question seeks to illustrate, the *Dodsworth* interpretation of the equitable award in *Inwards v Baker* is not the only possible view.

? QUESTION 17.10

Do you think that the equitable interest created by the equitable estoppel in *Inwards v Baker* could have been an interest under a resulting or constructive trust of the sorts considered earlier in this chapter?

An award of a resulting trust is not consistent with the facts of *Inwards v Baker*, for Baker junior did not get back an interest in the land equivalent only to that which he had put in by way of bricks, mortar and labour. On the contrary, he 'sowed' in bricks and mortar and 'reaped' a right to occupy his father's land for as long as he wished.

Perhaps, then, it was a constructive trust? That is a more plausible alternative. It will be recalled that Lord Bridge in *Rosset* held that to establish a constructive trust in land there must be either express agreement coupled with detrimental reliance thereon, or an agreement inferred from direct financial contributions to the purchase of the land. In *Inwards v Baker* the son would probably have qualified for an interest under a constructive trust on the former basis.

If a constructive trust is the remedy deemed to be appropriate to satisfy the proprietary estoppel, the claimant will end up with a trust which will be identical in its operation (if not its creation) to a constructive trust construed directly from the facts (that is, constructive trusts of the *Rosset* type). It is hardly surprising, therefore, that the use of the terms proprietary estoppel and constructive trust have frequently been confused in the courts.

Now it might be asked, why is there such a pressing need to distinguish proprietary estoppel from constructive trusts, if the facts of some cases will justify both conclusions? This is a question that has been debated in the courts and within the legal academy for many years.

Professor David Hayton regards the common intention constructive trust to be indistinguishable from equitable proprietary estoppel (D Hayton, 'Constructive Trusts of Homes—A Bold Approach' (1993) 109 LQR 485). He was responding to an article by Ms Patricia Ferguson ('Constructive Trusts—A Note of Caution' (1993) 109 LQR 114) who takes an opposing view.

Professor Hayton reasons that in both cases the court is involved in essentially the same exercise. It is analysing and assessing the conduct and relationship of (typically) the man and the woman up to the date of the trial to ascertain whether the circumstances make it unconscionable for the legal owner (typically the man) to be allowed to assert his formal 100 per cent ownership. The court then intervenes to alter the formal position and prevent the man's unconscionable retention of full ownership to the extent necessary to protect the woman's detrimental reliance.

Ms Ferguson, on the other hand, contends that a constructive trust must be different from a proprietary estoppel because the former arises independent of the courts' intervention, whereas the latter is merely a remedial jurisdiction, and any proprietary right arising from it is effective only as a result of and subsequent to the courts' order. On her view this leads to substantial evidential differences, there being higher evidentiary requirements in relation to the constructive trust.

Ms Ferguson's argument accords with orthodox constructive trust principles. We observed in the last chapter that in English law the constructive trust is an institution employed by the courts to vindicate pre-existing proprietary entitlements, and that English law does not yet recognize a remedial constructive trust (see, in particular, *Re Sharpe* [1980] 1 WLR 219). Ms Ferguson contends that where a proprietary estoppel is satisfied by means of a court-imposed (hence 'constructive') trust, what one ends up with is a 'remedial constructive trust'. This should be distinguished, she argues, from the genuine constructive trust, which is itself '*a means of creating a proprietary right*' without any need for an estoppel.

In his response to Ms Ferguson's article Professor Hayton confirmed that he accepts entirely that a distinction should be made between institutional and remedial constructive trusts. Nevertheless, he asserts that in many of the cohabitation cases (starting with *Gissing v Gissing*) the court is actually exercising its discretion in recognizing (one might say 'awarding') the constructive trust. In other words, in cases like *Gissing v Gissing* the courts have very often been exercising the sort of remedial jurisdiction that one normally finds in proprietary estoppel cases, but instead of recognizing the estoppel, the courts have described the outcomes in terms of constructive trust.

Some years earlier Sir Christopher Slade, who had sat as a judge of the Chancery Division between 1975 and 1982, urged a similar three-fold distinction: '(1) [I]mplied and resulting trusts arising by virtue of contributions to the cost of acquisition of land; (2) constructive trusts arising by virtue of the doctrine of proprietary estoppel; [and] (3) other cases of constructive trusts'. (*The Informal Creation of Interests in Land*, The Child & Co Oxford Lecture, 2 March 1984.) One cannot help but think that the law would have developed in an altogether more orderly way had Sir Christopher's three-fold division been enunciated in the superior courts. We would surely have had, at the very least, a reasoned explanation for the casual interchange in *Rosset* of the terms constructive trust and proprietary estoppel.

17.4.2 The impact of proprietary estoppel on third parties

The remedial flexibility attaching to proprietary estoppel has the potential to deter third parties from purchasing the land from the legal owner. Where the constructive trust is institutional, the theory is that a purchaser can discover from making a simple inquiry whether or not the legal title is encumbered by any beneficial interest under a trust, and this interest can be overreached by payment of the purchase monies to two trustees (perhaps the legal owner and a friend of the legal owner who has been appointed as a second trustee). Where the legal owner is subject to a proprietary estoppel it will not be clear until a later court hearing whether or not the equitable claimant has a proprietary right or not. It might be that an award of compensatory or restitutionary damages will suffice to satisfy the equity, it may be that nothing short of a conveyance of the legal fee simple will suffice (see *Pascoe v Turner* [1979] 2 All ER 945). Whether or not the ultimate award is proprietary in nature is of fundamental concern to the purchaser, because only proprietary interests will be binding upon him (see *National Provincial Bank v Ainsworth* [1965] AC 1175).

M P Thompson has argued that proprietary estoppels have the effect of introducing uncertainty into conveyancing ((1981) 125 Sol Jo 539).

He submits (at p 540):

> that the operation of proprietary estoppel should be limited to factual situations where money has been expended on the property, as a result of representations made: *Inwards v Baker* [1965] 2 QB 29; *Pascoe v Turner* [1979] 1 WLR 431. At least in this situation, when the fact of expenditure is disclosed to him, the purchaser can be certain that equities have arisen in favour of the person claiming the interest.

He referred approvingly to the judgment of Browne-Wilkinson J in *Re Sharpe (a bankrupt)* [1980] 1 All ER 198, at 204: 'Doing justice to the litigant who actually appears in court by the invention of new principles of law ought not to involve injustice to other persons who are not litigants . . . but whose rights are fundamentally affected by the new principles'.

Practically speaking, the prudent purchaser should probably work on the assumption that the estoppel will be remedied by the award of a constructive trust interest, and should therefore overreach that interest by paying purchase monies to all the trustees (being at least two in number or a trust corporation: s 2 of the Law of Property Act 1925). It would be perverse for a court of equity to award any larger proprietary right (such as the fee simple itself) to the prejudice of an innocent third party purchaser of the legal title.

If the purchaser pays the purchase monies to a sole legal owner this will not overreach any proprietary interest binding on that legal title in the form of a trust, if that is the sort of interest recognized by the court or awarded by the court in satisfaction of the estoppel. It is a moot point whether, in such circumstances, the inchoate (that is, nameless, not yet specific) equity raised by the proprietary estoppel can be registered as a pending land action (see Mark Pawlowski (1997) 141 SJ 64) or is capable of being an overriding interest in registered land where it is held by a person in actual occupation of the land (see s 70(1)(g) of the Land Registration Act 1925).

■ CHAPTER SUMMARY

We have seen that there are three basic situations in which A may successfully claim a beneficial interest under an informal trust of land to which B is legally entitled.

- (Lord Browne-Wilkinson's category (A) resulting trust—from the *Westdeutsche* case) A resulting trust is presumed to arise where A has contributed in whole or in part to the purchase of land which is vested in the name of B (albeit that it may be vested in the joint names of A and B). A resulting trust merely entitles A to an interest in the land equivalent to the proportion A's contribution bore to the whole purchase price. Because of this rigidity, a resulting trust solution will probably not be appropriate where A and B have agreed, expressly or by inference, that A will gain some larger interest in the land in return for A's contributions.
- (Lord Bridge's first basis for establishing a constructive trust—from the *Rosset* case) A constructive trust arises where A and B by express words 'agree' that A is to have a beneficial interest in the land, and A

has acted to her detriment in reliance upon that 'agreement'. In such circumstances B's conscience would be bound by A's claim, making B a constructive trustee for A. This constructive trust may be institutional, if one takes the view that at the date of the court hearing the court is merely vindicating A's existing proprietary right. An alternative view is that the express 'agreement' (it is often just an express representation) raises an estoppel, for where A has relied upon it to A's detriment, it would be unconscionable for B to assert his 100 per cent legal entitlement against A, and B would be estopped from so doing. This proprietary estoppel must be 'fed' (satisfied) by the minimum equitable award capable of achieving justice in all the circumstances (an award that frequently takes the form of a constructive trust). If the estoppel analysis is the correct one, it is clear that in most of the reported cases the courts, when awarding the constructive trust, do not explicitly refer to the estoppel stage. The better approach may be to limit proprietary estoppel to cases where A has effected improvements to the property after, or independently of, acquisition.

- (Lord Bridge's second basis for a constructive trust—from the *Rosset* case) Where there is no express 'agreement', a common intention can be inferred from direct financial contributions to the purchase price (either by way of deposit, other purchase capital or mortgage instalments). It might also be inferred, exceptionally, from later direct financial contributions (for example, building an extension). It might even be possible to infer agreement from indirect financial contributions, so long as they are referable to the purchase price (there are *dicta* in *Gissing v Gissing* (HL) to support this). The advantage of the constructive trust approach to financial contributions, over the resulting trust approach to financial contributions, is that an interest established by the constructive trust method will be quantified not merely at the level of the financial contribution, but at a level necessary to prevent the trustee taking unconscionable advantage of the equitable claimant. Hence a £10,000 contribution to the purchase of a £200,000 house might give rise to a half-share in the house if an agreement to that effect can be inferred from all the facts (including the £10,000 contribution) taken together.

SUMMATIVE ASSESSMENT EXERCISE

online resource centre

Mr and Mrs Brown bought a house for their daughter Jenny to live in during her time as a student at university. The house cost £130,000 and for tax reasons was conveyed into Jenny's sole name. Mr and Mrs Brown paid £30,000 in cash and Jenny took out a mortgage to cover the balance of £100,000. It was understood that Mr and Mrs Brown would make payments into her account each month to cover the mortgage instalments as they fell due. Jenny's only financial outlay was £3,000 to cover stamp duty, the expenses of the purchase, removals and home insurance, but it was understood she would not have to pay a penny thereafter apart from the usual bills for gas, electricity and so forth. After one year of her university course Jenny invited Pete to live with her in the house. Pete is Jenny's long-term boyfriend and he has a steady job. From the moment he moved in, he started to pay the mortgage instalments instead of Mr and Mrs Brown. However, the house remained in Jenny's sole name. Jenny explained that her parents had paid a lot of money towards the house and would not let her put the house in the joint names of her and Pete.

A year later Jenny and Pete split up. Advise the parties as to their likely interests in the house.

FURTHER READING

Bright, S, and McFarlane, B, *'Personal liability in proprietary estoppel'* (2005) Conveyancer and Property Lawyer.

Burles, D, 'Promises, promises—Burns *v* Burns 20 years on' (2003) 33 Fam LJ 834.

Clarke, P, *The Family Home: Intention and Agreement* [1992] Family Law 72.

Dixon, M, 'Resulting and Constructive Trusts of Land: The Mist Descends and Rises' (2005) Conv 79.

Ferguson, P, *Constructive Trusts—A Note of Caution* (1993) 109 LQR 114.

Gardner, S, *Rethinking Family Property* (1993) 109 LQR 263.

Glover, N, and Todd, P, 'The myth of common intention' (1996) 16 Legal Studies 325.

Hayton, D, *Constructive Trusts of Homes—A Bold Approach* (1993) 109 LQR 485.

Law Commission, *Sharing Homes*: A Discussion Paper (2002).

Law Commission, *Transfer of Land: Formalities for Contracts of Sale, etc* Report No 164 (1987).

Montgomery, J, *A Question of Intention?* [1987] Conv 16.

Probert, R, 'Trusts and the Modern Woman: Establishing an Interest in the Family Home' (2001) 13(3) Child and Family Law Quarterly 275–86.

Rotherham, C, 'The property rights of unmarried cohabitees: the case for reform' (2004) Conv 268.

Slade, Sir Christopher, *The Informal Creation of Interests in Land*, The Child & Co Oxford Lecture, [2005] Conv 40 , Jan/Feb, 14–31.

Thompson, M P, 'The obscurity of common intention' [2003] Conv 411.

Note that this chapter has not considered the operation of co-ownership trusts once they have been established, but has focused principally upon the routes to their establishment. To discover more about the operation of co-ownership trusts, it will be necessary to consult a specialist text on land law, such as Roger Sexton's volume in this series.

18 Tracing

OBJECTIVES

By the end of this chapter you should be able to:

1 Distinguish proprietary remedies from personal remedies
2 Identify the limits to common law tracing
3 Apply the rules for tracing in equity into unmixed funds, mixed funds and assets purchased with such funds

18.1 Introduction

We have already considered the extent of trustees' personal liability in an action for compensation or account (see **Chapter 15**). Now we ask, amonst other things, 'what should be done if the action proves worthless in practice because the trustees are impecunious or have been declared bankrupt, and are therefore unable to repay trust monies to the fund?' In such circumstances the beneficiaries may be able to trace the value of their trust property into bank accounts and into assets which have been bought with the trust property. It is important to realize that it is not the precise item of trust property itself which is sought in most cases, but the value of that property.

Tracing is often spoken of as being a remedy in itself—lawyers will refer to the 'tracing remedy'. In fact, this is not strictly accurate. Tracing is a process that leads to the ultimate remedy of recovering misapplied money or property.

It might help to imagine 'tracing' as a form of detective work. Take, for example, the following series of events: first, trustee Tim places trust monies in his private bank account and then, with monies from that account, buys some shares which he transfers to Sam and Sally. Later, Sam sells her shares and gives Tim the cash proceeds of sale, while Sally sells her shares and spends the proceeds on a party for her friends. Finally, Tim uses the money he had received from Sam and some of his own money to purchase a car. Where has the trust property gone?

The answer is far from obvious to the lay observer. It would be very helpful to have contemporaneous memoranda detailing the whereabouts of the trust property at every stage of every transaction, but without such documentary or other evidence it is necessary to rely on the presumptions raised by a number of rules of 'tracing'. It is these rules with which we shall be primarily concerned in this chapter.

The problem posed by the above scenario is not made any simpler by the fact that the cash may have been earning interest, the value of the shares may have changed (indeed, dividends, or a bonus issue, may have been declared on them) and the car may have depreciated in value. Nevertheless, we should be able to conclude with some confidence that, as a piece of detective work, it will be easier to try to trace and recover the 'value' of the original trust assets than to attempt to trace and recover the original trust assets themselves. Generally, this is the aim of tracing. (The process of tracing the original assets as they pass from person to person and place to place is simply referred to as 'following'.)

18.1.1 The artificiality of the distinction between common law and equitable tracing rules

Tracing may take place at common law or in equity, and, for convenience in handling the older authorities, this chapter is divided along those lines. However, it is hoped that in the future it may be possible finally to put aside the artificial distinction between the legal and equitable rules for tracing. As Lord Steyn observed in *Foskett v McKeown* [2000] 2 WLR 1299:

> In truth tracing is a process of identifying assets: it belongs to the realm of evidence. It tells us nothing about legal or equitable rights to the assets traced. In a crystalline analysis Professor Birks (The Necessity of a Unitary Law of Tracing, essay in Making Commercial Law, Essays in Honour of Roy Goode, (1997), pp. 239–258) explained that there is a unified regime for tracing and that 'it allows tracing to be cleanly separated from the business of asserting rights in or in relation to assets successfully traced': at p. 257. Applying this reasoning Professor Birks concludes at p. 258:
>
>> '... that the modern law is equipped with various means of coping with the evidential difficulties which a tracing exercise is bound to encounter. The process of identification thus ceases to be either legal or equitable and becomes, as is fitting, genuinely neutral as to the rights exigible in respect of the assets into which the value in question is traced. The tracing exercise once successfully completed, it can then be asked what rights, if any, the plaintiff can, on his particular facts, assert. It is at that point that it becomes relevant to recall that on some facts those rights will be personal, on others proprietary, on some legal, and on others equitable.'

In *Trustee of the Property of FC Jones and sons (a firm) v Jones* [1996] 3 WLR 703, Court of Appeal, Millett LJ had observed likewise that:

> [t]here is no merit in having distinct and differing rules at law and in equity, given that tracing is neither a right nor a remedy but merely the process by which the plaintiff establishes what has happened to his property. The fact that there are different tracing rules at law and in equity is unfortunate though probably inevitable, but unnecessary differences should not be created where they are not required by the different nature of legal and equitable doctrines and remedies. There is, in my view, even less merit in the present rule which precludes the invocation of the equitable tracing rules to support a common law claim; until that rule is swept away unnecessary obstacles to the development of a rational and coherent law of restitution will remain.

The facts of *Jones v Jones* were that the wife of one of the partners of a bankrupt firm of potato growers placed £11,700 from a joint bank account held in the name of her husband and another partner with brokers to invest in potato futures. When she ultimately realized her investment it was worth £50,760. She placed this sum in a deposit account with 'Raphaels plc'. The judge at first instance held that she had received the money in a fiduciary capacity and was a constructive trustee. It was held on appeal that the defendant was not a constructive trustee. She had neither legal nor equitable title to the property, but was merely the possessor of it. The claimant trustee in bankruptcy had to bring his claim at common law and trace his property into the proceeds of the defendant's dealings, equity had no role to play. The chose in action constituted by the deposit of the trustee's money with the brokers belonged to the trustee, it was not a right to the original deposit, but to the current balance of the account with the brokers. The defendant would be unjustly enriched were she able to retain the monies and the huge profits she had made on them. (See G McMeel, 'Misdirected Funds and Profits' [1997] Nott LJ 90.)

Lord Millett (as he now is) confirmed his objection to the distinction between legal and equitable tracing in the House of Lords in *Foskett* v *McKeown* [2000] 2 WLR 1299:

> Given its nature, there is nothing inherently legal or equitable about the tracing exercise. There is thus no sense in maintaining different rules for tracing at law and in equity. One set of tracing rules is enough . . . There is certainly no logical justification for allowing any distinction between them to produce capricious results in cases of mixed substitutions by insisting on the existence of a fiduciary relationship as a precondition for applying equity's tracing rules. The existence of such a relationship may be relevant to the nature of the claim which the plaintiff can maintain, whether personal or proprietary, but that is a different matter.

His Lordship was speaking *obiter* (he stated that this case was not 'the occasion to explore these matters further'), but despite his earlier belief that the distinction between legal and equitable tracing might be 'inevitable' (see *Jones* v *Jones* above) his Lordship would doubtless remove the distinction at the first opportunity.

18.2 Tracing at common law

18.2.1 General

As long as the distinction between tracing at common law and tracing in equity persists, common law tracing cannot be used to identify assets to be the subject of an equitable claim, and equitable tracing cannot be used to identify assets to be the subject of a common law claim. The significance of this shortcoming is potentially very great, because a common law claim is a personal claim against a person holding, or a person who has held, the property that is traced, whereas a proprietary claim in equity is a claim against the property currently held by the defendant. The latter is unaffected by the defendant's personal insolvency (see 18.3.1).

Common law tracing is possible where the defendant has received the claimant's property and that property still exists in an identifiable form, even if its precise form has changed. In *Banque Belge Pour L'étranger* v *Hambrouck* [1921] 1 KB 321 a cashier stole monies from his employer, paid them into a new bank account, and later made certain withdrawals. He paid some of the money to S, with whom he was living. S then paid these monies into her own deposit account. She spent the majority of the balance of this account. Only £315 remained in

S's account at the date of the court hearing. It was held that the bank was entitled to trace its money. The £315 could be identified as the product of, or substitute for, the original money.

Agip (Africa) Ltd v Jackson [1990] 1 Ch 265, Chancery Division

A senior officer of A Ltd innocently signed a payment order which was then forged and used by a fraudulent accountant in the employ of A Ltd. The accountant took the order to a Tunisian bank, who in turn requested a payment from Lloyds Bank plc, in accordance with the terms of the order. Lloyds Bank then made a payment over to the defendant's account, believing that it would be reimbursed by the recipient's New York bank. In doing so Lloyds took a delivery risk, as the New York bank had not yet opened for business. By the time the plaintiffs had discovered the fraud it was too late to stop the payment; nor could a refund be obtained from the defendants. The defendants claimed that they had acted innocently throughout and that the Tunisian bank, and not the plaintiffs, was entitled to bring the action.

Millett J:

> The common law has always been able to follow a physical asset from one recipient to another. Its ability to follow an asset in the same hands into a changed form was established in *Taylor v Plumer* 3 M & S 562. In following the plaintiff's money into an asset purchased exclusively with it, no distinction is drawn between a chose in action such as the debt of a bank to its customer and any other asset: *In re Diplock* [1948] Ch 465, 519. But it can only follow a physical asset, such as a cheque or its proceeds, from one person to another. It can follow money but not a chose in action. Money can be followed at common law into and out of a bank account and into the hands of a subsequent transferee, provided that it does not cease to be identifiable by being mixed with other money in the bank account derived from some other source. *Banque Belge pour l'Etranger v Hambrouck* [1921] 1 KB 321 . . .
>
> Nothing passed between Tunisia and London but a stream of electrons . . . and accordingly the plaintiff's attempt to trace the money at common law must fail. . . .
>
> There is no difficulty in tracing the plaintiffs' property in equity, which can follow the money as it passed through the accounts of the correspondent banks in New York or, more realistically, follow the chose in action through its transmutation as a direct result of forged instructions from a debt owed by the Banque du Sud to the plaintiffs in Tunis into a debt owed by Lloyds Bank to Baker Oil in London.
>
> The only restriction on the ability of equity to follow assets is the requirement that there must be some fiduciary relationship which permits the assistance of equity to be invoked. The requirement has been widely condemned and depends on authority rather than principle, but the law was settled by *In re Diplock* [1948] Ch 465 . . .

? QUESTION 18.1

In which of the following situations do you think that common law tracing could be used to trace the value of the £10,000 after the particular transaction has occurred? You should derive some guidance from the case of *Agip (Africa) Ltd v Jackson* [1990] 1 Ch 265 (above).

(a) Trustee Tim uses £10,000 of trust monies to purchase £10,000 worth of shares.

(b) Debbie pays £10,000 cash into Gold Bank plc which then transfers £10,000 in cash to Nunnery National Building Society at Debbie's request.

(c) Silver Bank plc transfers £10,000 by telegraphic transfer (think of it as a transfer over the telephone) to Banque Argent SA, France.

(d) X deposits £15,000 worth of krugerrands with Silver Bank plc with the instruction to pass them on to Banque Argent SA. In anticipation of the receipt of the krugerrands from Silver Bank plc, Banque Argent pays out £15,000 worth of krugerrands to Y.

The solutions are as follows.

(a) Tracing at common law would be permitted, because there is a clear transactional link between the original £10,000 and the £10,000 worth of shares. The shares clearly represent the original cash—they are said to be its 'exchange product'. So it can be said that the trust property still exists, but has merely changed its form. This result should come as no surprise. After all, it is precisely the sort of transaction which occurs when a trustee makes a legitimate investment with trust monies. The cash was trust property to begin with and the shares are the same trust property at the end, except that the precise form of the trust property has changed.

(b) Again, there is no difficulty here. This time the cash has changed hands, but it remains in an identifiable form. It does not matter that Debbie may have deposited £10,000 in £10 notes and that the bank might have transferred £10,000 in £50 notes. The property exists in an identifiable form throughout and can be traced through the various transactions. In theory, Debbie could point at the monies at any time and say 'they are mine'. Her trust property is a chose in action (a debt) which is good against the bank and then the building society.

(c) In this scenario common law tracing fails. This is because a telegraphic transfer involves the passing of electrons down a telephone line. The cash has ceased to exist in an identifiable form. The fact that there is £10,000 at one end of the telephone line and £10,000 at the other end will not suffice to permit tracing at common law. An onlooker might say 'there's the £10,000' when it is in the custody of Silver Bank plc, and 'there it is, again', when it reaches Banque Argent SA. However, common law tracing will not be possible, because it was not possible to identify the £10,000 in the intermediate stage. In this respect the common law appears to suffer from a Luddite inability to deal with the technological realities of the commercial world.

(d) In this situation Banque Argent are said to have taken a 'delivery risk'. They have made a payment out of monies before receipt of monies in. Clearly, the two sums of krugerrands must have been distinct. The transfer of krugerrands had yet to arrive when another £15,000 worth of krugerrands were paid out. It would therefore be impossible to identify the krugerrands paid out to Y as being the exchange product of the krugerrands originally held by X. Common law tracing would not be possible in this scenario.

This last example further illustrates the importance attached to identifying the thing itself, even if its form has changed, to trace at common law.

18.2.2 Defences to the common law restitutionary claim

We have so far considered tracing at common law from the point of view of the person attempting to trace their original property to an ultimate fund or asset. Generally, they do not wish to recover their original fund or asset, but wish to recover its value as represented in a new fund or asset which is identifiable as their original property in a new (substitute) form. Now we must put ourselves in the position of the defendant to a common law tracing action.

Suppose that the original owner of certain property claims to be able to identify property currently held by you as being their original property in a new form. What defences might you raise?

You should recall *Lipkin Gorman v Karpnale* [1992] 4 All ER 512 from **Chapter 1**, the facts of the case being that a partner in a firm of solicitors had used monies from his firm's client account to gamble at the 'Playboy Club' casino in London. The casino was the defendant to the action. Two defences to a restitutionary claim based upon common law tracing were identified (if either of these defences can be made out, the 'ultimate' property holder will not have to make restitution to the 'original' property holder, even though the latter had successfully carried out the tracing process).

First, the casino argued that it should not be required to make restitution to the claimant because it had provided consideration for the monies it had received, namely the provision of gambling services. It argued that because it had given consideration it had not been unjustly enriched by the receipt of the client account monies, and therefore should not have to make restitution. The court accepted that the provision of consideration could be a valid defence in certain circumstances, but it would not be so on the facts of the present case.

? QUESTION 18.2

Can you guess why this defence was unsuccessful on this occasion?

The defence did not succeed here because a contract for gambling services is not a legally enforceable contract. Even though consideration had been given it could not be treated as legal consideration and so the casino was held to have been unjustly enriched.

Secondly, the casino argued that if it must be liable to make restitution it should only be liable to make restitution net of winnings which it had paid out to the gambling solicitor. It would be unjust, it argued, to require it to repay all the money that it had received without taking account of the money that it had paid out. This time the court accepted the defence. The casino would be excused having to make restitution, to the extent that the casino had altered its finances in good faith by paying winnings to the solicitor. This has been described as the 'change of position defence'. If this defence develops in the UK in the way that it has developed in other common law jurisdictions it is probable that the defence will succeed only where the activity constituting the 'change of position' (for example, the paying out of winnings), would not have been undertaken had it not been for the receipt by the defendant of the monies which the claimant is seeking to recover.

? QUESTION 18.3

Can you imagine any other scenarios in which the 'change of position' defence might succeed?

One example might be where X receives £20,000 (in good faith) and builds (again, in good faith) a £20,000 swimming pool in his garden. X would not have built the swimming pool had he not received the monies; indeed, he could not have afforded to do so. Tracing might be possible at common law, inasmuch as the swimming pool can be said to represent the £20,000 fund in a new, but identifiable, form. But would it be just to require X to repay the £20,000 cash? Probably not. This sounds like a scenario in which the defence of change of position would succeed. X would say 'I have spent the money in good faith and I would not have done so were it not for the fact that I received the £20,000 in good faith. I have changed my position'. However, X has clearly been unjustly enriched by this process and it seems that the claimant would be entitled to a charge over the property to the extent to which its value has been increased by the swimming pool. So, if a £20,000 swimming pool adds, for example, £15,000 to the market value of the house and garden, the claimant would be entitled to a charge for £15,000 secured on the house and garden.

Having considered these possible defences to a restitutionary claim founded upon a tracing action at common law, it is worth noting that it will not be a defence for the defendant to show that they have disposed of the claimant's property. This is because the claim at common law is a personal claim and not a proprietary one. If the defendant has received, at some stage, my property in an identifiable form, I have a claim against him personally. It does not defeat my claim for the defendant to show at the date of the court hearing that they no longer hold that property. Only if the claim were proprietary would it be essential to show that the defendant still had the property in his hands. We will come to consider this distinction in more detail when we analyse tracing in equity.

18.2.3 Problems for common law tracing

The last section considered defences to the ultimate restitutionary claim brought when the common law tracing process has been successful, but the process itself can sometimes encounter difficulties and not infrequently fails. Some of those difficulties are considered in this section.

18.2.3.1 Mixed funds

It has been said that 'tracing runs into problems when it encounters mixing' (Professor Peter Birks, 'Mixing and Tracing' [1992] CLP 69). This is clear from the most primitive of examples.

Suppose I own a cow and it joins your herd of 1,000 cows. Will I be able to recover my cow if it is unmarked and indistinguishable from the majority of your herd? You now have 1,001 cows and you will have been unjustly enriched if you fail to return my cow. That I have a restitutionary right seems beyond doubt, but tracing my particular cow would appear to be impossible. The tracing process has run into difficulties. A similar problem arises in modern commercial arrangements. Suppose I mistakenly pay £5 into your bank account, the balance of which was previously £1,000. You were aware of my error and have been unjustly enriched to the tune of £5. Again, it is clear that I should be able to establish a restitutionary claim, but how could I possibly trace my £5? It is, after all, indistinguishable from all the other £5s in the account.

In each of the above situations, I am no more able to identify my property than I would be able to point to my share of the 'stream of electrons' passing on a telegraphic transfer. For this reason, common law tracing is not permissible through mixed funds. To trace through mixed funds we must attempt to trace in equity, to which we will shortly turn. It is often said that there is no tracing at common law into mixed funds. This is not true in a case where a fiduciary has mixed his own money with that of his principal. If it were true, a fiduciary could (by the simple expedient of paying his principal's monies into his own current account) escape personal liability at common law for the tort of conversion. (The tort of wrongfully 'converting' another's property to one's own use.) In such a case it is more accurate to say that at common law it is not possible to trace through a mixed account. So common law tracing would fail if monies were withdrawn from a mixed account to buy an item of property.

18.2.3.2 Trust beneficiaries tracing at common law

? QUESTION 18.4

Do you see any conceptual difficulty in permitting beneficiaries under trusts to trace their beneficial entitlements at common law?

There is a difficulty. Beneficiaries, as you will be aware, only have equitable interests and their rights are recognized only in equity. Accordingly, they will not be able to take advantage of the purely common law right to trace.

? QUESTION 18.5

Can you think of any way in which the beneficiaries might be able to take advantage of the common law right to trace?

One solution might be to compel the trustees to trace on behalf of the beneficiaries. The trustees hold the legal title to the trust property and are able to take advantage of legal, as opposed to equitable, rights of action. This will include the common law tracing action. But on what basis could the beneficiaries be entitled to compel the trustees to trace on their behalf?

One argument is that the right to trace is a *chose in action*, in other words, it is a form of property consisting of a right to sue. Because trustees cannot hold any trust property for their own benefit, the benefit of the right to trace at common law must belong, in equity, to the beneficiaries. Accordingly, the beneficiaries are able to enjoy the benefit of that right by compelling the trustees to sue on their behalf. However, the exercise of an exclusively common law right by indirect action in equity would be highly unorthodox. There is authority to suggest, however, that beneficiaries can be subrogated to the trustees' right to sue if the trustees themselves are unwilling to exercise that right (*Parker-Tweedale v Dunbar Bank plc* [1990] 2 All ER 577); in such a case the trustees would be joined as parties to the common law action. However, such an action will only succeed where the trustees do in fact have a common law right to sue.

? QUESTION 18.6

Can you think of a situation where the trustees would not have a right to sue for the recovery of property at common law?

A straightforward example is the situation where the trustees have themselves paid the trust monies away in breach of their trust. The beneficiaries want to recover the monies but may not do so via the trustees because the trustees are not permitted to 'derogate from their grant' to the third party against whom tracing is sought.

In conclusion, the tracing process at common law might not be available to beneficiaries, and even if it is available the process is liable to fail if it encounters a mixed fund. In addition, even if the tracing process is successful in itself, the claimant may fail to establish an ultimate restitutionary right if the defendant can show that he gave innocently consideration for it or changed his position by reason of receipt of the property. Should tracing at common law fail for any of these reasons it may be that the claimant will have more success with a tracing action in equity.

18.3 Equitable tracing

Equitable tracing reaches the parts that tracing at common law does not reach! There are three basic distinctions between the two forms of tracing.

First, the crucial advantage of equitable tracing is the fact that it is possible to trace in equity into mixed funds. This aspect is considered in depth in 18.3.3. Having said that, equitable tracing has its limits (see 18.3.2).

Secondly, another distinction is that beneficiaries under trusts are able to trace directly in equity, whereas they are not able to do so at common law.

Thirdly, the tracing action in equity is against identifiable property in the defendant's hands, whereas the tracing action in common law is against the defendant's general, personal funds. Whereas common law tracing may lead to a personal remedy, tracing in equity can lead to a proprietary remedy. It is to this last point that we now turn our attention.

18.3.1 Advantages of proprietary rights

Successful tracing in equity leads to a right in a thing (be it a bank account or a tangible asset, for example, shares). A right in a thing is known as a proprietary right, or a right *in rem*. This can be contrasted with tracing at common law, which leads to a personal claim against a person holding, or a person who has held, the property that is being traced. However, a proprietary right should not be confused with 'real' rights, such as those established in land law. A 'real' right allows the recovery of specific, one might call it 'original' property, whereas a proprietary right permits recovery of value as represented by original or substitute property or a charge over original or substitute property in the hands of the defendant.

? QUESTION 18.7

Proprietary remedies have certain advantages over personal remedies. Can you think of any?

There are several advantages:

(a) Proprietary claims do not depend for their success upon the personal solvency of the defendant. It does not defeat the proprietary claim to discover that the defendant may owe more money to his various creditors than he can possibly hope to repay from his personal assets, nor does it defeat the proprietary claim if the defendant is declared personally bankrupt on that basis. His personal circumstances are, in theory, irrelevant to the success of the claimant's tracing action in equity. This is by far the most significant advantage of the proprietary claim over the personal claim. This is not to say that a personal claim is useless in the event of a defendant's insolvency, merely that the claimant with only a personal claim will have to join the queue of creditors with personal claims against the bankrupt's estate. If the claimant is able to establish a proprietary right to property in the defendant's hands, the claimant will be able to avoid the queue of creditors. If the claimant's proprietary claim is successful, the property which the claimant is claiming is treated as if it had never become part of the bankrupt's personal estate.

(b) A proprietary claim to property in the defendant's hands has the added advantage that the claimant can recover the property even if it has increased in value. This is so, even if the defendant's shrewd investment was responsible for the increased value of the property. The claimant cannot be said to have been unjustly enriched by a windfall gained at the expense of the defendant's time or know-how, although it might be different if the windfall can be shown to have been acquired at the defendant's financial expense.

As Lord Hoffmann observed in *Foskett v McKeown* (for the facts see 18.3.3.4):

> Mr. Murphy's children, claiming through him, and the trust beneficiaries whose money he used, are entitled to share in the proceeds of the insurance policy in proportion to the value which they respectively contributed to the policy. This is not based upon unjust enrichment except in the most trivial sense of that expression. It is, as my noble and learned friend says, a vindication of proprietary right.

(c) In a proprietary claim, interest accrues from the date that the defendant acquired the property. In contrast, the claimant in a personal action may usually claim the interest only from the date that the defendant's personal liability is established—that is, the date of the court's judgment. Not infrequently the judgment will backdate the account for interest to the date of the writ, but no earlier.

(d) Whereas personal actions may be time-barred under the Limitation Act 1980 either directly or by analogy (see 15.3.3) the Act will usually have no application to a proprietary claim (see 15.3.2.2).

(e) Because the success of a proprietary claim depends upon the continued existence of the property in the defendant's hands it will often be possible to obtain an injunction preventing disposal of the property before the hearing. Such an injunction may be available under s 37(1) of the Supreme Court Act 1981.

> The main strengths of proprietary claims are summarized by the 'Four I's':
>
> **I**nsolvency is no bar to a claim
> **I**ncrease in value can be claimed
> **I**nterest accrues from the date that the defendant acquired the property
> **I**njunction can prevent disposition of property

18.3.2 Limits to equitable tracing

> **EXERCISE** 18.1
>
> As you have progressed in your study of land law and the law of trusts you will have acquired a cumulative understanding of equity and equitable concepts. With this understanding you might be able to think of some ways in which the claimant's ability to trace in equity may be limited. If you have any ideas jot them down and compare them with the following list.

18.3.2.1 Tracing against *bona fide* purchasers for value

It is well established that equitable tracing will not be permitted against a *bona fide* purchaser for value of the legal estate in property, if that purchaser had no notice of the claimant's equitable claim to the property. This is a concept with which you should be very familiar from your study of land law.

Such a purchaser has, by definition, given consideration for the property in their hands, but what if the property is being held by an innocent volunteer—someone who has not given consideration but has received the property without notice of prior equitable claims? This brings us to the next section.

18.3.2.2 Innocent volunteers

When a claimant claims to be able to trace into property held by an innocent volunteer, equity has a dilemma. We have already seen that when property comes to an innocent purchaser without notice of the claimant's rights there is no dilemma, because the presence of the consideration gives the purchaser an unanswerable claim at common law. Innocent volunteers have given no consideration for the property in their hands and can be said to have been unjustly enriched if it can be shown that the property in their possession properly belongs to another. The dilemma is choosing between two innocent parties.

EXERCISE 18.2

Read the following analysis of *Re Diplock* [1948] 1 Ch 465. How was the dilemma resolved in that case?

In *Re Diplock*, Lord Greene MR held that the volunteer should not be treated as strictly as a person standing in a fiduciary relationship to the person with the equitable claim. In fact, he went as far as to equate the equitable burden on the conscience of the volunteer with that of the equitable claimant. The result was that the volunteer did not have to treat the claimant's claim as paramount. The defendant volunteer (the charity in *Re Diplock*) was entitled to assert its own claims on the mixed fund to the extent that it was not unconscionable to do so. Put another way, equitable tracing will not be permitted against innocent volunteers who have mixed their own monies with those of equitable claimants, if it would be inequitable so to permit.

The rationale given in *Re Diplock* for permitting tracing against innocent volunteers was that equitable claimants have 'rights of property' in mixed funds containing their monies and that it would be unconscionable for the innocent volunteer to deny those proprietary rights. Hence the orthodox view is that the claimant must be able to prove that the funds they claim have at some time been held in the nature of property for them. In practical terms this has put on the claimant a requirement to show that the funds they claim have been held, at some stage, by some other person, in a fiduciary capacity. To show, in other words, that some other person has held the funds knowing they belonged to (were the 'property' of) the claimant.

In *Foskett* v *McKeown* the House of Lords confirmed that the rules of tracing 'through a mixed fund' should be distinguished from 'those regulating the position when moneys of one person have been innocently expended on the property of another':

> In the former case (mixing of funds) it is established law that the mixed fund belongs proportionately to those whose moneys were mixed. In the latter case it is equally clear that money expended on maintaining or improving the property of another normally gives rise, at the most, to a proprietary lien to recover the moneys so expended. In certain cases the rules of tracing in such a case may give rise to no proprietary interest at all if to give such interest would be unfair: see *In Re Diplock* [1948] Ch 465, 548.

It is clear from *Re Diplock* that the tracing rules operate less harshly against a wholly innocent volunteer. However, not every volunteer recipient is wholly innocent.

In *Boscawen v Bajwa* [1995] 4 All ER 769, the registered proprietor of a property charged it to a building society and exchanged contracts for the sale of the property to purchasers who had obtained a mortgage offer from a bank. The bank transferred cash to the purchasers' solicitors for the sole purpose of completing the purchase. The purchasers' solicitors transferred the money to the vendor's solicitors who then paid it on to the building society in repayment of the vendor's mortgage arrears. The building society duly discharged the charge and forwarded the title deeds of the property to the vendor's solicitors. However, the sale fell through. Later, the claimant (who was a judgment creditor of the vendor), obtained a charging order absolute against the property. The question was whether the claimant's charge had priority to the equitable claim of the bank.

The Court of Appeal held that, as the bank's money could be traced into the payment to the building society and had been used towards the discharge of the latter's charge, the bank was entitled to a charge on the property by way of subrogation to the rights of the building society to the extent that the money had been used to redeem the charge and in priority to any interest of the claimant. Millett LJ rejected the claimant's claim, based upon *Re Diplock*, that the vendor and the bank had both contributed to the discharge of the building society's charge, and should be entitled to the property in proportion to their contributions, allowing the claimant to assert its charge against the vendor's part. The present case, his Lordship declared, was very different from *Re Diplock*. In that case innocent volunteers had mixed trust monies with their own monies. In the present case the vendor and his solicitors were not innocent volunteers, although it was true that their actions fell short of dishonesty (because the vendor had relied upon the solicitors, and the solicitors had honestly believed that completion was imminent). The vendor must have known that any monies received by his solicitors would represent the balance of the proceeds of sale due *on completion*. He cannot possibly have believed that he could, at one and the same time, retain possession of the property and use and enjoyment of the proceeds of sale. Had he thought of the matter at all, he would have realized that the money was not his to mix with his own and dispose of as he saw fit. This was not wholly innocent behaviour and it followed that the more favourable tracing rules which are available to an innocent volunteer who unconsciously mixes trust money with his own could not be relied upon by the claimant in the present case. Incidentally, in *Boscawen*, Millett J indicated that he thought the defence to an action available after tracing property, whether at law or in equity, should be the 'change of position' formulation suggested by Lord Goff in *Lipkin Gorman* (see 18.2), rather than the 'inequitable' formulation applied in *Re Diplock*.

18.3.2.3 Need for a fiduciary

Equitable tracing will not be possible unless the property has at some stage been held in a fiduciary capacity (*Chase Manhattan Bank v Israel-British Bank (London) Ltd* [1981] 1 Ch 105).

If the property which is being traced is trust property it will readily satisfy this requirement, because the legal title to trust property is by definition always held in a fiduciary capacity. In fact, Professor Birks suggests that a 'proprietary base', and not the presence or absence of a fiduciary is the essence of the claim ('Mixing and Tracing' [1992] CLP 69). In modern commercial settings the presence or absence of fiduciary relationships seems to be an almost random factor, and the concept of what is and what is not a fiduciary relationship is surely too ill-defined to allow the right to trace in equity to turn upon it.

In fact the courts have shown a pragmatic willingness to 'discover' fiduciary relationships where the justice of the case demands that tracing succeed. The *Chase Manhattan* case illustrates this pragmatic approach. There, the claimant bank paid monies to the defendant bank by mistake. The monies had not previously been subject to any trust or fiduciary obligations, but Goulding J held that the conscience of the defendant bank became subject to 'a fiduciary duty' to respect the claimant's proprietary right upon receipt of the claimant's monies.

In *Nesté Oy v Lloyds Bank Plc* [1983] 2 Lloyd's Rep 658 at 666, Bingham J confirmed that 'the receiving of money which consistently with conscience cannot be retained is, in equity, sufficient to raise a trust in favour of the party for whom or on whose account it was received'. (Here his Lordship was actually quoting Story's pre-Judicature Acts *Commentaries on Equity Jurisprudence*.) But Lord Mustill has urged greater restraint in the 'discovery' of fiduciary relationships. In *Re Goldcorp Exchange Ltd* [1994] 3 WLR 199, his Lordship observed that:

> [m]any commercial relationships involve . . . a reliance by one party on the other, and to introduce the whole new dimension into such relationships which would flow from giving them a fiduciary character would . . . have adverse consequences . . . It is possible without misuse of language to say that the customers put faith in the company, and that their trust has not been repaid. But the vocabulary is misleading; high expectations do not necessarily lead to equitable remedies.

18.3.2.4 **Unjust enrichment**

As an alternative to the convenient 'discovery' of fiduciary relationships to trace successfully in equity, a more straightforward solution has been suggested. Namely, that equitable tracing should be permitted whenever a defendant has been 'unjustly enriched' by the claimant's monies. As long ago as 1914, in the case of *Sinclair v Brougham* [1914] AC 398, Lord Dunedin appeared to advocate claims based on unjust enrichment without any need to show that the funds had, at some stage, been held in a fiduciary capacity. However, English law has so far refused to reject fiduciary-based equitable tracing in favour of tracing based on unjust enrichment.

18.3.2.5 **Dissipation and destruction**

Equitable tracing will not be permitted where the claimant's property has been dissipated or destroyed (*Borden (UK) Ltd v Scottish Timber* (1981)). In *Re Diplock* it was held that successful tracing presupposes 'the continued existence of the money either as a separate fund or as part of a mixed fund or as latent in property acquired by means of such a fund. If . . . such continued existence is not established, equity is as helpless as the common law itself'.

This limitation on the right to trace in equity is probably the easiest one to grasp. Because equitable tracing leads to a proprietary claim it depends for its success upon the continued existence of property in the defendant's hands. If the defendant has dissipated or destroyed the property the tracing action must fail. It would be necessary to have recourse to a personal action against the defendant (where possible) to recover the lost value of the property.

EXERCISE 18.3

Briefly list some ways in which the property might be dissipated or destroyed.

Hopefully your examples were not too dramatic; property need not be dissipated and destroyed by explosion or such like. One could, for instance, spend the fund on a holiday, or on a meal for friends. You should now remember the example scenario with which we began this chapter, and be some way nearer to a solution to the problems it raised.

It is also possible to dissipate monies by paying off unsecured debts. This is because the creditor will be a *bona fide* purchaser for value without notice. Using the fund to pay off secured debts produces a very different result: in such a case payment of the debt releases property ('the security for the debt') to which the tracing claim can continue to attach.

EXERCISE 18.4

Would it be fair to permit tracing in equity, even after dissipation, against the general funds of the defendant? Try to list some of the arguments for and against such an approach.

Against such an approach is the fact that the equitable claimant would be given priority over the general creditors of the defendant in the defendant's insolvency. In favour of the approach is the fact that it might be fair in certain situations to allow the claimant to fix a charge or lien over the defendant's property where it would be unjust to allow the defendant to set up the dissipation as a defence. The justice or injustice of permitting dissipation to be set up as a defence might tie-in with the presence or absence of facts which show that the claimant has undergone a 'change of position' in dissipating the property in a way in which he would not have done had he never received the property in the first place.

Whether a general charge would be permitted after dissipation should, perhaps, depend upon whether or not the defendant is solvent. There would appear to be little injustice, with the availability of the defence of change of position, in permitting a charge against the general assets of a solvent defendant where this would cause no prejudice to the defendant's general creditors. Of course, the law instinctively recoils from making its conceptual coherence subject to the factual accident of solvency, but instances of result-led conceptualization are not unknown elsewhere (see, for example, innominate terms in contract law).

In *Space Investments Ltd v Canadian Imperial Bank of Commerce Trust Co (Bahamas) Ltd* [1986] 1 WLR 1072, a bank had deposited trust monies with itself, having been authorized to do so. Lord Templeman stated, *obiter*, that equity might permit beneficiaries to trace their trust property into *all* the assets of the bank by placing a charge over the bank's assets. This approach, it is arguable, runs contrary to the principles of insolvency law in that it has the effect of promoting the equitable claimant to the position of debenture holder with priority over general creditors, but it might achieve fairness in the case of a solvent defendant.

The major obstacles to tracing and claiming in equity are summarized by the mnemonic 'FIDE':

Fiduciary must hold property at some stage
Innocent volunteer recipients of misapplied trust property are not always bound by trust beneficiaries' claims.
Dissipation or destruction of trust property is a absolute bar to a proprietary claim in equity
Equity's Darling: the *bona fide* purchaser of a legal estate without notice of the trust has an unanswerable defence.

18.3.3 Equitable tracing into funds and assets

The rules for equitable tracing vary according to whether the tracing is into mixed funds or unmixed funds and according to whether the funds remain in a bank account or have been used to purchase property.

18.3.3.1 Tracing into unmixed funds in a bank account

Generally, equity follows the law. If I give you £10,000 which you then place in an empty bank account, I can trace into the £10,000 which has been deposited into that account. I can trace in law and in equity, provided that the prerequisites and limits to those respective actions are observed. We have already noted that one of the great advantages of the equitable tracing action in this context is that trust beneficiaries can use it directly.

18.3.3.2 Tracing into assets purchased with unmixed funds

Here, the beneficiaries may recover the original assets or their exchange products. The court will order the person currently holding the property to make restitution to the trustees, who will then hold the property on the original trusts for the beneficiaries. The beneficiaries will, in effect, be entitled to 'adopt' the new asset as if it were an authorized investment.

Further, because equitable tracing is a proprietary claim, the beneficiaries may also claim any increase in the value of the assets and any profits which have been made on the property whilst in the trustees' hands. On the other hand, if the trust property as represented in the current assets has decreased in value the beneficiaries will not wish to adopt the current assets as if they had been obtained by an authorized investment. Instead, the beneficiaries have the option of treating the new assets as security for the full value sought, by taking a charge over the new assets (see *Re Hallett's* (1880) 13 Ch D 696 at 18.3.3.3).

According to Lord Millett in *Foskett v McKeown* (for the facts see 18.3.3.4):

> The simplest case is where a trustee wrongfully misappropriates trust property and uses it exclusively to acquire other property for his own benefit. In such a case the beneficiary is entitled at his option either to assert his beneficial ownership of the proceeds or to bring a personal claim against the trustee for breach of trust and enforce an equitable lien or charge on the proceeds to secure restoration of the trust fund. He will normally exercise the option in the way most advantageous to himself. If the traceable proceeds have increased in value and are worth more than the original asset, he will assert his beneficial ownership and obtain the profit for himself. There is nothing unfair in this. The trustee cannot be permitted to keep any profit resulting from his misappropriation for himself, and his donees cannot obtain a better title than their donor. If the traceable proceeds are worth less than the original asset, it does not usually matter how the beneficiary exercises his option. He will take the whole of the proceeds on either basis. This is why it is not possible to identify the basis on which the claim succeeded in some of the cases.
>
> Both remedies are proprietary and depend on successfully tracing the trust property into its proceeds. A beneficiary's claim against a trustee for breach of trust is a personal claim. It does not entitle him to priority over the trustee's general creditors unless he can trace the trust property into its product and establish a proprietary interest in the proceeds. If the beneficiary is unable to trace the trust property into its proceeds, he still has a personal claim against the trustee, but his claim will be unsecured. The beneficiary's proprietary claims to the trust property or its traceable proceeds can be maintained against the wrongdoer and anyone who derives title from him except a bona fide purchaser for value without notice of the breach of trust. The same rules apply even where there have been numerous successive transactions, so long as the tracing exercise is successful and no bona fide purchaser for value without notice has intervened.

? QUESTION 18.8

How would you advise the beneficiaries of the trust to proceed if their trustee had misappropriated £20,000 from the trust and used the money to purchase:

(a) shares which have risen in value to £40,000?
(b) a new car?

In situation (a) the best advice would be to assert beneficial ownership of the shares as the direct exchange product of the misappropriated monies. This would give the beneficiaries a 'windfall' of £20,000.

In situation (b) the best advice, in the light of the rapid depreciation of new cars, would be to fix the trustee with personal liability to repay the £20,000 and to place a charge over the car to secure the repayment of the £20,000.

18.3.3.3 Tracing the trustee's and the beneficiary's monies into bank accounts containing a mix of monies

If a trustee, or other fiduciary, mixes his own money with that of a beneficiary (whether a beneficiary under an orthodox trust or a beneficiary of the obligations owed by a fiduciary), it will not be possible to trace at common law through the mixed fund that results (see 18.2.3.1). It is, however, possible to trace in equity.

According to *Re Hallett's* (1880) 13 Ch D 696, the beneficiary in such a case will be entitled to a first charge over the mixed fund to the extent of their claim to the fund. In *Re Hallett's* the trustee had died leaving enough money in his mixed bank account to satisfy the beneficiaries, but the trustee's general creditors claimed that they should be entitled to the fund. It was held that the balance in the account must be treated as belonging to the trust, because the trustee will be presumed to have withdrawn his own money first rather than to have withdrawn the trust money in breach of trust. (In the same way that the legal owner of land cannot assert at law that they have trespassed on their own land, a trustee cannot assert that they have done an act improperly which it is open on the facts to find that they have done properly.) This rule against 'improper assertion' appears to share the rationale of the maxim *equity imputes an intention to fulfil an obligation*.

By extension of *Re Hallett's*, a beneficiary will be entitled to trace into the 'lowest intermediate balance' in a mixed bank account. Trust monies will always be deemed to have been withdrawn from the account last (*James Roscoe (Bolton) Ltd v Winder* [1915] 1 Ch 62).

? QUESTION 18.9

What do you think would be the result if the balance in a mixed account was reduced to 'nil' and the trustee later paid £10,000 of their own monies into the account?

You might have thought that the courts would once again assume that the trustee had acted properly and decide that the payment into the account should be treated as a repayment of trust monies. In fact, payments into an account after a nil balance are not to be treated as repayments in of trust monies. This principle was confirmed in *Bishopsgate v Homan* [1994] 3 WLR 1270, one of the cases arising out of the Robert Maxwell scandal. In that case a pension account ended up in credit but the liquidators were not able to trace into those monies on behalf of the pensioners because there had previously been a nil balance in the account (in fact the account had been overdrawn), indicating that all the trust monies must have been paid out at some point. Equitable tracing, as has been said before, depends upon the continued existence of the property in the defendant's hands.

One legal analyst suggests that the presumption that the trustee has withdrawn his own monies first is made on the basis that the trustee has been culpable in mixing the fund in the first place and therefore should be the one who suffers the loss (see Simon Gardner, *An Introduction to the Law of Trusts*, Clarendon Press, Oxford).

However, in *Re Diplock* Lord Greene stated that the principle in *Re Hallett's* could be applied to mixed funds even where the mixing had been effected by an innocent volunteer. He disagreed with the view, adopted by the judge at first instance, that *Re Hallett's* could operate only where the mixing takes place in breach of trust, actual or constructive, or in breach of some other fiduciary relationship. Rather, Lord Greene MR stated that 'equity may operate on the conscience not merely of those who acquire a legal title in breach of some trust, express or constructive, or of some other fiduciary obligation, but of volunteers, provided that as a result of what has gone before some equitable proprietary interest has been created and attaches to the property in the hands of the volunteer'.

18.3.3.4 Tracing into assets purchased with mixed funds of trustees' and beneficiaries' monies

Here, because the assets have been purchased in part with the beneficiaries' monies and in part with the trustees' monies, the beneficiaries cannot claim the assets outright. Such cases are referred to as cases of 'mixed substitution'. This description applies where the substitute assets are purchased using a pre-mixed fund and where funds are mixed for the first time at the moment the 'substitute' assets are purchased.

In *Re Oatway* [1903] 2 Ch 356, the trustee bought shares with a mixed account, comprising his own monies and that of the trust. At the time of the purchase of the shares enough money remained in the account to meet the claims of the trust beneficiaries, but later the balance in the account was dissipated.

? QUESTION 18.10

Were the beneficiaries entitled to a charge on the shares?

It was held that the beneficiaries were entitled to a charge over the shares. However, this result is rather puzzling at first sight. After all, did not *Re Hallett's* decide that the trustee was presumed to withdraw his own money first? In which case, should not the shares in *Re Oatway* have belonged to the trustee? The apparent conflict can be resolved when one recalls the thinking which seems to underpin the decision in *Re Hallett's*, namely that *equity imputes an intention to fulfil an obligation*. It would be entirely in keeping with the maxim to require that the trustee in *Re Oatway* should satisfy the claims of the beneficiaries before setting up a personal claim to the shares. As Ungoed-Thomas J stated in *Re Tilley's WT* [1967] Ch 1179, 'If a trustee mixes trust assets with his own, the onus is on the trustee to distinguish the separate assets and, to the extent that he fails to do so, they belong to the trust'.

A burning question in this area of the law is whether beneficiaries who have successfully traced their property into assets in the hands of the defendant should be able to claim increases in the value of those assets if the assets were bought with a mixed fund.

It had been argued, on the authority of an *obiter* statement of the Master of the Rolls in *Re Hallett's*, that the beneficiaries should be permitted to enforce only the original value of their charge (or 'lien'). For example, suppose that trustee Tam placed £5,000 of trust money in her own account and later purchased a car worth £20,000 with monies from that account. According to *Re Hallett's* the beneficiaries would be entitled to a charge on the security of the car representing their misappropriated funds. The value of the charge would therefore be £5,000. If the car should later prove to be a collectors' item worth £100,000 the *obiter* statement in *Re Hallett's* suggested that the beneficiaries should still be entitled to recover only £5,000.

If you feel an instinctive unease with this approach, you should pause to consider whether you would be happy for a debt secured by a charge (mortgage) on your home to increase in value simply because your home has increased in value. The fixed value charge argument suddenly appears to be more attractive doesn't it? That, of course, is a quite different case, and the arguments against the fixed charge in the case of a trustee who has wrongfully mixed his own monies with those of the trust are quite overwhelming.

Indeed, an argument against the *Re Hallett's* approach appeared as early as the year that case was reported. Williston, in 'The Right to Follow Trust Property when Confused with Other Property' (1880) 2 Harvard Law Journal at p 29, argued that:

> If the trust fund is traceable as having furnished in part the money with which a certain investment was made, and the proportion it formed of the whole money so invested is known or ascertainable, the *cestui que trust* should be allowed to regard the acts of the trustee as done for his benefit, in the same way that he would if all the money so invested had been his; that is, he should be entitled in equity to an undivided share of the property which the trust money contributed... The reason in the one case as in the other is that the trustee cannot be allowed to make a profit from the use of the trust money, and if the property which he wrongfully purchased were held subject only to a lien for the amount invested, any appreciation in value would go to the trustee.

Re Tilley's WT [1967] 1 Ch 1179 was the first modern English authority to cast serious doubt upon the *Re Hallett's* fixed charge approach. It is authority for the recovery, in addition to the original value of the beneficiaries' property, of that proportionate part of the assets which is attributable to the beneficiaries' property. Ungoed-Thomas J stated that 'the beneficiaries are entitled to the property purchased *and any profits* which it produces to the extent to which it has been paid for out of trust moneys... it appears to me, however, that the trust moneys were not in this case so laid out' (emphasis added). On the facts of *Re Tilley's* the trust monies had not actually been 'paid out', strictly speaking, but had been used to reduce the trustee's overdraft at his bank, therefore the statement on this point was *obiter dicta*.

However, this '*pro rata*' solution has now been approved in the House of Lords in *Foskett v McKeown*. Lord Millett stated that:

> Where a trustee wrongfully uses trust money to provide part of the cost of acquiring an asset, the beneficiary is entitled at his option either to claim a proportionate share of the asset or to enforce a lien upon it to secure his personal claim against the trustee for the amount of the misapplied money. It does not matter whether the trustee mixed the trust money with his own in a single fund before using it to acquire the asset, or made separate payments (whether simultaneously or sequentially) out of the differently owned funds to acquire a single asset... The primary rule in regard to a mixed fund, therefore, is that gains and losses are borne by the contributors rateably. The beneficiary's right to elect instead to enforce a lien to obtain repayment is an exception to the primary rule, exercisable where the fund is deficient and the claim is made against the wrongdoer and those claiming through him.

In so stating the rule, his Lordship disapproved the *obiter dictum* of Sir George Jessel MR in *Re Hallett's Estate* (1880) 13 Ch D 696 (at page 709) where the Master of the Rolls appeared to suggest that in the case of a mixed substitution the beneficiary is *confined* to the lien (that is, the charge).

? QUESTION 18.11

Does this *pro rata* solution go far enough?

Arguably not. It might be asked why the trustee should be permitted to retain *any* of the profits made on the 'mixed asset' where they have been responsible for the mixing. This would appear to breach the 'inflexible rule' against allowing a fiduciary to profit from their trust (see 12.2). Certainly, if it can be shown that the trustee or fiduciary could not have obtained the profit 'but for' the use of the beneficiaries' monies in their hands, in other words, if the necessary causal or 'transactional' link can be made out, would the trustee not be profiting from their breach of trust by retaining any part of the profit made on the mixed asset?

On the other hand, if the beneficiaries are permitted to claim *all* profits made on the mixed fund or asset on the basis that the fiduciary must not profit from their breach, this could work great injustice against the fiduciary's general creditors in the event of the fiduciary's insolvency. As so often in this area of the law the formulation of a unified theoretical approach is thwarted by the vastly differing outcomes in solvent and insolvent scenarios.

In *Foskett v McKeown* [1997] 3 All ER 392, the Court of Appeal had to consider whether the claimant could trace into the proceeds of an insurance policy misappropriated funds which had been used to pay part of the insurance premium, and, if so, what they were entitled to recover. M misappropriated money entrusted to him by a number of purchasers for the purchase of land in Portugal. M used some of this money to pay part of the premium on a life insurance policy. However, prior to this, M had by deed divested the beneficial interest in the policy in favour of his three children. M later committed suicide. The claimant, who was one of the prospective purchasers, claimed to be entitled to the proceeds of the policy. The trial judge decided that the purchasers were entitled to 53.46 per cent of the proceeds of the policy. The children appealed, arguing that the purchasers were only entitled to trace their money into the proceeds to the extent they could recover plus interest.

The Court of Appeal held, by a majority, that since M did not have any beneficial interest in the insurance policy at the time the misappropriated money was used to pay the premiums, no resulting or constructive trust could be imposed upon the proceeds of the policy. The purchasers were only entitled to recover the money used to pay for the premiums plus interest.

The Court of Appeal stated that the authorities were against the conclusion that the payment of the premiums meant that the payer became the owner of the policy. Hobhouse LJ suggested that 'it did not follow that if the value of an innocent party's asset has been increased by an amount greater than the expenditure that had been made using trust money that the innocent third party should besides making full restitution account as well for the additional increase in value'.

When this case came for consideration before the House of Lords Lord Browne-Wilkinson stated that:

> The question which arises in this case is whether, for tracing purposes, the payments of the fourth and fifth premiums on a policy which, up to that date, had been the sole property of the children for tracing purposes fall to be treated as analogous to the expenditure of cash on the physical property of another or as analogous to the mixture of moneys in a bank account. If the former analogy is to be preferred, the maximum amount recoverable by the purchasers will be the amount of the fourth and fifth premiums plus interest: if the latter analogy is preferred the children and the other purchasers will share the policy moneys pro rata.

In the Court of Appeal Hobhouse LJ had preferred the analogy of improvement of land, but Lord Browne-Wilkinson (agreeing with Lord Millett's analysis of this point) held that the analogy of monies mixed in an account was the correct one:

> Where a trustee in breach of trust mixes money in his own bank account with trust moneys, the moneys in the account belong to the trustee personally and to the beneficiaries under the trust rateably according to the amounts respectively provided. On a proper analysis, there are 'no moneys in the account' in the sense of physical cash. Immediately before the improper mixture, the trustee had a chose in action being his right against the bank to demand a payment of the credit balance on his account. Immediately after the mixture, the trustee had the same chose in action (i.e., the right of action against the bank) but its value reflected in part the amount of the beneficiaries' moneys wrongly paid in. There is no doubt that in such a case of moneys mixed in a bank account the credit balance on the account belongs to the trustee and the beneficiaries rateably according to their respective contributions.

Lord Millett described the case as a 'textbook example of tracing through mixed substitutions':

> The claimants claim a continuing beneficial interest in the insurance money. Since this represents the product of Mr. Murphy's own money as well as theirs, which Mr. Murphy mingled indistinguishably in a single chose in action, they claim a beneficial interest in a proportionate part of the money only. The transmission of a claimant's property rights from one asset to its traceable proceeds is part of our law of property, not of the law of unjust enrichment. There is no 'unjust factor' to justify restitution (unless 'want of title' be one, which makes the point). The claimant succeeds if at all by virtue of his own title, not to reverse unjust enrichment. Property rights are determined by fixed rules and settled principles. They are not discretionary. They do not depend upon ideas of what is 'fair, just and reasonable.' Such concepts, which in reality mask decisions of legal policy, have no place in the law of property.

18.3.3.5 Tracing into mixed bank accounts containing beneficiary's monies and monies of another trust or innocent volunteer

If a trustee places £10,000 of trust A into a current account which already holds £10,000 of trust B, and later withdraws £10,000 and spends it on a luxury cruise, who can claim the £10,000 left in the account?

Here is equity's traditional dilemma. How should a choice be exercised between two innocent parties? From your land law studies you may recall the maxim of equity that 'where the equities are equal, the first in time prevails'. So, if a legal owner concludes a contract for land with X and then concludes another contract for the same land with Y, X's equitable estate contract will prevail (subject to the need to protect it by registration) because it was established first in time. This rule of 'first in time, first in right' is a rule of convenience. It is dispute-resolution at its crudest. A different rule of convenience exists which is designed to produce a solution to the problem of the competing claims of A and B to the residue of the mixed fund in the scenario with which we began this section. It is called the rule in *Clayton's Case* and was developed to deal with similar problems which frequently occur in the banking world. The rule is designed to allocate the balance of an account when there have been a number of payments in and payments out of the account and will not be applied to scenarios other than those involving simple, current accounts. The rule is that the first payment into the account is deemed to correspond to the first payment out of the account. Ironically, then, this rule of convenience achieves the opposite result to the maxim 'first in time, first in right'. The balance of a bank account will belong to the persons who made the most recent payments into it, so bringing about the result that the 'last in time is first in right'.

? QUESTION 18.12

If the rule in *Clayton's Case* were applied to the problem of A and B, which of them would be entitled to the £10,000 left in the account?

The answer is that A will be entitled to the balance, because B's money was the first money to be paid into the account and is therefore assumed to be the first money paid out. Does this result seem fair? Can you think of a fairer solution?

The result does not seem at all fair. A rule which was designed to achieve a convenient solution to the complex accounting problems arising where there are numerous and frequent payments into and out of simple bank accounts produces a palpably inequitable result in the context of our representative breach of trust scenario.

A fairer result would have been for A and B to share the balance in the account *pari passu* their contributions. In other words, they should share the balance in proportion to their contributions, which in the case of A and B would mean allocating the balance half and half. This fairer approach was adopted in the case of *Sinclair v Brougham* [1914] AC 398. In that case a building society had been wound up and the question of priority arose between outside creditors, shareholders and depositors. The assets remaining to be distributed could not satisfy all their claims and were divided *pari passu* between the claimants according to the amounts credited to them in the books of the society at the commencement of the winding up. (Note that

Sinclair v Brougham was considered by the House of Lords in the *Westdeutsche* case (see 1.3.7). Their Lordships declined to follow *Sinclair v Brougham*, but in relation to a different point.)

Jessel MR would have approved of this approach. In *Re Hallett's* he described the rule in *Clayton's Case* as 'a very convenient rule, and I have nothing to say against it *unless* there is evidence either of agreement to the contrary or of circumstances from which a contrary intention must be presumed' (emphasis added).

There has also been modern support for a more equitable solution to the problem of cases like that of A and B. In *El Ajou* v *Dollar Land Holdings plc* [1993] 3 All ER 717 it was stated that the rule of convenience (the rule in *Clayton's* Case) must yield to the contrary intentions of the parties involved. Likewise, in *Vaughan v Barlow Clowes* [1992] 4 All ER 22 the Court of Appeal stated that the rule would not be applied if it was contrary to the intentions of the parties; nor if its application would be impractical (it is, after all, a rule 'of convenience'); nor, in fact, if the application of the rule would produce an unjust result (confirmed in *Commerzbank AG v IMB Morgan plc* [2005] 1 Lloyd's LR 298). In other words, even though the rule still exists it has been emasculated and will apply in the future only to resolve otherwise irreducible accounting difficulties, and only then in current bank accounts. In one recent case the judge even suggested that the so-called 'rule' in *Clayton's Case* ought to be known as the 'exception' in *Clayton's Case*! (*Russell-Cooke Trust Co v Prentis* [2002] All ER (D) 22 (Nov), *per* Lindsay J.)

It is worth clarifying that if the fund contains a mixture of the trustee's own money and monies from more than one trust, the courts will first apply the rules in 18.3.3.3 above, for distinguishing between the trustee's and beneficiaries' money. Then, the rules we have just discussed will be applied to ascertain the entitlements of the beneficiaries *inter se*.

Lord Millett in *Foskett v McKeown* had this to say:

> The tracing rules are not the result of any presumption or principle peculiar to equity. They correspond to the common law rules for following into physical mixtures (though the consequences may not be identical). Common to both is the principle that the interests of the wrongdoer who was responsible for the mixing and those who derive title under him otherwise than for value are subordinated to those of innocent contributors. As against the wrongdoer and his successors, the beneficiary is entitled to locate his contribution in any part of the mixture and to subordinate their claims to share in the mixture until his own contribution has been satisfied. This has the effect of giving the beneficiary a lien for his contribution if the mixture is deficient... Innocent contributors, however, must be treated equally *inter se*. Where the beneficiary's claim is in competition with the claims of other innocent contributors, there is no basis upon which any of the claims can be subordinated to any of the others. Where the fund is deficient, the beneficiary is not entitled to enforce a lien for his contributions; all must share rateably in the fund.

CHAPTER SUMMARY

- We have seen that there is a difference between tracing misapplied trust property and actually recovering it. Tracing is the process of following the value of the misapplied trust assets into substitute assets (for example, the value of a coin can be traced into a book acquired with the coin) and since it is merely an evidential process (like detective work) it should not make any difference that the property one is seeking to recover is equitable property under a trust rather than property owned absolutely.

- Tracing having been completed, the ultimate claim the trust beneficiary brings to recover the misapplied trust property is an equitable proprietary claim.
    - A proprietary claim has certain advantages, summarized by the 'Four I's':
        - Insolvency is no bar to a claim
        - Increase in value can be claimed
        - Interest accrues from the date that the defendant acquired the property
        - Injunction can prevent disposition of property.
    - However, the fact that the ultimate proprietary claim is an equitable claim has reflex action on the tracing process leading to the claim, with the result that the courts still refer to 'tracing in equity', when it would be more logical to regard the evidential tracing process as neutral (or 'unitary') that is, having no distinction between equity and law. Because of the equitable nature of the claim, and because the equitable nature of the claim reflects an equitable character upon the tracing, there remain certain obstacles to tracing and claiming in equity. They are summarized by mnemonic 'FIDE':
        - Fiduciary must hold property at some stage
        - Innocent volunteer recipients of misapplied trust property are not always bound by trust beneficiaries' claims.
        - Dissipation or destruction of trust property is an absolute bar to a proprietary claim in equity
        - Equity's Darling: the *bona fide* purchaser of a legal estate without notice of the trust has an unanswerable defence.
- Apart from the problematic 'equitable' label attached to the tracing process, the process itself is a relatively simple and logical one. It is a series of factual presumptions, and the golden rule is that the presumptions always operate in favour of the innocent and against the wrongdoer so far as possible. So if, for example, a trustee misapplies trust money by placing it in his own bank account, it will be presumed thereafter that he spends his own money first and leaves the trust money in his account, unless he uses money in his bank account to purchase a highly profitable asset, in which case he will be presumed to have acquired the asset for the trust.

SUMMATIVE ASSESSMENT EXERCISE

online resource centre

Trevor is a trustee of two trusts, Black's Settlement and White's Settlement, each comprising £50,000 in cash. The trust monies are kept in separate bank accounts. Trevor also has a private bank account in which he holds £100,000. Suppose that the following events take place, in the following order:

- Trevor withdraws all the monies from the Black's Settlement account and places them in his own private account
- Trevor withdraws all the monies from the White's Settlement account and places them in his own private bank account
- Trevor withdraws £100,000 from his own account in order to purchase a piece of fine art
- Trevor withdraws £50,000 from his account and uses the monies to pay off the building society mortgage on his house
- Trevor withdraws the balance of his private account and spends the monies on a luxury world cruise

- Trevor finally pays £10,000 into his private account.

Trevor has just been declared bankrupt. His general creditors claim the work of fine art which is now worth £150,000, and the balance of monies in Trevor's private account. Advise the beneficiaries of the two trusts, who wish to recover the value of their misappropriated funds.

FURTHER READING

Birks, P, 'Establishing a Proprietary Base' [1995] Restitution Law Review 83.

Birks, P, 'Mixing and Tracing: Property and Restitution' (1992) 45 CLP 69.

Birks, P, 'The Necessity of a Unitary Law of Tracing' in *Making Commercial Law: Essays in Honour of Roy Goode* (Oxford: Clarendon Press, 1997) 239.

Matthews, P, 'The Legal and Moral Limits of Common Law Tracing' in P Birks (ed) *Laundering and Tracing* (Oxford: Clarendon Press, 1995) 23.

Matthews, P, '"Specificatio" in the Common Law' (1981) 10 Anglo-American LR 121.

Millett, Sir Peter, 'Tracing the Proceeds of Fraud' (1991) 107 LQR 71.

Pearce, R A, 'A Tracing Paper' (1976) 40 Conv 277.

Smith, L, *Tracing* (Oxford: Clarendon Press, 1998).

Smith, L, 'Tracing in *Taylor v Plumer*: Equity in the Court of King's Bench' [1995] LMCLQ 240.

Thomas, S B, 'Electronic Funds Transfer and Fiduciary Fraud' [2005] JBL 48.

19 The equitable liability of strangers to the trust

OBJECTIVES

By the end of this chapter you should be able to:

1 Explain the rationale behind liability as a constructive trustee due to the 'knowing receipt' of trust property
2 Distinguish 'knowing receipt' from 'inconsistent dealing'
3 Assess the nature of a stranger's liability for dishonestly assisting in (or procuring) a breach of trust
4 Advocate possible reforms of the law in this area

19.1 Introduction

> The equitable doctrine of tracing and the imposition of a constructive trust by reason of the knowing receipt of trust property are governed by different rules and must be kept distinct. Tracing is primarily a means of determining the rights of property, whereas the imposition of a constructive trust creates personal obligations which go beyond mere property rights.
>
> *Per* Sir Robert Megarry V-C in *Re Montagu's Settlement Trusts* [1987] Ch 264.

The above quote usefully ties in the subject matter of this chapter with that of **Chapter 18**, which considered the nature and limits of equitable and common law tracing. Common law tracing is a personal action against the persons who have received the property that is being traced, whether or not they have since parted with that property. Equitable tracing, we noted, is a proprietary claim, a claim to property currently held by the defendant. This chapter looks at other forms of personal liability, whereby 'strangers' may be made liable as if they were trustees because of their behaviour. When this so-called 'constructive trusteeship' is imposed upon them they are treated in many ways as if they were normal deed-appointed trustees. They cannot, for instance, make a profit from their trust.

19.2 'Strangers'

Suppose that trustee Tabitha and trustee Tim hold property on trust for Brenda and Bashir. The trustees appoint and pay a stockbroker to invest certain monies on behalf of the trust. If the stockbroker uses the monies for his own purposes he may be liable, *inter alia*, as a constructive trustee. The stockbroker was a stranger to the trust but became a trustee of the trust property because of the way he behaved in relation to the property subject to the trust.

Of course, this example illustrates that the imposition of personal liability as a constructive trustee may coincide with other liability. For one thing, there is likely to have been a breach of contract by the agent in the above situation for which the agent is liable to be sued by the trustees at common law. One major advantage of the imposition of liability as a constructive trustee is that the beneficiaries are able to take action against the stockbroker in their own capacity. The constructive trustee's personal liability is actionable in equity, giving the beneficiaries, and not just the trustees, a right of action.

With any type of personal action there is a risk that the defendant might be insolvent and unable to meet the judgment debt, but as Moffat has pointed out, the type of 'strangers' who may be held liable are often solvent, indeed affluent, corporations, such as banks and building societies. They are attractive defendants for aggrieved beneficiaries or principals to have within their sights. (Moffat, *Trusts Law Text and Materials* 3rd edn, Butterworths, 1999.)

Any commercial agent in a real dilemma as to the validity of a proposed course of action can apply to the court for a 'binding declaration' that the proposed course of action is proper, or apply for directions as to the best way to proceed. If the declaration is granted and the agent acts according to its terms the agent will effectively be immune to any subsequent action brought by a beneficiary (*Governor and Company of the Bank of Scotland v A Ltd and others* [2001] 1 WLR 751).

Barnes v Addy (1873–74) LR 9 Ch App 244, Court of Appeal in Chancery

Lord Selborne:

> Those who create a trust clothe the trustee with a legal power and control over the trust property, imposing on him a corresponding responsibility. That responsibility may no doubt be extended in equity to others who are not properly trustees, if they are found either making themselves *trustees de son tort*, or actually participating in any fraudulent conduct of the trustee to the injury of the *cestui que trust*. But, on the other hand, strangers are not to be made constructive trustees merely because they act as the agents of trustees in transactions within their legal powers, transactions, perhaps of which a Court of Equity may disapprove, unless those agents receive and become chargeable with some part of the trust property, or unless they assist with knowledge in a dishonest and fraudulent design on the part of the trustees.

19.3 Where tracing fails

In *Agip (Africa) Ltd v Jackson* [1989] 3 WLR 1367 common law tracing failed because money had been transmitted by telegraphic transfer—'nothing passed between Tunisia and London but a stream of electrons'—*per* Millett J. Further, equitable tracing was only partially successful in that case. Millett J stated that 'the tracing claim in equity gives rise to a proprietary remedy which depends on the continued existence of the trust property in the hands of the defendant'. The claimants could trace only into those monies which remained in the hands of the defendants. The judge continued, 'to recover the money which the defendants have paid away the claimants must subject them to a personal liability to account as constructive trustees and prove the requisite degree of knowledge to establish liability'.

The imposition of liability as a constructive trustee is frequently a last resort when tracing has failed. But it is also a remedy that can co-exist with the tracing process and is useful where tracing has been successful only in part.

This chapter examines three major bases for strangers' liability: liability as a 'trustee *de son tort*'; liability for knowing receipt; and liability for dishonest assistance in a breach of trust.

19.4 Trusteeship *de son tort*

> . . . if one, not being a trustee and not having authority from a trustee, takes upon himself to intermeddle with the trust matters or to do acts characteristic of the office of trustee, he may thereby make himself what is called in law a trustee of his own wrong—i.e., a trustee *de son tort*, or, as it is also termed, a constructive trustee (*per* Smith LJ in *Mara v Browne* (1896) 1 Ch 199 at p 209).

It is clear from this *dictum* that strangers who intermeddle in the business of a trust will be taken to have assumed a fiduciary duty to the beneficiaries of that trust. Indeed, they will be treated, for all purposes of liability, as if they had been expressly appointed to trusteeship of the trust. Of course, there would be no liability unless the stranger actually *breaches* the trust they have assumed.

19.5 Knowing receipt

A personal action is available in equity against a stranger to the trust who received trust property which they knew to be fixed with a breach of trust. In such a case, the stranger will be held personally liable as if they were a constructive trustee.

? QUESTION 19.1

Can you think of any circumstances where the personal action would be useful?

This personal action is most useful where the claimant's property cannot be traced or can be traced but has depreciated in value. The disadvantage of this personal action to recover lost value is that, even if judgment is given for the claimant, he will have to 'join the queue' of creditors if the defendant is insolvent. If there are creditors with priority over the claimant, the claimant might be unable to enforce their judgment debt.

> **? QUESTION 19.2**
>
> Suppose that a trustee uses trust monies, together with some of his own monies, to purchase shares as a gift to a favourite nephew. The nephew receives dividends on the shares over a period of two years before passing them on to his daughter as an eighteenth birthday present. In her hands the value of the shares plummets dramatically to the extent that they are nearly worthless. What actions may be open to the beneficiaries?

There is the personal action against the trustee for breach of trust (see **Chapter 15**). However, if judgment against the trustee proves worthless (perhaps because the trustee cannot be traced or has become insolvent) it should be possible to trace the value of the trust property through to the shares held by the daughter. Tracing would have to take place in equity because the shares were bought with a mixed fund. Of course, those shares are now practically worthless. It is at this stage that the lost value of the shares might be recovered from the daughter or the nephew by a personal action against them as constructive trustees. In addition, if it is established that the nephew is liable as a constructive trustee, he will be liable to account to the beneficiaries for some or all of the profits which he made on the shares while they were in his hands. The ultimate success of these personal actions depends in large part upon the personal solvency of the various defendants. If the daughter and nephew are insolvent, or impecunious, a judgment against them will be practically worthless. However, if in the event, it is worth taking action against the defendants, the success or otherwise of the action will depend upon whether the stringent prerequisites to liability as a constructive trustee can be made out. It is to these requirements that we now turn.

19.5.1 'Knowing'

Certain preliminary notes should be made. First, in *Agip (Africa) Ltd v Jackson*, Millett J stated that a recipient would not be liable as a constructive trustee for knowing receipt until they know about the breach of trust. (Recently confirmed in *Papamichael v National Westminster Bank plc* [2003] 1 Lloyd's Rep 341, 375 and *Criterion Properties plc v Stratford UK Properties LLC* [2003] 1 WLR 2108.) So, if a stranger receives trust property but does not find out that it was fixed with a breach of trust until a later date, the stranger will not be liable as a constructive trustee of the property until that later date. Secondly, it is clear that a stranger will not be taken to have knowledge 'of a fact he once knew but has genuinely forgotten'—*per* Megarry V-C, *Re Montagu's ST* [1987] Ch 264.

Knowledge that a trust is being claimed in litigation is generally insufficient to found liability. In *Carl Zeiss Stiftung v Herbert Smith & Co* [1969] 2 Ch 276, an action was brought against one of the United Kingdom's largest solicitors' firms alleging that fees which the firm had received from a West German company comprised property which the West German company held in trust for an East German company. Both of the German companies had been involved in litigation to decide which was entitled to the property. The Court of Appeal held that the solicitors' firm had actual knowledge of the claim made by the East German company, but knowledge of a claim that a trust existed was not enough to found liability as a constructive trustee (in that case liability was sought on the basis of knowing assistance (dishonest assistance as it is now)—but the same principle applies to knowing receipt).

Carl Zeiss was considered in *United Mizrahi Bank Ltd v Doherty* [1998] 2 All ER 230. There the judge accepted that it could not be right for solicitors to be looking over their shoulders when acting for a defendant in a suit for breach of trust. However, the learned judge stopped short of sanctioning in advance an act by the defendant solicitors which would allow them to take their own fees out of the monies claimed by the claimant. The solicitors would have to take the risk (albeit not very great) that the defendants might lose and the solicitors be found liable for knowing receipt of trust monies applied in breach of trust.

One of the more complex aspects of fixing liability on a stranger for knowing receipt of trust property is ascertaining the degree of knowledge that is required to give rise to liability. Is it essential that the stranger actually knew that they were in receipt of property which has come to them directly or indirectly by reason of a breach of trust? Or, is it sufficient that they 'turned a blind eye to the obvious', or even that they should have been suspicious?

Does a stranger, a bank for example, have to play detective in searching for evidence of fraud and money laundering in relation to monies it has received? Few would doubt that the bank should be liable if it had actual knowledge that the monies had come its way in breach of trust, but the difficult question is 'what degree of constructive knowledge should be sufficient to found liability as a constructive trustee'? This question will be addressed in the following sections.

19.5.1.1 The *Baden* categories

According to Peter Gibson J in *Baden v Société Générale* [1983] BCLC 325 knowledge is of five types.

(a) actual knowledge;
(b) wilfully shutting one's eyes to the obvious. This is sometimes referred to as 'Nelsonian blindness'—with allusion to the famous incident at the Battle of Copenhagen when Admiral Lord Nelson was reputed to have placed a spyglass to his blind eye, to avoid reading a signal calling him back from engagement with the Danish fleet. In recent cases it has been referred to as 'blind-eye knowledge' (*Credit Suisse (Monaco) SA v Attar* [2004] EWHC 374; *Manifest Shipping Co v Uni-Polaris Shipping Co* [2003] 1 AC 469, House of Lords). In the *Manifest Shipping* case Lord Clyde held that such knowledge requires 'a conscious reason for blinding the eye. There must be at least a suspicion of a truth about which you do not want to know and which you refuse to investigate';
(c) wilfully and recklessly failing to make such enquiries as an honest and reasonable man would make;
(d) knowledge of circumstances which would indicate the facts to an honest or reasonable man;
(e) knowledge of circumstances which would have put an honest and reasonable man on enquiry.

Of these five categories of knowledge, types (1), (2) and (3) can be loosely grouped together as 'naughty knowledge', while types (4) and (5) being 'constructive' forms of knowledge are more consistent with an innocent state of mind. Having said that, the reference to the 'honest' and 'reasonable' man in types (4) and (5) seems to import, or assume, an element of good faith.

19.5.1.2 Applying the *Baden* categories

For the purpose of fixing liability as a constructive trustee for knowing receipt of trust property, it had been thought that knowledge in any of the *Baden* categories would suffice. However, more recently there has been support for a more restrictive approach. In *Re Montagu's ST* Megarry V-C held that only types (1), (2) and (3) would suffice. In summarizing his findings the Vice-Chancellor doubted that *Baden* types (4) and (5) would suffice because, he stated, 'I cannot see that the carelessness involved will normally amount to want of probity'. For Megarry V-C there needed to be some evidence of bad faith on the stranger's part before the stranger would be held liable as a constructive trustee.

He further held that constructive notice as applied in property actions should not be applied to personal actions where it is sought to fix liability as a constructive trustee:

> It seems to me that one must be careful about applying to constructive trusts either the accepted concepts of notice or any analogy to them . . . [t]he rules concerning a purchaser without notice seem to me to provide little guidance on this and to be liable to be misleading.

To add further complication to this area, Vinelott J in *Eagle Trust Plc v SBC Securities Ltd* [1992] 4 All ER 488 expressed the view that liability based upon constructive knowledge of the *Baden* types (4) and (5) would be inappropriate to commercial transactions because the basis of commercial transactions should be trust and not suspicion (a view which receives support in the case of *Cowan de Groot v Eagle Trust plc* [1992] 4 All ER 700).

The courts had become preoccupied with the *Baden* categories and with questions about their precise relevance to different factual contexts. More recently, however, a more pragmatic approach has been supported in the Court of Appeal. Scott LJ in *Polly Peck International Plc v Nadir and others (No 2)* [1992] 4 All ER 769 pointed out that the *Baden* categories are not 'rigid categories with clear and precise boundaries. One category may merge imperceptibly into another'. For Scott LJ the real question is whether the stranger should have been suspicious. This pragmatic, less rigid approach was again adopted by the Court of Appeal in *Bank of Credit and Commerce International (Overseas) Ltd v Akindele* [2001] Ch 437, where their Lordships held that it need not be established that the defendant had acted dishonestly, but merely that his conscience was affected by what he knew. (Compare *Royal Brunei v Tan* (see 19.6).)

It is not every suspicion that should be entertained. Certainly a bank should be slow to refuse a deposit into a customer's account. In *Tayeb v HSBC Bank Plc* [2004] EWHC 1529, the court reminded banks that the proper way to respond to concerns about money laundering is to apply to court for a declaration of interim directions. That case concerned the transfer on 21 September 2000 of £944,114.23 to an account recently opened by a Libyan businessman at a Derby branch of the HSBC. The bank manager suspected money laundering which in the circumstances was a perfectly reasonable suspicion but his unreasonable response (as the court found it) was to send the money back to the transferring bank. In fact the transfer was perfectly legitimate and the claimant was awarded judgment debt in the sum of £944,114.23 with interest from 21 September 2000. The judge held that the anti-money laundering procedures to which banks are subject 'do not necessarily lead to the bank having to disengage from the transfer and they certainly do not normally involve the retransfer to the payor, a course which would be most unlikely to protect the rightful beneficiary of the fund and which might well involve tipping off those criminally responsible' and 'If banks are to be entitled to depart from their contracts with customers, on the basis of suspicion of unlawfulness and of general banking practice, that practice has to be clearly proved'. Of course, whether the court would have been quite so censorious had the bank followed the same course exactly one year later ('post 9–11') may be doubted.

19.5.2 'Receipt'

In *Agip (Africa) Ltd v Jackson* the judge at first instance, Millett J, stated that 'the recipient must have received the property for his own use and benefit'. The Court of Appeal in that case did not expressly deal with the issue. This raises the question whether a bank, which holds monies in an account into which monies had been placed by a trustee in breach of trust, will be liable as a constructive trustee for 'knowing receipt'.

? QUESTION 19.3

Do you think that when a bank receives a deposit of monies it has received those monies for its 'own use and benefit'?

Millett J decided that the answer depends upon whether the bank placed the monies in an account in reduction of an overdraft or whether the bank merely acted as a conduit for the monies. In the former case there is, his Lordship suggested, beneficial receipt, while in the latter there is not. A cynic might argue that any time a bank receives monies for whatever purpose it benefits from the receipt, or will use the monies for its own benefit. Indeed the receipt of monies to increase the credit balance of an account might actually be of greater benefit to a bank than the reduction of an overdraft. However, his Lordship argued that this apparently technical distinction was 'essential if receipt-based liability is to be properly confined to those cases where the receipt is relevant to the loss'.

It is not enough to establish the requisite degree of knowledge and the fact of beneficial receipt. It must also be shown that what is being received is, indeed, trust property.

? QUESTION 19.4

If a trustee divulges confidential information about the trust to a stranger, could the stranger be made a constructive trustee of that information and any profits made with it?

Nowadays, with the development of the law of patents and copyright and increased recognition of intellectual property there is strong support for the view that a monopoly of knowledge can be protected like property. However, there is little authority for treating information held by trustees in their official capacity as being property *per se*. The possibility was touched upon briefly in the House of Lords' decision in *Boardman v Phipps*. Lord Cohen stated that information held by a fiduciary was not property 'in the strictest sense of the word'. However, his Lordship held the fiduciary liable to account for profits which he had made with information gained in his fiduciary capacity. Information may not be property 'in the strictest sense', but in *some* sense it is.

19.5.3 Inconsistent dealing

A stranger might be liable as a constructive trustee for 'inconsistent dealing' with trust property. This category of liability is closely related to 'knowing receipt', as they have in common the receipt of trust property by a stranger, but there are also clear factual differences.

? QUESTION 19.5

Suppose trustees appoint an agent and transfer trust property to that agent within the terms of their trust, and that agent receives the trust property lawfully and not for his own benefit. Could the agent be liable as a constructive trustee for 'knowing receipt' if he later sells the trust property and in a moment of impetuosity gambles the proceeds at a casino and loses it all?

No, there are two important factors missing. First, there had been no original breach of trust. Secondly, the agent has been appointed to carry out a task not for his own benefit, but for the benefit of the trust. As we have seen, 'knowing receipt' applies only to strangers who have received property for their own 'use and enjoyment'.

It is fairly clear that an action for 'knowing receipt' would not apply to this scenario, but it is possible that the stranger (the agent) could be liable to account as a constructive trustee on the basis of 'inconsistent dealing' with the trust property.

For a stranger to be fixed with liability for inconsistent dealing they must have known that they had trust property in their hands, but need not have known the precise terms of the trust. The chances are, of course, that very few genuine strangers to the trust would know its precise terms!

It is important, however, that agents are not too readily fixed with liability as constructive trustees. Lord Selborne in *Barnes v Addy* [1874] 9 Ch App 244 stressed the need to protect agents who have acted honestly and within the terms of their agency. If such agents are not protected, persons may in the future be dissuaded from undertaking the role of agent to trusts.

19.6 Dishonest assistance in (or procurement of) a breach of trust

This area of law has been dramatically altered by the decision of the Judicial Committee of the Privy Council in *Royal Brunei Airlines Sdn Bhd v Tan* [1995] 3 WLR 64. It had previously been the law that where a dishonest and fraudulent venture had been undertaken by trustees, or other persons, in a fiduciary position, a stranger might be liable for knowingly assisting in that design.

Now it is clear that the original design of the trustees need not have been dishonest and fraudulent in order for the stranger to be liable as an accessory. On the contrary, the principal breach might have been quite innocently performed. The focus now is upon the accessory's (the stranger's) state of mind, whereas previously, strangers would have been liable only if they had known of the trustees' dishonesty.

Liability under this heading has never been dependent upon the receipt of trust property by the stranger. This is a crucial difference between liability under this head and liability for 'knowing receipt' or 'inconsistent dealing'.

? QUESTION 19.6

Do you detect any conceptual difficulty in creating liability as a constructive trustee for 'dishonest assistance'? (It might help to recall the 'certainties' requirements for trusts.)

If a stranger is fixed with liability as a constructive trustee by reason of their dishonest assistance in a fraudulent design they are a very 'strange' trustee indeed. As Millett J observed in *Agip (Africa) Ltd v Jackson*: 'The basis of the stranger's liability is not receipt of trust property but participation in a fraud'. If the strangers are truly 'trustees', it must be asked, 'what is the trust property to which they hold the legal title?' It may be simple enough, in most cases, to *identify* the trust property, namely the property held on the original trusts (or the property subject to the original fiduciary obligations), but this still begs the question whether the stranger can ever be said to have held or controlled the legal title to that property.

It may be that these unresolved conceptual difficulties are no bad thing as equity seeks flexible tools to rationalize the complex transactional environment of the modern commercial world (S Gardner, 'Knowing Assistance and Knowing Receipt: Taking Stock' (1996) 112 LQR 56).

EXERCISE 19.1

Read the following summary of *Royal Brunei Airlines Sdn Bhd v Philip Tan Kok Ming* [1995] 2 AC 378, Privy Council. Was the imposition of liability as a constructive trustee justified? Can you suggest any alternative remedies for the claimant airline?

***Royal Brunei Airlines Sdn Bhd v Philip Tan Kok Ming* [1995] 2 AC 378, Privy Council**

An insolvent travel agency owed monies (ticket receipts) to the plaintiff airline, and held those monies on an express trust for the airline. The present action was brought against the principal director/shareholder of the travel agency. The plaintiffs sought to fix the defendant with liability as a constructive trustee on the basis of the defendant's knowing assistance in a dishonest and fraudulent design. The 'design' was the use of the airline's monies by the travel agency for its own business purposes in breach of the trust under which those monies were held. It was held that the defendant would be liable on the basis of his dishonest assistance in, or procurement of, the breach of trust. Lord Nicholls observed disapprovingly that courts had restrained themselves within the 'straightjacket' of Lord Selborne's dictum in *Barnes v Addy* (see 19.2 above), with the result that liability for 'knowing assistance' had been confined to cases where the trustee had been dishonest. Lord Nicholls of Birkenhead considered the hypothetical case of an innocent trustee who is deceived into breaching his trust by a dishonest stranger and asked whether it could be right for the stranger to escape liability in such a case. His Lordship's conclusion was that the emphasis should be switched from the state of the trustee's mind to that of the stranger. Liability should not depend upon the *Baden* categories of knowledge (which his Lordship suggested should be forgotten), but upon whether the stranger had himself been dishonest. His Lordship made it clear that whereas dishonesty is a necessary and sufficient ingredient of accessory liability for breach of trust, ' "knowingly" is better avoided as a defining ingredient'. An objective test of dishonesty should be adopted, although his Lordship appeared prepared, in determining 'dishonesty' to consider the stranger's 'personal attributes . . . such as his experience and intelligence, and the reason why he acted as he did'.

We have suggested that the imposition of liability as a constructive trustee is inappropriate where the stranger does not control the trust property. Although the argument still holds good in the typical case of, for example, a solicitor advising a trust, on the peculiar facts of *Tan* the defendant stranger was actually the controlling director and the shareholder of the 'trustee' company. Accordingly, *Tan* itself is one of the few cases in which the stranger could genuinely be said to have been in control of the trustee, who in turn controlled the trust property. Accordingly, the defendant in *Tan* was sufficiently in control of the trust funds to justify the imposition on him of liability as a constructive trustee.

However, would an alternative be to extend tortious liability to cover civil wrongs of this sort? As Professor Peter Birks said some years before *Tan* (in the 1990–91 Butterworth Lectures) 'there is no respectable modern reason why "knowing assistance" should not be regarded as a tort' ('knowing assistance' was, of course, the precursor to the concept of 'dishonest assistance' introduced by *Tan*). Indeed, the similarity between equitable liability for dishonest assistance and tortious liability at common law has grown stronger with the recent acceptance by the House of Lords that the partners of a solicitor liable for dishonest assistance may be held vicariously liable where the acts of dishonest assistance were rendered in the ordinary course of the firm's business (*Dubai Aluminium Co Ltd v Salaam* [2002] 3 WLR 1913, HL).

Unfortunately, the Privy Council in *Tan* omitted to consider the potential of tortious liability as an alternative to liability as a constructive trustee in cases of assistance by strangers in breaches of trust. This omission is all the more surprising given that Lord Nicholls, delivering the opinion of the Judicial Committee of the Privy Council, made express reference to the related tort of procuring a breach of contract. As things stand at present, the tort of procurement of a breach of trust has not yet been acknowledged in the highest courts although Hoffmann LJ in *Law Debenture Corp v Ural Caspian Ltd* [1993] 2 All ER 355 added his support to the recognition of such a tort.

19.6.1 The four requirements for 'dishonest assistance'

The basic four requirements were set out in *Baden* v *Société Générale* [1983] BCLC 325, but they have since been modified by *Tan* (see J Snape and G Watt, 'A position of trust' (1995) 92(28) LSG 20), so they are now as follows:

19.6.1.1 Existence of a trust

It is not necessary to show that a formal trust exists, a fiduciary relationship is sufficient. So, for example, where a director of a company misappropriates company-owned property by passing it to a third party via the medium of the director's private bank account, the director's bank could be liable for dishonest assistance.

19.6.1.2 Breach of the trust

Before *Tan* it had to be shown that a dishonest or fraudulent design existed, and that the trustee or fiduciary had been a party to it. It had to be something more than a mere misfeasance or breach of trust, which, as we have seen from previous chapters, can be committed innocently. Since *Tan* an innocent breach of trust on the part of the principal fiduciary will suffice.

19.6.1.3 Assistance

It has to be shown that there was assistance in the breach of trust. This is a question of fact in each case. There is no requirement for the assistance actually to have caused the loss, but it must have been of more than minimal importance. The 'assistance' requirement could be satisfied by proving that the stranger had been involved in an intermediate step in the process leading to the breach of trust.

Assistance seems to mean some kind of purposive conduct designed to advance and promote the unlawful object which breaches the trust: *Brinks Ltd v Abu-Saleh and others (No 3)* (1995) *The Times*, 23 October. In this case, the claimants had been the object of a huge bullion heist which had been facilitated by the actions of one of its own employees who was in breach of his fiduciary relationship with the claimants. The claimants' case was that Mrs E, as part of the laundering of the proceeds, had accompanied her husband on trips to Zurich, at the instigation of P, one of those convicted of the robbery. The allegation was of accessory liability against Mrs E. Rimer J found as a matter of fact that Mrs E had simply accompanied her husband in the capacity of his wife and that this could not constitute 'assistance' for the purposes of accessory liability.

19.6.1.4 Dishonesty

Even before *Tan*, the view which generally prevailed in the courts was that a stranger must be shown to have had a dishonest intent to be fixed with liability for knowing assistance. As Millett J said in *Agip* at first instance, 'the true distinction is between honesty and dishonesty, and not between various levels of knowledge'.

? QUESTION 19.7

Tan has made the stranger's 'dishonesty' and not that of the principal/trustee/fiduciary, the trigger of liability. Can you think of any justification for this change of emphasis?

Lord Nicholls considered the hypothetical case of a dishonest solicitor who had induced a trustee to misapply trust property in a manner which the trustee honestly believed to be permitted by the terms of his trust, but which the solicitor was fully aware constituted a breach of trust. 'It cannot be right', said his Lordship, 'that in such a case the accessory liability principle would be inapplicable because of the innocence of the trustee'. In the past, the error has been, he said, to make the principal's state of mind a prerequisite to the accessory's liability. The better view is to establish the accessory's 'fault based' liability on the basis of the accessory's own state of mind.

The developments in *Tan* did not represent a wholly novel departure from the existing law, but did bring clarity to the conflicting views expressed in lower courts. Since *Tan* it is clear that dishonesty is a necessary ingredient of liability for 'knowing' assistance (as recently confirmed by the House of Lords in *Twinsectra Ltd v Yardley* [2002] 2 AC 164, which approved Lord Nicholls' analysis in *Tan. Twinsectra* is considered further at 19.6.3, where the definition of dishonesty is considered at some length), which is why the label 'dishonest assistance' is used in this chapter.

In fact, as long ago as 1969, the Court of Appeal had favoured an approach based on the defendant's dishonesty.

Carl Zeiss Stiftung [1969] 2 Ch 276 was a unanimous decision of the Court of Appeal. On the question whether constructive notice or knowledge (the court preferred the neutral term 'cognizance') would suffice to establish liability for knowing assistance, Sachs LJ stated that '[i]t does not . . . seem to me that a stranger is necessarily shown to be both a constructive trustee and liable for a breach of the relevant trusts even if it is established that he has such notice. As at present advised I am inclined to the view that a further element has to be proved, at any rate in a case such as the present one. That element is one of dishonesty or of consciously acting improperly, as opposed to an innocent failure to make what a court may later decide to have been proper inquiry'.

Of further note is the decision of the Court of Appeal in *Polly Peck International plc v Nadir and others (No 2)* [1992] 4 All ER 769. Nadir was the chief executive of Polly Peck. Polly Peck became insolvent and monies owned by it were passed through a bank controlled by Nadir to the Central Bank of the Turkish Republic of North Cyprus. Polly Peck brought an action against the Cypriot Bank on the basis of its knowing receipt of the monies which Nadir had passed on in breach of his fiduciary duty to Polly Peck. Knowing assistance was discussed to clarify its relationship with knowing receipt.

Scott LJ said, 'if liability as a constructive trustee is sought to be imposed . . . on the basis that the defendant has assisted in the misapplication of trust property' (knowing assistance), 'something amounting to dishonesty or want of probity must be shown'.

In *Polly Peck* Hoffmann LJ made an illuminating comparison between the actions for knowing assistance and knowing receipt, and also clarified their common law counterparts. Hoffmann LJ stated that:

> Although both knowing assistance and knowing receipt give rise to the equitable remedy of accountability as a constructive trustee, the two causes of action are very different. Liability for knowing assistance is based upon wrongful conduct, namely knowing participation in a fraudulent breach of trust or fiduciary duty. Its common law analogy is conspiracy to defraud. Liability for knowing receipt is restitutionary, based upon the beneficial receipt of money or property known to belong in equity to somebody else. The equitable remedy depends upon the existence of a trust or fiduciary duty, but the breach of trust or duty need not have been fraudulent. The nearest common law analogy is money had and received.

no more

Subject to the obvious changes following *Tan*, the above statement is still a highly informative comparison between equitable and common law accessory liability.

Any commercial agent (such as a bank) that is in doubt (a real dilemma) as to the propriety of a proposed course of action is well advised to apply to the court under CPR, r 40.20 which provides simply that 'The court may make binding declarations whether or not any other remedy is claimed'. (See also, for interim declaratory relief: CPR, r 25.1(1)(b).)

As Lord Woolf CJ observed in *Governor and Company of the Bank of Scotland v A Ltd and others* [2001] 1 WLR 751:

> ... it seems almost inconceivable that a bank which takes the initiative in seeking the court's guidance should subsequently be held to have acted dishonestly so as to incur accessory liability. The involvement of the court should . . . enable, in the great majority of cases, a practical solution to be determined which protects the interests of the public but allows the interests of a bank to be safeguarded.

19.6.2 The relationship between knowledge and dishonesty in cases of dishonest assistance

In *Tan* their Lordships substituted for the 'knowledge' requirement, a requirement that the accessory be shown to have been 'dishonest'. Lord Nicholls stated that 'their Lordships' overall conclusion is that dishonesty is a necessary ingredient of liability. It is also a sufficient ingredient . . . "Knowingly" is better avoided as a defining ingredient of the principle, and in the context of this principle the *Baden* scale of knowledge is best forgotten'. However, Rimer J in *Brinks v Abu Saleh (No 3)* held that it is still necessary to show that the defendant had knowledge of the existence of a trust fiduciary relationship, or at least of facts giving rise to such a trust. In *Heinl v Jyske Bank (Gibraltar) Ltd* [1999] Lloyd's Rep Bank 511, the Court of Appeal, purporting to follow *Tan*, held that 'dishonesty' means conscious impropriety and should be determined by reference to the third party's actual knowledge of the facts leading to the breach. However, where Lord Nicholls had urged that the *Baden* scale of knowledge should be forgotten, Nourse LJ suggested that the *Baden* scale might still be useful in distinguishing different shades of knowledge.

The reintroduction of a separate ingredient of 'knowledge' is to be resisted not least because chancery lawyers might confuse the concept with 'notice'. It is clear, however, that the knowledge of the defendant is bound to inform the determination of the defendant's honesty or dishonesty. Lord Nicholls himself stated that 'in most situations there is little difficulty in identifying how an honest person would behave . . . an honest person does not participate in a transaction if he *knows* it involves a misapplication of trust assets' (emphasis added).

19.6.3 Defining dishonesty

The test of 'dishonesty' adopted by Lord Nicholls is, he says, 'an objective standard', if a person knowingly appropriates another's property, he will not escape a finding of dishonesty 'simply because he sees nothing wrong in such behaviour'. Having said that, later on in Lord Nicholls' judgment subjective considerations enter into this 'objective test'. He says that 'when called upon to decide whether a person was acting honestly, a court will look at all the circumstances known to the third party at the time. The court will also have regard to the personal attributes of the third party such as his experience and intelligence and the reason why he acted as he did.'

Royal Brunei was followed in *HRT Ltd and others v J Alsford Pension Trustees Ltd and others* (1997) 11(2) TLI 48 (noted in (1997) 6(2) Journal of International Trust and Corporate Planning 83). However, Lindsay J voiced concern in relation to establishing dishonesty in commercial contexts. Lord Nicholls, when attempting to capture 'the flavour' of dishonesty in *Tan*, had approved Knox J in *Cowan de Groot Properties Ltd v Eagle Trust plc* [1992] 4 All ER 700 who had held that dishonesty is evidenced by 'commercially unacceptable conduct in the particular context involved'. Lindsay J in *HRT* suggested that this formulation could be misunderstood:

> It may, for example, be in one sense 'commercially unacceptable' for a bank to lend money without security or without investigating the title to the security it is offered by its borrower. It may thus be 'unacceptable' because too risky, but if the bank chooses to do so because, for example, it genuinely trusts the personal covenant of the borrower or is truly content to rely upon his assertion of his own beneficial title to the security he offers, that may involve conduct which is 'commercially unacceptable', if at all, only in relation to the bank's own position.

The complex question of the meaning of dishonesty in the context of accessory liability for 'dishonest assistance' finally came before the House of Lords in *Twinsectra Ltd v Yardley* [2002] 2 AC 164. Their Lordships held (Lord Millett dissenting) that the test to be applied is a combined subjective/objective test: a defendant will only be held to have been dishonest if it can be shown that *he knew* that ordinary honest people would have considered his actions to have been dishonest. Their Lordships were reluctant to apply a purely objective test when the outcome would be to stigmatize the defendant (often a professional person) as being 'dishonest'. Lord Millett seemed equally concerned to avoid the casual imposition of that stigma, but his solution was to suggest that dishonest assistance should revert to its former description 'knowing assistance', with knowledge being the primary test of dishonesty. He combined this suggestion with his belief that the test for dishonesty should be a purely objective one—the defendant should be measured against an objective standard, albeit allowing that the objective standard against which the defendant is measured may be varied according to the defendant's subjective characteristics (that is, a lower standard should be applied when judging the behaviour of a junior bank clerk than would be applied when judging a senior bank manager). All their Lordships purported to approve and apply the analysis adopted by Lord Nicholls in *Tan* so it may be somewhat surprising that they did not agree in their approach. It is this author's respectful submission that the test adopted by Lord Millett (an objective test appropriate to the subjective characteristics of the defendant) comes closest to that suggested by Lord Nicholls, but the majority were correct to conclude that Lord Nicholls intended to remove 'knowledge' as a defining ingredient. There is, however, much force in Lord Millett's argument (in spite of Lord Nicholls' apparent opinion to the contrary) that 'knowing assistance' would be a more appropriate description of this head of liability.

The facts of the case were fairly straightforward. Mr Yardley borrowed £1million from Twinsectra Limited. Leach, a solicitor, acted for Mr Yardley in connection with the loan, but did not deal directly with Twinsectra. Twinsectra dealt with another firm of solicitors,

'Sims', which represented themselves as acting on behalf of Mr Yardley. Sims paid the money to Leach and he paid it on to Yardley. Sims gave the following undertaking to Twinsectra:

(a) The loan monies will be retained by us until such time as they are applied in the acquisition of property on behalf of our client.

(b) The loan monies will be utilized solely for the acquisition of property on behalf of our client and for no other purposes.

(c) We will repay to you the said sum of £1,000,000 together with interest calculated at the rate of £657.53 such payment to be made within four calendar months after receipt of the loan monies by us.

Contrary to the terms of the undertaking, Sims did not retain the money until it was applied in the acquisition of property by Yardley. On being given an assurance by Yardley that it would be so applied, they paid it to Leach. He in turn did not take steps to ensure that it was utilized solely for the acquisition of property on behalf of Yardley. He simply paid it out upon Yardley's instructions. The result was that £357.720.11 was used by Yardley for purposes other than the acquisition of property. The loan was not repaid. Twinsectra sued all the parties involved, including Leach. The claim against him was for the £357,720.11 which had not been used to buy property. The basis of the claim was that the payment by Sims to Leach in breach of the undertaking was a breach of trust and that Leach was liable for dishonestly assisting in that breach of trust. Their Lordships allowed Mr Leach's appeal (Lord Millett dissenting).

Lord Hutton (with the majority) suggested that there are three possible standards which can be applied to determine whether a person has acted dishonestly:

> There is a purely subjective standard, whereby a person is only regarded as dishonest if he transgresses his own standard of honesty, even if that standard is contrary to that of reasonable and honest people. This has been termed the 'Robin Hood test' and has been rejected by the courts. [See, for example, Sir Christopher Slade in *Walker* v *Stones* [2001] 2 WLR 623] . . . Secondly, there is a purely objective standard whereby a person acts dishonestly if his conduct is dishonest by the ordinary standards of reasonable and honest people, even if he does not realise this. Thirdly, there is a standard which combines an objective test and a subjective test, and which requires that before there can be a finding of dishonesty it must be established that the defendant's conduct was dishonest by the ordinary standards of reasonable and honest people and that he himself realised that by those standards his conduct was dishonest. I will term this 'the combined test'.

Lord Hutton, approving 'the combined test' held that:

> for liability as an accessory to arise the defendant must himself appreciate that what he was doing was dishonest by the standards of honest and reasonable men. A finding by a judge that a defendant has been dishonest is a grave finding, and it is particularly grave against a professional man, such as a solicitor. Notwithstanding that the issue arises in equity law and not in a criminal context, I think that it would be less than just for the law to permit a finding that a defendant had been 'dishonest' in assisting in a breach of trust where he knew of the facts which created the trust and its breach but had not been aware that what he was doing would be regarded by honest men as being dishonest.

Lord Millett expressed the contrary view thus:

> In my opinion Lord Nicholls was adopting an objective standard of dishonesty by which the defendant is expected to attain the standard which would be observed by an honest person placed in similar circumstances. Account must be taken of subjective considerations such as the defendant's experience and intelligence and his actual state of knowledge at the relevant time. But it is not necessary that he should actually have appreciated that he was acting dishonestly; it is sufficient that he was.

And on the question of describing this head of liability, his Lordship asked:

> Should we return to the traditional description of the claim as 'knowing assistance', reminding ourselves that nothing less than actual knowledge is sufficient; or should we adopt Lord Nicholls' description of the claim as 'dishonest assistance', reminding ourselves that the test is an objective one?

He concluded:

> For my own part, I have no difficulty in equating the knowing mishandling of money with dishonest conduct. But the introduction of dishonesty is an unnecessary distraction, and conducive to error. Many judges would be reluctant to brand a professional man as dishonest where he was unaware that honest people would consider his conduct to be so. If the condition of liability is intentional wrongdoing and not conscious dishonesty as understood in the criminal courts, I think that we should return to the traditional description of this head of equitable liability as arising from 'knowing assistance'.

Because of the complexity and confusion in this area of the law, some commentators have proposed that wrongful recipients of trust property should be held strictly liable, subject to their being able to raise an adequate defence (Birks [1989] LMCLQ 296). This would have the result of aligning the approach of equity with that of the common law. We have already considered the common law tracing action in *Lipkin Gorman*, which was based on the action for money had and received. We saw there that liability does not depend upon degrees of knowledge, but that defences can be raised on the basis of consideration given and change of position.

The clear advantage of strict liability for 'knowing receipt' is certainty in the law, which is, perhaps, especially important in the commercial sphere. However, it is doubtful that the parties who would benefit most from certainty in this area (usually banks) would wish to reap the 'benefits' in the form of strict liability. Strict liability would mean that banks would not only be attractive targets to claimants (because banks are usually solvent and wealthy), but easy targets because they would be unable to raise the defence that they had acted honestly and did not 'know' that they had been involved in a breach of trust. In practice banks would have to take out massive insurance against the risk of action being brought against them.

Even if strict liability were introduced, uncertainties inherent in fixing liability on strangers as constructive trustees would remain. There are still conceptual difficulties to be resolved in the definition of a 'receipt' and on the question whether 'assistance' in a breach of trust should be remedied in the law of trusts or the law of torts.

CHAPTER SUMMARY

Personal equitable liability of strangers to the trust

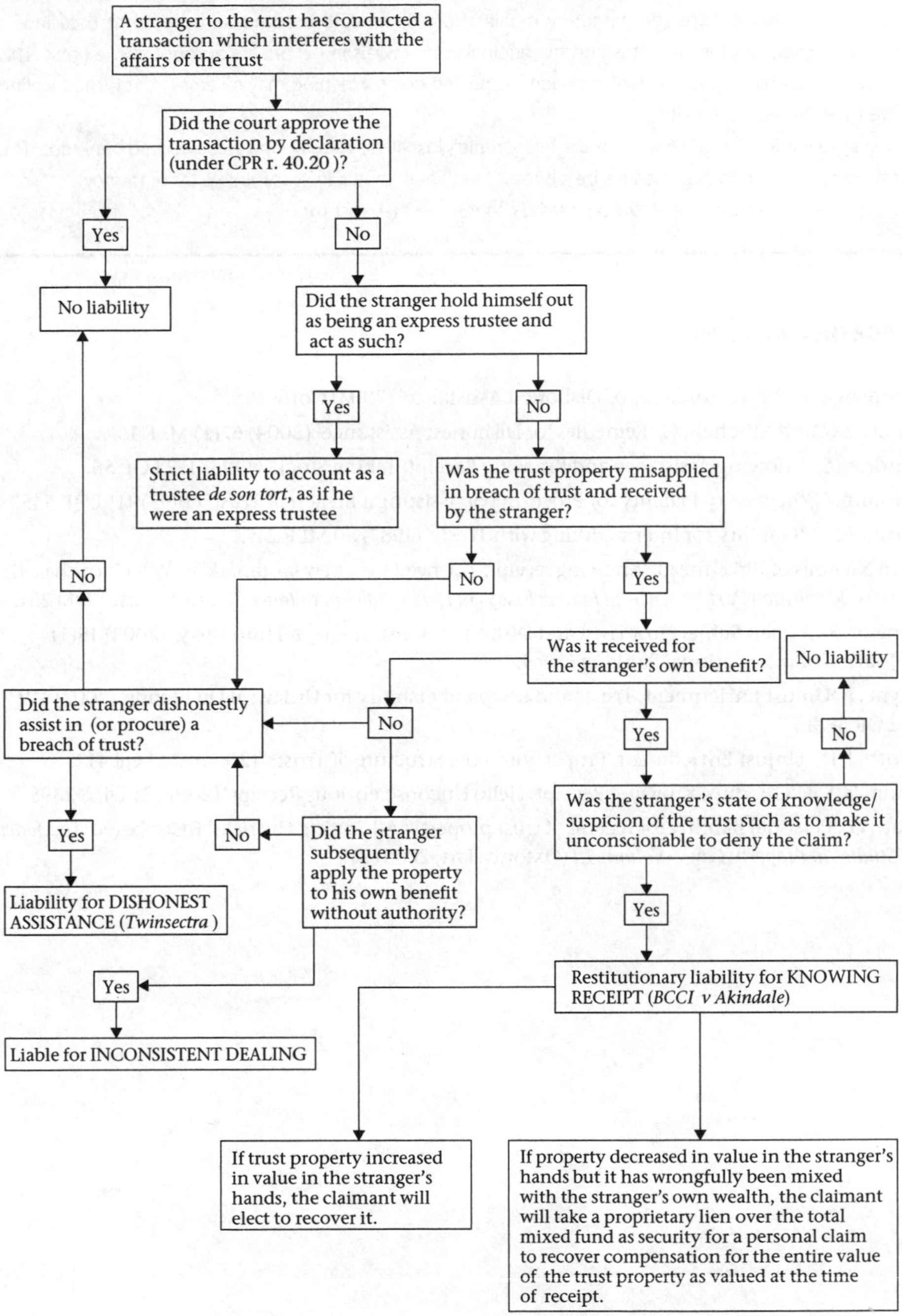

SUMMATIVE ASSESSMENT EXERCISE

online resource centre

Mr Sleeson, a solicitor, is a sole practitioner with access to his clients' accounts. He withdrew money from 'the client account' and placed it in his own private bank account which he holds with the Nelson Westminster bank. Later, he withdrew monies from his private account and played at a casino in the city. He placed the winnings and the original withdrawals in his private account at the bank. This happened regularly and the bank manager suspected that something may be amiss, but turned a blind eye to Mr Sleeson's activities.

Eventually, Mr Sleeson 'went for the big gamble', lost all his money, and was declared bankrupt. The casino manager had accepted his bets because he 'knew that solicitors made a lot of money'.

Advise Mr Sleeson's clients who now seek to recover their lost funds.

FURTHER READING

Andrews, G, 'The Redundancy of Dishonest Assistance' (2003) Conv 398.

Elliott, S B, and Mitchell, C, 'Remedies for Dishonest Assistance' (2004) 67(1) MLR 16.

Gardner, S, 'Knowing Assistance and Knowing Receipt: Taking Stock' (1996) 112 LQR 56.

Harpum, C, 'Accessory Liability for Procuring or Assisting a Breach of Trust' (1995) 111 LQR 545.

Harpum, C, 'Liability for Intermeddling with Trusts' (1987) 50 MLR 217.

Lord Nicholls of Birkenhead, 'Knowing receipt: The need for a new landmark' in W R Cornish et al (eds) *Restitution Past Present and Future: Essays in Honour of Gareth Jones* (Oxford: Hart, 1998) 231.

Panesar, S, 'A Loan Subject to a Trust and Dishonest Assistance by a Third Party' (2003) 18(1) Journal of International Banking Law 9.

Payne, J, 'Unjust Enrichment, Trusts and Recipient Liability for Unlawful Dividends' (2003) 119 LQR 583.

Smith, L D, 'Unjust Enrichment, Property and the Structure of Trusts' (2000) 116 LQR 412.

Thomas, S B, 'Goodbye Knowing Receipt, Hello Unconscientious Receipt' (2001) 21 OJLS 239S.

Watt, G, 'Personal liability for receipt of trust property: Allocating the risks' E Cooke (ed) in *Modern Studies in Property Law—Volume III* (Oxford: Hart, 2005) 91.

GLOSSARY

Account This is a procedure and a remedy. It involves the production of the trust's financial accounts and requires the trustee to give an account of his dealings with the trust property and make up any shortfall to the fund. A trustee will also be required to account for unauthorized profits made by reason of his trusteeship.

Acquiescence The decision by the injured party not to take action in response to a wrong done. Acquiescence may be a ground for barring a claim.

Advancement A statutory power granted to trustees (which may be altered, enlarged or removed by the trust instrument) under which the trustee can apply trust capital for the benefit of beneficiaries even though the beneficiaries are not yet strictly entitled to it.

Bona vacantia Assets having no ascertainable owner, with the result that they become property of the Crown.

Chancery The current Division of the High Court derived from the old Court of Chancery, which itself had its origins in the special jurisdiction of the medieval Chancellor to exempt the King's subjects from the King's common law where justice in the particular case required it.

Charitable trust A trust for non-political purposes exclusively beneficial to the public in which (with the exception of charitable trusts for the relief of poverty) the potential beneficiaries cannot be identified with any particular private group (class) of persons.

Constructive trust A trust imposed by the court on the legal owner of an asset to prevent that person asserting beneficial ownership of the asset in bad conscience to the prejudice of the true beneficial owner.

Cy-près Where it is not practical to apply charitable property to a specified charitable purpose it will be applied *cy-près* to another similar charitable purpose.

Discretionary trust (also 'trust power') An obligation upon the donee of certain property to distribute it amongst a certain class of objects (beneficiaries), but with discretion as to the manner of distribution.

Donatio mortis causa A gift made *inter vivos* in expectation of the donor's imminent death, but which is not fully effective until the donor's death.

Fiduciary Descriptive of a duty of exclusive loyalty owed in law by one person to another, and descriptive also of certain offices (the paradigm being trusteeship) under which a fiduciary duty is always one of the duties owed. Although a trustee is the paradigm fiduciary, the term 'fiduciary' is often used as shorthand to indicate 'a fiduciary other than a trustee'.

Hastings-Bass, the rule in Under this rule (exemplified in the case *Re Hastings-Bass*) a court may set aside an otherwise unreviewable trustee decision if it is clear that the trustees would not have decided as they did if they had taken all relevant factors (and only such factors) into consideration.

Investment The process by which trust assets are applied with the intention of producing income and/or capital growth over the medium to long term.

In personam A remedy operates *in personam* where it is enforced against a defendant in his personal capacity, thus it may be defeated by the defendant's personal insolvency.

In rem A remedy operates *in rem* where it is enforced against assets in the defendant's hands in which or over which the claimant has a proprietary interest, thus it is not defeated by the defendant's personal insolvency.

Inter vivos Of an instrument/document by which property is disposed: taking effect during the lifetime of the person making the disposition.

Laches A claim against a defendant will be barred by reason of the claimant's *laches* if there was such a delay in bringing the claim as is likely to prejudice the defendant's fair trial or otherwise offend the public interest in finality of litigation.

Maintenance A statutory power granted to trustees (which may be altered, enlarged or removed by the trust instrument) under which the trustee can apply trust income for the benefit of infant beneficiaries of the trust.

Maxim A traditional judicial principle of the Court of Chancery which serves as a guide to the exercise of discretion in the application of equitable doctrines and the award of equitable remedies.

Mutual wills Wills entered into by two or more persons in identical form and intended to be irrevocable upon the death of the first of them to die.

Perpetuity, the rules against Rules which prevent the disposition of property (eg by trust) from vesting in the donee at too remote a future date, and which prevent income from being accumulated and capital being rendered inalienable for too long a time.

Power of appointment A power given to the donee of certain property to distribute it if he sees fit amongst a certain class of objects.

Proprietary In the nature of property or appertaining to property.

Proprietary estoppel A doctrine which operates where B has been led to rely to his detriment upon a representation by A that A will dispose of property in favour of B, it operates by preventing A from acting unconscionably inconsistently with the representation made. A is said to be 'estopped'.

Protective trust A trust established by the settlor to protect the beneficiary (who cannot be the settlor) from the beneficiary's creditors. Sometimes called a 'spendthrift' trust, because it was traditionally employed to protect spendthrift children of the settlor.

Quistclose Trust Where property is transferred for a particular purpose, a trust imposed on property to prevent its misapplication for any other purpose. Exemplified by the trust in *Barclays Bank v Quistclose Investments Ltd* [1970] AC 567, House of Lords.

Restitution The reinstatement of wealth to a person who has been unjustly deprived of it by a person who has been unjustly enriched by it.

Resulting trust Where an attempt is made by the owner of an asset to dispose of the beneficial ownership of the asset, the benefit will return to the donor under a resulting trust whenever the attempt is for any reason unsuccessful, unless it is clear that the owner intended to abandon the entirety of his interest in the asset.

Secret trusts A trust binding on property passed under a will, but which does not comply with the formalities required by the Wills Act. It is effective because it binds the conscience of the person to whom the property passes under the will, that person having accepted the trust when the testator was still alive.

Settlor The person who sets up a trust *inter vivos* in furtherance of an express intention to do so.

Specific performance An equitable remedy taking the form of an order of the court requiring performance of a contract, it is awarded where the court will not permit the defendant to breach his contract and pay common law damages by way of remedy.

Testamentary Of an instrument/document by which property is disposed: taking effect on the death of the person making the disposition.

Tracing The process of following the value of an asset into substitute assets (eg. the value of a coin can be traced into a book acquired with the coin).

Trust A private trust is the legal relationship between the formal owner(s) of assets ('the trustee' or 'trustees') and the beneficial owner(s) of those assets ('the beneficiary' or 'beneficiaries'). The hallmark of the trust is that every trustee is obliged in equity to employ every incident of their formal (typically 'legal') ownership for the exclusive benefit of the beneficiaries, although a trustee might himself be one of the beneficiaries.

Trustee A legal owner of assets who is bound to hold and apply the assets for the exclusive benefit of other persons or to advance charitable purposes.

Trustee de son tort A person who takes it upon himself to intermeddle in the affairs of an express trust as if he were a trustee must account for the consequences as if he were indeed a trustee of the express trust. He is said to be a trustee *de son tort* ('trustee by his own wrongdoing').

Volunteer Where a promise is made voluntarily in favour of a person, the person claiming the benefit of the promise is said to be a volunteer. A volunteer does not give contractual consideration for the performance of the promise.

INDEX

D

E